What the Bible teaches

NAHUM
HABAKKUK
ZEPHANIAH
HAGGAI
ZECHARIAH
MALACHI

What the Bible teaches

NAHUM
P. Harding

HABAKKUK
P. Harding

ZEPHANIAH
P. Harding

HAGGAI
P. Harding

ZECHARIAH
J. J. Stubbs

MALACHI
P. Harding

SERIES EDITORS

W. S. STEVELY   D. E. WEST

JOHN RITCHIE LTD
CHRISTIAN PUBLICATIONS

ISBN-13: 978 1 904064 37 4
ISBN-10: 1 904064 37 X

WHAT THE BIBLE TEACHES
© 2007 John Ritchie Ltd.
40 Beansburn, Kilmarnock, Scotland

www.johnritchie.co.uk

Typeset by John Ritchie Ltd.
Printed by Bercker UK Ltd., London.

PREFACE

The publishers have commissioned this Old Testament series of commentaries to complement the completed set of New Testament commentaries issued under the general title "What the Bible Teaches". Together they seek to provide an accessible and useful tool for the study of, and meditation on, Scripture.

While there is no shortage of commentaries currently available on the various books of the Old Testament it was felt that there was no complete series that sought simply to apply the message of Genesis through to Malachi to the concerns of believers today.

The authors of these volumes are not scholars of the original languages and rely on others for guidance on the best modern views of word meanings and similar matters. However, all the authors share the conviction that the Bible in its entirety is the Word of God. They believe it to be reliable, accurate, and intended "for our learning" (Rom 15.4). This view has been explained further by Mr Stevely in a short series of articles that appeared in "The Believer's Magazine", also published by John Ritchie Ltd., in 1999.

The two Testaments fit together so that principles and illustrations from the Old are brought to bear on issues that arise on nearly every page of the New. Knowledge of the Old is therefore an indispensable aid to the proper understanding of the New. In particular the Lord Jesus can be seen in prophecy and picture again and again. He, Himself, as described in the Gospels, is an exemplar of this approach to the Old Testament through His constant reference to people and incidents whose histories are recorded for us, and to those prophetic statements that applied to Him.

Given this understanding of the nature and purpose of the Scriptures, the main lessons of the books are considered and applied to our circumstances today by authors experienced in preaching and teaching the Word of God.

Since no attempt is being made to produce an academic series the technical apparatus has been kept to a minimum. Where authors have judged it of value attention is drawn to linguistic and other issues. Transliteration, where appropriate, is accompanied by reference to the numerical system devised by Strong to allow the reader without knowledge of the original languages to gain access to the various lexical aids which have adopted this system. For clarity, numerical references to New Testament words only are given in italics, following the practice used in Strong's Concordance.

The system of transliteration generally used is that adopted by the *Theological Wordbook of the Old Testament* (TWOT), edited by Harris, Archer and Waltke, and published by Moody Press, Chicago, 1980. However, there are occasions when account has been taken of the commonly recognised English spelling of some Hebrew words.

References to Scripture without attribution are taken from the Authorised (King James) Version. Where other translations are quoted the source is indicated.

Biblical measurements are usually given in cubits. For ease of calculation the general assumption has been adopted that 1 cubit = 18 inches/46cms.

Since the commentaries do not necessarily follow a verse-by-verse approach, and to save space and cost, the text of Scripture is not included. It is assumed that all readers have available a copy of the Bible.

The complete Old Testament is expected to be covered in around fifteen to eighteen volumes. These will not appear in the order in which they are found in the Scriptures but simply in order of completion by the authors commissioned for the series.

W. S. STEVELY
D. E. WEST

CONTRIBUTORS

PHILLIP HARDING –
Nahum, Habakkuk, Zephaniah, Haggai, Malachi

Born and brought up in Port Talbot, South Wales, Phillip Harding was saved at the age of 19 in 1951 and was received into the assembly in Port Talbot, along with his wife Gwen. He moved to Yorkshire with secular employment and spent 20 years in Skelmanthorpe, being commended to the Lord's work by the assembly there in 1969. During his first years of service he was involved in tract distribution in North Wales, tent work in West Wales, and gospel campaigns in various assemblies. Since then he has been preaching the gospel and ministering the Word of God in the UK, Canada, USA, Australia, New Zealand, South Africa, and Botswana. He has previously completed a book on the Second Epistle to Timothy and contributed to the volume *The Person of Christ,* as well as writing articles for a number of magazines including Truth & Tidings, Words in Season, Believer's Magazine, and Present Truth. His ministry and preaching have been greatly appreciated over the years.

JOHN J. STUBBS – Zechariah

John Stubbs was born into a christian family in Co. Durham, England, saved as a boy of 11, and received into assembly fellowship in London at the age of 12. Three assemblies in Co. Durham and one in Shipley, Yorkshire commended him to the work of the Lord in 1965, his first labours being in Malaysia until 1969 when he returned to the UK where he continued to engage in gospel work and ministry. In 1972 he moved to Castle Douglas where he laboured for twelve years before moving to Mayfield assembly near Edinburgh. He has served the Lord in many parts of the UK as well as in Australia, New Zealand, USA, and Canada. He has written *Is the Bible the Word of God?; Misunderstood Texts of Holy Scripture; The Person of Christ;* and has jointly authored a further book on the Person of Christ. He has also written the commentary on the book of Numbers in this series, and has contributed many articles to magazines. He currently shares responsibility for the Question Box in the Believer's Magazine.

BIBLIOGRAPHY

The Bibliography for this Volume of "What the Bible Teaches" is in two sections. The first, General, section includes those books which cover more than one of the Prophecies under consideration. The second, Specific, section lists works which apply primarily to individual Prophecies.

GENERAL

Anstey, Martin. *Chronology of the Old Testament.* Kregel Publications, 1973.
  Basing his work solely on Scripture, the author traces the continuous line from Adam. He explains each period step by step, sometimes using diagrams and charts. After his conclusion he gives chronological data in tabulated form.

Baker, David W. *Tyndale Old Testament Commentaries: Nahum, Habakkuk and Zephaniah.* Inter-Varsity Press, 1988.
  A conservative work that gives a helpful and concise introduction to each prophecy. It considers each book section by section giving the main themes. It is a scholarly work and has useful additional notes.

Barber, C. J. *Everyman's Bible Commentary: Habakkuk and Zephaniah.* Moody Press, 1985.
  A scholarly work, providing detailed outlines and a section by section commentary. A helpful volume giving a background to certain passages.

Boyd, Robert T. *World Bible Handbook: Nahum - Malachi.* World Bible Publishers Inc., 1991.
  A comprehensive work giving an outline and summary of each book of the Bible. It suggests a key chapter, verse, word, phrase, and thought for each book. It is a helpful handbook giving useful Bible background information along with detailed cross references.

Coates, C. A. *An Outline of Some of the Minor Prophets.* Stow Hill Bible and Tract Depot.
  A brief exposition with good spiritual lessons, applying many principles and thoughts to the assembly.

Cook, F. C. *The Holy Bible with Commentary, Vol 6, Minor Prophets: Nahum - Malachi.* John Murray, 1876.
  An extensive work with much to amplify the text. Quite helpful, but with little application and void of spiritual depth. Many quotations in Hebrew and Latin.

Craig, P. C. *Daily Study Bible: Twelve Prophets.* Westminster/St Andrews Press, 1985.
  Helpful and interesting.

Darby, J. N. *Synopsis of the Books of the Bible, Vol 2: Nahum - Malachi.* Stow Hill Bible and Tract Depot, 1957.

A very useful outline of the whole Bible that encourages study of the Scriptures. It is helpful to the careful and thoughtful reader.

Davidson, A. B. *The Cambridge Bible for Schools and Colleges: The Books of Nahum, Habakkuk and Zephaniah.* Cambridge University Press, 1905. *The long introduction to each book is very helpful, but its text and notes are limited.*

Deane, W. J. *The Pulpit Commentary, Vol 14: Nahum - Malachi.* MacDonald Publishing Company.
A general commentary with homilies by various writers. A valuable help; suggestive, but requires care in accepting all the views expressed.

Dods, Marcus. *The Post-Exilian Prophets: Haggai, Zechariah, Malachi.* T. & T. Clark.
This is part of the series of "Handbooks for Bible Classes and Private Students", and, while not spiritual in content, is nevertheless helpful. At the end of each section considered questions are asked which certainly should lead to a better understanding of the Prophecies.

Driver, S. R. *The Century Bible: The Minor Prophets: Nahum - Malachi.* T. C. and E. C. Black, 1906.
A brief and compact commentary. To be treated with care.

Eaton, J. H. *Torch Bible Commentaries: Obadiah, Nahum, Habakkuk and Zephaniah.* SCM Press, 1961.
Referred to by David W. Baker in "The Tyndale Old Testament Commentaries: Nahum, Habakkuk and Zephaniah".

Feinberg, C. L. *The Minor Prophets: Nahum - Malachi.* Moody Press, 1976.
A scholarly work with much to commend it. The language is lucid and clear, enabling one to grasp the writer's meaning. It includes occasional spiritual exhortations.

Ironside, H. A. *The Minor Prophets.* Loizeaux Brothers Inc., 1981.
A readable work with much application to conditions today and some challenging statements. It is not a verse by verse exposition, but gives a general overview of the books.

Jamieson, Fausset & Brown. *Commentary on the Whole Bible: Nahum - Malachi.* Zondervan Publishing House, 1975.
A valuable and helpful work with an assortment of informative and suggestive thought. However, one must be careful not to imbibe all its views.

Keil, C. F & Delitzsch, F. *Commentary on the Old Testament, Vol 10: The Minor Prophets.* Wm. B. Eerdmans Publishing Co., 1980.
An academic and conservative work by German scholars with some helpful exposition of the text and instructive references. It has many Hebrew quotations.

Kelly, W. *Study of the Minor Prophets.* Hammond Trust Bible Depot, 1874.
Kelly's writings are generally wordy but also instructive. This short commentary contains some practical and challenging passages, although one does not accept all the author's prophetic views.

Merrill, Eugene H. *An Exegetical Commentary; Haggai, Zechariah, Malachi.* Moody Press.

This work concentrates on the text with a translation, and dwells much on giving the sense and use of Hebrew words. While this is helpful, it is more a book for the scholar than the ordinary reader.

Moore, Thomas V. *Haggai, Zechariah & Malachi.* The Banner of Truth Trust.

This commentary might be called a typical puritan work, but C. H. Spurgeon summarised the value of Moore's work in the highest terms. "A capital book", he wrote. "Most useful to Ministers".

Morgan, G. Campbell. *The Minor Prophets.* Fleming H. Revell Company, 1960.

Very brief but helpful, giving characteristics of the time of the prophet, an analysis and message of the book, and a practical application for today.

Morrish, G. *A New and Concise Bible Dictionary.* G. Morrish, 114 Camberwell Road, London.

Contains short articles on words, brief outlines on each book of the Bible, and other valuable information. Names of persons and places are included as are some helpful biblical doctrines.

Pentecost, J. Dwight. *Things to Come.* Zondervan Publishing House, 1960.

A comprehensive work bringing together systematically the whole scope of biblical eschatology. Many controversial issues are dealt with where the author gives the views of others as well as his own. An instructive and helpful work even though one cannot accept all his conclusions.

Poole, Matthew. *A Commentary on the Holy Bible.* Macdonald Publishing Company.

A large work seeking to give a verse by verse sense of the Scriptures. Its style is nineteenth century and its format and print do not make it an easy book to read. Although it is helpful and thought provoking, the reader must be careful in considering the views expressed.

Pusey, E. B. *The Minor Prophets.* Baker, 1953.

The reader will find this work helpful and instructive.

Rosenberg, Rabbi A. J. *The Book of the Twelve Prophets.* Judaica Press, 1992.

Contains the complete Hebrew text. Accompanying the English translation are translations of Hebrew commentaries. Contains quotations from Talmudic and Midrashic literature. Helpful in the meaning of some Hebrew words.

Smith, G. A. *The Expositor's Bible: The Book of the Twelve Prophets.* A. C. Armstrong/Hodder & Stoughton, 1898.

An orthodox exposition with some applications to circumstances in life. Most informative and generally helpful.

Smith, R. L. *The Word Biblical Commentary: Micah – Malachi.* World Books, 1984.

Referred to by David W. Baker in "The Tyndale Old Testament Commentaries: Nahum, Habakkuk and Zephaniah".

Spurrell, Helen. *A Translation of the Old Testament Scriptures from the Original Hebrew.* James Nisbet and Co, 1885; reprinted 1985 by University Press, Oxford.
A delightful, interesting, and thought provoking translation from the original Hebrew. In many passages her language is sublime. Valuable in the study of the Old Testament.

Stallan, F. E. *Things written Afore Time.* John Ritchie Ltd., 1990.
A measured exposition of every verse in the Old Testament quoted in the New Testament. It gives a valuable insight into these quotations. The writer expands the meaning and shows the importance of each quotation.

Watt, J. D. W. *The Cambridge Bible Commentary: The Books of Nahum, Habakkuk and Zephaniah.* Cambridge University Press, 1975.
Most instructive in its introductions, but brief in its text and notes.

SPECIFIC
Nahum

Cann, Cyril G. *The Minor Prophets: Nahum* (Ed I. Steeds). Precious Seed Publications, 1992.
A limited work. However, this commentary is helpful with some spiritual applications.

Tatford, F. A. *Prophet of Assyria's Fall.* Prophetic Witness Publishing House, 1973.
One of a fine series on the Prophets. Very helpful. Easy to read, and concise with good application.

Habakkuk

Armerding, C. E. *The Expositor's Bible Commentary: Habakkuk* (Ed F. E. Gaebelein). Zondervan, 1985.
A standard commentary with exposition of the text and some useful comments.

Barnes, H. *The Minor Prophets: Habakkuk* (Ed I Steeds). Precious Seed Publications, 1992.
A limited work but helpful. This commentary gives an overview of the book with historical and biographical notes. The reader will enjoy the spiritual content and appreciate the conclusions drawn.

Lloyd-Jones, D. M. *From Fear to Faith.* IVF, 1953; republished in *Faith Tried and Triumphant,* IVP, 1987.
A compact book that the reader will find helpful and easy to read. The author draws parallels between the message of Habakkuk and modern times. He suggests that in Habakkuk is the secret to the problems of life and shows that faith can triumph in every circumstance.

Tatford, F. A. *Prophet of the Watchtower.* Prophetic Witness Publishing House, 1973.
One of a fine series on the Prophets. Very useful and instructive. A sound, detailed and spiritual book, easy to read and helpful.

Zephaniah

Newell, David. *The Minor Prophets: Zephaniah* (Ed I. Steeds). Precious Seed Publications, 1992.

A limited work but most helpful. This commentary gives a useful introduction. The application of Judah's transgressions is most challenging. The spiritual content is clear and stimulating. Well worth reading.

Tatford, F. A. *Prophet of the Royal Blood: The Book of Zephaniah.* Prophetic Witness Publishing House, 1973.

One of a fine series on the Prophets. Very useful and instructive. A sound, detailed and spiritual book, easy to read and helpful.

Haggai

Jennings, A. C. *An Old Testament Commentary for English Readers, Vol 5: Haggai* (Ed C. J. Ellicott). Cassell & Co. Ltd., 1897.

An extensive work in five volumes by various writers, edited by C. J. Ellicott. It has been mentioned as one of the better commentaries. It is helpful, with comments on most verses although some are dealt with scantily. There is little or no practical application, and one must take care not to accept all the views expressed.

Steeds, Ivan. *The Minor Prophets: Haggai* (Ed I. Steeds). Precious Seed Publications, 1992.

A limited work but most helpful. This commentary gives a useful introduction and outline of the book with historical information. The reader will enjoy the spiritual content and clear application of each section.

Tatford, F. A. *Prophet of the Restoration.* Prophetic Witness Publishing House, 1973.

One of a fine series on the Minor Prophets. Very useful and instructive. A sound, detailed and helpful book. It is spiritual and practical with challenging passages to stir one's spirit.

Zechariah

Baron, David. *The Visions & Prophesies of Zechariah.* The Hebrew Christian Testimony to Israel, 1951.

A classic work often referred to by other authors. It has the advantage of being written by a converted Jew, a true lover of the Messiah and Israel.

Dennett, Edward. *Zechariah, The Prophet.* W. H. Broome and Rouse, 1888.

Probably one of the first books to be written on this prophecy by an assembly writer. A helpful work, clearly showing the order of future events in the prophetic programme.

Hartman, Fred. *Zechariah, Israel's Messenger of the Messiah's Triumph.* The Friends of Israel Gospel Ministry Inc.

A brief exposition of the book, but readable and sound in its view of Israel's future. The publishers have a great interest in, and support for, the Jewish nation.

Hocking, C. *The Minor Prophets: Zechariah* (Ed I. Steeds). Precious Seed Publications, 1992.
A good introduction and outline with very helpful brief notes on each section of the prophecy. It will give the reader an understanding of the book and its message for today.

Luck, G. Coleman. *Zechariah, A Study of the Prophetic Visions of Zechariah.* Moody Press.
This is a popular study of the "apocalypse of the Old Testament". Clear outlines, compact discussion, and pointed applications add to its value.

Meyer, F. B. *The Prophet of Hope; Studies in Zechariah.* Ambassador Publications Ltd.
The aim of this book is to give the salient features and lessons of each chapter with the object of leading the Bible student to a more searching and careful acquaintance with the prophet.

Smith, J. Denham. *The Prophet of Glory,* or, *Zechariah's Visions of the Coming and Kingdom of Christ.* James E. Hawkins.
This is pre-eminently a very devotional book, but it is full of lovely thoughts concerning Christ.

Tatford, F. A. *Prophet of the Myrtle Grove.* Prophetic Witness Publishing House, 1973.
A most helpful commentary from the pen of a very able and sound exponent of prophecy.

Unger, Merrill. F. *Zechariah, Prophecy Of Messiah's Glory.* Zondervan Publishing House.
This is a major work on Zechariah. Dr Unger, with vast insight and copious footnotes, has provided in this verse-by-verse study a valuable and scholarly commentary.

Wright, C. H. H. *Zechariah And His Prophecies, Considered In Relation To Modern Criticism: With A Critical and Grammatical Commentary.* Hodder & Stoughton
A large critical work in which the writer quotes from many previous authors. Believers looking for help in this commentary will find certain sections rather heavy. It is disappointing that the author does not accept that Zechariah 14.5 speaks of the second advent of Christ!

Malachi

Tatford, F. A. *Prophet of the Reformation.* Prophetic Witness Publishing House, 1972.
One of a fine series on the Prophets. Very useful and instructive. A sound, detailed and spiritual book which the reader will fine easy to read and helpful.

West, David E. *The Minor Prophets: Malachi* (Ed I Steeds). Precious Seed Publications, 1992.
A limited work because of space, this commentary is helpful and instructive with clear spiritual application to the present day.

ABBREVIATIONS

ASV	American Standard Version (the American variant of the RV)
AV	Authorised Version (known in USA as the King James Version)
JB	The Jerusalem Bible, published by Darton, Longman & Todd Ltd
JND	New Translation by J. N. Darby
LXX	The Septuagint: the ancient translation of the Old Testament into Greek. Often quoted in the New Testament
MT	Masoretic Text – the traditional Hebrew Old Testament
Newberry	The AV as edited by Thomas Newberry; also known as "The Englishman's Bible"
NEB	New English Bible
NIV	New International Version
RSV	Revised Standard Version (revision of the ASV)
RV	Revised Version, 1885 (published in England; a revision of the AV)
TWOT	*Theological Word Book of the Old Testament*, edited by Harris, Archer and Waltke

NAHUM

P. Harding

CONTENTS

INTRODUCTION

Unlike most of the prophetic books, Nahum does not commence by mentioning the author's name, but goes straight to the subject, "The burden of Nineveh". The sole theme of the book is to announce and describe the approaching overthrow of the evil city of Nineveh, and thus the fall of the Assyrian empire, since Nineveh, being its capital, was representative of the whole nation. Nahum is the seventh book of the so-called Minor Prophets. D. W. Baker notes that "All canonical traditions place it before Habakkuk and all place it after Micah, except the Septuagint, where it follows Jonah". It seems that the Septuagint places it after Jonah because in both books Nineveh is the subject. In Jonah the prophet proclaims coming judgment because of the wickedness of its inhabitants. This produced repentance and thus the judgment was averted. However, the city returned to its evil ways with increased wickedness, and Nahum unfolds the inevitable consequences.

The victorious Assyrian nation was not only proud and arrogant, but also cruel. Its treatment of the kingdom of Israel and its oppression of the kingdom of Judah brought it into opposition with Jehovah who had, in His longsuffering, waited until its true character was revealed. R. T. Boyd states that Nineveh's destruction in 612 BC by Cyaxares of the Medes and Nabopolassar of Babylon fulfilled Nahum's prophecy to the last detail! The city's aqueduct was destroyed and the River Tigris diverted to flood Nineveh (1.8; 2.6). "The flood waters dissolved the mud-brick foundations of houses and buildings, and the walls crumbled. Evidence also shows that, along with the flood, the city was burned (2.13; 3.13). Those in authority, as drunk as they were (2.5), and seeing their doom, mounted a funeral pyre and died as they were devoured by the flames. No one wept over her funeral, and she was no more heard of (3.7; 2.13). From 612 BC till AD 1845 it was a forgotten site. Since then, discovered evidence tips the scales in favour of God's word through Nahum."

Although there are no direct references to the Messianic Kingdom, one cannot remove the Messianic association from the prophecy. This association is woven into the book where statements such as those in 1.9, 12 & 15 can only have their complete fulfilment in a coming day. God's justice is asserted throughout the book, and the people of God could draw comfort from the announcement of coming judgment upon Assyria. As in Nahum's day so today: God is sovereign and is working out His purposes.

"Among the minor prophets Nahum holds the highest place. His prophecy is a poem, stately, orderly, and impressive, all the parts of which are well arranged and mutually conducive to the unity of the whole" (W. J. Deane). The majestic description of the character of God in the opening verses of the book is preparation for the elegance, forcefulness, and vividness of the prophecy. Nahum employs a variety of imagery which he conveys in a dramatic and powerful way. The language of the book has a certain originality which separates it from other writings. F. C. Cook declares that "Those who can read the prophet's own words will best understand their force, beauty and vivid imagery. Yet very much of this is retained in a good translation...'Nahum described the fate of the vast city in images which human imagination or human language has never surpassed.' (Milman, *History of the Jews)*".

The Prophet of the Book

Nothing is known definitely of the prophet Nahum except for the few words of v.1. Like many Old Testament prophets he is a man hidden behind the message he was given by God to proclaim. His name means Comforter, or Consolation, in keeping with the comfort for the people of God which is contained in the prophecy of the Assyrian oppressor's destruction. The name itself only occurs in v.1 of this book and in Luke 3.25 in the genealogy of the Lord Jesus Christ where it refers to another Nahum. The expression "the Elkoshite" does not indicate lineage, but refers to the place of his birth, i.e. a native of Elkosh or Elkesi. The name Elkosh does not occur anywhere else in the Holy Scriptures and thus its actual location is disputed. Three suggestions have been presented.

1. A late tradition adopted by some modern writers maintains it is the Assyrian village of Alkush situated on the eastern side of the River Tigris and north of the ancient city of Nineveh. This tradition states that Nahum was born in Assyria of parents who had been among the captives when Israel was carried away into that land. However, this village has no antiquity about it, and the tradition cannot be traced back beyond the sixteenth century. It probably arose from the similarity of the name and in order to account for the prophet's knowledge of Assyrian matters which supposes that he was an eye witness. This suggestion has not much authoritative support since there is no decisive evidence from within the prophecy itself of an Assyrian origin. Besides this, when Israel was taken into captivity they were placed in Halah, Habor, and the cities of the Medes (2 Kings 17.6; 18.11).

2. Another tradition states that it was situated beyond Bethgabre, of the tribe of Simeon, some 20 miles (32 kilometres) south-west of Jerusalem making Nahum a native of Judah. This seems to be more probable than the first since the prophecy was intended to comfort Judah and it seems that the prophet was there when he prophesied. However, this tradition has little support.

3. A third tradition suggests that Nahum was born in Galilee. C. F. Keil writes that "The statement of Jerome is older, and much more credible - namely, that 'Elkosh was situated in Galilee, since there is to the present day a village in Galilee called Helcesaei (others Helcesei, Elcesi), a very small one indeed, and containing in its ruins hardly any traces of ancient buildings, but one which is well known to the Jews, and was also pointed

out to me by my guide' - inasmuch as he does not simply base his statement upon the word of his guide, but describes the place as well known to the Jews". This has much to commend it since the prophecy mentions the northern territory of Bashan, Carmel and Lebanon (1.4). That Nahum was a native of Galilee may be implied in the name Capernaum which means "village of Nahum". It has been suggested that he lived in Capernaum although born in Elkosh not far away. Many commentators suggest that although Nahum was a native of Galilee he moved to Judah and prophesied there. For further discussion on the location of Elkosh see Keil & Delitzsch, D. W. Baker, W. J. Deane, and S. R. Driver. It is remarkable that both the prophets who prophesied against Nineveh were probably natives of Galilee. How prejudiced and ignorant the religious leaders were in their opposition to the Lord when they said, "Search, and look: for out of Galilee ariseth no prophet" (Jn 7.52).

The Period of the Book

There is no precise date given in the book and its period has been considered uncertain. Thus various dates have been assigned to it ranging from Hezekiah's reign to that of Jehoiakim. Those who set the prophecy in Hezekiah's day appeal to its place in the Hebrew canon which seems to support this view. A confirmation of this is supposed by referring 1.12 & 15 and 2.2 to the invasion of Judah by Sennacherib, 1.9 & 12 to the affliction brought upon Judah by the Assyrians of that period, and 2.13, "the voice of thy messengers", to Rabshakeh and others sent by Sennacherib to Hezekiah (2 Kings 18.19,27; 19.14; Is 36.4,12; 37.9). This would mean that Nahum was a contemporary of Isaiah and Micah. Confirmation of this, as to Isaiah, is supposed by the phrases that correspond with Isaiah (cp. 1.8 with Is 8.8; 1.15 with Is 52.7; 3.5 with Is 47.2-3; 3.7,10 with Is 51.19-20 – see Keil & Delitzsch and Jamieson, Fausset & Brown). The similarity of such passages does not on its own prove that Isaiah was a contemporary of Nahum.

The book itself contains sufficient internal evidence to determine the period, though not the exact date, when it was written. The reference to turning again (back) the excellency of Israel (2.2) refers to the captivity of Israel having taken place, and thus Nahum must have prophesied after that event. From the book one can gather that the Assyrian power was still strong at the time of writing (1.12; 2.11-13; 3.15-17), and so it must pre-date the decline of the Assyrian empire and the destruction of Nineveh its capital city in 612 BC. This suggests, according to D. W. Baker, a date prior to the death of Ashurbanipal (668-627 BC). The reference in 3.8 to the downfall of No (No-Amon), which is Thebes in upper Egypt, is another pointer to the date of the prophecy. W. J. Deane states that the cuneiform records show "that Assurbanipal, the son and successor of Esarhaddon, took that city in his second expedition against Urdamani, or Rud-Amon, the successor of Tirhakah, and carried the inhabitants away. This invasion took place soon after the death of Tirhakah (664 BC)". It would, therefore, have taken place in 663 BC. Thus the time of Nahum's prophecy, according to the internal evidence, falls within the period of 663-627 BC, which indicates that he prophesied in either the reign of Manasseh or in Josiah's reign. Since Assyria's greatest oppression of Judah was when Manasseh was on the throne, that seems the most probable period of the prophecy. This would limit the timing of the book to between 663 and 641 BC. Thus Nahum's contemporaries would have been Jeremiah, Habakkuk, and Zephaniah rather than Isaiah and Micah as favoured by some.

The Message of the Book

The opening expression, "the burden of Nineveh" (1.1), indicates that the prophecy of Nahum is taken up with the judgment of God upon the Assyrian nation, and in particular upon its capital city Nineveh. The certainty of this judgment upon the Assyrian oppressor would bring relief to the oppressed kingdom of Judah (1.12-15). The northern kingdom of Israel had already been taken into captivity by that power. Assyrian pride and idolatry, its oppression of Judah, and its defiance of God are all severely rebuked in the book, and its certain and complete destruction is announced. The book reveals the relationship of God to the whole world, not only to His people, and the opening verses describe His character which is the basis for the whole prophecy.

God, who is longsuffering, is a jealous and avenging God (1.2-3), and when He rises in judgment the whole world is affected (1.3-6). Every part of the earth and sea bears witness to His irresistible power and no one can withstand His might. Jehovah is indeed good and is a safe haven to those who put their trust in Him, but He visits with judicial vengeance those who oppose Him and oppress His people (1.7-15). Although God manifests patience, He is just and His righteous claims must be met or retribution will be meted out. D. W. Baker expresses it thus: "Yahweh is applying his universal standard against evil, no matter who is responsible (cp. Amos 1.3 - 2.16). Even though God has chosen Assyria to act as his instrument of punishment against the rebellious and recalcitrant Israel (Is 7.17; 10.5-6), he holds that nation corporately responsible for the excesses and atrocities committed in fulfilling this role (Is 10.7-19; cp. Zeph 2.14-15)". Over a century before Nahum's prophecy, Nineveh had hearkened to the preaching of Jonah and repented, but the guilty city had returned to its old sins and had increased in wickedness and idolatry. Its state was such that Nahum had no word of hope or comfort for it, but only of condemnation and judgment. The continuing existence of the Assyrian power was indeed a manifestation of the longsuffering of God. The withholding of judgment gave that nation an opportunity for repentance, but also allowed the extent of its wickedness to be revealed (cp. Gen 15.16). For many years Assyria had been the dread of the nations, and its complete guilt had now been displayed and the basis of the judgment pronounced was shown to be God's righteousness and justice. S. R. Driver writes, "The violence, the oppressions, the inhumanities of the tyrant, which have afflicted not Judah only but the then known world, must have their end; and the prophet for the moment will know nothing about his God, save that He is a God of vengeance. It is outraged humanity at large which calls for vengeance from his lips (2.13; 3.4-5,19b)".

Nineveh, its capital city and the largest city at that time, was situated by the River Tigris. It was a great commercial centre having been enriched by plunder from numerous military campaigns and was strongly fortified. It had, however, become like a lion's den full of prey (2.11-12) and there was no cure for it (3.19). Nineveh was now to suffer final and complete destruction. F. C. Cook describes it as, "...not conquest or overthrow only; it is annihilation: 'He will make an utter end of the place thereof' (1.8,9). 'There is no healing of thy bruise' (3.19). 'She is empty, and void, and waste' (2.10)". The city would be destroyed as an overflowing flood (1.8; 2.8); as being devoured like stubble (1.10); and burned with fire (3.13,15). When the judgment of God fell upon the city it would be unmitigating and would bring a complete end to it. Nineveh must be destroyed in spite of its wealth and power because it had exalted itself against God and ignored His claims.

In ch.2 the prophet details in vivid imagery the overthrow and destruction of the city. He depicts the approach of the invaders, the attack, the raging of the chariots (v.4), the plunder of the city (v.9), the emptying of the city (v.10), and the devouring of her ferocious soldiers (v.13). In His justice, God turns the splendour and power of Nineveh, and the nation, to devastation and oblivion.

In ch.3 Nahum gives the reason for Nineveh's judgment and develops further its downfall. Assyria's cruelty, violence, treachery, and idolatry are the cause of its destruction, and once more the prophet vividly depicts the attacking chariots and horsemen unmercifully spreading slaughter throughout the city, bringing terror to the inhabitants (vv.1-4). There would be no escape or protection for Nineveh despite its power, its influence, and its multitude of defenders. It would be powerless to prevent her doom just as the great city of Thebes, in Egypt, had been unable to avert its overthrow (vv.7-11). The strongholds of Nineveh would fall before the attackers like ripe figs when the tree is shaken; fire would devour the place; the defenders would be put to the sword; the normally crowded streets would be deserted as when locusts flee; the Assyrian power would crumble; the proud empire would pass away; and the result of its fall would be the rejoicing of all who suffered under its cruel and wicked oppression (vv.12-19). At the time of Nahum's prophecy the nations around would never have imagined that such a calamity could overtake the mighty city of Nineveh. Whereas in the prophecy of Jonah the mercy of God was emphasised, in this prophecy the emphasis is on the justice of God.

The teaching of the prophecy is surely that God is not only faithful to

His promises of blessing to His people, but is also faithful to His warnings of judgment and will certainly, in the end, punish all forms of wickedness.

The Background to the Book

It is certain that the predominant world power in Nahum's day was Assyria, and its supremacy continued for many centuries. Although it is mentioned in the Old Testament as early as Genesis 2.14 and 25.18, it is not referred to in Israel's history until the northern kingdom of Israel paid tribute to the Assyrian king (2 Kings 15.19-20). God used Assyria, as His instrument, to punish Israel for its sin and idolatry, and Israel was ultimately taken into captivity (2 Kings 15.29; 17.3-18). The southern kingdom of Judah was oppressed by Assyria in the reign of Hezekiah who also paid tribute to it (2 Kings 18.13-16). "Assyria was a cruel nation which dominated and oppressed weaker kingdoms demanding homage and tribute. Its religion consisted in the worship of a range of minor deities under the head of Asshur who was the deified patriarch of the nation (Gen 10.22). Conquest of a country by the Assyrians resulted in the establishment in that country of the 'Laws of Asshur' and 'Altars to the Great Gods' which were in opposition to the teaching and practice of Judaism. Herodotus, the Jewish historian, records that the Assyrians were 'Lords of Asia' for 520 years" (C. G. Cann).

The downfall of Assyria and its capital city, Nineveh, in fulfilment of prophetic Scriptures, came through the revolt of Babylon and its alliance with the Medes. Their allied forces besieged Nineveh, and ultimately the city fell in keeping with this prophecy. Some years after the city's fall and the collapse of the Assyrian empire, the prophet Ezekiel wrote, "Asshur is there and all her company: his graves are about him: all of them slain, fallen by the sword: Whose graves are set in the sides of the pit, and her company is round about her grave: all of them slain, fallen by the sword, which caused terror in the land of the living" (32.22-23).

The Purpose of the Book

The message of God, through the prophet, was to encourage and comfort Judah. Oppressed by the mighty Assyrian power, which had overrun the entire region from the Tigris to the Nile rivers and had already carried away into captivity the ten tribes, Judah was dependent upon God alone for deliverance. The opening verses of the prophecy, describing the character of God and announcing the judgment of Nineveh, were intended to remind Judah of the goodness of God and prove to it that He was a refuge to all who put their trust in Him (1.7). The yoke that Assyria had placed upon Judah would be broken by Jehovah (1.13), and His people would again be able to keep their solemn feasts and perform their vows (1.15).

Nahum makes no reference to the sins of Judah neither does he call upon it to repent, but is solely taken up with the wickedness and approaching judgment of Assyria. Assyria thus becomes a lesson to the nations of the world, emphasising the principle of accountability to the Creator and His demand for the righteousness which exalts a nation (Prov 14.34). The prophecy is intended to testify to the moral government of God among the nations of the world. The fall of the great Assyrian empire and its capital city, which represents the world in its opposition to God and His people, foreshadows the certain and complete judgment of the godless world when its kingdoms will become the kingdoms of the Lord (Rev 11.15). God will triumph over His enemies - good will triumph over evil.

OUTLINE OF THE BOOK

The Title of the Book (1.1)

The Proclamation of Nineveh's Judgment (1.2-15)
 A. The divine character (1.2-8)
  1. The passion of God (1.2)
  2. The patience of God (1.3a)
  3. The power of God (1.3b-6)
  4. The provision of God (1.7-8)
 B. The divine contrast (1.9-15)
  1. The certain downfall of Nineveh (1.9-11)
  2. The comfort for Judah (1.12-15)

The Imagery of Nineveh's Destruction (2.1-13)
 A. The siege of Nineveh (2.1-8)
  1. The attacking army (2.1-4)
  2. The defenders and fall of the city (2.5-8)
 B. The spoiling of Nineveh (2.9-13)
  1. The deserted city (2.9-10)
  2. The den forsaken (2.11-13)

The Reasons for Nineveh's Overthrow (3.1-19)
 A. Judgment because of sin (3.1-7)
  1. Their lies and robbery (3.1-3)
  2. Their lust (3.4-7)
 B. Judgment unavoidable (3.8-19)
  1. The example of God's judgment (3.8-10)
  2. The execution of God's judgment (3.11-19)
   a) Nineveh's inadequacy (3.11-13)
   b) Nineveh's preparation and collapse (3.14-17)
   c) Nineveh deserted and obliterated (3.18-19).

 The book unfolds the fact of the unchanging nature of God in His dealing with nations as well as individuals. People may change, but God's principles remain and abide eternally. He is ever the same in His dealing with men and thus, in His longsuffering, He gives men and nations the required opportunity to repent of evil and turn to Him. However, the solemn lesson of the book is that God will not always forbear, and that rejecting and despising His mercy inevitably brings judgment.

It is interesting to trace the history of Nineveh in the Scriptures. Its first mention is in Genesis 10 and is there linked with the name Asshur. Its reign as the capital of Assyria is found abundantly in the historical and prophetical books. Its repentance is found in Jonah and its final ruin is predicted here.

NAHUM 1

The book of Nahum contains a majestic and significant presentation of the character and greatness of God. He is seen as God, the covenant keeping God, who is interested in His people's relationship with the nations around them. In this instance the haughty and cruel Assyrian nation is in view, which is representative of the pride and arrogance of the world. The boast of its capital city Nineveh, with its 100 feet (30 metre) high walls and strong towers, was that it was impregnable. This claim of Nineveh would be shattered by the judgment of God, just as the world's attempt to oppose God and His Son will be brought to naught (Ps 2; Rev 19.11-21).

This chapter unfolds the truth that God is the source of strength and comfort for His people as well as being just in His dealings with men and nations. It opens with the title of the book, indicating the subject matter and the prophet who proclaims and pens it (v.1). The majesty of a jealous God, who is the avenger of evil, is next set forth, and, although He is slow to anger, the wicked will inevitably be punished (vv.2-3a). The power of His wrath is then pictured in great tempests and upheavals in the world of nature, showing that His might is irresistible (vv.3b-6). He is good to those who put their trust in Him and He is their place of safety in the day of trouble (v.7). In contrast to this, His judgment is proclaimed upon the oppressor of His people, Assyria, and its capital city, Nineveh, which are to be completely destroyed (vv.9-11). God would break the yoke Assyria had laid upon Judah (vv.12-13), and the message of Assyria's destruction would be a source of comfort to, and a cause for rejoicing in, Judah (v.14-15).

Verse 1: The Title of the Book
The title in the opening statement is peculiar to the prophetic books in that the substance of the book and its object are mentioned first. The Hebrew word for "burden" (MASSA - 4853) is translated in a number of ways, but generally signifies a burden or weight. Some, as Strong's Concordance, have taken the figurative meaning as "utterance". However, MASSA in itself, never means "…utterance, and is never placed before simple announcements of salvation, but only before oracles of a threatening nature" (Keil & Delitzsch). It is translated "burden" as a responsibility to be borne (Num 11.11), a weight to be carried (2 Kings 5.17), and iniquities weighing one down (Job 7.20; Ps 38.4). It is rendered "tribute" as a burden to be paid in silver (2 Chr 17.11), and "carry away" as spoil too heavy to be removed (2 Chr 20.25). It is also translated "they set" referring to the heart's desire in the lifting up of one's soul (Ezek 24.25). In 1 Chronicles 15.22,27 it is given as "song" and is linked with the burden of responsibility when the ark was moved. C. F. Keil states: "Even in Proverbs 30.1 and 31.1 MASSA does not mean utterance. The words of Agur in Proverbs 30.1 are a heavy burden, which is rolled upon the natural and conceited reason; they are punitive in their character, reproving human forwardness in the strongest

terms; and in ch. 31.1 MASSA is the discourse with which King Lemuel reproved his mother". Where the word occurs in prophetic passages it proclaims heavy judgment upon nations because of wickedness and idolatry (eg. Is 15.1; 17.1; 23.1; Mal 1.1). Here, in Nahum, the word indicates that the book unfolds the inevitable judgment upon the oppressor of Judah, His people.

The object of this burden is Nineveh and by implication Assyria, of which it was the capital city until its destruction in 612 BC. Nineveh is not mentioned again until 2.8 and its mention there removes all obscurity from the earlier part of the prophecy. Although the literal city is in view, it is representative, not only of the nation, but also of all who oppose God, His people and His purpose.

The second clause, which could be viewed as a second title, states the form, source, and channel of the prophecy. The prophecy is in the form of a book which contains the vision that Nahum had received from God. This unusual combination of book and vision is only found here and seems to indicate that Nahum committed the vision to writing before orally proclaiming it to the people. The noun translated "book" (SEPER - 5612) means a writing and is used of legal documents ("bill" - Deut 24.1,3; Is 50.1; Jer 3.8, and "evidence" - Jer 32.10-16), official records (Gen 5.1, and "register" - Neh 7.5), divine commandments (Ex 24.7; Deut 17.18; Josh 1.8; 2 Kings 22.8), official letters (2 Sam 11.14-15; 2 Kings 5.5-7; Jer 29.1,29), historical events (1 Kings 11.41; 2 Kings 24.5), and prophetic announcements as here (cp. Is 30.8; Jer 25.13). All these would have been in the form of scrolls as the word is translated in Isaiah 34.4. The word "vision" (2377) refers to the revelation, given by God, of the downfall of Nineveh. It seems evident that the designation "Elkoshite" refers to the birth place of the prophet (see Introduction - The Prophet of the Book).

Verses 2-15: The Proclamation of Nineveh's Judgment

God, who is slow to anger, hates oppression of His people and is inflexible in judgment upon His enemies (vv.2-8) which would result in the destruction of Nineveh (vv.9-11). However, He is faithful in His promise to His people and comforts them in the day of affliction (vv.12-15).

The divine character (vv.2-8)

Having stated that God's judgment upon Nineveh is the subject of his book, the prophet emphasises the justice of that judgment by describing the character of God. Although He is longsuffering He will not allow guilt to go unpunished, but will display His justice in meting out punishment to those who deserve it. His judgment is righteous in its character, slow in its manifestation, and dreadful in its execution. His irresistible power is vividly portrayed in His control over the mighty storms and earthquakes on earth which indicates how awesome and terrible is His judgment. None can escape or stand before His wrath and fury. Thus, over against the oppression and cruelty of the Assyrians, Nahum places before the people of God, in forceful terms, the majesty and power of God, showing His passion (v.2), His patience (v.3a), His power (vv.3b-6), and His provision for them (vv.7-8).

The passion of God (v.2)
   This verse has been paraphrased thus by S. R. Driver:

> *"A jealous and avenging God is Yahweh,*
> *Yahweh is avenging, and full of wrath;*
> *Yahweh is avenging towards his adversaries,*
> *And he retaineth (wrath) against his enemies".*

   The prophet commences his description of God's character with the use of His name El (God - 410) meaning strength (cp. Ezek 32.21) and might (cp. Ps 29.1) which permeates this section. As such He is called "the Great, the Mighty God" (Jer 32.18). He does wonders (Ps 77.14), He is great and terrible (Deut 10.17; Neh 1.5), and is to be feared (Ps 89.7). This name occurs first in Genesis 14.18-24 - in the phrase, "the most high God". Under "Divine Titles" in the Introduction to the Newberry Bible it is stated that the name is in the singular and that "It is the title which shows God to be the Mighty One, the First Great Cause of all", and that "...in nature and essence God is one". This name is included in many Old Testament names - Bethel, Elijah, Ezekiel etc.
   The structure of the opening expression "God is jealous" is peculiar in the sense that the Hebrew word translated "jealous" (QANNO - 7072) is a noun and is only found elsewhere in Joshua 24.19. It can be viewed as another name for God as in Exodus 34.14 where a related noun QANNA is used (cp. Ex 20.5; Deut 4.24; 5.9; 6.15). One must not view the word "jealousy" when used of God in the same sense in which it is used of men. The verb form expresses a strong emotion and has the sense of zeal. When used of God it always conveys the idea of zeal for what is rightfully His. When used of men it is used of zeal for what is one's own and for what is another's. Here it expresses that God is jealous for His people's devotion, allowing no rivals (Ex 34.14), jealous over His people's welfare and for His own honour as their faithful God. He is jealous for His own glory, which He will not give to another (Is 42.8). The source of such jealousy is His great love for His people. It indicates a burning zeal which will not endure the honour due to Him or to His people being permanently withheld. The thought here is that His jealousy is aroused by the continual mistreatment of His people and so He turns the burning zeal of His wrath upon those opposed to Him and His people. He is zealous to defend His character and honour against His enemies as One who loves His people and punishes their enemies. Thus the jealousy of God, who is infinitely holy, is linked with the vengeance of God that follows (cp. Rom 1.18).

Christians ought to have the same kind of zeal for the things of God and for His glory. In the New Testament the same Greek words are translated as "jealousy", "zeal", and "fervent". The Apostle Paul had this burning zeal for the assembly in Corinth (2 Cor 11.2). All believers should be fervent in spirit (Rom 12.11), and have a burning zeal for good works (Tit 2.14).

Having commenced his prophecy with God's name El, Nahum continues it with God's name Jehovah (the Lord - 3068) which he uses throughout the rest of the prophecy. This name indicates that God is the unchanging eternal One and is the covenant keeping God. The threefold repetition of this sacred name, which is the subject of the three clauses, adds authority and emphasis to the verse. There is also a threefold repetition of the Hebrew word NAQAM (5358) translated "revengeth" and "vengeance", giving an awesome solemnity to the judgment that follows.

The vengeance of God flows from His holiness and justice which cannot allow sin to pass unpunished. As the God of justice He avenges all injustice (Deut 32.41; Rom 1.18-19). God's vengeance against sin (upon His people or others) is not the result of prejudice or obsessive anger and has no malice in it, but is based upon His unchanging holy character. Thus His response to any action, good or bad, is always righteous and is never too much or too little. Here the judgment on Nineveh serves as an example of the holiness and justice of God. C. G. Cann writes, "It is important to understand that the judgment is not vindictive. Vindictive judgment is hasty and capricious. We have here a principle which is in harmony with the character of Jehovah, 'He will not at all acquit the wicked' (1.3). Because it is principle, the judgment can wait unchanging and unchangeable so that the mercy of Jehovah, which is also principle, may operate. Jehovah's judgment never falls without warning and opportunity for repentance". The vengeance of Jehovah against Assyria is further emphasised by the word "furious" (CHEMA - 2534) which means possessor of fury, or master of fury. His fury is at His command and is meted out in His time. It contains the idea of being aroused to great or wrathful heat indicating that Jehovah is the wrathful God to those opposed to Him and His people. The prophecy has in view the Assyrians' provocation of Jehovah to fury by their treatment of His people. God is ever watchful over those that are His and will not overlook any wrong done to them (2 Thess 1.6). The indication here is that the enemies of His people are His enemies. He watches over His people and although He allows many things for their discipline and benefit He will never ignore how others treat them. He takes up their cause, and upon this fact faith rests.

The verb "reserveth" (NATAR - 5201) denotes keeping, or guarding, and indicates here the withholding of wrath until His own appointed time (Acts 17.31; 2 Pet 2.9). Jehovah, in His longsuffering, waits, giving opportunity for repentance, but at length His judgment falls upon the unrepentant. This suspending of judgment does not mean that He is insensible to sin, or indolent, but manifests His patience and His sovereignty in reserving judgment until the time He has appointed.

The patience of God (v.3a)

The opening statement of this verse does not contradict the statements of the previous one, but indicates Jehovah's patience in the face of provocation. Literally the statement reads, "Jehovah is long of anger", in contrast to being "soon angry" (Prov 14.17), and is translated "longsuffering" in Exodus 34.6 (cp. Num 14.18; Ps 86.15). Anger attributed to God, who is infinitely holy, is not inappropriate. When used in relation to Him it is always a holy and righteous anger. Nineveh had experienced the longsuffering of Jehovah in Jonah's day when He stayed His judgment so that it could repent, but here one notes that He will not always bear with the wickedness of Nineveh. God is slow to anger, but not as men count slackness (2 Pet 3.9). The Lord Jesus Christ displayed righteous anger in casting out those who sold and bought in the temple (Mt 21.12-13; Jn 2.13-16), and it is recorded that He looked on the Pharisees with anger because of the hardness of their hearts (Mk 3.5). Christians, who are in harmony with God, will know righteous anger against all that dishonours Him. However, one must take heed to the exhortation, "Be ye angry, and sin not" (Eph 4.26). Longsuffering here is not failure to act, but a display of the love and mercy of God (cp. Rom 2.4). It is one of the features of true love (1 Cor 13.4) and of the fruit of the Spirit (Gal 5.22). It should characterise every child of God (Col 3.12), and is that quality of self-restraint which does not hastily retaliate in the face of provocation. The perfect example is the Lord Himself, "Who, when he was reviled, reviled not again; when he suffered, he threatened not; but committed himself to him that judgeth righteously" (1 Pet 2.23). This is opposite to the maxims of the world – "I'll get even", and, "I'll get my own back". It is not easy to suffer long at the hands of others without retaliating in one way or another, but this is what the Lord requires of His own (Mt 5.44; Rom 12.17-21).

The power of God (vv.3b-6)

The fact that Jehovah is great in power shows that His longsuffering is not an indication of weakness. Patience and power are two complementary features of Jehovah's character. It is suggested that what is in view here is Jehovah's power to "hold back His anger, not vent His rage immediately" (Rabbi Rosenberg and S. R. Driver). Numbers 14.17-18 would seem to support this view. However, the context would suggest that, although He is longsuffering, He also is omnipotent and has the ability to destroy His enemies at any time. This is evident from the next expression, "…and will not at all acquit the wicked". The language here is the same as Exodus 34.7. The word rendered "acquit" (NAQA - 5352) means to be clean, pure (similar to Dan 7.9), and spotless. It is translated "blameless" (Judg 15.3), "free" (Num 5.19,28), "guiltless" (Ex 20.7; 1 Sam 26.9), "innocent" (Prov

6.29; Jer 2.35), and "unpunished" (Prov 11.21; Jer 25.29). Jehovah cannot, and will not, treat the guilty as innocent, hold blameless the guilty, or set free the wicked from all punishment. This is a solemn warning for all, even for believers. God will not tolerate unjudged sin. The principle is the same for both believer and unbeliever. If there is no self-judgment by the believer then that person will be judged by God (cp. 1 Cor 11.28-32). "The wicked" would indicate hardened and persistent sinners - "Let the wicked forsake his way, and the unrighteous man his thoughts: and let him return unto the Lord, and he will have mercy upon him" (Is 55.7). Sin ultimately leads to ruin and death (Rom 6.23; James 1.15).

The prophet gives a description of the power of Jehovah in judgment in vivid terms and in the form of a theophany that continues to the end of the passage giving a sublime picture of His greatness and majesty. His power is irresistible in whirlwind and storm (v.3), dreadful in drought and barrenness (v.4), and destructive in earthquake and volcanic eruption (v.5). Although what is primarily in view is the strength of His fury upon Nineveh, the prophecy does look on to that future great judgment upon the enemies of God and His people at the manifestation of the Lord Jesus Christ (cp. Is 13.10-13; 29.6-7; Rev 18; 19.11-21). The imagery is similar to that of Psalms 18.7-15 and 29.3-9. Jehovah in His vengeance will remove the Assyrian oppressor like a great storm sweeping all before it. The word meaning "whirlwind" (SUPA - 5492) is derived from a root word SUP (5486) and has the thought of consuming by its ferocity. It is used of God's wrath which shakes the world (Is 66.17; Jer 8.13; Zeph 1.2-3). There could also be the idea here that the vengeance of God may be suddenly executed like the appearance of a swift moving whirlwind. Jehovah comes down on the clouds which are the dust of His feet. In the Scriptures clouds are associated with the giving of the law (Deut 4.11), with the majesty of God (Ps 18.11-12; 97.2), with His omnipotence (Ps 68.34; 104.3), and His judgment (Is 19.1; Mk 13.26; Rev 1.7; 14.14). Nahum emphasises the greatness and grandeur of Jehovah by using an uncommon Hebrew word for "dust" (ABAQ - 80) which means small or fine dust, or powder. However majestic and glorious the clouds appear to men, they are but as fine dust to His feet.

Jehovah's power is further demonstrated in His ability to intervene in nature by drying up the sea and rivers (cp. Is 50.2; Jer 51.36). If Judah was reminded of the greatness of God at the exodus and Mount Sinai in the closing statements of v.3, it was reminded of His power at the Red Sea and Jordan by the opening statements of v.4. The stormy sea and the rivers heed His command just as the sea of Galilee responded to the command of the Lord Jesus Christ (Mt 8.26), proving that He is God. However, here the rebuke of Jehovah is generalised and extends to every sea and every river which He smites in His wrath. This may well be symbolic of Jehovah, in His vengeance, smiting Assyria and in the end times the nations (cp. Is 17.12-13; 57.20). Nahum uses two Hebrew words, HARAB (2717) and

YABESH (3001), which are similar in meaning, to convey the affect of Jehovah rebuking the sea and rivers. "The synonym *harab* is almost equivalent to *yabesh* though *harab* is employed more frequently to indicate bodies of water becoming dry, whereas *yabesh* is employed more often to portray dryness of vegetation" (TWOT). The use of YABESH in relation to the rivers is clearly linked with what follows since when it is used in regard to judgment it indicates the withholding of rain thus drying up the land to make it barren (Is 42.15; Jer 50.38; 51.36).

The three regions mentioned were the most fertile parts of the land, abounding in fruitful vegetation and forests. They were situated at the eastern, western, and northern boundaries of the country. Bashan was noted for its rich pasture, Carmel was remarkable for its vineyards and olive groves, and Lebanon was famous for its cedar forests. These are chosen to show that the most fruitful and prosperous areas or people cannot escape the wrath of Jehovah. He can cause their fruitfulness to disappear, their beauty to decay, and their prosperity to vanish. This may well be a picture of the fruitful military campaigns of the Assyrians when they plundered other nations (2.9), and the prosperity and pride of its capital Nineveh (Zeph 2.15).

The word "languisheth" (AMAL - 535) means to droop, describing a state of exhaustion and is rendered "waxed feeble" (1 Sam 2.5) and "weak" (Ezek 16.30). It is used to express the state into which objects are brought by the discipline or judgment of God (Is 19.8; Jer 14.2; Hos 4.3). Jehovah would cause the Assyrian empire to wither in the blast of His wrath and the proud and prosperous Nineveh would become desolate (2.10). One is reminded of a future prosperous city that in its pride will glorify itself, but in the hour of God's judgment will be destroyed and become desolate (Rev 18). The picture here could embrace that future day.

The theophany continues in v.5 with the effect of Jehovah's presence upon the mountains, hills, and world at large. The foundations of the earth also react to His presence. The word translated "quake" (RAASH - 7493) occurs about 30 times in the Old Testament, 21 of which are found in the prophetic books. It is translated "make...afraid" (Job 39.20), "moved" (Jer 49.21), and "remove" (Is 13.13), but mainly "shake" (16 times, eg. Is 24.18), and "tremble" (9 times, eg. Jer 10.10). The mountains are emblems of stability and permanence. The thought here is that the mountains which seem to be stable and unmoveable will be shaken. They are personalised and viewed as trembling in fear or terror in the face of the vengeance of Jehovah. The description might well point to an earthquake as when Sinai shook at the presence of God (Ex 19.18; Ps 68.8) continuing the thought of the last part of v.3. The indication is that the world power, which seems firmly established and unmoveable, would be shaken and would crumble in the face of the judgment of God. The hills would also melt at His presence. The verb "melt" (MUG - 4127) means to wax soft and, figuratively, to faint or fear. It is used of people fainting in fear of an enemy (Josh

2.9,24; Ezek 21.15), and of the judgment of God (Jer 49.23). It conveys the effect of judgment - dissolving or melting the enemy (Is 14.31) or the earth (Ps 46.6; 75.3). The picture of the hills melting is therefore figurative of helpless terror and of panic-stricken conditions produced by the wrath of Jehovah upon His enemies, indicating its destructive effect which causes ruling powers to totter and disappear from the scene. The Assyrian empire would tremble and the hearts of the Assyrians would melt with fear.

The meaning of the last part of v.5 is disputed because of the Hebrew word given as "burned"' (NASA - 5375) meaning to lift, but with a variety of applications, literal and figurative, absolute and relative (Strong's Concordance). Three meanings have been suggested.

1. The earth lifted up as in an earthquake. F. C. Cook states, "Most of the Ancient Versions seem to have adhered to the ordinary meaning of the word, which suits the passage well. What is peculiar here is, that though used in the active voice, the context requires that it should be understood reflexively, *lifts itself,* or *heaves,* as we say - a word most appropriate to an earthquake, to which there seems to be an allusion" (see also Keil & Delitzsch).

2. The earth being laid waste. D. W. Baker writes: "The result will be the laying waste (RSV) of the earth and all creatures on it, showing God's complete and universal power for building and destroying" (see also S. R. Driver).

3. The earth burned as in the AV. F. C. Cook points out that in adopting the rendering "burned" the "translators have followed Jewish authorities, as they have in 2 Samuel 5.21, where the marginal translation is better. The verb is a very common one, and means *to lift, to raise.* It has been supposed here to mean *burn,* because a derived substantive is used for *the rising* of smoke and flame. See Judges 20.38,40. Both verb and substantive occur together in Jeremiah 6.1 - *set up a sign of fire*", and Rabbi Rosenberg draws attention to the fact that "The Torah defines this as the earth's being burned (Deut 29.23). Redak also suggests that the phrase may refer to real fire, like that which destroyed Sodom and Gemorah".

Although most commentators favour the first suggestion, there is no reason to set aside the AV since it is supported by the mention of fire in the following verse and in the judgment of Nineveh (2.13; 3.13,15; cp. Is 13.19; Rev 18.18). The Creator holds to account the whole world, and in His zeal (jealousy) to protect the honour that belongs to Him alone He will judge it and all mankind will experience the result of His offended holiness. The mention of "the world, and all that dwell therein" indicates that the prophecy goes beyond the fall of the Assyrian empire.

The vengeance of Jehovah is stressed in v.6 by four Hebrew synonyms (indignation, fierceness, anger, and fury) and by the use of rhetorical questions compelling the answer, "No one" (cp. Mal 3.2; Rev 6.17).† Since Jehovah can so affect the mountains, hills, and the earth with its inhabitants it is certain that no one can stand against or face His indignation (Jer 10.10), i.e. His intense anger (Ps 7.11) or rage (Jonah 1.15) because of sin. The design of the question is to awaken the conscience. The word rendered "abide" (QUM - 6965) means to rise, and could have the idea here of rising up against the fierce wrath of God and successfully enduring it (cp. Job 8.15, where QUM is translated "endure"). However, none can endure the ferocity of His wrath. The fury that He possesses (reserveth, v.2) is poured forth like fire (cp. Gen 19.24), or the liquid fire of a volcano spreading in every direction (cp. Jer 7.20). The picture seems to be of volcanic eruptions uprooting rocks with streams of destructive fire. God is a consuming fire (Deut 4.24; 9.3; Heb 12.29). The Hebrew word for "thrown down" (NATAS - 5422) means to tear down, and is used of pulling down a tower (Judg 8.17), a city (Judg 9.45), altars (Judg 6.28; cp. Jer 1.10), and the ripping out of teeth (Ps 58.6). It seems to be used here figuratively of breaking down the power of nations opposed to God and His people. The power of Jehovah is irresistible and is used, in keeping with His character, to destroy those who oppose Him, and to accomplish His purposes.

Foolish are they who ignore the judgment of God or think that they can stand unscathed before His fierce wrath. Those who are wise will acknowledge their guilt and seek forgiveness and peace with God. This, of course, can only be achieved through repentance and faith in the Lord Jesus Christ and the work that He accomplished upon the cross. The repentant sinner who trusts the Lord Jesus Christ will never face the judgment of God, since the matter of that person's sin was dealt with at Calvary.

The provision of God (vv.7-8)

The combination of the patience and grace of God with the power and wrath of God in vv.2-3 is again evident in these verses. His fury does not extend to those who trust Him, but falls only upon His foes who oppress His people. Thus Nahum prepares the way for the judgment upon Nineveh which is set forth in the rest of the prophecy.

Having described the vengeance of Jehovah in the terms of a theophany, the prophet assures those who trust in Jehovah that He is good and a place of safety. Jehovah is good ethically, morally, and practically - God is "good and doest good" (Ps 119.68). His goodness was made known to Moses (Ex 33.19; 34.6), declared in the Psalms (52.1; 106.1; 145.7), proclaimed by Jeremiah in a time of judgment (Lam 3.25), and was emphasised by the Lord Jesus Christ (Mt 19.17), who displayed that goodness in His life (Acts 10.38). Creation itself is a manifestation of God's goodness (Ps 33.5), and His benevolence to all mankind proves that He is good (Ps 145.9; Mt 5.45). Above all, the giving of His Son to be the Saviour of sinners, and the various blessings of salvation, are wonderful displays of His unfathomable goodness. Even in His just severity Jehovah is good. The Targum adds, "Jehovah is good *to Israel*". In these verses the goodness of Jehovah is displayed towards His people in two ways - in being a stronghold for them in a day of trouble, and in judging their enemies, thus bringing deliverance to them (cp. Prov 18.10). The "strong hold" (MAOZ - 4581) indicates a place or means of safety (TWOT). It is translated in five different ways in Daniel 11 - "strength" (vv.1,31), "fortress" (vv.7,10), "fort" (v.19), "forces" (v.38), and "strong holds" (v.39). It is mainly translated "strength" (cp. 3.11) and is used of relying upon a foreign power for protection (Is 30.2-3). However, human strongholds are not invincible, but are subject to destruction (Is 17.9; 23.11,14). Elsewhere in the Scriptures (Ezek 24.20-21) the people of Israel, instead of resting in God for refuge, placed their confidence in the sanctuary for their protection only to discover the error of doing so - they had left God out of their lives. Jehovah alone is the security for His people (Joel 3.16), not only in the time of trouble (Ps 37.39), but at all times (eg. 1 Sam 22.23; Ps 27.1; 28.8) – "God is our refuge and strength, a very present help in trouble" (Ps 46.1; cp. Prov 14.26). He is a refuge to all mankind generally if they avail themselves of it (Ps 91.9). God, in His grace, has provided a place of refuge from His judgment against sin. That place of refuge is His own beloved Son who bore the tempest of sin's judgment on the cross (cp. Is 32.2) and put away sin by the sacrifice of Himself (Heb 9.26). Now all who repent and receive the Lord Jesus Christ as their personal Saviour enjoy that refuge, being justified by God, receiving forgiveness and knowing peace with God (Rom 3.24-26; 5.1; Col 1.14). Jehovah's knowledge of His own is all embracive (Gen 18.19; Ps 1.6; 37.18; 2 Tim 2.19). C. F. Keil quotes Calvin: "To know is just the same as not to neglect; or, expressed in a positive form, the care or providence of God in the preservation of the faithful". He knows and searches the heart (Acts 15.8; 1 Thess 2.4). Nothing is hidden from His all-seeing eye (Jer 16.17; 23.24; Heb 4.13). This is both a comfort and a challenge to believers and is solemn for unbelievers. It is a comfort to those of His people who are passing through trying times knowing that He knows, understands, and cares (1 Pet 5.7). It is challenging for the Christian to know that every word, thought, and action comes under the all-seeing eye of the Father, who is no respecter of persons, and judges according to every man's work, so we should pass the time here in godly fear - fear lest there is anything in one's life contrary to His character and will, or fear that one brings dishonour to Him (cp. 1 Pet 1.17). How careful the believer must be in one's life for God.

The word translated "trust" (HASA - 2620) means to seek refuge, or to put trust in. The context here favours the thought of those who take refuge in Jehovah (Ps 2.12; 57.1; cp. 1 Pet 1.5). He lovingly and tenderly cares for those who commit themselves to Him and promotes their well-being.

There is a different portion for those who reject and oppose Jehovah. Because He is the refuge for His people He will destroy those who oppose and oppress them with an overflowing flood. The expression "overrunning flood" is figurative of the irresistible judgment of Jehovah sweeping over the land and carrying all before it. The judgment of Jehovah, like a mighty flood that disdains all that seek to check it, will sweep away His enemies. It is used of overwhelming hostile armies invading a land (Is 8.7-8; 28.15; Dan 11.40). There may be an allusion here to the way Nineveh would be captured and destroyed - through flood waters destroying the foundations (see Introduction) thus allowing the besieging armies to enter. This is an anticipation of what is more fully described in the following chapters. The designation "the place thereof" in Hebrew is feminine - her place thereof - referring to the city Nineveh which is the subject of the book (v.1). This can be looked at in two ways.

1. Nineveh is personified as a queen (2.7; 3.4), but a full end would be made of her power and position (cp. Zeph 2.15).

2. The city of Nineveh would be completely destroyed, never to be rebuilt, so that even the place where it stood would not be known (3.17; cp. Job 7.10; 20.9). Both views are admissible although the second seems to be more acceptable. The enemies mentioned in the closing statement of v.8 refer to the inhabitants of Nineveh or the Assyrians in general, initially, and then to the armies arrayed against Israel in the end times. This rendering and meaning of the statement, "…darkness shall pursue his enemies", is disputed.

1. As rendered in the AV, this could refer to the intense terror produced by the judgment that would fall upon them (cp. Joel 2.2), or to the severe and successive calamities that would overtake them. The picture is of a defeated enemy pursued by a victorious army as night falls in order to destroy them (cp. Gen 14.15). The thought of darkness following implies that there would be no dawn for them, i.e. they would rise no more. This would be the parallel to the previous statement.

2. Another view, which follows the RV rendering – "…will pursue his enemies into darkness" – considers that the enemies of Jehovah would be driven into darkness (cp. Ps 35.6), i.e. they would disappear from the earth. Thus, as the city would vanish leaving behind no trace of its existence so would its inhabitants also vanish without trace.

Whichever view is taken the conclusion seems to be the same. Those who pursue a life of evil today love darkness rather than light and are under the condemnation of God (Jn 3.19). Should they remain unrepentant they will reap what they sow (Gal 6.7), for they will be cast into outer darkness (Mt 8.12; 22.13; Jude v.13).

The divine contrast (vv.9-15)

This passage contrasts the calamities that would overtake Assyria (vv.9-11) with the consolation for Judah as a result of Nineveh's downfall (vv.12-15). The opening section commences with a question (v.9) and continues with the destruction of the Assyrians because of their wickedness (v.10). Those who plot evil against Jehovah and instigate the destruction of His people will ultimately fall (v.11). Jehovah would break the Assyrian's yoke from off His people and they would be afflicted no more (vv.12-13) for both the Assyrians' name and their gods would be cut off (v.14). The section closes with good tidings being proclaimed of the oppressor's utter destruction (v.15).

The certain downfall of Nineveh (vv.9-11)

These verses can be viewed as introductory to the description given in chs.2-3 of the ruin of Nineveh. The question is thus asked indicating the power of God both to destroy Assyria and to deliver His people (v.9), the announcement is made of Nineveh's downfall (v.10), and the charge against the Assyrian is made (v.11).

Verse 9 opens with a question, but to whom is it addressed - the Assyrians or the people of God? This is disputed. D. W. Baker takes the view that "The writer addresses Assyria directly as 'you' (see RSV; the Hebrew verb is in the second person plural). Whatever Assyria 'plots' (RSV; cp. Dan 11.24; Hos 7.13) in opposition to Yahweh will come to nothing as a result of God's action (see v.8). So complete is this end that Assyria will not be troubled again, nor will she cause further trouble, because she will be no more" (see also Jamieson, Fausset & Brown). On the other hand, C. F. Keil is of the opinion that "The question in v.9a is not addressed to the enemy, viz. the Assyrians, as very many commentators suppose...the last clause does not suit this view of the question...Consequently the question, 'What think ye with regard to Jehovah?' can only be addressed to the Judaeans", and F. C. Cook writes, "Our AV has the same preposition (*against*) here and in v.11; it is otherwise in the Hebrew, in which there are two prepositions, and of these the one here employed does not mean *against*, but *with respect to*. And it is most improbable that the prophet would have used two different prepositions with the same verb, yet with the same meaning". W. J. Deane includes both standpoints stating, "The prophet suddenly addresses both Jews and Assyrians, encouraging the former by the thought that God can perform what He promises, and warning the latter that their boasting (cp. Is 10.9, etc.; 36.20) was in vain". The word translated "imagine" (HASHAB - 2803) is of no help in determining who is addressed since its basic idea is that of the employment of the mind (TWOT), and thus has a variety of meanings. The different Hebrew prepositions translated "against" here and in v.11 favour the thought of the people of God being addressed and this is supported by the last statement in the verse. The question is addressed to those who were anxious regarding further oppression and plundering by the Assyrians, and it was to stimulate their trust in Jehovah. In order to strengthen their confidence and dispel any doubts the prophet repeats the statement of v.8 concerning Jehovah making a full end of Nineveh and thus of Assyria. As strong as it was, He was already arranging events that would result in its downfall. Its destruction would be so complete that it would be impossible for it to repeat its oppression of the people of God. The word for "affliction"

(SARA - 6869) is rendered "trouble" in v.7 and describes the anguish and distress of oppression by an enemy. Such would never again be Judah's experience. This is further emphasised in the following verse.

The details of Jehovah's judgment upon Assyria and the reason for it are now given in v.10. D. W. Baker states, "Difficulties in text and syntax make this verse one of the most difficult to interpret in the Old Testament". The opening clauses of this verse are conditional – "For though they be or were they even...they shall be...". The expression "folden together" (SABAK - 5440) is only found elsewhere in Job 8.17 where it is translated "wrapped about" and means closely entangled, or intertwined. The image of entangled thorns represents the Assyrians in their boasted strength as being untouchable (2 Sam 23.6), with a supposed impenetrable front to defy any attack (cp. Is 27.4). However, just as intertwined thorns are vulnerable to destruction by fire so the Assyrians would be unable to escape the fiery wrath of Jehovah (cp. 2 Sam 23.6-7). The image indicates not only that the Assyrians would be destroyed together in the judgment of Jehovah, but also the swiftness of their destruction. The combination of the Hebrew verb SABA (drunken - 5433) and the Hebrew noun SOBE (wine - 5435) conveys the thought of being drenched in wine and thus sodden drunkards (cp. Is 5.11). This allegory also expresses the boastful confidence of the Assyrians who considered that they were so invincible, and had such a sense of security, that they had nothing to fear. The Assyrian court was known for its luxury, revelry and gluttony. There may be an allusion to the drunken revelries during which the foe broke into the city of Nineveh (W. J. Deane; Keil & Delitzsch). The comparison to drunkards is appropriate, for, although they are exulting, self-confident and boastful, yet they are weak, vulnerable and easily overthrown. D. W. Baker notes that "The two metaphors of fire and drunkenness are mixed, and the syntax makes the exact nature of the comparison unclear, resulting in variations between different translations, but what is clearly portrayed is the certainty of God's punishment". The figure of being consumed by fire as dry stubble signifies utter destruction of what is worthless and refers to the Assyrians who are only fit for judgment. The tense here indicates the certainty of an event yet future. The adverb "fully" (MALE - 4392) is better taken with the verb "devoured" (AKAL - 398), but is placed at the end for emphasis - consumed fully, or altogether consumed, as dry stubble.

Most take v.11 as an allusion to Sennacherib, king of Assyria, who had invaded Judah and, through his general Rabshakeh, had blasphemed Jehovah (Is 36.13-20). However, since Nahum prophesied after Sennacherib's day (see Introduction - The Period of the Book) it cannot refer to him. The address of Rabshakeh in Hezekiah's day indicated the attitude of the Assyrian empire throughout its whole existence. This is also the attitude of the world today in its opposition to God and His people. The word "one" in the opening statement is not in the original text, and the pronoun "thee" is feminine which, in the context, must refer to Nineveh.

Although this could be a reference to the Assyrian king at the time of the prophecy, it seems rather to indicate the imperial power of Assyria represented by its capital city Nineveh. That power, in its arrogant idolatry, set itself against God and, having taken the kingdom of Israel into captivity, sought to oppress and destroy the kingdom of Judah. Although the Hebrew word for "imagineth" can be used in v.9 of "thinking", here it has the idea of devising, planning, or plotting evil. The devising of evil against Jehovah refers to the Assyrians' intention of destroying the people of God. Any design of evil against His people is evil designed against Jehovah Himself. One is reminded of the words of the Lord to Saul on his journey to Damascus to persecute the Christians there – "Saul, Saul, why persecutest thou me?" (Acts 9.4).

In this verse "wicked" (BᵉLIYAAL - 1100) means worthless or unprofitable, but it can express the idea of being unprincipled or villainous. Although it is used as a proper noun, "Belial", in a number of passages (eg. Deut 13.13; Judg 20.13; 1 Kings 21.10), it seems to be used here of the useless plans of Assyria to destroy the people of God. This premeditated, wicked attack upon God and His people is, in keeping with His justice, the reason for the destruction of Nineveh and the Assyrian empire. This verse may well be a picture of the last world power opposed to God and His people in the end times and in particular the Antichrist who will head that power.

The comfort for Judah (vv.12-15)

The same ground seems to be covered here as in vv.9-11, but now Jehovah is the speaker and the subject is approached from a different viewpoint. Whereas in vv.9-11 the emphasis is upon the destruction of Nineveh, the focus here is upon the encouragement and comfort of Judah. Jehovah addresses Judah first, giving it assurance of deliverance from the Assyrian oppression (vv.12-13). He then turns to Nineveh confirming emphatically the certainty of its destruction (v.14). The passage closes with the glad tidings of Judah's freedom to keep the Feasts of Jehovah and to fulfil their vows (v.15).

The opening expression of v.12, "Thus saith the Lord", gives both solemnity and certainty to the passage. It emphasises the solemnity of opposition to God and His people, and the certainty of the Assyrian's destruction and Judah's liberation from oppression. Therefore the passage is a message of hope to the people of God. Jehovah would take up their cause and fulfil His covenant promises. The word translated "quiet" (SHALEM - 8003) means to be complete or sound. It is given as "quiet" only here and is rendered once elsewhere as "peaceable" (Gen 34.21) which could give the idea here of the Assyrians being tranquil, free from fear, and having a sense of security. However, SHALEM generally has the idea of fullness or completeness and is used of iniquity being full (Gen 15.16), of a full reward (Ruth 2.12), of a complete weight (Deut 25.15 - perfect; Prov 11.1 - just), and of complete stones and a complete nation (Deut 27.6;

Amos 1.6,9 - whole). The thought here is that Assyria was in full strength, complete in all that was needful for battle, lacking nothing to give security. It stresses the might of the Assyrian empire and the strength of Nineveh's defences. The expression "...likewise many" adds another dimension in Assyria's favour indicating that the Assyrian army was not only fully equipped and strong, but it was also full in number, i.e. numerous. However, neither the might and completeness of its army nor the greatness of its numbers would avail in the day of Jehovah's judgment, for they would be cut down. "Cut down" (GAZAZ - 1494) means to shear, or to mow, and is used of shaving the hair (Job 1.20; Jer 7.29) and of shearing sheep (Gen 31.19; Deut 15.19). The idea here of the Assyrians being mowed down, in spite of their boasted might, is figurative of their complete destruction, bringing deliverance to the people of God. One is reminded of the sharp sickle used to gather into the winepress of the wrath of God in a coming day (Rev 14.17-20; cp. Is 63.1-4). There are different views as to the rendering and interpretation of the phrase "when he shall pass through".

1. Jamieson, Fausset & Brown state, "(The) English Version is better, 'they shall be cut down, when He (Jehovah) shall pass through' destroying by one stroke the Assyrian host. This gives the reason why they with all their numbers and power are to be so utterly cut off. Compare 'pass through' i.e., in destroying power (Ezek 12.12,23; Is 8.8; Dan 11.10)".

2. W. J. Deane writes, "'When he shall pass through'; better, *and he shall pass away*. The number is changed, but the same persons are meant, spoken of as one to show their insignificance and complete annihilation" (see also Keil & Delitzsch and F. C. Cook).

The Hebrew verb for "pass through" (ABAR - 5674) does not help as it contains both the thought of passing through and passing away. The fact that Jehovah is the speaker favours the second view for if the phrase referred to Him the personal pronoun would have been used. Also the thought of the Assyrians vanishing away enhances the mention of their destruction in the previous statement (cp. vv.8-10).

In the latter part of v.12 Jehovah turns to address Judah in words of comfort, assuring His people that they would not be afflicted again by Assyria. This looks on to the final judgment of the Assyrian in a future day (Is 10.24-11.16). It is evident that the oppression by Assyria was indeed the affliction of Jehovah Himself upon His people because of their departure from Him (Is 10.5-7). There are two elements of judgment in the verse - on the one hand judgment of what was wrong in His own people and on the other judgment upon their merciless oppressors. The first was a chastening judgment for the benefit of Judah, the other a judgment of destruction because of the wickedness of Assyria. The principle of punishment for sin is not set aside by God for His own people. It still operates, but in a different way and for a different purpose. To God, sin in the believer's life is as displeasing and unacceptable as in an unbeliever's life. In both, sin must be dealt with in order that His holiness might be satisfied. In the case of Assyria it was dealt with by complete destruction without mercy, but in Judah it was to chastise and bring about recovery. One notes that God used affliction to humble and prove the Israelites in the wilderness that they might walk in His ways and fear Him (Deut 8.1-6). In the unbeliever, where there is no repentance, it will ultimately mean eternal judgment. In the case of the Christian it is corrective chastisement for a measured time that the believer might live more faithfully in keeping with His word. The affliction that God allows in the lives of His people can be educational (Job 42.1-5), preventative (2 Cor 12.7), or retributive (1 Cor 11.30).

Verses 13-14 couple together the severity of the judgment of God upon Assyria and the blessing of God upon His people (cp. vv.7-8). Verse 13 gives the reason for the assurance of no further oppression upon Judah by confirming how it would be brought about. Jehovah would break the yoke Assyria had laid upon Judah. The word translated "yoke" (MOT - 4132) actually refers to the bar across an animal's neck which became a name for the whole yoke. The figure of a yoke implies some form of bondage that benefits another (cp. Lev 26.13; Jer 28.10-14). The yoke here refers to the burden of tribute laid upon Judah by the Assyrian kings right from the reign of Ahaz (2 Kings 16.7-8; 18.13-16). Although this yoke was relieved in Hezekiah's reign by the overthrow of Sennacherib, king of Assyria, it was never completely cast off as is seen in the reign of Manasseh (2 Chr 33.11). This yoke would only be completely broken by the overthrow of Assyria and the destruction of its capital, Nineveh. The following expression refers to the ropes that bound the yoke to the animals' necks and indicates here the firmness of Assyria's hold upon Judah. The unjust edicts were like strong bonds fastening the yoke to Judah. However, the burdensome tyranny of Assyria would be completely removed in the judgment of Jehovah as chains were snapped (Jer 30.8), and thus Assyria would vanish from the scene.

In v.14 the prophet addresses the enemies of Judah, announcing that a commandment from Jehovah had gone forth concerning them. The idea is that Jehovah had decreed the destruction of the Assyrians and that He would provide the means to accomplish what he had commanded. His purpose had already been formed and declared although its execution was still future. "Concerning (or against) thee..." - since the pronoun "thee" in Hebrew is masculine, some commentators state that Sennacherib, king of Assyria in Hezekiah's reign, is in view. C. L. Feinberg points out that "The prophet has not yet concluded his word of threatening to the God-defying Sennacherib. It is not a general word of judgment upon Assyria and Nineveh, but directly addressed to the king of Assyria. The Lord pronounces through Nahum the extinction of Sennacherib's dynasty. No future rulers will bear the name of his ruling house...Even the place of Sennacherib's death is here indicated: the temple of his gods. While worshipping his gods, his sons slew him (2 Kings 19.37; Is 37.38)" (see also Jamieson, Fausset & Brown). However, as stated in respect of v.11, the prophecy is post Sennacherib's day. Keil & Delitzsch take the view that "It is not the king of Assyria who is here addressed, but the Assyrian power personified as a single man". It is better to take the pronouns in this verse as the personification of the Assyrian people rather than a reference to the king of Assyria himself. The Assyrian empire would reach its end because its people would be annihilated so that there would be none left to perpetuate the name (cp. Deut 7.24; Is 14.20-22), thus it would become extinct.

Jehovah speaks to the Assyrians, declaring that not only would they be cut off, but also their temple worship and their many idols would be destroyed. Just as it was the practice of the Assyrians to desecrate the shrines and to destroy the idols of the nations they conquered (2 Kings 19.17-18), so their own temples and idols would be destroyed. The graven (PESEL - 6459) image is an idol carved out of wood or hewn out of stone (cp. Is 37.19), while the molten (MASSEKA - 4541) image is an idol made by pouring molten metal into a mould (Ex 32.4,24). Where these two Hebrew words are together as here, they denote every kind of idolatrous image (see Deut 27.15; Judg 17.3; Hab 2.18). It is stated that the Medes under Cyaxares hated idolatry, so that when they captured Nineveh, together with the Babylonians, they would have delighted in destroying its idols. Thus, the Assyrian power, along with its idolatry in which it trusted, would be utterly destroyed, i.e. the whole nation is viewed as doomed to be laid in the grave. The reason is given in the closing phrase, "for thou art vile". It seems that "vile" is used here in "...its now obsolete sense (derived directly from the Latin *vilis* - cheap) of *common* or *of small account*" (S. R. Driver). Here, "vile" (QALAL - 7043) means to be light or slight. It does not mean vile in the modern sense of morally detestable. It is also translated "curse" (Gen 8.21; Josh 24.9) and "light" (1 Sam 18.23; 1 Kings 16.31). The thought therefore could be that the Assyrians were cursed of God or that they had been found light in the balances of God (cp. Dan 5.27). It could also mean that they were lightly esteemed by Jehovah (cp. 1 Sam 2.30) because of their idolatry and opposition to His people. Whatever view is taken it is clear that the judgment of the Assyrians would be in keeping with the justice and holiness of God.

Verse 15 looks forward to what would happen after the destruction of the Assyrian empire at the fall of Nineveh. In the Hebrew text this verse begins ch.2. The destruction announced in v.14 is so sure that the prophet gives a description of the joyful proclamation of its fulfilment and an appeal to Judah to keep the feasts and to fulfil its vows with gladness. The opening word, "Behold", is an interjection demanding attention - Look, See! It draws attention to the fact of Nineveh's downfall and the joyful news of that fact. Nahum sees the messengers upon the mountains of Judah gladly hastening to bring good tidings to Jerusalem and the people of God. The glad tidings of the gospel are proclaimed in this day of grace, announcing deliverance from the bondage of sin and Satan through faith in Christ. Just as the destruction of Assyria meant peace for Judah, so the overthrow of the devil and the powers of darkness by the Lord Jesus Christ on the cross (Col 2.15) means peace for all who believe (Rom 5.1). It is suggested that the messengers appear on the mountains to indicate that their voice would be heard far and wide. "Publisheth" (SHAMA - 8085) means to hear, or to give attention to and indicates here that the messengers of peace would be joyfully welcomed and received. This first part of the verse is almost identical to Isaiah 52.7. Here it is linked with deliverance from Assyria; in Isaiah it is linked with deliverance from Babylon; it is descriptive of Messianic salvation (Is 40.9; Rom 10.15). These words also look to the end times when the world power, typified by both Assyria and Babylon, will be destroyed and when the Lord Jesus Christ Himself will proclaim peace which will never be broken. William Kelly states, "It would appear that Israelites will go out to the nations with the testimony of the kingdom after the destruction of the Assyrian and their settlement in the land. Thus the word of Jehovah will spread far and wide, backed by the power which has interfered on behalf of His people so conspicuously. For the knowledge of Jehovah and of His glory is to cover the earth, as the waters cover the sea; and Israel will be the messengers of it among the nations".

The prophet himself summons Judah to keep the feasts and perform the vows made. While the Assyrians oppressed Judah, it was not possible for it to keep the appointed feasts at Jerusalem, but now there is freedom once more to keep them and to offer thanksgiving to Jehovah for deliverance. Instead of terror and fear, the people of God would now have peace to fulfil their ceremonial obligations and to perform the vows they made when oppressed. This indicates the responsibility that rests upon those who have experienced the salvation of God. Deliverance from the bondage of sins gives believers the privilege of worshipping and serving God. Are Christians grasping the opportunity to express their gratitude to God for His salvation by living for Him now? Nahum, having summoned Judah in this way, gives his reason - the Assyrians would never again pass through the land as conquerors for they have been cut off. The Assyrian power is again personified as a single man, embracing the whole nation.

Notes

6 <u>Rhetorical Questions.</u> Different literary forms or genres serve different functions. That of prophecy is to persuade the hearers to a certain course of action in the light of God's revelation through the prophet. This persuasive function is also that of classical rhetoric, which used certain techniques to achieve its aims. Many of those techniques can also be discerned in Hebrew prophecy, including the use of rhetorical questions.

Unlike a regular question, which is soliciting information, a rhetorical question assumes the answer is already known by both the asker and the asked. Instead of the statement which could have been used in its place, the rhetorical question forces the hearer to become actively involved in the discussion. By his response in replying with the known answer, the hearer himself takes part in the process of persuasion. The technique is used elsewhere in Nahum (2.11; 3.7-8) and in other prophetic texts.

For further discussion in the use of rhetoric, including rhetorical questions, in other prophetic texts, see Y. Gitay, *Prophecy and Persuasion: A study of Isaiah 40-42* (Linguistica Biblica, 1981). See also D. W. Baker.

NAHUM 2

Verses 1-13: The Imagery of Nineveh's Destruction

In this chapter Nahum turns from the glad tidings of Judah's deliverance to the details of Nineveh's overthrow. The description of her destruction, which is the central theme of the prophecy, is vivid and graphic. Jehovah's supreme power and control of events on earth are evident in the chapter. God is sovereign and orders the various nations according to His eternal purposes, and none can resist His might. He sends a powerful army to conquer and destroy Nineveh, and to avenge the dishonour brought upon His people. Thus Nineveh would be besieged by a mighty army (vv.1-8). The prophet describes the attack upon the city (vv.1-4) and its defence which, although formidable, would be to no avail (vv.5-8). The plundering of Nineveh would follow its capture (vv.9-13), and it would become deserted (vv.9-10) and destroyed, leaving behind no trace of its existence (vv.11-13).

The siege of Nineveh (vv.1-8)

Assyria, which attacked and oppressed other nations, would itself be attacked and its capital city, Nineveh, would be besieged. The Assyrians would experience the same as they had mercilessly inflicted upon others. The invading army would surround the city bringing fear to its inhabitants (vv.1-4), but the attempt to defend it would fail and the Assyrians would flee from it (vv.5-8).

The attacking army (vv.1-4)

The prophet challenges Nineveh to defend itself in view of the judgment that was about to fall upon it because of the way Israel had been treated by it. Nahum depicts the invading army advancing openly towards Nineveh and the way in which it orders itself for battle. The onslaught of the enemy would be irresistible and its appearance would strike terror into the defenders of Nineveh.

Since chs.2 and 3 are taken up with the destruction of Nineveh, it must be the Assyrians who are addressed in the opening verse. Nahum sees, in vision, a mighty army "coming up against Nineveh, proudly resting in her glory on the banks of the Tigris. Founded by Nimrod, as was also the rival Euphratean city Babylon, the one sets forth the world in its grandeur and independence of God; the other, the religious world, the home of superstition and traditionary ritual" (H. A. Ironside). The invading army is personified as one that "dasheth in pieces", the word for which (PUS - 6327) is a primitive root meaning to scatter, to be dispersed, or to dash in pieces (Strong's Concordance). It is first used of the Canaanites being scattered (Gen 10.18 – spread abroad), and then of the desire of those at the tower of Babel and their being scattered abroad (Gen 11.4,8-9). It is most often translated "scatter", and is mainly used in the prophetic books, particularly in Jeremiah (ten times) and Ezekiel (eighteen times). Since it is rendered "breaketh" in Jeremiah 23.29 some commentators have linked it with the expression "battle axe" (Jer 51.20), applying it to Cyaxares and Nabopolassar, the leaders of the Medo-Babylonian army that destroyed Nineveh. However, in Hebrew the expression, "He that dasheth in pieces", is "The scatterer", which conveys the idea of one that devastates, indicating that Nineveh would not only be besieged by the invading army, but would also be destroyed and its inhabitants scattered.

The phrase, "come up before thy face", implies that the might of their enemies besieging the city would be evident to the defenders of Nineveh. The verb "come up" (ALA - 5927) is used elsewhere of military attacks (1 Kings 20.22; 2 Kings 18.13).

Nineveh is called upon to prepare herself for attack by making every effort to fortify herself. The Hebrew word for "munition" (MᶜSURA - 4694) refers to a stronghold (2 Chr 11.11) or the "fencing" of a city (2 Chr 11.10; 12.4; 21.3). Here it embraces all the fortifications of the city. The call to Nineveh to strengthen herself is considered by some as being ironic in view of her destruction because of her sin. However C. F. Keil takes the view that "This is not irony, but simply a poetical turn given to the thought, that Nineveh will not be able to repulse this enemy any more". The word "watch" (SAPA - 6822) conveys the idea of being fully aware of a situation and thus not being surprised by the enemy (TWOT). They were to be alert as to the way the enemy would approach so that they would be ready to repulse it and prevent it from gaining an entrance into the city.

The loins, indicating the seat of strength, were to be made firm for the conflict. The idea seems to be a call for courage in the face of the enemy's onslaught (cp. Jer 46.3-6). The last expression of v.1 reiterates what has been stated in order to emphasise the need for strength. They were to strengthen, or make firm, their ability to resist, displaying both physical power and intelligent strategy. However, no amount of preparation to defend the city would succeed in preventing a devastating defeat because Nineveh could not escape the richly deserved judgment of Jehovah. This call to preparation for the fight is a fitting introduction to the vivid battle scenes that follows in this and the following chapter.

It has been suggested that v.2 is misplaced and "would more naturally follow 1.15" (S. R. Driver). Verse 2 refers to the oppression of Judah and looks back to the invasion and captivity of Israel when God used the heathen nation Assyria as an instrument in His hand to punish His people because of their disobedience and departure from Him. However, the time had come for the punishment of Assyria for its idolatry and wickedness. Since God could not pass over the sin of His own people, He must deal righteously with the wicked nations. It is again the principle stated in 1 Peter 4.17-18. The opening word "For" is really linked with the opening statement of v.1. The thought in this verse is that Nineveh would be completely destroyed by the advancing army because Jehovah is about to restore the glory of Israel that Assyria had destroyed. The word translated "turned away" (SHUB

- 7725) means to turn or return. It has the thought here of turning or bringing back. It seemed that Jehovah had forsaken His people when He allowed Assyria to invade, remove, and oppress them. However, He was but using that nation to fulfil His purpose for His people and now He would avenge the wrongs done to them and restore them to their inheritance.

The root of the Hebrew word for "excellency" (GAON - 1347) means to mount up and the word itself is given elsewhere as "majesty" (Is 2.10,19; Micah 5.4), and "pomp" (Is 14.11; Ezek 32.12), but mainly "pride" (Jer 13.9; Hos 7.10). The reference here is to what Jacob, Israel, is justly proud of or glories in. It has been suggested (C. L. Feinberg; F. C. Cook; Keil & Delitzsch; and Jamieson, Fausset & Brown) that it signifies the land of Canaan as distinct from other countries (Ps 47.4), or all the privileges and honours Jehovah had invested in His chosen people and which the enemy had taken away (Amos 6.8; 8.7), or Jerusalem and the temple (Ps 87.2; Ezek 24.21). The word may include all the above. However, the dwelling of the glory of Jehovah in their midst would be Israel's greatest boast or honour. That glory departed from the temple and Jerusalem when Judah was taken into captivity, which Ezekiel saw in a vision (Ezek 8.2; 9.3; 10.18-19; 11.22-23), but will return in the Millennium, when Israel is restored to the land, to Jerusalem, and the rebuilt temple (Ezek 40.2; 41.1; 42.1; 43.1-5; 44.4). What a glorious day that will be for the nation of Israel (cp. Rom 11.26-27).

There are two suggestions in regard to the terms "Jacob" and "Israel".

1. That "Jacob" refers to the southern kingdom of Judah and "Israel" refers to the northern kingdom of Israel. D. W. Baker writes, "Yahweh's restoration of 'Judah's' (MT 'Jacob's') splendour is hoped to parallel that of Israel in the north. A rebuilding of the entire people of God is desired, since they had been completely 'plundered' (cp. Is 24.1,3) by Assyria and Babylonia. Thus, even after the fall of the northern kingdom, a complete restoration of the nation is desired (cp. Ezek 37.15-23; Zech 10.6-12) though not yet actualised in the form of a restored and unified nation", and S. R. Driver maintains that "Jacob - in poetry (e.g. Gen 49) and the higher prose style, a synonym of *Israel* - must here, (from the context) denote *Judah* (as Is 43.1; 44.1)".

2. That both terms refer to the whole nation of Israel. F. C. Cook states, "*Jacob* and *Israel* are taken by many as representing the kingdoms of Judah and Israel respectively, though it would not be easy to find another place where the two names are thus used. Perhaps Jacob and Israel are designations of the whole people, as in Ps 78.21 *Jacob* was the name given by man, *Israel* that conferred by God", and C. F. Keil contends that "*Jacob* does not stand for Judah, nor *Israel* for the ten tribes, for Nahum never refers to the ten tribes in distinction from Judah…Both names stand here for the whole of Israel (of the twelve tribes)…Jacob is the natural name which the people inherited from their forefather, and Israel the spiritual name which they had received from God". Whichever position is taken it is evident in the passage that the whole nation is in view and that Jehovah

will restore it to the excellence it had lost. He will exalt the nation, not only restoring what had been taken away by Assyria, but give to it a more lofty excellency by bringing it into the fullness of its inheritance as His chosen people which they had never before possessed.

The following clause, "for the emptiers have emptied them out, and marred their vine branches", gives the reason why God will restore His people. Although judgment would fall upon their enemies because they had behaved with cruelty, the reason given here for that judgment and for Israel's restoration is because those enemies had plundered them and removed them from the land, in particular the Assyrians. Their enemies, as God's instrument, had inflicted the full measure of the chastisement of God upon them because of their failure and departure from Him and so now He would restore them. The words "emptiers" and "emptied" (BAQAQ - 1238) mean to pour out and have the thought here of depopulate (cp. Is 24.1-3). In their spoiling of the people of God, their enemies had marred the vine branches.

The image of the "vine" refers to Israel as seen in Psalm 80 (cp. Is 5 and Jer 12.10). The branches may indicate families that populated the land given to Israel, but it is also suggested that they refer to the cities in the land.

Having given the divine reason for the judgment of Assyria, in v.2, the prophet continues in v.3 the theme of v.1 depicting the advancing army against Nineveh in its appearance with colourful uniforms, bright weapons, and the noise and flashing of its chariots. The mighty men refer to the heroes or champions of the army. Some take the pronoun "his" as a reference to the destroyer of v.1 while others believe it refers to Jehovah in v.2 who has summoned the army against Nineveh (cp. Is 13.3).

The word for "shield" (MAGEN - 4043) refers to the small shield carried by the light infantry, officers, or particular men as here. It is used of God as the protector of His people (Deut 33.29; Prov 30.5). There is uncertainty as to the shield "made red" and thus at least three propositions have been made as to its meaning. The suggestion that the shields are stained with blood because of the battle does not have much support and would not suit the context since the verse presents the appearance of the army and not the actual battle. Secondly, some think that the shields were made of, or overlaid with, copper giving them a reddish colour, particularly when reflecting the sun. Thirdly, "Calvin suggested that the ancient warriors dyed their bull's hide shields red to frighten the enemy and especially in order that the blood from their own wounds might not be seen to give confidence to the enemy" (C. L. Feinberg). This last suggestion is supported by the fact that the Hebrew word for "made red" (ADOM – 119) is translated elsewhere "dyed red" (Ex 25.5; 39.34). Whichever view is taken, the idea seems to be of that which strikes terror into the enemy. The invaders are not described as mere fighting men, but as mighty men of valour (valiant - HAYIL - 2428; cp. Josh 1.14; Judg 11.1; 1 Chr 5.24) clothed in scarlet or crimson (cp. vermillion - Ezek 23.14).

The word "torches" (PᵉLADA - 6393) is from an unused root (Strong's Concordance) and only occurs here in the Old Testament. It means iron or steel and some take it as a reference to steel scythes. C. L. Feinberg notes that "In order for the chariots to flash with steel, scythes were put at right angles to the axles of the chariots...At times they also projected from the ends of the axles...It is known that the scythed chariots were already in use among warring nations in the time of Nahum". However, F. C. Cook states, "More probably it means a fine kind of iron or steel, and the plural may be used to describe the parts of the chariots, or ornamental trappings made of this metal, which, when the light played upon them, flashed like fire: lit. the chariots (not 'shall be' but) are with fire of steel, i.e. sparkle and flash with steel". C. F. Keil supports this: "But *pᵉladoth* are not scythes, which would suggest the idea of scythe-chariots...for scythe chariots were first introduced by Cyrus, and were unknown before his time to the Medes". The thought seems to be that of chariots of metal flashing in the sunlight (cp. Josh 17.16).

The last clause refers to the spears made from the fir tree held up and shaken to show the eagerness of the warriors for battle and to bring fear to the enemy.

Verse 4 is a striking portrayal of the wild disorder that would prevail when the attacking army assaulted Nineveh. Once the battle had commenced the adrenalin would run high and the chariots would rage in the streets (cp. Jer 46.9). The idea in "rage" (HALAL - 1984) is that of madness and is translated that way in 1 Samuel 21.13 (cp. Jer 25.16). Here it indicates that the chariots would be driven furiously at a reckless speed (2 Kings 9.20). The phrase "justle one against another" (SHAQAQ - 8264), portrays people running or rushing to and fro (cp. Is 33.4) in such a way that they appear as if they crash into one another. The word for "broad ways" (RᵉHOB - 7339) is also translated "broad places" (Jer 5.1), "street" (Gen 19.2; 2 Chr 32.6), and "streets" (Jer 49.26; Zech 8.5). It refers to open areas like squares and market places which are public places, and here indicates those places in the suburbs surrounding the walled inner city of Nineveh as is evident from the following verse. The chariots with their gleaming metal parts, and occupied by colourful warriors, appear as flaming torches and flashing lightning as they speed around these open places.

The defenders and fall of the city (vv.5-8)

D. W. Baker includes v.5 in the attack on the city stating, "The soldiers, mustered by their leader, stumble in their haste to reach the wall, where they set up a protective shield ('mantlet', RSV), a portable cover to protect the besiegers from objects hurled from the walls under attack. Some interpret this as a reference to the defending forces (eg. AV), but the grammatical reference to the musterer ('he summons', NIV) appears best to have as its antecedent the 'scatterer' of v.1". However, it seems clear that the subject is different at the beginning of v.5 because of the change from

the plural in vv.3-4 to the singular. The pronoun "He" looks back to the
pronoun "thy" in v.1, indicating that the Assyrian, or the Assyrian king, is in
view. This is also confirmed by the context which indicates the attempt to
defend Nineveh from capture.

On seeing the enemy with their swift chariots attacking the walled city,
the king of Assyria brings to mind the courage and achievements of his
mighty warriors. He believed that they would be able not only to defend
the city, but also to defeat the invading army. However, his thoughts, like
many others, were wrong and not in keeping with the purpose of God.
How often is this true of the believer and the unbeliever? The word "walk"
(HALIKA - 1979) indicates the way or going, and refers to the defendants
rush to defend the city. The verb "stumble" (KASHAL - 3782) is generally
used of physical falling. When suddenly summoned, the defenders stumble
into one another either in their haste, or rather, like men panic-stricken
because of the ferocity of the attack. Most commentators accept that the
prophet's description passes from the defence of the city to the attack
upon it in the closing part of v.5. They take the word rendered "defence"
(SOKEK - 5526), which means to cover, as a reference to a moveable shelter
protecting the invading soldiers. However, the meaning of the root from
which SOKEK is derived is to block or stop something, and may well refer
to the preparation of the defenders in trying to prevent the attacking army
entering into the city. It could also be taken as a covering for the defenders.
C. L. Feinberg is of the view that "The protection of the wall of the city is of
paramount importance in any siege, so the leaders rush to take their place
there. Some understand the mantlet to be a covering of the besiegers which
they use to approach the wall, but it is rather the protection employed by
the defenders. It refers to some kind of breastwork of interwoven boughs
and branches of trees put up between the towers on the walls".

In vv.6-7 Nahum refers to the downfall of Nineveh. Although the AV uses
the future tense, some commentators and other versions prefer a tense
which views the event as complete in the purpose of God. When God reveals
a future event, whether near or far humanly speaking, its fulfilment is sure
and nothing can prevent it. Every attempt to defend the city of Nineveh
would be in vain and its utter destruction was certain.

There is a dispute as to the meaning of the opening expression of v.6,
"The gates of the rivers shall be opened". There are three suggestions.

1. "It is easy and natural to take the gates of the rivers to mean those
situated on the streams or canals, fed from the Tigris, which served as a
means of defending a portion of the walls. By diverting these, as was done
at Babylon...the channels would be left dry, and there would be no
obstruction to the advance of the enemy. By them the gates would be
opened by force" (F. C. Cook).

2. "Perhaps the most probable view on the whole is that the reference is
to the gates at the points where the Khushur and the canal passed through
the city walls...the effect of them being opened, as the prophet pictured it,

was that the city was at the mercy of the foe" (S. R. Driver; see also Keil & Delitzsch). The idea is that these gates were forcibly opened by the attackers without the channels being drained.

3. The reference is not to literal gates but is a metaphorical expression denoting a flood of water (cp. Gen 7.11). "In the third year of the siege, however, heavy rains brought on a flood which broke down the walls about the city. This is exactly the picture given by the prophet" (C. L. Feinberg; see also Jamieson, Fausset & Brown; C. G. Cann).

Most favour the last meaning which seems to be supported by historical accounts of the destruction of Nineveh. Professor Rawlinson states, "At the north-west angle of Nineveh there was a sluice or flood-gate, intended mainly to keep the water of the Khosr-su, which ordinarily filled the city moat, from flowing off too rapidly into the Tigris, but probably intended also to keep back the water of the Tigris, when that stream rose above its common level. A sudden and great rise in the Tigris would necessarily endanger this gate, and if it gave way beneath the pressure, a vast torrent of water would rush up the moat along and against the northern wall, which may have been undermined by its force, and have fallen in" (*Ancient Monarchies* ii, p. 397, edit. 1871). The collapse of a section of the city wall would allow the attacking forces to pour into the city and bring about its destruction. Some take the expression, "the palace shall be dissolved", to refer to the royal palace being overthrown by the flood, but that is untenable since the Assyrian palaces were built on the top of natural or artificial hills. The statement is to be taken metaphorically, i.e. the hearts of the royal household would be dismayed and would melt with fear on hearing the news that the enemy had entered the city. All was now lost, with little or no resistance, so the city would be at the mercy of the invaders. Once the defence was breached the city's fall was certain.

The Christian's battle is not physical but spiritual and, although it is against spiritual wickedness in heavenly places (Eph 6.12), it takes place first in the mind – "We do not war after the flesh: (For the weapons of our warfare are not carnal, but mighty through God to the pulling down of strong holds;) Casting down imaginations, and every high thing that exalteth itself against the knowledge of God, and bringing into captivity every thought to the obedience of Christ" (2 Cor 10.3-5). It is the mind that the devil tries to control: thus it must be protected – "Wherefore gird up the loins of your mind" (1 Pet 1.13). The believer must not allow this age to press him into its mould, and thus the exhortation is given: "Be not conformed to this world: but be ye transformed by the renewing of your mind, that ye may prove what is that good, and acceptable, and perfect, will of God" (Rom 12.2).

"Huzzab" (from NATSAB - 5324) in v.7 has been taken, by some, to be the name of the queen of Assyria, but there is no trace of this name elsewhere. It seems that in some marginal renderings the mention of the palace in the previous verse and the expression "her maids" has led to the suggestion that the Assyrian queen is in view. The fact that the pronouns and verbs are feminine in the verse does not support this opinion since the same gender is used in v.10 where the city itself is clearly the subject. Verse 7 views Nineveh metaphorically or personified as the queen or mistress of the nations, holding sway over them, but here she is removed from that lofty position. NATSAB means to establish, fix, or determine, and it appears as "appointed" (1 Sam 19.20), "establish" (Prov 15.25), "set" (Deut 32.8; Ps 74.17), and "settled" (Ps 119.89). Here it refers to the determined purpose of God in relation to Nineveh's downfall.

The word translated "captive" (GALA - 1540) means to uncover, or to remove, and is used in Isaiah 47.2-3 of the exposure and shame of Babylon. Thus the opening expression indicates God had determined that Nineveh would be stripped of her wealth, pomp, and finery to her ignominious shame.

The phrase "brought up" (ALA - 5927) is translated "gone up" (2 Sam 2.27), "cut off" (Job 36.20), and "broken up" (Jer 37.11). Thus the expression, "she shall be brought up", indicates a sudden removal. The idea might be that of being brought up for judgment, and therefore the making bare and the taking away of Nineveh would denote the complete annihilation of the city. Assyria lived by the sword, conquering and plundering nations, so she would perish by the sword and would herself be plundered, i.e. they would suffer what they had inflicted on others – "they have sown the wind, and they shall reap the whirlwind" (Hos 8.7). They sowed violence and oppression, they would reap violent destruction; they sowed greed and covetousness, they would be stripped of all they possessed; they sowed pomp and pride, they would be humiliated and put to shame; they sowed idolatry and blasphemy, they would reap the dreadful judgment of God. Even Christians must be careful as to what they sow for there will be a time of reaping for all men – "For he that soweth to his flesh shall of the flesh reap corruption; but he that soweth to the Spirit shall of the Spirit reap life everlasting" (Gal 6.8).

> Sow flowers, and flowers will blossom
> Around you wherever you go;
> Sow weeds, and of weeds reap the harvest,
> You'll reap whatsoever you sow.
>
> Sow blessings, and blessings will ripen,
> Sow hatred, and hatred will grow;
> Sow mercy, and reap sweet compassion,
> You'll reap whatsoever you sow.
>
> You'll reap whatsoever you sow;
> You'll reap whatsoever you sow.
> The harvest is certainly coming,
> You'll reap whatsoever you sow.

It has been stated, "As Nineveh is compared to a queen dethroned and dishonoured, so she has here assigned to her in the image handmaidens attending her with dove-like plaints (Is 38.14; 59.11). The image implies helplessness and grief suppressed, but at times breaking out" (Jamieson, Fausset & Brown). The inhabitants of the city are viewed as her maids who lament over what has overtaken their mistress – Nineveh's downfall. The city, over which the inhabitants had rejoiced in its pomp and splendour, would, when destroyed, become the cause of their mourning.

The verb "lead" (NAHAG - 5090) means to lead or guide, but the Theological Wordbook of the Old Testament states that in this case, because of the verb form, it means moan, lament. However, the AV is in keeping with the imagery of the previous statement, showing her maids leading her as a dethroned queen in lamentation. The idea seems to be that of the people, feeling the ignominy and shame of the city's fall, moaning audibly as doves coo at the complete downfall of the city (cp. Is 38.14; 59.11; Ezek 7.16). Their deep mourning and anguish is evident by the beating of their breasts (Mt 11.17, RVm; Lk 18.13). This is the result of the way they had taken - as Proverbs 13.15 states, "the way of transgressors is hard". It is important that men take heed to the instructions and warnings of the word of God. Examples are given in the Holy Scriptures of those who despised the warnings of God and suffered the consequences, eg. Pharaoh. "Whoso despiseth the word shall be destroyed: but he that feareth the commandment shall be rewarded" (Prov 13.13). Hebrews 10.28 reminds one that, "He that despised Moses' law died without mercy under two or three witnesses". Paul in proclaiming the gospel declared, "…that through this man is preached unto you the forgiveness of sins: And by him all that believe are justified from all things, from which ye could not be justified by the law of Moses. Beware therefore…Behold, ye despisers, and wonder, and perish" (Acts 13.38-41). Christians must also take heed not to despise the word of God for, although it would not alter their eternal destiny, it would have an affect upon their present lives as David experienced (2 Sam 12.7-14).

In v.8 Nineveh is compared to a pool of water which is a vivid picture of its security, wealth, and inhabitants, none of which would prevent its overthrow in the day of judgment. The city's antiquity is mentioned in the word "old" meaning from the earliest days of its existence (Gen 10.11). As to its security, it was well known for its situation by the River Tigris and for its wide moat forming a water barrier around it to ensure its safety. However, this barrier would be of no avail in the day of retribution and the inhabitants would be forced to flee from the city. The pool of water could also be a figure of the wealth and prosperity of the city teeming with many traders and which figure is suggested in Jeremiah 51.13: "O thou that dwellest upon many waters, abundant in treasures". The wealth and prosperity of Nineveh would be of no value in the day of God's judgment. The picture may also refer to the Assyrian warriors being like a pool of water that

evaporates in the heat rendering it of no use, which would signify the fleeing warriors being of no value in the defence of the city. The main idea in
the metaphor would be that of the vast population, including the soldiers,
of Nineveh (cp. Is 8.7; Jer 51.13; Rev 17.15). This population, proud of its
city and believing it to be impregnable, flee from it at the advance of the
enemy, like water being drained from a pool. The cry of the leaders, "Stand,
stand" (or "remain, remain" - repeated to indicate earnestness), goes unheeded as the citizens and warriors seek safety in flight. Confusion over-
takes the city and not one responds to the command. No-one looks or
turns back (cp. Jer 46.5; 48.39). Self-preservation is the order of the day
and flight is paramount in the mind of each one. If in v.7 the inhabitants are
brought to shame and dishonour, moaning over the city's downfall, in v.8
they are fleeing for their lives in hopeless despair.

In the Christian warfare believers should stand against the attacks of the
enemy. God's provision for the saints is complete and enables them to
stand at all times. Christians are responsible to "Put on the whole armour
of God, that ye may be able to stand against the wiles of the devil. For we
wrestle not against flesh and blood, but against principalities...Wherefore
take unto you the whole armour of God, that ye may be able to withstand
in the evil day, and having done all, to stand" (Eph 6.11-13).

The spoiling of Nineveh (vv.9-13)

This section describes the desolation of Nineveh, the most prosperous
and glorious city of its time, in graphic and unmistakable language. The
city is plundered and made waste in vivid contrast to its former glory.

The deserted city (vv.9-10)

Nineveh is deserted by its inhabitants who flee from the invading forces,
and God, through Nahum, calls upon the victors to plunder its vast treasures.
The fact that God calls upon the conquerors to spoil Nineveh further shows
that He has determined to avenge what Assyria inflicted on others and in
particular upon His people. The word translated "spoil" (BAZAZ - 962)
means to seize, plunder, or prey upon, and is found mostly in the prophetic
books - twelve times in Isaiah, seventeen times in Ezekiel, and twelve times
in the other books of prophecy. It is generally connected to warfare when
the victors take by force various goods, carrying them off to their own
country. The command of God, "Plunder silver, plunder gold", would be
completely obeyed by the conquering forces although they would be
unaware of the divine command. This would be the ultimate humiliation
of Nineveh, and thus of Assyria. Nineveh would be stripped of all the
treasures of silver and gold which were her pride and boast. One is reminded
of the vanity of all earthly glory – "Vanity of vanities, saith the Preacher,
vanity of vanities; all is vanity" (Eccl 1.2; 12.8). Historical accounts indicate
the great riches of Nineveh – "The riches of Nineveh are inexhaustible, her
vases and precious furniture are infinite, copper constantly occurs in their

weapons...Neither Botta nor Layard found any of that store of silver and gold and 'pleasant furniture', which the palaces contained; scarcely anything, even of bronze, escaped the spoiler (W. J. Deane). The vast amount of silver and gold would be of no value to the Assyrians in the day of God's judgment.

Silver and gold, although of value in this world, can never contribute to a person's acceptance by God or purchase eternal salvation. Whatever value is placed upon them it cannot be compared with the infinite value of the blood of the Lord Jesus Christ shed on the cross – "ye were not redeemed with corruptible things, as silver and gold...But with the precious blood of Christ, as of a lamb without blemish and without spot" (1 Pet 1.18-19). Apart from the shedding of His blood, there is no forgiveness (Heb 9.22).

The word translated "store" (T^{e}KUNA - 8498) only occurs twice more in the Old Testament (Job 23.3 – "seat"; Ezek 43.11 – "fashion"). The idea in the word is that of setting up, or establishing, although Strong's Concordance suggests the word in Job 23.3 comes from a different root from the other two. In Ezekiel 43.11 it refers to the setting up or establishing of the temple. In Job 23.3 it is used of the place where God's throne is established. Here it is applied to the furnishings and riches of Nineveh as the established dwelling place of the Assyrian monarchy or world rulers. Nahum indicates the extent of the furnishings and treasures by using the expression, "there is none end". C. L. Feinberg notes that, "Accounts of ancient writers, almost fabulous in their descriptions, narrate the great treasures of metals and vessels accumulated in Nineveh. They exceeded by far the enormous treasures of the Persian Empire. The Medes and the Babylonians, who conquered and plundered Nineveh, furnished Ecbatana and Babylon with gold and silver to a degree unequalled at any period in history". The word for "furniture" (K^{e}LI - 3627) has a wide application embracing precious vessels of different kinds, jewels, ornaments, and all kinds of furnishings. Thus the closing expression "glory out of all the pleasant furniture" indicates the magnificence or abundance of riches found in Nineveh (cp. Gen 31.1). However, what value are the riches of this world compared with God's salvation or, for the believer, with living for God? "For what shall it profit a man, if he shall gain the whole world, and lose his own soul? Or what shall a man give in exchange for his soul?" (Mk 8.36-37).

In graphic terms and in a combination of exclamations, Nahum describes in v.10 the desolation of the city to the distress of those who remained in it. The city, which was far above all others of its day, supreme among the nations in riches, power and influence, is now viewed as a wilderness. The picture given is not just of defeat, but of complete humiliation and total devastation (cp. Ezek 26.17). This is expressed in three Hebrew synonymous words without a verb, the first two from the same root word BWQ. The three words, BUQA, M^{e}BUQA, and M^{e}BULAQA (950, 4003, 1110), are similar in sound and meaning with the number of syllables increasing giving the idea of a climax that is reached. This emphasises the complete obliteration of the city. One has suggested that the structure of the Hebrew words could be likened to *sack, sacking,* and *ransacking* in English. Emptied of her inhabitants and stripped of her treasures she would become a total ruin. The riches, power, and pomp of this world are false and fleeting and are all destined to perish – "the world passeth away, and the lust thereof: but he that doeth the will of God abideth for ever" (1 Jn 2.17). In light of this fact, Christians are challenged: "Seeing then that all these things shall be dissolved, what manner of persons ought ye to be in all holy conversation and godliness?" (2 Pet 3.11).

Having described the utter ruin of the city, the prophet takes up the people that are left, indicating their miserable condition. All courage would disappear and great despondency would settle upon them. The word for "smite together" (PIQ - 6375) is only found here and means trembling, or tottering. Terror would take hold of them and they would hardly be able to stand (cp. Dan 5.6; Acts 24.25). Anguish would overtake them as the pains of a woman in childbirth (Is 13.8; 21.3). They had been bidden to make strong their loins (v.1), but all would be in vain and there would be acute pain and grief instead of courage. The closing expression of v.10 is similar to the last clause of Joel 2.6 where the only other occurrence of the word translated "blackness" (PARUR - 6289) is found. The Theological Wordbook of the Old Testament, along with others, states that the meaning of the word PARUR is uncertain, but Strong states in his Concordance that it comes from the root word PA'AR (6286) meaning to gleam, and that it probably means illumination, i.e. to glow. The expression "gather blackness" is translated by Calvin as "withdraw (lit., gather up) their glow" and by Spurrell as "withdraweth its shining", which has been taken as "turning or growing pale" by commentators. The primary meaning of the root word may well indicate a glowing or flushing of the face through distress and fear. Matthew Poole states, "The faces, which were wont to be haughty and scornful, and as it were sparkle with briskness of spirit, all gather blackness; now are clouded, sorrowful, and dejected".

What a solemn picture is presented here of God's judgment upon Nineveh. How solemn the coming day of God's judgment upon this world will be when "sudden destruction cometh upon them, as travail upon a woman with child; and they shall not escape (1 Thess 5.3; cp. Rev 6.15-17). Those who gloried in their wealth and position, and boasted, in their folly, of the invincibility of Nineveh would be suddenly brought down – "Boast not thyself of to morrow; for thou knowest not what a day may bring forth" (Prov 27.1). The power, pomp, and wealth of this world is transient and is but for a moment in God's reckoning. The Christian alone can glory, not in one's self (Rom 3.27), but in the Lord (2 Cor 10.17) and "in the cross of our Lord Jesus Christ" (Gal 6.14).

The den forsaken (vv.11-13)

Nahum now sees, in vision, Nineveh, not only captured and given over to plunder, but completely obliterated so that there is even doubt as to where it was situated. The prophet changes from simply describing the attack and downfall of the city to using a metaphor showing that it is as a den of lions from which the lions, known for their ferocity and cruelty, had been driven away. The lion is the emblem of majesty and power, but also, in the context here of violence, bloodshed, and the carrying off of prey to its den. The lion speaks of Assyria which is evident, not only in the passage, but by the figure of the lion on the monuments of Nineveh. The lions' den is an animated picture of the lordly position Assyria possessed among the nations up to its collapse.

The question in v.11 indicates that Nahum, having in spirit beheld the destruction of the city, now looks for the site upon which it stood, but is unable to see it. It is suggested that the question God asks through the prophet is a taunting rhetorical one concerning the place where the lion previously dwelt unopposed, for the answer was self-evident. It can, however, also be taken as a question expressing amazement, since it seemed so incredible that the city should be erased. The question covers the whole of the verse and therefore must be applied to each clause. The word "dwelling" (MAON - 4583) comes from the same root word as the plural word "dens" in v.12, and "den" would better suit the passage here. In viewing Nineveh as a den of lions Nahum is comparing the invading lust of Assyria's kings and armies who crushed and devoured nations, carrying plunder back to their capital city, with lions who carried their prey back to their dens. The lion is fittingly applied to Nineveh, being a beast that dominated others, brought fear to them and cared only for its own, for Assyria had these same features.

The word for "feedingplace" (MIREH - 4829) is translated "pasture" elsewhere (Gen 47.4; Ezek 34.14). This indicates that it was not only a dwelling place, but also a place of pasture which conveys the idea that Nineveh was a desirable place to satisfy the lusts, pleasures, and pride of the Assyrians. These are the features that are in the world today – "For all that is in the world, the lust of the flesh, and the lust of the eyes, and the pride of life, is not of the Father, but is of the world" (1 Jn 2.16). Such features should not characterise believers (Eph 5.1-12; Col 3.5-14). The Hebrew for "old lion" (LᵉBI - 3833) is the same as that translated "lionesses" in v.12, but here it is singular and would be better translated "lioness". The whole family of lions are mentioned, the lion, lioness, young lions, and whelps, indicating that all Assyria is represented in Nineveh. The closing expressions indicate the freedom of movement, security, and undisturbed power with which Nineveh ruled supreme over the nations (cp. Micah 4.4).

Continuing the same metaphor in v.12, the prophet describes the ferocity, destructiveness, and tyranny of the Assyrians. However, one must appreciate that the description given here is still governed, in thought, by the question of v.11 and would thus indicate what Assyria was like before its destruction. The primary meaning of "tear" (TARAP - 2963) is to seize the prey and tear its flesh in order to consume it - a vivid picture of the inhuman violence of the Assyrian kings in conquering and destroying nations during their military campaigns. This is seen today in terrorism and in many countries where life is counted as nothing. The recorded accounts of those exploits bear ample witness to the cruelty of these Assyrian monarchs. C. L. Feinberg records that "Tiglath-pileser I boasted that he had fought and conquered sixty kings. In the beginning of his reign in combat with five kings he made the blood of the warriors to flow in the valleys and on the high places of the mountains. He cut off the heads of his enemies and piled them up outside their cities like heaps of grain. City after city is reported as having been defeated, burned with fire, devastated, and destroyed. Twenty-five cities of one land were so treated in one campaign. Their troops were cut down like lambs. One boast of this king was that he dyed a mountain red with the blood of the slain". The lioness and the whelps seem to represent the citizens of Assyria who benefited from these military successes.

The word for "strangled" (HANAQ - 2614) means to throttle or choke, and is only found elsewhere in 2 Samuel 17.23 where it is translated "hanged". Here it involves action against another whereas in 2 Samuel 17 it is used of Ahithophel's action upon himself. It again indicates the violence and cruelty used by the Assyrian rulers to enrich their empire. At the close of the verse the mention of holes and caves as hiding places or store houses portrays them as robbers.

Verse 13 opens with the interjection, "Behold", which demands that attention be given to the statement, "I am against thee", making it emphatic and confirming all that has gone before (cp. 1.15). The Psalmist David writes, "The face of the Lord is against them that do evil, to cut off the remembrance of them from the earth" (Ps 34.16). How solemn are the words, "I am against thee", when spoken by the omnipotent and holy God in His righteous anger. How sobering for the sinner to know that God's judgment is approaching. How great is the need to flee to the Saviour for refuge from the wrath to come (Mt 3.7; 1 Thess 1.10). The idea here is that God is towards Nineveh in judgment. It is directly addressed to her thus sealing her doom – "Thou, even thou, art to be feared: and who may stand in thy sight when once thou art angry?" (Ps 76.7). Assyria had been entrusted with a measure of power and sovereignty over the nations, but had, in her wickedness, used it to oppress and destroy them in order to enrich herself. She had been an instrument in the hand of God to chastise His people, the kingdom of Israel, but had acted beyond what God intended by lifting her hand against Judah which God would not permit. Thus the cup of her iniquity was full with the inevitable result that the time of her judgment had come.

God was against the nation of Assyria because of her sin, but it is sobering to know that God is also against every individual who is without the Lord Jesus Christ as their Saviour because of their sins. The opposite is true of Christians, as God is for them – "If God be for us, who can be against us?" (Rom 8.31). No one can be successfully against the believer because, "He that spared not his own Son, but delivered him up for us all, how shall he not with him also freely give us all things?" (Rom 8.32).

The Jehovah title "the Lord of Hosts" (Jehovah Sabaoth) indicates His majesty and glory as the Lord of the hosts of heaven and earth, Sovereign over all, and therefore omnipotent. It occurs over 200 times in the Old Testament occurring first in 1 Samuel 1.3. In a number of passages it implies ultimate victory for Israel for He is the God of Israel and can do what He wills among the armies of the world. The title reveals the characteristic of God that is applicable to the situation. It is used here to encourage His people in the midst of oppression by the Assyrians, the idea being that He who is over all has determined the destruction of Nineveh and none can stay His hand in judgment. It is the Lord of Hosts who brings up the enemy armies against the doomed city of Nineveh, empowering them to overthrow the city and causing them to destroy it.

The change to the third person "her" in the next expression reveals a return to the prophetic description of what would take place, as in previous verses. One notes, in the rest of the verse, the mixture of direct address and prophetic description as well as a mixture of the battle scene, as in vv.3-10, and the metaphor, as in vv.11-12, thus bringing both together. The Assyrian chariots, which were renowned (Is 37.24) and their boast, would be destroyed. The chariots here seem to represent the whole military might of Assyria. The idea in the expression is that her chariots would be burnt into smoke indicating the utter destruction of Assyria as a military power. It also includes the idea that Nineveh would be swiftly reduced to nothing. Taking up the figure of the previous verse, the prophet predicts that as Assyria had slaughtered the forces of other nations so the sword would consume her warriors – "His mischief shall return upon his own head, and his violent dealing shall come down upon his own pate" (Ps 7.16; cp. Mt 7.2). The consequences of this would be that she would no more be able to subdue and pillage other countries. She would be recompensed for all that she had done to others. Her position of supremacy among the nations would be a thing of the past and all her pomp and grandeur would disappear from sight. The last clause implies the complete destruction of the Assyrian empire, for the voice of her officers carrying the Assyrian monarch's commands and demands would never again be heard. The messengers here are messengers of gloom, speaking of bondage, oppression, and conflict, in contrast to the messengers in 1.15 who bring glad tidings telling of freedom and peace. Her warriors would perish, her plundering would cease and her messengers would be silent, for she would disappear from the scene.

NAHUM 3

Verses 1-19: The Reasons for Nineveh's Overthrow
The theme of ch.2 is not only continued in this chapter, but is also further developed, thus confirming the doom of Nineveh. This is the last and longest chapter of the prophecy, announcing and vividly describing the city's inevitable destruction. Its coming doom is viewed from four different points of time - the prophet looking ahead to its downfall (vv.5-13), the city's preparation for the siege and its futile defence (vv.14-17), the actual battle (vv.2-4), and looking back to its defeat (vv.18-19). Nahum indicates that the coming doom of Nineveh would not be because of the superior might of the enemy, but because of its own treacherous and sinful ways (vv.1-7). It would suffer defeat as did the city of No and its defences would crumble before the invaders, in spite of its resources. The city, which seemed to be invincible, would be captured and brought to a terrible end to the rejoicing of those who had suffered at its hand (vv.8-19).

Judgment because of sin (vv.1-7)
The prophet announces in the opening woe that Nineveh, as the city of blood, would experience the dreadful slaughter it had inflicted on other nations. The awful bloodbath described in the opening verses is retribution for Assyria's deceitful and plundering ways (vv.1-3). Another reason given for its downfall is its relationship, as a harlot, to the surrounding nations (vv.4-7).

Their lies and robbery (vv.1-3)
The graphic description of the attack upon Nineveh is continued from 2.3-10 with the sights and sounds of the attacking enemy forcing its way through the streets of the city, spreading carnage as the army advances. However, the viewpoint is different. In ch.2 the particular reason given for Nineveh's downfall is Assyria's treatment of the people of God. It was also in order that the excellency of Israel might be restored (2.2). Here the reason given for its annihilation is its violence and deceit in relation to other nations. Assyria had plundered the surrounding nations and her hands were covered with blood (v.1), and thus her doom was sealed. In v.1 judgment is threatened and in vv.2-3 it is portrayed. The violent end of Nineveh would correspond to the violence which had characterised her. The lesson is clear, that one cannot set aside moral principles and pursue evil ways to gratify self, without retribution. The features evident in Assyria are similar to those that characterise Christendom in the last days (2 Tim 3.1-9), from which the child of God should be separated. These features will be seen in their fulness in Babylon religiously, commercially, and politically in a coming day (Rev 17 & 18). In many ways the city of Nineveh, in this prophecy, is a picture of the city Babylon yet to be rebuilt.
The opening word "woe" (HOY - 1945) is an interjection, usually of

lamentation, and is addressed to Nineveh. Except for 1 Kings 13.30, where it is translated "alas", it only occurs in the prophetic books. Although it is mainly rendered "woe" it is also given as "ah" (Is 1.4,24), "alas" (Jer 30.7), and "ho" (Is 55.1; Zech 2.6). It is used of mourning for the dead (Jer 22.18; 34.5), but mainly in regard to the threatened judgment of God (Is 5; Hab 2). Here it expresses the certainty of the destruction of Nineveh and indicates the lamentation that would accompany its downfall. It is suggested that this particular use is a form of irony since the fall of Assyria, represented in the capital city, would actually be rejoiced over and not lamented (v.19). Nineveh's cup of iniquity was now full and she was ripe for the judgment of God (cp. Gen 15.16; Joel 3.13; Rev 14.18). Nineveh is called "the bloody city, or "the city of bloods" for its barbarous cruelty and blood-shedding without any reservation, which is developed in the rest of the verse. It was founded and built up with strife and bloodshed. The words, "it is all", refer to every part of the city or the nation it represents. "Full of lies" indicates the treachery of Assyria in making fine promises, which were never kept, to further its conquests and expand its power (cp. Rom 3.13). It gained its unrighteous ends by deceit. It accepted readily the maxim that "the end justifies the means" however despicable the means might be.

For the Christian, nothing can justify secret, underhand activity for such belongs to Satan and the powers of darkness. It is only when the deeds and doctrines of men are contrary to the light that men act in underhand ways, being afraid to come to the light (Jn 3.20). Those who belong to Christ are the children of the light (1 Thess 5.5) and should walk as such (Eph 5.8). The believer should always do that which is honest (2 Cor 13.7), providing for honest things in the sight of God and men (2 Cor 8.21; cp. Rom 12.17; 13.13; Heb 13.18). Assyria's promises of help and protection were fraudulent (2 Chr 28.16-21; cp. Is 36.16) and were used to take advantage of weaker nations bringing them under its control. It was unreliable and untrustworthy and its truce-breaking was common practice. Its word was not to be trusted and it swiftly breached any agreement in order to further its purposes. It was totally self-centred and was not prepared to consider other nations.

This feature of self-centredness is becoming more prevalent today and the great danger is that the child of God can become tainted with it. It is important for Christians to remember that the child of God should "Look not every man on his own things, but every man also on the things of others" (Phil 2.4). Also the word of the Christian should be completely reliable (Mt 5.37; James 5.12). Anything but a straight forward and honest answer tends to evil.

The noun "robbery" (PEREQ - 6563) is rare and only occurs elsewhere in Obadiah v.14 where it is translated "crossway". It comes from a root verb PARAQ (6561) meaning to tear or rend in pieces (Zech 11.16), and so the idea here is that of violence (cp. Rom 1.29). Thus the wickedness of Assyria is summed up in a few words - blood-shedding, deceit, and violence.

The Hebrew words PEREQ and TEREP (prey - 2964) refer back to the metaphor in 2.11-13 indicating that Nineveh is like a lion's den full of torn prey. It has been suggested that the closing expression, "the prey departeth not", refers to the fact that Assyria had not restored the northern kingdom, Israel, to its land. However, "departeth" (MUSH - 4185) along with the negative "not" also carries the idea of not ceasing (cp. Is 54.10; 59 21; also Jer 17.8 where it is translated "cease"). The statement, therefore, seems to indicate that while Assyria remained in power it would go on in the same way, never refraining from violence and plunder, but increasing in it.

One is reminded of 2 Timothy 3.13: "But evil men and seducers shall wax worse and worse, deceiving, and being deceived". They proceed from bad to worse both morally and spiritually and, pursuing a path of deception, they are being deceived themselves. However, the believer is illuminated by the truth through the word of God and the indwelling Spirit of God.

Nahum now explains the threat of v.1 by transporting the reader into the coming battle for Nineveh describing, with the clarity of an eyewitness, the manner in which the enemy would storm and capture the city (v.2; cp. Jer 47.3). C. L. Feinberg observes, "This description of the siege of the city has been praised, and rightly so, as an unexcelled account whether in sacred or secular literature". He hears the charioteers cracking their whips as they urge the horses on and the unmistakable rumbling of the wheels of the war-chariots speeding to and fro in the city. The word translated "pransing" (DAHAR - 1725) is used only here in the Old Testament, but a derivative word is found in Judges 5.22 (DAHARA - 1726). Strong's Concordance gives the meaning as galloping, although the idea here seems to be that of dashing. "Jumping" (RAQAD - 7540) means to spring or jump, either wildly or for joy. It occurs ten times in the Old Testament and is translated elsewhere as "dance" (Job 21.11; Eccl 3.4), "leap" (Joel 2.5), and "skip" (Ps 29.6; 114.4,6). The idea in the closing part of the verse is of the horses pulling the chariots dashing wildly over the rough ground causing the chariots to spring over any obstacle in the way.

Having described the noise of the coming conflict in v.2, Nahum, in v.3, now views the battle field. The opening expression, "The horseman lifteth up", has been interpreted in a number of ways. F. C. Cook states that "...*lifteth up* is a participle in Hebrew, and belongs only to the word that goes before, not connected with what follows. *The charging horseman* is perhaps on the whole the simplest and most suitable rendering. As regards the meaning of the word, there is very great diversity of opinion. There are almost as many interpretations as interpreters. Amongst them may be mentioned *the rearing horse* or *horseman, the mounting horseman, the plundering horseman*". Since the word translated "lifteth up" (ALA - 5927) means cause to ascend, it is suggested that the horseman, by using a spur, makes the horse rise up and accelerate in speed. Some take the words "lifteth up" as referring to the horseman lifting up the sword and the spear as seems to be indicated in the AV, but most commentators accept that the

Hebrew text does not allow that interpretation. Whatever view is taken, it is clear that the verse first depicts the assault in three statements - the charging horseman, the bright sword, and the glittering spear - then gives the result of the attack. Although it is suggested that the horseman indicates the cavalry, and the sword and spear refer to the foot soldiers, the weapons are applicable to the warriors in general.

"Bright" (LAHAB - 3851) means flaming or gleaming. It refers to the blade of the sword and indicates its deadliness as well as its appearance. The warriors kept their swords in such a condition that they would be effective in wounding and killing, and that they would dazzle the enemy in the sunlight. The word rendered "glittering" (BARAQ - 1300) means lightning and is mainly translated in this way, but it is also used metaphorically to denote the gleam of a weapon (cp. Deut 32.41; Job 20.25; Hab 3.11). The spear (HANIT - 2595) or javelin (1 Sam 18.10-11) was a deadly weapon, usually short, and capable of being thrown. The idea here is that of a flashing spear that inflicts judgment upon the Assyrians. The result would be a multitude of slain. This word "slain" (HALAL - 2491) includes the act of wounding, whether fatal or otherwise, depending on the context. It is amplified by the following two Hebrew words for "carcases" (PEGER - 6297) and "corpses" (GᵉWIYA - 1472). PEGER contains the idea of death and is translated as "dead bodies" (2 Chr 20.24-25; Jer 31.40; 33.5) and "corpses" (2 Kings 19.35; Is 37.36), but mainly as "carcases" as here (cp. Is 66.24; Ezek 6.5). It always refers to the bodies of men after death and sometimes after decay and stench has set in (Is 34.3; Amos 8.3). It generally refers to death as a result of divine judgment and not by natural causes. GᵉWIYA refers to a body as an object and, apart from Judges 14.8-9 (carcase) and here (corpses), it is always translated "body". It is applicable to a body whether dead (1 Sam 31.10-12; Ps 110.6) or alive (Gen 47.18; Neh 9.37), and is used of the bodies of the "four living creatures" in Ezekiel 1.11,23, and the body of "a certain man" in Daniel 10.6. Whereas the word PEGER emphasises the mass of dead because of the judgment of God, GᵉWIYA emphasises the bodies being heaped together (cp. Ps 110.6) and so numerous that not only the fleeing inhabitants but also the invaders stumble over them and are impeded in their advance. It is a fearful thing to fall into the hands of the living and righteous God as these verses demonstrate (cp. Heb 10.31). The only way for any to escape His judgment, because of sin, is to avail oneself of His salvation through faith in the Lord Jesus Christ.

Their lust (vv.4-7)

The opening word "Because" in v.4 introduces the reason why God is against Assyria, indicating the justice of God's judgment. The cause of Assyria's collapse is given in this section in the form of another metaphor, that of a harlot (cp. Is 23.16; Rev 17.1-5) who debased other nations. Her relationship with the surrounding nations involved allurement as well as violence. Associated with her harlotry was witchcraft which indicated satanic influence and the activity of the powers of darkness. The result was not only the seduction of nations and the disregard of moral values, but complete opposition to God, the things of God, and the people of God. The immoral and amoral character of Assyria and its capital, Nineveh, would be the reason for her exposure, shame, and destruction. Since Assyria was never in covenant relationship with God or a follower and worshipper of Him, "whoredoms" here cannot refer to apostasy, the turning away to other gods, as in the case of Israel and Judah (Ex 34.15-16; Zeph 1.4-5). Jehu accused Jezebel of such conduct in his answer to Joram: "What peace, so long as the whoredoms of thy mother Jezebel and her witchcrafts are so many?" (2 Kings 9.22). Also Jehoram, king of Judah, made Judah to go a-whoring, as the house of Ahab (2 Chr 21.12-13). However, it is scarcely possible that idolatry is not included in the figure used since Assyria carried out her military exploits in the name of her gods and attributed their successful conquests to them. Also, as stated, whoredom is used in regard to Jezebel who was a Gentile (1 Kings 16.31; 18.4,19), and the prophet has already pronounced that Assyria along with its idolatry would be destroyed (1.14).

Idolatry, which is deceptive because of the falsehood linked with it, was clearly a characteristic of the Assyrian empire. Idolatry ignores responsibility to the one true God and gives licence to lust and every kind of evil. It can take various forms and does not necessarily involve worshipping idols made of wood, stone, or various metals. Any thing that replaces God in one's life can become an idol. There is a danger of allowing achievements or possessions to become objects of affection and thus one's idols. In the world there is much emphasis on these things and it would be well to remember that whatsoever Christians do should be done heartily as unto the Lord and for His glory (Col 3.23-24).

The figure here mainly speaks of the deceptive friendship, and the superficial and plausible promises through which Assyria allured the nations in order to subject them to herself. It has been suggested that her commerce is in view, but the idea here is of her treachery, crafty politics, and deceitful ways in seeking to snare the weaker nations. Nineveh is likened to a well-favoured harlot because of her greatness, splendour, and brilliancy with which she amazed and bewitched the nations as she lusted after power and possessions. The splendour of her temples, idols, and idolatrous ceremonies may well be indicated. She was externally attractive, but her motives were to deceive, ensnare and to glorify herself. The unwary were enticed by her as in 2 Kings 16.7-10 when Judah under Ahaz called upon Tiglath-pileser, king of Assyria, for aid and became tributary to him.

The noun "witchcrafts" (KESHEP - 3785) is in the masculine and only occurs six times in the Old Testament. It is always in the plural form and is translated elsewhere as "witchcrafts" (2 Kings 9.22; Micah 5.12), and "sorceries" (Is 47.9,12). It indicates trafficking in the occult which is often linked with idolatry and is used, supposedly, to determine the will of God (cp. Is 47.12-13). It is inevitably linked with the worship of demon-gods. However, the term may be used metaphorically here, in a similar way to "whoredoms", of the secret wiles and arts she employed to achieve her own end. The term "mistress" emphasises her skill and success in beguiling and charming the nations, corrupting them with her idolatry and sorcery. The expression "selleth nations" can be viewed in two ways – depriving nations of their freedom, and literally selling the inhabitants as slaves to others (Joel 3.3, 6-8; Amos 1.6,9); and robbing nations of their liberty and bringing them into slavery by making them tributary (Judg 1.30,33,35; 2 Kings 23.33). Although both may be included in the expression, F. C. Cook takes the view that "...the figurative language of the context makes it probable that *selling* is to be taken metaphorically; treating nations brought under her power simply as articles of merchandise, abandoning them to misery and ruin with utter indifference".

Nineveh was a city of bloodshed, deceit, seduction, and oppression. The word translated "families" (MISHPAHA - 4940) mostly refers to a circle of relatives, but is also often used, as here, of a subdivision of a larger group like a tribe or of a smaller nation (Jer 25.9). It is suggested that in this verse it is used of smaller groups to indicate that none escaped her seductive influence.

Because of such wickedness and ungodliness the Lord is against Nineveh and would heap upon her the judgment she deserved. Here in v.5 the Lord of hosts directly addresses Nineveh with the same statement of 2.13: "I am against thee". It is repeated to emphasise the certainty of His judgment upon her. She had blasphemed the God of Israel (Is 37.23) and thus He was against her. Although the downfall of Nineveh would be inflicted by man, yet man is but an instrument in the hands of Jehovah carrying out what He has purposed.

The word rendered "discover" (GALA - 1540) means to uncover, or to remove. Here it may well have the meaning of removing that which served as a covering, i.e. exposing the true character of Nineveh. The borders or hem (skirts) of the long flowing dress, which depicts Nineveh's pomp and beauty, would be removed before her or lifted up over her face (cp. Is 47.2-3; Ezek 16.37; Hos 2.3). The idea here is that Nineveh would be stripped of all that made her attractive to the nations. Thus the glory of Nineveh would be removed and, to her shame, she would be exposed to the derision of the nations (cp. Jer 13.22,26). As a harlot she had exposed herself, in a certain way, to achieve her own ends, but now her true nakedness would be revealed to the nations. So her judgment would be certain, shameful, and evident to all. This thought is carried on in the following verses.

In v.6 Jehovah continues to address Nineveh declaring what He would do to her. The shame of Nineveh would be widespread and the nations would show their disgust. The figure of a harlot is continued although

Nineveh is now viewed not as an attractive and beautiful woman, but as a vile woman exposed to the ridicule and ill treatment of others. "Abominable filth" (SHIQQUS -8251) means disgusting or detestable things and is used in connection with idolatrous practices. It is translated elsewhere "abomination" (Dan 11.31; 12.11), "abominations (Jer 4.1; Ezek 20.7), and "detestable things" (Jer 16.18; Ezek 7.20). C. F. Keil notes that the word "is used most frequently of idols; but here it is used in a more general sense for unclean or repulsive things, dirt and filth. Throwing dirt upon one is a figurative expression for the most ignominious treatment or greatest contempt". However, "The 'abominable filth' of Nahum 3.6 is *shiqqus*. It seems likely that, since *shiqqus* is everywhere else clearly related to idolatrous worship, the same would be true here. It is important to recognize that by the use of such a strong word as *shiqqus* God wants his people to recognize the extreme seriousness and wickedness of this sin, however attractive and popular it might be" (TWOT). Thus the expression would mean that Jehovah would cast upon Nineveh the consequences of her idolatrous ways to her open shame. The word "vile" (NABEL - 5034) means to wilt or wither, and is often translated "fade" (Ps 18.45; Is 64.6; cp. Is 34.4 - fall, falleth, falling). It signifies disgrace (Jer 14.21) and dishonour (Micah 7.6; cp. Deut 32.15 - lightly esteemed). Nineveh had made herself attractive to the nations, but was morally evil, so God would bring disgrace upon her. It indicates here that Nineveh would be made a spectacle for contempt and abuse. The last expression, "will set thee as a gazing stock", is translated "will make thee a public example" (LXX; cp. Mt 1.19). Thus the expression conveys the thought that Nineveh would become an astonishment (cp. Lam 4.12), exposed to public ignominy and shame as an example to other nations.

The opening expression of v.7, "And it shall come to pass", adds certainty and solemnity to what follows, as well as linking it with the previous verse. There seems to be a play in this verse on the Hebrew word ROI (gazingstock - 7210) in v.6 and the root word RAA (look - 7200) from which it comes. Such will be the repugnance of the spectators who would behold the spectacle of Nineveh's downfall that they will flee in horror and hatred. The word for "waste" (SHADAD - 7703) means destroy, ruin, or spoil, and is found mainly in the prophetic books. It is generally given as "spoil" (Jer 47.4) and "waste" (Is 15.1), and indicates here that Nineveh would be plundered and emptied of her inhabitants. The savagery of SHADAD is indicated in Jeremiah 5.6 where it is linked with a wolf. Since "flee" (5074) is used it has been suggested that those who flee do so out of fear in order that they may not partake of her judgment. However, the thought of abhorrence and disgust seems to be more suitable to the context as is evident from the following rhetorical questions. The clear answer to these questions is in the negative. The sight of Nineveh wasted would be one of aversion and scorn. The word translated "bemoan" (NUD - 5110) basically denotes a going back and forth and is applied in a number of ways, one of

which is the shaking or nodding of the head signifying pity or sympathy.
Thus it is rendered "mourn" (Job 2.11), "take pity" (Ps 69.20), "be sorry"
(Is 51.19), and, as here, "bemoan" (Jer 16.5; 22.10). No one would mourn
for the devastated city, not only because its fate was well deserved, but
also because of what it had inflicted on others. The closing question is
similar to the closing question of Isaiah 51.19 where the answer is also in
the negative. Here the answer is, "Nowhere", because there is none to
comfort her. Her violent and cruel ways, befriending no one with sincerity,
would leave her friendless among the nations – "A man that hath friends
must show himself friendly" (Prov 18.24). She had sought only her own
enhancement, and in no way the welfare of those she had subjugated. She
would learn that "Righteousness exalteth a nation: but sin is a reproach to
any people" (Prov 14.34). She would also learn that "the most High ruleth
in the kingdom of men, and giveth it to whomsoever he will" (Dan 4.25,32).
Thus not one of the nations would lament her destruction or seek to
comfort her, but all would heap scorn upon her.

Judgment unavoidable (vv.8-19)

Nahum looks back to a time prior to the assault on Nineveh and presents
another capital whose strength did not save it from destruction in order
to stress the certainty of Nineveh's ruin and to further demoralise the
Assyrian capital. The Assyrians knew full well what had happened to No,
and what happened there gave them an example of God's judgment (vv.8-
10). In comparison to that city Nineveh was feeble, and in relation to the
execution of God's judgment (vv.11-19) its defences would be like ripe
figs falling to the ground (vv.11-12). It would be totally destroyed as
cankerworms and locusts consumed all that was before them (vv.13-17).
Her proud nobles would be remembered no more, there would be no
remedy for her condition, and the oppressed would rejoice at her downfall
(vv.18-19).

The example of God's judgment (vv.8-10)

The example of the fate of No indicates that Nineveh should have learned
the consequences of ungodliness, and that God is no respecter of persons
or nations. The chastisement of Israel showed that it is impossible for God
to be partial, for He cannot act contrary to His holy character. Men, through
unbelief, do not acknowledge this fact and refuse to accept that the
inevitable consequences of sin must be the judgment of God. They consider
that things will continue as they are and scoff at the thought of judgment
(2 Pet 3.3-4). They will discover, to their horror, that they have deceived
themselves and, because of their unbelief, there will be no escape from
the just judgment of God. Since sin was punished in No, so it would be
dealt with in Nineveh. Thus the proud and mighty capital of Assyria would
share the same fate as No, or rather, as the Hebrew, No-amon. S. R. Driver
states, "No-amon. Rather, No of Amon, or Amon's No. Amon (or Ammon)

was the name of the tutelary god of No, in whose honour had been built the immense temple...The expression thus suggests that No was specially under Amon's protection. 'No' is the Egyptian *Net*, "city"; and the city here referred to was called by the Egyptians...sometimes *N.t rs.t,* "southern city," sometimes *N.t Ymn*, "city of Amon," as here, sometimes simply *N.t*, the "city" *par excellence* (so Jer 46.25; Ezek 30.14,15,16). By the Greeks it was called Thebes: it was the great and celebrated capital of Upper Egypt...the capital of the brilliant rulers of the 18th, 19th, and 20th dynasties, who constructed there the great temples...on a scale of imposing magnificence, to which there is probably no parallel in the world".

The comparison with No-amon is more fitting since it had been the capital of great conquering kings who had poured the wealth gained by military exploits into it just as the Assyrian kings had done to Nineveh. The use of this comparison implies that what the prophet relates would be fresh in the memory of Assyria and the nations. The rhetorical question, "Art thou better?", in v.8 may be viewed morally, materially, or militarily. If morally, it indicates less guilty, less deserving of judgment; if materially, it means more prosperous; and if militarily, it implies being stronger or more powerful. All three may be indicated, but in the context the latter seems to be in view. Was Nineveh stronger, more able to repel any attack, and more powerful to defeat any enemy than No-amon was? Was she better placed and better protected? These verses, by describing No-amon and its might, emphasise the negative answer to the question – "No, not at all". Thus Nineveh could perceive her fate in that of No-amon for she was not superior to the Egyptian capital. It claimed to be impregnable, like Nineveh, although, it is said, it had a hundred gates.

The use of "populous" indicates that the large number of citizens in No-amon was of no value in the day of its destruction and this would also be so in relation to Nineveh. The situation of No-amon enhanced its defence more than Nineveh's situation did. The word "situate (YASHAB - 3427) means to sit, or to dwell. Here No-amon is personified as one that had dwelt proudly, securely, and peacefully upon the rivers. The plural refers to the Nile with its streams and canals (cp. Ex 7.19; 8.5; Is 19.6-8) which surrounded the city as the following expression "the waters round about it" indicates. Thus it had natural water defences similar to, yet more effective than, Nineveh. Its "rampart" (HEL - 2426) indicates the fortification of the city which, as stated, was the sea - the reference here also seems to be to the Nile and its streams. It is stated that the Nile itself appears as a sea when it overflows its banks. Thus the Nile and its streams were the protection of the city. The last expression, "her wall was from the sea", is viewed in two ways: either a literal wall rose up from the sea - a protecting wall on the banks of the Nile and its streams surrounded the city, or, her wall consisted of the sea - the great river and its streams were a wall to her. Although the latter view seems to be a repetition of the previous statement it is more in keeping with the Hebrew text and the historical records.

No-amon was better off than Nineveh for, added to its natural defences was the strength of powerful nations to defend it. Unlike the Egyptian capital, Assyria had alienated the surrounding nations and so there would be no help from them when Nineveh would be attacked. Ethiopia and Egypt are closely linked, forming the Egyptian empire and at one time the Ethiopians ruled that empire. They were rulers at the time of No-amon's destruction which may be the reason why here they are mentioned first. Ethiopia (KUSH - 3568) inhabited the land to the south and south-west of Egypt. The Ethiopians were the descendants of Cush the first son of Ham (Gen 10.6) and their land is mentioned as far back as Genesis 2.13. Egypt (MISRAYIM - 4714) is one of the great powers of the Old Testament and is referred to first in Genesis 12.10. It seems that the Egyptians were descendants from Mizraim the second son of Ham (Gen 10.6). Thus both Ethiopia and Egypt were descendants of Ham the son of Noah. A brief Egyptian history is given in the Theological Wordbook of the Old Testament. "Egyptian history may be conveniently divided into and highlighted by the following important periods: (1) The Old Kingdom/Pyramid Age/third - sixth Dynasties (2700-2200 BC); (2) The Middle Kingdom, especially the twelfth Dynasty (2000-1800 BC); (3) The New Kingdom or Empire Age, eighteenth - twentieth Dynasties (1570-1090 BC); (4) The Ethiopian period, especially the twenty-fifth Dynasty (715-663 BC); (5) Saitic/twenty-sixth Dynasty (633-525 BC); (7) Dynasty of the Ptolemies (306-30 BC)."

"Strength" (OSMA - 6109) is a feminine noun which means powerfulness, or full might, and is found elsewhere only in Isaiah 40.29 and Isaiah 47.9 (translated "abundance"). The whole power of the renowned Egyptian empire had been at No-amon's disposal to defend it. The word "infinite" (7097) either indicates that the Egyptian army was numberless or that there was no end to its resources. Both are probably in view. Added to this was the help of Put and Lubim, both North African countries. It is suggested that they refer to two sections of the Libyans. C. F. Keil identifies them as "*Put, i.e.* the Libyans in the broader sense, who had spread themselves out over the northern part of Africa as far as Mauritania (see at Genesis 10.6); and *Lubim = L^ehabbim*, the Libyans in the narrower sense, probably...of the ancients (see at Genesis 10.13)". However, C. L. Feinberg indicates that "Some have tried to identify Put with the Libyans, but they are evidently distinguished in this verse. Present opinion relates Put to Punt, the present Somaliland in Africa". "Put" (6316) is also translated "Libya" (Ezek 30.5; 38.5), and "Libyans" (Jer 46.9),which could be the reason why some have considered it a section of Libya. However, Strong's Concordance indicates that the word should be translated "Put" in these verses. The people of Put were descendants from Ham's third son Phut (Gen 10.6; cp. 1 Chr 1.8). It is associated in various passages with Ethiopia (Jer 46.9), Persia and Lud (Ezek 27.10), Egypt and Ethiopia (Ezek 30.4-5), and with the hosts of Gog (Ezek 38.3-5). It is suggested that the people of Lubin were descendants from Lehabim the son of Mizraim (Gen 10.13) and from these the Libyans derived their name. Should this be the case, all four countries mentioned here were the descendants of Ham.

The word translated "helpers" (EZRA - 5833) means support, and here denotes military aid which is to no avail (cp. Is 31.1-3; Jer 37.7; Lam 4.17).

The opening words of v.10, "Yet was she...", are emphatic. Notwithstanding its might, the multitude of its defenders, and its majestic position No-amon suffered defeat and captivity. This historical event took place when Sargon, king of Assyria, captured it in his campaign against Egypt and Ethiopia, which was foretold in Isaiah 20. The significance of No-amon's downfall here is that Assyria was the power, used by God, to bring about its destruction. Thus Assyria knew how the greatest city or power could fall when God was against it, and she also knew that a city could not be overcome when God was for it (Is 37.33-37). In spite of this, Assyria continued in her cruel and violent ways, which God hated. No-amon was an example showing that no power could resist or stand before the judgment of God. The cruelty mentioned in this verse - children dashed in pieces, gambling for those brought into slavery, and exhibiting the nobles fettered - was common in ancient warfare (2 Kings 8.12; Is 13.16; Hos 13.16). Assyria in her conquests resorted to the mass removal of people in order to ensure the complete subjugation of the lands they conquered. The expression "at the top of all the streets" indicates that the slaughter of the young children took place in public view, bringing anguish and terror to the inhabitants (cp. Is 51.20; Lam 2.19). It seems that these public places were where several streets met. It is suggested that this was done to avoid trouble and inconvenience on the journey of the people into captivity. These acts of barbarity were carried out without mercy, showing the depravity of man's heart (cp. Jer 17.9; 50.42). Such cruelty is still displayed today in many places and particularly in warfare, for the depravity of man is unchanged. The honourable men of the city were treated as plunder, becoming slaves and being divided among the victors by lot (cp. Joel 3.3; Obad v.11).

The verb "bound" (RATAQ - 7576) only occurs here in this form, and means to fasten. The nobles were fastened with chains and made a spectacle to all in order to emphasise the subjugation of the city.

The execution of God's judgment (vv.11-19)
Having described the downfall of No-amon, the prophet addresses Nineveh once more. Nineveh, and thus Assyria, would fall more easily than No-amon, showing her inadequacy (vv.11-13). In spite of all her preparation, fire and the sword would swiftly devour her (vv.14-17). In concluding the prophecy, Nahum declares that the inhabitants would disappear from the scene and the city would be erased with no hope of restoration (vv.18-19).

(a) Nineveh's inadequacy (vv.11-13). The parallel between Nineveh and No-amon is emphasised in the prophet's message to Nineveh that the

same fate awaited her. The inhabitants of Nineveh boasted in their defences, but they would be shaken like fig trees by the judgment of God and they would fall like ripe figs to be consumed.

There seems to be an intended comparison between the description of No-amon's destruction (v.10) and that of Nineveh's (v.11) in the use of the Hebrew word GAM (1571), translated "yet" and "also", which is used twice in both verses. The thought would be: "as No-amon, so thou Nineveh". Thus the fate of No-amon was a prophecy of the certain fate of Nineveh which would be an encouragement to Judah who was oppressed by Assyria. As Jehovah dealt with the Egyptian capital so He would deal with the Assyrian capital. He is no respecter of nations or persons, but deals righteously with all.

This is also true in relation to His people. Christians must remember the words of 1 Peter 1.17 – "And if ye call on the Father, who without respect of persons judgeth according to every man's work, pass the time of your sojourning here in fear". The verse is in relation to children in the family of God and shows that the Father deals alike with each one in the family, on a righteous basis. Thus believers should order their lives in keeping with the character and claims of the Father, having a reverential fear. That demands a constant watchfulness that nothing is done or said that will bring dishonour on the Father or grief to His heart.

The opening expression in v.11, "Thou also shalt be drunken", has been taken to be a reference to "the last drunken orgy, to which, history tells us, the whole city was given up on the night of its awful fall" (H. A. Ironside). However, this does not suit the context. The word "drunken" (SHAKAR - 7937) should be taken here as metaphorical and not literal. In this instance the intoxicating drink would be the cup of divine wrath (Is 51.17; Jer 25.15; Hab 2.16). Nineveh would be compelled to drink it because of its wickedness. The metaphor indicates the effects of a great catastrophe that stupefies and terrorises men. Drunkenness here is a figure of the helplessness of Nineveh, powerless under the paralysing effect of the judgment of God. None can resist or stand before that judgment. Some have taken the following clause, "thou shalt be hid", to refer to Nineveh's action in seeking safety when under attack – "Thou who now vauntest thyself, shalt be compelled to seek a hiding-place from the foe" (Calvin). Although this interpretation may suit, what follows it does not agree with the metaphor of drunkenness. The word translated "hid" (ALAM - 5956) means to veil from sight, or to conceal (2 Kings 4.27; Job 28.21). It is generally rendered "hid" (Lev 4.13; 5.2-4), but is also translated "secret" (Ps 90.8; Eccl 12.14) and conveys the idea of something being out of sight. The thought here, similar to 2.11, is that the great city of Nineveh would be obliterated. F. C. Cook writes that the expression is "Better as an imperative, 'be thou hidden'. It is not a simple verb, but a combination of the substantive verb with a participle. And so the force of the expression is to remain, continue hidden, become obscure, unknown, blotted out; cp.

1.8; 2.11, and Obadiah v.16. And it is only in recent times that by excavations beneath the mounds that mark the site of Nineveh the buried city has been brought to light".

The word translated "strength" (MAOZ - 4581) indicates a place or means of safety (cp. 1.7 - strong hold). "Thou also, as No-amon, shall seek protection and help" - Nineveh, the terror of the nations, would seek refuge, in some stronghold, from the attacking enemy, but she would seek in vain. When the day of judgment arrived there would be no reprieve and all hope would be lost. It will be the same for this world when the day of God's wrath comes, when men will seek a place of safety but find none (Zeph 1.18; Rev 6.16-17). One is reminded of the solemnity of not seeking for the salvation God has provided until it is too late.

> Out of Christ, without a Saviour,
> Oh! can it, can it be?
> Like a ship without a rudder,
> On a wild and stormy sea!
>
> Oh, to be without a Saviour,
> With no hope or refuge nigh!
> Can it be, Oh blessed Saviour,
> One without Thee dares to die?
>   (F. M. Davis)

There is salvation for all who will repent and trust the Lord Jesus Christ, the Son of God, but salvation is only offered now in this life – "behold, now is the accepted time; behold, now is the day of salvation" (2 Cor 6.2).

The inadequacy of Nineveh to defend itself in that coming day, is illustrated by likening her defences to fig trees with ripe figs that, when shaken, immediately fall into the mouths of those who shake the trees (v.12). The word translated "strong holds" (MIBSAR - 4013), which means fortifications, is not limited to the fortified wall of the city, but includes the fortresses and watch-towers in the land that guarded the approach to the capital city, as the word "All" indicates. These fortifications would be of no value to those who trusted in them in the day of God's fury. They would be easily and rapidly overthrown and their occupants destroyed as ripe figs being consumed as they fall from the trees. The word "firstripe" indicates the early and tender figs which were considered a delicacy and thus highly esteemed (cp. Jer 24.2; Hos 9.10). The choice of this metaphor may be to indicate the prized achievement of the enemy in overthrowing Nineveh as well as the ease of victory over her.

The opening word "Behold" (HINNEH -2009), in v.13, is an interjection demanding attention and is employed as an indicator. Here it is used to point out what the condition of Nineveh would be when under attack, which condition seems incredible. Nahum introduces another metaphor, likening the people of Assyria to women. Some have taken this to indicate scorn heaped upon the might of Assyria. The word translated "people" (AM - 5971) does not mean the people in general, but refers to the warriors of Assyria. This seems to be borne out by the expression "in the midst of thee", implying the very place where strength and courage should be present. The purpose of the figure here is not to indicate cowardliness, but to highlight the weakness and inadequacy of the defenders to resist successfully the enemy's attack. Her brave warriors would become weak and timid as women, their hearts would fail them from fear (Jer 48.41; 51.30). The last thing Nineveh would have expected was that her warriors, once invincible, would become faint-hearted and that her fortifications would be so easily overrun.

How brave men can be when things are in their favour, but that can change rapidly when circumstances alter. Many people today blaspheme and ridicule God, ignore the claims of God, and think all is well in doing so, but their confidence will be shattered in the day of reckoning. The warlike Assyrians who had conquered and terrorised the nations would be reduced to helplessness under the judgment afflicted on them by God, through their enemies. This metaphor is used in the same way in regard to the Egyptians (Is 19.16) and the Chaldeans, the mighty men of Babylon (Jer 50.37; 51.30).

The last part of the verse is viewed differently by commentators. C. F. Keil holds that "The gates of the land are the approaches to it, the passes leading into it, which were no doubt provided with castles...The bolts of these gates are castles, through which the approaches were closed". However, D. W. Baker suggests that the might of Assyria was "also founded on the false protection of *open gates* for the towns, with their ruined cross-bars (cp. Deut 3.5; Judg 16.3). None of these are able to carry out their defensive function. Security is gone". However, it may be taken as a metaphoric picture of the ease with which the enemy would overcome the defence and having entered the capital city would destroy it with fire.

(b) Nineveh's preparation and collapse (vv.14-17). Nahum ironically calls upon Nineveh to lay up supplies and to strengthen her defences in preparation for the siege, but her preparation would be in vain. Her dependence upon the numerical strength of her population would be dashed to pieces when they flee away as locusts. These verses illustrate the futility of human effort to thwart the purpose of God. Assyria should have learned this lesson when Sennacherib sought to overthrow Jerusalem (Is 37.33-38). The will of God here was that at last the haughty and cruel rule of Assyria should be terminated, and Nahum unfolds how that would take place. Every effort of Assyria and its capital to prevent it would fail. Every hostile action against God, His purpose, and His people cannot in the end succeed. Christians should seek to know the will of God, through His word, and, having obtained that knowledge, seek to live in keeping

with it. To ignore or set aside the will of God results in spiritual loss for the believer.

The imperative mood is used in v.14 giving, ironically, four commands. Although Nineveh's doom was sealed, she was commanded to store water which refers to the priceless drinking water necessary for every city to survive in a siege. The implication here is that Nineveh would experience a long and trying siege before her downfall. There may be a play on the word translated "draw" (SHA'AB - 7579) with the metaphor of "women" in the previous verse since SHA'AB is used in the Old Testament in connection with the daily work of women drawing water (Gen 24.11,13; 1 Sam 9.11).

The city was also commanded to make every provision for attack by strengthening her defences. This would involve repairing any breaches and securing every position on the approach to the city and at the city itself, making them as strong as possible. The means of achieving this is signified in the rest of the verse. The expression "go into clay" is a command to make bricks in order to repair old fortifications and to construct new ones - set the brick-makers at work to supply bricks. It is stated that the words "clay" (TIT - 2916) and "morter" (HOMER - 2563) are used synonymously here (cp. Is 41.25). The word TIT has two basic meanings:- mud, or mire and clay used for making bricks – "to *be sticky...mud* or *clay*" (Strong's Concordance). The word HOMER means mortar or clay – "a *bubbling* up...*mire* or *clay*" (Strong's Concordance). W. J. Deane notes that "The soil round Nineveh was of a tenacious quality; and when moistened with water and kneaded either with feet or hands, with the addition usually of a little chopped straw, was easily formed into bricks. These, even without the aid of fire, became dry and hard in the course of a few days. But it is plain from the investigations of ruins that the Assyrians used both kiln-burnt and sun-dried bricks, though the mass of the walls was usually composed of the latter, the more durable material being employed merely as an accessory (see Bonomi, *Nineveh and it Palaces;* Layard, *Nineveh*)". The last expression is viewed in two ways because of the uncertainty of the meaning of "brickkiln" (MALBEN - 4404). It only occurs elsewhere in 1 Samuel 12.31 and Jeremiah 43.9. The first view takes MALBEN to mean a brick-mould translating the expression as, "lay hold of the brick-mould". This would then refer to the shaping of bricks prior to leaving them to dry and harden in the sun or baking them in a kiln. The second view accepts the AV translation of MALBEN and takes the expression as a command to put in order or repair the brick-kiln to make bricks. The second view seems more likely, although both views indicate the necessity of making bricks to repair and strengthen Nineveh's defences. The implication is again that the siege of Nineveh would be severe and long.

Though for very different reasons, Christians have the responsibility to strengthen themselves "in the grace that is in Christ Jesus" (2 Tim 2.1). There is ever sufficient in Christ to support believers, enabling them to live for God whatever the circumstances. The strength is available, through grace, but believers are responsible to avail themselves of it by being continually in touch with the risen Lord, in whom resides all power. Fellowship with Christ is absolutely essential.

The prophet, in the use of the opening word "There" in v.15, declares the certainty of Nineveh's doom stating that the coming siege, for which she would make great preparations, would end in her destruction. In the very place which had been strengthened and made secure the fire would devour all. Fire would destroy the city and its fortifications, the sword would destroy the inhabitants including the warriors. It has been suggested that the word "fire" is used metaphorically of the enemy's fury, but the context, along with the word "sword", indicates it should be taken literally. It is evident from ancient historians that fire played a major part in the destruction of Nineveh, and this is confirmed by the discovery, in modern times, of the remains of the city. It is also claimed that the last king of Assyria, in despair, set fire to his palace and perished, along with his household, in the flames. The phrase "cut thee off" (KARAT - 3772) contains the thought of destruction or bringing to an end and is used of terminating a person's life. Nahum introduces here the simile that the destruction of Nineveh and its inhabitants by fire and sword would be like a swarm of locusts consuming all before it. This devouring by the locusts would also be a symbol of devastation and destruction.

The word for "cankerworm" (YELEQ - 3218) comes from an unused root meaning "to *lick* up; a *devourer*" (Strong's Concordance). It represents the larval and nymph stages and occurs nine times in the Old Testament. It is translated elsewhere as "cankerworm" (Joel 1.4; 2.25), and "caterpillars" (Ps 105.34; Jer 51.14,27). In Joel 1.4, and 2.25 it is considered that the young larval stage of the locust is represented. In Jeremiah 51.27, where it is described as being "rough", the hornlike sheath covering the wings of the nymph stage is in view. In the following verse here (v.16) they are viewed at the stage when the wings are unfurled. This mention of the cankerworm may also include the thought of the plundering of Nineveh by its enemies. Nahum changes from the locusts consuming all as a simile of Nineveh's destruction to the locusts being a figure of the Assyrians or inhabitants of Nineveh. "The thought is this: fire and sword will devour Nineveh and its inhabitants like the all-consuming locusts, even though the city itself, with its mass of houses and people, should resemble an enormous swarm of locusts" (Keil & Delitzsch).

The expression, used twice, "make thyself many", comes from one Hebrew word KABED (3513) meaning to be heavy or weighty. The literal meaning is rarely used, but the figurative is used in a variety of senses. It is stated that here it is firstly in the masculine gender and then in the feminine. There are two suggestions as to the use of these two genders.

1. The masculine gender represents the inhabitants of Nineveh and the feminine pictures the city itself. The thought would then be that even

though defenders were many and the city had many defences yet both would be destroyed.

2. The masculine gender refers to the advancing army and the feminine refers to Nineveh. Since the word "cankerworm" is used in relation to the enemies earlier in the verse and in the following verse it is feasible that it could refer to them here. If this is the case then the enemies are commanded to make themselves strong (weighty) to accomplish the overthrow of Nineveh. Christians today can do all things, in keeping with the will of God, through Christ who strengthens them (Phil 4.13). However, the two genders can be used in a general way.

The word translated "locusts" (ARBEH - 697) is the word generally used in the Old Testament and is derived from a root RABA (7235) meaning to become numerous. Some have distinguished the two Hebrew words for "locusts" namely YELEQ "the licking locusts" and ARBEH "the swarming locusts". Jamieson, Fausset & Brown explains it as, "However 'many' be thy forces, like those of the 'swarming locusts' or the 'licking locusts', yet the foe shall consume thee as the 'licking locust' licks up all before it". Whereas in previous statements the devastation of the locusts (cankerworm) is in view, in the last clause it is the actual multitude of the locusts. The thought in the last clause is that though Nineveh made herself as numerous as locusts, yet she would be devastated. When Nineveh had done all that she could, she would still be completely and suddenly destroyed.

Nineveh is reminded of her commerce in v.16 for she not only depended on her numbers, but also upon her wealth. Nineveh, with its canals and the River Tigris giving access to the Persian Gulf, was a great commercial centre. "Although the site of Nineveh afforded no special advantage for commerce, and although she owed her greatness rather to her political position as the capital of the empire, yet, situated upon a navigable river communicating with the Euphrates and the Persian Gulf, she must have soon formed one of the great trading stations between that important inland sea, and Syria, and the Mediterranean, and must have become a depot for the merchandise supplied to a great part of Asia Minor, Armenis, and Persia" (Smith's Bible Dictionary). Again, "Nineveh was most favourably situated for carrying on commerce with other countries. The roads from Asia Minor, Syria, Egypt and Phoenicia, that led into Media, Persia, and the interior of Asia, converged at Nineveh, and brought thither merchandise from all lands; and the Assyrians themselves exported their own produce and manufactures to the far West. Among these are enumerated textile fabrics, carpets, dyed attire, and embroidered work, carvings in ivory, gems, spices" (see Rawlinson, *Anc. Mon.*; Layard, *Nineveh*). The opening words, "Thou hast multiplied", imply that Nineveh sought to increase her commerce, encouraging the merchants so that she might benefit from their trade. This increase of merchants and their enterprises greatly enhanced Nineveh's wealth. However, she would not ultimately benefit from the riches she had stored up from her commerce.

Material wealth in itself is not evil, but when it is one's sole ambition or boast it becomes the object of one's affections and this is a root of all evil (1 Tim 6.10). Material wealth is transient and uncertain, but spiritual things are eternal and sure – "Lay not up for yourselves treasures upon earth, where moth and rust doth corrupt, and where thieves break through and steal: But lay up for yourselves treasures in heaven" (Mt 6.19-21).

The latter part of v.16 here has been interpreted by commentators in two different ways because the word "spoileth" (PASHAT - 6584) has two basic meanings - one, to strip off, and the other, to invade. Those who take the first meaning, to strip off, consider that it refers to the young locusts stripping off their horny sheaths and quickly flying away. They apply this figure to Nineveh. "It suits the context better to regard it as a symbol of Nineveh. After all the plundering expeditions she had made, she would vanish like the locust"; and, "The rapidity with which a swarm of such locusts flies off is here a symbol of the rapidity with which the busy merchant population of Nineveh will melt away" (F. C. Cook and S. R. Driver). Those who take the other meaning, "to invade", apply the figure to the besieging army which, after plundering the city and stripping it of all its treasures, leaves it in ruins – "*Pashat* never means anything else than to plunder, or to invade with plundering...In the passage before us we cannot understand by the *yeleg*, which 'plunders and flies away'...the innumerable multitude of the merchants of Nineveh, because they were not able to fly away in crowds out of the besieged city. Moreover, the flying away of the merchants would be quite contrary to the meaning of the whole description, which does not promise deliverance from danger by flight, but threatens destruction. The *yeleg* is rather the innumerable army of the enemy, which plunders everything, and hurries away with the booty" (See Keil & Delitzsch and W. J. Deane). The second view seems to suit the comparison with v.15 and would contrast the wealth of Nineveh with the devastation that awaited her, as the prophet does in previous verses. Nineveh, who had so often plundered other nations, would herself be plundered and stripped of her wealth, which would be considered an act of just retribution. As soon as the invading forces entered and captured the city they would begin to plunder and speedily remove the spoil.

The word rendered "crowned" (MINZAR - 4502) in v.17 which occurs only here is of uncertain meaning. There are two schools of thought as to its derivation and thus as to its import.

1. Some scholars think it is derived from the Hebrew word NAZAR (5144) which means to set apart - to separate or consecrate - and consider that it refers to the multitude selected or conscripted to fight and defend Nineveh. They object to the terms "crowned" or "princes" on the ground of the simile "as the locusts". This simile they take as indicating a multitude which, they say, could not refer to a comparatively small number. However, the simile could well refer to the swiftness of the locusts' flight rather than their actual numbers.

2. Other scholars believe the word is derived from the Hebrew word NEZER (5145) which also means "to set apart" - separation, consecration, crown. It is used of "the crown of the anointing oil" in relation to the High Priest (Lev 21.12), and of "the consecration of his God" being on the head of the Nazarite (Num 6.7). The word here indicates the princes, nobles, and officers of the Assyrian empire who are distinguished by the head crown or band. F. C. Cook explains that "The Hebrew word is unusual in its form, but its etymology is clear, and there is no good reason for disputing the meaning assigned to it by Jewish interpreters, who are followed in our AV. It describes what is corroborated by Assyrian monuments on which 'high officers of state were adorned with diadems, closely resembling the lower band of the royal mitre, separated from the cap itself...Very commonly the head was encircled with a simple fillet or hoop, probably of gold, without any adornment' (Gosse, *Assyria*)". The Hebrew word MINZAR has been translated "princes" by Jewish translators (See Rabbi A. J. Rosenberg and Helen Spurrell).

The word for "captains" (TIPSAR - 2951) refers to military officers and is only found elsewhere in Jeremiah 51.27 in regard to a commander in chief. It is generally accepted that it is not of Hebrew origin, but probably an Assyrian name for soldiers of a special kind, i.e. officers. It is to be noted that the last syllable of the words MINZAR and TIPSAR - *zar* or *sar* - which means "prince" - is also the last syllable of the names Nebuchadnezzar, Belteshazzar, and Belshazzar (Dan 1.1,7; 5.1). One considers that there is no reason to dispute the rendering of MINZAR and TIPSAR as "crowned" and "captains" as is seen in the AV.

The words "great" and "grasshoppers" are the singular and plural of the same Hebrew word (GOB, GOBAY - 1462) which is only found elsewhere in Amos 7.1. It refers to some kind of locust - there are a number of Hebrew synonyms for "locusts" denoting either different species or different stages of development. The expression "great grasshoppers" is literally "locust of locusts" which has been taken to mean the largest of locusts and thus leading to the AV rendering "great". The image of locusts camping in the hedges in the cold day and flying off in the warmth of the sun depicts the order of the Assyrian leaders and army that would be in place to defend the city, but who would, in the heat of battle, flee away. The idea is that they would be put to flight and disappear. The last expression, "their place is not known where they are", indicates the complete annihilation of the Assyrians. Thus the overthrow of Nineveh and the end of the Assyrian empire is portrayed in the flight and disappearance of a swarm of locusts.

(c) Nineveh deserted and obliterated (vv.18-19). These verses are conclusive and solemn as the prophet is looking back to the defeat of Nineveh. He describes the scene of death and destruction inflicted by the hostile invading army, having captured, plundered and left the city as a heap of ashes, without hope. The pronouns from vv.11-17 are all in the

feminine because the city Nineveh is addressed, but now they are masculine as the king of Assyria himself is the focus of attention, although he is
viewed here as the representative of the whole Assyrian empire and its
power which was centred in Nineveh. His leaders sleep, his nobles are
brought down to the dust, and his people are scattered. The holiness
and justice of Jehovah are vindicated and His voice is heard through
the fulfilment of the prophecy.

Assyria's shepherds, in v.18, are the rulers who were responsible for
governing the people and upon whom the safety of the city depended
(cp. Jer 3.15; 23.1-4; Ezek 34). The nobles are the mighty men that the
king relied upon to defend the city (cp. 2.5 - worthies). Some commentators
have taken these two companies as being careless and indifferent, feeling
secure and thus providing no help in the coming attack. However, that
would not be suitable to the context nor to the object of the whole
prophecy. The word translated "slumber" (NUM - 5123) is not used here
of natural sleep nor used figuratively of carelessness and neglect as in Isaiah
56.10, but of the sleep of death (cp. Jer 51.39,57). "Twice the verb is used
to denote the sleep of death. In the one instance (Ps 76.5), men have been
rebuked by God and have fallen into sleep. In the second instance (Nah
3.18), the rulers of the king of Assyria slumber or are dead" (TWOT). The
princes and rulers would be slain and lie still in the slumber of death.

The word "dwell" (SHAKAN - 7931) contains the idea of a long or
permanent stay and is used of God dwelling among His people Israel (Ex
25.8; 29.45-46), doing so forever (Ezek 43.7-9), as well as dwelling in the
high and holy place (Is 57.15). SHAKAN is also used of Israel dwelling to
move no more or forever (2 Sam 7.10; 1 Chr 17.9; 23.25; Ps 37.29). It is
elsewhere rendered "abode" of the cloud upon the Tabernacle (Ex 40.35;
Num 9.17-18), "place" where God chose to place His name (Deut 14.23;
16.2; 26.2), and "rest" (Ps 16.9; 55.6).

The expression "dwell in the dust" has been given as "are at rest" referring
to death. The mighty men would be smitten and lie down beneath the
dust of death. Neither the rulers or the mighty warriors would survive the
attack upon the city. Thus the high hopes and confidence of Nineveh in its
own strength and ability would be shattered. The result would be that the
people, like sheep, would be scattered upon the mountains with no one
to gather them (cp. Num 27.17; 1 Kings 22.17). Even in this last expression
there is the thought of death - the people scattered would perish for there
would be none to help them. Thus arrogant Nineveh, the proud capital of
Assyria, would become desolate. The power that had for centuries
dominated and oppressed nations would be silent.

Many there are, today, who place their hope and confidence of being in
heaven at the close of life upon their good works, religious observances,
or their own opinions, but such hope and confidence will be shattered.
Without repentance one will perish (Lk 13.3,5), without faith one cannot
please God (Heb 11.6), without shedding of blood there is no forgiveness

(Heb 9.22), and without Christ there is no hope (Eph 2.12). Nothing of human achievement can fit a person for heaven - repentance and faith in the Lord Jesus Christ and His finished work alone can do that. Although believers are eternally secure, there is a similar principle that is true in relation to how they live - those who seek to live for God in their own strength and ability will certainly fail, but those who live in the power of the Spirit will succeed (Rom 15.13,19; Eph 3.20).

Nineveh's devastation would be irreparable and its downfall would be rejoiced over (v.19). It is stated that "healing" (KEHA - 3545) is a noun formed from the adjective and has the thought of extinction or softening. Strong's Concordance gives the meaning of weakening and, figuratively, alleviation, i.e. to cure. Thus the word does contain the thought of healing although some reject this and think it should be read with the Hebrew word GEHA (1456) which means to cure and is translated "medicine" (Prov 17.22). "Bruise" (SHEBER - 7667) means fracture and is translated "breach" (Is 30.26; Jer 14.17; Lam 2.13), "broken" (Lev 21.19), and "breaking" (Is 30.13-14). Figuratively it means ruin and thus is mainly given in the Old Testament as "destruction". So the expression "no healing of thy bruise" indicates that Nineveh's ruin would be irreparable - there could be no restoration for the city. The reason for this is given in the next expression, "thy wound is grievous", referring to the stroke of divine judgment.

The word "bruit" is archaic, commonly used by writers in a past day, meaning a report or rumour. The idea here is that all who hear the news of Nineveh's collapse, and thus the destruction of the Assyrian empire, would clap their hands with joy, as well as in derision. All the nations would rejoice because they had suffered from the tyranny, cruelty, and oppression of Assyria. Among those rejoicing would be Judah at the fulfilment of this prophecy and the vindication of the character of Jehovah. Although the nations might gloat with revengeful joy, the people of God should not gloat, but should rejoice in the righteous dealings of Jehovah against sin and rebellion towards Him and His people. The closing word "continually" implies God's longsuffering and thus the enormity of Assyria's guilt. God could not and would not allow Assyria's cruelty and violence to continue unabated. He would, in His time, in His way, and in keeping with His word intervene and deal righteously with Assyria in judgment. One can but add the words of C. L. Feinberg: "The nations had suffered so much and so long from her cunning and cruel dealings, that they rejoice now that she has come to her well-deserved end. But we do God an injustice if we think this is what He preferred for Assyria. God delights to bless and only judges when He must. Far rather would God have heaped upon Nineveh blessing and prosperity instead of shame and ruin. But she chose the contrary part and her doom is writ large in the annals of the world's history. The fulfilment of the prophecy took place about a half-century after the prophet Nahum. The Medes entered an alliance with the Lydians (against whom they were fighting) to form a common front with Nabopolassar (at Babylon) against

Nineveh. The city fell in 612 BC, a fact definitely confirmed by the Babylonian Chronicles".

Conclusion

The prophecy of Nahum is centred upon Assyria and its capital city, Nineveh, which was characterised by tyranny and cruelty. In particular its opposition to God and His people, displayed in its removal of Israel from its land and its oppression of Judah, is in view (2.2). Unlike most prophetic books there is no condemnation of the people of God, although there is a reference to God using Assyria, as His instrument, to chastise His people (1.12-13). The prophecy directs the attention of the people of God to the destruction of Assyria and Nineveh to indicate the faithfulness and mercy of God in removing their oppressor. It was also to encourage them to remain faithful in affliction and to keep His word. However, they failed to respond and therefore were later taken into captivity by the Babylonians.

The book deals with moral principles which are applicable to all nations and individuals, whether or not they recognise the claims of God. It also shows that sinful practices, rebellion against God, and hostility to His people may appear to pass with impunity, but this is not the case. God, who is eternal and longsuffering, can patiently wait until the appointed time of His righteous judgment. It must be appreciated that however dark and difficult the day might be, and however much evil might abound, good will ultimately overcome evil because God's judgment operates in keeping with His holiness and justice. Thus the people of God, in every generation, should be encouraged knowing that God is upon the throne, that He is righteous, and that His purpose will be fulfilled. However, one must also appreciate that God is love and that He is merciful and gracious. Thus He always acts within the context of love and His love always operates in keeping with His righteousness. The people of God today should act likewise pursuing righteousness and love – "...follow righteousness, faith, charity, peace, with them that call on the Lord out of a pure heart" (2 Tim 2.22).

As stated, Nahum's prophecy was totally fulfilled even to the disappearance of the existence of Nineveh, but one must not restrict the prophecy to this one historical event. Since Nineveh also represents the opposition of the world to God and His people, the prediction of Nineveh's destruction also applies to world powers of a future day. In end times there will be a world power, a ten kingdom confederacy, with its capital city symbolised by Nineveh, which will dominate the world in the spirit that characterised Assyria in Nahum's day. The destruction of that power and its capital city is prefigured in this prophecy.

HABAKKUK

P. Harding

CONTENTS

INTRODUCTION

It appears that the prophecy of Habakkuk was addressed to a people who had experienced political, social, and religious change. The peace and prosperity of the reign of Josiah soon passed away. They were the result of Josiah's reforms and a turning again to the Lord. Although those reforms seemed only to affect the outward observances of Judah, God nevertheless honoured the faithfulness of Josiah (2 Chr 34.26-28). After Josiah's death, the kingdom of Judah forgot the reason for their peace and prosperity and soon returned to their evil ways (2 Kings 21.16-26; 23.29-32). They also ignored the teaching of Deuteronomy 29.25-28 and the message of Huldah the prophetess to King Josiah (2 Kings 22.14-20). The results of Josiah's reformation must have been short lived, for the next and last kings of Judah did evil in the sight of the Lord (2 Kings 23.31-32,36-37; 24.8-9,18-19). Thus the spiritual condition of Judah when Habakkuk prophesied was one of apostasy with violence, lawlessness, and perverted judgment (Hab 1.2-4).

The value of the book is not in its size but in its unique structure which unfolds the way in which Habakkuk progresses from perplexity of mind to praising God. God used Habakkuk, with his burden concerning the prevailing conditions, to reveal that He was not complacent about evil, and to show His righteous dealings with men. The prophet learned that God, in His sovereignty, was working out His own programme for the punishment of evil and the ultimate blessing of His people. Habakkuk was amazed to learn that God was going to use, as His instrument, a nation more wicked than the Israelites to punish and chastise Judah. God revealed to him that the very nation He would use would itself come under the judgment of God for its cruelty, and that the righteous, those who lived by faith, would be preserved. Thus Habakkuk learned that in every circumstance of life one can rest and depend upon God and His word. In this book, therefore, we see the prophet transformed from a perplexed and questioning man to a rejoicing and confident one who rests upon the majesty and word of God.

The Prophet of the Book

Nothing definite is known of the personal history of Habakkuk. His generation, lineage, family, and place of abode are not mentioned in the Scriptures. Less is stated in the Old Testament concerning Habakkuk than almost any other prophet. Some scholars state that the prophet's name is apparently not Hebrew but comes from the Akkadian word for some plant or fruit tree (D. W. Baker). Other scholars accept that his name comes from the Hebrew word HABAQ (2263) which means to embrace (C. L. Feinberg). This word occurs in some passages in the Old Testament (eg. Gen 29.13; 33.4; Prov 4.8) and denotes an expression of love by the position or action of one's hands or arms. Martin Luther stated that Habakkuk was "one who takes another to his heart and [into] his arms, as one soothes a poor weeping child, telling it to be quiet" (C. J. Barber). Habakkuk embraced God by prayer in his bewilderment (1.2,12); by faith, expecting a solution to his problem (2.1); in praise (3.1-15); and with confidence (3.17-19). He wrestled with the perplexities, problems, and difficulties of his day by laying hold upon God and embracing His word. The safest course for the believer in every circumstance of life today is to lay hold upon God in prayer.

Jewish tradition states that Habakkuk was the son of the Shunammite woman who was blessed by Elisha. He was called "Habakkuk" as an expression of "embracing", because the prophet used that term when he blessed the woman – "About this season, according to the time of life, thou shalt embrace a son" (2 Kings 4.16). The double "k" of Habakkuk is said to represent the two embraces, that of his mother and that of the prophet. Again, tradition and the Apocryphal book of "Bel and the Dragon" states that Habakkuk brought Daniel his supper when he was in the lions' den (Rabbi A. J. Rosenberg). Such traditions are fanciful and are not in keeping with the book itself nor the times in which Habakkuk lived.

The book takes its name from the author who designates himself "the prophet" (1.1) which some take to indicate that he was a professional temple prophet (D. W. Baker). There is support for linking the prophet with the Levitical order as liturgical connections are suggested in ch.3. The expression "upon Shigionoth" (3.1) is a musical ascription (see Ps 7), and the closing expression of 3.19 along with the use of "Selah" (3.3,9,13) appears to indicate that Habakkuk was competent enough to compose and to take part in the singing in the temple. Therefore, it seems that he belonged to one of the Levitical families who were responsible for the maintenance of the temple music (1 Chr 15.16; 2 Chr 5.11-14). He was a man familiar with the Scriptures and in particular the Psalms. It appears that Habakkuk was called to prophesy while serving in the Levitical service, in relation to singing, in the temple just before the captivity of Judah. Being a Levite he was from the same tribe as Jeremiah (Jer 1.1) and Ezekiel (Ezek 1.3).

The Period of the Book
Habakkuk does not date his prophecy as some of the other prophets do (Is 1.1; Jer 1.1-3; Hos 1.1; Zeph 1.1), and so there are various suggestions as to the period in which he prophesied and wrote his book. Some Jewish chronologers place his ministry during Manasseh's reign along with Joel and Nahum (see Rabbi A. J. Rosenberg). E. B. Pusey also places the prophecy during Manasseh's reign (696-641 BC), but C. J. Barber states that "such an early date is too soon for the Babylonians to have become well known for the atrocities described in chapters 1 and 2". Campbell Morgan states that he probably "prophesied during the closing years of Manasseh or during the reign of Amon or earlier than Zephaniah in the days of Josiah". Others have suggested a date between Josiah's reformation (622 BC) and

the fall of Nineveh (612 BC). However, a number of commentators have dated Habakkuk during the reign of Jehoiakim (609-598 BC).

The period when Habakkuk prophesied may well be indicated in the book itself. The conditions mentioned in 1.2-4 could never have prevailed during the reign of Josiah (640-609 BC) when Assyria was the dominant power. Jehoahaz succeeded Josiah but had only reigned for three months when he was deposed by Pharaoh-nechoh who placed Eliakim on the throne, changing his name to Jehoiakim (2 Kings 23.30-34). It appears from 1.6 that the invasion of Judah by the Chaldeans (Babylonians) was about to take place. The Babylonian empire gained power under Nabopolassar around 625 BC increasing in strength in 612 BC when it destroyed the Assyrian capital, Nineveh. It reached its peak in 605-604 BC when Nebuchadnezzar defeated Egypt at Carchemish in Syria (Jer 46.1-2). A suitable period for Habakkuk's prophecy would be the reign of Jehoiakim because it was during that period that the Babylonian presence was increasingly felt (see J. Bright, *A History of Israel*). The personal knowledge of Babylonian cruelty recorded in 1.12-17 also agrees with this. There are a number of passages in Jeremiah which correspond with 1.3-4, again pointing to the same period (Jer 11.9-12; 14.10-12). Although the destruction of Jerusalem did not occur until the eleventh year of Zedekiah's reign (587-586 BC), the first invasion of Judah by the Babylonians took place in the third year of Jehoiakim's reign, when Daniel and his companions, along with the vessels of the House of God, were taken to Babylon (605 BC - see 2 Kings 24.1; Dan 1.1-7). A possible date then for the writing of the book would be prior to the first invasion by the Babylonians as seems to be suggested in 2.2-3. From the above, we glean that Habakkuk was a contemporary of Jeremiah, Nahum, and possibly Zephaniah. The warnings of these prophets were ignored by the leaders and most of the people who preferred the bright picture painted by the false prophets (Jer 5.31; 14.14; 23.32). It seems that God first revealed to Habakkuk that the end for Judah was near.

The Message of the Book

The book of Habakkuk is similar to the book of Jonah in the sense that both open with the prophet's perplexity and close with God's solution. However, Jonah seeks to avoid the perplexity by running away, whereas Habakkuk takes his to God for an answer. Habakkuk differs from most of the prophetic books as it records the prophet's own experience of soul before God. Generally the prophets spoke for God to the people, whereas Habakkuk speaks to God about His dealings with the people. There is no record in the book of the prophet speaking for God to the people, although his prophecy is for the people of Judah. Most of the book is devoted to dialogue between Habakkuk and God.

The structure of the book revolves around two dialogues, with a concluding Psalm and the rejoicing of Habakkuk. Chapter 1 dwells upon

Habakkuk's search for answers, and the invasion of the Chaldeans. Chapter 2 pronounces the judgment of the Chaldeans and chapter 3 records the prophet's prayer and praise. Habakkuk opens the prophecy with the complaint that, although the godly in Judah are oppressed, suffering all kinds of affliction, and the wicked prosper, there is no intervention by God. Why? This is a question that has been asked down the ages. In answer, God reveals to Habakkuk that, far from being indifferent to evil, He was going to send the Chaldeans to invade the land because of Judah's rebellion and idolatry. This puzzles Habakkuk exceedingly and further distresses him since he considers the Chaldeans to be far more wicked than Judah. Habakkuk is not expressing any patriotic objections to this revelation, but his distress of spirit is in view of the cruel and unrighteous behaviour of the Chaldeans. His problem was, first of all, the suffering of the godly at the hands of the ungodly in Judah, but now his difficulty is in the choice of the Chaldeans by God to punish Judah, which is relatively innocent in contrast to them. As Habakkuk waits for an answer to his dilemma, God unfolds His righteousness in His judgment upon the Chaldeans and in His salvation. This results in the prayer, praise, and rejoicing of Habakkuk. Thus the book unfolds the righteous dealings of God and the development of the prophet's faith. God was indeed sovereign and in control in spite of the prevailing conditions.

The book, in a sense, is a defence of God's sovereignty, omnipotence, and goodness in view of evil, and illustrates the way in which the just can live by faith.

"A comparison of 1.2 with 3.19 gives us an indication of the true value of the book. Opening in mystery and questioning, it closes in certainty and affirmation. The contrast is startling. The first is almost a wail of despair, and the last is a shout of confidence" (Campbell Morgan).

Whereas Nahum prophesied the destruction of Assyria, the power that took into exile the kingdom of Israel, Habakkuk prophesied the destruction of Babylon, the power that took into exile the kingdom of Judah. Like Nahum, Habakkuk does not arraign his own people, but sees them, in comparison with the Chaldeans, as relatively innocent. However, he goes further than Nahum in his insight into the issues that surround God using the Chaldeans as an instrument to chastise His people.

It is generally acknowledged that the book has a high place among the Hebrew prophets and that its literary quality is unsurpassed in the Hebrew Scriptures. Delitzsch states, "His language is classical throughout, replete with rare words and idiomatic phrases peculiar to him. His manner of presentation bears the impress of independent power and consummate beauty. That his thoughts rush swiftly onward and soar to the greatest heights, does not, however, interfere with the clarity of organisation and artistic form of the entire book. Like Isaiah, Habakkuk is comparatively much more independent of the former prophets" (see also F. A. Tatford).

The poetry of ch.3 has been considered the most magnificent of Hebrew poetry, and the language of the book is very beautiful. M. F. Unger writes, "The magnificent lyric ode of ch.3 contains one of the greatest descriptions of the theophany in relation to the coming of the Lord which has been given by the Holy Spirit, awaiting fulfilment in the Day of the Lord (cp. 2 Thess 1.7-10)" (Unger's Bible Handbook).

The book teaches that the people of God should wait patiently for their vindication and retain their loyalty and faith whatever circumstances or doubts may arise. Through faith and confidence in God the people of God can maintain faithfulness in the midst of suffering and injustice.

The lessons of the book are: the just live by faith; God does not overlook sin; evil does not ultimately triumph; believers should wait patiently upon God; and God is sovereign and in control in the universe.

The Purpose of the Book

The main purpose of the book is to encourage those who are truly the people of God to have confidence in Him whatever the surrounding circumstances. Its design is to comfort those under severe afflictions and encourage them to live by faith and patiently wait upon God. The book reveals that God is unchanging and unchangeable and that He is working out His own purposes notwithstanding all appearances to the contrary The keynote of the book is, "the just shall live by his faith" (2.4). Confidence in God, despite adverse circumstances, is emphasised, and the self-consuming nature of a self-centred life is condemned. Believers should be living for God, not for self, and have their eyes upon the unseen. The will of God is all important to the child of God, knowing that God is upon the throne whatever the circumstances. The message of Habakkuk is an encouragement and a stimulation of faith for the people of God. In embracing them he comforts them with the assurance of their preservation despite their captivity, and sets them an example of living by faith. The theme of the book is therefore "Faith: its Trial and Triumph".

OUTLINE OF THE BOOK

The Title (1.1)

Problems and Answers (1.2-2.20)
A. The first dialogue (1.2-11)
    1. The perplexity of Habakkuk (1.2-4)
      a) The silence of God (1.2)
      b) The problem of unjudged sin (1.3-4)
    2. God's answer - The Chaldean invasion of Judah (1.5-11)
      a) God's activity (1.5)
      b) God's instrument (1.6-11)
B. The second dialogue (1.12-2.20)
    1. The problem of the Chaldean invasion (1.12-17)

2. The attitude of Habakkuk (2.1)
3. The answer of God (2.2-20)
    a) Instructions to Habakkuk (2.2-3)
    b) The divine principle (2.4)
    c) The judgment upon the Chaldeans (2.5-20)
        (i) For their aggression and exploitation (2.6-8)
        (ii) For their covetousness (2.9-11)
        (iii) For their brutality (2.12-14)
        (iv) For their debauchery and atrocities (2.15-17)
        (v) For their idolatry (2.18-20)

The Prayer, Psalm, and Praise of Habakkuk (3.1-19)
    A. The prayer (3.1-2)
    B. The psalm - future deliverance (3.3-15)
      1. The majesty and glory of God (3.3-7)
      2. The power and purpose of God (3.8-15)
    C. The praise - The fear and faith of Habakkuk (3.16-19)
      1. Habakkuk's conception of God (3.16)
      2. Habakkuk's confidence in God (3.17-19).

In ch.1 we have the Problems of Habakkuk, in ch.2 we have the Prophecy of Habakkuk relative to the judgment of the Chaldeans, and in ch.3 we have the Prayer of Habakkuk. The key verse seems to be 2.4 – "the just shall live by his faith." Other notable verses are: 2.2 - "make it plain...that he may run that readeth it"; 2.14 - "the earth shall be filled with the knowledge of the glory of the Lord"; 2.20 - "the Lord is in his holy temple: let the earth keep silence before him"; 3.18 - "Yet will I rejoice in the Lord, I will joy in the God of my salvation". Habakkuk quotes much from other parts of the Old Testament, and is quoted in the New Testament: 1.5 in Acts 13.40-41; 2.4 in Romans 1.17, Galatians 3.11, and Hebrews 10.38.

HABAKKUK 1

Verse 1: The Title

This opening verse gives no indication of the lineage of Habakkuk nor of the time of his ministry, but it is a title which indicates the serious nature of the prophecy. It prepares the people for the solemn details that follow.

The Hebrew word translated "burden" (MASSA - 4853) occurs in the Old Testament with two different meanings: load or burden, and oracle or utterance, the latter being a figurative meaning derived from the former. It is used of a burden or weight to be carried (Ex 23.5; Num 4.15); of a responsibility to be borne (Num 11.11); of tribute (2 Chr 17.11 - silver being carried to the king as tribute); of sin as a burden (Ps 38.4); and of the heart's desire in the sense of lifting up one's soul (Ezek 24.25 – "set"). In 1 Chronicles 15.22,27, where it is translated "song", it is linked with bearing the ark. It has been stated that, "In prophetic passages such as the book of Habakkuk, it announced heavy judgments upon the people" (C. J. Barber – see Is 13.1; Zech 12.1; Mal 1.1). Here the word indicates that the prophecy unfolds the solemn consequences of departure by Judah from the word of God and also judgment upon the Chaldeans because of their wickedness. Habakkuk would no doubt have felt the weight of this ministry intended for the people of Judah. His ministry was not palatable, but it was necessary. Even today faithful men, with burdened spirits, are compelled to minister that which is not palatable but yet is necessary in order to stem the tide of declension and to produce something for God in the people of God. How important it is for those who minister to feel the weight of divine truth in their own souls first before faithfully conveying that truth to others.

This title is unusual in the sense that Habakkuk actually refers to himself as a prophet, unlike the authors of most of the other prophetic books. A prophet is one who has been chosen by God to receive direct revelation from Him, along with His authority to convey that revelation to others, either orally or in written form. Thus to ignore the prophet's proclamation was to set aside the word of God to them.

The Hebrew word HAZA (2372) is rendered "see", "look", "behold", and "Prophesy" in the Old Testament Scriptures. It is used of literal sight (Job 23.9; Prov 22.29); of the Lord beholding men (Ps 11.4,7; 17.2); of men beholding or contemplating God and His works (Ps 17.15; 27.4; 46.8; 63.2); and of prophetic sight or vision (Is 13.1; and here). This revelatory vision was given by God to the prophets that they might prophesy to the people either in an oral or written form. Here the Lord causes Habakkuk to see the impending punishment of Judah and the judgment of the Chaldeans. Both divine foreknowledge and divine revelation are indicated in this verse.

Verses 1.2-2.20: Problems and Answers

There are two problems in the opening verses of ch.1 (vv.2-4), the one springing out of the other. The first is the oppression and affliction of the godly while the perpetrators prosper. This has been a problem throughout human history and in every country of the world, and is because of sin. Because of such conditions in Judah Habakkuk cried to God in prayer. How good to know that the believer can always have recourse to prayer in every circumstance of life. However, another problem arose for Habakkuk since there seemed to be no answer to his cries. The apparent silence of God was a sore problem to him. How many believers down the centuries have felt like Habakkuk, thinking that God had not answered their prayers? God always hears and answers the prayers of His people, but in His own time and in His own way. When God did answer the prophet it was not as he had anticipated (1.5-11). This again has been the experience of many of the Lord's people. The answer Habakkuk received became another problem to him. How could God, who was infinitely holy, use such a wicked nation to chastise His people (1.12-17)? Such problems arise because we do not see the full picture or we lack perception and are impatient. God is too wise to make a mistake and He always works for the ultimate blessing of His people. Habakkuk waits for God to speak (2.1). It is always better to wait upon God than to come to hasty conclusions. God's answer included confirmation of the chastisement of Judah, encouragement to the just, who lived by faith (2.2-4), and a revelation of His justice in judging the Chaldeans for their wickedness (2.5-20). God is indeed in control and His purposes will be fulfilled despite the opposition and unbelief of men.

The first dialogue (vv.2-11)

Habakkuk, distressed in spirit because of the conditions prevailing in Judah, expresses his perplexity to God because of His silence and apparent inactivity in neither delivering the righteous nor punishing the wicked (vv.2-4). God's answer, when it comes, is most unexpected and deepens the concern of the prophet, although it was truly an answer to his cry. His plea was for God to manifest His justice and righteousness by dealing with the wickedness of Judah. This God was about to do, using the Chaldeans as His instrument of chastisement, much to Habakkuk's amazement (vv.5-11).

The perplexity of Habakkuk (vv.2-4)

These verses show the moral and spiritual depravity in Judah, in their departure from God and His word. Violence and iniquity abounded in a people who should have been characterised by holiness. The law of God had been set aside and thus justice was perverted. The deep concern of the prophet because of the dreadful conditions prevailing is expressed in his cry to God to intervene. He knew those conditions were contrary to God's character and word. This reveals that Habakkuk was concerned about the glory of God and that he believed that intervention by God was necessary in order to display His character. He also desired to see righteousness flourishing in the land. Is there that attitude among the people of God today? Believers should be concerned about moral conditions and pray for the good of society. Those who have a deep desire for righteousness will be marked by practical righteousness (1 Cor 15.34; 1 Pet 2.24). These verses take the form of a lament or complaint where the need is described and help is sought from the Lord. The prophet was to learn that God's thoughts were not the same as his thoughts and that God's ways were different from his ways (Is 55.8). Every child of God needs to learn this important truth. One may be perplexed about many things, but, like the prophet here, it is to be accepted that God's ways are always best.

(a) The silence of God (v.2). The expression "O Lord, how long" echoes the cry of the Psalmists, particularly that in Psalm 94.3 (see also Ps 6.3; 13.1). Most prophets, unlike Habakkuk here and unlike the Psalmists, did not normally question God as to His silence and apparent inactivity (H. Barnes). Habakkuk generally uses in his prophecy the name Jehovah (Lord), the unchanging eternal One, the covenant keeping God. The expression indicates that the prophet had called upon Jehovah concerning the existing situation in Judah on more than one occasion. "How long", is Habakkuk's lamenting cry as he questions the long silence of God which has only deepened his concern. Time very often seems long when one is taken up with the problems, difficulties and trials of life. Circumstances and conditions can so often distract and distress. The hymn writer expressed this:

> Oh, what peace we often forfeit,
> Oh, what needless pain we bear!
> All because we do not carry
> Everything to God in prayer.
> (J. Scriven).

His meaning was that we should take everything to God and leave it there, resting completely on Him. This is easier said than done, but is the only way to enjoy His presence and peace in the changing situations of life.

The prophet's desire here is for Jehovah's intervention in punishment upon the wicked of Judah. There are two Hebrew words rendered "cry" and "cry out" in this verse. The first, SHAWA (7768), occurs mainly in Job (eight times) and Psalms (nine times). The other four occasions are in the prophetic books (Is 58.9; Lam 3.8; Jonah 2.2; and here). It is used mainly with the personal pronoun "I" (eg. Job 30.20; Ps 28.2) and indicates the intensity of the petition. The second, ZAAQ (2199), is used more often, and here it is an expression of the need felt. Habakkuk cries out of a heart disturbed because of the wickedness in the land. The short tense, "shall I cry", indicates decision and determination, whereas the long tense, "cry out", suggests a continual action. The prophet was continually distressed by what was taking place and so continually cried out intensely to Jehovah for His intervention. He groaned in his own spirit and he groaned to God. To God alone Habakkuk made his plea as he recognised that Jehovah knew the state of Judah far better than he did, and Jehovah alone could change the situation by punishing the wicked and saving the godly. The salvation mentioned here is deliverance from oppression and freedom from distress. He had not only witnessed the hostility of the ungodly but more than likely he had, like Jeremiah (Jer 18.18,23), personally experienced it. Thus he pours out his heart to Jehovah, beseeching Him fervently to intervene because he desired that justice and righteousness should prevail. However, his cry and complaint were not merely personal but on behalf of the faithful in Judah who had the same desire.

Conditions in Judah at that time (during the reign of Jehoiakim) were characterised by evil (Jer 25.1-7). Jeremiah, like Habakkuk, cried to God because of them (Jer 12.1; 20.8). The apparent silence of God regarding Habakkuk's plea caused him to question God. Why silence? Why no intervention? His knowledge of the character of God did not correspond to his present experience. The apparent silence of God is still hard to understand. When evil and sin abound, as in today's society, why does God not intervene? The same questions have been asked down through the centuries by the people of God. Why does God allow His people to suffer and the ungodly to prosper? Why does He not answer prayer? How long will God allow wickedness to prevail? Even unbelievers ask, "Why does God allow such wickedness to continue?". However, this does not mean that there is no answer and that God is not capable of dealing with every situation. He is sovereign, all is under His control and we must accept this. It is not for Christians to know the reason why, but to wait patiently upon Him and to rest in Him. The apparent silence of God to our petitions can often be to test our faith and sincerity. True prayer involves an appreciation of the greatness of God and an acceptance of His will.

(b) The problem of unjudged sin (vv.3-4.) The prophet's complaint is in regard to the grief and suffering of the poor and godly who are being victimised and exploited (see Ps 10). He unfolds the reason for his distress and concern in these two verses. Daily he came face to face with these appalling situations. He could not understand why such conditions should prevail among those who claimed to be the people of God. "Why dost thou shew me iniquity?", was a cry of incredulity that iniquity prospered in the place where God had placed His name and where justice and righteousness should have been displayed. That the nations around should be iniquitous would have been no surprise, but that iniquity was prevalent in Judah without being judged was distressing. It is sad to see similar conditions in the world today but that is to be expected. However, it is distressing to see them among those who profess to belong to Christ.

Habakkuk's deep distress and the severity of the wickedness are emphasised by three couplets in v.3 - iniquity and grievance; spoiling and violence; strife and contention. Habakkuk had witnessed the wickedness of those in positions of influence and power (Jer 2.8; 10.21; Zeph 3.3-4). He had seen exploitation, oppression, violence and injustice, but was powerless to intervene and so had cried to God for His intervention. However, his troubled spirit had not been calmed. The prophet's expectancy of God's intervention was in keeping with the history of the nation (Num 16; Judg 7; 1 Sam 7; 2 Kings 19) and with God's promise to hear the cries of the needy (Ex 22.23,27). David had stated in Psalm 34 that "The eyes of the Lord are upon the righteous, and his ears are open unto their cry" (v.15), and that "The righteous cry, and the Lord heareth, and delivereth them out of all their troubles" (v.17). The words of the prophet Nathan to David the king in 2 Samuel 7.10 along with his own experience (2 Sam 22.7) would justify this expectation. The prophet would also be aware of Isaiah's prophecy that there would be no more violence in Jerusalem but righteousness and praise (Is 60.18; 61.11). Habakkuk's experience was so different from this and it seemed to suggest that God was tolerating the evil which abounded in Judah. He, like us, was a creature of time and expected an immediate answer to his cries. He, like us, thought that God would solve the problems in the way he expected. As he viewed the conditions he might well have felt that the foundation of Jewish society (the law, justice, and righteousness) was being destroyed (Ps 11.3), and he could well have used the language of Psalm 12.1, "Help, Lord; for the godly man ceaseth; for the faithful fail from among the children of men".

How many believers today feel like Habakkuk? The result of such wickedness was a weakening of the law, and perverted judgment. The law was given by God to Israel to control and govern them so that there might be justice and righteousness in the land. There was no nation that had statutes and judgment so righteous as the God-given law (Deut 4.8), and judges in Israel were charged with judging righteously in every case (Deut 1.16). There should have been righteous judgment without partiality (Lev 19.15) so that the righteous might be justified and the wicked condemned (Deut 25.1). However, in Habakkuk's day the law was ineffectual (set aside) because of unrighteous judges who perverted judgment and because of the manipulation of the wicked. The righteous and poor were being mistreated and robbed by the ungodly and unruly, and thus righteousness and justice were thwarted. Miscarriage of justice and the perversion of right and honesty were the order of the day. There was no respect for either persons or property so that neither were safe. Are not these conditions prevailing in many countries today? Has not the word of God been set aside by many who profess to be Christians? Once God's standard is set aside then there is a lowering of standards in society. We can truly sympathise with Habakkuk here and enter into his feelings a little.

The opening question in v.3 may well be a complaint by the prophet that by allowing evil to continue unjudged God was compelling him to look upon iniquity and witness grievance. There is a contrast here to Numbers 23.21, "He hath not beheld iniquity in Jacob, neither hath he seen perverseness in Israel", where both verbs are used. It seems that wickedness was openly practised without any control or punishment. The primary meaning of the Hebrew word for "iniquity" (AWEN - 205) "seems to have two facets: a stress on trouble which moves on to wickedness, and an emphasis on emptiness which moves on to idolatry" (TWOT). Here it seems to indicate physical trouble, wickedness. "Grievance" (AMAL - 5999) means effort, whether of body or mind, hence labour or worry, toil or grievance. The first is the actual action of the ungodly, who have no thought of God and no respect for His claims, and the second is the result of their actions upon the victims - grief and sorrow.

This first couplet, iniquity and grievance, occurs a number of times in the Old Testament although translated differently, e.g. iniquity and wickedness (Job 4.8); iniquity and mischief (Ps 7.14); vanity and mischief (Job 15.35). The second couplet "spoiling (SHOD - 7701) and violence (HAMAS -2555)" also occurs in Jeremiah 6.7; 20.8; Ezekiel 45.9 and is translated "violence and robbery" in Amos 3.10. This couplet is "of special significance because of the import of the word 'violence' (*hamas*). This word designates the type of sin preceding the deluge, 'the earth was corrupt and filled with violence' (Gen 6.11). What is meant by 'violence'? We tend to agree with Cassuto (*Commentary on Genesis*, II, p. 52) that *hamas* does not refer to deeds of outrage and violence, that is, lawlessness perpetrated by force. Rather, *hamas* refers to anything that is unrighteous, e.g. injustice or social unrighteousness. Perhaps this sheds some light on the meaning of *shod*. It is clear, however, that *shod* is not only a cause for destruction but also may be the destruction itself (Hos 7.13; 10.14)" (TWOT). Here it appears to suggest the destruction of social life by robbery and exploitation. Thus Habakkuk seems to feel that the very fabric of society was unravelling, a feeling that many share today. Because of these things "strife and contention" were before him. This last couplet is also found in Proverbs 17.14 and Jeremiah 15.10, and is translated "contentious…strife" (Prov 26.21); and "strife…strife" (Prov 15.18). "Strife" (RIB - 7379) is contrasted with quietness (Prov 17.1), and could be either physical or verbal, personal or legal. "Contention" (MADON - 4066) has the thought of contesting or contending. The idea is that of strife-raising contention and may well refer to the abuse of the law by grasping and quarrelling men in authority. Strife and contention in any society, even in a company of believers, divides and impoverishes. This is seen in the church at Corinth (1 Cor 1.11; 3.1-3). These things are unprofitable (Tit 3.9).

"Law and judgment" (v.4) is another couplet which occurs often in the Old Testament (Deut 33.10; Ps 89.30; Is 51.4). The law (TORA - 8451) revealed the character of God and gave instruction to Israel about approach to God and social responsibility. It embraced both ceremonial and moral law although here only the moral side is in view. The Hebrew word rendered "slacked" (PUG - 6313) is translated "fainted" (Gen 45.26), and "feeble" (Ps 38.8), and means to be sluggish, to grow numb, or to become paralysed. The wicked evaded the claims of the Lord and manipulated the law to serve their own unrighteous aims and activities. Through corruption, the legal claims of the victims were denied. This is also the case in many countries today. Thus "judgment doth never go forth" or to its right end, i.e. on to victory - the punishment of the wicked and the protection of the innocent. The implication is that of a total cessation of justice. The wicked† (RASHA - 7563) are frequently contrasted with the righteous in the book of Proverbs where they are described as cruel, deceitful, evil, loathsome, and violent. Here they compass (surround) the righteous - as by a siege, preventing justice by bribery and false witness. The righteous are deprived of their rights and limited in their influence for good. Justice could not be carried out as the wicked were able to hem in the righteous on every side so that they could not receive just judgment. Thus we have the idea of the triumph of injustice in the cloak of law. The wicked ensnared the righteous by fraud, bribery, and other means, thus perverting honesty and uprightness. Wrong (AQAL - 6127) or perverted judgment was the result, with the innocent being condemned and the guilty acquitted. In this way miscarriage of justice prevailed. The words of Proverbs 29.16, "When the wicked are multiplied, transgression increaseth", and Proverbs 28.4, "They that forsake the law praise the wicked", were evident in Habakkuk's day and are true in every age and in every country.

The wickedness mentioned in these verses was public and not secret and was practised by those who claimed to be the people of God. Mere profession is valueless unless it is supported by a life lived in keeping with the claims and character of God – "Wherefore by their fruits ye shall know them" (Mt 7.20); "Let your light so shine before men, that they may see your good works, and glorify your Father which is in heaven" (Mt 5.16).

God's answer - the Chaldean invasion of Judah (vv.5-11)

Jehovah did not answer the prophet's questions as he thought He would, but we must remember that He is sovereign and does not need to explain His actions. The answer to Habakkuk's pleas came in a way he least expected. How often is this the experience of the people of God? How often believers question the apparent answers to prayer. However, "the foolishness of God is wiser than men" (1 Cor 1.25). Often men cannot understand the way of God's dealings with them, neither do they have the wisdom to fathom fully His actions. It is true that God, in wondrous grace, has revealed to His people certain events which are hidden from the world, but His ways are past finding out (Rom 11.33). Habakkuk should not have thought that the silence of God was an indication of His indifference to the conditions in Judah. Had not God continually challenged (Jer 7.5-7;

22.3-5), rebuked (Jer 2.13; 23.14), and warned (Jer 5.15-17; 16.13) Judah through His servant Jeremiah? God is far from being unconcerned or indifferent when sin and ungodliness increases. This section confirms this and reveals that God had already been working in answer to the prayers of Habakkuk and the godly in Judah. However, instead of alleviating the affliction and oppression of the poor and godly, as the prophet anticipated, God was going to deal in judgment. This was not because Jehovah ignored his petitions but because He was showing that Habakkuk's cry was really an appeal to God to display His justice and righteousness. This inevitably involved judgment. Despite Jehovah's rebukes and warnings the people of Judah had provoked Him to anger with their wickedness and idolatry. They had trifled with His word despite His longsuffering, but now their day of opportunity for mercy was past (Jer 8.19-20; 11.11). Now Habakkuk, who had been taken up with the conditions in Judah, was directed to look at what was taking place in the surrounding nations. The Babylonian empire was increasing in power. The Assyrian kingdom had been destroyed (612 BC) and Egyptian power had diminished. God's answer was to be seen among the nations. The answer was not only for Habakkuk but also for Judah.

That God was behind the rise to power of the Babylonian empire is shown in Daniel 2.37-38. The prophet and all Judah should have marvelled at this rapid rise to power, understanding that it was because God was at work. The Chaldeans were invading and conquering nation after nation. They were now to be His instrument to chastise Judah in fulfilment of the prophecy in Manasseh's reign (2 Kings 21.11-14) and the prophecy of Jeremiah (Jer 5.9; 15.14). Thus, instead of Jehovah being indifferent, He was active in a way they could scarcely believe, since it was unthinkable to them that He would allow the heathen to destroy Jerusalem and the temple where He had placed His name. It has also been suggested, "that probably at this time the Babylonian nation was still friendly (2 Kings 20.12-19)" (C. L. Feinberg). The message not only unfolds the coming invasion of Judah by the Chaldeans but also describes their supremacy, swiftness, cruelty, and idolatry. However, the people would not believe such a message and did not think that there was such danger. They considered the true prophets to be alarmists who warned of judgment which never seemed to come, and, furthermore, false prophets soothed them with words of safety and peace (Jer 4.10; 14.13-15).

Down through the centuries men have set aside the truth of God and willingly believed that which is false to ease the conscience. Today, evolution is eagerly accepted since it seems to relieve man of his moral responsibility and accountability to God, the Creator. People are not prepared to accept that accountability or the fact that their sin exposes them to the judgment of God. Therefore they adopt any teaching that takes God out of their lives, falsely believing that by doing so they can avoid being responsible to Him.

(a) God's activity (v.5). Although the speaker is not specifically mentioned, the context and use of the personal pronoun "I" indicates that the speaker is Jehovah. This message from Jehovah is not only addressed to Habakkuk but also to Judah through the prophet. The opening statement would arrest them as they were called upon to behold among the nations and regard events unfolding before them. The Septuagint translates it, "Behold, ye despisers". Judah deserved to be considered among the nations because of its iniquity and would be judged like the nations in answer to Habakkuk's prayers. The people were not only to see but to contemplate carefully what was taking place.

The first two verbs, "behold" (RAA - 7200) and "regard" (NABAT - 5027), used in v.3 link the message of Jehovah with the cry of Habakkuk. Judah was called upon to consider the unexpected events taking place among the nations that should have caused it to wonder or be astounded. The words "wonder" and "marvellously" are translated from the same Hebrew word "TAMAH" (8539). "The root meaning is 'be astounded, dumfounded, bewildered,' with an element of fear, whether because of an amazing or fearful sight..." (TWOT). The repetition of the word emphasises the effect their contemplation of what God was doing among the nations should have had upon them - they should have been overwhelmed with astonishment. This was Jehovah's work - bringing judgment upon the heathen nations because of their wickedness. Jehovah was revealing that He was not indifferent to lawlessness and idolatry in these nations, and neither was He unconcerned about these same things in Judah, but He was going to chastise it. The chastisement may have seemed strange, but it would certainly come and come suddenly. Great changes had been taking place among the surrounding nations and a great change was about to take place in Judah. God would not defer His work but would begin, continue, and finish this work of judgment, thus displaying His justice in their day. The course of action which he was about to take would be such that they, the people of Judah in general, would not believe it even though it was told them. The idea that God would use the Chaldeans to chastise them was nonsense to them. This indicates the strength of the opposition of the wicked in Judah to Jehovah and His word. They had hardened their hearts against God, rejected His word and were bent on going their own way. This is characteristic of the world today where self-centeredness and self-advancement is prevalent. However, God is still working today despite the opposition of men.

The words "told you" refer to the message which had been proclaimed to them both by Habakkuk and Jeremiah. The expression "in your days" indicates that this work of judgment would take place during the lifetime of Habakkuk and of the people who were then living in Judah. This was the answer to the prophet's cry, "O Lord, how long" (v.2). The Apostle Paul quoted from this verse in Acts 13.41 regarding the work of redemption, when he warned the Jews against ignoring or rejecting the truth of the gospel. There the Jews were in danger of refusing to believe the good news of God's salvation, but here the Jews were refusing to believe the warnings of God's impending judgment. Although it was a message of judgment to the wicked, it was also intended to comfort the godly, giving them confidence in the word and character of God. Even in the darkest trial the believer should remember that God is still in control. He knows what every child of God is going through and He cares. He is Sovereign.

(b) God's instrument (vv.6-11). In these verses Jehovah continues to unfold His intention of using the Chaldeans as His instrument. A full account is given of the chastening to come and of the characteristics of the Chaldeans who were known for their impulsiveness and cruelty. In vv.6-7 we have the characteristics of the Chaldeans; in v.8 the particulars of the invasion; in v.9 the purpose of the invasion; in v.10 the attitude of the Chaldeans; and in v.11 the folly or idolatry of the Chaldeans.

Jehovah now declares (v.6) what is involved in the work He has mentioned. The expression "I raise up the Chaldeans" does not refer to the rise of the Babylonian empire but to the invasion of Judah as Moses had warned Israel (Deut 28.49). The verse shows that the message is very precise as it specifically mentions the Chaldeans who were the driving force of the Babylonian empire. The Chaldeans "were originally a semi-nomadic desert tribe. They had settled in southern Babylonia, where they gradually increased in power" (C. J. Barber). C. L. Feinberg states, "The Chaldeans were the inhabitants of Babylonia and were of Semitic origin from Kesed (*Chesed*), son of Nahor, brother of Abraham (Gen 22.22). The mention of the Chaldeans in Job 1.17 shows they were an ancient people (see Jer 5.15). The Chaldeans are mentioned throughout Jeremiah's prophecy in relation to Judah as well as here in Habakkuk. The invasion of Judah by the Chaldeans was the plan of God although this was unknown to the Chaldeans or appreciated by Judah".

Every nation today is in truth under the control of God since He "ruleth in the kingdom of men, and giveth it to whomsoever he will" (Dan 4.25,32; 5.21), "he removeth kings, and setteth up kings" (Dan 2.21; see Ps 75.7), and "the powers that be are ordained of God" (Rom 13.1). These verses should comfort us as the people of God. Still, today, the world is unaware that God is working behind the scenes to accomplish His own purpose. The people of Judah would never have related this invasion to the purpose of God, but it was His plan. The word of God gives clear instruction as to how believers are to live for Him in this world. Even if there are many things one is unable to relate to the plan of God, the believer is expected to acknowledge that He is in control and everything is according to His permissive will. The people of God may not know what the future holds, but they do know who holds the future.

Jehovah uses various expressions here to describe the character of the Chaldeans. They were bitter, cruel, showing no mercy – "they are cruel, and have no mercy" (Jer 6.23). They were swift (hasty, MAHAR – 4116; see Prov 6.18), quick in carrying out their purpose of conquest and impulsive in their actions. The expression "shall march through...the land" indicates that their object would be to conquer completely. They would go through Judah plundering and nothing would escape their conquering power and cruelty. Their intention would be not only to spoil but to possess the land, cities, towns and villages. These rightfully belonged to the people of Judah as an inheritance from the Lord (Deut 4.21; 12.10) which could never be taken from them as long as they cleaved to Him and walked in His ways (2 Kings 21.14). However, in turning away from the Lord and His word and turning to idolatry they had forfeited the right to enjoy that inheritance. Thus this invasion and dispossession were intended to chasten them and to teach them the folly of their lawlessness, unbelief and idolatry.

It must be remembered that God still chastens His people today – "For whom the Lord loveth he chasteneth, and scourgeth every son whom he receiveth" (Heb 12.6). His chastening is not always because of sin in the believer's life, but it is always an evidence of His love. It is also that we might be "partakers of his holiness", and that it might produce "the peaceable fruit of righteousness unto them which are exercised thereby" (Heb 12.10-11). God uses unwelcome and unexpected circumstances to teach us important lessons and produce certain features in our lives. The trials of life test the reality of faith and produce something for God in our lives (1 Pet 1.7). It is good to be exercised before God in the varying circumstances of life and to ask, "What lessons are there to learn?"; "What features can be produced in us that would further His work and bring pleasure to Him?". Since even the people of God come under the government and judgment of God, unbelievers cannot escape His judgment (1 Pet 4.17-18).

Jehovah now describes the effect the Chaldeans had upon the people they invaded (v.7). "Terrible and dreadful" speaks of their power and cruelty; "judgment" speaks of their purpose in carrying out their own will and, in so doing, the purpose of God; and "dignity" speaks of their pride. The Hebrew word translated "terrible" (AYOM - 366) denotes terror or dread caused by a great army. It is only found elsewhere in the Song of Solomon 6.4,10 where it is used figuratively. The Chaldeans struck terror into the hearts of their victims. The second word, "dreadful" (YARE - 3372), may well be an actual description of them and of their actions. It is used elsewhere to describe the Day of the Lord (Joel 2.11,31) and the attitude of the heathen to the name of the Lord (Mal 1.14). The word also indicates the fear that is produced in those they invade as they anticipate what is about to take place (see 1 Samuel 7.7 - afraid). The Chaldeans were arrogant, setting themselves up as the sole authority. Power and pride often go together. The only laws or authority they acknowledged were their own. Their own desires and laws were their rule of judgment and they acted accordingly. They had no respect for the laws of others and refused to acknowledge a higher authority than themselves. History has revealed that aggression, arrogance, cruelty, and disrespect for others has characterised many nations. However, although God has permitted these things to take place with what seems to be impunity, He will eventually call each nation to account and judge their actions as is shown here in ch.2 in relation to the Chaldeans. The Chaldeans exalted themselves and forced others to honour and reverence them. They considered that they had all that was to be desired and that there was nothing lacking in themselves. The word for "dignity" (S^{e}ET - 7613) is translated "excellency" in Psalm 62.4 and "highness" in Job 31.23, and means exaltation or elation. Their dignity proceeded from themselves as they assumed their supremacy and superiority. Thus they were governed by self-will, self-gratification, and self-exaltation.

How prevalent this is in the world today! Self is foremost in these last days, even among those who claim to be Christians, as described for us in 2 Timothy 3.1-5. Selfish people abound in every nation but, in contrast to this, the believer should be characterised by humility and selflessness (Rom 12.16-21; Phil 2.3-4) and seek to display the fruit of the Spirit (Gal 5.22-23).

In v.8 Jehovah describes the coming invasion in metaphorical terms to show the Chaldean's rapidity of conquest and ravenous activity. They would come with ferocity greater than wolves at evening which, having had no food during the day, fiercely pursue and tear their prey. Judah's princes had been as roaring lions and her judges as evening wolves (Zeph 3.3 - see Ezek 22.27). Now they themselves would experience the ferocity of the Chaldean invasion which would be "swifter than the leopards" and "more fierce than the evening wolves". The message indicates that the Chaldeans would be upon them sooner than they expected and that when the invasion took place they would be unable to escape. So rapid would it be that it would be futile to send for help. The Chaldeans would come to kill, loot, and spread terror through the land consuming all before them. The expression "their horsemen shall spread themselves" is translated "their riders shall increase" in Targum Jonathan (Rabbi A. J. Rosenberg). The expression indicates that the horsemen would be so many that they would spread through the whole land and that all would fall into their hands. They would come from a remote country and would thus carry away captives to that far off land. They would hasten to kill just like the eagle swooping down with rapidity to kill and consume its prey (Job 9.26). Thus the invasion would be sudden, rapid, fearful, and complete. We know that God is slow to anger and plenteous in mercy (Ps 103.8). However, He must deal with sin, and after warning Judah over and over again through His servants the prophets, without response, judgment was inevitable.

In this day of grace God is longsuffering "not willing that any should perish, but that all should come to repentance" (2 Pet 3.9), yet so many refuse the good news of the gospel and ignore the solemn warning of coming judgment. When judgment comes, as with Judah, it will be swift and sure – "Be not deceived; God is not mocked: for whatsoever a man soweth, that shall he also reap" (Gal 6.7). Here is an abiding principle that is not only true in the agricultural world but also in life. We cannot live as we like without reaping the harvest. Hosea tells us, "They have sown the wind, and they shall reap the whirlwind" (8.7), and, "Sow to yourselves in righteousness, reap in mercy" (10.12). This principle is applicable to the believer as well as the unbeliever. The believer comes under the government of the Father (1 Pet 1.17). Therefore we should be careful how we live and seek to be "steadfast, unmoveable, always abounding in the work of the Lord" (1 Cor 15.58).

The swift and fierce Chaldeans, each one of them, would have one purpose in mind: that of violence, or to get all that they could by violence (v.9). Habakkuk had cried to God because of violence in Judah (vv.2-3). How startling it was for him to hear that in answer to his cries God was going to send more violence, the violence of a savage and fierce army invading the land. The opening expression can be viewed as the Chaldean's coming to repay the violence of which Habakkuk had complained and would therefore be God's answer to his cry, "Violence" (v.2). What the people of Judah had practised would be meted out to them (Deut 19.21). There would be no pity and no mercy. When the judgment of God falls upon men there is no mercy (2 Thess 1.8-9; 2.11-12; Rev 20.11-15). Now is the day of God's grace, "now is the accepted time, now is the day of salvation" (2 Cor 6.2). How solemn it is for sinners today to miss the opportunity of listening to the gospel and trusting the Saviour of sinners. However, it must be remembered that now is also the opportunity for believers to live for God in a godless society. One should seek to fulfil this responsibility out of love for Him and in godly fear.

There are different opinions as to the meaning of the middle clause of v.9. Some render it, "the look or design of their faces is to the east". Another rendering gives, "The yearning of their faces is to the east; they think only of plundering their enemies and returning to their land, which is east of Eretz Israel" (Rabbi A. J. Rosenberg). Although the meaning of the Hebrew word translated "sup up" (MᶜGAMMA - 4041) is debated, many agree that in the context the idea is that of hordes (TWOT; Strong's Concordance gives "accumulation") whose faces are set forward or set to advance. Their countenances would be as a withering and blasting east wind. The east wind is used to symbolise judgment and devastation in other prophetic books (Jer 18.17; Ezek 17.10; Hos 13.15). They would be formidable and irresistible, carrying all before them. The last clause of the verse can be viewed in two ways - (a) As they rapidly conquer the land they would gather captives with as much ease as scooping up sand, or (b) The result of their conquest would be the gathering of captives so numerous that, like the grains of sand, they could not be counted. The latter seems to be more in keeping with the message. Remember also that the same metaphor is used elsewhere of Israel (Gen 22.17; Is 10.22).

The Chaldeans would be so confident of their supremacy and power that they would scoff at the kings through whose territory they would pass (v.10). The Hebrew word translated "scoff" (QALAS - 7046) means to disparage or belittle, and "scorn" (MISHAQ - 4890) means object of derision. So they would belittle the kings, counting them and their armies as valueless and would make the princes (rulers) a laughing stock. C. J. Barber states, "It was a Chaldean custom to put captive rulers in cages and exhibit them as public spectacles". The fortified cities (strong holds) would be no barrier to their conquest and they would ridicule the helplessness of those who opposed them. These fortified cities would be breached by making (heaping up, SABAR - 6651) earthen (dust, APAR - 6083) ramps or bulwarks against the city walls (see 2 Kings 19.32; Jer 6.6). No one and nothing would withstand the invasion, and so they would scoff at the feeble attempts made to hinder their progress. Here is seen the weakness of those who try to withstand the judgment of God. The folly of man's attempt to oppose God and His anointed is noted in Psalm 2. Revelation 19 also tells of the futility of those gathered together to make war against the Lord when He returns to the earth as King of kings and Lord of lords.

In v.11 the change from the plural *they* and *their* in the previous verses to the singular *his* and *he* has resulted in two methods of interpretation. The one takes the singular as representative of the Chaldeans as a whole and the other applies it to Nebuchadnezzar.[†] The first is used here. The word "then" indicates both the time and the result of what would take place. After the Chaldeans' success and triumph a change of mind takes place and they become proud and pompous.[†] Success can produce a spirit of pride in men which is opposite to the spirit of humility seen in all its perfection in Christ and which should characterise every Christian.

It has been suggested that the middle clause of the verse refers to the Chaldeans passing on to new areas of conquest. However, it is closely linked with the first clause and therefore seems to refer to the Chaldean's change of attitude. The Hebrew word translated here "pass over" (ABAR - 5674) is translated in numerous ways and could mean passing on to another place (Gen 18.5). However, it also has the idea of going beyond certain bounds as in Deuteronomy 17.2 where it is translated "transgressing". It could be translated here "he transgresseth". Thus, this change of attitude in the Chaldeans would step over the limit, offend or be guilty, as in their pride they attribute their power and success to their idol god or they made their power their god.[†] This would ultimately lead to their downfall – "Pride goeth before destruction, and an haughty spirit before a fall" (Prov 16.18; see also Dan 11.37-38; 2 Thess 2.4). D. W. Baker states, "The last clause is grammatically difficult, but it takes note of the already mentioned arrogant pride of the Babylonians (v.7), in that they deify their *own strength,* thereby making themselves *guilty,* a common fault among major powers who attribute their position on the world stage to their own doings (cp. Is 47.8,10; Zeph. 2.15)". They would be an offence to God in whose hand they were simply an instrument to chastise Judah. They would fail to appreciate they were simply instruments or channels through whom God was working out His own plan and purposes. Believers must always remember that if God deigns to use them in various ways to fulfil His purpose and for His glory they are still only instruments in His hand. There is no place for pride in the christian life, including the service of God.

Although these verses refer to the invasion of Judah by Nebuchadnezzar they can also be viewed as a picture of what is to take place in a coming day (Joel 3.2; Zech 14.2). However, here there is no intervention by God whereas in the future the Lord will intervene and deliver His people.

The second dialogue (1.12-2.20)

The first dialogue involved Habakkuk's two problems, namely the affliction of the godly and prosperity of the wicked, and God's apparent silence (1.2-4). God's answer indicated that He was not indifferent to what was taking place in Judah, but was already at work to use the Chaldeans as His instrument of chastisement (1.5-11). This answer intensified the prophet's anxiety leading to this second dialogue in which he seems to suggest that the use of the Chaldeans in this way would be inconsistent with the character and covenant of God (1.12-17). However, Habakkuk is willing to wait for God to further enlighten him (2.1) which He does by revealing His judgment upon the Chaldeans (2.2-20).

The problem of the Chaldean invasion (1.12-17)

Instead of alleviating the perplexity of Habakkuk, the answer he received from God simply intensified it. The prophet now contemplates another problem - how can a holy and righteous God use such a wicked people as the Chaldeans, who have no relationship with Him, to punish and chastise those who were in covenant relationship with Himself? Habakkuk again appeals to God, placing emphasis upon His character and expressing his faith by stating his conviction that the people of God would not die. In referring to the Chaldeans as the divinely appointed instrument of chastisement, the prophet seems to question how this could possibly relate to the holiness and justice of God.

In v.12 we see a mixture of Habakkuk's confidence, faith, and perplexity. His confidence in God and His character, his faith in God that His people would not be utterly destroyed, and his perplexity over God's use of the Chaldeans. His confidence and faith are clearly indicated in his use of the personal pronouns "my" and "mine". Habakkuk now uses two names of God – "O Jehovah my Elohim" (O Lord my God). Elohim is plural and indicates the triune God. The prophet commences his plea with a rhetorical question, not to receive an answer, but to indicate his confidence and faith in God. He knew that the inevitable answer to such a question was the affirmative. This was the basis of Habakkuk's confidence and hope in spite of the coming Chaldean invasion. The God of Israel was the eternal God (Deut 33.27; Ps 90.2), the Ancient of days (Dan 7.9) who inhabits eternity (Is 57.15), in contrast to the Chaldean's god which was but the product of their pride. The God of Israel was the only true and living God (Is 45.21-22) as distinct from, and to the exclusion of, the multiplicity of the gods of the heathen nations. Habakkuk not only referred to God as the eternal One, but mentioned again the covenant name of God's relationship with Israel - Jehovah (vv.1.2,12 – "O Lord"; see also Ex 6.2-8). The fact that God was eternal indicated that men and nations may come and go but supreme over all is the everlasting God and Israel was His chosen people in covenant with Him. They had been set apart to God (Deut 7.6-7; 14.2). They were chosen, in keeping with God's promise to Abraham, to be His earthly people with an earthly inheritance (Gen 12.1; 13.15). Believers in this day of grace are also a chosen people but to be a heavenly people with a heavenly inheritance (Eph 1.3-4; 1 Pet 1.3-4).

The expression "mine Holy One" indicates the intrinsically holy nature of God, His moral perfection in contrast to the wickedness of the Chaldeans. God alone is intrinsically holy (Rev 15.4). He is glorious in holiness (Ex 15.11). God was holy and He would therefore act righteously in keeping with His word and His covenant with Israel: "The Lord is righteous in all his ways, and holy in all his works" (Ps 145.17). Since God is infinitely holy, sin in every form, whether in his people or in unbelievers, must be dealt with. It is well to remember this solemn and sobering fact. Habakkuk had confidence in the knowledge that God was eternal and unchanging in His holiness. Thus the prophet confidently stated that, "we shall not die".[†] The prophet drew encouragement and comfort from the Person and character of God. Believers in every age and in every circumstance can do the same. Habakkuk was confident that Judah would not be utterly cut off but would continue since it was part of the nation of Israel. This would be in keeping with the covenant God made with Israel and in keeping with His faithfulness (see also Mal 3.6). God is unfailingly faithful to His word and His promises, whether of blessing or of judgment. Believers have confidence from the word of God that they will never perish because of the finished work of Christ and that they are now seen in Christ without spot or stain.

The prophet's confidence was indeed vindicated as seen in Jeremiah 5.18: "Nevertheless in those days, saith the Lord, I will not make a full end with you" (see also Jer 46.28). God limits the severity of the judgment and in so doing not only manifests His justice but also His mercy. Since God limits the extent of His judgment upon Judah, the Chaldeans would not be allowed to utterly destroy them. Habakkuk seems now to submit to the righteousness and wisdom of God in this matter of judgment although he is still unable to understand it. It is better to rest upon what we are certain of rather than jump to conclusions. Some writers suggest that the expression "ordained them for judgment" has reference to judgment upon surrounding nations and that only the expression "established them for correction" refers to the people of Judah. However, in the context, both expressions seem to be used in relation to Judah. The people of Judah had rejected correction (discipline), hardened their faces and refused to return to the Lord (Jer 5.3). Thus God said, "Shall I not visit for these things? saith the Lord: and shall not my soul be avenged on such a nation as this?" (Jer 5.9). Jehovah, the covenant-keeping God, had appointed the Chaldeans to execute judgment upon the covenant-breaking Judah. This corresponded to His word (Lev 26.15-25) and the prophecy of Moses (Deut 28.49-51).

The Hebrew word translated "mighty God" (SUR - 6697) means rock and is often used metaphorically (1 Sam 2.2; 2 Sam 22.32). It indicates that God is unchangeable, totally reliable, and a sure source of strength, power, might, and security. God is immutable in His nature (Mal 3.6) and thus unchangeable in His promises and His dealings with men. His unchangeable character is a source of comfort and encouragement to believers but a warning and a source of terror to unbelievers. He is referred to as the Rock of salvation (Deut 32 15; Ps 89.26), the Rock of safety or refuge (Ps 94.22), and the Rock of defence and strength (Ps 62.6-7). The unchangeable mighty God, who could be absolutely relied upon, had established the Chaldeans (or founded, YASAD - 3245, them as a kingdom) to correct or reprove Judah. This indicates the justice of that reproof and the security of the nation. The Chaldeans would be but a rod in Jehovah's hand to be used for the ultimate benefit of His people.

The prophet in v.13 contrasted the purity of God with the wickedness of the Chaldeans. God's purity was, and still is, ethical and not ritualistic as Israel's was. D. W. Baker points out that "Israel's purification laws were to ritually cleanse themselves from defilement due to external contact with uncleanness (see Lev 11-12; 15; Num 19), though cleanliness of the heart from sin is the ultimate goal (see Ps 51.7; Ezek 36.25; Heb 1.3; 9.14)". Since God is infinitely pure He abhors sin of every kind and thus cannot look upon iniquity without judging it (Ps 5.4-6). The purity of God is not measured in relation to evil. It is completely separate from evil and thus not compared with it at all. The word "eyes" is used metaphorically to indicate both the omniscience and the omnipresence of God: "The eyes of the Lord are in every place, beholding the evil and the good" (Prov 15.3). His understanding is infinite (Ps 147.5), and nothing can be hid from Him (Jer 23.24; see also Ps 139.7-12). The omniscience and the omnipresence of God are both a comfort and a challenge to the believer. When trials and afflictions come, the child of God can say like Job, "He knoweth the way that I take: when he hath tried me, I shall come forth as gold" (Job 23.10). In sickness and weakness, in anxiety and perplexity, the believer can rest in the knowledge that the Lord knows, He loves and He cares (Ps 103.14; 1 Pet 5.7). However, the fact that nothing is hid from God is not only a comfort to believers but is also a solemn reminder that they should live in keeping with the claims and character of God. In vv.12-13 Habakkuk has enumerated that God is eternal, holy, faithful, immutable, omnipotent, omniscient and omnipresent.

The prophet was emboldened to speak of the Chaldeans in relation to the character of God. He was fully aware of what kind of people they were (Jer 6.22-24), and thus his problem was in reconciling God, who was of purer eyes than to behold iniquity, with His looking at the Chaldeans with apparent favour, from a human assessment. The Chaldeans were successful and prosperous although they were treacherous (unfaithful, BAGAD - 898). They were unfaithful because they broke agreements made with other nations. They dealt treacherously with Judah by acting in a friendly way towards them while planning to attack and plunder them. Fraud and force were the tools they used. At the beginning, Habakkuk questioned the silence of God to his plea for the oppressed faithful in Judah. Here he questions God's silence in regard to the Chaldeans devouring (swallowing up, BALA - 1104) those more righteous than themselves. "Wicked" here refers to the Chaldeans, whereas in v.4 it refers to the unrighteous and unfaithful of Judah. Habakkuk seems to imply that the faithful as well as the unfaithful of Judah would suffer at the hands of the Chaldeans which would be inconsistent with the character of God. Since God was infinitely holy, how could He possibly use a nation more corrupt than Judah to punish them? The eternal God was in covenant with Israel and He was absolutely holy. Why then will He use such a wicked nation as His instrument to judge the people of Judah, who were, relatively, more righteous, and particularly so the godly in Judah? Why does He allow the Chaldeans to prosper? Why was God silent when such wickedness was taking place? (However, God's silence does not indicate His approval of the actions of the Chaldeans [Ps 50.21]). Habakkuk's faith in the holiness of God was challenged by His choice of the Chaldeans to carry out the judgment that Judah righteously deserved.

The prophet had a problem that he could not solve because he was short sighted. He was trying to reconcile things at that present time and was seeking to compare different forms of evil. He was to learn that God in His sovereignty chooses whoever He will to carry out His purpose, yet He will hold those He uses responsible for their actions and will ultimately judge them for their wickedness. Asaph had the same kind of problem (Ps 73) in regard to the prosperity of the ungodly until he went into the House of the Lord and understood their end. We cannot see as God sees but we know that, however inconsistent things may seem, God never acts contrary to His righteous and holy character, and that all will be revealed one day.

Habakkuk's concern (v.14) is not only that God had chosen the Chaldeans to punish Judah but also that He had allowed men to be treated like fish or creeping things, by permitting the Chaldeans to go unpunished. Some suggest that these creeping things are also creatures of the sea such as crabs or lobsters etc. (Ps 104.25). The image here can be looked upon in two ways.

1. Like fish or creeping things where the greater live off the smaller or weaker, swallowing them up as food. This would link with the previous verse.

2. Like fish which could be caught in quantity, without opposition, and removed from their environment. This would link with the following verse.

Whichever way it is taken, the image indicates the supremacy and power of some and the oppression of others. The prophet was suggesting that the Chaldeans were treating men as fish, as creeping things which were defenceless with no ruler to protect them or to restrain the oppressor. There was certainly no true and righteous ruler in Judah to uphold the law of God, maintain justice, and support the poor and righteous. However, Habakkuk might be complaining that if Judah was to be cruelly treated by the Chaldeans, it would seem as if they had no God who was capable of protecting them.

In the following verse, Habakkuk continues to use the allegory of fish to show the violent and callous way in which the Chaldeans would treat, and take captive, the people. Life to them would mean nothing and there would be no consideration for the suffering of their victims. They would be like fishermen gathering in the fish but instead of the angle, the net, and the drag they would use their military weapons to ensnare, subdue and capture their victims. The angle (hook, HAKKA - 2443), the net (HEREM - 2764), and the drag (dragnet, MIKMERET - 4365) describe three ways of catching fish, indicating that the Chaldeans would use all conceivable means to conquer and capture Judah. It has been suggested that these three methods symbolise the conquest of different nations by Nebuchadnezzar.[†] They are used symbolically of judgment in the Scriptures - the angle (Is 19.8), the net (Ezek 32.3), and the dragnet (net, Is 51.20). The Chaldeans would remove the people of Judah from their land (2 Kings 24.12-16; 25.11-21) as fish in a net would be dragged from the sea against their will, and as they had done to other nations. The Chaldeans rejoiced in their success and in their gain as well as in the plight of their victims. They delighted in prosperity gained by their oppression of other nations, and were glad that they had such ability and power. This can be seen even today in the battle for supremacy among modern day nations. Not all use aggression, but all take pride in their standing in the world, giving no thought to the God who allows them to be there.

The two words "rejoice" (SAMAH - 8055) and "glad" (GIL - 1523) could refer to what was felt inwardly and also to what was expressed outwardly. The root of the word SAMAH "denotes being glad or joyful with the whole disposition as indicated by its association with the heart (cp. Ex 4.14; Ps 19.8; 104.15; 105.3), the soul (Ps 86.4); and with the lighting up of the eyes (Prov 15.30)" (TWOT). The root meaning of GIL is "'to circle around' from which such ideas as 'to circle in joy' are readily derived. The root meaning is more applicable to vigorous, enthusiastic expressions of joy" (TWOT). The Chaldeans delighted in their victories but were never thankful to God, not appreciating that they were simply instruments in His hand. The people of God should appreciate what God has done for them and what He has bountifully bestowed upon them, so they should be characterised by thanksgiving to Him. "Enter into his gates with thanksgiving, and into his courts with praise: be thankful unto him, and bless his name" (Ps 100.4); "In every thing giving thanks: for this is the will of God in Christ Jesus concerning you" (1 Thess 5.18); "...be ye thankful" (Col 3.15). The Chaldeans were empowered by God to carry out His purpose of judgment upon certain nations including Judah. However, it must be remembered that God did not sanction or condone their excessive violence and cruelty although it was permitted by Him. He is the sovereign Creator and all men are ultimately responsible to Him whether they accept this or not.

The Chaldeans, because they were able to rejoice in their triumphs, sacrificed to the means of their success and prosperity (v.16). The net and the drag are suggested to be symbolic of the Chaldeans' idols. "All of the Babylonian deities, at one time or another, were pictured holding or dragging a net in which they had captured their enemies" (C. J. Barber). Others think that they symbolize their military prowess (C. L. Feinberg). Both could be indicated if the Chaldeans attributed their success in subjugating so many nations to their power and plans which they believed had been given them by their gods. In this sense they worshipped themselves and their idol gods. However, it seems from the context that their weapons, might, and methods were actually the object of their worship, not the gods themselves. The prophet is taking up what Jehovah had said (v.11) to show the gross idolatry and pride of the Chaldeans as justification for His judgment upon them. The use of "sacrifice" and "burn incense" together often refer to idolatry (2 Chr 28.4; Hos 4.13; 11.2) which Habakkuk uses to condemn the Chaldean practice before God.

There is a danger today of allowing prosperity to develop into materialism and of turning the things that one uses into actual objects of worship, as the Chaldeans were doing. Believers need to take care not to allow anything to come between their hearts' affections and the Lord. It is perilously possible to be taken up with seeming successes, even in the spiritual life, and fail to give the Lord His rightful place as the object of worship. After all, if there are any seeming successes in our lives it is only by His grace and goodness.

The expression "their portion is fat" indicates their enrichment. Their dominion had been enlarged, their revenue had increased, and they had been enriched by their plunder and the taking of captives. The word "meat" (MAAKAL - 3978) is used frequently of delicacies and the food of kings (2 Chr 9.4; Job 33.20; Dan 1.10) which, with "plenteous" (BARI - 1277), corresponds with the word "fat" (SHAMEN - 8082), and indicates richness.

The allusion might be to the sumptuous feasts and rich banquets they enjoyed after their victories and triumphs. The Chaldeans were pompous, arrogant and self-centred. These features are prevalent in the world today.

Having used the analogy of fish and fishing in vv.14-16 to illustrate the activity and cruelty of the Chaldeans, Habakkuk, in v.17, resumed his questioning by asking, "Would such activity and cruelty continue unchecked?; Would the Chaldeans continue to prosper from their oppression and violence?; Would the Lord allow them to go on in this unmerciful and idolatrous way?". The prophet seems to say, "Since they attribute all their success to themselves and not to Thee, wilt Thou allow them to continue to succeed?". Habakkuk knew that the Chaldeans would continue their onslaughts if they could, but he also knew that for God to allow this would be inconsistent with His character. Jewish tradition translates this opening statement as, "Is it because of this that he empties his net?".† The idea here is that of emptying a full net in order to use it again and again to catch more and more fish. Leaving the metaphor, Habakkuk's question then goes on to address the conduct of the Chaldeans. Would they continue to slaughter whole nations unmercifully? Whereas the prophet fully expected the answer to his first question in this section (v.12) to be in the affirmative, he now expected a negative answer to this last question. God could not and would not allow the Chaldean onslaughts to continue unabated. Jehovah would, in His time and in His way, intervene and deal righteously with the Chaldeans.

Although the revelation given to Habakkuk had intensified his perplexity, his faith in God and his view of God's character remained the same. He had besought God to deal with the wicked in Judah who oppressed and exploited the innocent (vv.2-4), so that Judah might prosper both spiritually and materially. God had then revealed that He was going to judge Judah by using the wicked Chaldeans since He had the eventual restoration of His people in view. The prophet's view in this was short sighted but God was looking on to the ultimate restoration and blessing of Israel as mentioned in Isaiah 26 (see Is 11; 60.18). Here at the end of the first chapter Habakkuk wondered if there would be an end to the wickedness of the Chaldeans as things looked very bleak indeed. However, there is an end but God allows nations to continue in their evil ways until their cup of iniquity is full (Gen 15.16). Believers can take comfort today even as they look around and see the awful wickedness on every hand - God is still in control and will intervene in His own time. Man *will* reap what he sows (Gal 6.7).

The characteristics of the Chaldeans in this chapter will be seen in the last Gentile power, the ten kingdom confederacy yet to arise, of which the Chaldeans are a picture (cp. Dan 7.7, 23-24; Rev 17.12-14).

Notes

4 The wicked of v.4 and the wicked of v.13 must be differentiated. The wicked of v.4 refers

to the wicked in Judah, whereas the wicked of v.13 refers to the Chaldean invaders. The righteous of v.4 refers to those in Judah who experienced the injustice and oppression of the wicked in Judah, whereas the righteous of v.13 refers to the whole of the nation of Judah in contrast to the much more evil Chaldeans.

11 C. L. Feinberg states, "It has been suggested that when the Chaldean is exulting in his victories, his mind will change (he will lose his reason), and he will pass over all restraints to his destruction. This passage would then be a prophecy of the disease that came upon Nebuchadnezzar when his reason was unseated". Howard Barnes states, "From vv.10 and 11 the rendering should be in the singular and refer to *he, his* and *him*, not *they* etc, and could well refer to Nebuchadnezzar, the prototype Chaldean who led the Babylonian army and as we have seen showed scant consideration for any members of royal families. Also in v.12, Jehovah is said to have ordained 'him' for judgment; and 'thou...hast appointed him for correction', JND. So powerful would he be that eventually 'this his power is become his god', v.11, JND". Rabbi A. J. Rosenberg writes of v.10 that, "Redak interprets the verse as a metaphor meaning that Nebuchadnessar gathers an army as numerous as grains of earth, and he conquers the fortified city".

11 "Then shall his mind change." Of this expression W. J. Deane states: "From the ease and extent of his conquests the Chaldean gains fresh spirit. But it is best to translate differently, *Then he sweepeth on as a wind.* The Chaldean's inroad is compared to a tempestuous wind, which carries all before it".

11 Rabbi A. J. Rosenberg states, "Use of the singular form for a deity is somewhat unusual in Scripture. Some commentators interpret use of this singular form as means of derision and belittling. Ibn Ezra and Redak, however, believe that since the singular is sometimes used in Scripture, it doesn't necessarily convey a particular intention".

12 "Rabbinic tradition sees this verb as an example of scribal emendation, changing the unthinkable 'you shall die' " (D. W. Baker). "Some explain that the scribes mentioned are the Sages of the Talmud. They explain certain Scriptural verses as 'emendations': i.e., Scripture worded the verse euphemistically rather than accurately. This definition is offered by Rabbi Elijah Mizrachi in his supercommentary on Rashi's commentary on the Torah (Gen 18.22, Num 11.15). However, Gur Aryeh (Gen 18.22) explains that Rashi's intention is that the verse is written in the manner followed by the scribes, that they euphemize rather than use harsh expressions. It does not mean, however, that the scribes alter the text" (Rabbi A. J. Rosenberg).

15,16 "*Malbin* explains that the prophet is describing three types of fishing tackle, with which the fisherman catches three sizes of fish: The fishing hook is used to catch the largest fish; the nets are used to catch the middle-sized fish, for which many nets are spread; the trawl is spread over the surface of the water to catch all those fish that enter it. These symbolise the three methods Nebuchadnezzar would use to conquer countries of different sizes. He would conquer the great kingdoms one by one, with great effort, as a fisherman pulls up the fish with a fishhook. Then he would gather the smaller kingdoms that are scattered over the earth; this is easier than conquering the great kingdoms. Finally, he would take all the nations captive like one who traps all the fish in a net spread over the water" (Rabbi A. J. Rosenberg).

17 "Is it because he attributes his power to his god that he succeeds in emptying his net daily when he returns home laden with spoils, like the fisherman who comes home with his net full of his catch and empties it in his house? The prophet complains to God: Since he attributes his power to his god, how do You permit him to prosper? How do You grant him power and success when he denies Your existence, attributes his power to his god, and slays nations without pity?" (Rabbi A. J. Rosenberg).

HABAKKUK 2

Verses 1.2-2.20: Problems and Answers (continued)

Habakkuk, waiting patiently for God to answer his questions (2.1), received a revelation which was certain to be fulfilled although not immediately (vv.2-3). Thus, by faith, God's people were to wait humbly for this fulfilment, in contrast to the pride of the enemy (v.4). The revelation unfolded God's judgment upon the Chaldeans (vv.5-20).

The attitude of Habakkuk (v.1)

Initially Habakkuk was perplexed because God, with seeming indifference, allowed the wicked of Judah to prosper by exploiting and oppressing the godly (1.1-4). However, he learned that God was fully aware of the conditions and would use the Chaldeans to punish Judah (1.5-11). Habakkuk's distress was now intensified as he viewed the problem of the wicked prospering at the expense of the righteous in the wider sphere, for he considered Judah relatively righteous in contrast to the wicked Chaldeans. How could God, in His intrinsic holiness, use such a wicked and cruel nation to chastise and afflict His people (1.12-17)? Habakkuk was confident that God had the solution to this greater problem and that, in His faithfulness, He would convey that to him and alleviate his distress. Faith accepts there is an answer, although it does not know that answer. There is a remedy to every problem in the christian life and, although that remedy might not be evident, the believer should rest upon God in tranquillity. Far better to leave all with God and to be in the enjoyment of His peace than to know the reason why (Phil 4.6-7). The prophet, sure that God would answer him, used figurative language to describe his determination, patience and expectancy as he waited for God's response to his questions.

Perhaps this is where most Christians fail, as one of the hardest things for the believer is to wait patiently upon the Lord. The restlessness of the flesh hastens one on, thinking that delay is time lost. However, waiting time is not wasted time but time to be spent in the sanctuary alone with God – "Be still, and know that I am God" (Ps 46.10).

Habakkuk is now no longer looking at the problem or the conditions but is looking to Jehovah and waiting to see what He will say to him. How good to look beyond the prevailing conditions to God and to wait to hear His voice in His word. One must believe that God is always faithful to His word and so, having committed any problem to Him, one must wait with expectancy and certainty for God's answer. The prophet viewed himself as a watchman upon the watchtower waiting with vigilance for Jehovah to speak to him. The prophets were often called watchmen (Is 21.6-8; Jer 6.17; Ezek 3.17) being responsible to warn the people of danger (Ezek 33.1-9) and to convey the word of God to them (Is 21.11-12; Jer 31.6-7). There are two Hebrew words translated "watch" in this verse, the first

(MISHMERET - 4931) indicating a place of waiting or observation (Keil & Delitzsch), and the other (SAPA - 6822) meaning the act of watching or of being alert. The figure of a watchman, looking from the heights of the tower into the distance, is intended to express the spiritual preparation of Habakkuk to receive the word of God. It involved withdrawing from mundane things and fleshly thoughts to wait upon God. How vital for believers today to learn this important lesson from Habakkuk. In this attitude of heart and alertness of spirit the prophet would be ready to receive the answer of God. In spite of what God had revealed, which was beyond his understanding, the prophet had no doubt as to the character and wisdom of God. The expression "what he will say unto me" is literally "what he will speak in me". The idea here is of divine revelation and illumination when God speaks inwardly. Thus Habakkuk is waiting to see how God will answer his complaints (1.12-17). Although God does not speak by revelation today He does speak to His people inwardly when they meditate upon His word.[†]

There are three suggestions as to the meaning of the last clause.

1. The reproof of God because of Habakkuk's complaints – "the reproof which I anticipate from God on account of the liberty of my expostulation with Him" (Jamieson, Fausset & Brown; Howard Barnes).

2. The reproof of men - "when I am reproved - For they reprove me to my face that one should criticize the Divine standard of justice" (Rabbi A. J. Rosenberg; see also Matthew Poole and C. J. Barber).

3. The reference is to his complaint – "Habakkuk refers not to a reproof addressed to himself, but to the charge, or plea, which he had urged in controversy, so to speak, with God. The expression is legal; in a suit the plaintiff is the reprover, and his plea is the reproof (TOKAHAT – 8433), the word here used. The prophet has to consider what answer he was to give himself and others, touching the words which seemed to impute injustice or inconsistency to God" (F. C. Cook; see also C. L. Feinberg and Keil & Delitzsch).

The third seems to be more in keeping with the context, for there is no record of any reproof or complaint against Habakkuk. The prophet does not challenge, criticise or condemn the actions of God, but wishes to know the reason for His choice of the Chaldeans that he might reconcile the character of God, of which he is confident, with His choice.

The answer of God (vv.2-20)

Jehovah did not disappoint Habakkuk but vindicated his confidence by answering him, although it was not in the way the prophet expected. Instead of responding to Habakkuk's question as to why the Chaldeans were chosen to chastise Judah, Jehovah revealed His intention to punish them for their pride and cruelty.

(a) Instructions to Habakkuk (vv.2-3). The vision was not just for the benefit of Habakkuk but also for the people's benefit, therefore he was to

make known the revelation to the people. The message was to be written in a permanent form; it was to be made plain that it might have a practical affect upon the people, although its fulfilment was still future.

As Habakkuk maintained his patient watch (v.2) Jehovah answered (responded, ANA - 6030) by instructing him to write the vision (revelation, HAZON - 2377) on tables (tablets, LUAH - 3871) so clearly that it might be easily read, for it was of paramount importance. Some commentaries state that these tablets were of wooden material with a waxed surface although the word LUAH can refer to writing surfaces of stone (Ex 24.12), and is also used figuratively of the heart (Prov 3.3; 7.3) (TWOT). It is widely thought that these tablets were to be placed in public places for all to see: "Inscribe it upon tablets and place them in a public place"; "Certain tablets placed in public places"; "Shown in the marketplace on which public notices were written" (See C. J. Barber; W. J. Deane; C. L. Feinberg). However, C. F. Keil takes it figuratively stating, "The words simply express the thought, that the prophecy is to be laid to heart by all the people on account of its great importance, and that not merely in the present, but in the future also. This no doubt involved the obligation on the part of the prophet to take care, by committing it to writing, that it did not fall into oblivion" (Keil & Delitzsch). Whichever view is taken it is clear that the revelation was to be written down in a permanent form, not only for the benefit of that generation but also for future generations.

The spoken word is soon forgotten because of human frailty, but the written word is a continual reminder of that which God has revealed. The apostles' doctrine of Acts 2.42 was verbal and partial at that time, but it later became complete and enshrined permanently in the New Testament Scriptures to guide and direct the saints of this present dispensation. It is essential for the people of God today to take heed to the vital, inspired instruction of the Holy Scriptures which builds and beautifies christian character. The vision was to be written or engraved clearly for all to understand. This indicates the importance of the word of God. It is so necessary that it must not be misunderstood. How careful men must be in conveying the word of God so that its meaning is not obscured, since its truth is intended to guide and govern the lives of believers. There is a sufficiency in the word of God to direct the Christian in every circumstance of life.

The expression, "that he may run that readeth", is viewed in different ways.

1. It was a warning to the people so that they could flee before Jerusalem was invaded.

2. It was a message of hope that those who read it might run and inform others.

3. The writing should be so clear that even those running past would be able to read the message, i.e. read it easily (See C. J. Barber; C. L. Feinberg; Keil & Delitzsch).

The expression clearly indicates the authoritative nature of the revelation and that it should have a practical effect upon the reader. The word of God should have a practical effect upon the lives of the people of God today. Christians should not only be readers or hearers of the word of God but also doers of the word (James 1.25). It has been said that Bible teaching should grow legs and walk.

The reason why the vision was to be written down was because it was prophetic, true and sure (v.3). The fulfilment was not immediate but would take place at the time appointed (determined, MOED - 4150) by God. MOED is translated "feasts" in Leviticus 23 referring to the God appointed times for the various feasts. The complete fulfilment of the vision will take place at the time fixed by God and not before. The purposes of God cannot be hastened or delayed. One can rest assured, knowing that what God determines He will carry out. It is a comfort for the Christian to know that God's purposes and promises are sure and that they will be fulfilled.

The expression "at the end" looks beyond the fall of the Babylonian empire to the destruction of the last Gentile power when Israel's true Messiah, the Lord Jesus Christ, comes back to earth in glory as the King of kings and Lord of lords (Rev 19.11-21). Similar expressions, referring to the same period, are used in Daniel: "at the time of the end shall be the vision" (Dan 8.17); "at the time appointed the end shall be" (Dan 8.19); "yet the end shall be at the time appointed" (Dan 11.27; see also 11.35 & 12.4,9). Only in that coming day will Israel experience true deliverance and come into the enjoyment of full and final pardon. Although there are dark days ahead for Israel, there is a bright future for them when their history of transgression will be brought to an end and they are brought into the fulness of the Day of Atonement (Dan 9.24). Then Israel will be brought into the good of the New Covenant (Jer 31.31-34) and will never again depart from the Lord, for they will be cleansed and given a new heart and a new spirit (Ezek 36.25-26).

The word translated "speak" (PUAH - 6315) means to breathe or puff, and can refer to breathing out words (Prov 12.17 - speaketh) or breathing out air (Song 4.16 - blow). It is suggested that the prophecy in its fulfilment will speak in judgment. However, many believe that the idea is that of panting or hastening, "panteth or hastening towards the end" (see W. J. Deane and F. C. Cook). The revelation will not deceive or fail, but will certainly come to pass. God is sovereign and, despite the sin and rebellion of men, He will carry out His purposes in His own time and way (2 Pet 3.7-10). The answer of God, revealing what was going to take place, was intended to comfort and encourage Habakkuk and Judah.

A knowledge of what is going to take place in future days is intended to mould the believer's life now. Faith lays hold upon the truth of God and lives in the light of a coming day (2 Pet 3.11-14).

The last clause of the verse is quoted in Hebrews 10.37, but the neuter pronoun (*it*) is changed to the masculine (*he*) thus personalising the statement. Here the reference is to the full and final fulfilment of the prophecy, whereas in Hebrews it is primarily a reference to the coming Messiah. This will be a precious promise to the Jewish remnant who, in the midst of suffering, will be waiting and watching for His coming. However, believers today can take its promise to themselves and apply it to the soon return of the Lord for His Church at the Rapture (Jn 14.3; 1 Thess 4.16-18). In view of the Lord's coming Christians should serve Him faithfully while they wait and watch with expectancy for His return (1 Thess 1.9-10).

Twice the word "tarry" occurs in this statement, but in the Hebrew there are two distinct words. The first (MAHAH - 4102) means linger or delay which may cause anxiety or perplexity; the second (AHAR - 309) means delay or defer without hope and implies being behind time. The thought seems to be, "If it tarry, wait for it, for it will surely come and not be behind its time". The complete statement is intended to remove the anxiety and perplexity of the prophet. The Christian today is assured of the ultimate fulfilment of all the word of God. Christians are to wait patiently, doing the will of God, "For yet a little while, and he that shall come will come, and will not tarry" (Heb 10.36-37). The promise of the Lord (Jn 14.3) will be fulfilled at the appointed time.

(b) The divine principle (v.4). Some consider that this verse is the answer to Habakkuk's perplexity. "Behold" (HINNEH - 2009) is "An interjection, demanding attention, 'Look!' 'See'" (TWOT). It draws attention to the important principle in the verse which is shown in the contrast between the proud and the righteous. Taken in context, the contrast in the verse is between the proud independence of the Chaldeans and the humble trust and submission to God of the godly remnant of Judah. However, we have here a divine principle which is applicable to all mankind. The implication is that there are only two classes of people in the sight of God, with two different ends in view. "Lifted up" (APAL - 6075) means to swell or to be puffed up indicating a person who is proud, presumptuous, self-centred, self-sufficient and self-willed. Such a person is not upright before God, i.e. the person has deviated from the standard of God and does not acknowledge or respect His claims. "Upright" (YASHAR - 3474) means to go straight, and indicates a manner or way of life in keeping with the claims of God (Ps 94.15; Prov 15.21) and of departure from sin (Prov 16.17). Here the opposite manner of life is in view. The Theological Wordbook of the Old Testament states, "...his soul is not upright within him and this leads to pride and failure". The end of such is judgment and destruction. This end is not specifically stated here, but it is implied by the contrasting statement, "the just shall live by his faith". It is also implied by the quotation of this verse in Hebrews 10.38, followed by the statement, "But we are not of them who draw back unto perdition" (v.39).

The last expression of the verse, "the just shall live by his faith", is considered by some as the key to the book of Habakkuk and is one of the central themes of the Scriptures. It is certainly the key to the christian life. The word translated "just" (SADDIQ - 6662) comes from a root word (SADEQ - 6663) meaning to be just or righteous, i.e. to conform to an ethical or moral standard. That standard, in the Scriptures, is the nature and will of God (TWOT). Righteous standing before God and righteous conduct is the result of the work of God in the national or individual life (Is 32.15-17; Ezek 36.25-27). In New Testament terms it is the result of "Being justified freely by his grace through the redemption that is in Christ Jesus" (Rom 3.24). It has been suggested that, "In this context, therefore, the life promised is political and national, in contrast to the imminent national demise of the oppressor" (D. W. Baker). However, the expression is intended to encourage Habakkuk and the godly of Judah in their complete trust in God and His promises, despite the conditions. It therefore has a deeper meaning than physical, political or national life. "Faith" (EMUNA - 530) is mainly translated as "faithfully" (2 Kings 12.15) and "faithfulness" (1 Sam 26.23; Ps 89.1). Because of this, and the fact that it contains the idea of firmness or steadfastness, it is stated that "faithfulness" rather than "faith" is the meaning here. However, the root word (AMAN - 539), which has the thought of certainty in it, has already been used by Habakkuk of those who believe not (1.5; see also Gen 15.6). Most commentaries accept the word "faith". W. J. Deane renders the expression: "As to the just, through his faith he shall live".

Faith is necessary to make good the promises and predictions in the word of God to the soul before they actually come to pass. Faith is living in the good of what is yet future and allowing that to affect the life now. The statement here is quoted on three occasions in the New Testament although the pronoun "his" is left out.

In Romans 1.17 the emphasis in the expression is upon the word "just" in keeping with the righteousness of God and the great truth of justification unfolded in the epistle, which answers the question of Job: "How then can man be justified with God?" (Job 25.4). Justification means being cleared of every charge of guilt or sin and reckoned righteous by God. This epistle teaches that it is through faith that a person is justified (Rom 3.22,28; 5.1).

In Galatians 3.11 the emphasis in the expression is upon the word "faith" in contrast to works or law-keeping emphasised by the Judaisers. Paul, in order to combat this teaching, shows in this epistle that law is not of faith (3.12), and that law and faith are actually opposed to one another (4.21-31). Whereas in Romans the believer's position before God is in view, here it is the principle of faith that is emphasised.

In Hebrews 10.38 the emphasis in the expression is upon the word "live" in keeping with the trials, difficulties and dangers of the pilgrim life unfolded in ch.11. It is faith that enables and encourages the believer to live for God in every circumstance of life. It looks beyond the present to the fulfilment of the promises and purposes of God. "Faith is the substance of things hoped for, the evidence of things not seen" (Heb 11.1).

Here in Habakkuk, the fact that the word "his" is included may suggest that the compensation of faith is, to the individual, both being just and having life.

(c) The judgment upon the Chaldeans (vv.5-20). Jehovah would have Habakkuk to look beyond the immediate circumstances to future events and lay hold upon them by faith so that he might be encouraged instead of perplexed. Likewise, at the present time the days seem to be darkening, with moral conditions deteriorating and there is much to discourage and distress the child of God. However, the believer must look beyond the present to a future day, with glad anticipation, holding fast the word of God by faith. The eyes of the prophet were opened to see the future both of the godly and the ungodly. He is given a further description of the Chaldeans and Jehovah indicates His righteousness by pronouncing judgment upon them. The Chaldeans, who were but an instrument used to chastise Judah, would be recompensed fully for their wickedness. Intoxicated with wine and their own achievements they would discover that the day of reckoning would soon overtake them. Verse 5 is clearly linked with the first part of v.4, developing the expression and applying it to the Chaldeans. This prepares the ground for the judgment of vv.6-20 which consists of five woes detailed in five sets of three verses.

The opening words of v.5, "Yea, also", indicate an addition to a previous statement, and here they add a new feature to the first statement of v.4. The construction of the opening statement is somewhat difficult and some place the emphasis upon the character of the wine (wine is treacherous or deceitful) while others place the emphasis upon the character of the Chaldeans. Both emphases are in view, indicating that the proud Chaldean gives himself over to the treachery of wine – "Wine is a mocker, strong drink is raging: and whosoever is deceived thereby is not wise" (Prov 20.1). Since the singular is used some suggest that the reference is to the Chaldean king. However, the context seems to indicate that either the nation is embraced in the person of the king or all the Chaldeans are referred to as one collective group. That the Chaldeans were addicted to wine is confirmed by ancient writers and it is also implied in Daniel 5.1-4.

The treachery of wine and strong drink leads away from God and gives a false confidence in one's self. Those who give themselves to wine and strong drink are mocked by them, and have sorrow and suffering (Prov 23.29-32). Drunkenness has caused havoc and heartache throughout the world and in every generation, and is still doing so today. The modern tendency, by some Christians, to partake of the occasional social glass of wine is not only a danger to themselves but is also a dangerous influence upon others.

"Proud" (YAHIR - 3093) means haughty or arrogant, and its only other use is in Proverbs 21.24. It has been suggested that the expression "neither keepeth at home" indicates that the Chaldeans would not continue as a nation or power in the world. However, in the context, the idea of restlessness seems to be indicated. Their pride and haughtiness stimulated their desire for further exploits and conquests, and thus their unwillingness to settle down and be satisfied with their possessions. They were not only intoxicated with wine but also with power and victories which stirred them up to further conquests (see 1.16-17). However, they were never satisfied.

Greed and discontent are often linked together. Christians are to be content with what they have, for, on top of their possessions, they have the guarantee of the Lord's presence and help (Heb 13.5-6). Having the essential things of life, food and raiment, the believer should be content, remembering that godliness with contentment is great gain (1 Tim 6.6-8). Discontentment with material wealth and a desire to have more will affect one's usefulness in the things of the Lord. If one is taken up with one's material possessions then spending more time to increase them means that less time is devoted to the Lord's things. This is a materialistic age and there is a great temptation to follow the trends that abound. It takes determination to be different.

The Chaldeans' desire to conquer and possess more was enlarged as hell (SHᶜOL - 7585; see Is 5.14), i.e. just as hell, the abode of the dead, was never full and always ready to take more, so they desired to possess more. Thus their desire was like death itself. This insatiable desire resulted in the continual conquest of nations which they gathered in (ASAP - 622) like grain at harvest time (Ruth 2.7; Is 17.5), and assembled together (heapeth, QABAS - 6908) all peoples. Their passion was never satisfied, they pursued their own impulses and considered themselves superior to others. They thought that their needs could only be met by themselves, and were marked by the spirit of independence which is the product of pride.

Many today have great desires or ambitions and, in their pride, seek to fulfil them, considering that they themselves are most important, and as long as they achieve what they want then all is well. How different to the christian principle in Philippians 2.3: "…in lowliness of mind let each esteem other better than themselves".

This verse further describes the guilt of the Chaldeans rather than their punishment, which is elaborated and condemned in the following verses. Thus it serves as a transition from the opening statement of v.4 to the five woes of judgment pronounced upon the Chaldeans in vv.6-20. Judgment because of their aggression and exploitation (vv.6-8); their covetousness (vv.9-11); their brutality (vv.12-14); their debauchery and atrocities (vv.15-17); and their idolatry (vv.18-20). These seem to be divided into two sections by the sudden reference to the earth in relation to Jehovah - full of the knowledge of His glory and the command to keep silent before Him. It must also be noticed that this division is further indicated in the fact that the fourth woe ends in the same way as the first one. The first section (vv.6-14) seems to focus on judgment because of the Chaldeans' greed and violence while the last section (vv.15-20) seems to deal with judgment because of their attitude and pride. As in ch.1, the characteristics of the Chaldeans and their judgment unfolded in the following verses points forward to the world power, its head and judgment in a coming day (Dan 7.7-8, 23-26; 8.9-12, 24-25; 2 Thess 2.3-8; Rev 13.1-8; 19.19-21).

(i) Judgment for their aggression and exploitation (vv.6-8). Jehovah showed Habakkuk that the Chaldeans would fall at the hands of those they plundered, who would mock them by a parable or taunting song. The first woe is proclaimed because of the pride, aggression and greed of the Chaldeans. They had swept through the lands plundering and exploiting the nations but just retribution would be inflicted upon them.

The first part of v.6 is really an introduction to the passage, showing that it is viewed as a poem or song. The first expression looks back, as the words "all these" refer to all nations and all people of v.5, as well as looking forward to the actual destruction of the Chaldeans. It is suggested that, since this is prophetic, a believing remnant of these nations is in view (Keil & Delitzsch). The thought seems to be that those who suffered under the tyranny of the Chaldeans would rejoice at their downfall. The word "parable" (MASHAL - 4912) is translated in a number of ways in the Old Testament and thus, "to define the exact meaning of MASHAL in some of its uses is very difficult" (S. R. Driver). Many commentaries suggest that the meaning here is a taunting or derisive song. The expression "taunting proverb" comes from two Hebrew words. The former (MᶜLISA - 4426) has the idea of scorn or mockery in it although it is also translated "interpretation" in Proverb 1.6. Strong's Concordance states that it is an aphorism (a pithy observation which contains a general truth); also a satire (ridicule, irony). The latter (HIDA - 2420) means an enigma or puzzle. The expression, therefore, indicates a speech or poem incorporating enigmas or having a double meaning. Thus the idea in this opening section is that of a poem, song, or sayings which contain symbols to convey the retribution upon the Chaldeans because of their wickedness.

Each woe relates to some specific offence and pronounces its appropriate penalty. This first woe is directed against the aggression and exploitation of the Chaldeans and highlights their greed and dishonesty. Their avarice drove them on to plunder as much as they could of the possessions of others. They sought to amass wealth by any means possible. However, the plunder did not really belong to them. A person can only truthfully call something his own if it is obtained honestly. There are people today who have increased in wealth by dishonest and devious means because of a desire to be rich – "But they that will be rich fall into temptation and a snare, and into many foolish and hurtful lusts, which drown men in destruction and perdition" (1 Tim 6.9). As mentioned earlier, believers must be on their guard regarding wealth and materialism since there is a danger of being led away from spiritual things and into many sorrows (1 Tim 6.10).

"How long?" comes as an interjection and is in the form of a sigh because of the seemingly unending exploitation and plundering by the Chaldeans. How long shall the groans of those under oppression continue? Here is an echo of the prophet's opening cry in 1.2. The expression could also be looked at in relation to the Chaldeans' plunder - "How long will they continue to enjoy their ill-gotten possessions?" This would then be a rhetorical question implying the inevitable answer, "Not long".

Three different suggestions have been made regarding the last clause of the verse.

1. The Chaldeans load themselves with wealth like thick clay which becomes a burden or which will soon be removed (Jamieson, Fausset & Brown; Matthew Poole; and Rabbi A. J. Rosenberg).

2. The extortion of the Chaldeans through the accumulation of pledges (D. W. Baker).

3. The Chaldeans compared with an unmerciful and dishonest usurer, and their wealth compared to pledges in their hands (Keil & Delitzsch; S. R. Driver).

The last two are taken from the fact that the word translated "thick clay" (ABTIT - 5671) comes from a root word (ABOT - 5670) which means to pawn or to lend. Thus comes the thought of pledges or heavy pledges (see Deut 24.10-13). The third suggestion seems to be more in keeping with the passage and would thus be an illustration or symbol of what has already been stated.

The punishment of the Chaldeans described in v.7 is commensurate with their wickedness, for as they have spoiled others so they will be spoiled and their victims will be victorious over them. Those who had been exploited and cruelly treated would suddenly revolt, rise up and exact retribution. The word "suddenly" may well be the answer to the question "How long?" in the previous verse. As a serpent suddenly strikes its victim so will God's judgment, inflicted by the surrounding nations as the instrument of God, strike the Chaldean nation (see Jer 8.17). The venom of the bite would thus cause the vexation or trembling of the following statement. However, the word translated "bite" (NASHAK - 5391) is also used metaphorically of "to oppress with interest on a loan" (Strong's Concordance - see Deut 23.19). This would continue the illustration of the previous verse, where the Chaldeans are viewed as the creditor exacting an excessive and unbearable interest from the conquered nations, who are viewed as the debtor. However, the roles are reversed here so the Chaldeans are viewed as the debtor and the nations they plundered as the creditor demanding the capital, with interest, of what the Chaldeans had unrighteously taken from them. Many feel that the Medo-Persian power is the exacter of this debt, but the context seems to suggest a wider application. The thought is that as the Chaldeans oppressed others so they would be oppressed by their victims.

The exploited nations would not only rise up and bite them but would also awake and vex them. "Vex" (ZUA - 2111) means to tremble, to quiver, or to be in terror. The victimised nations will awake, as out of a sleep, to seize upon the Chaldeans causing them to tremble, just as a debtor is seized by the creditor to pay back every part of the debt (see Mt 18.28,34). The word translated "booties" (MᶜSHISSA - 4933) means plunder or spoil and is in the plural. "The plural, an unusual form in the Hebrew, as in English, denotes the vast amount and variety of the spoils to be wrung from the oppressor" (F. C. Cook; see also S. R. Driver). Thus the last statement indicates not only that the Chaldeans' lands, houses and possessions would be the spoil but also their own selves, implying that they would become slaves just as they had made slaves of the peoples they conquered and plundered. The day of reckoning would surely come for them.

One must remember that the great day of reckoning will come for every individual, whether unbeliever or believer, when they stand before God. For unbelievers it will be at the Great White Throne, when the solemn consequences of their unbelief and life of sin will result in the lake of fire forever (Rev 20.11-15), and for believers it will be at the Judgment Seat of Christ when their lives will be solemnly reviewed resulting in reward or loss (Rom 14.10; 1 Cor 3.13-15; 2 Cor 5.10). All should review their lives in the light of that coming day of reckoning.

The reason for the retribution to be inflicted upon the Chaldeans is now given in v.8. Here we have the law of retaliation, and the relationship between exploitation and recompense is clearly in view. This is righteous retribution as it is the proclamation of God. The Chaldeans had plundered many nations but they would reap what they had sown. There are two suggestions in regard to "the remnant".

1. It refers to the nations which had not been conquered and plundered by the Chaldeans. Those who accept this view consider that the Medes and Persians were among those nations.

2. It refers to those remaining of the nations subjugated and exploited. Those who take this view believe that Media and Persia were conquered by the Chaldeans. For a discourse on this subject see Keil & Delitzsch.

The second view is taken here. All who had been plundered, cruelly treated, and yet had survived would ultimately plunder Chaldea. "The agents in the overthrow of the Babylonian empire were Media, Persia, with confederate tribes, all whom had been attacked and spoiled by Nebuchadnezzar, but existed as a powerful remnant ready when 'awakened' to exact revenge" (F. C. Cook). Having been given the general reason for the coming judgment, their greed in plundering the nations, the prophet is now given more specific reasons. It may well be that although these grounds may be applicable to all the nations plundered, the reference is really to Judah and Judea. The specific reasons refer to the unwarranted slaughter of the people of Judah (it is suggested that this is a reference to the slaying of the sons of Zedekiah and the princes of Judah - Jer 52.10);

the unnecessarily violent oppression and plundering of Judea; the unjustifiably violent burning of Jerusalem; and the unreasonable cruelty inflicted upon the inhabitants of Jerusalem. Habakkuk was given not only a view of crimes the Chaldeans had committed but also a preview of crimes they would commit and of their punishment. Since God was revealing His righteousness, Habakkuk would understand that the principle here was not that of revenge but of justice as in the law – "Eye for eye, tooth for tooth, hand for hand, foot for foot" (Ex 21.24).

This principle of God's justice is operative today. Although people may not be aware of this, it will be fully manifest in a coming day. The passion of pride will bring its recompense as is evident in Daniel 5.18-31. It is profitable to remember the word of the Lord Jesus Christ: "For whosoever exalteth himself shall be abased; and he that humbleth himself shall be exalted" (Lk 14.11).

(ii) Judgment for their covetousness (vv.9-11). Whereas the first woe was in relation to the Chaldeans' aggression and exploitation, this second woe is in regard to their covetousness. The Chaldeans sought to enforce dominance and authority over many nations. Although some feel that Nebuchadnezzar and his desire to establish his dynasty is in view, all the Chaldeans are clearly embraced in these verses. The Chaldeans sought to enrich themselves, driven by covetousness and self-exaltation and at the expense of others. They did not consider the sufferings of others as long as they themselves were enriched, nor were they concerned as to how they enlarged their possessions. Their covetousness drove them on to increase materially so that they might be set on high and all who stood in their way be removed so that their greatness and glory might be established. In so doing they sought to obtain for themselves what they considered to be a place of security. This is illustrated in the eagle's nest being in a high, inaccessible place and protected from all harm or attack (see Obad v.4). However, their plan and purpose would be brought to naught for their dominance, power, and authority would collapse and they would be brought down.

Many in the world today are motivated by covetousness, and, sad to say, many who profess to belong to Christ will do almost anything to advance materially or to obtain a position in the world. All such activities will be brought to the light for, one must realise, God is a witness to every desire, motive and action of one's life. How solemn. Unrighteousness often springs out of covetousness, "For the love of money is the root of all evil" (1 Tim 6.10). Covetousness seems to be prevalent today. Subtly it takes hold even of Christians, and has proved to be the stumbling block to their spiritual progress. Covetousness is really the unsatisfied craving for more and more temporal things. Believers need to be constantly on their guard against it. It is the opposite of the contentment which the believer is exhorted to display (1 Tim 6.8; Heb 13.5).

In addition therefore to the Chaldeans' plunder and exploitation there is added the underlying evil of covetousness (v.9) which forced them on in their wickedness and resulted in their ruin. The verse begins with covetousness and ends with self-exaltation or self-confidence. Some have translated the opening expression as, "that gain an evil gain". However, "coveteth (BASA - 1214) and "covetousness" (BESA - 1215) have the idea of "cutting off" in the sense of taking away from another's property. Where the two words occur together they emphasise lust for personal gain which is opposite to unselfish devotion to God, and will bring ruin to all who succumb to it (TWOT). Covetousness involves one in the endless and feverish pursuit of material things to either enrich or to promote one's self. It shows a reliance upon material things and a lack of dependence upon God (Lk 12.15; Col 3.5). The addition of the word "evil" (RAA - 7451) strengthens and emphasises the dreadfulness of the Chaldeans' covetousness which brings the judgment of God upon them.

There are three different views as to the expression "his house".

1. It is a reference to the palace or fortress of Nebuchadnezzar which was built and beautified with material plundered from other nations. In this view Nebuchadnezzar and his palace can be compared with Jehoiakim and the woe proclaimed against him (Jer 22.13-19).

2. It is figurative of the dynasty which the Chaldeans sought to establish and permanently secure through the subjugation of surrounding nations, and by the amassing of wealth through plunder.

3. It refers to the actual houses and buildings of the Chaldeans which had been erected, enlarged and made fast with stolen property.

Although most scholars favour the second view, all three could be applicable. The Chaldeans, in their covetousness, had plundered many nations, using the stolen property to enrich themselves and their families and to make themselves more comfortable and secure. The dreadfulness of this sin is that it encourages robbing others of what is rightfully theirs in order to enrich one's self, even though it may bring those robbed to poverty. As in 1.8 the Chaldeans are compared to the eagle but here it is in relation to its building its nest in a high inaccessible place rather than its swiftness in taking its prey (see Job 39.27-28). The metaphor is used to denote the security and self-confidence of the Chaldeans who employed violence and subtlety to establish their power. It is suggested that the thought is that of securing the monarchy and government of the nation against any form of calamity. Thus the exploitation of other nations was in order to ensure that power and authority might never be wrested from the Chaldean dynasty. Some see here an allusion to the fortifications raised by Nebuchadnezzar to protect Babylon. The last expression indicates that the Chaldeans thought that their harsh treatment of the nations they conquered would ensure their immunity to every kind of harm or evil.

Verse 10 gives the result of the Chaldeans' covetousness, self-exaltation, and self-confidence. The action they take to secure their position will prove to be their downfall (see Prov 15.27). Many who put their trust in riches and prosperity, thinking that they will bring satisfaction and happiness, discover that they only bring misery and ruin.

The word "consulted" (YAAS - 3289) means counsel, purpose, or determine. Thus their determination to consolidate and secure their power, authority, and dynasty would bring shame upon them. In seeking to establish and exalt themselves by evil gain they would disgrace themselves and, instead of securing lasting supremacy and safety, they would be brought to ruin. It is suggested that the shame and ruin of the royal family under Belshazzar is in view. The word "shame" (BOSHNA - 1322) carries the idea of shame and disgrace because of defeat at the hands of an enemy. However, the reason given here for their ultimate shame or disgrace is their treatment of other nations. Their determination to cut off many peoples in order to establish and secure their position and power would be the means of bringing shame upon them.

The expression "cutting off" (QASA - 7096) indicates the taking of life (2 Kings 10.32) and thus the annihilation of many peoples. Their strategy of destroying nations by the slaughter of the people, in order to prevent a challenge to their dominance, would fail. In their resolve to cut off many people they were sinning against their souls in the sense of bringing guilt and thus retribution upon themselves (see Prov 20.2) – "he that sinneth against me wrongeth his own soul" (Prov 8.36). Those who treat others in a wrong way are at the same time harming themselves. The thought here may well be that by cutting off the lives of others they forfeited their own lives. The Chaldeans, in their treatment of the nations, demonstrated that they were lacking compassion and mercy.

Whereas in v.10 the result of the Chaldeans' sin and self-exaltation is in view, in v.11 the reason for the judgment is mentioned. Inanimate things are personified in order to condemn their wickedness and to cry out for vengeance or retribution. The very material of their buildings, be it houses, palaces, or fortresses, would bear testimony to their cruelty and wicked plundering. Just as the stones would witness to the righteous claims of the Lord Jesus Christ (Lk 19.40), so the stones here would bear testimony to the need for the righteous judgment of God. The stone crying out (ZAAQ - 2199), as with the prophet's cry (1.2), indicates the need for action felt and desired. This cry reveals the abhorrence with which their violence, cruelty and plundering were viewed, especially in relation to their buildings. These buildings had not only been built with plundered materials, but also with the enforced labour of captives who were despised and ill-treated. Some suggest that this crying out of the stone of the wall was literally fulfilled in the writing upon the plaster of the wall at Belshazzar's feast (Dan 5). The cry of the stone out of the wall (the main outside walls are in view) is answered by the beam (tie-bar or rafter). The word translated "answer" (ANA - 6030) has the idea here, not of an answer to a question, but of a response. The thought could well be that the stone commences the cry and the beam responds by taking up the same cry for punishment of the perpetrators. Thus every part of the building, which the Chaldeans prided themselves in, would testify to their evil which would ultimately bring upon them righteous retribution.

(iii) Judgment for their brutality (vv.12-14). This third woe is pronounced upon the Chaldeans because of their ruthlessness and brutality. Their determination to establish themselves and their dynasty through wickedness was also shown in the building of towns and cities using the blood and toil of the people they conquered. However, they would be held responsible and punished for carrying out their building programs in such a violent and merciless way. Their plan was to build something for themselves and their own glory. It mattered not how it was done as long as it was achieved, even if iniquitous means were necessary.

Pride and covetousness always seek to establish something for self and will make plans in order to fulfil that desire even though it might be through force or fraud. This spirit is prevalent in the world today, but should never be seen among the people of God. How sad when Christians use devious methods to further their own desires and interests. How solemn when they plan to establish their own ways by violating the word of God. It is possible to use the tongue in a subtle way, not caring about another's feelings or character, in order to establish something for one's self. The children of God should never seek their own advancement without a thought for others or at their expense – "Let no man seek his own, but every man another's wealth (or welfare)" (1 Cor 10.24). The third woe (v.12) is against the Chaldeans in the use they made of the wealth they acquired by violence. It is also against the brutality and ruthlessness they demonstrated during the carrying out of their building programme with slave labour. It was their pride, as displayed by their monarch (Dan 4.30), which urged them on in their inhumanity to others in building and fortifying their cities for their glory. The majority of the inscriptions of Nebuchadnezzar which have been discovered relate to buildings, the cost of which had been met by war against and plundering surrounding nations. Many of the ancient capital cities were founded through violence and bloodshed (Micah 3.10; Nah 3.1). The features of violence and ruthlessness were also displayed by Jehoiakim (Jer 22.17-18).

The Hebrew words for "town" and "city" seem to be synonymous here and being in the singular suggest indefinite generality (Keil & Delitzsch). The verbal adjectives are intended to indicate that the brutality used in building these cities was not unique to that occasion but was characteristic of the Chaldeans. Sadly, this has been true of many nations and individuals throughout history and is still present today in some parts of the world. It is opposite to the love, compassion and tenderness which are seen in all their perfection in the Lord Jesus Christ and which should characterise every Christian.

The stress in the verse is upon the means they employed to carry out their purpose - the shedding of blood and iniquity. The use of "blood" (DAM - 1818) here implies the guilt of blood shedding, i.e. murder. The prophecy views the multitude of captives brutally treated under the taskmasters, wounded by the lash and even losing their lives, as they were compelled to build, enlarge and fortify the cities. The thought could well be that the blood shed was really the material that erected these buildings. "Iniquity" (AWLA - 5766) denotes an action that is against or opposite to what is right, i.e., behaviour contrary to the character of God. Thus, seen in the light of God's righteousness, the Chaldeans' building programme was iniquitous since it involved not only plunder but also loss of human life and suffering. In contrast to this, the believer should "live soberly, righteously, and godly, in this present world" (Tit 2.12).

In the preceding woes the central verse continued or expanded the wickedness of the Chaldeans or stated the result of that wickedness, but in v.13 something different is introduced. The word "behold", as in v.4, draws attention to the important principle in the verse which is the sovereign ordering of Jehovah. The expression "the Lord of hosts" is a Jehovah title (Jehovah Sabaoth) indicating His majesty and glory as the Sovereign over all (see Ps 24.10; Is 6.5). It is first mentioned in 1 Samuel 1.3 and occurs over 200 times in the Old Testament. In many passages it implies that ultimate victory belongs to Israel since the God of Israel is Jehovah of the hosts of the universe and so able to do what He wills among the armies of this world. The thought in this verse is that Jehovah, who is over all, has righteously determined the destruction of the Chaldean empire.

The expression "labour in the very fire" has the idea of labouring for the fire. The word translated "very" (DAY - 1767) means sufficiency or enough. Thus the expression is literally "to suffice the fire". The word translated "labour" (YAGEA - 3021) means working until tired or exhausted, and indicates the wearying toil of the captives to the point of complete exhaustion. All the toil, blood, and sweat of the Chaldeans' captives or slaves were only producing material for the fire (Jer 51.58). The fire would destroy the cities and the Chaldean empire would fall into ruin. All the self-exaltation and glorying of the Chaldeans would then be terminated.

All the plans and labour of men are of no lasting value if they are not in keeping with the character and will of God. The Christian ought to remember that expending energy on worldly things, or in amassing material goods, has no lasting profit. This world is not going to last forever and, "Seeing then that all these things shall be dissolved, what manner of persons ought ye to be in all holy conversation and godliness" (2 Pet 3.11).

The last expression of the verse expresses the consequence of the destruction of the cities. All the wearying toil in their construction was to no purpose and ultimately wasted, since they would soon be destroyed. Solemn judgment would fall upon the Chaldeans, and their empire would fall. This is also a picture of the destruction of the coming ten kingdom confederacy, the last great Gentile power, after which the Messianic Kingdom will be manifested. This verse indicates that vengeance belongs to Jehovah (Deut 32.35; Ps 94.1; Rom 12.19).

Verse 14 is the reason for the previous verse since the events described here cannot take place until the preceding one comes to pass. The darkness and foreboding of the preceding woes are suddenly changed to the brightness of the glory of Jehovah. This verse describes the result of the judgment upon the Chaldeans, and it passes from their temporary self-glorying to the abiding glory of God. In contrast to the passing away of man's establishment, the kingdoms of men, what is of the Lord is for ever. The link with the previous verses is that the glory of Jehovah will be manifested in His judgment and overthrow of the Chaldean empire (see Ezek 39.21-22). It has been stated that "Here the sense is, 'The Jews shall be restored and the temple rebuilt, so that God's glory in saving His people, and punishing their Chaldean foe, shall be manifested throughout the world', of which the Babylonian empire formed the greatest part" (Jamieson, Fausset & Brown). However, this is a Messianic prophecy and looks on to the establishing of the Kingdom of the Messiah, so the judgment of the Chaldeans looks beyond the fall of the Chaldean power of Habakkuk's day. The features of Babylon seem to run through the Scriptures from its first references (Gen 10.10; 11.1-9) to the manifestation of Christ and the setting up of the Messianic Kingdom (see Rev 17-19). The ultimate result of God's judgments upon the powers of the world opposed to Him will be the display of His glory and peace throughout the world in keeping with His promise (Num 14.21; Is 11.9). This will necessitate the destruction of the kingdoms of men – "The kingdoms of this world are become the kingdoms of our Lord, and of his Christ; and he shall reign for ever and ever" (Rev 11.15). The promise in this verse is linked with the intimation of God's judgment upon the Chaldeans whose presumed glory shall be destroyed that the glory of Jehovah might fill the earth, but the promise in Numbers 14.21 is linked with pardon - the pardon of Israel. The passage in Isaiah 11.9 is slightly different. The statement in Isaiah closes the description of the coming Messianic Kingdom when there will be peace on earth and it will be full of the knowledge of Jehovah. However, here in Habakkuk the statement indicates that it is only through the judgment and overthrow of the enemies of God and of Israel that there will be lasting peace and a knowledge of His glory. In Isaiah it is linked with the knowledge of Jehovah, but in Habakkuk it is linked with the knowledge of the glory of Jehovah, i.e. the display of His majesty and power. Only through the manifestation of His majesty and omnipotence in judgment upon the evil powers of this world will the earth be filled with the knowledge (or acknowledgement) of the glory of Jehovah.

The last expression of the verse denotes an overflowing abundance of that glory. This verse not only indicates the necessity of the judgment and destruction of the Chaldeans, but it also aims to encourage Habakkuk and the godly remnant of Judah. It does this by reminding them that there is a bright future for the nation of Israel, in keeping with His covenants (Gen 12.1-3; Jer 31.31-40). Habakkuk had a glimpse of the brightness and glory of a coming day.

(iv) Judgment for their debauchery and atrocities (vv. 15-17). The fourth woe follows the brief glimpse of what Jehovah purposed for the distant future. Woe is now pronounced on the Chaldeans because of their treatment of other nations in vivid contrast to the Messianic Kingdom of v.14. Verses 15 and 16 can be viewed either literally or figuratively in relation to the Chaldeans' treatment of other nations.

1. Literally. The Chaldeans are condemned, not only for their own excessive drinking, but also for leading the neighbouring nations into debauchery by encouraging the people to consume intoxicating drink. However, not only did they encourage them to take alcohol, they actually compelled them to take more and more by forcing the bottle (skin) upon them until they became senseless and helpless in drunkenness. Although the influence and forcefulness of the Chaldeans in causing others to drink excessively to the point of loathsome drunkenness was totally evil, their purpose in doing so was far more wicked. It was to enable them to gaze shamelessly upon the nakedness of their drunken victims. Such perverse gloating over the sight of indecent exposure was to their condemnation and would bring just retribution (Gen 9.22-27). The idea would be that of disgraceful and immoral corruption. The Chaldeans' design was to satisfy their base desires and to expose their victims to scorn and derision. The Chaldeans' guilt was increased by their deliberate actions to humiliate and expose their neighbours. As a consequence of their evil intentions and actions they would be punished and filled with disgrace instead of honour. Just retribution would be meted out to them by Jehovah. Whereas the Chaldeans used a literal cup of intoxication to stupefy others, Jehovah would use a figurative cup of wrath to bring shame and destruction upon them.

2. Figuratively. The description is figurative, being taken from the idea of intoxicating drink being given to another to take delight in their drunken state. This metaphor is used elsewhere in the Old Testament (Ps 75.8; Jer 25.15). The thought would be of reducing the nations conquered to a state of helpless prostration like a person who is drunk. The sensual desire to gaze at nakedness would indicate metaphorically the Chaldeans' lust for power and the complete subjugation of those conquered. The result of such barbarous treatment would be their own shame and destruction.

Whichever view is taken, the principle of the corruption and abuse of others for pleasure or profit can be lifted from these verses. The persuasion or compulsion of another to deviate from what is right for one's own pleasure or benefit is condemned, and will ultimately result in loss. It is dreadful to influence others to take a wrong course and then to take pleasure in their doing so. Some, who are not taking the right course in life, seek to influence others to take that same course in order to justify themselves. The child of God should always seek to influence fellow believers in the right pathway by example as well as by instruction from the word of God – "be thou an example of the believers, in word, in conversation, in charity, in spirit, in faith, in purity" (1 Tim 4.12).

In this study the figurative view is being taken in vv.15-16. In v.17 the wickedness of the Chaldeans seems to be brought to a climax in their violence against the forests and wild life of Lebanon.

The description in v.15 is assumed to be figurative and is taken from the practice of the Chaldeans mentioned in v.5 in order to indicate their treatment of the nations they had conquered. They are depicted as a man giving intoxicating liquor to his neighbour with the express purpose of bringing shame and ridicule upon him. In this instance the intoxicating drink was the cup of the Chaldeans' fury. It was given to the conquered nations to bring them more easily into subjection. "Drunkenness is here a figure of the prostration and helplessness of a conquered people, powerless under the stupefying or paralysing effects of a great catastrophe: cf. Nahum 3.11" (S. R. Driver). Some suggest that the thought here is that of the Chaldeans, in their desire for power and supremacy, alluring neighbouring nations into campaigns of war to plunder, but in the end exposing them to shame and loss. The second clause is a strengthened form of the preceding one by adding a further ingredient. The Hebrew in the clause is said to be textually difficult and so is viewed in different ways. The word translated "puttest" (SAPAH - 5596) means to attach or to join together, and can have the idea of adding. Thus some have suggested the expression "adding thy poison thereto". The thought would then be of adding some drug to the wine to speed up the intoxicating process. It has been stated that "'pour out' may underlie the difficult crux here" (TWOT). The idea would then be of the Chaldeans pouring out their fury. It is suggested that the Hebrew word for "bottle" (HEMET - 2573) should really be HEMA (2534) which signifies heat, or figuratively "anger or poison" and is translated "fury" (Gen 27.44; Nah 1.6) and "poison" (Deut 32.24; Ps 58.4) (see S. R. Driver and F. C. Cook). Whatever the construction of the clause it is evident that the end in view was to produce drunkenness which is figurative of the complete subjugation and helplessness of the conquered nations. The expression also indicates the atrocious manner and the violent nature of the Chaldeans in subjugating the nations. The helpless drunkard, grovelling about, without control of his faculties, is a graphic picture of the nations subdued and plundered by the Chaldeans.

The last statement gives the reason for producing drunkenness - so that they could gaze with delight upon their nakedness. The word translated "nakedness" (MAOR - 4589) is only found here in the Old Testament and means to be exposed or be bare. The metaphor here indicates that the Chaldeans delighted in the pitiful condition to which the conquered nations were reduced and in the ignominy which came upon them. These nations became the object of mockery and scorn. How dreadful to delight in the ruin of anyone, let alone to be the instrument in bringing about that ruin. One must note that the actions of the Chaldeans mentioned in this verse are also seen in the mystic and literal Babylon of Revelation 17.2 and 18.3.

The Chaldeans barbaric treatment of those they subjugated in order to bring them to shame only demonstrated their own shamefulness and degradation (v.16). They sought to glorify themselves by debasing others, but they would discover they could not succeed ultimately. The delight with which they beheld the conquered nations would turn to misery. Instead of the glory of supremacy they would be brought into the shame of ruin and destruction. The exalting of themselves would result in their humiliation, as with Israel (Hos 4.7 - see also Prov 4.19). Many today seek to exalt themselves, but the Lord said, "For whosoever exalteth himself shall be abased; and he that humbleth himself shall be exalted" (Lk 14.11; 18.14). The Chaldeans would be filled with dishonour instead of honour, and receive the opposite of what they sought through their inhumane behaviour. There could be an allusion here to the contrast between the grandeur of Nebuchadnezzar's reign and the shame and drunken orgy of Belshazzar's feast at the fall of the empire. The punishment of the Chaldeans would be in keeping with their wickedness. What they sought to do to others would be done to them in keeping with the principle that "whatsoever a man soweth, that shall he also reap" (Gal 6.7).

The expression "let thy foreskin be uncovered" has the thought of "show thyself as uncircumcised", which is intended to indicate that they would be held in utter contempt, particularly in the eyes of the Jews. They had given other nations the cup of wrath so Jehovah would give them the cup of wrath or judgment (Ps 75.8). The Chaldeans were the cup of judgment in Jehovah's hand making all nations drunken (Jer 51.7 - see also Jer 25), and that cup would be given to Judah to drink (Lam 4.21) even as Israel had to drink of it at the hands of the Assyrians (Ezek 23.33).

The cup of Jehovah's right hand refers to His wrath and judgment which would be passed to the Chaldeans and which they would be compelled to drink (see Rev 16.19). "The Lord's right hand" speaks of His power and indicates that none, not even the mighty Chaldean empire, can escape His righteous judgment. Just as vomiting follows excessive drinking of intoxicating liquor, bringing disgrace upon the drunkard, so complete disgrace would cover the glory of the Chaldeans (see Jer 25.27). It is suggested that "shameful spewing" may indicate that the Chaldeans would be compelled to disgorge the spoil taken during their conquests. The Hebrew word for that phrase (QIQALON - 7022) is only found here and means intense disgrace or ignominy.

Some commentators continue the symbolic view into v.17, taking "Lebanon" as referring to either the land of Palestine (Is 33.9; 37.24) or to Jerusalem (Jer 22.23). However, this section is dealing with the Chaldeans' treatment of the conquered nations and thus this verse should be taken literally. Here we have another reason for the threat of judgment upon the Chaldeans mentioned in the preceding verse. Their violence refers to the stripping of the well known forests of Lebanon, and their brutal treatment of the animals. The Chaldeans cut down vast quantities of fir, cedar, and cypress, desolating the land, in order to build and adorn their extravagant buildings and palaces. The verb "cover" (KASA - 3680) has the idea of overwhelming (see Ps 55.5; 78.53). The same devastation which they inflicted on Lebanon would completely overwhelm them. There may well be an illustration of this in Isaiah 14.8: "Yea, the fir trees rejoice at thee, and the cedars of Lebanon, saying, Since thou art laid down, no feller is come up against us". The "spoil" (SHOD - 7701) denotes the destruction of the wildlife, although some include domestic animals. They meticulously hunted the wild animals which they unsparingly slaughtered. Not only did the Chaldeans commit atrocities against men but also against nature. It has been stated that it was not just their inhuman atrocities which were condemned, but also their ecological excesses. Is there not a greater awareness today of what is being done to the environment? Are not men realizing that they are responsible for natural resources and the maintenance of wild life? Will not men, today, be accountable to God for their treatment of the environment?

The expression "which made them afraid" is acknowledged as being difficult. Some apply it to the Chaldeans – "'the slaughter of beasts shall terrify thee'...The meaning appears to be that the Chaldean will be terrified by the vision of the beasts which he had slaughtered" (F. C. Cook; see also W. J. Deane). Others apply it to the animals – "the devastation which terrified the animals" (Keil & Delitzsch). The stripping of Lebanon and the extermination of its wildlife may well be indicative of what the Chaldeans did to every land they conquered.

The latter part of this verse is a repetition of the latter part of v.8. As in that verse, the general reasons for judgment upon the Chaldeans change to the more specific reasons which centre upon Judah. Although the three statements of this latter part can be applied to all the nations conquered, they really refer to Judah and Jerusalem. Thus in both sections of these woes, which unfold judgment upon the Chaldeans because of their treatment of the conquered nations, there is a reference to the consequences of the Chaldeans' treatment of Judah and Jerusalem (see v.8).

(v) Judgment for their idolatry (vv.18-20). The last woe in the judgment of the Chaldeans is in relation to their idolatry. Unlike the preceding four woes it does not commence with the pronouncing of retribution for the Chaldeans but it first indicates the basis for all that has gone before, and

prepares the ground for this final word of woe. Idolatry ignores responsibility to the living and true God and gives licence to all forms of evil. The opening verse reveals the worthlessness of idols and their impotence, as well as the folly of the idolaters, strengthening this last judgment upon the Chaldeans. Idolatry is not only senseless but also deceptive because of the falsehood linked with it. Throughout the Scriptures every form of idolatry is condemned. The folly of idolatry is demonstrated by the inability of idols to respond to cries for help in the time of need. They are but dumb and lifeless. They may have outward beauty, being overlaid with gold or silver, but they have no life and therefore no power. Verses 18 and 19 show that idolatry is absurd, a fraud, and brings ruin to its adherents. In contrast to the lifeless and powerless idols, there is a true and living God who sits in holiness upon the throne in His holy temple. Unlike the sightless images, He sees all and is ruler and judge over all. When the day of reckoning comes, the Chaldeans, who put their trust in their idols, would be unable to escape His righteous judgment. However, He will deliver and bless those who have placed their trust in Him. Although the living God is invisible and enthroned in His heavenly temple, He is sovereign and omnipotent, and therefore it behoves all the earth to be silent when He speaks and to submit reverently to Him.

The Chaldeans resorted to their gods for direction and power (v.18), putting their trust in their idols and attributing to them their successful conquests. Thus the inability of the idols to deliver them from the judgment unfolded in the previous verses is an appropriate introduction to this last woe. The folly of the Chaldeans is indicated in the opening ironical question - "what profit"? The word translated "profiteth" (YAAL - 3276) is generally used in a negative way in the Old Testament, e.g. "My people have changed their glory for that which doth not profit" (Jer 2.11). This indicates that the question is not only ironical but also rhetorical with the inevitable answer in the negative (cp. Is 44.10). There are three references to idols in this verse. The first two are in regard to their construction - the graven image and the molten image. The third reference is in regard to their inability and worthlessness. The graven image (PESEL - 6459) is an idol carved out of wood or hewn out of stone (Is 37.19). The molten image is an idol made by pouring molten metal into a mould (Ex 32.4,24). Of what value is all the time, skill, and effort of the maker since it is but a false god and has no power?

The expression "a teacher of lies" can be looked at in two ways.

1. It is a reference to the priests or prophets of the idol who made predictions and gave direction to the adherents. However, what they proclaimed was false. The idol was supposed to speak through priests and prophets and so the deception of it being a god was maintained.

2. It refers to the molten image itself, since it signified a false object of worship and was called a god although it was nothing (1 Cor 10.19-20) in contrast to the true God. It also deluded men and encouraged false

instruction in contrast to the truth of God (Zech 10.2). This second view is more in keeping with the context since it would enhance the following clause.

How absurd for the maker of the idol, who gave it shape and size, to put his trust in it for instruction and help. Idols were the product of man's art and yet the hope of man's soul. The folly of worshipping those things which one's hands had made is emphasised - his work and yet his god. The folly of trusting or worshipping one's own achievements is clearly implied. The proud person sets up his own accomplishments to be idolised and considers they are the best and most important. There are those who consider that their ways, ideas, designs, and work are the best and should be held up for all to see. Very often things are done to draw attention to self. One can think of the Pharisees who fasted, prayed, and gave alms to draw attention to themselves in order that men might praise them. One must be careful of this kind of spirit. There is a danger of allowing achievements or possessions to become objects of affection and thus become one's idols. It would be well to remember the expression,

> Only one life, 'twill soon be past,
> Only what's done for Christ will last.

Whatever the believer does should be done heartily as to the Lord and done for His glory (Col 3.23-24).

It has been stated that "idols" (ELIL - 457) "applies specially to little images employed in divination, or consulted as oracular. It is of course always used contemptuously as contrasted with God (*elilim* not *elohim*)" (F. C. Cook). The word means a "worthless thing" (Job 13.4 – "physicians of no value"; Jer 14.14 – "a thing of nought"). These idols, expected to give divine directions, were dumb (1 Cor 12.2). Men can indeed make idols, but they are unable to give them life or make them speak.

In v.18 the uselessness of the idol itself is emphasised whereas in v.19 judgment upon the Chaldean idolaters is introduced. In v.18 the idol itself is in view, but here the material of the idol is emphasised in order to stress the absurdity of idolatry.

Woe is pronounced upon those who expected help from that which was inanimate (Ps 115.4-7; 135.15-18). To address a piece of wood, whatever shape may be given to it, and to expect it to wake out of sleep and hearken to their cries, was folly since it remained just wood. The same applied to stone. "Arise" (UR - 5782) has the thought here of arousing one's self from inactivity. The expression "it shall teach!" has been viewed in three different ways: "it teach?" - a rhetorical question demanding a negative answer - absolutely not; "shall this teach?" - a question of astonishment at so great a deception; and "it shall teach!" - used in the same sense as "a teacher of lies" in v.18 - although dumb stone it directs its worshippers away from the true and the living God to the gross error of idolatry (Rom 1.25). The language in this verse seems to be derisive and ironical, similar to Elijah's taunting of the prophets of Baal: "Cry aloud...peradventure he sleepeth, and must be awaked" (1 Kings 18.27).

Although overlaid with gold and silver, giving it earthly splendour and beauty, it still had no ability to help the worshipper because it had no breath in it, i.e. no life (Jer 10.14). In this last clause there seems to be a note of contempt for the deluded Chaldean idolaters in light of the following verse. This verse shows that whatever men may do with the works of their hands, and however they may address what they have made, the material remains the same and their gods remain lifeless. Such is the folly, dreadfulness and delusion of idolatry. A more detailed description of the condemnation heaped upon idolatry is found in Isaiah 44.9-20 and Jeremiah 10.1-16.

Idolatry is still widely practised today as is evident in the various shrines found in the different religions, including Christendom. In fact it is on the increase with the spread of Occultism, Theosophy, Astrology, Satanism and many other false cults. There are more subtle forms of idolatry that the believer can fall into, e.g. materialism, being taken up with academic achievement or social status. Idolatry will be prevalent in a coming day when there will be worldwide worship of the beast and his image (Rev 13.14-15; 14.9,11; 19.20).

The woes of judgment upon the Chaldeans end in v.20 with this note of encouragement for the godly remnant of Judah. As in v.14 the gloom and forewarning of the woes suddenly changes to the light and glory of Jehovah, but here that contrast is between the dumb, lifeless idols and the majesty and glory of the living God (Jer 10.10) enthroned in His holy temple (Micah 1.2). He and He alone was worthy of honour, praise, and worship. Habakkuk had heard the voice of Jehovah and had received His revelation; thus the prophet's anxieties were removed and he was overwhelmed by the greatness, majesty, and glory of Jehovah, the God of Israel. He was the true source of revelation and the fountain of life, and, in spite of the Chaldeans' claim to great power, He alone was the source of all power and would ultimately bring deliverance and salvation to Judah. The events that faced Judah when the invasion of the Chaldeans took place would emphasise that the just live by faith. For the godly remnant of Judah faith would sustain them through the calamities that would overtake them. The fact that Jehovah was enthroned in His holy temple would be the key to triumph in the midst of violence and oppression for those who lived by faith.

Faith is the key to knowing that God hears and answers prayer in His own time and way, and that He will recompense those who diligently seek Him (Heb 11.6). Through faith believers acknowledge that God is sovereign and that all things work together for good (Rom 8.28). Faith accepts that ultimately the wicked will be punished and the righteous will be recompensed, and that the Lord will one day reign in righteousness on the earth.

The expression "his holy temple" does not refer to the temple in Jerusalem, but to the heavenly temple where Jehovah is eternally enthroned (Ps 11.4; Is 66.1) as supreme Sovereign over all. Nothing escapes His all-seeing eye and, in righteousness, He dispenses judgment to the wicked, but bestows blessing upon His people, who trust Him. His throne is a throne of judgment (Ps 76.8; Rev 4.5) and He will come forth to punish the wicked of the earth (Is 26.21). This is implied by the expression "holy temple". It is holy and eternal in contrast to the corrupt and temporary thrones of earthly monarchs. It is a throne of abiding glory (Is 6.1; Jer 14.21) unlike the passing glory of the Chaldean empire and the fading earthly splendour of its idols. It is also a throne of grace (Heb 4.16) from which He hears the cries of His people (Ps 18.6) who receive grace from Him to help in every circumstance of life.

The idols were dumb, but now the whole earth is to be silent before Jehovah for He is going to intervene in judgment (Is 41.1; Zech 2.13). The word translated "keep silence" (HAS - 2013) is an interjection and has a strong imperative meaning - "be silent", or "hush". The inference could well be that Jehovah was about to act in judgment and the solemnity of the moment or occasion was not to be broken (see Rev 8.1). The action He would take would be in keeping with the cries of His people and in keeping with the holiness of His throne and temple. Silence is also a token of reverence in His presence and an indication of subjection to Him. This latter clause looks on to the Day of the Lord (Zeph 1.7). In that coming day all the ends of the earth shall turn to the Lord and all nations shall go up to the temple in Jerusalem to worship before Him (Ps 22.27; 86.9; Is 66.23) and to receive instruction (Is 2.2-3; Micah 4.1-2). Believers now have the opportunity and privilege to praise and worship the Lord and to submit reverently to His will. Christians are to worship the Father in spirit and in truth (Jn 4.23-24) and should offer the sacrifice of praise to God continually (Heb 13.15).

This verse is the link between the woes and the next section as it turns from the negative view of the Chaldeans' wickedness to the positive view of God in His grandeur and glory. The last statement may be the transition to ch.3.

Notes

1 It is clear from Matthew 5.17-18, 1 Peter 1.10-12 and 2 Peter 1.20-21 that the Old Testament writers received divine revelations and were divinely inspired. The New Testament apostles and prophets were given special abilities to receive divine truth directly from God and to communicate that truth accurately to others. At first it was verbal and partial (the apostles' doctrine - Acts 2.42), but later it became complete, and by divine inspiration it was written down, making it permanent - "the faith which was once delivered unto the saints" (Jude v.3). With this completion of the divine revelation these revelationary gifts ceased. In the Scriptures we learn that we are built upon the foundation laid by the apostles and prophets (Eph 2.20). To claim that there are apostles and prophets today is to say that the Scriptures are not complete, which is contrary to such passages as 2 Timothy 3.16 and Revelation

22.19. Prophecy, which was a foundational gift, must not be confused with teaching, which has continued down to the present time. Prophets revealed that which had not been disclosed, whereas teachers teach what is revealed in the completed Scriptures. Space will not permit an exposition of 1 Corinthians 13.8-13 save to say that the word "perfect" has reference to the completed revelation of divine truth. The Old and New Testaments contain the full revelation of divine truth and are God's final words to men. Thus God no longer speaks or communicates truth by direct revelation, but through His written word alone.

HABAKKUK 3

Verses 1-19: The Prayer, Psalm, and Praise of Habakkuk

It has been suggested that Habakkuk did not write this chapter but that it was added later to the rest of the book. However, there is no proof of this and no reason to deny his authorship. When the chapter is viewed in the light of the preceding chapters, it shows the triumph of faith in the midst of affliction and adversity. It unfolds the progress of Habakkuk's attitude, so that instead of looking at the prevailing conditions he looks above them to the Lord and beyond them to the day of deliverance and reward. Having received answers to his pleas in chs.1 and 2, Habakkuk concludes his prophecy with prayer and praise. This chapter has for its title "A prayer of Habakkuk the prophet" although most of it takes the form of a lyric poem or song and gives a description of a theophany that the prophet had experienced. The answers (1.5-11; 2.2-20) to his pleas (1.2-4; 12-17) deeply concerned Habakkuk as he contemplated the judgment of God which would first overtake Judah at the hands of the wicked Chaldean nation and then would fall upon the Chaldeans because of their brutality. Thus he petitioned the Lord to carry out His work and yet to show mercy in the manifestation of His wrath (v.2).

The prophet describes in wonderful language and imagery the theophany of the coming of the Lord in judgment to execute vengeance upon the enemies of His people and to bring salvation to them (vv.3-15). Much of this theophany corresponds with the exodus and the past history of Israel, and harmonizes with such passages as Deuteronomy 33.2 (see also Josh 10.12-14; Judg 5.4-5; Ps 68.7-8; 77.18-20; 97). Verse 2, which contains the only petitions of the chapter, seems to be the theme from which the rest of the chapter is developed. The first petition is that the Lord would carry out His work of judgment as announced in 1.5. The fulfilment of this is shown in the Lord's coming as both judge and deliverer (vv.3-15). The second petition is that the Lord would remember mercy in the display of His wrath, which links with the effect the theophany had upon Habakkuk (vv.16-19). This effect was twofold, causing the prophet to fear and tremble in contemplation of the wrath of God (v.16) and then to rejoice in the God of salvation as he thinks about the mercy of the Lord (vv.17-19). The close of the chapter contains one of the greatest examples of faith in God. The chapter is called a psalm since it commences with a musical note or melody (Shigionoth - v.1; see Ps 7) and ends with the accompanying instruments (v.19), as well as containing the word "Selah" which is found elsewhere only in the book of the Psalms.

The prayer (vv.1-2)

At the close of ch.2 there is a contrast between the dumb and lifeless idols and the Lord who is the fountain of life, power and salvation for His people. The Lord was in His holy temple and all the earth was to be silent before Him. However, Habakkuk broke into prayer which really assumes the form of a song or psalm. The purposes of God for Judah and the Chaldeans had been revealed to the prophet and powerfully brought home to his soul. Thus Habakkuk prostrates himself before God in earnest prayer and worship. The prayer of Habakkuk, which takes up the whole of the chapter, is considered to be one of the choicest Hebrew poems in the whole of the Old Testament.

The opening expression in v.1, "A prayer of Habakkuk", is similar to those psalms which are specifically called "a prayer" in the superscription (Ps 17; 86; 90; 102; 142) which would indicate that the prophet's prayer was probably designated as a hymn of praise. It would then be sung by the Levite singers in the temple (2 Chr 5.12). This indicates that the chapter would have been separated from the rest of the book for this purpose and could well be the reason why some have doubted or denied that Habakkuk was its author. F. A. Tatford has pointed out that "There is a symmetrical arrangement in the hymn, viz. (a) 7 lines (2-3b), (b) 14 lines (3c-7), (c) 7 lines (8-9b), (d) 14 lines (9c-13), and (e) 7 lines (14-15), although most expositors do not recognise this arrangement".

"Prayer" (TᵉPILLA - 8605) is used in the widest sense, containing not only fervent supplication to God, but also occupation with the majesty and power of God, and confidence in God. It is really the outpouring of Habakkuk's heart and soul to God. Although petitions are only mentioned in v.2 one can see the development of the prayer in the whole chapter. The expression "Habakkuk the prophet" reveals the prophetic nature of the prayer and indicates that it was uttered and written under divine inspiration.

The word "Shiggionoth" (7692) is only found here and is the plural form of "Shiggaion" which is only found in Psalm 7. Its meaning is obscure although most agree that it refers to a musical tempo or rhythm. It does not refer to the contents of the psalm, but either to how it is to be sung or to its structure. The verb SHAGA (7686) means to go astray (Prov 5.23), to wander (Deut 27.18), to err (Is 28.7), and thus there is a suggestion that "Shiggionoth" indicates a Psalm of irregular rhythms, rapid transitions, and vivid imagery. Strong, in his Concordance, suggests it means "a rambling poem". The verb SHAGA also means, by extension, to reel (see Strong's Concordance) which could indicate that "Shiggionoth" refers to the rapid change of emotions either in the writer or in the musical tempo. These are only conjectures. However, it is generally agreed that the psalm was set to music and would be sung during the temple worship. How good to link one's petitions with praise and thanksgiving – "Be careful for nothing; but in every thing by prayer and supplication with thanksgiving let your requests be known unto God" (Phil 4.6).

As at the beginning of the previous chapters, Habakkuk in v.2 pours out his heart before God and looks to Him for an answer. He was, without doubt, a concerned and caring servant of God, longing that the will of

God be carried out and that the people of God be blessed. He was concerned about the spiritual state of Judah and desired that the godly remnant be spiritually prepared for the coming events. The revelation he received stirred his soul and spirit, and thus he unburdened himself in the presence of God.

Believers should have a deep concern about spiritual conditions, but often the spirit of indifference characterises the lives of so many. What effect has the word of God upon Christians today? Does it stir the soul and spirit, and affect the daily life, or are its claims soon forgotten? The word of God is not only intended to reveal the mind of God to Christians, but also to burden their souls as to the will of God and enable them to live for God in every circumstance of life.

The word translated "speech" (SHEMA - 8088) means report (Jer 50.43) whether good or bad, and also fame (2 Chr 9.1). Some commentators suggest that Habakkuk is referring to the report (Deut 2.25) or the fame (Num 14.15) of what had taken place at the exodus when Israel was delivered from the bondage of Egypt and the wondrous works of God were seen. However, in the context Habakkuk is referring to the declaration of God in chs.1 and 2 regarding the chastisement to be inflicted upon Judah by the Chaldeans and the ultimate judgment meted out to the Chaldeans themselves. The Septuagint gives a double translation: "I have heard thy report, and was afraid: I considered thy works, and was amazed", which has been used to embrace the declaration in the preceding chapters and the wonderful works of God in the history of Israel. This is very unlikely as the prophet had before him the impending judgment of God. Habakkuk had been given a preview of the punishment of Judah and of His just retribution upon the Chaldeans which made him afraid or filled him with awe.

"Afraid" (YARE - 3372) indicates awe or reverential fear. The prophet had come to appreciate that God's plan far exceeded his comprehension. Also, the revelation of God's judgment, not only of Judah but also of the powerful Chaldean empire, filled him with awe. Habakkuk, now informed of the Lord's intentions, supplicates Him to revive His work. This petition indicates that Habakkuk had acknowledged the justice of God in His coming chastisement of Judah. The repetition of "O Lord" emphasises the petitions of Habakkuk.

"Revive" (HAYA - 2421) basically means to live or have life, thence giving or restoring life, and is translated in a number of ways in the Old Testament. The expression "revive thy work" has been looked at in three ways.

1. That the Lord would renew or give fresh strength or import to His work in His people. Habakkuk had seen the departure from the things of God in Judah. The great requirement was for the Lord to renew His work and produce in the lives of His people that which would be for His glory. What a great need there is today for revival amongst the people of God and for a fresh fervour in the work of God. Ezra felt the need for reviving

in his day (Ezra 9.8-9). The Psalmist mentions the result of reviving – "Wilt thou not revive us again: that thy people may rejoice in thee" (Ps 85.6). Revival will always result in glory to God and rejoicing for His people. Revival must be the work of God, for anything that is of the flesh will be false, fleeting, and doomed to failure. Although looking at the expression in this way can be intensely practical it does not really suit the context here.

2. That the Lord would renew or re-enact His mighty deeds of a past day by intervening on behalf of His people; that He would give a fresh demonstration of that power displayed in the deliverance of Israel from Egypt and in the conquering of their foes in Canaan. Habakkuk recognised that wonderful work of God in a past day needed to be repeated if God was going to intervene for Judah. It has been suggested that the prophet's request is that, as God sustained His people in the midst of crisis in the past, He would do so during the coming invasion of the Chaldeans. We know that God will always sustain His people and give grace to endure the difficulties of life. This view of God renewing His work is taken by some because it seems that, in the theophany (vv.3-15), the past work of God for Israel is being recalled.

3. That the Lord would make His promised work (1.5) become a living action. The verb is used in this way in Deuteronomy 32.39 (see also 1 Sam 2.6). The work that God promised to accomplish was twofold - first the chastisement of Judah, and second the judgment of the enemies of the people of God. The prophet prays that God would make that work alive, i.e. active, for it would not only deal with the present situation, but ultimately result in the destruction of their enemies and bring salvation to His people as well as make known His omnipotence and glory. This last view would seem to be more in keeping with the context.

The expression "in the midst of the years" seems to indicate that Habakkuk's desire was that God would not delay His work of judgment, but bring it to fruition in His appointed time (2.3). Thus He would make it known that He was the God of Israel, and that they were His people. The expression "make known" can be taken in a wider sense - make known Thyself and Thy works, make known Thy truth, Thy wisdom, Thy power, Thy sovereignty. This can be applied to the desire to have a greater appreciation of God, His word and His ways. The Scriptures unfold much of God and of His ways, yet, generally, there seems to be little appreciation of His blessed Person and little understanding of His ways. God has given His word to make believers spiritually wealthy, but they must make it their own (2 Tim 2.15; 1 Pet 2.2).

Although the prophet prays that God would not delay His work of judgment, he also desires that in His wrath He would remember mercy. The thought is of showing mercy to Judah in the midst of the wrath of God upon them. This would be shown in the softening or shortening of the Chaldeans' cruelty and by the hastening of their destruction. The prophet links himself with Judah despite their waywardness and lawlessness and prays for mercy.

The psalm - future deliverance (vv.3-15)

This section is viewed in different ways. Some have seen it as a vision given to Habakkuk "of the God of Israel in His triumphal march with His people, bringing them out of Egypt; going via Sinai and the southern parts into Canaan; through the day of the sun standing still in the days of Joshua, into Canaan and fighting with His people" (H. Barnes). However, although there is clear reference to the past history of Israel, this is only to illustrate the coming of God in a future day. C. F. Keil states, "The description of this theophany rests throughout upon earlier lyrical descriptions of the revelations of God in the earlier times of Israel. Even the introduction (v.3) has its roots in the song of Moses in Deuteronomy 33.2; and in the further course of the ode we meet with various echoes of different psalms (compare v.6 with Ps 18.8; v.8 with Ps 18.10; v.19 with Ps 18.33,34; also v.5 with Ps 68.25; v.8 with Ps 68.5,34)...Habakkuk depicts a coming redemption under figures borrowed from that of the past". The coming of God in majesty and power to judge the world and to bring salvation to His people, is described in terms of remarkable natural phenomena. In the theophany the prophet views the dazzling brightness and splendour of the presence of God, the measuring of the earth, the scattering of the mountains, the sinking of the hills and the terror stricken nomadic tribes (vv.3-7). Habakkuk's rhetorical questions (v.8) are followed by his view of God as the great warrior King, moving on to crush His enemies and deliver His people in keeping with His purpose and promise (vv.9-15). Thus the prophet views the ultimate answer to his prayer for God to act and also to show mercy (v.2).

The majesty and glory of God (vv.3-7)

The prophet describes the coming and presence of God in sublime language and views the effect of His presence upon nature and people.

Verse 3 introduces the coming of God. Just as in a past day the God of Israel came in glory to make a covenant with Israel after their deliverance from Egypt (Deut 33.2; Judg 5.4), so also will He come in a future day to execute judgment and deliver them from their enemies. The verb "came" (BO - 935) is actually in the future tense. Thus, at the commencement, the prophet indicates that a future coming is the subject of the theophany. Both Moses and Deborah looked back to the exodus and stated that Jehovah came, but Habakkuk looks forward to a future event and uses the name "Eloah" (God - 433) for the coming One. Eloah is the singular of "Elohim" and is found mainly in the book of Job. It is found first in Deuteronomy 32.15 and is not found elsewhere in the prophetic books except in Isaiah 44.8 and Daniel 11.37-39. It is considered as belonging mainly to the poetic sections of the Old Testament. Under "Divine Titles" in the Introduction to the Newberry Bible, it is stated that the word Eloah comes from "AHLAH, to worship, to adore, [and] presents God as the one supreme object of worship, the Adorable One". However, the Theological Wordbook of the Old Testament states that "Three times it occurs in parallel to 'rock' as a descriptive term for God (Deut 32.15; Ps 18.31; Is 44.8). Once it is found in a context in which God is described as a shield to those who take refuge in him (Prov 30.5). Three times it is used in a context of terror for sinners (Ps 50.22; 114.7; 139.19). This would suggest that the term conveyed to God's people comfort and assurance while conveying fear to their enemies". This would better suit the context here, where God is coming as the supreme Sovereign to intervene on behalf of His people. He comes as the Holy One, who cannot behold iniquity (1.12-13), to judge the world and deal with all who fill the world with lawlessness and rebellion. The expression "the Holy One" emphasises that aspect of His deity and character which is in keeping with the judgment He is about to execute (Jer 51.5; Ezek 39.7).

Teman was a grandson of Esau, who is Edom (Gen 36.1,11), and the territory of Teman was the southern mountainous district of Edom. Mount Paran was also in southern Edom, separated from Teman by a deep valley. The mention of Teman and Mount Paran does not indicate the starting point of God's coming, but rather the direction of His coming. Whereas the Chaldeans came from the north to invade and terrorise Judah, God will come from the south bringing salvation to His people. Both Moses and Deborah mentioned Sinai in relation to the coming of Jehovah, as there the law was given, bringing bondage and condemnation to Israel. Habakkuk does not mention Sinai, since the coming of God in that future day will, for Israel, be in mercy and grace bringing them salvation. Although there might be a near fulfilment to some of Habakkuk's prophecy, it really looks on to a complete and final fulfilment when Israel's Messiah, the Lord Jesus Christ, comes to destroy Israel's enemies and establish His Kingdom (Is 62.11-63.6; Zech 14.1-4; Rev 19.11-21).

The word "Selah" (5542) is thought to mean pause, or lift up and is regarded as being of musical significance. It is considered, by some, to indicate a pause in the music to give time for worshippers to reflect upon the truth of what has gone before.

The outward manifestation of the presence of God in His majesty is described as covering the heavens and is reflected over the earth. Some have suggested that Habakkuk saw a great thunderstorm coming from the south with the lightning illuminating the heavens and the earth. The idea here is that the glory of God's appearance affects the whole of creation which reflects that splendour. The last expression does not mean that all the inhabitants of the earth will praise at His appearance, but that God and the manifestation of His glory deserve the praise of all creation. The word translated "praise" (TᵉHILLA - 8416) is a noun and indicates that praise belongs to God and that His glory and acts merit praise.

Whereas in v.3 we have the extent of the glory of God, in v.4 we have the magnitude of that glory. That His glory shall shine forth as the light corresponds with His coming as the Holy One (v.3) since light is a fitting emblem of His spotless purity and holiness. Just as light spreads across the sky and the land at sunrise so at the coming of the Lord His glory will spread throughout creation (2.14; Ps 72.19). However, the dazzling brightness of the glory of God surpasses the brightness of the sun in its fulness (Acts 26.13). In a past day Israel saw the evidence of the presence of God in the pillar of cloud by day and the pillar of fire by night, but in a coming day they will see the splendour of His glory covering the heavens and radiating throughout the earth. God is light (1 Jn 1.5) and light shines from Him - He covers Himself "with light as with a garment" (Ps 104.2). "Brightness" (NOGAH - 5051), brilliancy, brings to mind one of the statements concerning the Son of God, "Who being the brightness of his glory" (Heb 1.3), and that of His coming as the Sun of righteousness (Mal 4.2; see also 2 Thess 2.8). The unparalleled and impenetrable light will shine in all its splendour at His coming and presence.

The word "horns" (QEREN - 7161) primarily denotes the horns of various animals, but can also indicate rays of light. The verbal form of the word (QARAN - 7160) is translated "shone" in Exodus 34.29-30, 35 indicating the rays of the passing glory of the old covenant radiating from the face of Moses (2 Cor 3.7-11).

"Hand" (YAD - 3027) is also translated "side" (Dan 10.4). Thus many commentators feel that Habakkuk saw the brilliancy of God's glory from which rays of light streamed out from either side. It is suggested that the rays were like flashes of lightning coming from both sides, i.e. from each hand, and illuminating the scene. Whichever view is taken, whether horns from the hand, rays of light from His hand, or rays of light from either side, the thought conveyed is of the display of the majesty and power of God. The very light that shines out is the light that also hides. The manifestation of the majesty and glory of God is yet the hiding place of His power. The display or the acts of His power are seen but not Omnipotence itself. Whereas darkness generally represented the covering of God in Israel's history (Ex 20.21; 1 Kings 8.12; Ps 18.11), here it is light as suitable to His coming righteously to execute judgment upon the world. God dwells in light unapproachable for He is the invisible God (1 Tim 1.17; 6.16). The wonder is that God has now been fully revealed in the Person of the Lord Jesus Christ, the Son of God (Jn 1.18; 14.9) – "God was manifest in the flesh" (1 Tim 3.16).

Having mentioned the extent and intensity of the glory and power of God in His coming, the prophet now deals in v.5 with the effects of His coming as the Holy One in judgment. The thought is that of the cleansing of the world and the bringing in of righteousness. "Pestilence" (DEBER - 1698) refers to any kind of plague which destroys, i.e. results in death. Almost all uses of the word in the Old Testament refer to plagues sent by

God as punishment. The word translated "burning coals" (RESHEP - 7565), which indicates flame or heat, is also given as "burning heat" (Deut 32.24), and "hot thunderbolts" (Ps 78.48). Although it has been viewed here as lightning inflicting sudden death, or fire consuming His enemies (Ps 97.3; see also Ps 18.12-13), it is generally believed that the reference is to fever heat. The latter blends more with pestilence. Both pestilence and fever were regarded by "the Babylonians as the chief malignant spirits, in accordance with the old Accadian system" (F. C. Cook; TWOT). Pestilence and burning fever, as coming from God in judgment, are personified and viewed as His attendants or servants, over which He has control. Here the idea seems to be that pestilence goes before Him and burning fever follows after Him. This verse not only indicates the effect of the coming of God upon the world but also prepares the way for what follows. Both pestilence and burning fever are mentioned in regard to the exodus (Ex 9.15; Deut 32.24; Ps 78.50). As various diseases were used by God as instruments of judgment in a past day, so the Lord will use them in a future day when He comes in judgment (Zech 14.12; Mt 24.7; Rev 6).

God, having come from the south, draws near and stands, or positions Himself, to take dealings with the earth (v.6). The expression "measured the earth" can be explained in two ways.

1. The thought of measuring or surveying. He measures the earth with His eye or with a glance, surveying it to determine the degree of judgment to be meted out; measuring as a General the forces of the enemy, or surveying all the actions and intentions of men, to recompense them accordingly.

2. The thought of shaking or trembling. The Septuagint translates the expression as "the earth stood at his feet and trembled", while others have rendered it "He stood and rocked the earth", or "the earth shook". The idea suggested is that of a great earthquake as a result of the presence of God. Regarding the Hebrew word translated "measure" Strong's Concordance states it is "a primitive root; *to shake*:- measure".

Commentators are divided with regard to these two views. Whereas C. F. Keil writes that it "cannot mean to measure here", W. J. Deane states that although the second view is admissible "it is not so suitable as the other". It seems that either is admissible, but the latter is more in keeping with what follows.

The look of God results in the nations being scattered or caused to tremble with terror. The fact that nations are mentioned indicates that this event goes far beyond the events of the exodus, as the following statements prove. The expression "drove asunder" (NATAR - 5425) can also be rendered "move" out of place in relation to the heart (Job 37.1). It refers to a sudden shock and may well indicate here the sudden terror of the nations through the condemnatory look of God, the sovereign Judge of the universe. However, not only the nations but also the mountains and hills are affected by that look. The term "everlasting mountains" show that they are ancient and have been in the same place since creation (Deut 33.15). These primeval mountains, lofty objects of God's creative power, were emblems of stability and permanence, yet at the glance of the Creator they are scattered, or shattered. The word "scattered" (PUS - 6327) is a primitive root meaning "to dash in pieces" (Strong's Concordance) although it is mostly translated scatter. However, it is translated "shaken to pieces" (Job 16.12), "breaketh in pieces" (Jer 23.29), and "dasheth in pieces" (Nah 2.1). The thought here is that the mountains which seem to be stable, permanent and unmoveable will be shaken as with an earthquake, be shattered into pieces, and scattered as dust. The hills of old are brought low in submission to the God of creation. It is suggested that they sink to the level of the plains. These catastrophic events intensify the trembling of the nations.

The adjective "everlasting" (OLAM - 5769) at the close of the verse is translated "perpetual" earlier in the verse and has the thought of being old (Jer 6.16; Mal 3.4) or ancient (Prov 22.28). Thus the ways of God are the same as of old. He is the same, unchanging and unchangeable. The believer can take comfort from this. As God acted on behalf of Israel in the past at the exodus, so He will act again for their salvation. As the earth trembled and the mountains were affected at His presence in the past (Judg 5.4-5) so will the mountains and hills be affected at the coming of God in a future day, but to a greater degree (cp. Is 13.13; Heb 12.26; Rev 11.13; 16.18). As the peoples trembled when they heard of what God had done (Ex 15.14-16), so nations will tremble to a greater degree and extent when He comes to judge the world.

The opening expression of v.7, "I saw", shows that Habakkuk is the speaker and it is he who experiences the theophany. The prophet here turns from the general aspect to certain particular details. With prophetic vision he saw the effect of the Lord's presence upon two of the nations mentioned in the previous verse. It seems that these are particularly identified because they were from the south and would be affected first by the coming of God. This section therefore closes, as it began, in the south. Whereas in v.3 the mountainous territory of Teman and Mount Paran are mentioned, here specific tribes are in view. The reference to tents and curtains indicates that the tribes mentioned are nomadic in character.

Cushan itself is found only here, but has been linked with Chushan-rishathaim, king of Mesopotamia (Judg 3.8,10), the first oppressor of Israel in the land of Canaan. The thought would be that as Israel was delivered from the oppression of Chushan-rishathaim by Othniel (meaning lion of God) of the tribe of Judah, so Israel will be delivered from oppression by their Messiah, the Lord Jesus Christ, the Lion of the tribe of Judah (Rev 5.5). Although this may be appealing, it does not suit the context since Mesopotamia was to the north and outside the territory in view here. Since Cushan is not found elsewhere in the Old Testament it is suggested that either it refers to an unknown Arabian tribe or it could be a subgroup of the Midianites. The latter seems to be supported by the fact that the wife of Moses (Zipporah) was the daughter of the Midian priest, Reuel (Ex 2.16-22), and yet was called an Ethiopian woman (Num 12.1; see also Strong's Concordance - 3569). However, it does not state that Reuel (or Jethro, Ex 3.1) was himself a Midianite. Most commentators believe that Cushan is a poetical form of Cush which is the same as Ethiopia. This last view is more acceptable as both Cush and Ethiopia are translations of the same Hebrew word (KUSH - 3568).

The word "affliction" is rendered "iniquity" in 1.3. There the prophet complains of God allowing him to behold iniquity, but here he sees the result of iniquity, i.e. the trouble or affliction of those who were iniquitous. The land of Midian was on the opposite side of the Red Sea to Ethiopia. The prophet sees the inhabitants of the land trembling with fear. Thus the nations around the Red Sea are visited in judgment at the coming of God which again shows that the ways of God are as of old (v.6).

The power and purpose of God (vv.8-15)

This section commences with rhetorical questions and also with the name Jehovah (the Lord). This is in contrast to the last section that commenced with the name "Eloah" (v.3 - God). Instead of the subject of the theophany being "God", as in the previous section, Jehovah is addressed in the second person singular, "Thine", "Thy" and "Thou". Although both sections have links with the exodus, the previous section emphasises the effect of the presence of God on nature and people, whereas this section emphasises the power of God. Jehovah is seen as the Divine Warrior fulfilling His covenant with Israel by destroying their enemies and bringing to them salvation. Thus this section gives the reason for the theophany, i.e. the salvation of His people. Although there may be reference to a near fulfilment, the passage really looks on to the end times when Israel will experience full and final deliverance with the appearance of their long looked for Messiah, the Lord Jesus Christ, and the setting up of His earthly Kingdom.

In what seems, in v.8, to be an interruption to Habakkuk's description of the theophany, he questions the reason for the apparent judgment upon nature. Here the name Jehovah is introduced. Jehovah is not really addressed in the opening clause and the questions are intended to introduce this section in which the purpose of the coming of God is stated - the salvation of His people. Thus the prophet has the final answer to his cry in 1.2-4. Deliverance from violence, oppression, and exploitation is coming for the godly remnant. Habakkuk did not expect a reply to his questions. Nevertheless they are answered within the scope of the theophany. These questions, which are poetical in character, emphasise the power of the wrath of God and seem to invigorate the passage. The scene changes from the dwelling places of nomadic tribes (v.7) to the rivers and the sea.

"Displeased" (HARA - 2734) means to kindle or burn. Was Jehovah kindled against the rivers (in His anger)? The next question may supply the sense of the first by the use of "anger" (AP - 639) which frequently occurs with HARA (TWOT). However, the first question may well be general as to the wrath of God followed by the double-claused question indicating the subject matter. Although there is doubtless an allusion to the miraculous events of the Red Sea and the River Jordan (Ex 14.19-22; 15.1-9; Josh 3.13-17), the rivers of the earth and the sea in general are in view here (Nah 1.4). The supremacy of Jehovah, as the Divine Warrior, over creation is depicted. There were horses and chariots at the crossing of the Red Sea, but they belonged to the enemy and were overthrown (Ex 14.23-25). Here in Habakkuk they are part of Jehovah's forces (cp. Jer 4.13) as He comes as the Judge of the world to destroy the enemy and deliver Israel.

The expression "thy chariots" is an explanation of "ride upon thine horses", indicating riding in chariots to which horses have been harnessed. Some take the reference to horses and chariots to be symbolic of storm clouds (Ps 104.3; Is 19.1). The phrase "thy chariots of salvation" is translated by the Septuagint as, "thy chariots are salvation". However, the same thought is conveyed whichever rendering is accepted. Although glorious triumph will be the result of the coming of the Lord, the emphasis here is upon the salvation of Israel (Is 46.13; Joel 2.32; Obad v.17).

In v.9 Habakkuk continues the description of Jehovah as the Divine Warrior, not only riding forth, but with His bow withdrawn from its sheath ready to shoot His arrows at all who are opposed to Him and His people.

Although the word "bow" (QESHET - 7198) is used in Genesis 9 for what is commonly called a rainbow, it is generally used of the hunter's or warrior's bow. The verb "made naked" (UR - 5783) is only found here in the Old Testament and means to expose. It indicates here that the bow has been removed from its cover in order to be used in battle. Thus God is depicted as a man of war attacking His enemies.

Most scholars agree that the middle clause of the verse is obscure. C. L. Feinberg states, "There are but three words in the Hebrew, but as yet they have not been explained satisfactorily. One eminent Old Testament scholar counted more than one hundred translations of these words. With such diversity of opinion, it is foolhardy to be dogmatic at this point". One can but state the main views about this clause.

1. The word translated "oaths" (SHᵉBUA - 7621) comes from a Hebrew root that "is identical in its consonantal root to the word *sheba*" which means seven (TWOT). D. W. Baker points out that, "Sevenfold volleys were known in Israel's warfare, although no evidence is found for the period under discussion. In Baal mythology, the deity's arrows are lightning (seven in number in one text), so we could have here another echo from Canaanite poetry. Arrows used by Yahweh in punishment and judgment are common in poetry (cp. v.11; Deut 32.23; Ps 7.13; 18.14). The concept of 'dedicating' the weapons, using the alternative meaning of the word 'seven', is also

known in Israel (Deut 32.40-42) and appears to fit the context better. Here the dedication is done orally, by a 'word' (AV)". It seems unlikely that the number "seven" would be suddenly introduced into the passage.

2. F. A. Tatford writes: "The second clause has been variously translated. The AV rendering, 'according to the oaths of the tribes, even thy word', does not follow logically upon the first clause, and the RSV rendering, 'put the arrows to the string', is probably nearer the intention of the writer. The image of the eternal God as a man of war, with bow taut and arrows fitted to the string, is a remarkable one, but extremely pertinent to the circumstances".

3. This and the following view are based upon the translation of the Hebrew word MATTEH (or MATTOTH - 4294 - AV, tribes). C. F. Keil is of the opinion that, "Of the two meanings which may be given to *mattoth*, viz. branches, rods, or staffs, and tribes of the people of Israel, the latter can hardly be thought of here, since *mattoth* would certainly have been defined by either a suffix or some determining clause, if the tribes of Israel were intended. On the other hand, the meaning staffs or sticks is very naturally suggested both by the context - viz. the allusion to the war-bow - and also by v.14, where *mattim* unquestionably signifies staves or lances...*Matteh*, a stick or staff with which blows were struck, might stand, as an instrument of chastisement, for the punishment or chastisement itself (cp. Is 9.3; 10.5), and in Micah 6.9 it denotes the rod...The expression, 'chastising rods (chastisements) are sworn through the word', points to the solemn oath with which God promised in Deuteronomy 32.40-42 to take vengeance upon His enemies, and avenge the blood of His servants" (Keil & Delitzsch; see also W. J. Deane).

4. F. C.Cook states, "Our version follows Jerome, who explains it to mean 'the oaths which Thou spakest to the tribes', a rendering accepted, as on the whole presenting least difficulty, by Rosenmuller, and by Dr Pusey, who observes, 'the oath, the word or promise of God, to His people, was *that they should be saved from their enemies and from the hand of all that hate them*'" (see also Jamieson, Fausset & Brown). The expression "according to the oaths of the tribes" would be a confirmation that Jehovah's bow was unsheathed on their behalf, and would be a source of encouragement and comfort to them. This view seems to be more feasible than the other three and quite in keeping with the context.

The introduction of "Selah" here, indicating a pause before introducing a new series of images, seems to support the fourth view of the previous clause. The pause to ponder the foregoing statements was intended to encourage and to give confidence to the godly remnant. The last clause commences the series of effects which the power and presence of the Divine Warrior and Judge had upon the world of nature. The effect here is the trembling or shaking of the mountains resulting in wide cracks through which water from beneath gushes out in power forming rivers.

The first two verbs of v.10 have the relationship of cause and effect.

There is a link back to v.6. Whereas that verse presents the general effect of the presence of God, here specific effects are described when judgment is executed. The mountains are personified and viewed as trembling before the supreme Judge. "Trembled" (HUL - 2342) contains the idea of physical movement and is used of a woman writhing in labour pains (Is 13.8; 26.17). Since the mountains are personified it indicates a trembling in fear or terror. The description may well point to an earthquake as when Sinai shook at the presence of God (Ex 19.18; Ps 68.8), continuing the thought of the last clause of v.9. It is suggested that the earthquake resulted in great waves of the sea pounding the land. However, the following expressions suggest a similar judgment to that which took place at the flood, although not as extensive. The language could also be linked with the crossing of the Red Sea.

"Overflowing" (ZEREM - 2230) means a gush of water and is translated "flood" (Is 28.2), "storm" (Is 4.6), and "tempest" (Is 28.2; 30.30). The words "water" (MAYIM - 4325) and "deep" (TᵉHOM - 8415) are both used in Genesis 7 (see also Ps 77.16-17). The waters of the deep gush forth and the torrents pour down – "the same day were all the fountains of the great deep broken up, and the windows of heaven were opened" (Gen 7.11). The deep is personified and the roaring of the waters pouring forth is likened to the sound of a voice. The surging of the water from the deep, causing high waves, is referred to as the lifting up of the hands on high. Thus the waters from beneath meet the rain from above. Some have likened the waves of water to a suppliant with uplifted hands imploring for mercy or help. The whole picture speaks of terror and anguish.

The terrifying phenomena which take place on earth are matched by cosmic changes at the coming of the Lord in judgment (v.11). The two great lights, the sun and the moon, become obscure. Darkness envelopes the scene which is only illuminated by the brightness of the Lord's coming and by His weapons of war.

"Habitation" (ZᵉBUL - 2073) means a dwelling or an abode, and only occurs five times in the Old Testament (1 Kings 8.13; 2 Chr 6.2; Ps 49.14; Is 63.15; and here). All these occurrences are linked with splendour. Some consider that the habitation of the sun and the moon refers to the place where the sun spends the night and the moon spends the day as suggested in Psalm 19 – "In them hath he set a tabernacle for the sun, Which is as a bridegroom coming out of his chamber" (vv.4-5). The sun retires to its chamber for the night and the moon retires to its chamber during the day. That both retire at the same time would indicate some calamity. However, there is no suggestion of retiring in the passage. This verse has been linked with Joshua when the sun and moon stood still, lengthening the day (Josh 10.12-14), but on that occasion it was to extend the light of the sun whereas here we have the obscuring of that light. Darkness rather than light seems to be the sign of the presence and judgment of God (Joel 3.15; Amos 5.20; Mt 24.29). It is suggested that storm clouds obscure the light of the sun and the moon as the tempest continues to rage, but the expression "stood still in their habitation" rules out the continuation of their orbit. Neither does the clause indicate that the brightness of the Lord's presence or weapons causes the sun and moon to pale into insignificance. As the mountains were personified in v.10 so the sun and moon are personified here. The idea is either that they refuse to shine in the face of the overpowering splendour of God, or that in fear and dread they withdraw and hide themselves, which would be in keeping with previous statements. The following clause also points to the sun and moon withdrawing themselves in terror as the Lord's arrows are discharged. Some take both the arrows and the spear as symbolic of lightning (Ps 18.14; 77.17-18). However the arrows and spear are so described to indicate they come from the One who is as the light (v.4). The swiftness of His arrows as they bombard the enemy, and the brilliancy of the glittering spear that metes out punishment are indicated. It is true that the word translated "glittering" (BARAQ - 1300) is mainly translated "lightning", but here it is descriptive of the spear and not an explanation of the spear. It is the terror of judgment that is being emphasised (see 2 Thess 1.8-9).

After describing the effect of the presence and power of Jehovah upon nature, in v.12 the prophet begins to describe His judgment upon the nations. Habakkuk sees Jehovah, the Mighty Warrior, striding through the land in His fury - marching through the land at the head of His hosts meting out judgment upon the nations, among them the Chaldeans (Babylonians - Is 13.1-6). It must be appreciated that only the nations opposed to God and His people are in view. As Gentile nations experienced the might of Jehovah in bringing Israel into their inheritance in a past day (Deut 4.38), so will they in the end times when Israel will finally be restored to the land. The figure of threshing grain by the trampling or treading upon it by oxen (Deut 25.4; 1 Chr 21.20-23) is used here in the judgment of the nations. Jehovah is pictured here trampling the nations in His fierce anger. The same idea is presented in the treading of the winepress in Isaiah 63.1-6, which looks on to the final judgment of God carried out by the Lord Jesus Christ. This will take place when the nations are gathered together to eradicate God's people and oppose the claims of the rightful King (Ps 2.6-9; Joel 3.13-16; Rev 14.19-20).

The purpose of these manifestations, displaying the power and indignation of Jehovah, is clearly stated in v.13. It was in order that salvation might be brought to His people in contrast to the destruction of the nations arrayed against them. It has been suggested that these closing verses of the theophany return to the past, as an assurance of deliverance for Israel in the future. However, C. F. Keil states, "The perfects in vv.13-15 are prophetic, describing the future in spirit as having already occurred". As brought out before, what has taken place in the past can be linked with the future events unfolded in this theophany. Thus, as Jehovah went forth to smite Israel's enemies in the past (2 Sam 5.24; cp. Is 42.13), so He will go forth to destroy their enemies and bring salvation to them again. Habakkuk is thus reminded that, although the Chaldeans would be used by God as His instrument to chastise Judah, He would nevertheless hold them accountable. He would execute judgment upon them for their oppression, brutality and inhumanity, and bring deliverance to Judah. Here, along with 2.5-20 is God's answer to the prophet's complaint (1.12-17). But, as noted before, the theophany also looks on to that future deliverance and salvation at the manifestation of their true Messiah, the Lord Jesus Christ.

The expression "thine anointed" is interpreted in two ways - as representing the godly remnant of Israel, and as representing the Messiah. D. W. Baker states, "They are also called his *anointed* (Messiah), a term which usually refers to an individual. It could here be speaking of the King, one who is customarily anointed (eg. 1 Sam 10.1; 16.12-13; 24.6,10; 2 Sam 12.7). He is the representative of the people (cp. Is 7.8-9) and therefore his consecration by anointing would also be theirs". However, W. J. Deane states, "The 'anointed one', again, is not the nation of Israel, for the term is always applied to a single individual and never to the people collectively; so here it is the theocratic king who is meant - first, the representative of David; and secondly, the Messiah" (see also Keil & Delitzsch). Most commentators accept that it refers to the Messiah. The word "with" indicates that God will bring salvation to Israel in association with or through the Messiah, and many passages in both the Old and New Testaments confirm this. Just as in the past God used certain individuals to bring deliverance to Israel (Judg 2.16; Is 63.11), so He will deliver Israel in a coming day through His anointed Son and King (Ps 2.2-9). The bringing of salvation necessitates the destruction of Israel's foes and this is why there is the imagery of wounding the head (cp. Ps 68.21). Thus Jehovah is again viewed as the Divine Warrior.

The expression "house of the wicked" is used metaphorically, first of the Chaldean empire and its king, then of the opposing nations and their leader in a coming day. That an individual is also in view is clear from the word "head" which points, not only to the Chaldean king, but also to that great apostate leader who will be destroyed at the coming of the Lord (2 Thess 2.8). The allegory of a house is continued in the closing expression to show that judgment would be executed in such a way that the house would be completely destroyed from the foundation to the roof (neck). Nothing will remain standing when that judgment falls. The allegory indicates that both the nations and their leader (the beast), gathered together against the Lord and His people will be utterly destroyed (Zech 14.2-3; Rev 19.19-21).

In v.14 the prophet continues to describe the destruction of Israel's foes. That there are difficulties in the first clause of the verse is evident in the various ways it has been interpreted. The word "head" (ROSH - 7218) meaning head, literally or figuratively, is translated "captain" (Num 14.4;

Neh 9.17) and "captains" (Deut 29.10; 1 Chr 4.42; 11.15). Some take it as singular, referring to the same individual as in v.13, while others take the plural form, meaning either heads or mighty princes as representative of the nations.

The meaning of "villages" (PRZ or PARAZ - 6518) is also disputed. Of this word W. J. Deane states, "The Septuagint renders it, 'Almighty men'; Jerome, 'warriors'; Chaldee, 'army'; Delitzsch and many modern critics, 'hordes' or 'inhabitants of the plain'; others again, 'rulers' or 'judges'. The most probable version is either 'warrior' or 'hordes'". Again, opinions differ as to why the pronoun "his" is used instead of "thy" with staves (spears). Both C. L. Feinberg and C. F. Keil take it to indicate that the enemy will fall by their own weapons, slaying one another (1 Sam 14.20; 2 Chr 20.23-24). F. A. Tatford writes, "This runs counter to the tense of the whole picture, however. It is the supreme might of the Eternal that has been demonstrated and there seems no reason to interpret the closing strophe in any other way". The thrust of the opening clause seems to be that the opposing nations, with their leaders and king, were gathered together in order to destroy the people of God, but Jehovah, as it were, pierced them through. Thus the annihilation that they had intended for Israel was turned back upon themselves. The destruction of the hostile nations is necessary for the salvation of Israel and it is carried through to the end of the theophany. Habakkuk identifies himself with his people as he views the nations storming in against them, scattering them as stubble before the wind (Jer 13.24), but suddenly things are turned around, and instead of triumphing the enemy is destroyed (Is 66.15-16). The nations anticipated an easy victory and a successful campaign, but they completely failed and suffered the consequences of their opposition to God and His people. The last clause seems to liken the enemies of Israel to highway robbers or murderers who anticipated with delight exploiting and devouring (murdering) their victims (Ps 10.8; Prov 30.14). The idea is that they hide in some secluded or dark place waiting with anticipated rejoicing to rob and kill the helpless. However, this anticipated delight or rejoicing would never take place because they would be overtaken by the judgment. The poor here represent the nation of Israel, the people of God.

Verse 15 brings to a close the theophany in the triumph of God, in the utter destruction of the enemies and salvation of Israel. This section closes as it began with the sea and God's horses. Again there is a link with Israel's past deliverance from the bondage of Egypt. Fittingly, this closing verse of the theophany is reminiscent of the crowning triumph over Egypt at the Red Sea when Pharaoh and his army were destroyed (Ex 14.27-31). As Jehovah marched through the Sea leading the children of Israel and overthrowing the Egyptians, destroying them in the waters, so He will tread down the waters with His horses, destroying the hostile nations, bringing salvation to Israel. As in v.8, the horses are harnessed to chariots, which are a part of Jehovah's forces, or are representative of the might and power of Jehovah.

Some have taken the heap of waters as figurative of the surging mass of the hostile nations rushing towards the people of God as in the middle clause of the previous verse. Others take it as literal, and consider it to be parallel to Psalm 77.19-20. Whichever view is taken, the verse intends to convey that nothing can prevent the complete triumph of Jehovah, the utter destruction of the enemy, and the salvation of His people. It would be profitable in closing this section to quote the words of F. A. Tatford: "Perhaps the believer today may also draw strength from the picture. If the forces of evil seem stronger and more prevalent than ever before, the Eternal is unchanged and the ultimate victory is in His hands. In a past day He came forth for the deliverance of His earthly people, Israel, as He will again in the future at the close of their sufferings through the Great Tribulation. But He changes not and His people of today may just as confidently rely upon Him and His delivering power as ever did His chosen of old. The storm-clouds may gather, but Habakkuk's message is that Almighty God is in the storm".

The praise - the fear and faith of Habakkuk (vv.16-19)

The theophany experienced by Habakkuk was ended and the impact of it, along with previous events, had left him in a state of shock or complete exhaustion. These closing events are full of emotion. The prophet's true heart is revealed as he recognises the inevitability of the Chaldeans' invasion of Judah and the ultimate deliverance of Israel. Habakkuk had come a long way spiritually since he first cried to God (1.2-4) and complained of the Chaldeans being used as God's instrument to chastise Judah (1.12-17). He had waited upon God (2.1), viewed the Chaldeans' destruction (2.5-20), and had requested mercy in spite of God's wrath (3.3). God had fully answered his petitions in showing him that He was indeed the covenant keeping God who would come to bring full and final salvation to Israel and to destroy all their enemies. In these closing verses the prophet uses the first person singular, "I", "my", "myself", and "mine". He is recording his own experiences. His questions had been answered in such a way that he was left without any strength, yet his faith shone out in all its brightness. Faith lifts a person beyond themselves and the circumstances of life to rest completely upon God and His word.

Habakkuk's conception of God (v.16)

This verse seems to revert back to v.2. Habakkuk was filled with dread as he contemplated the coming invasion of Judah by the Chaldeans and the anguish that this would bring upon his people. Undoubtedly the theophany also had an effect upon him. The prophet describes his personal reactions to the purpose and power of God in emotional and physical terms. He records how his belly, lips, bones, and his nervous system were affected by the revelations of God. However, Habakkuk's reactions did not end with fear and dread, but passed beyond that to faith and confidence in God.

Most commentators take the expression "I heard" in v.16 to indicate that Habakkuk is referring back to "I have heard" in v.2 and not to any audible noise occurring in the theophany (cp. v.10). C. F. Keil states, "This address goes back to its starting point, to explain the impression which it made upon the prophet, and to develop still how he 'was afraid'". Others feel that the prophet's reaction is to the phenomenon he had seen. Both seem to be in view here. There is certainly a reference back to what the prophet had heard from God about the invasion of Judah by the Chaldeans, which Habakkuk realised must precede the events of the theophany. When that invasion came, God would be against them instead of being for them. Thus, what he had heard from God and what he had been shown produced the reaction described in this verse. As he contemplated the coming invasion by the Chaldeans, whose cruelty, violence, and inhumanity had already been described, he was overpowered with dismay and fear. Although he knew that Judah deserved the chastisement, he nevertheless felt deeply for his land (the inheritance of God) and for his people, and his whole being was affected. This description of the effect upon him commences and ends with trembling. The primary meaning of "trembled" (RAGAZ - 7264) is "to quake or shake, from which ideas such as shaking in anger, fear, or anticipation are derived" (TWOT). The result of what the prophet heard before the theophany (v.2) was reverential fear, but here, afterwards, the result was trembling in anticipation of God's judgment upon Judah.

Some take "belly" as a reference to the inward parts while others feel it refers to the seat of the emotions (the heart). The word for "quivered" (SALAL - 6750) is only found elsewhere in 1 Samuel 3.11, 2 Kings 21.12 and Jeremiah 19.3 where it is translated "tingle" in relation to the ears. The idea here is of the lips uncontrollably vibrating together so that the prophet could scarcely cry out. Such was the effect of what he had heard from God.

The expression "rottenness entered into my bones" is symbolic of utter weakness, the bones being the strongest part of the body. He felt as if rottenness (RAQAB - 7538, decay) had penetrated his bones weakening and paralysing him so that he had no strength in himself. The prophet's whole system trembled through the shock. Having described the effect of what he had heard and seen, he suddenly expresses his confidence that he would rest when the Chaldeans invaded the land, for he had seen the ultimate end. Both the declaration concerning the Chaldean invasion and the theophany prepared Habakkuk to rely completely upon God and His word. The prophet rested unreservedly on the promise and purpose of God, and on the sovereignty of God. He was submissive to God's will. It is important for the child of God today to do the same. Even in the most difficult and painful situations in life the believer can rest in the Lord, knowing that He is sovereign and that there is a bright future ahead.

Habakkuk's confidence in God (vv.17-19)

Here Habakkuk contemplated the devastation of the land through the invasion of the Chaldeans. Although this would be a grief to his soul yet he was confident that he would rejoice and rise triumphantly above the distress and tribulation. This will also be true of the faithful remnant in a coming day as they pass through the Great Tribulation (Rev 12.17).

Habakkuk knew full well what the immediate future would bring with the invasion of the land by the Chaldeans (v.17). They would not only slaughter the people of the cities and towns, but they would consume the harvest and livestock. They would carry off people as captives, strip the land of its produce, cut down the trees, and remove from the land what livestock remained. The impending offensive of the Chaldean army would bring ruin to Judah since it was mainly an agricultural country and depended upon its produce for sustenance. Figs, grapes, olives, and grain were greatly valued. They were part of the inheritance of the land (Deut 8.8). The fig tree, the vine, and the olive tree are used symbolically in the Scriptures of Israel (Is 5.1-7; Jer 11.16-17; Rom 11.17; Mt 24.32). The fruitlessness of these would be a fitting picture of the condition of Judah in Habakkuk's day. The land that flowed with milk and honey (Deut 11.9) would be stripped and left bare. There would be no bud on the fig tree, indicating barrenness. The vines would be fruitless and there would be no produce from the olive. The labour of the olive refers to its produce - the olive fruit. Since the word translated "fail" (KAHASH - 3584) can convey the idea of deceive or disappoint, some take the view that what is described in this verse is the result of natural causes - failure of the harvest, famine. However, the majority of scholars agree that the description is of the land after its devastating conquest by the Chaldeans. The cornfields would be overrun and remain unsown, thus yielding no grain. The folds and the stalls would be empty through the slaughter for food and confiscation of the flocks and herds by the hostile troops. This description is similar to Jeremiah's prediction (Jer 5.17). The gloom and darkness of this verse highlights the gleam of the following verse.

There is a clear link in v.18 with the previous verse indicated by the first word in both verses – "Although...Yet". This verse is in contrast to the preceding one and is intended to emphasise the faith and confidence of Habakkuk referred to in v.16. As the prophet faced the future he did so with faith and confidence. Although he anticipated the devastation of the land and the loss of all earthly prospects, he was confident that he would rise above it all. His eyes had been turned from the circumstances and conditions of earth to the living and true God, the covenant keeping God, who, in His sovereignty, would fulfil His promise. Habakkuk knew that Jehovah was in control in spite of the coming invasion. He was their Saviour

God (vv.8,13; Ex 15.2) and would bring deliverance to His people. Having experienced shock at what he had heard and seen, described in v.16, the prophet now experiences inward calm as he rests in God. This is surely the pinnacle of faith. The answer to all his problems and perplexities was found in God. In the light of the majesty and presence of God earthly events and prospects were insignificant and transient.

Such faith and confidence should characterise Christians today. Trials will come and they may lose things that are valued, but God remains the same and in Him they have all. The passing things of life are valueless in comparison with what is eternal. The believer should walk by faith and not by sight (2 Cor 5.7) for "the things which are seen are temporal; but the things which are not seen are eternal" (2 Cor 4.18).

The verb "rejoice" (ALAZ - 5937) means to exult, and indicates the prophet's unbounded joy in Jehovah because of what He is in Himself. God is the source of true joy. This first clause has its echo in Philippians 4.4 – "Rejoice in the Lord alway: and again I say, Rejoice". Believers should never allow the varying circumstances of life to rob them of rejoicing. All their blessings are in Christ and are eternal, and so they ought to rejoice in the sphere of His Lordship. Habakkuk would shout with joy, or rather would express his enthusiastic joy (see 1.15, glad) in the God of his salvation. This verse is one of the greatest and most forceful displays of the power of faith in the Scriptures, and it can be linked to 2.4. The prophet, in the midst of adverse circumstances, can speak of "the God of my salvation". Salvation here embraces eternal salvation. Habakkuk rested upon God for his salvation and realised that He would uphold him in all the trials of life, including the coming devastation. Believers today have the same assurance and can look beyond the difficulties and trials of life knowing that "our light affliction, which is but for a moment, worketh for us a far more exceeding and eternal weight of glory" (2 Cor 4.17). "If God be for us, who can be against us?" (Rom 8.31).

The closing verse, v.19, is very similar to some of David's expressions in Psalm 18. The first clause readily corresponds with v.32: "It is God that girdeth me with strength" (see also v.39). The next two statements correspond with v.33: "He maketh my feet like hinds' feet, and setteth me upon my high places".

In the opening expression the prophet introduces another name of God (ADONAY - 136) which is the plural form of ADON (113) and always refers to God. It "might also be called an intensive plural or plural of majesty" (TWOT). It means Lord or Possessor and signifies sovereignty. Thus the opening words are "Jehovah Adonay" or Jehovah the Lord. Habakkuk, who had no power in himself (v.16), declares that Jehovah the Lord is his strength. When one appreciates one's weakness then one can experience the strength of the Lord – "for when I am weak, then am I strong" (2 Cor 12.10). It is suggested that Habakkuk viewed Jehovah the Lord as a stronghold, but the basic meaning of the Hebrew word (HAYIL - 2428) is "strength". The thought here might be that Habakkuk's strength of confidence was in Jehovah the Lord. However, it seems more likely that the prophet means that his source of strength in every circumstance was Jehovah the Lord. Paul declared the same truth: "I can do all things through Christ who strengtheneth me" (Phil 4.13). Paul, like Habakkuk, was declaring his confidence because of the sufficiency found in Christ. Here is a continuing supply of spiritual strength for every believer whatever the circumstance or trial. It is for them to avail themselves of this provision in Christ – "be strong in the Lord, and in the power of his might" (Eph 6.10). The prophet's strength in Jehovah the Lord not only enabled him to endure afflictions, but would also provide him with vigour and vitality to reach and abide in high places. In the strength of the Lord he could surmount every obstacle.

The hind (or gazelle) was sure footed, enabling it to move safely in difficult terrain. God would give Habakkuk, and those he represented, security in difficult circumstances. The figure of the hind is used to signify the power that enables one to reach the heights – "But they that wait upon the Lord shall renew their strength; they shall mount up with wings as eagles; they shall run, and not be weary; and they shall walk, and not faint" (Is 40.31).

The expression "upon mine high places" may well describe the hills and mountains of the land (Deut 11.11; 2 Chr 27.4) and thus convey the thought that Habakkuk was confident that God would restore Israel to the land. C. F. Keil states, "The figure must be taken as a whole; and according to this, it simply denotes the ultimate triumph of the people of God over all oppression on the part of the power of the world...The prophet prays and speaks throughout the entire ode in the name of the believing congregation. His pain is their pain; his joy their joy". It can be applied to believers today and the question asked as to what the trials and difficulties of the present pathway are compared with the enjoyment of spiritual things and the future glory – "For I reckon that the sufferings of this present time are not worthy to be compared with the glory which shall be revealed in us" (Rom 8.18). Are Christians today, like Habakkuk, bearing one another's burdens (Gal 6.2; see 1 Cor 12.26)?

Habakkuk closes this chapter, in one sense, as he began (v.1), indicating that the poem or psalm was to be used in the temple worship accompanied with stringed instruments. Thus this closing clause does not form part of the sublime poem or psalm, but is a subscription answering to the heading in v.1 and giving direction as to how the psalm should be accompanied with stringed instruments in the temple worship. The expression "my stringed instruments" affirms that the prophet himself was qualified to take part in this accompaniment and thus belonged to the Levites. Joyful praise and worship is a fitting end to the prophecy which emphasises the triumph of faith. Christians today should be marked by joyful praise and worship in spite of the difficulties and problems of life.

Conclusion

The book of Habakkuk unfolds the great change that takes place in the experience of the prophet, replacing concerns and perplexity with trust and rejoicing. At the beginning, Habakkuk was full of questions which at first increased, but then he discovered that the all-sufficient answer to all these was found in God. This transformation takes place through waiting, in faith, upon God to reveal Himself and His purposes. In this book, therefore, we have the triumph of faith displayed. Although the outward conditions and circumstances had not changed, Habakkuk's understanding of God's ways changed as did his appreciation of God's greatness and power. He had learned that despite the conditions and circumstances on earth God was still in control, and ultimately the people of God would be triumphant through Him. The prophet learned the importance of resting in the faithful, unchanging, omnipotent God who would accomplish His purposes in His own way and at His appointed time. By turning his eyes from the problems of earth to the living God he could rise above difficulties and rejoice in the Lord.

It is possible for believers today to be so occupied with the problems of this life that they are robbed of the joy of the Lord. The vision that God gave Habakkuk of His greatness and purpose satisfied his heart and gave him tranquillity. The closer one draws to the Lord and the more one is occupied with His word the stronger one becomes spiritually, and the more one is able to rest in the Lord and to rejoice in Him. The forces of evil might seem to be growing stronger, and iniquity might be increasing today, but remember that God is still on the throne. He will ultimately fulfil His purpose in destroying the powers of evil and bringing His people into eternal blessing. With this assurance the believer can rejoice in the Lord in every circumstance of life. Habakkuk found that, although he was weak in himself, he could be strong in the Lord. This can be the experience of every child of God.

ZEPHANIAH

P. Harding

CONTENTS

INTRODUCTION

The prophecy of Zephaniah is set in the time of Josiah (1.1) who began to reign at the early age of eight (2 Chr 34.1). At the age of sixteen "he began to seek after the God of David his father" (2 Chr 34.3), and later sought to purge Judah of idolatry. Thus a time of restoration and spiritual renewal took place during his reign of thirty-one years (2 Chr 34.1). It seems evident that Zephaniah's prophecy was contemporary with the first part of Jeremiah's prophecy, for both condemn the idolatrous practices of Judah during the same period (1.4-5 with Jer 2.8; 8.2). The existence of those practices, along with the conditions unfolded in Habakkuk, which were condemned by these prophets, indicate that the reformation under Josiah was neither widespread, deep, nor lasting.

Among the prophets, Zephaniah "is conspicuous for the comprehensiveness of his words" (F. C. Cook). C. L. Feinberg writes, "A sixteenth-century writer indicated: 'If any one wishes all the secret oracles of the prophets to be given in a brief compendium, let him read through this brief Zephaniah'. He has affinities in his prophecy with the message of earlier prophets".

The prophecy commences with universal judgment before stating the threats of specific judgments. The kingdom of Judah is the first to receive such a threat with particular reference to Jerusalem (1.4,12), which was called the city of David, and Zion (2 Chr 5.2). The temple was there and it was called the city of God (Ps 48.1,8) since it was the place where God had set His name. Because of the evil practices which took place there, this status was going to be removed, yet, through God's grace, it would be once more restored and God would again dwell in their midst (3.15-17). When the prophet mentions judgment upon other nations he moves from the west (Philistia, 2.4-7) to the east (Moab and Ammon, 2.8-11), and from the south (Ethiopia, 2.12) to the north (Assyria, 2.13-15). These are chosen, not only because of their relationship to Israel, but also to emphasise the universal character of God's judgment with which the book commences (1.2-3). God is indeed the Judge of all nations. His judgments, as well as His blessings, are directed to the whole world (2.11; 3.8-9).

Although there is no prediction of the coming Messiah in the book, Zephaniah prophesied of a coming day when God would be in the midst of Israel (3.15-17) and when all nations would call upon the name of the Lord and serve Him (3.9). His style is vivid in detail, and parts of his prophecy show a familiarity with other prophets (1.5 with Jer 8.2; 1.7 with Joel 1.15; 2.14 with Is 34.11; 2.15 with Is 47.8). This shows that he is only one of a number of prophets and that his prophecy is linked with other prophecies.

The Author of the Book

There is very little known about Zephaniah apart from his note in the opening verse. There is no information within the prophecy as to his personal life. There are three others with the name Zephaniah in the Old Testament: a priest (2 Kings 25.18; Jer 21.1; 52.24), a Kohathite (1 Chr 6.36), and another Israelite (Zech 6.10,14). The name Zephaniah means "whom Jehovah hath hidden or guarded". It is suggested that as such he is representative of the saved remnant of the end times with which his prophecy is concerned. Out of that remnant God will preserve (hide) a nucleus through all the terror of the Day of the Lord in order to build the new nation of Israel (cp. 2.3). From the meaning of his name, "it has been deduced that he was born during the latter part of the reign of Manasseh (686-642 BC; cp. 2 Kings 21.16)" (C. J. Barber). The prophecy of Zephaniah is the ninth in the minor prophets and has the longest stated genealogy of all the prophets, going back to the fourth generation. The fact that Zephaniah traced his line back to his great-great-grandfather implies that he was a noteworthy person in the history of Judah.

It is generally accepted that the name Hizkiah is a reference to King Hezekiah although there is no designation here and there is no record in the Old Testament of his having a son named Amariah. However, Ibn Ezra states that "Amariah is Manasseh's brother" (see Rabbi A. J. Rosenberg). It is suggested that the reason why Hizkiah is not called "king of Judah" is because that title is used of Josiah, the reigning king at that time. The name Hizkiah is synonymous with the names Hezekiah and Hizkijah (see Strong's Concordance at 2396, and compare Nehemiah 7.21 with Nehemiah 10.17). The only other persons of this name in the Old Testament lived after the captivity of Judah (1 Chr 3.23; Ezra 2.16) so they cannot be in view here. The objection that it cannot be King Hezekiah who is being referred to, because there are only two generations in the genealogy of the kings, is not sustainable since there are 57 years between the end of Hezekiah's reign (Manasseh - 55 years; Amon - 2 years: 2 Chr 33.1,21) and the commencement of Josiah's reign. Thus it seems evident that Zephaniah was of royal descent. It has been suggested that "Zephaniah's knowledge of the geography and demography of Jerusalem (1.10-13; 3.1-4) implies that he was a long-time resident, if not a native, of the capital city" (D. W. Baker).

The Date of the Book

It is clear from the opening verse of the book that Zephaniah prophesied during the reign of Josiah, the son of Amon. Josiah was the sixteenth monarch of Judah (2 Kings 22.1-23.30) and he reigned from 640 to 609 BC. This dating is widely accepted and is said to agree with the position of the book in the Minor Prophets, between Habakkuk and Haggai. The content of the prophecy also corresponds with this period. The reign of Josiah was generally characterised by peace and prosperity, with no opposition or hostility from other nations. It was also marked by a measure of restoration and spiritual renewal. Idolatry was rampant when Josiah came to the throne at the early age of eight.

The reforms of his great-grandfather, Hezekiah (2 Kings 18.4-6), were set aside by Hezekiah's son Manasseh who reinstated idolatrous practices to an even greater degree (2 Kings 21.1-9). These practices were continued by Manasseh's son, Amon (2 Kings 21.19-22). Josiah, during his reign, sought to cleanse Jerusalem and Judah from these (2 Chr 34.3-7). Since most scholars accept that Zephaniah prophesied during Josiah's reign it is evident that his ministry could not have been prior to 640 BC.

The prophet predicts the destruction of Assyria and the desolation of Nineveh, its capital city (2.13), which indicates that the Assyrian empire and Nineveh were still in existence. Assyria had defeated Israel, the northern kingdom, had taken it into captivity (2 Kings 17.1-6; 18.9-12 - 722-720 BC), and in Josiah's time it was a dominant power. Nineveh was conquered about 612 BC and the complete Assyrian empire crumbled at the hands of the Babylonians a few years later. Thus Zephaniah's ministry must have been before 612 BC.

There are two significant periods of Josiah's reign recorded, the twelfth year of his reign when he began to cleanse the land of Judah (2 Chr 34.3-7), and the eighteenth year of his reign when he had the temple repaired (2 Chr 34.8), the book of the law was found (2 Chr 34.14-19), and when he made a covenant before the Lord (2 Chr 34.29-33). There is a dispute as to whether the prophecy belongs to the first or the second half of Josiah's reign. D. W. Baker states, "It was only in the course of Josiah's reign (c. 621 BC) that Yahwism was again officially restored and the pagan practices proscribed. It could be argued that in the light of this proscription and the evidence in (Zephaniah) 1.4-9 of continued pagan influence the prophecies must have predated Josiah's reform. This is possible, but not certain, since official policy was not always and everywhere evidenced in public practice, even among the rulers of the nation". C. J. Barber gives the view of most modern scholars which is that "Internal evidence is useful in establishing more specifically when the prophet ministered. The idolatrous practices of 1.4-6 parallel those spoken of in 2 Kings 23.4-14, and thus Zephaniah's prophecy may have been given shortly before Josiah began to purge Jerusalem and Judah in 628 BC (cp. 1.8-9,12). On the other hand, from a historical point of view, Zephaniah's predictions could easily have been uttered between 624 and 620 B.C. and could have provided

the impetus for the king's reforms". However, the expression "I will
cut off the remnant of Baal from this place" (1.4) presupposes that
Josiah's reformation had already begun and that Baal worship had
received such a blow that only a remnant remained, and that
remnant would ultimately be cut off. It seems that certain forms of
idolatry were still practised during and after the eighteenth year of
Josiah's reign (2 Kings 23.24). Thus the worship of Jehovah and
idol worship existed together for at least a part of Josiah's reign if
not throughout it (1.5). Some take the threat to punish the king's
children (sons, 1.8) to indicate a late date for the prophecy since
Josiah was so young in coming to the throne. However, there is no
solid ground for this conclusion for the reference may be to
Manasseh and Amon's sons, or it could be a general threat of
judgment to all who are of royal blood. C. F. Keil states, "Now, as
Zephaniah's prophecy presupposes the maintenance of the temple-
worship, it can only have been uttered after the purification of the
temple from the abominations of idolatry that were practised in its
courts, and in all probability was not uttered till after the completion
of the repairs of the temple, and the celebration of the solemn
passover in the eighteenth year of Josiah's reign. The time cannot
be determined more exactly". Although it does not seem possible
to fix the exact date of Zephaniah's prophecy it does seem to fall
between 622 and 612 BC.

The Message of the Book
   Zephaniah's prophecy provides a panorama of coming events.
The whole picture of the book embraces both judgment and
salvation in their totality. Generally prophetic ministry has its basis
in the days in which the prophet lives. Here the conditions prevalent
in Zephaniah's day are used as the basis of prophetic ministry
concerning the end times. The moral and spiritual conditions which
were about to be judged by God, using Nebuchadnezzar (though
not named), are intensified in the end times. This will bring far more
dreadful judgments and suffering under the last and most bitter
oppressor of Israel, the "man of sin" (2 Thess 2.3), of whom
Nebuchadnezzar is but a picture. Zephaniah looks beyond the near
view to a still future outpouring of God's judgment upon the world
which will take place at the Lord's glorious return to set up His
Kingdom.
   The book commences with universal judgment out of which arises
judgment upon Judah because of its departure from God, and
judgment upon the nations because of their hostility to the people
of God. However, the severity of judgment has in view the establishing
of the divine presence in the midst of Israel and of divine righteousness
upon the whole earth. Although the book commences with the threat

of judgment and contains an exhortation to repent, it ends with the promise of salvation and blessing for the remnant.

The main theme of the prophecy is "the day of the Lord" which is first mentioned by Joel (Joel 1.15) whose prophecy is earlier than all of the other prophetic books except, perhaps, the book of Jonah. Zephaniah was neither the first nor the last to write of "the day of the Lord", but he uses this expression more than any other prophet. The word "day" occurs twenty-one times in the prophecy and is governed by its first occurrence: "the day of the Lord is at hand" (1.7). The expression is used in the Old Testament both for local, national, and universal events, and has both a short and a long term significance. It is used relative to the dealings of Jehovah in judgment and in deliverance. It seems that the people of both Israel and Judah thought that the expression referred to the intervention of God, on their behalf, in judgment upon their enemies in order to bring deliverance to them. They did not seem to understand that they themselves would be involved in that judgment. C. J. Barber states, "To those living in Old Testament times, the concept of the 'day of the Lord' looked forward to the time when Yahweh would intervene in history on behalf of His chosen people, Israel. Israel would then become the head of the nations of the world and the channel of God's blessing to all people...The concept of the 'day of the Lord' that was popular initially was shown to be in error, however, for between the eighth and sixth centuries BC different prophets arose to correct the distorted view. They predicted that judgment would start with God's people, Israel (Is 2.5-3.26; Ezek 13.4; Joel 1.15; 2.1,11; Zeph 1.7,14; Zech 14.1). They showed that the Day of the Lord would begin with a battle cry (Ezek 30.2-3; Is 13.6; Joel 1.15), as the Lord summoned His enemies to prepare for battle (Is 13.2-5). It would be a day of darkness (Ezek 30.3) and fire (Zeph 1.18; Mal 4.1), and of cataclysmic events (Is 34.4) when those on earth would tremble (Joel 2.1-11). Babylon (Is 13.1,6,9), Egypt (Jer 46.10-11), Edom (Obad vv.1,15), and other nations (Joel 2.31; 3.14; Obad v.14) would be laid waste as God intervened to punish sin that had come to a climax".

However, judgment is not the only feature of the Day of the Lord, for salvation and blessing also characterise it (Zeph 3.9-20). The Day of the Lord will be both a time of judgment (1.14-18) and a time of blessing (3.14-17). It commences with judgment (Is 13.6-18) and includes the Great Tribulation (Mt 24.21-29), the manifestation of Christ and His triumph over His enemies (Zech 14.1-3; Rev 19.11-21), the restoration of Israel (Is 14.1-3; Ezek 37.12-14; Amos 9.11-15), all the events of the Millennium when Christ will be in the midst of Israel (Zeph 3.11-17), and the passing away of the heavens and the earth (2 Pet 3.10).

The prophecy is, in a sense, supplementary to Habakkuk's prophecy. Habakkuk foretold the punishment of Judah through the instrumentality of the Chaldeans, whereas Zephaniah indicates that the judgment of Judah would also affect the whole world. Unlike Habakkuk, Zephaniah does not name the Chaldeans as the instrument in God's hand in judgment so that God's hand alone can be seen universally. One learns in the prophecy that chastisement, retribution, and blessing all come from the hand of God. In the all-embracing character of the prophecy one sees the reason why the prophet does not name the instruments used by God to execute His judgment. The fact that it speaks of universal judgment manifests both the sovereignty of God and His holiness and justice. Through the pouring out of His judgment upon the nations God will give to the people, or turn them to, a pure language that they may all call upon His name (3.9).

One must not miss the serious moral and spiritual condition in Judah generally that is viewed in this prophecy. Serious declension had taken place since the reforms of Hezekiah's days showing that each generation is responsible for its own moral and spiritual condition, and for carrying out the word of God. This is true today as we see the departure from divine truth and the increase in evil. Believers are responsible before God to maintain divine principles and to allow the truth of God to mould their lives. The truth (doctrine) of God is according to godliness (1 Tim 6.3; Tit 1.1) and godliness is developed in the lives of believers by the truth. The truth should affect believers' lives practically and develop their characters in true godliness after the likeness of Christ who is Himself the very essence of truth.

The unity of the book is seen in that the mention of judgment in the opening verses (1.2-6) links with the Day of the Lord (1.7) which embraces both the judgment detailed (1.8-3.8) and the coming blessing (3.9-20).

The Purpose of the Book

Like Habakkuk, the main purpose is to encourage the faithful remnant in Judah at that time and to show them that Jehovah was sovereign and was faithful to His covenant. Whatever the circumstances of life, God is in control and He is unfailingly faithful to His people. The prophecy also exposed the moral and spiritual depravity of Judah and reminded Judah, in general, that Jehovah was holy and just, and that He would visit their iniquity in judgment. How important it is to be daily conscious of the infinite holiness of God. The book unfolds the ultimate dealing of God with the world and its outcome in universal peace, stability, and righteousness with Jehovah in the midst of the restored and blessed Israel.

OUTLINE OF THE BOOK

Introduction, or Personal Identification (1.1)

The Severity of Jehovah's Judgment, and His Exhortation (1.2-2.3)
A. Universal judgment (1.2-3)
B. Judgment upon Judah (1.4-18)
    1. The reasons for judgment (1.4-13)
        a) Spiritual depravity (1.4-6)
        b) Moral and social depravity (1.7-13)
    2. The description of judgment (1.14-18)
        a) Its imminency (1.14)
        b) Its intensity (1.15-18)
C. The exhortation to Judah (2.1-3)

The Subjugation of Israel's Enemies, and Jehovah's Exposure of Judah's Sin (2.4-3.8)
A. Judgment upon the nations (2.4-15)
    1. Philistia (2.4-7)
    2. Moab and Amon (2.8-11)
    3. Ethiopia (2.12)
    4. Assyria (2.13-15)
B. Jehovah's exposure and judgment of Judah's sin (3.1-8)
    1. Jerusalem's condition (3.1-7)
    2. The nations gathered (3.8)

The Sure Purposes of Jehovah Fulfilled (3.9-20)
A. The nations converted (3.9)
B. The remnant preserved (3.10-13)
    1. Restoration (3.10)
    2. Redemption (3.11-13)
C. The Lord in the midst (3.14-17)
D. The promise of God, or Israel's reward (3.18-20).

In one sense the book is divided into three sections by the expressions "the fire of his jealousy" (1.18) and "the fire of my jealousy" (3.8). Looking at it in this way the first section covers ch.1 in which the prophet first pronounces judgment upon the world (1.2-3) and then upon Judah (1.4-13) unfolding its character (1.14-18). The second section covers 2.1-3.8 in which Zephaniah exhorts Judah to repent (2.1-3) and encourages this by declaring the judgment of God upon the nations (2.4-15), His condemnation of the ungodly in Jerusalem (3.1-7), and the pouring out of His fury upon all (3.8). The final section covers 3.9-20 in which the ultimate end of God's dealings is reached -

the blessing of the Gentiles (3.9), the restoration and redemption of the scattered remnant (3.10-13), and the fulfilment of the covenant with Jehovah in the midst of Israel (3.14-20). The "Woe" of 2.5 pronounces judgment on the nations, and the "Woe" of 3.1 pronounces judgment on Jerusalem, the capital of Israel.

The key expressions are "the day of the Lord" and "the fire of my jealousy". The key verse seems to be 3.17. Although there is no direct quotation from Zephaniah in the New Testament it seems as if 1 Thessalonians 5.1-3 looks back to this book.

ZEPHANIAH 1

The thought that this world is ripening for judgment is scorned by most in the present society. The two predominant ideas put forward today are either that men will destroy themselves and the world or that society will continue in its present lifestyle with some improvement. That God should intervene in judgment never enters the minds of these exponents of modern culture. Present day sociology manifests a rejection of God and His word. This may be because much of the word of God reveals that judgment is inevitable since God is holy and just. To those who value the word of God, this prophecy, with its predictions of judgment and blessing, reveals the righteousness and love of God. Although Zephaniah has been considered one of the most difficult prophetic books, it is clear that the prophet's message seems to be centred on the Day of the Lord. This opening chapter predicts that judgment will come upon the whole world (vv.2-3), that it will destroy the godless and idolaters in Judah and Jerusalem (vv.4-7), and that it will fall upon various social classes (vv.8-13). The chapter ends with the imminency and description of the great Day of the Lord (vv.14-18).

Verse 1: Introduction, or Personal Identification

The prophecy opens with the expression "The word of the Lord (Jehovah) which came unto Zephaniah", indicating that Zephaniah was the recipient, but God was the source of the prophecy. The whole book has the stamp of divine inspiration upon it as do the rest of the prophetic books (2 Pet 1.21; see also Jer 1.2; Hos 1.1; Zech 1.1). The absolute authority behind the prophecy, assuring the fulfilment of its predictions, is seen in every chapter by the emphatic statement, "saith the Lord" (1.2,3,10; 2.9; 3.8,20). Since it is the infallible word of God, men do well to take heed to the warnings and message of the book. Its warnings are that sin of every kind brings the judgment of God, and its message is that repentance toward God and trust in Him and His provision is the only way to escape that judgment. Zephaniah is identified by the longest genealogy of any of the prophets. Two reasons are suggested for the genealogy being extended to four generations.

1. To highlight his royal ancestry being the great-great-grandson of the godly and well known king Hezekiah (another rendering of Hizkiah - see Introduction - The Author of the Book) which would add weight to the pronouncement of judgment upon the princes and king's sons (1.8).

2. To "indicate that the writer was an Israelite rather than an Ethiopian, as one could translate the name of his father, Cushi (cp. Gen 10.6; 2 Kings 19.9; Is 18.1). His nationality is clear, however, since all of the other names in the genealogy, including the prophet's own, contain a form of the name of Israel's God, Yah(weh)" (D. W. Baker).

It might also be to link the recovery under Hezekiah with the reformation which was taking place at the time of Zephaniah's prophecy. The verse indicates that the prophet ministered during the reign of Josiah who was the great-grandson of Hezekiah. The reformation during the reign of Hezekiah did not continue after his day. Declension made rapid progress during the reign of Josiah's grandfather (Manasseh) and father (Amon) who were both ungodly men. Their idolatry, witchcraft, and corruption soon replaced the good wrought in Hezekiah's time (2 Chr 32-33). Although Josiah was the son and grandson of ungodly kings, he, himself, sought the Lord early in his life (2 Chr 34.3) and did all that he could to remove idolatry from the land (2 Chr 34.3-7). Thus one can see that the background of a person is not a barrier to spiritual development or godliness. David Newell states, "Although no son can entirely escape the influence of his parents, neither spirituality nor wickedness is automatically inherited...Whether we come from good or bad stock, all must stand as individuals before God, and make His truth our own possession".

It seems that the reformation under Josiah was neither deep nor widespread, and had touched only a section of the people. Although he sought to remove idolatry from the land, a remnant of Baal worshippers remained along with the worshippers of the host of heaven (1.4-5). Thus the majority, marked by materialism, were ripe for judgment. In spite of the earnest endeavours of Josiah, along with other godly men, the majority remained untouched. Although there might have been an outward adherence by many, their hearts remained unmoved. That is also true in a considerable number of places today. Unless there is repentance and genuine faith in Christ there can be no real and lasting change in a person's life. Mere profession gives a false sense of security, but it never changes the life or brings salvation to a person.

Verses 1.2-2.3: The Severity of God's Judgment, and His Exhortation

The first section opens with God's prediction of judgment upon the inhabitants of the world (1.2-3) because He is Lord and Judge of the whole earth (Gen 18.25; Ps 94.2; Zech 4.14). Nothing can stay His hand when it is stretched out in judgment (Is 14.26-27). The judgment announced narrows and focuses upon Judah and Jerusalem on account of their spiritual and moral depravity (1.4-18). This announcement of judgment is followed by an exhortation to Judah to repent and turn to the Lord (2.1-3).

Universal judgment (vv.2-3)

Zephaniah's prophecy suddenly commences with the declaration of God that He would completely consume everything from off the face of the earth. Although some take the word "land" as a reference to the land of Judah, the opening expression of v.4 indicates that these verses have a universal connotation in view. The word translated "land" (ADAMA - 127) in vv.2-3 differs from the word translated "land" (ERETS - 776) in the rest of the book (eg 1.18; 2.5; 3.19) and indicates here the whole earth in contrast to a specific land.

"Consume" (SUP - 5486) has the thought of sweeping or taking away (cp. Jer 8.13). Thus the AV marginal rendering, "By taking away I will make an end", is quite accurate. The fact that this verb is used more than once in these verses emphasises the comprehensiveness of the judgment. The emphasis is also strengthened by the different objects of the verb in these verses.

While v.2 speaks of utter destruction in a general way, v.3 gives the details of what is involved in that destruction. The description is all embracive and reminiscent of Genesis 6.7 when God pronounced universal judgment because of man's wickedness. The similarity intimates that the judgment threatened here would be as extensive and as dreadful as the flood when there was a sweeping away of all from the face of the earth. It has also been suggested that this judgment would be a reversal or the undoing of the work of God in creation since the same things are mentioned here as in Genesis 1. Whereas there God created and populated the earth, here the work of that creation is to be swept away from the face of the earth in judgment. The animals, fowls, and fish - all creation is linked with man and suffers with him awaiting a coming day when the curse, pronounced because of man's sin, will be removed (Rom 8.19-22).

It is evident in this prophecy that the judgment predicted will culminate in the conversion of the nations and of Israel (3.9-13). This coming universal judgment will be as predicted in Revelation (6.12-17; 9.20-21; 16.1). There will be the most dreadful and fearful intervention of God in judgment upon the satanically inspired rebellion against God (Rev 16.13-16) which will end with the manifestation of the Lord Jesus Christ and the destruction of all who are gathered against Him (Rev 19.11-21). It has been pointed out that the tragedy of the present generation is that men are greatly concerned about global pollution, nuclear arms, and rogue countries yet disregard the accurate and clear warnings concerning the coming wrath of God contained in His word (Mt 3.7; Rev 16.1). Believers can rejoice that they will never experience the coming wrath (1 Thess 1.10) because they do not belong to this doomed world (Jn 15.19; 17.16). They are waiting for the Lord to come to take them out of this world (1 Thess 4.13-18) and to take them to heaven where they rightfully belong (Jn 14.1-3; Phil 3.20-21). With such a glorious prospect before them believers should live in keeping with their heavenly calling and conduct themselves as children of light (Eph 4.1; 5.8; 1 Thess 5.5-10).

The specific details of judgment include the removal of the stumbling-blocks along with the wicked. Although some feel that the stumbling-blocks refer to the wicked themselves, the structure indicates that the stumbling-blocks are separate from the wicked yet linked with them. The word translated "stumbling-blocks" (MAKSHELA - 4384) is only found elsewhere in Isaiah 3.6 (ruin) and represents that through which a person or nation is brought to a fall or to ruin (Keil & Delitzsch; C. J. Barber). The reference is to anything that turns someone away from God. Here it could particularly indicate idolatry although sinful ways could also be in view (cp. Ezek 14.3-4,7). A similar prediction is made by the Lord in Matthew 13.41-42. Christians must take care that by their conduct they do not become a stumbling-block to fellow believers (Rom 14.13; 1 Cor 8.9). They should avoid anything that may cause another to fall.

Man is particularly singled out in relation to this judgment being mentioned twice - first and last in v.3. The word translated "cut off" (KARAT - 3772) contains the thought of destruction or bringing to an end, and is used of terminating one's life (cp. Ex 31.14).

The last expression seems to be a play on the Hebrew words for man and land - "I will cut off man (ADAM - 120) from off the land (ADAMA - 127)". In this way prominence is given to man whose wickedness and rebellion against God is the reason for such devastation of the earth. The repetition of the phrase "saith the Lord" adds certainty and solemnity to the declarations as well as emphasising the severity of the judgment.

Judgment upon Judah (vv.4-18)

Having opened with Jehovah's proclamation of universal judgment, Zephaniah now focuses on Judah. The northern kingdom, Israel, had been taken into captivity about a century before by the Assyrians because of their departure from God and their continued idolatry. Judah, in spite of this knowledge, and in spite of the times of reform and blessing under certain of their kings, was now itself characterised by departure and idolatry. The prophecy of Zephaniah turned from the general denunciation of wickedness to the specific depravity of Judah and exposed the true condition beneath the outward reform. Judah's guilt was intensified through their continued departure and sin and also because of their privileged position in having the oracles of God. The reason for the judgment proclaimed is pinpointed in v.17: "...because they have sinned against the Lord". This is always the reason for divine judgment (Ps 51.4). The judgment proclaimed in this prophecy exceeded anything that Judah might have contemplated. The prophet fused together the near and far prophecies so that the impending judgment of God upon Judah, using the Chaldeans, prefigured a more extensive time of judgment and trouble for the world (Is 24.1-6; 26.20-21; Dan 12.1; Joel 2.1-2; Mt 24.21-22; 1 Thess 5.1-3) and clearly embraces the coming Great Tribulation and the terrors of that period. However, one must see the structure of the book which leads from judgment to blessing. The judgment of God in that coming day will pave the way for Israel's final and full restoration in keeping with the word of God (3.14-20; cp. Jer 30.8-9; Amos 9.11-15; Zech 14.16-21; Rom 11.25-26). The lesson in view is that, because of sin, the only way to blessing is through judgment. Recognition of the righteousness of God's judgment will lead Israel to repentance and blessing on the basis of the work of Christ upon the cross.

This principle of blessing through judgment is not only applicable to Israel but to all nations and indeed to every individual. Through the judgment of sin at Golgotha salvation is now offered to "whosoever" (Jn 3.16; Rom 5.8). The ground of salvation for mankind is the death of the Lord Jesus Christ. On the cross He, through bearing the judgment of God against sin, laid a righteous basis which enables God not only to justify the sinner who repents and trusts Christ, but also to bring in new heavens and a new earth where righteousness dwells. Sin must be judged before one can experience the blessing of God.

Since the prophecy has the Chaldean invasion in view, the expression "the day of the Lord" can be viewed as "a day of the Lord" when God's hand is stretched out against Judah. However, this impending chastisement of Judah, for departure from God, is illustrative of coming events during the Day of the Lord in the end times. Just as a remnant would be preserved during the imminent terror of the Chaldean invasion, so a remnant will be preserved during the greater terror of the Day of the Lord (the time of Jacob's trouble - Jer 30.7) yet to come.

The reasons for judgment (vv.4-13)

One must not lose sight of the fact that Judah, as the people of God, had been blessed above other nations. They were the most privileged in having the law of God, yet had turned their backs upon Jehovah. They boasted of their covenant relationship with God, but worshipped Baal and the host of heaven. Since judgment begins with the people of God (1 Pet 4.17), one is not surprised at such a solemn warning. Judah would have understood the anger of Jehovah against the Gentile nations around them, but did not expect such a severe pronouncement upon themselves and their capital city. They would have recognised and acknowledged that there had been declension since the reign of Hezekiah, but some reform had taken place since Josiah had come to the throne. They were therefore unprepared for such severe censure upon them. They had lost a sense of the holiness and justice of God, and the dreadfulness of their true condition before God. Thus they were taken unawares by the pronouncement of judgment upon them. In these verses Zephaniah unfolds the spiritual and moral depravity that demanded such judgment.

(a) Spiritual depravity (vv.4-6). Judah and Jerusalem are now the objects of divine judgment since they had turned away from Jehovah to idolatry. The enormity of Judah's guilt is seen in the idolatrous practices taking place in Jerusalem, the place where God had placed His name. The opening expression in v.4, "I will also stretch out mine hand", is similar to expressions used when God is going to do something significant, as in creation (Jer 27.5; 32.17), in deliverance (Ex 6.6; Deut 26.8; Ezek 20.34), or in judgment

(Ex 3.20; Jer 6.12; Ezek 6.14). Here the hand of Jehovah is stretched out in judgment against Judah and its capital city. It seems that the inhabitants of Jerusalem are particularly mentioned because that was where the temple was, and thus idolatry would be more heinous there than elsewhere. There, in Jerusalem, the true worship of Jehovah should have been maintained and defended. How solemn when people who claim to be Christians live like heathens.

There is clearly a connection between the universal judgment in vv.2-3 and the judgment here since the verb form in v.3 is repeated here. Judah and Jerusalem would be swept away in judgment. Through this judgment the worship of Baal would be completely removed. The expression "the remnant of Baal" does not indicate that Baal-worship had almost disappeared through the reforms of Josiah, but that the very last trace of it would be exterminated. However, the expression does imply that Josiah's reformation had already begun. C. F. Keil states: "The emphasis lies upon 'the remnant', all that still exists of the Baal-worship or idolatry, even to the very last remnant; so that the emphasis presupposes that the extermination has already begun, that the worship of Baal no longer exists in undiminished force and extent. It must not be limited, however, to the complete abolition of the outward or grosser idolatry, but includes the utter extermination of the grosser as well as the more refined Baal-worship". Baal was the God of the Canaanites and the worship of Baal had been a snare to Israel from the time of the Judges (Judg 2.13; 6.25). Baal-worship became prevalent in the northern kingdom, Israel, during the reign of Ahab (1 Kings 16.30-32) and in Judah, the southern kingdom, in the reign of Manasseh, who built idolatrous altars in the House of the Lord (2 Chr 33.1-5). Baal was considered to be the god of fertility. The goddess linked with Baal was Ashtoreth (1 Kings 11.5,33; 2 Kings 23.13) and associated with the worship of both was the practice of gross immorality.

In the last clause of v.4 two classes of priests are mentioned: the Chemarim(s) and the priests. The word translated "Chemarims" (KOMER - 3649) only occurs elsewhere in 2 Kings 23.5 and Hosea 10.5 and it refers to the idol priests. Some have suggested that the word means black or black robed from the black garments these priests wore. The second class of priests refers to the priests of Jehovah who had corrupted the worship of Jehovah and had violated the law (cp 3.4), and secretly or openly, practised idolatry. Both groups would be cut off and the very name of the Chemarim would be obliterated. The solemn fact here is that the very people who had been set apart by God for Himself had turned from Him to idol worship. One must remember that an idol is not only an image of stone or wood which men bow down to, but anything that takes the place of that which alone belongs to God. Believers can, unwittingly, allow legitimate things, such as material possessions, family, academic achievements, and business, to take the place of the Lord in their lives. The first place in the affections and lives of believers should belong to the

Lord (Lk 14.26; Phil 1.21). It is essential and profitable to take heed to the exhortation, "Little children, keep yourselves from idols" (1 Jn 5.21).

In keeping with the two classes of priests in v.4, two classes of worshippers are mentioned in v.5: the worshippers of heavenly bodies and the mixed worshippers. The worship of the sun, moon and stars was an ancient practice (see Deut 4.19; Job 31.26-28) and may well be indicated in Genesis 11.4. It was partly linked with Baal-worship since the heavenly bodies were viewed as bearers of the power of nature worshipped in Baalism (see 2 Kings 21.3; 23.5). This form of idolatry looked upon the stars as the originators of events on earth. It was practised on the flat roofs of the houses as this gave the worshippers a clearer stellar view. Thus every housetop became an idolatrous sanctuary where incense was burnt and drink offerings poured out (see Jer 19.13; 32.29). This form of idolatry had also invaded the temple itself (2 Kings 23.4). David Newell states, "A particular manifestation of this was astrology (1.5). When people turn from God they inevitably turn to lies, and the star worship of Judah is not far removed from our twentieth-century obsession with spiritism and the occult, lately invigorated by the repackaged paganism of the New Age Movement. Sinful man will believe anything rather than God".

The second class of worshippers were characterised by compromise, giving allegiance to both Jehovah and Malcham. One has likened them to the Israelites in Elijah's day who halted between two opinions (1 Kings 18.21). These worshippers sought to combine the worship of Jehovah with idol worship. They had embraced idolatry, but had not outwardly renounced the worship of Jehovah. It is suggested that to swear by or to Jehovah was to bind one's self to His service, whereas to swear by Malcham was to call upon him as god. Some take Malcham to be the same as Moloch (Amos 5.26) and Milcom the god of the Ammonites (1 Kings 11.33). Others consider that Malcham (MALKAM - 4445) refers to "their king" (taking it from the root word MALAK [to reign – 4427] or MELEK [king – 4428]) who was Baal. Whichever way it is interpreted the main thrust is upon the strong condemnation of mixing truth and error, i.e. compromising the truth. To give only part to God is really robbing God and in fact is giving nothing to Him for, "No man can serve two masters: for either he will hate the one, and love the other; or else he will hold to the one, and despise the other" (Mt 6.24). Compromise of truth in any form inevitably involves rejecting the truth. God demands complete allegiance and total commitment to His truth. The message of Zephaniah is relevant today when there is so much emphasis on Christian unity without adherence to all the truth of God. Ecumenism seeks a uniformity, claiming tolerance, while at the same time setting aside much of the truth of God. To compromise any part of that truth is to dishonour Him. Union with any undermining of truth is detrimental to the Christian's spiritual welfare. One cannot compromise with divine truth as revealed in His word.

Two further types are mentioned in v.6 who would come under

judgment - those who apostatised and those who were completely indifferent to the claims of Jehovah. The first had known the truth and had seemingly followed Jehovah. It is suggested that they first responded to Josiah's exhortation to repent, but turned back to their idolatrous practices. To "turn back" (SUG - 5472) implies that they once professed to be followers of Jehovah, but there was no reality in their profession. The proof of genuine faith is continuance in the things of God (Mt 7.16; Lk 9.62; Col 1.23). God demands genuine faith, purity of heart, and adherence to His word. The second, while not being opposed to God, were characterised by indifference to spiritual things and to the claims of Jehovah. The word translated "sought" (BAQASH - 1245) conveys the thought of earnestly seeking, thus "'have not sought Jehovah, indeed have not sought Him' cp. Deut 4.29" (TWOT). Their indifference is further stressed by the fact that they had not even inquired after Jehovah. It must be pointed out that some commentators consider that there is only one class in v.6 who turned back from Jehovah and no longer sought Him or inquired after Him, while others consider there is a range of religious response in the verse. However, it is more than likely that two classes are in view following the pattern in v.4 and v.5.

Indifference to the gospel and eternal matters is characteristic of the present generation. People, in general, have no time for God or His word. The solemn consequence of this spirit of indifference is inevitably judgment. The danger for believers is that such a spirit of indifference could influence them and result in a decline of spiritual interest. Believers must not allow the spirit of the world to affect their lives and thus rob them of spiritual progress and blessing.

(b) Moral and social depravity (vv.7-13). When one considers the indictments of the previous section, the longsuffering of God is evident in the withholding of His judgment. Judgment is God's strange work (Is 28.21) for He is "slow to anger, and plenteous in mercy" (Ps 103.8), "not willing that any should perish, but that all should come to repentance" (2 Pet 3.9). However, judgment will not always be delayed. There is a command for silence, because the Day of the Lord is at hand, before the prophet unfolds the moral and social depravity that demands judgment. The judgment would fall upon the wicked of every rank, and not one of them in Jerusalem would escape. It seems that three classes of people, differing in rank and in attitude to God, would come under this judgment - those who were of royal blood and who imbibed foreign customs (vv.8-9), the merchants who had enriched themselves from trade and usury (vv.10-11), and those who were apathetic and atheistic (vv.12-13).

The expression "Hold thy peace" in v.7 is the same in Hebrew as the closing expression of Habakkuk 2.20 and the opening expression of Zechariah 2.13. The word translated "peace" (HAS - 2013) is an interjection and a command meaning, "Be silent", or, "Hush". It is used in the Old

Testament seven times and is translated "silent", "silence", or "keep silence" (Judg 3.19; Amos 8.3; Hab 2.20; Zech 2.13), "hold...peace" (1.7; Neh 8.11), "hold...tongue" (Amos 6.10), and "stilled" (Num 13.30). The thought here is to let all be silent with awe and reverence before the great and supreme Judge. It is suggested that the expression confirms the threat in vv.2-6 and summons men to be in silent submission to the judgment of God. The nation of Israel (Judah in this context) should have separated themselves from every form of idolatry and kept themselves wholly for God. Since they had not kept themselves pure in this way God would Himself ultimately bring about that purity (cp. Mal 3.2-4).

Believers today should take heed to the exhortation, "Keep thyself pure" (1 Tim 5.22), for "every man that hath this hope in him purifieth himself, even as he is pure" (1 Jn 3.3). This is only possible through separation (see 2 Cor 6.14-7.1).

The prophet uses two names for God in this opening expression: Adonay (Lord - 136) and Jehovah (God - 3069). Adonay is the plural form of Adon (113), and indicates the majesty and sovereignty of God. When it is used in the Old Testament it is always used in relation to God. Thus both names together indicate the Sovereign Lord whose sovereignty would be seen in His execution of judgment upon the earth and upon His covenant people. He alone has the right to mete out vengeance (Deut 32.35; Ps 94.1; Rom 12.19), and every challenge to that right and every charge that He has not intervened in the events of earth will be silenced. The reason for the command to silence is given in the next expression, "for the day of the Lord is at hand". C. J. Barber states, "The definite article is not used with YOM, 'day', and must be supplied in translation. Its absence seems to underscore the fact that before the final 'day of the Lord' comes there will be other occasions when He will intervene in history". It is evident that various divine interventions in judgment would take place leading up to the Day of the Lord (see Introduction - The Message of the Book). Although the invasion of the Chaldeans would be a partial fulfilment, the prophecy had in view the full and final fulfilment also prophesied by others (eg. Is 13.6; Joel 1,15; Obad v.15). That day will be a day of anger (Is 13.9), darkness and gloom (1.15; Joel 3.15), destruction and desolation (1.15; Is 13.6,9; Joel 1.15), distress (1.15; Obad v.14), trouble (1.15; Jer 30.7), vengeance (Is 63.4), and wrath (1.15; Is 13.9). It will be a day when God will act in righteousness and justice, and yet in grace and mercy (3.11-12). When one thinks of this day of reckoning, not only for Israel, but also for the world, one is reminded of the day of reckoning or review of believers (Rom 14.10-12; 2 Cor 5.10).

The initial experience of Israel and the nations of the Day of the Lord would be the judgment of God. The severity of God's judgment will be a manifestation of His holiness and hatred of sin. Do believers today appreciate the infinite holiness of God and His hatred of sin in any form? The nearness of the Day of the Lord is indicated by the fact that Jehovah had prepared a sacrifice for it and that He had already bidden the guests. The metaphor here may have been taken from the sacrifices where the offerer invited others to partake of the sacrifice (see 1 Sam 9.12-13; 20.6). The defeat of Pharaoh-neco, king of Egypt, by Nebuchadnezzar is referred to as a sacrifice (Jer 46.1-10) as is also the judgment upon Idumea (Is 34.6). The judgment upon the armies gathered against the Lord at His manifestation is called the supper of the great God, when the fowls are the bidden guests (Rev 19.17-18; cp. Is 18.6; 56.9; Ezek 39.17; Mt 24.28). However, here the sacrifice prepared by God is the nation of Israel and the guests are the Gentile nations. In the near view Judah is God's prepared sacrifice and the Chaldeans the guests. The identities of the sacrifice and the guests are deliberately withheld as the prophecy blends together the near and far views.

The word translated "bid" (QADASH - 6942) means sanctified or consecrated ones, and the word translated "guests" (QARA - 7121) means called ones. Those called by God to execute His judgment are termed sanctified ones, since they are God's instrument, set apart, to carry out His purpose (Is 13.3).

In v.8 the first class to be punished in the day of Jehovah's sacrifice could be designated the upper or ruling class - those in authority and those of royal blood. The word translated "princes" (SAR - 8269) is used of those with civil authority (1 Kings 22.26 - governor), religious authority (1 Chr 15.16; Ezra 8.24 - chief), and military authority (Judg 4.2; 1 Sam 17.55 - captain). It is also used of the rulers in Israel (Ex 18.21; 2 Chr 29.20) and of the tribal heads (1 Chr 27.16-22). It has been suggested that these leaders or officials might be those who exercised authority during the early years of Josiah's reign (2 Chr 34.1) and who lacked piety. However, in the light of Zephaniah 3.3, the reference is more than likely to the rulers and judges who were responsible to maintain righteousness (Deut 1.16) and justice (Ps 82.3). They were to judge righteously and without partiality (Lev 19.15), and had the responsibility of alleviating the oppression of widows and the fatherless (Ex 22.22). The fact that punishment was pronounced upon them indicates that they had not only failed miserably in their responsibility, but were the actual leaders in wickedness and idolatry. They should have been examples in righteousness and devotion to Jehovah, but instead they were promoters of evil and paganism. Since, as rulers, they were first in dignity and responsibility, they were also foremost in punishment. Those who take the place of leadership among the people of God have a great responsibility, not only to direct believers in the right pathway, but also to be examples of godliness. How solemn it is to misdirect or be a bad influence upon the people of God.

Linked with these rulers in punishment are the king's children (sons). There are different suggestions as to who this means. Some think that Josiah's sons are not referred to since they would have been too young to incur such guilt and merit such punishment. However, others think that

Josiah's sons are meant and that the prophecy is fulfilled in 2 Chronicles 36.2-6. Some consider that the sons of the king reigning when the judgment falls might be particularly in view (2 Kings 25.7). The term seems to refer to the royal family and would embrace all those of royal blood. In pronouncing this punishment Zephaniah was "dealing with his own family connections. How often in a local assembly has the truth of God been sacrificed on the altar of family loyalty! But Zephaniah was faithful to his trust. Perhaps he appreciated the meaning of his name, 'Jehovah will hide'. The believer who knows he has a safe shelter in the Living God will find it easier to stand alone for truth, however unfashionable and unpalatable" (David Newell). The king himself (Josiah) is not mentioned as being subject to the punishment, since he was of tender heart and had humbled himself before the Lord (2 Kings 22.19-20). Thus one sees that both the rulers and those of royal blood would fall in the day of judgment.

Some take the last clause of v.8 as the introduction of a new group, whereas others take it as referring to those already mentioned in the verse. C. F. Keil states, "The princes and king's sons are threatened with punishment, not on account of the high position which they occupied in the state, but on account of the ungodly disposition which they manifested. For since the clauses which follow not only mention different classes of men, but also point out the sins of the different classes, we must also expect this in the case of the princes and king's sons, and consequently must refer the dressing in foreign clothes, which is condemned in the second half of the verse, to the princes and king's sons also, and understand the word 'all' as relating to those who imitated their manners without being actually princes or king's sons".

The word translated "strange" (NOKRI - 5237) has the idea of being alien or foreign; thus the apparel referred to was alien to the Israelites. The clothing of the Israelites was to indicate that they were the people of God, consecrated to His service and separate from all others (Num 15.37-41). Believers today should not follow the fashions of the world, but should be governed by the word of God. The foreign dress adopted by the princes and king's sons and those who imitated them showed that they had violated the command of God and indicated that they had also adopted the customs, manners, habits, and idolatrous practices of the nations. They were no longer separated from the nations and consequently had lost their distinctiveness of character. In order to preserve Christian character believers must separate themselves from worldly pursuits and desires.

The opening expression in v.9 is regarded by some as condemnation of either some pagan superstition or some idolatrous activity. This is taken mainly from the practice the Philistines had of leaping over the threshold on entering the temple of Dagon which began when they found the head and palms of that idol cut off there (1 Sam 5.4-5). "The presence of the severed parts was said to sanctify the threshold...The Israelites, however, jumped over the threshold in a ritual of adoration to the idols" (Rabbi A. J.

Rosenberg). However, the closing expression of v.9 makes this very unlikely, since the condemnation here seems to be in relation to servants who fill their masters' houses with violence and deceit. What appears to be in view is the violent and deceitful activity of the servants of those mentioned in v.8. Rabbi Joseph Kimchi writes that, "when the servants of the princes or the attendants of the king would see a valuable article in a poor man's residence, they would virtually leap over the threshold of the poor man's house to obtain the article and fill their masters' homes with all these coveted prizes" (see Rabbi A. J. Rosenberg). The expression "leap on (or, over) the threshold" seems to refer to a sudden or unexpected entrance into houses to carry away by force or fraud property that would enrich their master's house (cp. Amos 3.10; Jer 5.27). Such property is referred to as "violence and deceit" having been obtained by such means. The implication is that the masters were involved in the guilt by either instructing or encouraging their servants to engage in such plundering. The actions of these servants, along with the actions of their masters, had not escaped the eye of Jehovah and thus punishment would be meted out upon them.

The prophet continues unfolding the solemn events of the day of Jehovah's sacrifice by describing the response of the inhabitants of Jerusalem. In contrast to the silence demanded in v.7, there will be loud noises at the execution of judgment. In vv.10-11 the merchants and usurers, who have increased their wealth by wicked practices, are in view. However, the prophet indicates that every class will be affected by the judgment since cries and mourning will arise from every part of Jerusalem. Once more the certainty of the judgment is emphasised by the expression, "saith the Lord".

The word translated "noise" (QOL - 6963) refers primarily to sound by the vocal cords either actually or figuratively. This is borne out by the following word translated "cry" (SᵉAQA - 6818) which has the meaning of calling out for help when under distress (Ex 3.7; 12.30; 2 Kings 4.40). It describes a strong outcry which frequently indicates that judgment is being meted out (Jer 48.3). The idea is that a loud cry of anguish will resound in Jerusalem. The fish gate is mentioned on three other occasions in the Old Testament (2 Chr 33.14; Neh 3.3; 12.39), but although its relationship to other sections of the wall is implied in Nehemiah its exact location is not given. Commentators place it either in the north or north-eastern part of the city and it was most probably the main gate in that section. It was so designated because there was a fish market in that vicinity and the fish were brought from the River Jordan and the Sea of Galilee through that gate. The north of the city of Jerusalem was the most vulnerable as the other sides were protected by steep slopes. It seems that the Chaldeans entered from that side and through the fish gate because Zedekiah and his company fled towards the south (2 Kings 25.4; Neh 3.15; Jer 39.4). Some think that the fish gate was later called the Damascus Gate. Not only will there be a loud cry of anguish from the fish gate when the enemy approaches and enters the city, but there will be a great howling as the foe advances through it (cp. Jer 25.36). The idea seems to be that of a deep mourning as death and destruction approach them.

Most agree that "second" identifies the second or lower part of the city which was an extension to the old city, and probably corresponds with the northern part enclosed by Manasseh (2 Chr 33.13-14). This extension was built upon the hill Acra. Some suggest that it is referred to in Nehemiah 11.9 and insist that the expression there, "second over the city", should be translated "over the second city". The closing expression of the verse seems to refer to the final collapse of the city.

The word "crashing" (SHEBER - 7667) is mainly rendered "destruction" (Prov 16.18; Is 1.28) and here refers to the turmoil and uproar at Jerusalem's collapse. The hills from which the crashing radiates are not specified, but might indicate Zion and Moriah with other hills upon which the main part of Jerusalem was built. This seems to be so since the verse appears to follow the progress of the advancing enemy from their entrance into the northern part and through the city until its final collapse. "The point made by the Lord was that when the day of reckoning came, the victorious shouts of the invaders would be coupled with their ruthless slaughter of the inhabitants of Jerusalem. That would bring about the kind of wailing, lamentation, and destruction described in the verses" (C. J. Barber).

Maktesh does not seem to be a proper name, but rather a description of a place in Jerusalem. The Hebrew word MAKTESH (4388, 4389) is translated "hollow place" in Judges 15.19 and "mortar" in Proverbs 27.22. It means a depression, dell, or valley. Although the Targum states that the valley of Kidron is meant here, others suggest the Tyropaeon valley. The reference seems to be to a lower area in the southern part of Jerusalem where the traders and merchants carried out their business. This is borne out by the development noted in v.10 and by the following expression. Loud mourning or wailing would come from this section of the city because the merchant people would be cut down which means that they would come to a violent end, to be destroyed. "Merchant people" could be translated "people of Canaan" since the word translated "merchant" (KᵉNAAN - 3667) refers to the land of Canaan. Not that those in view were actual Canaanite traders, but rather that the merchants of Judah were Canaanitish in their greed for gain, and unscrupulous in their transactions. They were completely engrossed in their business in order to increase their wealth. This is borne out by the closing expression of v.11. The verb "bear" (NATIL - 5187) only occurs here in the Old Testament and, in the context, means laden with silver. The reference is to the merchants who amassed wealth by iniquitous means. The same connotation is found in Hosea 12.7-8. However, the riches they had amassed would perish with them for they would not escape the day of judgment (v.18).

Silver and gold can never fit a person for heaven (1 Pet 1.18-19). The warning of coming judgment here links with James 5.1-6 where the menace and madness of materialism is condemned. This spirit of materialism is a danger to all who are taken up only with this life. Believers should recognise that material things are transient and should be looking beyond this life to a coming day (1 Pet 3.10-12). Here the collapse of Judah's commerce, which seemed so vital to them, is in view. There is a great emphasis upon commerce today and the spirit of materialism seems to permeate the world. In the pursuit of wealth conscience and truth are sacrificed and self is exalted. Wealth has become a god. Believers need to be preserved from such an unholy spirit and be content with such things as they have (Heb 13.5). The judgment upon Judah's commerce may well look on to the final judgment of God on the commercial city of Babylon (Rev 18).

Attention is drawn to Jerusalem as a whole in v.12, for Jehovah will meticulously search the city. Whereas in Ezekiel 9.4 the city was to be searched to set a mark on the foreheads of all who sighed because of the abominations done in Jerusalem, here the city is searched in order to punish the wicked. The Chaldeans, the instrument in Jehovah's hand, will leave no corner unexplored (cp. 2 Kings 10.23). C. F. Keil comments that, "Jerome observes on this passage: 'Nothing will be allowed to escape unpunished. If we read the history of *Josephus*, we shall find it written there, that princes and priests, and mighty men, were dragged even out of the sewers, and caves, and pits, and tombs, in which they had hidden themselves from fear of death.' Now, although what is stated here refers to the conquest of Jerusalem by Titus, there can be no doubt that similar things occurred at the Chaldean conquest". The seeking with candles, or lamps (NIR - 5216), denotes the minuteness of the search (cp. Lk 15.8) for those opposed to God and His people. The clear implication is that no one can escape the judgment of God and no sin can escape His all-seeing eye (cp. Ps 90.8; Lk 8.17). The only place of safety for the sinner is in the Saviour, the Lord Jesus Christ, who bore sin's judgment on the cross.

Those who are particularly mentioned for punishment are viewed figuratively as settled on their lees. This metaphor is taken from the fermentation process of wine when the solid particles settle to the bottom and form a sediment. This sediment is called the lees (SHEMER - 8105), also translated "dregs" in Psalm 75.8. The wine was normally strained by pouring the liquid from one vessel into another (Jer 48.11), but if left too long on the lees the wine thickened (Is 25.6). The metaphor is used here to indicate those who, being prosperous, were guilty of the sin of omission - indifference to the claims of Jehovah.

The apathy of Zephaniah's day is echoed today by the widespread prosperity all around and the resulting spiritual indifference. It seems that material prosperity and apathy go together, although prosperity should actually result in thanksgiving to God and brings greater responsibility in the use of what God has bestowed. The apathy of today can so easily affect

Christians inevitably stunting spiritual growth and preventing spiritual activity. Believers need to be on their guard against this spirit of indifference.

The more solemn element is the atheistic spirit linked with such apathy. In their indifference and carelessness they denied that God intervened in the affairs of men and thus placed Jehovah on the same level as idols. They might not have denied the existence of God theoretically, but they denied the moral government of God (cp. Mal 2.17) and attributed all to chance. Outwardly they assented to the claims of Jehovah but in their hearts they denied Him. Man looks at the outward appearance but God looks on the heart (1 Sam 16.7; cp. Jer 17.9-10). In spite of the warnings given by the law and earlier prophets they still persisted in believing that God would not intervene in either blessing or judgment. They had cast aside the teaching of the law and the history of Jehovah's intervention in the affairs of the nation. They had really rebelled against God and His word, and had cast Him out of their thoughts and lives. This, too, is characteristic of today's society in the so called western world of prosperity. Men no longer believe that God will intervene in the affairs of the world even if they acknowledge that God exists.

The fact that men are responsible to God for their actions, that the Bible sets forth a moral standard to be adhered to, and that God hears and answers prayer is deemed out of place in this scientific age. Today the theory of evolution is accepted as fact and the Creator is cast out. Christianity, to many, belongs to the past unenlightened age. However, God and His word remain the same. The day will soon dawn when men will come to know the reality of their accountability to God, but it will be too late then to escape the judgment of God.

Punishment is pronounced upon those who were indifferent to Jehovah's claims and who had lived only for self, but they were to learn that He was indeed the ruler and judge of the world. Their belief that God did not intervene in the affairs of men would be shattered when they experienced the curses of the law pronounced upon those who hearkened not to Him (Deut 28.15,30,39). The prosperity which they trusted in would be torn from them in the judgment of Jehovah, whose power and hatred of sin they had consistently ignored, for their wealth, houses, and vineyards would no longer be theirs to enjoy (cp. Amos 5.11).

The word translated "goods" (HAYIL - 2428) has the basic meaning of strength (Ps 18.32; Joel 2.22) but here it is in relation to wealth, i.e. their strength lay in their possessions which would become plunder or spoil (MᶜSHISSA - 4933). The closing expressions of v.13 seem to imply that they would go on building and planting to the last, but they would not benefit from this activity. The foolishness of living only for this world is clearly conveyed in this verse as it is in the parable of the prosperous farmer (Lk 12.16-21). It is the fool who says in his heart, "There is no God" (Ps 14.1), and it is fools who "make a mock at sin" (Prov 14.9). Thus one sees that indifference to the claims of God and of eternal realities will ultimately bring disaster.

The description of judgment (vv.14-18)
   In these verses the prophet describes the terrors of the Day of the Lord which have already been mentioned (v.7) with intensity and in vivid detail. It will be a day which will affect the world and from which no section will be able to escape. Although primarily Judah is in view, the whole world is also envisaged in this day of judgment. Thus this prophecy, in one sense, passes from the national to the universal warning of coming retribution. Zephaniah moves from the various sections of society that would come under judgment in vv.4-13 to the specific details that would characterise the great Day of the Lord. In that day all false ideas would be swept aside and all complacency would disappear. The prophet indicates that the day was near and that all would be terrified. The conditions described in these verses are so dreadful that the near fulfilment, in the invasion of the Chaldeans, seems to be passed over swiftly in order to get to the end times of unparalleled tribulation and the pouring out of the wrath of God upon the world (cp. Dan 12.1; Mt 24.21; Rev 6.15-17; 15.1; 16.1-21). David Newell states, "The unleashing of judgment (1.14-17) is described so graphically as to make even the saints tremble. Those saved by the precious blood of Christ are, of course, exempt from these terrors (Rom 8.1), but how we should mourn for a world running headlong into destruction".

   (a) Its imminency (v.14). The warnings of Zephaniah may well have seemed empty threats to the people of his day. For Judah it was a day of prosperity and peace and all seemed to be bright with nothing to fear. Thus the people, in general, were complacent and self-assured. The prophet therefore stressed the imminence of coming wrath so that they might take heed and repent before the storm clouds of judgment broke upon them. In the Hebrew text the word translated "near" (QAROB - 7138) is emphatic and stands at the commencement of the opening expressions - "Near is the great day of the Lord, it is near, and hasteneth greatly". It can indicate nearness in distance (Ex 13.17), in family relationship (Ruth 2.20), and in time (Is 13.22). The nearness in time of the coming judgment is here emphasised by the repetition of the word "near" and is strengthened by the term "hasteth greatly". What was stated in v.7 is now amplified in this verse. "Divine intervention in the lives of men was imminent (1.7,14). In 612 BC, the Babylonians annihilated Nineveh...And in 605 BC, only 17 years after Josiah rediscovered the Law, and perhaps 15 years after Zephaniah was writing, Jerusalem itself became the victim of Chaldean aggression (Dan 1.1,2). God's discipline of Judah was not an event in the remote future. Yet we must carefully distinguish between the immediate and the long term fulfilment of these prophecies. Like many Old Testament seers, Zephaniah telescopes events so that the Babylonian invasion of Judah

blurs with that final eschatological eruption of judgment which will rock the entire planet at the coming Day of the Lord" (David Newell). That day is called "great" because of its importance in the purposes of God, the terrible judgment poured out and its universal effect (cp. Joel 2.11,31; Mal 4.5). It will be accompanied by the voice, roar, or shout of Jehovah in judgment on the guilty (Jer 25.30; Amos 1.2). Those who refuse to listen to His voice through His prophets will hear His voice in judgment. Some take the expression as an interjection clause - "Hark! The day of the Lord...". It is also suggested that the battle cry of Jehovah as the Divine Warrior is in view (Is 42.13). The link with the previous expressions may well indicate that the Day of the Lord is so near that its voice can be heard.

Christians today are not listening for the voice of *that* coming day, but for the Lord's shout when He descends from heaven to take away His own from this world before the wrath of God is poured out upon it (1 Thess 1.10; 4.16-17). The coming of the Lord for His own is indeed imminent. How many believers can say from the heart, "Even so, come, Lord Jesus" (Rev 22.20)?

The word translated "mighty man" (GIBBOR - 1368) refers to the mighty men in Judah, the champions or heroic men of the army who were fearless in battle. So dreadful would that day be that even these men would cry in bitter anguish and fear in the face of divine judgment.

(b) Its intensity (vv.15-18). The prophet now provides one of the most condensed summaries of the Day of the Lord in the Old Testament. In describing the dreadfulness of the day of judgment, Zephaniah accumulates various expressions of terror, horror and calamity. The word "day" is repeated in six expressions describing the Day of the Lord. These could well be contrasted with the six days of creation (Gen 1). The first reveals that it would be a day of the fierceness of the wrath of God (Ps 78.49). "Wrath" (EBRA - 5678) indicates here God's wrath overflowing and consuming all that is opposed to Him and His word (cp. Is 13.9; Ezek 22.31) for He is angry regarding sin and rebellion. All who sin against God and refuse to repent and accept His provision in Christ will receive what they deserve to the full.

The result of this outpouring of His wrath in regard to men is described in the following five couplets (vv.15-16) in which the two words are closely related. The first couplet is in relation to inward emotions. "Trouble" (SARA - 6869) indicates intense inner turmoil (Ps 25.17) and describes the anguish of those exposed to God's wrath. "Distress" (MᶜSUQA - 4691) points to inward distress caused by pressure from without, and here the pressure in view is divine judgment. Thus it will be a day of anguish and distress. A similar couplet occurs in Job 15.24 (trouble and anguish).

In the second couplet, "wasteness and desolation", both words come from the same root, which indicates destruction, devastation, or ruin, and are found together in Job 30.3; 38.27. They indicate the swiftness of the destruction and devastation in the Day of the Lord. The third couplet, "darkness and gloominess", indicates a supernatural darkness which characterised one of the plagues upon Egypt (Ex 10.21-22). This darkness intensifies the terror of God's judgment. The same couplet is found in Joel 2.2 where the judgment of the Day of the Lord is also the subject.

The fourth couplet, "clouds and thick darkness", is also found in Joel 2.2 and in Ezekiel 34.12 (cloudy and dark). It may well refer to the clouds of judgment and the deepening darkness of that day. These words "clouds" (ANAN - 6051) and "thick darkness" (ARAPEL - 6205) were used by Moses relative to the giving of the covenant (Deut 4.11). Here they are used to describe the penalty for the violation of that covenant. Concerning the word ARAPEL, the Theological Wordbook of the Old Testament states, "Because the same term is used of God's enveloped glory and his awesome judgments, the term is paradoxical: it bespeaks terror, wonder, fear, majesty awe, and reverence".

The final couplet, in v.16, "trumpet and alarm", seems to convey the idea of a battle as in Amos 2.2 (shouting and trumpet). Trumpets were used in Israel for the calling of an assembly, for a festival, and to signal a battle against an invading enemy (Num 10.2,9; 29.1). The word translated "alarm" (TᵉRUA - 8643) is used in four distinct senses. "It is used for 'signal' (Lev 25.9)...for the blowing of the *shofar* on the day of atonement. It is also used for 'alarm' as in case of attack (Josh 6.5; Jer 4.19)...In addition, it is used for the trumpet in the tumult of the battle (Amos 2.2). Lastly, the noun is used for the exultation of praise to God (Ps 150.3)" (TWOT). The trumpet sound and the battle cry, bringing turmoil and terror will characterise that day as the Divine Warrior moves into battle against all who have rebelled against Him and despised His claims. In the near fulfilment the Chaldean invasion is in view which would bring terror to Judah. The final fulfilment will not only involve Israel, but also the Gentile nations when God will hold to account the whole world. The strongest fortresses, with their lofty towers, will succumb to the irresistible attack (cp. Hos 8.14; Micah 5.11-15). These (corner) towers (PINNA - 6438) are turrets built at the angles of the wall of the city to give the defenders an advantage over the invaders (2 Chr 26.15). However, they will not be able to withstand the wrath of God. Man's sin leads to the judgment of God when tranquillity gives way to distress and anguish, prosperity gives way to desolation and ruin, light gives way to darkness, safety gives way to calamity, and God's longsuffering gives way to His wrath. In that day sinners will perish without hope.

Jehovah again speaks personally in v.17 emphasising the certainty of coming judgment and revealing that it affects the whole of mankind. The word translated "distress" (SARAR - 6887) is not the same as that translated "distress" in v.15, but is the root word of the one rendered "trouble" in that verse. It means to bind or to cramp and the idea here is of being brought into the utmost straits. Since it appears as "besiege" in

Deuteronomy 28.52 many take the opening expression as an allusion to that prophecy. In view of the previous verse, this is confirmed by the association of the following expression, "they shall walk as blind men", with Deuteronomy 28.29. God who had bidden His guests to the sacrifice He had prepared (v.7) would lay siege to the wicked and bring great distress upon them. In their helplessness and sore distress (cp. Jer 10.18) they would be like blind men groping and seeking for a place of refuge, but unable to find one (cp. Is 59.10).

In the middle of v.17 a change takes place from Jehovah personally speaking to the inspired statements of the prophet. Zephaniah gives the reason for coming judgment, as unfolded in vv.4-12, which is the only reason for the judgment of God. The expression "their blood shall be poured out as dust" seems to indicate that the life blood of men would be treated as worthless. The comparison here is not in the abundance of dust but in its worthlessness. Just as dust, trodden under foot, is of little value, so the shed blood of the wicked would be viewed as worthless (2 Kings 13.7; Is 41.2). The term "poured out" is used metaphorically of the slaughter of men and this corresponds with the idea of a battle. This verb must be taken with the last two clauses of the verse. The word translated "flesh" (LᶜHUM - 3894) is only found elsewhere in Job 20.23 (while he is eating) and thus different views are taken as to the meaning of the clause. D. W. Baker states, "The exact identity of this second, valueless object is unclear. The only other use of the word (Job 20.23) provides no help for the present context, and the English versions appear to derive their translations ('flesh', AV, RSV; 'corpses', JB; 'bowels', NEB; 'entrails', NIV) from the context. Another option which merits consideration is to read the revocalized word as 'sap', the life fluid which parallels 'blood' in the sentence". However, F. C. Cook points out that "The word rendered *poured out* is applied to solids as well as liquids. Thus the second clause is equivalent to *their flesh* shall be heaped *as the dung*. The Hebrew for *flesh* occurs only in one other place, but the ancient Versions agree in giving it this meaning". The idea may well be that the dead bodies, being considered of no value, would be left unburied to rot and thus be as dung (cp. Jer 8.2; 9.22).

Verse 18 indicates that there would be no escape from the wrath of Jehovah and thus His judgment would be just, for the rich and the poor alike would suffer the consequences of their sin (cp. Ezek 7.9). The rich would find that their wealth would not appease the righteous anger of God (cp. Prov 11.4). It is suggested that the reference to silver and gold has in view idols which were made or covered with this material (Is 2.20; 30.22; Hab 2.19). The thrust would then be that their lifeless idols would be of no value in the day of wrath. Some take the word "land" as a reference to the land of Judah, whereas others view it as being the whole earth. In Hebrew (ERETS - 776) it "designates either (a) 'the earth' in a cosmological sense, or (b) 'the land' in the sense of a special territorial designation, primarily the land of Israel" (TWOT). The crowning error of Judah, like the kingdom of Israel, was turning away from God to idols and spurning Jehovah's love. The result of this spiritual adultery would be the judgment of God devouring the whole land in the fire of God's jealousy (cp. Deut 4.23-24; 32.21-22; Ezek 38.19). Judah should have known that God was jealous over His people, zealous for His honour as the covenant-keeping God (Ex 20.5; Josh 24.19). God, the Creator, holds to account the whole earth and in His jealousy - the zeal of protecting the honour that belongs to Him alone - He will utterly consume the earth because of sin. His fiery indignation will remove all the chaff as all mankind will experience the result of His offended holiness.

The closing expression indicates that the inhabitants of the earth are particularly in view. "Riddance" (KALA - 3617) has the idea of bringing a process to completion, and thus means a full or complete end (cp. Jer 46.28; Ezek 11.13). Earth's inhabitants will be brought swiftly to an end (cp. Nah 1.8). Thus the chapter ends as it began with universal judgment (vv.2-3).

David Newell writes, "And this, let us remember, is but the earthly prelude to the miseries of eternal torment (2 Thess 1.9). It is a proof of divine mercy, however, that this period of vengeance, for all its terrors, is called a day whereas the present season of gospel opportunity is the 'acceptable year of the Lord' (Is 61.2). Our longsuffering God is 'not willing that any should perish' (2 Pet 3.9)". The complacency and wickedness of Zephaniah's time are prevalent today with the wrath of God abiding upon unbelievers (Jn 3.36). It is, therefore, vital that gospel preachers make clear the solemn consequences of sin before a holy God, as well as making known the offer of salvation made possible by the love of God (Jn 3.16; Rom 5.8).

ZEPHANIAH 2

The Severity of God's Judgment, and His Exhortation (continued)

In the previous chapter the prophet proclaimed universal judgment and judgment upon Judah in particular because of their departure from God. Since that retribution was imminent (1.7,14), Zephaniah exhorted the nation, in general, to repent, and encouraged the godly to seek Jehovah and to pursue righteousness and meekness, so that they might be hidden in the day of judgment (2.1-3). One of the reasons for this call to repentance is the judgment of the surrounding Gentile nations. The Philistines, Moabites and Ammonites would be destroyed, all the gods of the earth would be exterminated, and the isles of the heathen would worship Jehovah (2.4-11). The Ethiopians would be put to the sword and Assyria along with its proud capital city, Nineveh, would be destroyed (2.12-15). The exhortation to repentance in view of the threat of judgment upon the Gentiles is enhanced by the mention that the judgment would lead to the acknowledgement and worship of Jehovah. Another, more striking, reason is the severe retribution upon polluted Jerusalem with its corrupt and treacherous leaders (3.1-7) and the gathering of the nations to receive the indignation of God (3.8).

The exhortation to Judah (vv.1-3)

This is the final part of the first section and is a call to repentance and a promise of shelter for the godly from the coming wrath. After the setting forth of the dreadful judgment of God, with no indication of escape, one would think that there was no hope for any. However, God does not warn men of coming judgment without opening a way of escape from it. Thus the prophet, who had faithfully declared divine judgment, appeals to those estranged from God to return to Him in repentance. The very announcement of judgment was intended to turn Judah from its evil ways and turn them to God. The preaching of the gospel today is not intended to terrorise men, but to warn them of coming judgment and to produce repentance toward God and faith in the Lord Jesus Christ.

The call in v.1 is addressed to Judah and is clearly a summons to repent. The word translated "gather...together" (QASHASH - 7197) means to gather stubble or sticks. Although it has been suggested that the gathering together was to a religious gathering in order to supplicate God to turn away His judgment (Joel 2.16), the meaning of QASHASH suggests otherwise. The word may well have a metaphorical sense indicating that the people were to bow down in repentance before Jehovah as one would bow down in gathering stubble. It would necessitate a searching of their hearts, a consideration of their ways and an acknowledging of their sins. Repentance is a change of mind and means agreeing with God leading to a change of life. It leads to a judgment of self and an acceptance of God's provision and ways. Repentance was essential if they were to avoid the judgment of God and the urgency of this is emphasised by the double use of the verb. The next expression indicates the necessity of contrition since Judah had become like the pagan nations.

The word translated "nation" (GOY - 1471) is not usually used of Judah or Israel, but is generally applied to the Gentile nations. Its use here conveys the thought that Judah had become just like those nations. "Once the descendants of Abraham had become a distinct, recognized, political, and ethnic group of people who were in a specific covenant relationship with Yahweh, the term *goy* and *goyim* increasingly takes the meaning of 'gentiles' or 'heathen', in reference to the non-covenant, non-believing peoples considered as national groups. However, Israel is still repeatedly spoken of as *goy* also, eg. when Israel is spoken of as taking possession of territory (Josh 3.17) or when foreigners speak of her (Deut 4.6)...However, the rule is that the un-circumcised are the *goyim* (Jer 9.25)" (TWOT).

"Desire" (KASAP - 3700) is translated elsewhere as "longedst, longeth" (Gen 31.30; Ps 84.2) and "greedy" (Ps 17.12). Strong's Concordance gives the meaning, "to become pale" and by implication "to pine after". Some have taken the primary sense of becoming pale, along with the negative, to indicate that Judah was a shameless nation. It had become so hardened by its continual departure from God and His word that it had no shame about its wickedness and idolatry. There is no doubt that continual rejection of the word of God hardens the heart. Thus the exhortations: "To day if ye will hear his voice, harden not your hearts, as in the provocation" (Heb 3.15), and, "He, that being often reproved hardeneth his neck, shall be suddenly destroyed, and that without remedy" (Prov 29.1). However, there is not sufficient evidence to reject the AV rendering for which there is strong support. The indication from the AV is that Judah was a nation not desired because of its idolatry, or rather without desire. They had no longing after Jehovah, His word or His ways. The people were satisfied with themselves and with their condition and thus had no desire for anything better (cp. Hos 8.12). They had no wish to change their ways and did not see any necessity to repent (1.12). How like so many today who are self-satisfied or self-righteous and see no necessity to repent and trust the Lord Jesus Christ. How sad, for the day will come when it will be too late as the next verse indicates.

The reason for emphasising the appeal to repent is given in v.2 which is the imminent fulfilment of the declaration of coming judgment (ch.1). The threefold repetition of "Before" is intended to emphasise the solemnity of failing to respond quickly to the call to turn from their wicked ways. Zephaniah did not try to pacify the people by giving them a false hope, but warned them of the nearness of the day of judgment. If they refused to repent, the storm clouds of divine wrath would engulf them. One needs to take heed to the warning, "Because there is wrath, beware lest he take thee away with his stroke: then a great ransom cannot deliver thee" (Job 36.18).

The word translated "bring forth" (YALAD - 3205) is used to describe childbirth (Ex 1.19; 1 Kings 3.17-18). Here it is used figuratively of the decree of God hastening on to its fulfilment (cp. Prov 27.1).

It is suggested that the expression "the day pass as the chaff" is parenthetical and that it explains the previous statement. "Pass" (ABAR - 5674) has the idea of movement although it is translated in various ways in the Old Testament. The expression can be viewed in two ways.

1. That the opportunity, the time given, for repentance would pass swiftly by just as chaff is suddenly removed by a strong wind. Thus they were to grasp the opportunity at once.

2. That the day of judgment would arrive rapidly just as chaff is driven by the wind, so they must make haste to respond to the call to repent.

The second view is more in keeping with the previous statement, but both emphasise the need for swift repentance. Also the "day" mentioned must refer to the Day of the Lord (1.7,14) which swiftly approaches just like chaff before a driving wind (Is 17.13). The fierce or burning anger of Jehovah will characterise that day (cp. Num 25.4; Nah 1.6). The anger of God is especially related to the departure and sin of His people who dishonoured and displeased Him (Judg 2.13-14; 2 Kings 13.2-3). The arrival of the day of Jehovah's anger, and its issues, are by His decree. After much longsuffering and many warnings His wrath would be poured out upon the unrepentant. Historically, Judah did not turn to the Lord, but spurned the call to repentance and thus were taken into captivity.

Within Judah there was a remnant who listened to the voice of God through the prophet, and it is this remnant that is addressed in v.3. Since judgment would come swiftly, they are exhorted to seek the Lord in contrast to the others (1.6). The meek in Judah depended upon God and were opposite in character to the proud, self-satisfied and arrogant majority who would not escape the wrath of God (cp. Is 2.11-17). Although the exhortation seems to be particularly addressed to the humble in Judah, it nevertheless embraces the meek world-wide since the Day of the Lord is in view (cp. Ps 37.11). "Meek" (ANAW - 6035; see also its associated word ANI - 6041 and their root word ANA -6031) stresses the moral and spiritual condition of the godly remnant. In the word is contained the idea of affliction implying that affliction is intended to produce meekness. The outcome of being meek would be persecution by the ungodly. The word can be translated "poor" (Job 24.4; cp. Mt 5.3) and is seen in perfection in the Messiah, Israel's King (Zech 9.9; Mt 11.29). It also has the thought of willing submission to the will of God. Thus they submit to God's chastisement, but the ungodly become more hardened by it. Meekness should characterise every believer today. The lowly are further described as seeking to carry out the law, yet they are entreated to strive after piety.

The primary appeal is to seek the Lord and it is applicable to all (Is 55.6)

- to unbelievers so that they might obtain His salvation, and to believers so that they might have a deepening sense of His presence and an increasing appreciation of His Person. Christians should take heed to the Lord's exhortation, "Seek ye first the kingdom of God, and his righteousness" (Mt 6.33). It is suggested that, in the context, seeking the Lord is explained by seeking righteousness and meekness. However, it seems that seeking righteousness and meekness is the inevitable outcome of seeking the Lord, i.e. seeking the Lord in reality expresses itself in right living and submission to the word of God (cp. Is 51.1,7). Although the earnest seeking of the meek would not divert the wrath of God they would find shelter in the One who was their refuge (Ps 27.5; 46.1; 76.9). The meaning of the prophet's name (whom the Lord hides) could well be an encouragement to the faithful (Amos 5.14-15). Despite the awful conditions prevailing and the dark outlook for Judah there was a remnant faithful to God and His word. However discouraging things might be today, with widespread indifference to eternal issues and lukewarmness in many believers, there are those who fear God and seek to obey His word.

The word translated "it may be" (ULAY - 194) seems to convey an element of doubt. In regard to this D. W. Baker states, "The theologically significant word concerning God's help in this verse is *perhaps* (cp. Ex 32.30; Amos 5.15). It could be suggested that 'perhaps' refers to the possibility of Judah's repentance and subsequent salvation, the uncertainty then being about the people's response rather than being about God…'Perhaps' safeguards God's sovereign freedom, but the fullness of who He is relieves this 'perhaps' of any anxiety of uncertainty, since God, as the just Judge of all creation, can be counted on to do what is right (Gen 18.25)…The response to God by his sinful people is commanded of them, and His response to them can safely be left in His own hands".

Verses 2.4–3.8: The Subjugation of Israel's Enemies, and Jehovah's Exposure of Judah's Sin

This new section of the prophecy is connected with the previous one by the word "For". The resumption of the theme of judgment, but now upon the surrounding enemies of Judah, is a further warning to the nation and is a fresh reason for repentance. Their pagan neighbours from every quarter would not escape the judgment of God (2.4-15). Since God will deal with the sin of His people, how much more will He punish the wickedness of their enemies (cp. 1 Pet 4.17-19). Nations from four directions are mentioned to indicate, once more, the universality of God's judgment and to emphasise that He is not only the God of Israel, but also of all nations. The proclamation of judgment on their enemies was a gracious warning to Judah, which went unheeded. Thus there is in this section the severe condemnation of Jerusalem (3.1-7). The section closes with the gathering of the nations to experience the fierce anger of the Lord (3.8).

Judgment upon the nations (vv.4-15)

Although God would use Gentile nations to chastise His people He would not disregard the excess cruelty used by them or their wickedness. Their inhumanity and delight in inflicting suffering upon the people of God would bring the severe judgment of God upon them. This is clearly seen in these verses in the judgment of Philistia (vv.4-7), Moab and Ammon (vv.8-11), Ethiopia (v.12), and Assyria (vv.13-15).

H. A. Ironside has stated, "This is all a picture of the time of the end. Judah then will be much in the position she occupied in Zephaniah's day - in the land, surrounded by enemies, a feeble remnant, crying, 'How long, O Lord?' the mass, apostate and swayed by Antichrist - and all this because of their rejection of Messiah when He came in grace. Therefore they must drink the cup of retribution to the dregs; but that cup emptied, the Lord will arise in His might as their Deliverer, and their enemies who have gloried over their helplessness shall become the objects of His avenging wrath, preparatory to the ushering in of the world-kingdom of our God and His Christ".

Philistia (vv.4-7)

The word "For" in v.4 not only connects what follows with the exhortation to repentance, but it also serves to introduce the threat of judgment upon the Gentiles which is stressed by the use of "Woe" in v.5. One of the ancient enemies of Israel is mentioned as the first nation upon which the coming judgment would fall. These verses not only relate to the overthrow of the Philistines, but also to the deliverance of the despised remnant of Israel which would return from captivity (v.7).

Zephaniah names only four of the main cities of the Philistines (1 Sam 6.17) just like Jeremiah (25.20; Azzah another name for Gaza), Amos (1.6-8), and Zechariah (9.5-6). There are two reasons suggested as to why Gath is left out.

1. Four were only necessary for the parallelism of the verse and to harmonise with the number of Gentile nations from the four points of the globe which represents the whole world (Keil & Delitzsch).

2. Gath had never fully recovered from the crushing defeat inflicted by Uzziah (2 Chr 26.6) and was, therefore, no longer a place of importance (F. C. Cook; Jamieson, Fausset & Brown).

The prophet begins with Gaza, in the south, and moves northward. Zephaniah makes a play on the names of the first and last of the cities to express the fate that awaited them (D. W. Baker; C. L. Feinberg). The basic meaning of "forsaken'" (AZAB - 5800) is to abandon, depart, or leave. Here the thought is that Gaza would be abandoned through the coming judgment and left desolate (cp. Jer 4.29). Ashkelon would be left waste as a result of the wrath of God (cp. Mal 1.3).

"Drive out" (GARASH - 1644) denotes expulsion and is used to express the divine wrath (cp. Hos 9.15). Here the human instruments that God will use in executing His judgment are viewed driving out the inhabitants of Ashdod. The time note "noon", being the hottest part of the day, implies a sudden and unexpected attack on the city (cp. 1 Kings 20.16-20; Jer 15.8). The unsuspecting inhabitants would be swiftly overcome and driven out of the city (cp. Num 22.6). It has been suggested that noon might indicate that the attack upon Ashdod and the expulsion of its inhabitants would be so rapid that it will only take half a day.

The word translated "rooted up" (AQAR - 6131) is used seven times in the Old Testament and is elsewhere translated "dig down" (Gen 49.6), "hough" (Josh 11.6,9; 2 Sam 8.4), and "pluck up" (Eccl 3.2). It seems to convey the idea of both removal and destruction. Ekron that appeared to be strong and unmovable would be destroyed in the outpouring of the indignation of God. There appears to be a parallel development in the verse moving from the forsaking of Gaza to the desolation of Ashkelon, and from the expulsion of Ashdod to the uprooting of Ekron.

It is not only the cities which are in view for judgment, but also the whole land of the Philistines as the "Woe" of v.5 clearly indicates. The "coast" (HEBEL - 2256) means a rope or line which may be used to measure (Zech 2.1) and so, by implication, comes to mean the portion of land measured (1 Chr 16.18; Ps 78.55). Here it refers to the strip of land by the Mediterranean Sea which was occupied by the Philistines. Their occupation of this coastal region dates back to at least the time of Abraham (Gen 21.32-34). Zephaniah refers to the inhabitants of the land as Cherethites (cp. Ezek 25.16). From 1 Samuel 30.14-16 it seems that the name is linked with the Philistines and may well be a province of Philistia. A section of David's special warriors, probably his bodyguards, were called the Cherethites (2 Sam 8.18; 15.18). Although it would seem unlikely that these were Philistines it is probable that during his stay in their land (1 Sam 27-30) a band of Philistines attached themselves to David and were loyal to him. Many commentators have suggested the name refers to the people of the Cretans thus linking them with the island of Crete (Caphtor - 3731; Deut 2.23; Jer 47.4; Amos 9.7). This would correspond with the suggested meaning of Philistine (an emigrant). However, C. F. Keil states, "The origin of this name, which is selected both here and in Ezekiel 25.16 with a play upon the appellative signification, is involved in obscurity; for...there is no valid authority for the derivation which is now current, viz., from the island of *Crete*". It is suggested that Cherethites (3774) means executioners, coming from the root word KARAT (3772) meaning to cut off.

The nature of the word of the Lord against the Philistines is described at the close of v.5. How dreadful to hear these solemn words. God will hold responsible those who ignore His word (Deut 18.19) and they will be judged by that very word which is despised and rejected (Jn 12.48). Here the implication is that the destruction of the Philistines is announced by God Himself.

The name Canaan is used to indicate that Philistia would suffer its fate by the extermination of its inhabitants and the possession of the land by Israel (Ex 6.4; 15.15). They considered themselves secure, but the judgment of God would swiftly pass through the land, from the south to the north, with catastrophic effect, leaving it desolate (cp. Jer 47.4-7; Ezek 25.15-17).

The land which would be depopulated by the judgment of God (v.5) would not remain completely desolate. It would become the habitation of nomadic shepherds and be a place of pasture and folds for their flocks.

The middle part of v.6 presents a difficulty because of the word "cottages" (KARAH - 3741). It only occurs here in the Old Testament and seems to be of doubtful meaning, but it is suggested that the word is derived from the verb KARA (3738) meaning to dig (Gen 26.25; Ex 21.33). Thus, it is suggested that, "to protect themselves from the heat of the sun, Nomadic shepherds would make themselves shelters out of caves or huts dug out of the ground" (see C. J. Barber and Keil & Delitzsch). However, because it might be derived from a word used in regard to digging wells, F. C. Cook states that it "may then be understood of such *wells* as shepherds would sink who felt that the land was secure, or trenches dug for the greater safety of sheep-folds. Such a meaning is simpler than that given by some of *digging* underground dwellings as shelters from the heat. It would, perhaps, be better translated by *wells* or *diggings*". The land which was then so thickly populated and full of activity would only be occupied by wandering shepherds tending their flocks.

The mention of the remnant of the house of Judah in v.7 manifests both the severity of God's judgment and the faithfulness of God to His covenant with Israel. The severity of the judgment of God would not only leave the land of the Philistines desolate, but would also reduce Judah to only a remnant, just a small company. The facet of hope for Judah is implied in the remnant, since God's punishment would not totally obliterate the nation. Destruction would come, but not annihilation. Thus grace and mercy is extended to Israel. The word translated "remnant" (SHᵉERIT - 7611) means the remaining portion. It generally refers to the remnant of Israel although it is sometimes used of other nations (1 Chr 4.43; Jer 25.20). It is used of a historic remnant - a remnant out of Israel which was in existence during the life time of the speaker or writer (Is 37.4,32). However, the word "finds what may be its most intriguing usage as a prophetic technical term representing the final future remnant of Israel, namely, those Jews who survive to the end of this present age upon whom God showers all of the blessings which have been promised to Israel through the centuries" (TWOT). While having a near application, the passage also looks on to its final fulfilment which is yet future (Jer 23.3; Micah 2.12; Zech 8.6,12). The Philistian land by the sea would become the possession of those who remained of Judah after the judgment (cp. Obad v.19). It is suggested that the remnant is viewed here as the Lord's flock which, under His care, would feed upon the land and lie down in the houses of Ashkelon. Under the guiding hand of the divine Shepherd they would be led to green pastures where their needs would be fully met and their security assured. The expression "they shall feed thereupon" may well indicate that the land would become a pasture where the remnant would feed their flocks.

Ashkelon, which would be made desolate (v.4), is mentioned as representative of all the cities. The remnant would possess all the dwelling places and rest in safety in their ancient enemy's land. The reason for such a change is given as the visitation of Jehovah their God, which also brings the section (vv.4-7) to a close. Here the prophet introduces another name of God, Elohim (430), which represents the plurality of Persons in the Trinity of the Godhead.

The basic meaning of "visit" (PAQAD - 6485) is to exercise oversight, and contains the thought of taking action which brings about a considerable change. The change for the remnant would be a change from oppression, turmoil and danger to tranquillity and safety (cp. Ex 4.31; Zech 10.3). At the close of this section of judgment upon the Philistines the prophet predicts the captivity and restoration of the people of God, and their possession of the promised land of which the land of the Philistines was part. Such a promise has not yet been fulfilled, but awaits its fulfilment when Israel will be restored and blessed at the coming and in the reign of their Messiah, the Lord Jesus Christ.

Moab and Amon (vv.8-11)

God continues to speak through Zephaniah, but the threat of judgment now focuses on Moab and Ammon, nations to the east of Judah. Both nations had a shameful beginning, being descendants from Lot, Abraham's nephew, which meant that they were thus ethnically related to Israel (Gen 12.4-5; 19.30-38). However, they were opposed to Israel and manifested their hostility on many occasions. As far back as Moses, before Israel entered into the promised land, Balak, king of Moab sought to curse Israel, through Balaam (Num 22.4-6, 15-17). When Israel was in the land both nations sought to oppress Israel separately (Moab - Judg 3.12-14; 2 Kings 3; Ammon - Judg 10.6-9; 11.4-5; 1 Sam 11; 2 Sam 10.1-6) and together (2 Chr 20.1). Even on their return from captivity Tobiah the Ammonite was opposed to Judah (Neh 2.10,19; 4.3). It is only here that they are jointly the subject of divine judgment although judgment is pronounced upon them separately in other prophetic passages (Moab - Is 15-16; Jer 48; Ezek 25.8-11; Amos 2.1-3; Ammon - Jer 49.1-6; Ezek 25.1-7; Amos 1.13-15).

The attitude and actions of these nations towards Israel had not gone unnoticed for, unknown to men, God had taken notice of their opposition to his people. "Heard" (SHAMA - 8085) not only indicates listening to or paying attention to something, but also involves a fitting response as in this passage (cp. Ezek 21.28). Because God did not immediately punish Moab and Ammon it did not mean that He had overlooked their treatment of Israel. God will always deal righteously with those who oppose His people - "Seeing it is a righteous thing with God to recompense tribulation to them that trouble you" (2 Thess 1.6).

The believer should not be characterised by a spirit of retaliation, but should seek to live peaceably with all and seek the blessing of those who oppose (Lk 6.28-31; Rom 12.17-21; 1 Thess 5.15). It is important to appreciate that God will judge sin in His own time. It must also be appreciated that God is not only a witness to the words and actions of men, but also to the intents of the heart - the desires and motives of men (Phil 1.8; 1 Thess 2.5,10). Men look on the outward appearance but the Lord looks on the heart (1 Sam 16.7), for He alone is able to search the heart of man (Jer 17.9-10). This is true not only in relation to the ungodly but also in regard to believers whose motives will be brought to light at the Judgment Seat of Christ (1 Cor 4.5). It is also true in relation to local assemblies (Rev 2 & 3).

In regard to the reproach and revilings of these nations C. F. Keil states, "The charge refers to the hostile attitude assumed by both tribes at all times towards the nation of God, which they manifested both in word and deed, as often as the latter was brought into trouble and distress". The verbal scorn and revilings against the people of God (1 Sam 11.1-2; Neh 4.3-5) were really against the living God (2 Kings 19.4,16; cp. 1 Sam 17.10, 45-46). They were not to fear such reproach from men (Is 51.7) for God would visit these nations with judgment and would remove all reproach from His people (Ezek 36.15). Thus, although God would allow His people to be abused with verbal reviling (Is 43.28) He would nevertheless comfort and encourage them when it took place (Is 51.7).

It is stated that the last clause of v.8 could also be verbal, but the mention of "borders" suggests encroachment upon the land of Israel. These nations exalted themselves by violating the borders of Israel, invading the land to enlarge their own territory (Jer 49.1; Amos 1.13). The land of Israel was given to them by God (Josh 2.9) and their borders were determined by Him (Num 34). In violating those borders to enlarge their coasts, Moab and Ammon were challenging Israel's right to the land and were rebelling against the decision of God who had "divided to the nations their inheritance" (Deut 32.8). The pride and haughtiness of Moab and Ammon in exalting themselves above the people of God is emphasised and condemned by the prophets Isaiah (16.6; 25.11) and Jeremiah (48.29-30). The sin of pride is still prevalent today and is the cause of many evils and many a downfall.

The resulting judgment of these two nations is announced in solemn terms, revealing that they would be completely destroyed. The solemn oath, "as I live", emphasises here the irrevocable sentence passed by God. This specific oath is only found in the prophetic books in the Old Testament, and out of nineteen occurrences in total, sixteen are found in Ezekiel. It is only found once in the New Testament where the Apostle Paul quotes from Isaiah 45.23 (Rom 14.11). Similar oaths are found in Numbers 14.21,28 and Jeremiah 49.13. The certainty of retribution is further stressed by the use of the title "The Lord of hosts" which indicates that He is the Divine Warrior with the power to carry out His threats. It is a Jehovah title (Jehovah Sabaoth) indicating majesty and sovereignty and is first used in 1 Samuel 1.3. The Lord, who is over all, had righteously determined the destruction of those nations. His love for, and His faithfulness to, His people is shown in the expression "the God of Israel", and thus He would avenge the insults and wrongs done to them. The use of both titles shows that He is the universal Sovereign who has covenant relationship with Israel. The comparison used in relation to the judgment of Moab and the children of Ammon is very apt since it goes back to their origin in the days following the destruction of Sodom and Gomorrah. It would also be a forceful threat since they dwelt in the vicinity of the ruins of these cities which would be a vivid reminder of the solemn consequences of sin. This prediction did not mean that these nations would be destroyed in the same manner, by fire from heaven, but that their judgment would be complete (cp. Is 1.9; 13.19; Jer 49.17-18; Amos 4.11). It is clear from its connection with the following verses that this judgment is still future. Their land would no longer be fruitful, but would become desolate. The three aspects of the lands of Moab and Ammon mentioned are intended to link with the simile of Sodom and Gomorrah - vegetation (Gen 13.10-12; 19.25), salt (Gen 19.26), and desolation (Jer 49.18).

The word "breeding" (MIMSHAQ - 4476) only occurs here and means possession. Thus the possession of nettles indicates a land overrun with them (cp. Job 30.7; Prov 24.31). It is stated that the stinging nettle, which flourishes in waste places, is in view. The mention of salt pits suggests land sterile and barren (Judg 9.45; Jer 17.6). The prophecy further states that the lands would not be restored to productivity again, but would remain desolate for ever, as a reminder of the end of all who magnify themselves against God - "And whosoever shall exalt himself shall be abased; and he that shall humble himself shall be exalted" (Mt 23.12; Lk 14.11; 18.14).

Whereas the first part of v.9 is taken up with the lands of Moab and Ammon, the latter part refers to the people who will be taken as a possession by the remnant of the people of God. As C. F. Keil points out, it is not likely that land left to perpetual desolation would be considered as spoil or as a possession. The thought here seems to be the same as in Isaiah 14.2 implying that the people of Moab and Ammon would become the possession of the Israelites in the sense of being their servants (cp. Is 60.9-10; 61.5). As with the Philistines (v.7) so here the remnant of the people of God will be the beneficiaries of the judgment meted out to their enemies.

In v.10 Zephaniah summarises the threat of Jehovah, recalling that judgment is pronounced because of pride. Thus the details of v.8 are reiterated. It was pride which caused the Moabites and Ammonites to revile Israel and led them to magnify themselves against the chosen people of God. This pride would be their downfall - "Pride goeth before destruction, and an haughty spirit before a fall" (Prov 16.18). This is applicable to individuals as well as nations (Prov 29.23). Pride, which is a characteristic of the ungodly (Rom 1.30), is hateful to God (Prov 6.16-19) and should not be found in the believer (Phil 2.3; cp. James 4.6; 1 Pet 5.5). Pride is opposite to meekness which characterises those who will inherit the earth (Ps 37.11; Mt 5.5). One notes that in vv.8-9 the expression "my people" occurs three times, but now they are called "the people of the Lord of hosts". David Newell states, "Amazingly, the very people God has condemned for idolatry and departure are now described as 'the people of the Lord of hosts' (2.10)! Like David (1 Sam 17.36), Zephaniah can see that faithless nation as God sees them, in the light of His irrevocable purpose. Truly, 'the gifts and calling of God are without repentance' (Rom 11.29), and, as He will faithfully keep His promises to Israel, despite their failure, so too will He keep His word to the believer in Christ...That He is able to fulfil His word to the letter is implicit in the glorious title 'the Lord of hosts' (one sadly and irreverently mangled by translations like the NIV)". As previously noted, the title "the Lord of hosts" indicates the universal sovereignty and power of God, and here it intimates that the judgment predicted is part of His universal dealings with the world which is confirmed by v.11. Thus, although there may have been partial fulfilment in the past it must await the time of Israel's complete restoration and conversion at the coming of their Messiah for its final and complete fulfilment.

Although the first clause of v.11 continues with the judgment of the two eastern neighbours of Judah it prepares the way for encompassing the whole world in the rest of the verse. It not only concludes the previous threat of judgment, but also introduces the purpose for it before judgment upon the northern and southern neighbours of Judah is introduced. Jehovah would be awesome as He revealed Himself as the supreme Judge in power and majesty. The expression "unto them" indicates that He would come in judgment thus driving terror into the hearts of the Moabites and Ammonites who would share the fate of all who oppose God and His people. One needs to be continually reminded that God records man's actions and discerns his thoughts, and no one can escape the consequences of their sin apart from faith in Christ. The prophet's vision widens as he reveals the ultimate purpose of such judgment. It was to overthrow wickedness and idolatry, and to remove ungodly men in order to bring peace to a troubled world. Just as in the exodus Jehovah executed judgment upon the gods of the Egyptians (Ex 12.12), so He will do worldwide.

The verb "famish" (RAZA - 7329) is rare in the Old Testament and means to make lean, or to impoverish. The idea seems to be that as a result of judgment there would be no more idolaters found to offer sacrifices to the idol gods and thus the gods they worshipped would disappear. Jehovah thus would demonstrate the emptiness and lifelessness of such gods (Micah 5.12-13). Men make idols which have no existence apart from in the minds of those who worship and serve them (1 Cor 8.4-6). The expression "gods of the earth" implies that their existence was only on earth in contrast to the true and living God whose dwelling place was heaven. The removal of all idolatry will result in the universal worship of God, since the "isles of the heathen" denotes the far distant regions of the pagan nations. All false gods will be removed and all men will worship the one true God. In regard to the phrase "every one from his place" C. F. Keil explains that, "The meaning [of *mimm^eqomo*, coming from his place] is not that the nations will worship Jehovah at their own place, in their own lands, in contradistinction to Micah 4.1; Zechariah 14.16, and other passages, where the nations go on pilgrimage to Mount Zion (Hitzig); but their going to Jerusalem is implied...though it is not brought prominently out, as being unessential to the thought". However, W. J. Deane is of the view that "Everyone shall worship God in his own place and country; the Lord shall be universally recognised, and His worship shall no longer be confined to one temple or one land, but wherever men dwell there shall they offer their homage and adoration (cp. Is 19.18,19; Mal 1.11, where the same truth is signified)", and C. L. Feinberg states, "Then will men worship the one true God, each from his place, that is, each in the place where he lives, thus making worship of the Lord universal" (see also Jamieson, Fausset & Brown). D. W. Baker acknowledges the possibility of either. It seems that the second interpretation is more in keeping with the context.

The prophet looks on past this present period and past the events of the Great Tribulation to the end of Daniel's 70th week, to the millennial reign of Christ and foresees that time when worldwide worship will ascend to God. This is only made possible by the death of the Lord Jesus Christ. Every blessing bestowed upon man displays the grace of God and is based upon the finished work of Christ at Calvary. It does not mean, as is true today, that worship ascends to God from every country, but that all in every nation will worship Him. After the coming again of the Lord Jesus Christ to the earth, conditions will exist so that the whole world will be united in worship and in serving the one and only God.

Ethiopia (v.12)

After the reason given in the previous verse for the famishing of the gods of the earth, two other nations are mentioned in vv.12-15 to confirm that all the pagan nations of the world will come under the judgment of God. Jehovah now turns from the west and east of Judah and directs His attention towards a nation to the south. Because of the close link between Ethiopia and Egypt, and the fact that the Ethiopians ruled Egypt (720-654 BC) some commentators think that Egypt is in view here. D. W. Baker gives as his opinion that "This is probably a reference to Egypt, one of the two major powers, who had herself been subject in the late eighth and early seventh centuries BC to the Ethiopian Twenty-fifth Dynasty (cp. 3.10; Is 11.11; 18; 20.3-6). It could, however, refer to the defeat of Egypt by Cambyses II of Persia in 525 BC". However, most commentators agree that

Ethiopia (KUSH - 3568), whose people inhabited the land south and south-west of Egypt, is in view (the area known today as Sudan, Somalia, and Eritrea). Since Zephaniah's prophecy is dated in Josiah's reign this also favours Ethiopia. The Ethiopians were the descendants of Cush, the son of Ham (Gen 10.6). The land is mentioned as far back as Genesis 2.13. They were the most southerly nation in contact with Judah, and as such they are representative of the pagan nations dwelling in the south. The expression "Ye Ethiopians also" indicates that, just as the nations in the west and east of Judah had been before the tribunal of God and judgment had been passed, so it was with them. Ethiopia had indeed threatened and invaded Judah (2 Chr 14.9-13) showing its hostility against God's chosen people. There is a sudden change in the verse from Jehovah addressing the Ethiopians to His statement declaring what would be the result of His judgment - a change from the second person to the third person, since the literal rendering would be, "Ye Ethiopians also, slain by (or the slain of) my sword are they". Similar instances of a sudden change are found in the Old Testament (cp. 3.18; Zech 3.8). The second person is used at the tribunal and the third person in the execution of the judgment passed.

Jehovah's sword speaks of the instrument He uses to carry out His judgment (Is 34.5-6; 66.16). The idea is that the land would be ravished and the Ethiopians would perish. However powerful they may have been they would learn that Jehovah was sovereign and no nation or individual could escape His righteous judgment. Although only one short verse deals with the Ethiopians, it pinpoints the important fact that, whatever the instrument used, God is the executor of all righteous judgment. Men may not be aware of God's involvement in the affairs of this world, but Christians know that God is upon the throne and that He will fulfil His purposes. However, it is possible to have this knowledge without living in the good of it by not allowing it to have a practical affect upon one's life. The children of God should appreciate that in the varying circumstances of life God is in control and His grace is sufficient to enable them to live for His pleasure and glory.

Assyria (vv. 13-15)

The prophet now turns his attention away from the south of Judah and directs his gaze northward. It was from that direction that the invading armies of Syria, Babylon, and Assyria came. Assyria and Babylon took advantage of the fertile land north of Israel and Judah when they invaded the people of God rather than attempt to cross the desert. The major power of that day, Assyria, which was still flourishing, together with its capital city, now becomes the focus of the prophecy. Its invading hordes had already taken into captivity the kingdom of Israel (2 Kings 17.1-6). This prophecy brings to an end the summary of God's vengeance against the Gentile nations from every quarter. God had used Assyria in the past as His instrument in chastising Israel, but they themselves were guilty before God (Is 10.5-12). The significance here is that divine judgment is not only general in embracing all, but is also specific in that it responds to the particular guilt of each nation. The Lord, who is righteous, will deal righteously with each nation and each individual (Gen 18.25).

Just as in ch.1, so here Jehovah stretches out His hand in judgment (Is 5.25; Jer 15.6; Ezek 6.14), but here against the Gentile power of the north instead of against Judah (1.4). It is stated that the Hebrew verbs in v.13 are in the optative mood which means that the statements are expressed in the form of a wish. Since Zephaniah was writing under the inspiration of the Holy Spirit (2 Pet 1.21) it could not mean that there was any doubt as to the fulfilment of these statements, but may imply that the prophet's desire was in harmony with the divine purpose. Although Assyria was to the north-east of Judah it was regarded as a northern power. Its destruction is predicted in other prophetic passages (Is 10.12; Ezek 31.11). The prophecy of Nahum gives a more detailed treatment of Assyria's capital city, Nineveh. Here it is briefly mentioned, but its judgment would be decisive. The inhabitants, known for their bestial brutality, would suffer the consequences of their actions. The desolation of the city, one of the oldest cities of the world (Gen 10.11), would result in it becoming dry and like a wilderness. "Dry" (SIYA - 6723) and "wilderness" (MIDBAR - 4057) are used together several times in the prophetic books (Is 41.18; Jer 50.12; Ezek 19.13). They are also given as "solitary" and "wilderness" in Isaiah 35.1, and "drought" and "wilderness" in Jeremiah 2.6. The idea seems to be that the land, being dry, becomes uninhabited. It has been pointed out that this is remarkable since at the time of Zephaniah's prediction Nineveh's boast was its irrigation scheme - "Assyria was greatly indebted for its remarkable fertility to a very successful system of artificial irrigation, and when this was not maintained, great tracts soon relapsed into a wilderness" (W. J. Deane; C. L. Feinberg).

The grandeur of Nineveh would be reduced to ruin and its desolation is emphasised in v.14 with the city becoming a dwelling place for animals and birds. Concerning the occupants of the city, D. W. Baker includes domestic flocks and wild creatures stating that "The two groups are apparently meant to comprise the totality of the animal realm, both domestic and wild (cp. Gen 1.24; Ps 50.10)". However, F. C. Cook states, "In the absence of man the site is taken possession of by *flocks*, here, not sheep or oxen, but herds of wild beasts (cp. Is 13.20-22), as is intimated in the phrase that immediately follows, *all the beasts of the nations*, literally, *all the beasts of nation*, which may mean, such as herd together. So *nation* is used of locusts in Joel (1.6), who calls them also a *people* (2.2) (cp. Prov 30.25,26). The form of the word for *beast* is ancient, the same as that found in the place in which it first occurs (Gen 1.24). It always means wild animals" (see also Keil & Delitzsch and W. J. Deane).

The description of the city's devastation favours wild beasts making it their habitation. The wild beasts are joined by other inhabitants of the sky. The identity of the birds mentioned is disputed, but both are also associated with waste and uninhabited land in Isaiah 34.11. "Cormorant" (QAAT - 6893) only occurs as such elsewhere in Isaiah 34.11, and both Strong's Concordance and the Theological Wordbook of the Old Testament suggest the probable meaning as "pelican" which most commentators accept. The word for "bittern" (QIPPOD - 7090) only occurs in Isaiah 14.23 and 34.11. Strong's Concordance states that perhaps the meaning is bittern, the Theological Wordbook of the Old Testament gives porcupine, and some commentators prefer hedgehog as its meaning. However, it seems clear from the following statements that both words refer to some kind of bird which make its resting places in the ruins of the city. The picture of general destruction and desolation is now changed to specific details - the upper lintels, windows, thresholds, and cedar work (panels). The upper lintels refer to the capitals (tops) of columns (pillars) which may have been left standing when the temples, palaces and mansions were destroyed. The fact that birds, which in normal circumstances would not dwell in cities, inhabit the deserted city emphasise again the desolation of Nineveh. Their melancholy singing or calling would be heard from the windows of the ruined buildings. Answering to the desolation in the upper parts of the ruined city is desolation in the lower parts – "in the thresholds". The buildings would be deserted and no human would pass over the thresholds since they would be covered with ruin and rubbish. The last statement of v.14 connects with the opening statement of v.13 indicating the complete destruction of Nineveh under the hand of Jehovah stretched out in judgment.

The word translated "cedar work" (ARZA - 731) is only found here and refers to the costly cedar panels in stately buildings which would be torn away from the walls and ceilings exposing them to the weather. The prediction of such devastation was intended to be both a warning and a consolation to Judah. Jehovah would not overlook the guilt of the Gentile nations, neither would He overlook sin in His own people. Since He has power to destroy the major power, Assyria, and its capital city, He is able not only to avenge His people, but also to protect and deliver them from such powers. How good to know that, "greater is he that is in you, than he that is in the world" (1 Jn 4.4).

Verse 15 opens by contrasting the uninhabited ruined city of v.14 with what it was before its destruction. A similar contrast is made by Isaiah in regard to Zion (22.2) and Tyre (23.7-9). There seems to be, in these opening statements, a measure of irony or scorn and also the reason is given for the overthrow of Nineveh. "Rejoicing" (ALLIZ - 5947) describes "an emotion of joy which finds expression in singing and shouting...When applied to the wicked (Ps 94.3) and Israel's foes (2 Sam 1.20; Is 23.12; Jer 50.11) it depicts a kind of gloating" (TWOT). This exulting and gloating was linked with a false sense of security which is implied in the expression "dwelt carelessly". While "carelessly" (BETAH - 983) is used of the safety God gives to those who trust Him (Ps 4.8; Jer 32.37), it is also used of a temporal sense of security resulting in carelessness (Is 47.8; Ezek 30.9). In Nineveh's godlessness she boasted, "I am, and there is none beside me" (cp. Is 47.8), which not only implied her false sense of security and self-sufficiency, but also her uniqueness. Her claims were, therefore, blasphemous for they usurped attributes that belong to God alone (Is 45.5-6, 21-22). Thus Nineveh deified herself, but just like the coming king of Babylon (Is 14.4-23) she would be brought down and destroyed. The greatness and power of Assyria and its capital city was known worldwide, but she would soon be ripe for judgment.

Nineveh is a picture of man in his self-sufficiency and arrogance, indifferent to God. She is a picture of man's pride and independence, as he lives in pleasure, self-centred and self-satisfied. However, man cannot succeed or know true satisfaction without God. In his pride man seeks supremacy, but, just like Nineveh, he will be brought to ruin and will learn that God alone is sovereign and omnipotent. As sovereign, God can do what He likes when He pleases, but it will always be in keeping with His holy character. Men, including Christians, have no right to question Him as to His will and ways. This spirit of pride and self-sufficiency, which is hateful to God, can characterise Christians - "I am rich, and increased with goods, and have need of nothing..." (Rev 3.17). It was a spirit of spiritual self-sufficiency that marked the Laodiceans which revealed that dependence upon the Lord was absent. Self-satisfaction not only results in one becoming self-centred and independent of God, but it also blinds the mind to one's true spiritual condition before God - "...and knowest not that thou are wretched, and miserable, and poor, and blind, and naked" (Rev 3.17). It is sad when a believer, through worldliness or materialism, becomes proud and self-sufficient, but tragic when one is characterised by spiritual pride and self-satisfaction. There will always be a need, down here, for spiritual development in a believer's life and thus dependence upon the Lord. His word and the gracious Spirit of God are essential.

Because of pride and arrogance the rejoicing city would be reduced to such desolation that it becomes a place for wild beasts. The suddenness and extent of its destruction would cause even passers-by to be amazed and to pour scorn upon it. The wagging of the hand indicates contempt and is a gesture of dismissal, indicating that judgment was deserved. The section begins in v.13 with Jehovah's hand stretched out in judgment and it closes here with man's hand raised at its fulfilment.

C. J. Barber states, "The exactness with which God's word has been fulfilled in ages past gives valuable clues as to how it will be fulfilled in the future. God's judgments are precise. His knowledge is absolute. His will is all-powerful. The pride of Nineveh was abased. As soon as the cup of her iniquity was full, she perished. The exactness with which this prophecy was fulfilled provides a startling preview of the overthrow of nations and kingdoms at the end times. Such contemplation should fill each God-fearing believer with reverential awe. All that the Lord has spoken of will assuredly come to pass. And it will happen exactly as He said it would". Believers can have absolute confidence in God and in His word.

This chapter shows that God, who is infinitely holy, cannot overlook sin. His judgment upon the Gentile nations, just as upon Judah and Jerusalem, is because of their guilt, and is thus in keeping with His righteous character. This solemn fact is not only applicable to nations, but also to individuals. All are sinners (Rom 3.23) and are guilty before God (Rom 3.19), thus every person is exposed to His righteous judgment. However, God, in His infinite love (Jn 3.16), has provided a way whereby the sinner can escape the righteous judgment deserved. The coming of the Lord Jesus Christ, the Son of God (Israel's true Messiah), into the world and His death upon the cross has met the righteous claims of God in regard to sin. This enables God to justify all those who repent and put their faith in His Son, the Lord Jesus Christ (Rom 3.24-26; 5.1).

ZEPHANIAH 3

Verses 2.4–3.8: The Subjugation of Israel's Enemies, and Jehovah's Exposure of Judah's Sin (continued)

After declaring the judgment of God upon the Gentile nations around Judah in the previous chapter, the prophet now returns to the people of God. Since Judah, and particularly Jerusalem, was so privileged by having the law of God and His dwelling place, the temple, in their midst, much more was required of them - obedience to the law, and reverence. However, their continued rebellion and sinful condition demanded the judgment of God (vv.1-7). His justice, manifested in His dealings with His people, will also be displayed in the pouring out of His wrath on all the nations (v.8). The result of such judgment upon all will be salvation for the Gentiles (v.9) and the restoration of Israel to a place of favour and blessing (vv.10-20).

Jehovah's exposure of Judah's sin (vv.1-8)

The prophecy retraces the same ground covered in the previous chapters in pronouncing judgment, first upon the people of God and then upon the Gentiles. The emphasis seems to be upon the necessity of judgment to bring salvation and security to Israel. God's dealings with His earthly people in righteousness (vv.1-7) will also involve His judgment upon all nations (v.8).

Jerusalem's condition (vv.1-7)

Jehovah, having unfolded what He was about to do to the nations surrounding Judah, now showed grace towards His people by warning them of approaching judgment. In this way He further appealed to them to repent. The solemn message of judgment was, therefore, not yet finished. The identity of the city here is not mentioned, but the context clearly indicates that it is Jerusalem. The disobedience and lack of trust in Jehovah (v.2) who is in their midst (v.5), indicates a close association with Him, which supports identifying the city as Jerusalem. It is suggested that the city is not named so that the recipients of the prophecy, the people of Judah, would at first believe that Nineveh was still in view and would thus acquiesce with the condemnation. However, they would soon realise that it was their own capital city, Jerusalem, which was referred to and that they themselves were being condemned, not their enemies. The claims of Jehovah upon His people were being ignored and the time had come to confront them with their rebellion (vv.1-4), their shamelessness (v.5), and their refusal to repent (vv.6-7). Instead of being in contrast to Nineveh, and faithful to God and His word, Jerusalem was the equal of that pagan city in its sinfulness (Is 1.21; Jer 2.20). The moral and spiritual conditions prevailing in the very place where God had set His name were now contrary to His unchanging character and to His claims upon His people.

It is one thing for these conditions to prevail in the nations around, but how solemn to see these conditions in Jerusalem. Today these conditions are prevalent in the world, but how dreadful to see them in believers or in a local church where believers claim to be gathered to His name. Surely the conditions prevailing among the people of God in Zephaniah's day are a voice to Christians today and there are solemn lessons to learn. Here Zephaniah gives the reasons for the dreadful condition of the nation.

The city of Jerusalem, being representative of the nation, is described as being no better than Nineveh, showing how far she was from God and how low she had become morally. Instead of being the city of peace she had become the city of oppression. It is not surprising then that the prophet begins with the emphatic expression, "Woe to her". This main section begins with woe upon the Gentiles and ends with woe upon the people of God. The utterance of "Woe" (HOY - 1945) indicates a lamentation over the dreadful condition of Jerusalem before God which calls for His judgment.

The word "filthy" (MARA - 4754) is from "a primitive root; to *rebel*" (Strong's Concordance). C. F. Keil demonstrates that as used here it has the idea of holding one's self straight against another, indicating opposition. Thus the rebellious spirit of Judah in holding herself against the claims of God is in view (cp. Jer 4.17; 5.23). It stresses the defiance of the nation in the face of His appeals through the prophets (Jer 6.17; 26.4-6; 44.16).

"Polluted" (GAAL - 1351) means to be stained or defiled. Here it is the thought of being irrevocably stained by setting aside the word of God (cp. Jer 25.3-4) and by sinful practices (Neh 13.29; Is 59.2). The inevitable consequence of rebellion is the practice of sin resulting in a loathsome state. Although GAAL here must be distinguished from the word GAAL, to redeem (1350; see also TWOT at 301, 300), it can be linked with it, showing that the very people who had been in the good of God's redemption (Ex 15.13) had now rebelled against Him. They had continued in their departure from His precepts to the point of becoming abhorrent in His sight, and had thus incurred His condemnation and judgment. Their true moral condition was in direct contrast to the holiness professed by their outward ceremonial observances. It is one thing to profess faith in Christ, it is another to demonstrate the genuineness of that faith in one's life (James 2.17-18,26). David Newell states, "If Nineveh was stained by carnal joy and carelessness, Jerusalem was worse still, guilty of wilful disobedience to her God (3.1). Greater light brings greater accountability (Lk 12.48b). It is sadly possible to possess truth without practising it, and the faithful ministry of the word is today becoming increasingly marginalised by the drift towards entertainment, easy-going compromise (usually paraded under the banner of 'love'), and religious respectability". The city in her defilement becomes characterised by oppression. One has translated the verse as: "Woe, rebellious and polluted! Thou oppressing city!"

The word translated "oppressing" (YANA - 3238) means to vex, oppress or do wrong to someone. It is used particularly in relation to strangers (Ex 22.21) and the poor (Ezek 18.12; 22.29), but also of one's neighbour (Lev 25.14,17). In setting aside the teaching of the law their moral standard was removed which resulted in lack of respect for others. Thus the rich exploited the poor, the strong took advantage of the weak, and strangers were mistreated (cp. Jer 22.3).

The word of God not only deals with man's relationship and responsibility to God, but also with his relationship and responsibility to others. To set aside the moral standard set out in the word of God is to destroy the true structure of society. The inhabitants of Jerusalem were rebellious because they would not submit to the law of God, they were polluted in themselves because they persisted in sinful practices, and they were oppressive because they disregarded the rights of others. These charges against Jerusalem are vindicated and the cause of them explained in vv.2-4.

A fourfold reason for the moral and spiritual condition of v.1 is given in v.2. They were disobedient, defiant, distrusting, and at a distance from God. How intensely solemn are these indictments. The four statements indicate the extent of Jerusalem's departure from the divine intention. The city of God's dwelling place on earth which should have reverenced Him and His word had degenerated into lawlessness and indifference. God's dwelling place today, the local assembly, should be characterised by unquestioning obedience to the word of God. The opening expression, "She obeyed not the voice", clearly refers to their refusal to give attention to the law and the word of God spoken to them through the prophets (cp. Jer 3.13; 22.21). All their ceremonial observances were of no value before God as their wilful disobedience annulled them - "Behold, to obey is better than sacrifice, and to hearken than the fat of rams" (1 Sam 15.22). God speaks to men through His word and most, even some believers, ignore His voice with a "We don't care" attitude. Disobedience is a characteristic of fallen man and is dreadful in the sight of God. It is the habit or principle of the life received from Adam (Eph 2.2). When people are saved they receive a new kind of life, the habit or principle of which is obedience (1 Pet 1.14). Christians ought to have a reverential fear for the word of God and should be swift to obey it - "to this man will I look, even to him that is poor and of a contrite spirit, and trembleth at my word" (Is 66.2). Well might believers search their hearts before God in relation to this and ask themselves, "Have we that reverence, and do we obey the word of God?".

"Correction" (MUSAR - 4148) means discipline which is intended to educate, and so it is also translated "chastising" (Prov 3.11) and "instruction" (Prov 1.7-8; 15.32). Thus the discipline of God is not to be considered in a negative way, but as beneficial (Prov 13.24). Such instruction is despised by fools (Prov 1.7) which results in poverty (Prov 13.18), but is received by the wise (Prov 13.1; 19.20). "Behold, happy is the man whom God correcteth: therefore despise not thou the chastening of the Almighty" (Job 5.17). When God's hand was upon Jerusalem in chastisement she refused to accept it (Prov 15.10) and therefore failed to learn the lessons He was seeking to teach (cp. Jer 2.30; 5.3; 17.23; 32.33). They deliberately refused instruction as to the right path and rejected correction as to the wrong path. Consequently, spiritual, social and moral degradation followed and they remained unrepentant.

In many lands long enlightened by the gospel the same attitude prevails, with God set aside and His word unheeded. Do all Christians today gladly accept correction from the word of God and willingly receive the chastening of God? The danger is that believers become insensitive to sin and fail to accept the discipline of God. The result being that they can scarcely be distinguished from unbelievers. The children of God ought not to despise the discipline of God since it is profitable, so that they might partake of His holiness (Heb 12.10). Chastisement is not pleasant, but to the exercised soul it yields the peaceable fruit of righteousness (Heb 12.11).

The first two statements of v.2 are also found in Jeremiah 7.28 and unfold the attitude of Jerusalem towards the demands of the word of God, whereas the next two statements reveal its attitude to God Himself and to His promises. Jehovah, who had entered into a unique relationship with Israel through His covenant with them, was now rejected by His people. They did not trust Him and refused to draw near to Him. The word translated "trusted" (BATAH - 982) expresses a sense of security resulting from confidence in someone. Jerusalem, in her defiled and rebellious state, no longer had confidence in God or His promises made to Israel. They had lost all sense of dependence upon God, but put their trust in man (Jer 17.5-7) in whom is no help (Ps 146.3); in their idols, but they would become ashamed (Is 42.17); in their ways (Hos 10.13) showing their folly (Prov 28.26); and in their work and wealth (Jer 48.7; 49.4) which would bring their downfall (Prov 11.28). When danger threatened they put their reliance upon Assyria (2 Kings 16.6-10) and upon Egypt (Is 30.2-3; 36.6,9; cp. Jer 2.18,36). Their confidence should have been upon Jehovah because He, and He alone, is the eternal God, Almighty, gracious, great in goodness, pardoning iniquity, plenteous in mercy and slow to anger (Ps 86.5,15; 103.8; 145.7-8). God is unfailingly faithful (Deut 7.9; Is 49.7; 2.Tim 2.13) and will keep his promises (Heb 10.23), and will do as He has stated (1 Thess 5.24). One can have complete confidence in Him. Well might the Christian take heed to the words of Proverbs 3.5-6: "Trust in the Lord with all thine heart; and lean not unto thine own understanding. In all thy ways acknowledge him, and he shall direct thy paths".

They distanced themselves from Jehovah by not serving and worshipping Him as they ought. Their ceremonial activities were a mere formality and in heart they were far from Him. The word "near" (QARAB - 7126) has a primary meaning here of being in close proximity to God, but also a secondary meaning of being in actual contact with God. However, they sought not Jehovah in repentance, but were estranged from Him, no longer worshipping Him or supplicating Him in their need. They were at a distance from the One who should have been the object of their trust and worship. How many Christians today are at a distance from God? Believers ought to ask if our confidence really is in God and whether we are living near to God. It is important for the child of God to enjoy close and constant fellowship with Him. It is clear from 2.3 that, in spite of the general dreadful condition in Judah, there was a remnant (3.13), Zephaniah being part of it, which was faithful to God and His word. As in Zephaniah's day there is a remnant today among the many who profess to belong to God, who still strive to carry out the word of God in their lives and seek His face.

Zephaniah, having given the reasons for the deplorable moral and spiritual conditions of the city, now turns to the guilt of both the civil and spiritual leaders (vv.3-4). They were responsible for maintaining moral standards and for upholding spiritual values, but here they are accused of practices which were inconsistent with their positions. Those who should have maintained righteousness in the city were marked by lawlessness, and those who should have preserved truth promoted error. The conduct of the leaders shows why the city was defiant, blemished, and cruel. As were the leaders so were the people. In the same way the spiritual condition of a local church depends upon the spirituality of its elders. Those who would take up leadership among the saints must take heed to the teaching of 1 Timothy 3.1-7 and to the exhortation of Acts 20.28.

The princes here do not refer to those of royal blood but rather to the civil rulers. They have been linked with the Sanhedrim, the Jewish rulers who crucified the Lord Jesus Christ (Ps 22.12-13; 1 Cor 2.8) and also with those who threatened and persecuted the apostles (Acts 4.21; 5.40). The princes were as roaring lions terrifying, pillaging and devouring all in their power (Ezek 22.27; Nah 2.12), tearing their prey to satisfy themselves (Prov 28.15; Mic 2.2). They had no thought for the people they ruled over, but sought their own profit. Rather than leading and protecting those entrusted to them they treated them mercilessly for gain. Thus, they forfeited the right to rule over the people of God. Their greed led them to use their power to abuse the privilege and responsibility of their position (Jer 10.21; 23.1; Ezek 34.2). The princes were characterised by pride and pomp seeking to promote themselves in their position over the people with no concern for them and no respect for the claims of God. The judges were like wolves at evening, which, having had no food all day, ferociously pursue and devour their prey during the night (Jer 5.6; Hab 1.8). The idea may well be that the judges secretly consumed all they could while professing to uphold justice. They were just like Abimelech who, through treachery, was pronounced king (Judg 9.1-6), and just like Absalom who secretly stole the hearts of the people for his own ends (2 Sam 15). The metaphor of ravenous and fierce wolves emphasises the merciless and cruel character of the judges who should have been an example of equity and virtue. Instead of encouraging the people to respect the righteous judgments of the law they instilled fear into them. The responsibility of protecting the innocent, the exploited and the oppressed by righteous judgment, in punishing the guilty, had been committed to them, but in their insatiable greed they set aside justice in order to gratify self.

"Gnaw" (GARAM - 1633) is only found elsewhere in Numbers 24.8 and Ezekiel 23.34 where it is translated "break". The verb in itself does not have the meaning of to lay up till the morning, and thus most commentators accept that the emphasis in the statement is upon the ravenous hunger of wolves which leave nothing until the morning (see Keil & Delitzsch). The morning is a time associated with legal justice or judgment (v.5; Jer 21.12) and so the idea here would be that the judges did not bring matters to righteous judgment, but dealt with them swiftly for their own advantage and benefit. Paul warned of the danger of such leaders - "...after my departure shall grievous wolves enter in among you, not sparing the flock. Also of your own selves shall men arise, speaking perverse things, to draw away disciples after them" (Acts 20.29-30). Today, in many companies of the Lord's people there is a failure in leadership, and godly elders seem to be scarce.

The religious leaders (v.4) were no better than the civil leaders. Those who claimed to be prophets (Micah 2.11; 3.5) engaged in activities they should have condemned instead of fulfilling the role they claimed. They should have conveyed precisely and courageously the word of God to the people, but they spoke words of their own composition leading the people astray while they pursued their evil ways (Jer 23.14).

The word translated "light" (PAHAZ - 6348) only occurs elsewhere in Judges 9.4, referring there to persons hired by Abimelech. It means to boil up or boil over and conveys the ideas of vainglory, recklessness and frivolity. The prophets were guilty of levity, trifling with solemn things, and handling the word of God wrongfully to deceive the people (Jer 14.13-14). There was no sobriety or stability in their lives or teaching. They were unprincipled men since they proclaimed a message claiming that it was from God while it was their own concoction, having no foundation or benefit. A derivative of PAHAZ is found in Jeremiah 23.32 where the false prophets are charged with causing the people of God to err by their lies, and by their lightness (PAHAZUT - 6350). By their deceit they subverted the word of God to serve their evil ends (Jer 6.13). The clear teaching of the Holy Scriptures was replaced by treacherous lies and thus the nation of Judah was misled (Jer 5.31). They were treacherous, being unfaithful to the God they claimed to represent, because they encouraged the people in their rebellion against God. How solemn and serious wrong teaching is.

In New Testament times there were men like these prophets who corrupted the word of God (2 Cor 2.17; 4.2). The Apostle Peter also warned the saints of God that, as there were false prophets in Israel, so there would be false teachers amongst them (2 Pet 2.1-2). Today is no different, with the Scriptures being twisted, misinterpreted and set aside by many. There is a great need in these days for pure, plain, pointed teaching of the wholesome, health giving word of God which alone can produce godliness in the lives of the people of God.

Not only were those who claimed responsibility in making known the mind of God treacherous, but those who were responsible for representing and maintaining the people before God were also corrupt. The priests, whose duty it was to make a difference between what was holy and profane, and between what was clean and unclean (Lev 10.10; 20.25), profaned the sanctuary by their unholy practices. They should have been examples of holiness as representatives of God whose exhortation through Moses was, "Ye shall be holy: for I the Lord your God am holy" (Lev 19.2). The same exhortation is given to Christians who should be holy in all manner of behaviour (1 Pet 1.15-16). However, these priests were like Eli's sons whose actions caused the people to abhor the offerings of the Lord (1 Sam 2.12-17, 22-25) and brought judgment on Eli's house (1 Sam 2. 27-31).

"Sanctuary" (QODESH - 6944) refers to that which belongs to the sphere of the sacred in contrast to what is common or profane. It refers to whatever is dedicated to, or set apart for, God including the service, sacrifices and worship as well as the priests themselves (Lev 21.6). Here it does not refer exclusively to the temple although it would be included. Being unclean themselves, the priests profaned the sacred, and consequently defiled the temple itself (Jer 7.9-11). Rather than keeping and teaching the law they violated the law of God by treating as profane what was holy and making no difference between what was clean and unclean (Ezek 22.26). They despised the law and redefined what God had commanded instead of teaching the truth (Lev 10.8-11; Deut 31.9-13). In order to promote themselves they distorted the meaning of the law and manipulated the truth. One is not surprised that the prophet Jeremiah strongly denounced the priests (Jer 2.8; 5.3).

The failure and corruptness of the leadership was all the more solemn because of Judah's great privilege of having the presence of Jehovah in her midst (v.5). Judah alone, of all the nations, had this privilege (Ex 29.45), and in spite of the dreadful conditions His presence remained with them (1 Kings 6.13). His faithfulness to the covenant had been demonstrated throughout their history and His mercies were indeed new every morning (Lam 3.22-23). His presence was associated with the temple in Jerusalem, but they had failed to appreciate the dignity of His presence and had despised the privilege that had been bestowed upon them. Is this true today of believers gathered to the name of the Lord Jesus Christ? The privilege and dignity of being gathered to His name (Mt 18.20) carries with it the solemn responsibility of obedience to His word and moral conformity to His holiness. Although the character of the leaders was also seen in the people of Judah in general, the prophet indicates that God was not without a witness because there was a faithful remnant who made known His righteousness. Thus the corruption and injustice of the leaders were rebuked by Jehovah's faithful prophets (Zephaniah among them; cp. Jer 25.4; 29.19; 35.15; 44.4) who daily proclaimed His justice and His law, and so their lawlessness was without excuse. Although one cannot rule out the idea of swift retribution, the expression "in the midst thereof" really emphasises the vivid contrast between the awful moral and spiritual state of the city and the characteristics of Jehovah (Deut 32.4).

The adjective "just" (SADDIQ - 6662) seems here to express the righteousness of Jehovah's conduct and refers to the fact that He does no wrong. This is confirmed by the following expression, "he will not do iniquity". Thus His righteousness is in contrast to their evil deeds; His truthfulness is in contrast to their lies, and His holiness is in contrast to their pollution. Being just, it inevitably follows that the rebellious and guilty would not be left unpunished. The word translated "judgment" (MISHPAT - 4941) is used of different aspects of both civil and religious government, but "When therefore the Scripture speaks of the *mishpat* of God, as it frequently does, the word has a particular shade of meaning and that is not so much just statutes of God as the *just claims* of God" (TWOT). Thus every morning (morning by morning) Jehovah publicly made known His just claims through the teaching of His true prophets demanding holiness and obedience to the law which condemned the nation's lawlessness. Some commentators include here judgment upon the ungodly in the nation. However, C. F. Keil states, "It is at variance with the context to take these words as reference to the judgments of God. These are first spoken of in v.6, and the correspondence between these two verses and vv.7 & 8 shows that we must not mix up together v.5b and v.6, or interpret v.5b from v.6" (Keil & Delitzsch). Jehovah did not fail to make known His claims on the leaders as well as the people, but all this was lost on the unjust and thus those claims were ignored.

The noun "unjust" (AWWAL - 5767) only occurs elsewhere in Job (18.21; 27.7; 29.17; 31.3 – wicked, or unrighteous) and is used to label persons who are evil, but it may be used here of Judah in general. The perverse and unrighteous were not shamed into repentance by the declaration of the just claims of Jehovah and thus they continued in their corrupt state (Jer 6.15; 8.12; cp. Eph 4.19). Christians know that today "evil men and seducers shall wax worse and worse, deceiving, and being deceived" (2 Tim 3.13) and that the mystery of lawlessness is already working (2 Thess 2.7). Although wickedness abounded in Zephaniah's day it will not reach its zenith until the Day of the Lord and just before the Lord Jesus Christ, Israel's Messiah, returns to sit upon the throne of His glory and set up the Messianic Kingdom. Then righteousness will reign and wickedness will be swiftly dealt with. Then morning by morning His just claims will be proclaimed throughout the world.

Verse 6 introduces judgment upon the nations in order to re-enforce the righteous character of Jehovah. In v.5 it is demonstrated by His just claims being proclaimed to His people so that they might accept correction (v.7) and repent, but here it is demonstrated in His judgment upon the sinful nations. To emphasise this, Jehovah is introduced here as the speaker and the judgment is viewed as devastating. It is evident that the judgment mentioned in 2.4-15 is not in view since that is still future, whereas the judgment here has already taken place. Some think that the destruction of the Canaanites is in view, but the thought seems to be that of nations in general which have experienced the judgment of God. There could also be an allusion to the ten tribes, the kingdom of Israel, which had been carried away captive by the Assyrians. His people only needed to look back over their history and recall the many nations that had been devastated by the judgment of God.

The verbs used in v.6 are strong verbs indicating momentous destruction. God had given many examples throughout their history of His justice in the way he had dealt with the various nations that surrounded them. Towards Israel God had been longsuffering, but Jehovah had cut off the wicked nations as an example of His righteousness and as a warning to Judah and Jerusalem. The fact that the characteristic of longsuffering as well as of righteousness belongs to God is clearly made known in the Scriptures (Ex 34.6; Num 14.18; Ps 86.15; Rom 2.4; 2 Pet 3.9,15). Their towers or fortifications in which they trusted for protection were shattered and lay in ruins. True safety is of the Lord (Prov 21.31) who makes His people dwell in safety (Ps 4.8). Some suggest that "streets" refer to the cities which were left deserted while others consider they refer to roads, indicative of the countries which were left devastated. The expression "that none passeth by" would favour the idea of cities in ruins with streets covered with rubble so they could not be used. "Waste" (HAREB -2717) means to be in ruin, and refers to the desolation of waste places which could favour the thought of desolate countries. The word for "destroyed" (SADA - 6658) is rare and means to lay waste, emphasising the desolation of the cities, confirmed by the following expression, "so that there is no man". The last expression sums up the whole picture indicating that no one was to be seen anywhere. The description of total destruction is given for Judah's benefit to remind them that God had removed those who rebelled against Him. God intended that through these past visitations of judgment Judah should take heed to the present threat of judgment and learn to fear Him and receive correction. History and the existing conditions in Judah which were continually condemned by His servants, the prophets, indicated Jehovah's displeasure with lawlessness. However, Judah failed or refused to learn the lessons.

With so many examples of Jehovah's justice and with continual warnings from His prophets, the people of Judah should have realised the need to repent in order to avert the judgment threatened. The opening words of v.7, "I said", may well refer to the constant bringing to light of the justice of God mentioned in v.5. Jehovah condescends to man's level by representing Himself as reasoning like man, although He was not ignorant of their response or of future events. Surely, knowing the holiness and power of God, Judah would fear Him and repent. They should have been swift to respond to the instruction and correction so that they might escape judgment (Jer 22.3-5). The word "thou" indicates that the appeal is actually made to Jerusalem and reminds one of the words of the Lord Jesus Christ: "O Jerusalem, Jerusalem, which killest the prophets, and stoneth them that are sent unto thee; how often would I have gathered thy children together, as a hen doth gather her brood under her wings, but ye would not!" (Lk 13.34). In both instances Jerusalem failed to grasp the opportunity of the day of God's visitation in grace and mercy (Lk 19.42-44). The city was called to fear Jehovah by living in awe of Him. This was not to be merely an emotional reaction, but a change in conduct by accepting His correction (Ps 55.19; 111.10).

The word translated "instruction" is rendered "correction" in v.2 and again has the thought of discipline or chastisement by instruction. Some commentators take the expression "their dwelling" as a reference to the place where God dwelt in their midst, the temple, and the possibility of the removal of His presence, linking it with Matthew 23.38, "Behold, your house is left unto you desolate" (see F. C. Cook and Jamieson, Fausset & Brown). However, the temple, which was God's dwelling place, is never called the dwelling place of the people and so the city of Jerusalem must be in view (see W. J. Deane and Keil & Delitzsch). If there was repentance the city would not be cut off from being a dwelling place. What was said of Jerusalem, the centre of Judah, was also true of the whole nation. They continued in their stubborn rebellion, deaf to every warning, and indifferent to the evidence of God's judgment upon surrounding nations (Jer 11.7-8). Nothing seemed to have an impact upon the people of Judah. Grace offered was spurned, and so Jehovah committed them to the punishment He had already appointed if there was no repentance. Instead of turning to God they became more fervent in their evil pursuits.

The expression "rose early" signifies activity with zeal and purpose. David Newell notes that "Abraham may have risen up early in the morning to obey Jehovah (Gen 21.14; 22.3), but his descendants 'rose early, and corrupted all their doings', slothful in spirituality but enthusiastic in evil". In defiance against Jehovah they earnestly and deliberately continued in their sinful practices and corrupted their ways (cp. Gen 6.12; Is 5.11).

The nations gathered (v.8)

The prophecy of judgment that has taken up most of what has gone before now ends where it began, with universal judgment (1.2-3). Thus the prophet completes a circle of judgment as he focuses on the nations gathered for judgment before the establishing of the Messianic Kingdom (cp. Rev 19.11-21). David Newell very helpfully points out that "While John sees this global mobilization before the Lord's return as a climactic expression of human defiance (Rev 19.19), Zephaniah, like other Old Testament prophets (Zech 14.2), views it all from the heavenly angle. Therefore the emphasis falls on God's activity: He will 'rise up', 'gather', 'assemble', and 'pour' His judgments on the nations (3.8). All man's boasted freedom is seen to be but the fulfilment of God's eternal plan".

The use of "Therefore" strengthens the exhortation of Jehovah. In view of the coming punishment of Judah, because of its spurning of Jehovah's grace and longsuffering, He exhorts them to "wait ye upon me". The exhortation here cannot be addressed to Judah in general upon whom the warnings and longsuffering of Jehovah had had no effect, since the verb "wait" (HAKA - 2442) contains the thought of hope and confidence (Ps 33.20). Also the idea of exhorting the nation to wait upon Jehovah for the punishment threatened is untenable. Just as a faithful remnant is addressed in 2.3 after the threat of judgment in 1.4-18 so that remnant, which God will spare, is addressed here. The future well-being and restoration of the nation is contained in that remnant. The exhortation is intended to comfort and encourage the godly not to despair, but to patiently endure affliction and confidently wait for Jehovah's intervention. So believers today are encouraged, in the word of God, to wait with patience and earnest expectation for the Lord's coming. Despite the coming judgments the faithful remnant, which waits for Jehovah, is blessed for it anticipates, with confidence, the promised glorious restoration of Israel (Is 30.18-26). The time of waiting is only until the day that Jehovah rises (Hab 2.3) - as some translate, "wait for me...for the day".

The word translated "prey" (AD - 5706) only occurs elsewhere in Genesis 49.27 and Isaiah 33.23. It has been viewed in three ways.

1. Following the RSV translation, "as a witness", Jehovah will arise in judgment to testify against the nations (Mal 3.5) (D. W. Baker).

2. Jehovah will rise up as a savage beast greedy for the prey implying the devastation and destruction of the nations (Mt 24.28) (Jamieson, Fausset & Brown; C. L. Feinberg).

3. The prey refers to those who, through the judgment, confess His name and are saved (Keil & Delitzsch; W. J. Deane).

The three occurrences of the word in the Hebrew text do not support the first opinion, and although destruction will take place when the nations are gathered for judgment, as the verse indicates, the result stated in v.9 supports the third position. In order to achieve the object in view Jehovah's judicial sentence must be carried out and the wicked must be destroyed.

"Determination" (MISHPAT - 4941) is translated "judgment" in v.5 and 2.3, and means justice, or right. Here it indicates Jehovah manifesting His justice in gathering the nations for judgment. The verb "assemble" (QABAS - 6908) refers primarily to gathering together into one place. The same event mentioned here is referred to in Zechariah 14.2 where Jehovah gathers the nations together against Jerusalem. However, the emphasis there is upon the intention of the nations to exterminate Israel, whereas here the emphasis is upon Jehovah's purpose to pour out His fury and burning anger upon them that the wicked might be destroyed (cp. Joel 3.2; Zech 12.9; 14.3). In concluding the prophecies of judgment, similar language is used to that in 1.18 in giving the reason for this universal judgment. The depravity and wickedness of man calls for the wrath of

God who is intrinsically holy. He will not tolerate continual rebellion and will not allow His purposes to be thwarted. Thus, in the intensity of His jealousy judgment will be meted out and deliverance brought to His people. The whole earth will experience the fiery indignation of God. Those who oppose Him will be removed in judgment, Israel shall be delivered, and the saved among the Gentiles brought through the judgment to be worshippers of Him.

Verses 9-20: The Sure Purposes of Jehovah Fulfilled
The book of Zephaniah does not end with gloom, for Jehovah is not only holy, just and righteous, seen in His intolerance of sin, but He is also gracious and merciful. As already mentioned, the Day of the Lord extends beyond the fiery judgment on both Israel and the Gentile nations to the Lord's coming to earth and His Messianic Kingdom. The closing part of this chapter glows with the promises of the Messianic times. Both the Old and New Testaments have many promises of the Lord's return to earth and His righteous rule during the Millennium. The subject is mentioned in 40 out of the 66 books of the Bible. In these verses the prophet outlines what will be the result of the pouring out of the wrath of God. Jehovah will turn Gentiles to Himself (v.9), restore and preserve a remnant of Israel (vv.10-13), and bring rejoicing to Israel in whose midst He will dwell (vv.14-20).

The nations converted (v.9)
The use of "For" connects the promise of v.9 with the judgment upon the nations predicted in v.8. As a result of the pouring out of the wrath of God a remnant of the Gentiles will be brought to Him. The word translated "language" (SAPA - 8193) "refers to the organ of speech. The lips are the gates of speech, and hence the gates of honesty or deception, righteousness or wickedness, wisdom or folly...Because speech is uttered through the lips, it was only natural that the lips should be used as a metonymy for language" (TWOT). Since the word has various shades of meaning the opening expression has been viewed in three different ways.
1. That the lip of God, which He will turn to the nations, is in view, i.e. the preaching of His servants in a clear, easily understood language that the people be converted and call upon Jehovah's name and serve Him.
2. That the statement "turn to the people a pure language" refers to the reversal of what took place at Babel (Gen 11). This would bring about the restoration of the earth's unity of language and worship.
3. That the impure speech of the nations would be cleansed and with pure lips they will call upon the name of Jehovah. The third view seems more in keeping with the passage and is developed here. For further consideration of these views see Keil & Delitzsch, Jamieson, Fausset & Brown, C. J. Barber, D. W. Baker, and C. L. Feinberg.
The word "people" (AM - 5971) is plural here and refers to all of the

Gentile nations. As a result of Jehovah's judgment upon the nations a remnant from among those nations will be converted as indicated in Revelation 7.9-17 and in the "sheep" of Matthew 25.32-46. "Pure" (BARAR - 1305) has the thought of purify or purge as in Ezekiel 20.38 and Daniel 12.10. Jehovah will turn to the peoples a pure lip by purifying their sinful lips through converting them. The change wrought in the saved Gentiles is such that their impure lips will become purified, which indicates a complete change in their lives (cp. Is 19.18). This is always the case when a person is saved (2 Cor 5.17; 1 Thess 1.9). The inward thoughts are imputed to the lips and mouth, so idolaters and the wicked, having taken the names of idols, blasphemy, and error upon their lips are deemed as having unclean lips (cp. Ps 16.4; Rom 3.13-14). Having learned of the righteousness of God through His judgments, the saved Gentile will worship Him sincerely and heartily with pure lips. The expression "call upon the name of the Lord" implies public worship coming from the heart. Not only will they worship Him, but they will also serve Him with oneness of heart and purpose. "Consent" (SHᵉKEM - 7926) has the meaning of shoulder (Gen 24.15; Josh 4.5; Is 22.22) and thus the expression is literally "serve with one shoulder" which indicates serving together or serving as one. The metaphor seems to be taken from a burden carried between two upon their shoulders (cp. Num 13.23). Thus we have the expression - shoulder to shoulder. It refers to harmony in serving Jehovah. Whereas the nations were united in opposition to God, thus bringing His judgment upon them (Ps 2.1-5), the saved Gentiles will be united in their worship and their service for Him. Harmony among believers today is an important element in their testimony for God (Ps 133.1) particularly in the collective testimony of a local church (Phil 1.27; 2.2; 3.16; 4.2). Idolaters and the wicked will be removed, and the nations united in spirit will enter into the Messianic Kingdom.

The remnant preserved (vv.10-13)

The remnant of Israel will be restored to the land, and their idolatry and wickedness, described in earlier passages of this prophetic book, will be removed. Then they will be characterised by worship and service (v.10), confidence and lowliness (v.11), dependence upon Jehovah, satisfaction, and security (v.13). They will not only experience restoration (v.10), but also redemption (vv.11-13).

Restoration (v.10)

Verse 10 turns from universal blessing to the restoration of Israel. Two interpretations have been given to this verse, one based upon the RV margin and the Chaldee version, the other upon the AV. F. C. Cook states, "From beyond the rivers of Ethiopia, they shall bring mine offering, my suppliants, the daughter of my dispersed. The Chaldee paraphrast understood the passage thus, and many modern scholars construe it in the same way. This interpretation suits the context (vv.8,9) in which the heathen nations are spoken of. They are first punished, then converted, and the fruit of their conversion is to restore the Jewish exiles to their own land. The Jews themselves are the offering which the Gentiles bring in token of their faith in God. And this agrees remarkably with a prediction in Isaiah (66.20), in which the Jews are spoken of as an offering brought by the Gentiles". Rabbi A. J. Rosenberg states the verse is paraphrased: "From the other side of the rivers of Cush the exile of My people who were exiled shall return with mercy, and they [the nations] shall bring them to you like sacrifices". Although most modern scholars accept this interpretation there is no clear proof to set aside the AV rendering which indicates, in keeping with the promises of God, that Jehovah Himself will restore scattered Israel to their land (Is 11.11-12; Ezek 28.25-26; 37.21-23; Joel 3.1). This is supported by the closing verse of the prophecy (3.20) and by the words of the Lord in Matthew 24.30-31. The lands from which the dispersed of Israel will be brought are described as being beyond the rivers of Ethiopia, a reference to the River Nile and its branches. Ethiopia is mentioned to indicate the parts of the earth distant from the land of Israel. Israel will be brought back to her land, not through passionate nationalism as in the twentieth century, but through being spiritually awakened. H. A. Ironside states, "From all the lands of their scattering He will bring His redeemed earthly people home to Zion, purging out pride and haughtiness, and making them willing in the day of His power (vv.10,11)".

The word "suppliants" (ATAR - 6282) means incense, or those who burn incense, and hence worshippers. These worshippers are identified in the expression "the daughter of my dispersed" which clearly refers to the dispersed of Israel - those who were geographically separated from their land and from God's chosen centre, Jerusalem. The re-gathered remnant of Israel will bring to Jehovah what is rightfully His. It is stated that "offering" is a reference to the meat (meal) offering (Lev 2) which speaks of a life lived for the pleasure and glory of God. Whatever the thought here the word of God teaches that those who are saved should yield their lives as a holy sacrifice to God (Rom 12.1) - "For ye are bought with a price: therefore glorify God in your body, and in your spirit, which are God's" (1 Cor 6.20), and, "...they which live should not henceforth live unto themselves, but unto him which died for them, and rose again" (2 Cor 5.15).

Redemption (vv.11-13)
In vv.11-12 Jehovah addresses the restored remnant of Israel with the prophet re-iterating their condition and adding the assurance of blessing in v.13.

Although the expression "In that day" (v.11) is linked with the Day of the Lord, it is most likely a reference back to the event mentioned in v.8 as suggested by some commentators. At the return of the Lord the remnant of Israel shall look upon Him "whom they have pierced, and they shall mourn for him, as one mourneth for his only son, and shall be in bitterness for him, as one that is in bitterness for his firstborn" (Zech 12.10; cp. Rev 1.7). Their contrition and repentance will lead them to redemption resulting in all their sins being removed.

"Ashamed" (BOSH - 954) primarily means to fall into disgrace through one's attitude and actions. Israel brought shame upon herself by her idolatry (Is 1.29), her trust in Gentile nations (Is 30.3,5), and her persistent rebellion against God and His word. The transgression mentioned here could be a reference to the rigid refusal of Jehovah's correction because of her pride and haughtiness as mentioned in the next expression. The faithful remnant had been exposed to that shame, being part of the nation. However, the restored remnant of Israel will have no cause to bear disgrace because, not only would they have repented and been converted, but Jehovah, through His judgment, would have removed the ungodly and wicked from among them. The impure attitudes and actions (vv.1-7) will no longer exist, and only purity and genuine worship of Jehovah will remain. Thus they will not be ashamed before the Lord (cp. Is 54.4), but will be confident in their acceptance before God and their place in His purposes.

The believer today should be diligent in the word of God, handling it rightly to earn the approval of God and not to be ashamed (2 Tim 2.15). The Apostle Paul's earnest desire was that he should be ashamed in nothing, but that Christ might be told out and glorified in his life (Phil 1.20). Devotedness to God and obedience to His word will inevitably bring suffering (2 Tim 3.12), but, rather than being ashamed, believers glorify God in this since His purpose for them is being fulfilled. Christians should live in such a way as not to be ashamed before the Lord at His coming (1 Jn 2.28).

The latter part of v.11 may well be a reference to the princes, judges, prophets, and priests who gloried in their sinful and selfish practices in violation of the law of God (vv.3-4). God will remove all who glory in their position, power, and earthly possessions with no thought of Him or consideration for others - those who boast that they can please themselves, do whatever they choose and are only accountable to themselves. Their pride lies at the root of their wicked ways and thus they will be cut off. The temple mount (Is 2.2; 11.9) will be free from the haughtiness that once prevailed, for the remnant will not be lofty because of the privilege of having the dwelling place of God in their midst.

In contrast to the proud and haughty of v.11, Jehovah will leave as a remnant in the midst of the land those who are lowly, dependent upon Him and owned by Him (v.12). This remnant, preserved through the Great Tribulation, will be the nucleus of the new nation of Israel.

"Afflicted" (ANI - 6041) primarily means one suffering some kind of disability or distress (Deut 15.11). C. F. Keil states that it "signifies bowed down, oppressed with the feeling of impotence for what is good, and the knowledge that deliverance is due to the compassionate grace of God alone; it is therefore the opposite of proud, which trusts in its own strength, and boasts of its own virtue". However, it is used of the Messiah, the Lord Jesus Christ (lowly - Zech 9.9), and of one who is of a contrite spirit (poor - Is 66.2), so the thought of being lowly, poor in spirit (Mt 5.3), is more applicable here. The remnant will be like their Messiah, characterised by humility. They will be in the enjoyment of the presence of God (Is 57.15) and will be in the good of the Kingdom (Mt 5.3). The throne will be set up in their hearts and the rule of their Lord seen in their lives. This should be true of believers today. Christians are to humble themselves in the sight of the Lord (James 4.10; 1 Pet 5.6), and be clothed with humility (1 Pet 5.5). They are not to be high-minded (Rom 11.20; 12.16; Gal 6.3). God requires His people to "do justly, and to love mercy, and to walk humbly with thy God" (Micah 6.8).

The word "poor" (DAL - 1800) means one that is low. It denotes the lack of material wealth (Prov 10.15) and social strength (Amos 2.7). The words ANI and DAL are closely linked in meaning and are translated in the Septuagint as "meek and lowly" - similar to that found in Matthew 11.29. Rabbi A. J. Rosenberg gives as a translation: *"A humble people that submits to humiliation"*. The thought here seems to be of a humble people who have endured humiliation - a lowly people looked down upon. However, such will put their trust in Jehovah (Ps 14.6). Their confidence will not be in themselves or religious ceremonies, but in the name of the Lord which is a place of refuge - a strong tower (Prov 18.10). Again, they will be like their Messiah who, while here, was characterised by perfect trust in God (Mt 27.43; Heb 2.13). Christians should not trust in themselves, but in God (2 Cor 1.9). Trust in God is one of the characteristics of true humility and holiness.

Verse 13 portrays the moral and spiritual integrity of the restored remnant. Their moral duty towards God is first described showing it is indeed in keeping with the divine intention for the nation (Ex 19.6). These are also the characteristics of the 144,000 mentioned in Revelation 14.1-5. It is clear that the verse looks forward to that coming day of peace and prosperity. The remnant will display the features of Jehovah Himself, in contrast to the ungodly who will perish under His judgment, because a fountain for the cleansing of sin and uncleanness will be opened for the house of David (Zech 13.1). They will not practice iniquity (Zeph 3.5) and thus their actions towards men will be just and their service for God will be pure in contrast to the unjust judges (v.3) and the impure priests (v.4). They will be free from falsehood, worshipping Jehovah with pure hearts and words, and always speaking the truth to men, in contrast to idolatry (1.5) and the lies of the prophets (3.4). There will be no fraud or deceit with them in contrast to those mentioned in 1.9 and the nation in former times (Jer 8.5; 14.14).

Righteousness and truth are features of the new life in Christ and should characterise Christians today. They should be "a pattern of good works" (Tit 2.7), practising them with zeal (Tit 2.14; 3.1), and serving God with piety, being conscious of His holiness. That service should be marked by dignity and the deportment suitable to the holiness of God (Heb 12.28). Believers should avoid anything that is improper, even in appearance, and "walk honestly toward them that are without" (1 Thess 4.12; Rom 12.17; 2 Cor 8.21), for honesty enhances one's testimony. There should be uprightness, sincerity and trustworthiness in every department of the Christian's life - honesty should be the hallmark of the believer (Rom 13.13; 1 Pet 2.12). Truth is the very essence of the new life in Christ who Himself is the truth (Jn 14.6), and thus all lying should be put away (Eph 4.25). Although lying is really a sin of the tongue, actions can also deceive and thus the child of God must act in a transparent way.

Zephaniah turns from the features of the remnant to their prosperity and peace by employing the figure of a shepherd with his sheep. The word "for" implies that their sustenance and safety are both a proof of, and the result of, their fidelity (cp. Lev 26.6; Ps 3.5; 4.8). As a result of their humility and godliness they will benefit from rich pasture, blessing from Jehovah (Ps 23.1; Is 40.11), rest (Ps 23.2), and freedom from fear (cp. Micah 4.4; 7.14). Under the protection of Jehovah they will enjoy material prosperity in the Messianic Kingdom. Today believers in Christ can enjoy the rich spiritual blessings already bestowed upon them (Eph 1.3). They can also look forward to the inheritance laid up for them knowing that not only is that reserved for them, but they are kept for it by the power of God (1 Pet 1.3-5).

The Lord in the midst (vv.14-17)

In the picture of millennial blessing in v.13 Zephaniah prepares the ground for what follows. He expands the description to indicate that the Messianic Kingdom will involve great rejoicing for Israel (v.14), the removal of judgment (v.15) and fear (v.16), and Jehovah rejoicing over them (v.17). The basis of their rejoicing will be the casting out of their enemy, the presence of Jehovah their King, and assured security. After the gloom of judgment and woe in most of the prophecy, this view of Israel's restoration and blessing is intended to encourage and stimulate the faithful in Judah. These verses have been looked at as a call to praise, a psalm of joy, and have been likened to Psalm 98 and Isaiah 12.

Zephaniah is projected, in spirit, to Messianic times and calls upon the remnant in that day to rejoice, not in themselves or their own achievements, but in Jehovah and all that He has done for them. This is emphasised in the same thought repeated in v.14 by the use of three different words. They are to sing (Zech 2.10), shout (Zech 9.9), and gladly rejoice (Ps 149.2,5; Is 25.9). The word "sing" (RANAN - 7442) reminds one of the Psalter, the song book of Israel, and thus the reason for designating vv.14-17 a psalm. The remnant is described in two ways: as the daughter of Zion, and as Israel. "Daughter of Zion" is a poetical personification of Jerusalem, as the closing expression of the verse indicates, and it is geographical. It stands for the city of God and indicates the spiritual centre of the nation, and the centre of God's purposes for His earthly people. The phrase is first used in 2 Kings 19.21 and occurs twenty-six times in the Old Testament, with Jeremiah using it eleven times (three in his prophecy and eight in Lamentations), and Isaiah using it six times. "Israel" is the ethnic description and embraces all the tribes joined together. The re-gathered remnant from every tribe will sing praises to God, shout with joy, and exult in the fulness of their salvation.

"Glad" (SAMEAH - 8056) means to be joyful, and "rejoice" (ALAZ - 5937) means to exult and indicates an emotion of joy which is expressed in singing or shouting. The two linked together and associated with the "heart" give the idea of joyfully exulting with one's whole being, i.e. emotion that cannot contain itself so that every part of the being is pervaded with joy. Believers have the same cause for exulting since their sins have been forgiven and they have peace with God (Rom 5.1).

There had been those who rejoiced in their pride (v.11), but here the rejoicing is for all the blessing the remnant will receive from Jehovah. David Newell's comments on the verse are helpful and pointed. "Complete restoration leads inevitably to rejoicing 'with all the heart' (3.14). Only those who have experienced the infinite mercy of God have any real reason to sing. Biblical joy is no irrational or hysterical exuberance but an intelligent response to the revelation of the Lord's goodness. If our joy is in God (Rom 5.11), then it must be worthy of Him. Much so-called 'joy' in Christian circles today seems little more than fleshly excitement instead of a thoughtful delight in the living God."

The reason for the rejoicing is given in v.15 indicating that God, acting in grace, established the new covenant promised to Israel (Jer 31.31-34; Heb 8.8-12). The word translated "judgments" is the same as the word translated "judgment" in v.5 and refers to the judicial sentence of God upon His people and the carrying out of that sentence. That sentence of chastisement upon His people was executed by their enemy. However, Israel's days of punishment for her sins would come to an end and Jehovah who had sent the punishment would remove it. Whereas Israel had turned away from Jehovah, in a coming day He will turn away their chastisements, for the removal of their sins (v.13) will inevitably lead to this. When the cause of such punishment ceases so does the punishment itself. Not only will their chastisements be taken away, but their enemies, who were appointed by God to execute His judgments, will be "cast out". That phrase (PANA - 6437) contains the idea of putting in order by clearing away anything disorderly. It is used of clearing out a house (Lev 14.36 - empty), and of preparing something (Gen 24.31; Is 40.3; 57.14). Here the thought seems to be that Jehovah will prepare the way for His dwelling in the midst of His redeemed people by clearing away every enemy. As long as Israel was subject to the power of the enemy the presence of Jehovah as King in their midst could not be realised. That is true of a company of believers gathered to the Lord's name today, for His presence cannot be enjoyed if there is unjudged sin in the company. With their judgments removed and the enemy cast out there will be nothing to hinder their enjoyment of the presence and reign of their true King, Jehovah, in their midst (Zech 6.12-13). He was once despised, rejected and crucified on a Roman cross with "set up over his head his accusation written, THIS IS JESUS THE KING OF THE JEWS" (Mt 27.37), but in that coming day, when He comes as the King of glory (Ps 24.7-10), they will acknowledge His right to the throne (Ps 2). He will not only be the centre of Israel's life (Ezek 37.26; Joel 2.27), but He shall reign over Israel (Is 52.7) and over the whole earth (Is 24.21; Zech 14.16) as the King of kings (Rev 19.16) sitting upon the throne of His glory (Mt 25.31).

Although some think the prophet turns back to the day of judgment in v.16 the expression "In that day" refers to the time indicated in the previous verse, the time of blessing when their Messiah, the King of Israel is in their midst. The expression "it shall be said" has been variously interpreted as referring to the prophets, the enemies of Israel, the Israelites encouraging each other, and the Gentiles. It seems most unlikely that it refers to the prophets since the Millennium is in view and it cannot refer to Israel's enemies for they have been cut off (v.15). Although it could possibly refer to the people of Israel, the reference is most likely to the Gentile nations. Such will be the favoured and secured position of Israel under Jehovah's rule that others will observe it and say to the once down trodden city of Jerusalem, "Fear thou not" (cp. Is 62.2-4; Lk 12.32). It is stated that Jerusalem will be so secure that she shall be called the fearless one. Jerusalem, once exposed to the onslaught of her enemies (1.10-13), will be absolutely secure with Jehovah the King in their midst. Believers today are eternally secure knowing that God is for them and that no one can lay a charge against them or condemn them (Rom 8.31-34). Jerusalem will not only be a place of safety, but also a place of service and thus the appeal not to be fainthearted.

"Slack" (RAPA - 7503) has the thought of being despondent or disheartened. It is translated "feeble" (Jer 50.43; Ezek 7.17; 21.7), and "faint" (Prov 24.10), indicating despair through fear and anxiety (Is 13.7). Drooping hands are an indication of a fainting heart. The thrust of the verse seems to be that the day of Jerusalem's fear will be past and so they should be diligently serving God. Slack hands are idle hands. In a time of apathy and indifference Christians tend to become lukewarm in spiritual things and idle in the service of God. One must be aware of this danger and constantly remember the debt of love owed to the One who loved us and gave Himself for us. In this day of indifference one can become despondent in the service of God. However, the Lord will sustain and grant strength to those who cast themselves on Him.

The promises and blessings reach their pinnacle in v.17 where Jehovah's presence in the midst of Israel is repeated (v.15). The source of their confidence, joy and safety is His presence. Zephaniah uses two names of God here - Jehovah thy Elohim (cp. 2.7, 9;3.2). Jehovah will not only be in their midst as their King (v.15), but also as God, who is mighty. This word "mighty"' (cp. 1.14) is used of Boaz, "a mighty man of wealth" (Ruth 2.1), who redeemed the destitute and distressed family of Elimelech. It is also used of Jephthah, "a mighty man of valour" (Judg 11.1), who delivered Israel from Ammon. Here both redemption and deliverance for Israel in their perfection and fulness are attributed to Jehovah. He is seen as the mighty Redeemer (Is 1.27; 59.20) and the mighty warrior, victorious over His people's enemies (Ps 24.8), and bringing deliverance to them (Jer 23.6). Although the word "save" (YASHA - 3467) is mainly translated "save" and "deliver", it is rendered "victory" in Psalm 98.1. It means to be brought from a state of distress (either physically, materially, or spiritually) into one of safety which is generally accomplished by an outside party. Here its fulness is in view, including national and individual, physical, material and spiritual salvation. The mighty God to whom the remnant will return (Is 10.21) is none other than the Lord Jesus Christ upon whose shoulder will rest the reigns of government (Is 9.6-7). Not only will Israel rejoice in Jehovah, but He will rejoice over His people with joy. David Newell states, "Verse 17 excited the comment of Spurgeon, 'I think this is the most wonderful text in the Bible in some respects - God Himself singing!' At creation the morning stars sang together (Job 38.7), but at the repentance and blessing of Israel God Himself will sing. The whole verse throbs with divine pleasure as Jehovah, in the midst of His ancient people, is so moved with joy that He is 'silent in His love' (Newberry margin). Would that our periods of quietness when we gather to remember the Lord were so eloquent! Silence, you see, may indicate a heart so full that it cannot speak, or a heart so empty that it has nothing to say".

The first word translated "joy" (SIMHA - 8057) refers to genuine joy, joy from the heart, but the second word so translated (GIL - 1523) indicates enthusiastic expressions of joy. Although there will be that silent joy which is too great for words to express, the last expression of the verse indicates that there will be the breaking of that silence with singing. The idea that the joy will be because God will no longer have cause to rebuke and chastise His people is secondary to the fulfilment of His purpose for His people and their joy in His presence. The joy is the joy of His love for His redeemed people and that love is unspeakable. The joy of God here has been linked with Isaiah 62.5 where the rejoicing of God is compared to the rejoicing of a bridegroom over his bride. As a bridegroom is delighted to gaze upon his bride without uttering a word, and at another time rejoices over her with singing, so Jehovah's love for His people cannot be fully expressed and yet it is demonstrated in His rejoicing.

The promise of God, or Israel's reward (vv.18-20)
One would have thought that the prophecy would have ended on the high note of Israel and Jehovah rejoicing (vv.14-17). However, it turns from the future Messianic Kingdom to what immediately faced Judah while still

giving further promises of blessing to encourage and comfort the godly in the nation. They would be driven from Jerusalem and Judah would be brought into captivity (1.13-14; cp. Hab 1.5-11; 2 Kings 25) just as Israel had been (2 Kings 17). The godly among them would mourn, not being able to keep the solemn assemblies, but God would fulfil His promises of blessing just as He would fulfil His threat of judgment. There would be future relief from suffering and separation, for there would be a restoration to the land of those who are scattered and who pine for Zion. In these closing verses Jehovah Himself is the speaker just as at the beginning of the prophecy. The prophecy opens with a sixfold "I will" of judgment (1.2-4), but ends with a sixfold "I will" of blessing (3.18-20), although the personal pronoun "I" occurs six times in the opening passage and eight times in the closing passage. Thus Jehovah is the source of both judgment and blessing in keeping with His holiness and His love.

The love of God is demonstrated in v.18 by His care and concern for the godly who, because of their exile from Jerusalem with its temple and ceremonial worship, are sorrowful for the solemn assembly. They would no longer be able to take part in the joy of gathering before Jehovah, keeping His feasts, and this would be a grief to them. "Sorrowful" (YAGA - 3013) refers to the troubling of the mind which is the result of some affliction. Here it indicates the grief and anguish of being separated from Jerusalem and thus being unable to carry out the ceremonial law (cp. Lam 1.4). Jehovah will restore the faithful who mourn to the land of their inheritance. Their mourning will be over and Israel will once again keep the appointed feasts. The faithful and true worshippers of Jehovah in Judah could take comfort from this promise although they would be taken into captivity - it was like good news from a far country (Prov 25.25). The expression "who are of thee" indicates that the godly among the scattered Jews, who grieve, belong to Zion, not only because they are citizens of the land, but because they are spiritually in harmony with Zion, i.e. true Israelites who worship Jehovah. It also signifies origin - such are from Zion, her true children, whose delight is in the worship of God and thus who pine for the temple and its sacred worship. How many Christians today have a deep longing after God and spiritual things (Ps 42.1-2)? The godly remnant among the exiled Jews will not only mourn for the solemn assembly, but will also bear the reproach of slavery heaped upon them by their enemies (cp. Ps 137). The word "reproach" (HERPA - 2781) is also translated "shame" (2 Sam 13.13; Is 47.3), and "rebuke" (Is 25.8; Jer 15.15), and has the thought here of scorn and mockery (cp. 2 Kings 19.22; Ps 119.42). The burden of reproach is another reason for the promise of restoration - "the rebuke of his people shall he take away from off all the earth: for the Lord hath spoken it" (Is 25.8).

Verse 19 begins with an interjection, "Behold", which demands attention and is used to emphasise what follows. Much in this verse corresponds with Micah 4.6. In that coming day, the Day of the Lord, Jehovah will deal in retribution with all those who have inflicted pain and suffering upon His people (Ps 60.12). He will recompense them for their ill-treatment of His people. The judgment of God upon those heathen nations which oppress His scattered people will precede the restoration of the godly remnant. He will not only deal with the oppressors, but will have compassion upon the weak and feeble, those who limp and stumble: "The afflicted of Israel, here compared to a lame and footsore flock of sheep" (W. J. Deane). Jehovah, as the great Shepherd, will gather His flock and, in grace, restore it to its own pasture and tend it there. Their weakness will not be a barrier or hindrance to Jehovah who will bring salvation to them. Those who are driven out in weakness will be restored in power (Ezek 34.16).

The closing expression is an allusion to Deuteronomy 26.18-19 and 28.1. Not only will they be restored and cared for, but their shame and reproach will be reversed, and instead of being reproached and ridiculed they will be the object of praise having a name of renown. This will not be because of their own merit, but through the grace of God and for His glory. Concerning this last expression F. C. Cook states, "When the people of Israel recognized the hand of God in their chastisements, returned to Him, and kept His laws, He would fulfil to the letter His part of the ancient covenant. Not only would He restore them and bless them, but make them famous in every land of their shame, or, as the words may be rendered literally, in all the earth, their shame, i.e. the scene of their shame. Wherever the Jews in their dispersion had been treated with indignity, they should one day be honoured and praised". Throughout the nations where Israel was scattered there will be the acknowledgement of what God has done for her and of the place He has given to her as the head of the nations (Deut 28.10-13).

The word "time" mentioned in v.19 is mentioned twice in v.20 emphasising that it is firmly fixed in the divine counsel and purpose, and it is identified as the time of Israel's restoration. The certainty of that restoration is stressed by its repetition in the closing expression of the prophecy. The glory of Israel's restoration is intended in the opening statement - "At that time will I bring you again", or "I will lead you home". The idea is that Jehovah will lead them as a flock, out of the lands where they have been scattered and into the verdant pastures of their own land (cp. Num 27.17). The shepherd care of Jehovah is thus continued from the previous verse. The word "gather'" (QABAS - 6908) also supports this, indicating the tender care of the shepherd as in Isaiah 40.11: "He shall feed his flock like a shepherd: he shall gather his lambs with his arm, and carry them in his bosom, and shall gently lead those that are with young". The thought here is of restoration to their former place and position rather than the release from captivity mentioned later. As in v.19 the promise of restoration is followed by the glorification appointed for Israel although here it is given as a reason for that restoration. However, here Israel's fame spreads throughout the world ("all people") not only to the nations to which they were dispersed as in v.19. ("Name" (SHEM - 8034) is translated "fame" in v.19.) Then will be fulfilled the promise of Deuteronomy 28.10 and Israel will occupy the place intended for her from the beginning (Deut 26.19). David Newell states, "Just as Israel will be universally honoured, so too will the faithful believer of this age. Many of the Lord's dear people have been savagely persecuted, often in the name of apostate religion. Their vindication is announced in the Lord's own words to Philadelphia, 'I will make them to come and worship before thy feet, and to know that I have loved thee' (Rev 3.9)". Israel's fame will be when their captivity is brought to an end.

The word "captivity" in Hebrew is plural and embraces all the captivities of Israel (both kingdoms) in her history and the different places to where they were dispersed. It thus implies the full and final restoration of the nation (Deut 30.3). Such an event may seem to be impossible, but will certainly take place to their joy and delight. The promises are sure and will be fulfilled because it is Jehovah, the covenant-keeping God, Himself who has made them - "saith the Lord". The prophecy with its message of judgment, its appeal for repentance, and its promised blessing ends where it began, in its source - Jehovah (1.1; 3.20). It ends with divine love and with the pleasure He takes in His people. This should be a joy and encouragement to believers today.

Conclusion

The end of God's ways with Israel will be blessing for her, in spite of her failures. Israel's blessings and fame are earthly, the Church's are heavenly. Both will contribute to the glory of God and both will display the wonders of His grace. Throughout the prophecy the fact that God is light (1 Jn 1.5 - intrinsically holy, righteous, and just) and God is love (1 Jn 4.7-8 - showing grace and mercy) is demonstrated by His judgments and His salvation. Zephaniah's prophecy centres around judgment and particularly that of the Day of the Lord with no country or nation being exempt. Glimpses of His grace are given in the prophecy which ends with promised salvation and blessing, not only for Israel, but also for the nations. The salvation of the nations and their blessing are linked with those of Israel and both are only possible because of the finished work of the Lord Jesus Christ. At Calvary He laid a righteous foundation that enables God to justify believers today, to bring salvation and blessing to Israel and the nations in a coming day, and to bring in a new earth and new heavens in which righteousness shall dwell.

HAGGAI

P. Harding

CONTENTS

INTRODUCTION

This prophecy is one of a group of three that belong to the period following Judah's captivity in Babylon - Haggai, Zechariah, and Malachi. These books contain the last messages of God to the nation and bring to an end the Old Testament Scriptures. The three prophecies are addressed particularly to the small remnant that had returned from Babylon to their land and to the ruined temple and forsaken city of Jerusalem. Haggai is the first of the post-exilic prophetic books. It is profitable to read the books of Ezra, Nehemiah, and Zechariah in the study of Haggai since they cover the same period. Ezra particularly deals with the period prior to Haggai and the rebuilding of the temple. The destruction of the temple by Nebuchadnezzar (587 BC) and the years of captivity meant that there was no earthly temple as the dwelling place of God among His people. However, through the edict of Cyrus, king of Persia, a remnant of Jews returned to the land in order to rebuild the temple which had been destroyed by the Chaldeans (Ezra 1.1-2). Their attempts to rebuild the temple and the opposition to their project are recorded in the book of Ezra (ch.4). It is also evident from Haggai 1.4 that the zeal of the remnant for building the temple had dwindled until they ceased in order to provide for their own necessities and comfort. As soon as they experienced opposition and disappointment they became indifferent to the House of God. Thus they willingly accepted the prohibition imposed by Artaxerxes (Ezra 4.23-24). The first message of Haggai shows that indifference and lukewarmness were the real reasons for not continuing to build the temple.

There is that same lukewarmness and lack of zeal in the things of God in our day. Love for Christ can soon ebb, and service for the Lord can simply become a lifeless form. Zeal for the truth and longing for holiness can wane. The moral declension of today demands that Christians be steadfast in the truth and in the spread of the gospel. God is still on the throne and the gospel is still "the power of God unto salvation to every one that believeth" (Rom 1.16).

Thus Haggai begins his prophecy with reproof and warning, then goes on to assure the people that Jehovah would be with them in the renewed work of building the temple. He outlines the glory of the future temple and sets forth the principles of sin and holiness. He also assures them of God's continual protection and blessing.

The Date of the Book

There is no question as to the period of the prophecy since Haggai gives the dates of his messages - "In the second year of Darius the king" (1.1) which is 520 BC. Unlike most prophetic books, Haggai, like Zechariah, commences with a Gentile date and the days are counted by the reign of a foreign king, Darius the Persian, although it is thought that the months quoted are those of the Jewish calendar. The messages of Haggai fall approximately within a four month period in the second year of Darius, seventeen years after the return of the Jewish remnant from Babylon in the first year of Cyrus (537 BC). Darius reigned from 522 BC to 486 BC during which time both Haggai and Zechariah prophesied, their messages intertwining together:

> The first day of the sixth month in the second year of Darius - Haggai's first message (Hag 1.1).

> The twenty-first day of the seventh month in the second year of Darius - Haggai's second message (Hag 2.1).

> The eighth month in the second year of Darius - Zechariah's first message (Zech 1.1).

> The twenty-fourth day of the ninth month in the second year of Darius - Haggai's third and fourth messages (Hag 2.10,20).

> The twenty-fourth day of the eleventh month in the second year of Darius - Zechariah's second message (Zech 1.7).

> The fourth day of the ninth month in the fourth year of Darius - Zechariah's third message (Zech 7.1).

God raised up these prophets to challenge the people and produce a positive reaction.

Haggai was given the task of making known the actual condition of the people and of bringing them back to what they had been. His messages brought home to the leaders and the people the importance of God's dwelling place among them. How important it is for believers gathered to the name of the Lord Jesus Christ to have a deep sense of His presence in their midst. The result of the ministry of Haggai and Zechariah was that the rebuilding of the temple began (Ezra 5.1-2). This gave rise to fresh opposition from their enemies who sought to prevent them building. Although not recorded in this prophecy, Ezra 5-6 recounts the opposition and the search for the decree of Cyrus. It gives Darius' decree, after Cyrus' decree was found, which authorized the continuation of the work and the provision of materials and sacrifices. From that time the work continued and within five years the temple was complete (Ezra 6.14-15).

The style of Haggai is not poetic like earlier prophetic books, but is simple prose given added force by the use of interrogating questions (1.4,9; 2.3, 12-13, 19). Jamieson, Fausset & Brown states, "The style of Haggai is consonant with his messages: pathetic in exhortation, vehement in reproofs, elevated in contemplating the glorious future. The repetition of the same phrases (eg. 'saith the Lord', or 'the Lord of hosts'", - 1.2,5,7; and thrice in one verse - 2.4; so 'the spirit', thrice in one verse - 1.14) gives a simple earnestness to his style, calculated to awaken the solemn attention of the people, and to awaken them from their apathy, to which also the interrogatory form, often adopted, especially tends".

Criticism of Haggai's style is not justified in the light of the effect of his messages which stimulated the people to renewed activity. There has never been a challenge as to Haggai being in the canon of the Old Testament. It was accepted into that canon as a part of what is called the "Minor Prophets" (The Book of the Twelve).

The Author of the Book

There is very little said of Haggai in the Scriptures. His genealogy, the tribe he came from, and the place of his birth are not mentioned, so his personal history is unknown. He seems to appear suddenly on the scene, with no credentials, but with definite messages from God. He is the only person in the Scriptures with the name Haggai and is only spoken of elsewhere in Ezra 5.1 and 6.14. Because of this some have thought it was a pseudonym. The name Haggai (2292) means the festive one and comes from the Hebrew word HAG (2282) meaning festival. He is the first of the post-captivity prophets to bring God's message to the returned remnant, and thus his prophecy is first in the order of the minor prophets after the captivity. Between Zephaniah and Haggai there is the gap of the seventy years of exile. F. A. Tatford states, "Tradition declares that he was born in Babylon during the exile, but the more general view is that he was among those carried away captive by Nebuchadnezzar and was one of the few survivors who returned to the land...He is said to have been a member of the Great Synagogue and an eminent scholar, who took part in the settling of the canon of the Old Testament. Ezra 3.2 to 6.22 (except 4.6-23 and 6.14) are said to have been written by him and edited later by Ezra. The authorship of certain of the Psalms is also attributed to him". The Septuagint attributes Psalms 137 and 146-148 to Haggai and Zechariah. Having been in exile Haggai was a contemporary of Daniel, and if he was among those carried into captivity by Nebuchadnezzar he would have been a contemporary of Jeremiah and Ezekiel. He would also have been present at the setting up of the altar (Ezra 3.2), the laying of the temple foundation (Ezra 3.10), and of its completion (Ezra 6.15).

The People of the Book

For seventy years Judah had been in captivity in Babylon. The result of that bondage, when they were slaves to idolatrous masters, was the removal of their tendency to idolatry. After the downfall of the Babylonian empire, Cyrus, the Persian ruler, in fulfilment of Isaiah's prophecy (Is 44.28), issued a decree allowing the Jews to return to their land to rebuild the temple (Ezra 1). Faced with the decree, the Jews were compelled to decide whether to respond to it and carry out the will of God or to remain in Babylon. It is recorded in Ezra and Nehemiah that, sadly, only a remnant, led by Zerubbabel the governor of Judah and Joshua the high priest, returned to their land, while the majority chose to remain where they were. Most of those who returned were from the tribes of Judah and Benjamin. The journey was dangerous and difficult and took about four months (Ezra 7.9), but they rejoiced because they were returning home with the freedom to obey the word of God. On their return the exiles settled in the cities of the land (Ezra 3.1). That remnant was in the good of the love of God since He had fulfilled His promise (Jer 29.10-14). They had a concern for the honour of His name (Neh 1.9,11; 9.5), knew the claims of God (Ezra 3), and had an earnest desire to rebuild the House of God (Ezra 1). However, by the time of Haggai's prophecy they had forgotten the goodness of God shown to them, had fallen into spiritual apathy and had lost their zeal in building the House of God. This was the condition of those who had returned when Haggai challenged them with messages from God. Nevertheless, they were still different in character to the people addressed by Jeremiah prior to the captivity who were an apostate generation and who rejected and derided the message that Jeremiah brought. Their hearts were hardened against the word of God and their consciences were seared. However, the message of Haggai to this returned remnant was received and acted upon. It seems that although their zeal had diminished and they had neglected to build the House of God they had a heart for the word of God. This is seen in their immediate response to the first message of Haggai and the fruitful result.

The Background to the Book

One must appreciate that when moving from one book to the next in the Bible we may be passing over a long period of time as we do from Zephaniah to Haggai. In the intervening years things had changed. When Zephaniah preached Assyria was still in power, but in Haggai's day Assyria had then fallen, Babylon had come to prominence and in turn had been replaced by Medo-Persia. Judah had experienced exile during which a great number of Jews had become settled as many of those who had hung their harps on the willows and had wept by the rivers of Babylon (Ps 137.1-2) had been attracted by the lifestyle of the Babylonians. Also a new generation had arisen, had been born and brought up in Babylon, and in general had become indifferent to their home land. To understand the condition of the remnant of Jews in Haggai's day one must go back to their return from exile in the first year of Cyrus (Ezra 1). On that return they found the temple in ruins and the walls of Jerusalem broken down into piles of stone and rubble. Having arrived in the land they first cleared the rubble in the former court of the destroyed temple in order to restore the altar of Jehovah. On the first day of the seventh month, which was the day they celebrated the Feast of Trumpets (Lev 23.24-25), they erected the altar upon its bases (Ezra 3.3). Although that day was to be a Sabbath with no servile work done, the altar was essential for the offering made by fire to the Lord.

It might seem peculiar to commence building the temple by erecting the altar first, but the altar was the foundation of temple activity. F. A. Tatford stresses that, "The application to the Christian is obvious. There can be no acceptable service for God until first the altar has been built: in other words, until the individual has first been in spirit to Calvary and viewed the supreme sacrifice there and experienced practically the efficacy of that atoning blood. The unbeliever has no part in the service of God: it is only the blood-washed believer who can engage in that ministry. Even after conversion, there must still be the altar before there can be acceptable service for Christ". They had hardly started to build when their adversaries offered to assist them in their work, but their offer was rejected (Ezra 4.1-3). These adversaries had no part in erecting the altar so could have no part in the building of the temple. The application is clear, only those who are in the good of Calvary can engage in service for God. The rejection of the adversaries' offer resulted in their bitter opposition and determination to prevent the Jews building the temple. This resulted in the Jews concluding that the time had not come to carry out this work (Hag 1.2). The difficulties dampened their zeal and soon they became lethargic and neglected the House of God. It is true that the Persian king, Artaxerxes, commanded the Jews to cease building, but that was thirteen to fourteen years after the foundation of the temple was laid. In that time they could have completed the temple, but lukewarmness and indifference had set in and they ceased to build. C. F. Keil suggests that there were those among the returned remnant who were motivated by earthly hopes instead of faith in God and when disappointed in their expectations they became idle and indifferent in regard to the temple.

The Particulars of the Book

In all probability Haggai's prophecy was first given orally (Ezra 5.1), and its object was to further the building of the temple. The fidelity of the nation was shown in its zeal for the House of God because it signified the presence of their covenant God in their midst. Thus one sees the importance of rebuilding the temple. Haggai not only deals with the condition of the remnant, but also refers to the coming glory of the Lord Jesus Christ. Most commentators consider that, in keeping with the dates mentioned, there are four sections in the book while some think there are five.

In the first chapter the prophet, on the first day of the sixth month, addresses the leaders and the people and condemns their inactivity and indifference in regard to the building of the temple. They were zealous in building their own luxurious houses which showed that their neglect of the temple was not due to the lack of materials. He states that the failure of the crops, the drought, the poverty and the other calamities they were experiencing were the result of leaving the House of God waste, and were also an evidence of divine displeasure. They were therefore called upon to consider their ways and, if they desired to regain the favour of the Lord, to go up to the mountain to fetch timber to recommence building the temple. In so doing they would bring pleasure to God and He would be glorified. This solemn message produced such an effect upon the people that they, along with their leaders Zerubbabel and Joshua the high priest, immediately submitted to the appeal and willingly recommenced building the temple on the twenty-fourth day of the same month. Haggai assured them that the presence of God would be with them in the work.

In 2.1-9 the prophet, on the twenty-first day of the seventh month, again addressed the leaders bringing to them a message of encouragement in order to dispel the despondency of those who had seen the glory of the first temple (Ezra 3.12-13). They were disheartened by what they deemed to be the poverty of the new building in comparison to Solomon's temple. They wondered if the splendour and magnificence of Solomon's temple could ever be restored. Haggai called on the leaders and the people to be strong, and assured them that the Lord would keep the covenant He had made with them when they came out of Egypt. He predicted that God would shake the heavens, the whole world, and the nations, and would give a greater glory to the future temple. This would take place when the desire of all nations came, which is taken by some commentators to refer to the second coming of the Lord Jesus Christ to the world. In that coming Messianic day the temple would be more glorious than Solomon's temple and the present hostility and unrest of the nations would be changed into peace and prosperity.

On the twenty-fourth day of the ninth month (2.10-19) Haggai emphasised the importance of pressing on with the restoration of the temple by means of illustration. Using questions and the priests' answers in regard to ceremonial uncleanness he showed the foolishness of only a partial obedience to God, and indicated that while the temple had remained unbuilt they were tainted with guilt and the curse of God was upon them. Their outward observances could never remove their guilt in neglecting the House of God. However, the material had been collected and they were building once again so the taint of disobedience and indifference would be removed. The consequences of their former neglect of the House of God would be replaced by the favour of the Lord. The previous curse upon the land (1.11; 2.17) would cease and would be succeeded by the abundant blessing that God promised if they continued the work of rebuilding the temple.

On the same day the prophet had a word of encouragement specifically for Zerubbabel (2.20-23), the representative of the Davidic dynasty, in regard to the throne of Israel. He declared again that there would be a tempest that would shake the heavens and the earth. He predicted the overthrow of the thrones of the kingdoms of the world and the destruction of the military and political power of the heathen. Zerubbabel was assured of the stability of the throne of Israel in the midst of the coming turmoil during God's judgment upon the world. Zerubbabel is here undoubtedly a representative of the Messiah, the Lord Jesus Christ, who at His manifestation will destroy those opposed to Him and set up His kingdom (Dan 2.44; 7.13-14; Rev 19.11-21). His divine authority to sit upon the throne of David and rule the world is indicated in the signet ring.

The Purpose of the Book

The historical purpose of the book was to exhort the returned remnant to rebuild the destroyed temple at Jerusalem. Haggai was God's messenger to stir up the hearts of those who, although privileged by God, had grown cold and indifferent in the work of God. Their zeal for the House of God had waned and they had forgotten the reason for returning to their land. The prophet did not merely predict future events, although he did this, but mainly he sought to arouse the people from their apathy and indifference. Thus the primary object of the prophecy was to challenge the people as to their true spiritual condition, to convict them of their neglect of God's dwelling, and to stir them up to recommence the rebuilding of the temple that Nebuchadnezzar had destroyed. They were to forget about self and be occupied with Jehovah and His claims. Christians today should remember that God has the first claim upon them.

Another purpose for the prophecy was to encourage the people in that work by reminding them of the covenant of God and of the promised future blessing and glory. Thus the book commences with the need to rebuild the temple and ends with the coming of the Messiah and His millennial reign. The key word for the people is "Consider" (1.5,7; 2.15,18), and the key expression to encourage them seems to be "I am with you" (1.13; 2.4). The practical purpose of the book is to show that God will chastise His people when they are disobedient to bring them back to Himself, and that they will only enjoy His presence and blessing when they put Him first in their lives. The book also indicates that the people of God should never weary in His service (Gal 6.9), and shows that God's promise as to the future is our hope in the present day.

The Outline of the Book

As already stated, most commentators divide the book into four sections, but it can be divided into five messages. The first message is one of reasoning as to the time of building the temple (1.2-4) and of rebuke in regard to their negligence (1.5-11). The second gives assurance of the presence of God with them in their building (1.13). The third is a message of exhortation to be strong (2.4) and of encouragement (2.7). The fourth recalls the blight they had experienced (2.17), and yet is also one of promised blessing (2.19). The final message predicts the overthrow of Gentile dominion (2.22) and final victory for the nation (v.23).

OUTLINE OF THE BOOK

A Message of Reasoning and Rebuke (1.1-11)
  A. The leaders addressed (1.1-2)
      1. The responsibility of the leaders (1.1)
      2. The excuse of the people (1.2)
  B. The people addressed (1.3-11)
      1. The challenge of God (1.3-4)
      2. The call to consider (1.5-6)
      3. The appeal of God (1.7-8)
      4. The discipline of God (1.9-11)

A Message of Assurance (1.12-15)
  A. Their obedience (1.12)
  B. Their assurance (1.13)
  C. Their activity (1.14-15)

A Message of Exhortation and Encouragement (2.1-9)
  A. The despondency of the people (2.1-3)
  B. The promise of Jehovah (2.4-5)
  C. The glory of the future temple (2.6-9)

A Message of Blight and Blessing (2.10-19)
  A. The teaching of the law (2.10-13)
  B. The application to the nation (2.14-17)
  C. The promised blessing (2.18-19)

A Message of Vision and Victory (2.20-23)
  A. The omnipotence of Jehovah (2.21-22)
  B. The faithfulness of God (2.23).

HAGGAI 1

The Babylonian captivity of Judah took place in three stages: the first during the reign of Jehoiakim (2 Kings 23.36-24.4; 2 Chr 36.5-7), the second in the reign of Jehoiachin (2 Kings 24.8-16; 2 Chr 36.9-10), and the third in the reign of Zedekiah (2 Kings 25; 2 Chr 36.11-21). The restoration of Judah to the land was also in three phases: the first under Zerubbabel and Jeshua (Ezra 2), the second under Ezra (Ezra 7-8), and the third under Nehemiah (Neh 2). The spiritual needs of the returned remnant were met, in part, by the ministry of Haggai and Zechariah as shown in the historical books of Ezra and Nehemiah. This ministry was intended to motivate the people to rebuild the temple, restore its institutions, and unfold the glorious future of Israel. The returned remnant needed encouragement since they had come back to a ravaged land, a ruined city, and a destroyed temple. The historical setting of Haggai is found in the first six chapters of Ezra. The object of Haggai was to urge the people to complete the temple without delay. In this chapter the prophet first gives a word of exhortation to those who were negligent in the Lord's work and who had allowed material things to take priority over spiritual things. It was a challenging message of reason and rebuke (vv.1-11). Haggai then encourages them with a consoling message because of their response in recommencing the building of the temple (vv.12-15).

Verses 1-11: A Message of Reasoning and Rebuke

The prophecy commences with a date, Haggai's admonishment of the civil and religious leaders who were responsible for the condition of the people, and a charge to the people who had excused themselves from rebuilding the House of God (vv.1-2). The prophet then uses the people's excuse to challenge them as to their diligence in building their own houses but neglecting God's House. He also reminds them of the consequences of their actions and appeals to them to recommence building the temple (vv.3-11).

The leaders addressed (vv.1-2)

Haggai begins his prophecy by giving the time of his first message and the persons to whom it was addressed. He dates his message with a reference to the reign of a Gentile king since there were no Jewish kings due to both the kingdoms of Israel and Judah having been taken into captivity. This clearly indicates that the "times of the Gentiles" were in progress (Lk 21.24). The king referred to was Darius of Persia (Ezra 4.5) who reigned from 521-486 BC. Haggai began to prophesy eighteen years after the remnant returned from exile in Babylon under Zerubbabel (Ezra 2) and 16 years after the foundation of the temple had been laid (Ezra 3.8-11). A period of lethargy and materialism had set in which was only removed by the ministry of Haggai and Zechariah. This ministry was given to stir the consciences of the people. Darius was a common name of the Persian kings in the same way as Pharaoh was a common title of the Egyptian rulers. Here Darius Hystaspes is referred to, being the first in the line of Persian rulers to bear that name. He was the king who reaffirmed the right of the Jews to rebuild the temple and provided the means to continue the project.

Although the prophet dated his messages with reference to the reign of the Gentile king he used the months of the Jewish calendar, as did Zechariah (Zech 1.7; 7.1). The sixth month is Elul which in our calendar is August/September. Two months later Zechariah commenced his prophetic ministry, thus supporting Haggai's appeal to the people (Zech 1.1). These two prophets stood shoulder to shoulder preaching in harmony so that out of the mouth of two witnesses the word from God was established. Whereas Haggai was concerned with the completion of the temple, Zechariah had a broader view which took in the world and in particular the end times. The first day was the day of the new moon when special sacrifices were offered (Num 28.11-15) and when the people gathered together (cp. 2 Kings 4.23; Is 1.13; Ezek 46.1-3). Thus this was an opportune time for proclaiming the message of God, to charge the people to rebuild the temple and to keep the feasts in the correct way. The day itself was an incentive to commence building the House of God. It is probable that this first message was given at the time of harvest.

The title of God in this opening verse is His covenant name Jehovah (the LORD) indicating His unchangeable character and His faithfulness in keeping His promise to His people. The expression "by Haggai, the prophet" is unique among the prophetic books. Generally the prepositions to, or unto, are used (Micah 1.1; Zech 1.1). In the Hebrew, the expression "by Haggai" is literally "in the hand of Haggai", and is an apt description of the prophet as the messenger of Jehovah carrying His message. It also indicates that Jehovah was the speaker and the prophet was only the instrument through whom the divine message was conveyed.

The responsibility of the leaders (v.1)
The message was sent to Zerubbabel and Joshua who were the civil and religious leaders of the returned remnant. Zerubbabel was of princely birth being of the line of David and the grandson of Jehoiachin (1 Chr 3.16-19). He is mentioned here as the son of Shealtiel, but is referred to as the son of Pedaiah, the brother of Shealtiel, in 1 Chronicles 3. To add to this difficulty he is mentioned in the New Testament as the son of Salathiel (i.e. Shealtiel) and the grandson of Neri (Lk 3.27). An adequate and full explanation is given by C. F. Keil, part of which is quoted here - "...according to the genealogical table given by Luke, inasmuch as Shealtiel's father there is not Assir or Jeconiah, a descendant of David in the line of Solomon, but Neri, a descendant of David's son Nathan, it follows that neither of the sons of Jeconiah mentioned in 1 Chronicles 3.17,18 (Zedekiah and Assir) had a son, but that the latter had only a daughter, who married a man of

the family of her father's tribe, according to the law of the heiresses (Num 27.8; 36.8,9 - namely Neri, who belonged to the tribe of Judah and family of David. From this marriage sprang Shealtiel, Malkiram, Pedaiah, and others. The eldest of these took possession of the property of his maternal grandfather, and was regarded in law as his (legitimate) son. Hence he is described in 1 Chronicles 3.17 as the son of Assir the son of Jeconiah, whereas in Luke he is described, according to his lineal descent, as the son of Neri. But Shealtiel also appears to have died without posterity, and simply to have left a widow, which necessitated a Levirate marriage on the part of one of the brothers (Deut 25.5-10; Mt 22.24-28). Shealtiel's second brother Pedaiah appears to have performed his duty, and to have begotten Zerubbabel and Shimei by his sister-in-law (1 Chr 3.19), the former of whom, Zerubbabel, was entered in the family register of the deceased uncle Shealtiel, passing as his (lawful) son and heir, and continuing his family" (see also F. A. Tatford).

The name Zerubbabel means born in Babylon, but he also had a Chaldean name, Sheshbazzar (Ezra 1.8; 5.14,16), which was indicative of his having some position under the Persian king. He had been appointed governor of Judea by Cyrus (Ezra 5.14).

Joshua, the first high priest after the restoration, was the son of Josedech (Jehozadak) who was high priest at the time of the Babylonian invasion and was carried away captive to Babylon (1 Chr 6.15). He was also the grandson of Seraiah the high priest who was executed in Riblah (2 Kings 25.18-21). Zerubbabel and Joshua, as leaders of the people, were responsible for the people's welfare, for guiding and directing them, as well as for their spiritual condition. Today, elders in a local church are responsible for the spiritual well being of the saints and ensuring that the assembly functions in keeping with the word of God. Therefore they should be spiritual and priestly men, chosen by the Spirit of God (Acts 20.28), with a deep concern for the spiritual condition of the saints. Those elders who faithfully discharge their responsibilities and are examples to the saints will be rightly recompensed (1 Pet 5.1-4).

The excuse of the people (v.2)
God now speaks, through Haggai, as "the Lord of hosts" (Jehovah Sabaoth - 3068, 6635). This name is one of the Jehovah titles and first occurs in 1 Samuel 1.3. It is used many times in the prophetic books, but is particularly common in the last three books where it occurs ninety times: fourteen in this book, fifty-two in Zechariah, and twenty-four in Malachi. It indicates His majesty and glory as the Lord of the hosts of heaven and earth. It signifies His sovereignty, and thus He demands complete obedience.

The expression "this people" is contemptuous, and is one of displeasure and a reproof to them indicating their distance from Him. It also implies that they had forfeited the right to be called His people because of their indifference to rebuilding His House. Their excuse for not building the temple was indefensible and a pretext to cover over their moral and spiritual state. For sixteen years the temple had lain in ruins. They had turned away from the work of God and had lost interest in spiritual things. They had commenced well in raising the altar and laying the foundation of the temple, but had failed to continue the work. It is one thing to commence a work for God, it is another thing to continue in that work. This is a voice to Christians today. One does well to take heed to Paul's exhortation: "And let us not be weary in well doing: for in due season we shall reap, if we faint not" (Gal 6.9). One can suggest reasons why they claimed that it was not the right time to build the temple.

1. It was not time because of the opposition (Ezra 4.1-4). Their attitude could have been, "If it was the time to build the temple we would not have this opposition". Their eyes were on their enemies instead of on Jehovah. They were hindered because of their lack of faith. As long as they looked to Jehovah and were dependent upon Him they were secure, but when they ceased to look to Him their adversaries filled their gaze and thus they said it was not the time. By this they sought to cover over their spiritual condition and justify their inactivity.

2. It was not time because of the edict of Artaxerxes (Ezra 4.17-24). Their spiritual condition was such that they readily ceased building the temple. Had they been steadfast in faith and faithful to God the decree of Artaxerxes would have been no hindrance. First the commandment of Artaxerxes was in relation to the city and contained no reference to the temple (Ezra 4.21). Second, since the law of the Medes and Persians was that no decrees could be changed (Dan 6.8,12,15), the decree of Artaxerxes was invalid. Thus ceasing to rebuild the temple was unjustified.

3. It was not time because the seventy years of chastisement had not been completed. However, there were two periods of seventy years that overlapped. First, the seventy years of captivity commencing with Jehoiakim being carried away captive in 606 BC (2 Chr 36.5-7) and ending in 536 BC when the remnant returned to the land (Ezra 1; Jer 29.10). Second, the seventy years of desolation commencing when Jerusalem and the temple were destroyed in Zedekiah's reign (590 BC; 2 Chr 36.17-21) and ending in the second year of Darius' reign (520 BC; Hag 1 & 2). Any inference that the temple could not be built because the seventy years had not run its course was merely an excuse. The real reason was their apathetic indifference to the claims of God and their own self-centeredness.

The people addressed (vv.3-11)

Jehovah replies to the people's excuse by pointing out that they were dwelling in their cieled houses while His House was lying desolate (vv.3-4). They were to consider their ways and were reminded of the years of crop failure (vv.5-6). Jehovah then urged them to commence building the temple, declaring that the failure they had experience was because of their neglect of His House (vv.7-11). They should have known from their history that neglecting the things of God would result in the hand of God upon them in chastisement.

The challenge of God (vv.3-4)

Jehovah speaks again, through Haggai, challenging and rebuking both the people and the leaders. The people had clearly expressed their intentions and had made their excuse to Zerubbabel and Joshua as to the rebuilding of the temple. The fact that the work had ceased for sixteen years implies that the civil and religious leaders were content to leave things as they were and had made no serious effort to stir the people from their lethargy in regard to the House of God. This was an indictment upon these leaders. It was their duty, as it is the duty of elders in local assemblies today, to encourage God's people to build for God. Haggai used the words of the people to expose their ingenuous excuse and their true spiritual condition. The repetition of the pronoun and the interrogative form of v.4 emphasise the challenge and rebuke of Jehovah. Their own argument, "The time is not come", is turned back upon them by the question, "Is it time for you, O ye...?". The contrast here is between their ornate luxurious homes and the desolate condition of God's House.

"Cieled" (SAPAN - 5603) means hidden by covering, i.e. wainscotted, panelled. They were not content with modest stone houses, but they had to have panelled walls and ceilings. They would have nothing but the best, yet the temple was still in ruins. The people found time and resources to build their own houses elaborately, but they had no time or resources to build God's House. It is inevitable that one must be either occupied with one's own things or with the Lord's. "No man can serve two masters...Ye cannot serve God and mammon" (Mt 6.24). Since they lived in comfortable houses their actual living conditions could not be so oppressive as to be a sufficient excuse for not building the House of God. The evidence was there to see what their money and energy had been used for over the years. Their sense of values was completely wrong. The Apostle Paul refers to this in Philippians 2.21: "For all seek their own, not the things which are Jesus Christ's". The same is true in many lives today. They showed no remorse for their conduct. Their attitude was opposite to that of David who was concerned for a dwelling place for God and could say, "See now, I dwell in an house of cedar, but the ark of God dwelleth within curtains" (2 Sam 7.2). Their attitude seemed to be, "Anything will do for God". They were robbing Him of His due.

God demands, and is worthy of, first place in the lives of His people. Is not this a voice to the people of God today? Would it be out of place to quote and apply to believers the words of the hymn:

> Room for pleasure, room for business;
> But for Christ the crucified -
> Not a place that He can enter
> In the heart for which He died?
> (D. W. Whittle).

Does the Lord Jesus Christ have first place in our lives? One does well to take heed to the exhortation, "But sanctify the Lord God in your hearts" (1 Pet 3.15). How many believers are prepared to spend long hours to promote their own things, but have little or no time to spend for the things of God. It is surprising how much energy some Christians expend for their own advancement yet how little is spent on spiritual things. Every child of God should take to heart the words of the Lord Jesus, "But seek ye first the kingdom of God" (Mt 6.33). Believers should be "Redeeming the time, because the days are evil" (Eph 5.16), i.e. be willing to pay the price of grasping the opportunity to live for Christ and to further His cause. Christians must remember that the Judgment Seat of Christ is before them. The words of the hymn are a challenge to all –

> Must I go, and empty handed?
> Thus my dear Redeemer meet?
> Not one day of service give Him,
> Lay no trophy at His feet?
>
> Up, ye saints, arouse, be earnest!
> Up and work while yet 'tis day;
> Ere the night of death o'ertake you,
> Strive for souls while yet you may".
>   (C. C. Luther).

The call to consider (vv.5-6)

The people were called on to consider their ways. This word "consider" is used four times by Haggai (1.5,7; 2.15,18). It is an exhortation to look back at their activities and their consequences. The word (SIM - 7760) has the idea of setting one's heart upon something. The plural nature of the word "ways" implies the conduct and its result. There was to be self-judgment, an honest assessment of their actions. The prophet's intention was to stimulate them to look back at their experiences and give thought to the reason behind them. Here the expression seems to be a rebuke about their past behaviour toward the things of God. There was nothing in their lives that glorified God. This is all very solemn, and Christians today should take it to heart. It may well be the reason for the failures in the lives of believers. It behoves Christians to take stock of their lives to ensure that there is that which brings glory to God. One can but quote H. A. Ironside: "We may look at it as entering every ramification of the life. Consider your ways, ye who have to do with the commercial world in its present conditions. How much is often tolerated among us that would not bear the all-searching eyes of Him who seeth not as man seeth! The covetous spirit of the age is eating the very life out of many companies of the Lord's people…Consider your ways in the home life. What place do you give the things of God there? Is the Bible habitually neglected, and the knee seldom bowed in prayer before the children? What wonder then if they grow up to think lightly of what you seem to place so slight a valuation upon!...Consider your ways in connection with the service of the Lord and the assembling of His people. Do trifles keep you from the assemblies of God's people for the remembrance of our Lord in His sufferings for us? Or do you neglect the preaching of the Word?...Are you generally missed at the prayer meeting, and seldom found at the Bible-reading?".

The Apostle Paul looked back and was able to say, "I count not myself to have apprehended" (Phil 3.13). The word "count" in that verse means to take an inventory (3049). It has the thought of coming to a settled conclusion after looking back and considering. After doing this there was, for Paul, but one thing to do and that was to "press toward the mark for the prize of the high calling of God in Christ Jesus" (Phil 3.14). Every believer should take stock and, whatever the conclusion, should press on in the things of God, striving to become more like Christ. They should not allow the past to hinder them, but, learning lessons from it, endeavour to live for the pleasure and glory of God. God is fully aware of our ways, but expects us to engage in self-assessment and acknowledge our failures. The Jews, rather than benefiting from ceasing to build the temple, had suffered because of their neglect. They had been robbing God, and in doing so had robbed themselves. They had been sowing to the flesh and had reaped the consequences (Prov 13.7; 2 Cor 9.6; Gal 6.8). This principle applies, in a spiritual way, to believers today who neglect spiritual things.

The results of their conduct are stated in v.6. The verbs in this verse are infinitives indicating a continued condition over a long period. The period implied is the sixteen years of neglect in building the temple. In that period the Jews sowed bountifully, but reaped little; they ate, but had not enough to satisfy them; they drank, but were not filled; they clothed themselves, but were still cold; they earned wages, but the money soon disappeared. Their expectations were never reached, and their self-centredness had robbed them of God's blessing. The causes of their calamities might have seemed natural ones, but the hand of God was behind them. "The blessing of the Lord, it maketh rich, and he addeth no sorrow with it" (Prov 10.22). The five statements in this verse can be applied to, or be typical of, Christians today who neglect spiritual things.

"Ye have sown much, and bring in little" - much activity, but no spiritual increase, no spiritual development. Carnality and neglect of the things of God results in stunted growth and barrenness of soul. Paul wrote to the Corinthians, "And I, brethren, could not speak unto you as spiritual, but as unto carnal, even as unto babes in Christ" (1 Cor 3.1). There was no spiritual growth because of fleshly desires, but the child of God should put on "the Lord Jesus Christ, and make not provision for the flesh, to fulfil the lusts thereof" (Rom 13.14).

"Ye eat, but ye have not enough" - some spiritual appetite, but neglect of the word of God results in no spiritual satisfaction. Saints today can experience spiritual hunger because of lightness in the ministry given instead of sound teaching that builds and beautifies christian character (cp. 2 Tim 1.13; 2.2; Tit 2.1). It is the unchanged and unadulterated teaching of the inspired word of God that enriches and satisfies the child of God (cp. 1 Cor 4.2). The Christian should have an intense desire for the Scriptures - "As newborn babes, desire the sincere milk of the word, that ye may grow thereby" (1 Pet 2.2), and "grow in grace, and the knowledge of our Lord and Saviour Jesus Christ" (2 Pet 3.18). The Psalmist wrote, "For he satisfieth the longing soul, and filleth the hungry soul with goodness" (Ps 107.9).

"Ye drink, but ye are not filled with drink" - thirsting but no quenching of the thirst because of worldliness and neglect of the word of God and communion with Him. The world can never satisfy the heart as the hymn writer signifies:

> I tried the broken cisterns, Lord,
> But Ah! The waters failed!
> E'en as I stooped to drink they'd fled,
> And mocked me as I wailed.
>
> Now none but Christ can satisfy....
>   (B. E.).

The Lord Jesus said to the woman of Samaria, "But whosoever drinketh of the water that I shall give him shall never thirst" (Jn 4.14; cp. Jn 7.37).

"Ye clothe you, but there is none warm" - no warmth of devotion to the Lord or genuine love for His word. One thing the Lord had against the church at Ephesus was that it had left its first love (Rev 2.4). This was a solemn and serious charge. The first place in the affections of the people of God belongs to the Lord. He must have the first place in the believer's heart (cp. Mt 10.37). It is devotion to Christ that compels one to carry out the word of God - "For this is the love of God, that ye keep his commandments: and his commandments are not grievous" (1 Jn 5.3). The Lord Jesus said, "If ye love me, keep my commandments" (Jn 14.15; cp. 2 Jn v.6).

"He that earneth wages earneth wages to put it into a bag with holes" - striving for earthly wealth, which is but temporal, results in spiritual poverty. The things of this life are passing, "for the things that are seen are temporal; but the things which are not seen are eternal" (2 Cor 4.18). For the believer to lay up treasure on earth is folly (Mt 6.19). The Christian should be laying up treasure in heaven (Mt 6.20; cp. Lk 12.33). The wise man states, "Labour not to be rich: cease from thine own wisdom" (Prov 23.4; cp. 1 Tim 6.9-10). "But godliness with contentment is great gain" (1 Tim 6.6). Their bitter disappointment was the result of living for themselves rather than living for God, and failing to rest in Him.

The appeal of God (vv. 7-8)

The exhortation "Consider your ways" is now repeated, but here it is a prospective exhortation and not a retrospective one as in v.5. Whereas in v.5 there was an element of rebuke as to their past behaviour, here it is intended to encourage them to think upon their responsibility to build for God. They were not to dwell upon their previous conduct and its consequences, but choose the way that was pleasing to God. The choice was between their own houses and the House of God, between the discipline of God and the blessing of God. Christians today have the choice of living for God or for self, of material or spiritual things, of pleasing God or pleasing self. The Lord Jesus said, "Labour not for the meat which perisheth, but for that meat which endureth unto everlasting life" (Jn 6.27). The principle in that statement is applicable to believers today. Spiritual things are more important than material, Christlikenesss and godly living are more important than worldly attainments. The exhortation is forceful in light of the previous rebuke and the calamities they had experienced. It is followed by clear instructions to build the temple. They had worked hard and purchased materials at considerable cost to build their own luxurious houses, but now they were called upon to do so in building the House of God, which they had so long neglected. This was the remedy to all their troubles and suffering. They were (i) to go up to the mountain, (ii) to bring wood and (iii) to build the House.

There are different opinions in regard to the expression "Go up to the mountain". F. C. Cook states, "According to Druisius and Rosenmuller, the mountain on which the temple was built. Others think that the word is used collectively of any neighbouring mountains, from which timber was procured, as in Nehemiah 2.8; 8.15. But it most probably refers to Lebanon (Ezra 3.7)". C. F. Keil takes the view that *"Hahar* (the mountain) is not any particular mountain, say the temple mountain...or Lebanon...but the article is used generically, and *hahar* is simply the mountain regarded as the locality in which wood chiefly grows (cp. Neh 8.15)". The reference to wood only has led to some suggesting that "the walls of the temple had been left standing when it was destroyed", and that "possibly the external walls and stone-work were considerably advanced" (Keil & Delitzsch; F. C. Cook). That neither of these could be the case is clear from the fact that a new foundation had been laid (Ezra 3.10; Zech 8.9), and also that the hand of the Lord had been upon the Jews since then because they had neglected building the temple (2.18-19). Besides this, the letter to king Darius from the adversaries of the Jews, states that they were building the temple "with great stones, and timber is laid in the walls" (Ezra 5.8).

Although Haggai specifies wood, it does not exclude other materials. The expression "bring wood", in light of the following expression, "and build the house", may well imply all building materials. It was time for them to take action and that is true for saints today. They were to go to the high places for building material and believers today should rise to the spiritual realm to enjoy communion with God and receive stamina and material to build for Him. As servants of God Christians must be active in the work of God, but in building for God one must be careful as to the material used (1 Cor 3.12-15). Believers must rise above an apathetic generation that stifles christian growth and activity. So often the work of God is neglected because of personal ambition or selfish pursuits. One must give the Lord Jesus Christ the first place in one's life.

If there was a positive response by the Jews to the exhortation of God, He would take pleasure in the rebuilt temple although it would not have the splendour of Solomon's temple. While His House remained desolate God was displeased with it, but when rebuilt He would take pleasure in it or be pleased with it. God is always displeased with the apathy and disobedience of His people, but finds pleasure in their obedience and their living for Him. The word translated "pleasure" (RASA-7521) is translated "accept" in relation to offerings (Ps 119.108; Mal 1.10,13), so the thought here could be that Jehovah would accept the rebuilt temple as an offering, showing His pleasure. Furthermore, Jehovah would be glorified or He would glorify Himself. There could be two thoughts in the expression, "I will be glorified". First, that Jehovah would be glorified by the people's obedience in building His dwelling place in their midst, and, second, that Jehovah would glorify Himself by once more pouring out His blessing upon His people. Every Christian should seek to live for the pleasure and glory of God.

The discipline of God (vv.9-11)

The prophet, with the thought of cause and effect, returns to the theme of the discipline of God (cp. v.6). Jehovah reveals why past events had been disastrous for the people. He declares that His hand had been upon them in chastisement, and in doing so He showed that, as the Creator, He was in complete control of nature.

"Looked" (PANA - 6437) has the idea here of turning one's eyes in expectation. The Hebrew infinitive indicates a continual process. Every year they anticipated rich and large harvests because of their labours, but when they gathered in the harvest it was scanty and their expectations were shattered. They might have at first considered that it was due to the land lying idle over the long years of exile, but the continual smallness of the harvests would have soon revealed that that was not the reason. The emphatic statements of Jehovah in this section would nullify any natural causes they might have in their minds. Not only were the harvests small, but the little harvest they brought home to store yearly God blew upon, i.e. caused it to be scattered as before a wind and it was blighted. It is suggested that God caused strong winds to shatter the barns and dissipate the harvest.

There is a double curse here. First instead of a bountiful harvest it was scant, then the little brought home soon disappeared. Did they wonder why harvest after harvest failed and all their hopes had been dashed? In order to arouse the people, and to emphasize the reason for such calamities the question, "Why?", is introduced, i.e. Why has this taken place?; Why has Jehovah done this? The question comes from the Lord of hosts, the Sovereign of the universe, so that the people may lay to heart the answer that follows.

"Saith" (NᶜUM - 5002) means oracle and is a term indicating that the question and response came directly from Jehovah. The clear and simple answer was that they had allowed the House of God to be desolate. The expression "mine house" is mentioned first to emphasize its importance as Jehovah's dwelling place amidst His people and to stress the seriousness of the people's neglect. The contrast between "mine house" and "his own house" is vivid, and intended to drive home the solemnity of the situation and to accentuate the enormity of the people's guilt.

"Run" (RUS - 7323) contains the idea of haste (Gen 41.14 – brought…hastily), of zeal and eagerness in anything. The preposition, unto, in the expression "ye run every man unto his own house" denotes the object of the running (cp. Prov 1.16; Is 59.7), which here is "his own house". It indicates the swiftness of each one of them in pursuing their own selfish interests. While the House of God was desolate no one took interest in it and there was no move to rectify the situation, but, at the same time, the people moved swiftly where their own houses were concerned. Their priorities were opposite to what they should have been, and because their hearts were in the wrong place Jehovah could not bless them but only chastise them. This was necessary too for their good and to bring them back to Himself.

The chastisement of God upon His people, however severe it may seem, is always a proof of His love and is always for their benefit (Heb 12.6, 10-11). It was also proof that the eye of Jehovah was upon them and that He cared about their spiritual welfare.

Because Jehovah was not given His rightful place and His House remained waste His curse, which was His chastisement for His people's neglect, is further described in vv.10-11. In these verses there is an evident link with the punishment for disobedience threatened in the law (Lev 26.19-20; Deut 28.15-24). The preposition "over" (AL - 5921) in v.10 is translated in a number of ways in the Old Testament. Here it could have the sense of "over" in keeping with the threat mentioned in Deuteronomy 28.23 (cp. Ezek 32. 8; Zech 5.3), or the sense of "because of" giving intensity to the reason for Jehovah's discipline mentioned in v.9 (cp. Ezek 33.29; Micah 6.13).

In both clauses of v.10 the idea behind the verb "stayed" (KALA - 3607) is that the heaven and earth are personified implying that, in obedience to Jehovah, the heaven withheld the dew and the earth withheld its produce. This was the result of His chastisement of the people's disobedience (cp. Hos 2.9-11). F. A. Tatford states, "'The dews of the Syrian nights are excessive', says Sir George Adam Smith *(Historical Geography of the Holy Land)*; on many mornings it looks as if there had been heavy rain, and this is the sole slackening of the drought which the land feels from May to October...the Creator had withheld the copious dew from their fields". The dew was indispensable for vegetation in the hot rainless summers and is therefore referred to frequently in the Scriptures as a blessing from God (Gen 27.28,39; Deut 33.13,28; Zech 8.12). This necessary dew being withheld resulted in the loss of the produce, and was further evidence of Jehovah's displeasure.

The involvement and concern of Jehovah in the welfare of the returned remnant is evident by the frequent use of the personal pronoun "I". It is found twenty times in the prophecy, five in this chapter (vv.8,9,11,13), and fifteen times in ch.2 (vv.4,5,6,7,9,15,17,19,21,22,23). Jehovah called for a widespread drought on the land and mountains so that the corn, wine, oil and other produce suffered. This resulted in hardship for men and cattle, and the labour of the people produced nothing.

The opening expression "I called" indicates that the heaven and the earth (v.10) were but instruments in His hand which brought drought and famine (v.11). It is also intended to contrast the prompt response of nature to Jehovah's call with the apathetic and indifferent response of the people regarding the temple. Famine in the Scriptures is often an indication of God's chastisement or His judgment (Ps 105.16; Is 24.3; 51.19; Jer 14.15-16; Ezek 14.13). "Drought" (HOREB - 2721) refers, strictly speaking, only to the land, but here it is extended to men and cattle because of the affect it has upon them. The idea here may be that of desolation. There seems to be a play on the Hebrew word for "waste" (HAREB - 2720) in v.9 and that for "drought" in v.11. Because Jehovah's House was waste or desolate (HAREB) through the neglect of His people, He punished them with drought (HOREB). The Septuagint replaces "drought" with the word "sword" (HEREB - 2719) presuming that the punishment referred to was the result of Jehovah smiting them with His sword. Undoubtedly the widespread drought was an indication of His displeasure and an act of His discipline.

The word translated "corn" (DAGAN - 1715) means grain and refers to a variety of crops. The Hebrew word for "new wine" (TIROSH - 8492) is not the general word for wine in the Old Testament. Strong's Concordance refers to it as *"must* or fresh grape-juice (as just *squeezed* out); by implication (rarely) fermented *wine"*. The grain, wine, and oil were the main crops of the land and are frequently mentioned together as the products of the land (Deut 8.8; 11.14; 2 Chr 31.5; 32.28; Hos 2.8,22). The expression "labour of the hands" refers to all the cultivation and preparation necessary to reap a rich harvest. The word for "labour" (YᵉGIA - 3018) comes from a prime root word (YAGEA - 3021) meaning wearied or exhausted. Thus the idea here is of toiling to the point of weariness without anything to show for it. F. A. Tatford states, "Jehovah made it clear that He had not abdicated and that He was still concerned with His people's conduct. Moore writes, 'God has not abandoned the universe to the sightless action of general laws, but is so related to that universe as to be able to direct its laws to the fulfilment of His purposes, whether in rewarding the good, punishing the evil, or answering prayer, without deranging or destroying the normal action of those laws themselves'. It is important to realise that the throne is still occupied and that the doings of men are all under the eye of the Omniscient".

Verses 12-15: A Message of Assurance
The message Haggai gave was undoubtedly given in the power of the Spirit of God. This message, with its rebuke of the people, could not be righteously challenged since it was supported by the law of God. It also fell upon attentive ears. The response to Jehovah's proclamations through the prophet was swift and unanimous. In particular, the initiative was taken by the leaders, Zerubbabel and Joshua, who had been singled out at the commencement of the message. Bearing the responsibility for the people, they led them in their response to Jehovah's claim. Within a month they commenced to rebuild the temple which had lain in ruins for so long.

Their obedience (v.12)
Zerubbabel, Joshua, and the rest of the people took heed to the message, and the effect of Jehovah's protestations became evident. There was no disobedience or division among the people, for they realized that what the prophet Haggai had proclaimed was the message of Jehovah to them. The expression "with all the remnant of the people" does not refer to the rest of the nation apart from its leaders, but to that section of the nation that had returned from exile in Babylon (Zech 8.6; cp. Neh 7.72). It also implies the frailty of the people (cp. Is 16.14) as it was but a fraction of the nation which had at one time been great and numerous (Gen 22.17; Deut 4.6-8; 1 Chr 27.23). "Remnant" (SH°ERIT - 7611) means residue, or portion and with its related words is used frequently in the Old Testament of that portion of the people left after some devastation (2 Kings 19.4; Is 37.31-32; Ezek 9.8), of the small company who returned from exile (Ezra 3.8; 9.8,14; Neh 1.3), and of the nucleus of the nation in a coming day (Is 10.20-22; 11.11,16; Jer 23.3; Micah 2.12; Zech 8.12). They responded to the message of God in a twofold way by obeying the voice of Jehovah and fearing Him. "Obeyed" (SHAMA - 8085) means to hearken, or to take heed, i.e. to fully intend to carry out. The AV rightly represents their purpose of heart which, in the sight of Jehovah, was obedience although it was not exercised until v.14. The task ahead would take all their resources and energy, but Jehovah was with them. The obedience of a believer is the outward expression of love for Christ - "If ye love me, keep my commandments" (Jn 14.15). Obedience should be a principle of life for the believer. The expression "As obedient children" in 1 Peter 1.14 is literally, "As children of obedience", and implies that obedience belongs to Christians

as a mother belongs to her children. Obedience should be the nature or the ruling disposition of believers. It is the opposite to what they were before being saved. Then they were "the children of disobedience" (Eph 2.2) and disobedience was a principle of that life. However, a change took place and believers received a new kind of life, the life of God, which is seen in obedience and in other ways.

The test of a Christian's spirituality is the extent of his or her obedience to the word of God. Samuel said, "Behold, to obey is better than sacrifice, and to hearken than the fat of rams" (1 Sam 15.22). Hearkening to the voice of God goes hand in hand with obeying His word.

The expression "the Lord their God" (Jehovah their Elohim), used twice in this verse, implies that they now had a greater appreciation of the greatness and holiness of God, and a closer intimacy with Him than before Jehovah's message was proclaimed by Haggai. This was the reason for their rapid response. The closer believers are to the Lord Jesus Christ and to the Father the more eager they will be to obey the word of God. The greater the appreciation believers have of God and His Son the more ready they are to live for them. The name Elohim is plural and refers to the three Persons in the Godhead, i.e. the Triune God. It only occurs here and in v.14 in this book. The juxtaposition of the expressions "the voice of the Lord their God" and "the words of Haggai the prophet" indicate that the message given by Haggai was divinely inspired and had divine authority. This is in keeping with the fact that "the Lord their God had sent him". As a result the people feared before Jehovah. They saw their sinful condition in His sight and realized that the drought was the judgment of God upon them. Godly fear was created in their hearts by Haggai's message. No other prophet to the people of God experienced such a positive and wholehearted response to his preaching.

The fear of God is often linked with the service of God in the Scriptures (Josh 24.14; Ps 2.11). It does not imply a terror or dread of God's judgment, but a reverential respect and awe in appreciation of the greatness, grandeur, and glory of the Omnipotent God. This fear is the beginning of knowledge (Prov 1.7), it gives strong confidence, and is the fountain of life (Prov 14.26-27).

Their assurance (v.13)

Immediately after the people's response to Jehovah's message He gave them a short, though sufficient, word of encouragement in order to stimulate them for the work ahead. He speaks again through the prophet who is described as "the Lord's messenger in the Lord's message". Only Haggai of all the prophets is designated in this way although all the other genuine prophets were also Jehovah's messengers, sent by Him to make known His word and will (cp. Mal 2.7 where it is used of the priest). The word for "messenger" (MALAK - 4397) is mainly translated "angel", or "angels", who are God's messengers, but it is also translated "ambassador"

(2 Chr 35.21; Is 30.4; Ezek 17.15) as well as "messenger" from which the author's name of the last prophetic book, Malachi, (MALAKIY - 4401) comes. As the messenger of Jehovah, Haggai was invested with divine authority and spoke by His command and in His name. The word he proclaimed was not by impulse or through human reasoning, but it was the word of Jehovah. The message here was short, "I am with you, saith the Lord", but it had depth of meaning. It was exactly what they needed, i.e. the assurance of Jehovah's favour instead of His displeasure and chastisement. This short message indicated the genuineness of their repentance and their determination to build the House of God. They were only a remnant with limited resources and were surrounded by enemies. They had failed and grieved Jehovah, but these few words gave them hope and guaranteed them His presence and protection. The work was His and everything that was necessary to build the temple would be provided by Him. They could ask for no more, because the presence of Jehovah was the greatest of blessings and was all-sufficient assuring them of complete success in the project. That presence was the answer to all their problems and difficulties. Where Jehovah was, nothing could be lacking. How gracious He was to assure them of His presence.

The people of God, down through the ages, have rested upon this promise in every circumstance and trial. It was the stay and strength for Joseph (Gen 39.2,21); assurance and certainty for Moses at the burning bush (Ex 3.12); courage and strength for Joshua as the new leader of Israel (Josh 1.5,9); the might and victory for Gideon in the battle (Judg 6.16); and defence for Jeremiah in his stand for God (Jer 1.8,19). This promise is reiterated by the Lord Jesus Christ to His disciples: "Lo, I am with you alway, even unto the end of the world" (Mt 28.20). This is the assurance Christians have today as they go forth in the Lord's work. The power, ability and necessities are supplied by God, and His presence is assured to each one until the end of the pathway. Every believer can rest on this promise "for he hath said, I will never leave thee, nor forsake thee. So that we may boldly say, the Lord is my helper, and I will not fear what man shall do unto me" (Heb 13.5-6). Faith lays hold of this promise and all the difficulties, problems and trials of life recede into insignificance in the enjoyment of His presence.

Their activity (vv.14-15)
It was Jehovah who stirred or awakened the spirits of the leaders and the people and through the message of the prophet they were heartened and prepared to toil in building the temple. He gave them the desire and the energy to rebuild His House. This is still true today for believers, "For it is God which worketh in you both to will and to do of his good pleasure" (Phil 2.13). God, the Holy Spirit, works effectually in the saints to produce spiritual desires. Every spiritual desire is produced by the Holy Spirit, through the entrance of the word of God. However, those spiritual desires

can be stifled by self-ambition, materialism, worldliness, and other fleshly lusts. Not only does the Spirit of God create these spiritual desires, but He also imparts to the believer the ability and strength to carry them out to the pleasure of God. One must appreciate that every work of grace can be attributed only to divine power operating by the Holy Spirit. The contrast to this is "the spirit that now worketh in the children of disobedience" (Eph 2.2). The devil works in unbelievers, influencing and encouraging them in a life of disobedience, bringing displeasure to God. The Jews, as a result of being stirred up, "came and did work in the house of the Lord of hosts, their God" (v.14). There was no more hesitation; they left their own occupations and exerted their energy in the rebuilding of Jehovah's House.

The expression "the house of the Lord of hosts" implies the great privilege granted to them in serving One so majestic, great and glorious. At that stage the temple was still desolate, but they would rebuild it. This reminds one of the great privilege and dignity of being part of a local assembly which is referred to as "house of God" (1 Tim 3.15), but also of the responsibility to order one's life so that one's behaviour is suitable to and worthy of the House of God. This work began on the twenty-fourth day of the sixth month in the second year of Darius' reign (v.15), which was twenty-three days after they were challenged by Jehovah's first message proclaimed by Haggai (v.1). Doubtless that period was spent in removing the debris, gathering material, and preparing to build. It is evident from the parallel passage in Ezra that this commencement of rebuilding the temple was met by opposition from their enemies who notified King Darius, hoping that he would stop the work. However, the Jews did not wait for the sanction of the king because they had heard the message of Jehovah. They simply acted on the word of the Lord and confidently carried on with the work. Darius, to the enemies' disappointment, confirmed the decree of Cyrus and ordered them to allow the work to continue and forbad them to interfere with the rebuilding (Ezra 5.1-6.12). This was an evidence that, because of their positive response to Jehovah's claim, He was with and for them. How blessed are the people of God who willingly respond to His word, who allow the Spirit to direct them and are faithful in His service!

HAGGAI 2

This chapter contains three messages from Jehovah to the people in the seventh and ninth months of the second year of Darius' reign. These messages were to strengthen and encourage the people in the rebuilding of the temple and to remove any despondency. The first message was proclaimed about four weeks after the building work commenced and refers to how this new building would compare with the splendour of the temple that Solomon built (vv.1-9). The second, uttered two months later, was of a different character, an illustration through questions to and answers from the priests in order to expose the condition of the people while the temple was neglected, yet promising blessing from that day onward (vv.10-19). The concluding message, delivered on the same day as the previous one, is addressed particularly to Zerubbabel and it pronounced the future overthrow of the Gentile kingdoms and the establishing of the Messianic age (v.20-23). The Lord is seen in the chapter as the Restorer of the temple's glory (vv.7,9), the Remover of the throne of the kingdoms of this world (v.22), and the Glorious King of the Messianic Kingdom (v.23).

Verses 1-9: A Message of Exhortation and Encouragement
There were those among the people who remembered what Solomon's temple was like before it was destroyed by the Chaldeans (2 Kings 25.10-17; 2 Chr 36.17-19). Whatever had been achieved in the past month, the temple in its present state was still a sorry spectacle and they were convinced that it was impossible to restore it to its former magnificence and glory (vv.1-3). Thus they were disheartened and despondent, but Jehovah called upon them to be strong and reiterated His promise to be with them (vv.4-5). To encourage them and to rally them to maintain the momentum of the work, Jehovah stated that the glory of the future temple would be greater than Solomon's (vv.6-9).

The despondency of the people (vv.1-3)
Approximately one month after the commencement of rebuilding the House of God, Haggai delivered another message from Jehovah. This message was intended to encourage them and to exhort them to continue in the work. It was proclaimed shortly before Zechariah's first message to the remnant. The day selected to deliver the message, the twenty-first day of the seventh month, was significant. It was the seventh day of the Feast of Tabernacles (Booths) when the people should have been rejoicing before the Lord their God (Lev 23.39-44; Deut 16.13-15). The seventh month in the Jewish calendar was called Ethanim (1 Kings 8.2), but in the Jewish Talmud it is called Tishri. In regard to this date, Ivan Steeds, noting the heavy emphasis of the number seven, states, "Not only would this remind us of the impeccability of God's timing as He intervenes to meet any crisis of confidence in our affairs, but also it would remind us

that all God's purposes concerning His House bear the hallmark of perfection". ·

This was the time of the final ingathering of the harvest. Thus it was not only called the Feast of Tabernacles, but also the Feast of Ingathering. The event would make them conscious of the failure of past harvests. The sacrifices during the Feast of Tabernacles were numerous, exceeding those of any other Jewish feast. It was a feast of thanksgiving to God and of rejoicing because of His blessing. The message was to the governor (Zerubbabel), the high priest (Joshua) and all the people who had returned from exile. As mentioned previously, the word for "residue" is given as "remnant" in ch.1 (vv.12,14). When the foundation of the temple was laid there was the sounding of trumpets and cymbals to praise Jehovah, and singing and thanksgiving and joyful shouting of the people because of the commencement of the restoration of the House of God (Ezra 3.10-11). However, there were also loud lamentations from the older generation who remembered the splendour and greatness of the temple. One does not know how much construction had occurred during the previous weeks, but it is evident that enough had taken place for a comparison to be made between the temple being built and Solomon's temple. Since it was the feast time it would be only natural for the older generation, though smaller in number than when the foundation was laid eighteen years before, to compare the meagre beginning of this temple with the glorious temple of Solomon overlaid inside with pure gold. It was also natural to compare the prosperity and abundance of sacrifices in Solomon's day with the scanty harvests and poverty of the present feast time.

These comparisons and their present circumstances seem to have diminished their zeal and confidence, resulting in a gloomy frame of mind. Thus this message was given to console and assure those who were in despair. Jehovah Himself draws attention to the comparison being made by the opening question of v.3: "Who is left among you that saw this house in her first glory?". This was addressed to the few who were left of the generation which had seen the glorious temple of Solomon about seventy years before (Zech 1.12). The glory of the temple Solomon built was renowned, glistening as it was with precious stones and gold. The holy of holies was overlaid with pure gold and contained the golden altar, the golden lampstands and the golden table of shewbread (1 Kings 6.20-21; 7.48-51; 2 Chr 3.8-13; 4.19-22). It is not surprising therefore that the older people, remembering the magnificence of the former temple, were dismayed.

The second question followed immediately after the first: "…and how do ye see it now?". Although comparison was being made between the temple Solomon built and the one now being built, the expression "this house" in the first question and the pronoun "it" in the second indicates that Jehovah viewed them as only one house of the Lord, i.e. He only had one place where He dwelt in the midst of His people. Jehovah's House had been seen in all its glory, then in ruin, but now was being rebuilt. This temple is identified with Solomon's as fulfilling the same purpose, built upon the same hallowed ground, and being central in the nation's life. The word translated "nothing" (AYIN - 369) in the final question of v.3 has the idea of nonentity, or as not existing, i.e. worthless and of no value. C. F. Keil translates the expression as "so is it, as having no existence," or "as not existing (nothing), so is it in your eyes". The comparison emphasised the limitations, weakness and impoverishment of the remnant who were working to rebuild the House of God. It could be that, not only the few who had seen Solomon's temple, but others also joined in the criticism of the work, making matters worse. Restoration could only be sustained by the enthusiasm of all the people. The reminder of weakness and poverty would have affected their confidence and stifled their willingness to continue building.

Some of the older generation of believers today are inclined to dwell on past days and belittle those of the younger generation who are seeking to live for God. They speak of the good old days, of the godly believers in those days, and of the achievements of faithful preachers. However, one must appreciate that it is the present that Christians must live for and not dwell on the past. Believers today can live godly lives as much as they did heretofore and they can serve God just as faithfully and leave the results with Him. One must not become despondent because of what took place formerly, but grasp the opportunity to live for God, to obey His word and serve Him faithfully out of love to Him. Despondency can be experienced by Christians engaged in the work of God today, but the anticipation of a coming day and a longing to be faithful labourers will often dispel such a feeling of being downcast.

It might also have been that the older people were dismayed because of the absence of certain items, such as the ark and mercy seat which were in Solomon's temple (See F. A. Tatford). Should this comparison be used to prevent the people continuing to rebuild the temple? The answer is "No" as the following verses show. The comparison was not introduced by Jehovah to discourage them, but to show them that His estimation was different to theirs (cp. Is 55.8-9) and to encourage them to depend solely upon Him. Ivan Steeds states, "Surely the lesson, then and now, is that God would have His people assess their circumstances in realistic fashion. Nothing is to be gained by resting on delusions…Here was a remnant-people, living in the midst of hostile nations…made conscious of their weakness and inadequacy, and of having to live under the shadow of past glories. What they needed to realise was that God looks for His people to work in connection with His House at all times, whatever the circumstances, and whatever the results of their labours".

The promise of Jehovah (vv.4-5)
The people needed a word of encouragement, and this message was

aimed at bringing stability to them as well as tranquillity. This could only be achieved if God was given His rightful place in their hearts and in the completing of the temple. They needed to be strong and courageous in carrying out the Lord's work in His way. Thus, to the discouraged and despondent comes the threefold exhortation, "Yet now be strong, O Zerubbabel...be strong, O Joshua...be strong, all ye people of the land". The repetition of the exhortation "be strong" emphasises the need for strength in the work of rebuilding. They were not to look to the past, but be courageous in the present work of building Jehovah's House. The idea here is for them to work on bravely and finish the work they have begun. It is often easy to begin a work, but it is more difficult to continue in that work. They had a work to do in their day, and the complaints of the older generation ought not to be allowed to hinder them in that work. They had the opportunity and privilege of working for Jehovah at that time and ought to engage in that work without fear of men. Believers today should grasp the opportunity and privilege of engaging in the Lord's work knowing that He could come at any moment - "Occupy till I come" (Lk 19.13).

The exhortation to the people, "be strong", has been used to and by the people of God down through the ages. It was used to stimulate Israel to enter and possess the land (Deut 11.8), to encourage Joshua as the new leader of the nation (Deut 31.7; Josh 1.6-7,9,18), and by Joshua to the nation (Josh 10.25). It was used by David to Solomon (1 Kings 2.2; 1 Chr 22.13; 28.10,20), by Azariah to Asa (2 Chr 15.7), and by Hezekiah to the people (2 Chr 32.7). The double exhortation "be strong, yea, be strong" was used to encourage Daniel (Dan 10.19) who wrote, "the people that do know their God shall be strong, and do exploits" (Dan 11.32). The exhortation was also used by Zechariah to the same people as Haggai (Zech 8.9). It does not refer to human resources, but to strength received from Jehovah, the omnipotent One, who assured them of His presence, "for I am with you, saith the Lord of hosts". They may have returned to ruin and desolation, and failed to rebuild the temple, but they now had the assurance and joy that Jehovah was with them, and this was their greatest strength. The consciousness of Jehovah's presence would give them might and confidence. The power of Jehovah would be made known in their weakness.

The Apostle Paul learned this from the reply to his request that the thorn in the flesh might be removed: "My grace is sufficient for thee: for my strength is made perfect in weakness" (2 Cor 12.9). The power of Christ upon Paul was more beneficial than physical health. Thus the apostle could go on to write, "Most gladly therefore will I rather glory in my infirmities, that the power of Christ may rest upon me". Christians are exhorted to "be strong in the grace that is in Christ Jesus" (2 Tim 2.1). The power that resides in Christ is available to Christians, through grace, but is only experienced in the measure in which they are in touch with the risen Lord Himself. There is a sufficiency in Christ to strengthen believers continually in the pathway, enabling them to serve Him faithfully whatever the circumstances. The enjoyment of fellowship with the Lord is therefore absolutely essential to being strengthened. Self judgment is necessary in order to prevent anything hindering the enjoyment of fellowship. The strength is available, but the responsibility rests with believers to avail themselves of it by being continually in touch with the risen and glorified Lord. Paul was in the good of this and therefore could say, "I can do all things through Christ which strengtheneth me" (Phil 4.13). One has delightfully rendered it as, "I can do all things through Christ Who continues to pour His strength into me". Strength that is used up in the christian pathway and conflict is replaced by fresh strength poured in by the Lord. What an encouragement, along the road, for Christians to know that they have a continual supply of strength, from the Lord, to enable them to remain faithful amidst departure and ever changing circumstances and conditions. They are exhorted, "Watch ye, stand fast in the faith, quit you like men, be strong" (1 Cor 16.13).

Although it is claimed that there are difficulties in the translation of the first clause in v.5, the import seems plain, and its link with the end of v.4 is clear enough (see S. R. Driver and F. C. Cook). To confirm the promise of His presence in v.4 Jehovah takes them back to the exodus and His promise made there by solemn covenant. Thus the thought is, "I am with you as I covenanted with you when you came out of Egypt". The promise of divine help was confirmed by reference to the past covenant. At the exodus God had been with them in the pillar of cloud by day and in the pillar of fire by night (Ex 13.21; 40.38; Neh 9.12). The same power manifested then was available to them now and this assurance would have been a comfort to them. The covenant at Sinai is referred to here, when Jehovah bound Himself to make Israel His own, separating it from other nations (Ex 19.5-6; Deut 14.2). The covenant promises of God were unchangeable and unfailing. Although the Israelites sinned in worshipping the golden calf, Jehovah still said to Moses, "My presence shall go with thee" (Ex 33.14). Jehovah's power had been demonstrated in their deliverance out of Egypt and His faithfulness had been manifested in the fulfilment of His promise down through the centuries. The covenant He had made with them had never been rescinded, and although there was no visible Shekinah cloud Jehovah was still with the remnant in the land. The word of Jehovah was true and certain. Thus they could depend completely upon it.

In the same way the Christian's word should be reliable. There is a saying, "an Englishman's word is his bond", but on numerous occasions that has proved to be false. However, the believer's word should always be his or her bond. The principle that should govern the Christian is "But let your communication be, Yea, yea; Nay, nay: for whatsoever is more than these cometh of evil" (Mt 5.37; James 5.12). The thrust is that the Christian's word should be constantly and utterly trustworthy. Anything but a straightforward answer tends to evil.

As well as having the favour of Jehovah's promise (cp. Ex 29.45-46) the Jews were assured of the abiding presence of the Holy Spirit in their midst enabling them to carry out the work of Jehovah - "Not by might, nor by power, but by my spirit, saith the Lord of hosts" (Zech 4.6). The implication is that His presence had been continually with them. This is true of the people of God in the present who are indwelt by the gracious Spirit of God. Ivan Steeds states, "Believers today should be conscious that the Spirit of God is as much with us, indwelling every true Christian, and dwelling in the midst of each local assembly of Christians, as He was with those of the early church after Pentecost (1 Cor 6.19; Eph 2.22, RV)". The evidence of the divine presence was in the messages of both Haggai and Zechariah. The presence of Jehovah and the working of His Spirit in their midst should dispel any despondency and fear. Thus the exhortation, "fear ye not". Jehovah would carry out His word and His purpose would be fulfilled.

The glory of the future temple (vv.6-9)

Here there is a sudden change in the subject of prophecy from the rebuilding of the temple to the prediction of future events. Although it may seem irrelevant to the circumstances at the time, this section is intended to encourage, comfort and assure the remnant by reminding them of the nation's glorious future. The Jews had failed in the rebuilding of the temple through fear of the Medo-Persian power, but this prophecy assured them that Jehovah would ultimately deal with all world powers. These prophetic predictions should be compared with the contemporary prophecies of Zechariah (eg. Zech 1.14-15,21; 2.7-9; 9.9-10) as well as other prophecies. This passage is difficult to study because of the various views expressed by different commentaries. The opening verse is viewed as particularly controversial because of its difficult construction. Although different opinions will be noted, one is convinced that the verses are clearly Messianic and deal with events prior to and including the millennial reign of the Lord Jesus Christ. The title "the Lord of hosts" is prominent in this section. Indeed it commences and ends with this title. It occurs five times and is mentioned in each of the four verses. The indication is that the future is under His sovereign control, and that the events predicted are in keeping with His will and purpose. One notes the power of Jehovah - v.6, the pleasure of Jehovah - v.7, the possession of Jehovah - v.8, and the purpose of Jehovah - v.9.

The meaning of the Hebrew word for "once" (EHAD - 259) in v.6 is generally disputed. It has been taken by some commentators to refer to the indefinite article - "The Hebrew for 'once' expresses the indefinite article 'a'", - while others take its meaning as "once, and only once" thus only alluding to the future (see Jamieson, Fausset & Brown, Keil & Delitzsch, and A. C. Jennings). However, the quotation of this verse in Hebrews 12.26, "Yet once more I shake not the earth only, but also heaven", indicates that there is a reference to a past shaking as well as a future one. This is supported by the Theological Wordbook of the Old Testament which states, "In Haggai 2.6 the Lord warned that he would shake heaven and earth 'once more in a little while'". C. F. Keil agrees and explains that, "In the verse before us it is used with reference to the previous shaking of the world at the descent of Jehovah upon Sinai to establish the covenant with Israel, to which the author of the Epistle to the Hebrews has quite correctly taken it as referring (Heb 12.26)", and so does F. E. Stallan who writes, "If at Sinai the earth shook they should remember the words of the prophet Haggai, 'Yet once more I shake not the earth only but also the heavens'. The writer is obviously reminding the readers that there is a limit to God's patience" (see also F. A. Tatford).

It is evident from the opening word "For" of v.6 that there is a link with the previous verse, that link being the covenant given at Sinai and the shaking that took place then. This has been objected to by some commentators who claim that only the earth was shaken at Sinai and only in the Sinaitic region (see Jamieson, Fausset & Brown and Keil & Delitzsch). In view of the following statements, "the earth trembled, and the heavens dropped" (Judg 5.4), and, "The earth shook, the heavens also dropped at the presence of God" (Ps 68.8), that claim is difficult to justify.

There are also different views about the expression "it is a little while". One can do no better than quote F. A. Tatford. "Many commentators lay stress on the phrase 'it is a little while' and maintain that the fulfilment of the prediction must have occurred at an early date after the announcement…This argument, of course, ignores the possibility of more than one fulfilment of a prediction. But the fact remains that no event comparable with the earthquake and Divine revelation of Sinai took place in the near future after Haggai's utterance of prophecy. Some writers interpret the prophecy as relating to the imminent destruction of the Medo-Persian Empire by Greece and as possibly also anticipating the conflicts of the Ptolemies and the Seleucids and the ultimate government of the world by the Romans. Calvin and others, however, see the universal convulsion as symbolic of the spiritual effect of the preaching of the gospel on the nations of the world. Neither of these alternatives is really a satisfactory explanation, and the only possible conclusion is that the reference is to the events described in the New Testament, following the Great Tribulation." Tatford's conclusion is correct, for the shaking of the heavens and the earth by God is apocalyptic in character and is confirmed by the Lord Jesus Christ (Mt 24.29; Lk 21.25) and in the book of the Revelation (6.12-17; 11.13; 16.17-18). This is also confirmed in other Old Testament prophecies (Is 13.9-13; Joel 2.10-11, 30-31; 3.13-16; Nah 1.5). It is clear from these various passages that physical and natural convulsions are indicated. The final fulfilment and the steps that lead to it are blended together in the passage.

The use of the expression "it is a little while" seems to emphasise the reality and certainty of the events predicted. The brevity of time in such predictions is not unusual in the prophetic books, although the end times are in view - "The great day of the Lord is near, it is near, and hasteth greatly" (Zeph 1.14; cp. Ezek 30.3; Obad v.15); "for the day of the Lord cometh, for it is nigh at hand" (Joel 2.1; cp. Is 13.6; Joel 1.15; Zeph 1.7). It is "a little while" in the eyes of Jehovah and in view of the eternal future. The clear link with v.5 is that as the earth trembled and the heavens were moved at Jehovah's presence in the past at Sinai, even so will they be affected by His presence in a future day, but to a greater degree. Also, just as in the past the God of Israel came in glory to make a covenant with Israel after their deliverance from Egypt (Deut 33.2), so He will come in glory in a future day to execute judgment and deliver Israel from its enemies in order to fulfil His covenant. As Jehovah acted on the behalf of the Israelites at the exodus so He will act again to bring them salvation. This would be a comfort and an encouragement to the remnant seeking to rebuild the temple. Christians today may experience problems and opposition, like the remnant of Haggai's day, but they know that the Lord who delivered them from the bondage of sin will, in a coming day, deliver them from this sinful world. Only then will they enter into the fulness of salvation. In the meantime believers know, in spite of the difficulties and trials of life, that "greater is he that is in you, than he that is in the world" (1 Jn 4.4), and that nothing can separate them from the love of God, which is in Christ Jesus our Lord (Rom 8.35-39) - "If God be for us, who can be against us?" (Rom 8.31).

There will also be a future shaking of all nations (v.7) which is linked with the shaking of the elements. The shaking of the nations by Jehovah refers to His judgment upon them. This also can be linked to Israel's deliverance from Egypt when the Egyptians were shaken by the plagues and also to their overthrow and the fear of other nations (Ex 15.12-16). The word "nations" refers to the Gentile nations. There will be social and political unrest and conflict culminating in the most dreadful and fearful intervention of God in judgment (cp. Zeph 1.2-3). This future universal judgment will be the result of man's wickedness and rebellion against God (Rev 9.20-21; 16.1). C. F. Keil states, "But if the shaking of heaven and earth effects a violent breaking up of the existing condition of the universe, the shaking of all nations can only be one by which an end is put to the existing condition of the world of nations, by means of great political convulsions, and indeed, according to the explanation given in v.22, by the Lord overthrowing the throne of the kingdoms, annihilating their power, and destroying their materials of war, so that one falls by the sword of the other, that is to say, by wars and revolutions, by which the might of the heathen world is broken and annihilated" (see also F. A. Tatford). The period in view is the time that God's judgment will fall upon the satanically inspired rebellion against all that is of God and will be brought to an end with the manifestation of the Messiah who will destroy all who oppose Him (Rev 16.13-16; 19.11-21).

The shaking of nature and of the nations will usher in the coming of "the desire of all nations". There are many different opinions and much controversy over this expression because of the various renderings of it. It is given as, "the choice portions of all the nations shall come" (LXX), "the desirable things of all nations shall come (RV), and "so that the treasures of all nations shall come in" (RSV). C. L. Feinberg states, "Much difference of opinion has centred about the interpretation of v.7, especially the words 'the desire of all nations' (AV), or 'the precious things of all nations' (ASV). Some of the translations offered are: 'the precious possessions of the heathen', or 'the Gentiles shall come with their delightful things'...The interpretation in these renderings is pretty much this: the lack in this Temple by way of outward adornment would be more than compensated for by the precious gifts which all nations would yet bring to make the Temple of the Lord glorious. This they will do in homage to the true God. This interpretation is supposed to square with the fact that the feminine singular subject has a plural verb. It is suggested that reference is being made to 'the good things' of the new covenant. We do well to remember that from earliest times the majority of christian interpreters have referred this passage to the coming of Christ. Jewish tradition also referred it to the Messiah...In Hebrew an abstract noun is often placed for the concrete, so this could refer to the Messiah. The plural verb is no argument against the Messianic interpretation, because the verb sometimes agrees with the second of two nouns...the prophecy relates to the glory of His second coming (Mal 3.1)" (see also Jamieson, Fausset & Brown and W. Kelly). In spite of different renderings and views one can only concur with Feinberg and the majority of christian commentators. One has come to the conclusion that the AV rendering of the expression "the desire of all nations shall come" is correct and refers to the manifestation of the Lord Jesus Christ in glory (Is 63.1-3; Mt 24.30; Lk 21.27). In fact this is the rendering of ancient Jewish expositors, the Chaldee Targum, and the Vulgate. The whole creation groans and travails in pain together waiting for that day of the Lord's manifestation (Rom 8.19-22). The coming of the long awaited Messiah is immediately followed by Jehovah filling His House with glory.

The commentators who take "the desire of all nations" to mean the precious things or treasures of all nations also say that these precious things or treasures will be used to fill the temple with glory (Is 60.5-7). Although it is true that those left of the nations will go up to Jerusalem yearly to worship (Zech 14.16-17) and bring offerings (Zeph 3.10), there is no indication that those offerings are used to beautify the House of God. On the contrary, it seems from Zechariah 14.14 that the Jews themselves will gather the spoil of the nations rather than the nations bringing their wealth to Jerusalem. Jehovah Himself will fill His House with glory in the Person of the Messiah. Just as the presence of Jehovah had filled the tabernacle with His glory (Ex 40.34) and His presence had filled Solomon's temple with His glory (1 Kings 8.11), so also will the presence of the Messiah, the Lord Jesus Christ, in the millennial temple fill it with His glory.

Some expositors see the fulfilment of this prophecy in the Lord's first advent. C. F. Keil states, "The majority of the commentators have referred these words to the glorification of the temple through the appearance of Jesus in it". Although there was a partial fulfilment then, the prophecy is actually looking on to the second advent of the Lord Jesus Christ when He will return to the earth in all His majesty and glory as the King of kings and Lord of lords (Rev 19.11-16).

Verse 8 is also taken by some commentators to refer to the riches of the nations - "The 'wealth of the nations' is Mine; and they will offer to Me of it willingly and abundantly" (see S. R. Driver and F. C. Cook). However, the verse was intended to give further assurance and encouragement to the Jews who would be unable to beautify the temple with precious things. The comparison made between the temple they were building and Solomon's temple, embellished with so much gold, would have disturbed them, but Jehovah declared that the silver and gold was His. All the wealth of the world is Jehovah's and He disposes of it as He wills. They were not to be disturbed by the absence of silver and gold because Jehovah could easily supply them if they were required. Their inability to adorn the temple was irrelevant, for Jehovah was going to beautify His House. Its embellishment was not going to be precious metals or treasures, but the glory of the coming Messiah whose preciousness would outshine all of earth's treasures. Although Solomon's temple had glorious materials, the closing verse of this section states that the glory of the future temple will outshine that. Jehovah views all the temples, in different periods, as one (cp. v.3), as His House in the midst of His people. The Jews themselves viewed the House of God built by Solomon, destroyed by the Babylonians and rebuilt by Zerubbabel as the same House (Ezra 5.11-13). Thus, "this latter house" does not refer to the temple built by Zerubbabel or by Herod, but to the temple in Jerusalem in the Messianic age. The emphasis, in v.9, is upon the former and latter glory of His House, and the expression "The glory of this latter house shall be greater than of the former" has been rendered, "The latter glory of this house shall be greater than the former" (see A. C. Jennings, S. R. Driver, and also F. C. Cook).

Those of the older generation who were looking back to the temple of Solomon are now encouraged to look on to that future day when the glory of Jehovah's House will exceed that of Solomon's day. The reference here is to the millennial temple described in Ezekiel 40-44. In that coming day, the Lord Jesus Christ, who said that "in this place is one greater than the temple" (Mt 12.6), will fill the temple with His glory, which surpasses its glory at any other time (Ezek 44.4). He is "the brightness of his glory" (Heb 1.3), the effulgence of the glory, i.e. the shining forth of divine splendour, the majesty of His Person. While stating that the prophet was anticipating the millennial temple, F. A. Tatford continues, "...or even the ultimate fulfilment in the eternal state, when the Lord God Almighty and the Lamb are the only temple needed and the glory of God illuminates the whole city (Rev 21.22,23)". The presence of Jehovah in the Sanctuary, which He condescendingly occupied, was the glory of God in the midst of Israel. However, the glory departed from Israel (Ezek 9.3; 10.4,18-19; 11.22-23). It departed because of the idolatry and disobedience of the nation. God cannot compromise with the sin and disobedience of His people.

There can be no lowering of God's standard. His claim upon His people is unchanged and unchangeable. It is possible today for believers and assemblies to lose the sense of the Lord's presence because of departure from His word and from the principles of gathering. Note that although the departure of the glory of God from Israel was lingering, the return of that glory is swift (Ezek 43.2-5). This indicates the character of God for He is "slow to anger, and of great mercy" (Ps 145.8; Ps 103.8). The slowness of the glory in departing and its swiftness in returning is surely a display of the love and mercy of Jehovah. God is longsuffering (2 Pet 3.9) and so should every believer be for it is a fruit of the Spirit (Gal 5.22). It was displayed in all its perfection in the Lord Jesus Christ (1 Pet 2.23). The return of the glory of God will be at the second advent of Christ and then will be fulfilled, "Arise, shine; for thy light is come, and the glory of the Lord is risen upon thee. For, behold, the darkness shall cover the earth, and gross darkness the people: but the Lord shall rise upon thee, and his glory shall be seen upon thee. And the Gentiles shall come to thy light, and kings to the brightness of thy rising" (Is 60.1-3). Then the earth will shine with His glory (Ezek 43.2). The millennial temple will be Jehovah's dwelling place where "he shall be a priest upon his throne" (Zech 6.13). It shall be the centre from which His glory and power radiates, not only through Israel, but to the utmost ends of the world. Thus the glory of Solomon's day will recede into insignificance in comparison with the future glory.

The added blessing to the future glory of Jehovah's House is peace given by Jehovah. The expression "this place" could either refer to Jerusalem, which will be the metropolis of the world, or to the millennial temple. The latter seems to be more in keeping with the context, as the temple will be the throne of Jehovah, the Messiah. Primarily this embraces Israel to whom Jehovah will give peace from all their enemies. Although at the second advent the Lord will come in judgment He will, as the Prince of Peace, establish peace, not only in Israel, but in the whole world. In His first advent He "made peace through the blood of his cross" (Col 1.20), but in the second advent "he shall speak peace unto the heathen: and his dominion shall be from sea even to sea, and from the river even to the ends of the earth" (Zech 9.10; Ps 72.8). The peace will not only be an inward peace, peace between God and men, but also external peace between man and man, nation and nation. "Violence shall no more be heard in thy land" (Is

60.18; cp. Is 11.9); "nation shall not lift up a sword against nation, neither shall they learn war any more" (Micah 4.3; cp. Is 2.4). That day will be a glorious era of peace the centre of which will be the temple, Jehovah's House, filled with His glory. Jehovah will reign supreme on earth and the world will be abundantly blessed. Such predictions would remove the people's fear and doubt, and would stimulate them in the work of rebuilding the temple. There is a glorious future for Israel, which will surpass all that is past, for Jehovah has reserved the best for that coming day, the day of universal peace when the Lord Jesus Christ will reign in righteousness.

Verses 10-19: A Message of Blight and Blessing
Haggai received two more messages for the people on the same day. The first is recorded in vv.10-19 and the second in vv.20-23. The first message is different in character to the previous messages as it is interrogative as well as instructive. By referring them to the law the prophet shows that while they were disobedient in their neglect of the temple they were as men unclean and so Jehovah's blessing was withheld from them. Haggai reminded them that uncleanness (sin) was contagious (vv.10-13). They were contaminated with sin and their disobedience brought His chastising hand upon them (vv.14-17). However, although their neglect of the temple had brought suffering to them, their obedience in rebuilding His House would guarantee Jehovah's blessing (vv.18-19).

The teaching of the law (vv.10-13)
Some time had passed since the comforting promises of the last message (vv.6-9) which had dispelled the people's despondency. This message now underlined the moral requirements Jehovah demanded. The reference to the law was intended to show the low moral state of the people which was really the reason for their past disobedience.

In the twenty-fourth day of the ninth month in the same year of Darius' reign this message was proclaimed to the people through the prophet Haggai. It was exactly three months after they had commenced rebuilding the House of God (1.15). No doubt in this interval the Jews had made considerable progress in this work. It was also about two months after the third message proclaimed by Haggai (2.1). Between these two messages falls, chronologically, the first message of Zechariah exhorting the people to turn to Jehovah from their evil ways (Zech 1.1-6). Haggai embraces another way of encouraging the people to continue in the rebuilding by pointing out the consequences of their neglect in past days. The ninth month in the Jewish calendar is Chisleu which corresponds to the last part of November and the first part of December in our calendar. It falls after the Feast of Tabernacles and after the sowing of the winter crops. It was the time of the early rain which was necessary to water the newly sown crops. In view of the failure of past harvests there would be anxiety because of their difficult circumstances. Abundance of rain at this time would assure them of Jehovah's blessing.

Jehovah's exposure of the past condition of the people and the inevitable consequences of this was shown by reference to the law. Two questions, concerning holiness and uncleanness, are proposed for the priests to answer (v.11ff). They were the authorised teachers of the Law of Moses (Lev 10.11; Deut 17.8-9; 33.10). Malachi 2.7 states that, "the priest's lips should keep knowledge", and that the people should seek the law at his mouth because he is called "the messenger of the Lord of hosts". As Jehovah's messengers they were the appointed teachers of the Law of Moses and were responsible to faithfully instruct the people in that Law. This was a solemn responsibility. To do this they needed to read the Law, earnestly and carefully, in dependence upon Jehovah, in order to convey it to the people accurately and faithfully. Those who minister the word of God today have the solemn responsibility to clearly make known the truth of God. How vital for such men to spend time in the word of God and in the presence of God. They will have to give account as to their ministry at the Judgment Seat of Christ - "Study to show thyself approved unto God, a workman that needeth not to be ashamed, rightly dividing the word of truth" (2 Tim 2.15).

We learn here in Haggai that, although the priests knew the law, they failed to convey it and to act in keeping with it. Their teaching had been superficial, leaving the people untouched as to their true condition before God. Verses 11-13 describe the remnant as it had been. It seems that the people had been sacrificing in keeping with the requirements of the law and had considered that this was sufficient to satisfy the claims of Jehovah. The priests had offered the sacrifices the people brought, assuming that because they conformed to the legal requirements of the law they would have been accepted by Jehovah. Both the people and the priests had neglected the House of God which had remained in ruins. They had ignored their disobedience yet had continued the ceremony of offering their sacrifices upon the altar. In order to impress upon the hearts of both the people and the priests that their past assumption was folly and that their sacrifices were unacceptable, the two questions are put to the priests.

The word for "law" (TORA - 8451) comes from a primitive root YARA (3384) meaning to teach, direct, or point out. Although used by the Jews to denote the law as in the Pentateuch, and also of the whole of the Old Testament, here it is used in its primary sense of the teaching of the law.

The first question (v.12) was in relation to that which was ceremonially holy coming into contact with other objects. If a person was carrying holy flesh in a fold (pocket) in the skirt of his garment and other food touched the fold would that food become holy? "If" (HEN - 2005) is also translated "Behold" (Nah 2.13) and "lo" (Hab 1.6; Zech 2.10). Although it demands attention and emphasises what follows, here it points to an action being possible and is equivalent to the word "suppose". The first word translated "holy" (QODESH - 6944) means sacred and comes from the second word translated "holy" (QADASH - 6942) which is a root word meaning to pronounce or observe as ceremonially or morally clean. Thus "holy flesh" refers to the flesh of an animal which was set apart to Jehovah, and was sacrificed to Him (Jer 11.15). The reference here seems to be to the Peace Offering because the offerer and his family were given part of the animal sacrificed (Lev 7.15-18). According to Leviticus 6.27 whatsoever touched holy flesh was constituted holy and so the skirt in which it was carried was reckoned holy. However, it could not transfer that holiness to anything else, neither could it make the offerer clean. Thus the answer given by the priests to the question was a correct and decisive, "No". Holiness could not be imparted in that way.

The second question (v.13) is in contrast to the first one. It is in relation to uncleanness, not holiness, and refers to the spread of ceremonial or legal defilement. The defilement in view is that of uncleanness through contact with a dead body (Lev 21.1; 22.4). This kind of uncleanness was the gravest of all, lasting for seven days, and could only be removed by a double sprinkling of running water placed in a vessel with the ashes of a burnt red heifer (Num 19). Fellowship with Jehovah was impossible with such uncleanness and could only be restored when the contamination had been ceremonially removed. This uncleanness seems to indicate that death and sin are closely linked together - "Wherefore, as by one man sin entered into the world, and death by sin; and so death passed upon all men, for that all have sinned" (Rom 5.12). The inevitable consequence of defilement, if not removed, was to be cut off from the people of God - "But the man that shall be unclean, and shall not purify himself, that soul shall be cut off from among the congregation, because he hath defiled the sanctuary of the Lord: the water of separation hath not been sprinkled upon him; he is unclean" (Num 19.20). The provision was there for him to remove his uncleanness, but if he failed, or refused, to accept it he would thus suffer the consequence. This reminds one of the gospel that declares that "all have sinned, and come short of the glory of God" (Rom 3.23) and are therefore unclean in His sight and thus unfit for heaven. However, God has provided, in the death of His Son the Lord Jesus Christ, a way whereby all men can be cleansed and made fit for heaven - "For God so loved the world, that he gave his only begotten Son, that whosoever believeth in him should not perish, but have everlasting life" (Jn 3.16). The Lord Jesus Christ gave Himself a ransom for all (1 Tim 2.6) so that all might be cleansed from the defilement of sin (1 Jn 1.7). However, only those who repent and accept the Lord Jesus as their own Saviour are made fit for heaven. The provision of God is there for all, but those who neglect or reject it will suffer the consequences not only now but eternally in Hell and the Lake of Fire (Rev 20.15). The answer of the priests to the question was emphatically positive in keeping with Numbers 19.22: "And whatsoever the unclean person toucheth shall be unclean; and the soul that toucheth it shall be unclean until even." W. J. Deane states, "It was owing to the defilement that accompanied contact with the dead that the later Jews used to whiten the sepulchres every year, that they might be seen and avoided (Mt 23.27). The two questions in these verses reveal that ceremonial uncleanness is more easily transmitted than ceremonial holiness. The lesson learned is that sin has a greater infectious power than purity; that holiness is not catching, but uncleanness is. A healthy person cannot impart his health to an unhealthy person, but a sick person can infect one who is healthy.

The application to the nation (vv.14-17)
In v.14 Haggai applies the principles of the two cases of the law addressed in the previous verses to the condition of the people in the sight of Jehovah - "So is this people, and so is this nation before me, saith the Lord". The fact that the past is in view is evident from the expression "this people" used in 1.2 and here. In this latter verse it indicates distance from Jehovah because they were unclean. The expression "this nation" is significant since the Hebrew word for "nation" is generally applied to the Gentile nations and so here it could be a term of rebuke. The first question and answer (v.12) is cited to illustrate the principle that the sacrifices offered to Jehovah could not make the disobedient, and thus unclean, offerers holy. The second question and answer (v.13) is cited to illustrate the principle that the defilement of the Jews, because of their neglect of Jehovah's House, affected their work and their offerings. F. C. Cook explains that, "The scope of the questions propounded and of the answers given in vv.12 & 13 is that no ceremonial obedience would be acceptable to God, so long as His will respecting the temple was being set at nought; and that disobedience on this one point was a contamination for which no ceremonial observances could atone (James 2.10)". The guilt of impiety had tarnished their work and offerings. They were utterly unclean like someone who had touched a corpse. Whatever defilement was on the people it had affected all their activities. Everything they planted and cultivated was under the curse of their uncleanness. It is evident that although the remnant had neglected the temple they had been offering sacrifices to Jehovah. The expression "offered there" indicates that their sacrifices were presented on the altar built on their return to the land (Ezra 3.3). The priests and the offerers had ignored their neglect of the work of God in rebuilding the temple. They thought that the restored ceremony of offering their sacrifice on the restored altar of Jehovah in Jerusalem would satisfy the claims of God and make them acceptable to Him. However, their disobedience polluted their sacrifices and therefore they were unacceptable to Jehovah. How could sacrifices made by such people be acceptable? There must be personal cleanness before one's offering is acceptable to God. The consequence was that Jehovah withheld His blessing. Just as one ceremonially unclean person polluted all he touched so the Jews' long disobedience tainted the

work of their hands. Their ceremonial sacrificing was but an outward show with no real meaning to it. Their offerings could never remove their guilt of neglect and reconcile them to God. Their sin of disobedience remained upon them.

This is applicable to believers today. One cannot ignore the sin of disobedience, thinking that outward show, plausible words, and giving to the Lord's work removes that guilt. The believer is to guard against defilement - "Let every one that nameth the name of Christ depart from iniquity" (2 Tim 2.19). The proof of genuineness is seen in a life that is separated from evil and which manifests holiness. The heart of the Christian is to be riveted to Christ and the life should be in keeping with the character of Christ. The child of God must avoid anything that would defile in order to be a vessel of honour fit to be used by the Lord in His service (2 Tim 2.21). There are things which believers should flee from and there are virtues to follow - "Flee also youthful lusts: but follow righteous, faith, charity, peace, with them that call on the Lord out of a pure heart" (2 Tim 2.22). Thus there is to be separation from all that dishonours the Lord, and fellowship with those who own the Lordship of Christ out of a pure heart. The purpose here of looking back is to guard them from reverting to what they were. They were not to return to their former disobedience, and their past experience was to be a warning to them. The very presence of Jehovah in their midst demanded holiness in their lives and obedience to His word.

In Jehovah's governmental dealings with His people He had chastised them in various ways. In vv.15-17 the prophet draws their attention to their past experiences calling upon them to recall all that happened during the time of their neglect of the House of God. They were to consider their plight during that period. Thus their own experience should be a lesson to them as well as a warning not to return to their past ways. The consequence of their apathy towards the temple was a succession of scanty harvests, and only now, when they had submitted to Jehovah's claim and commenced rebuilding His House, could He promise to bless them. The expression "from this day upward" has been viewed in two ways.

1. The word translated "upward" (MAAL - 4605) should be rendered "backwards". C. F. Keil states, "Here it is used not in the sense of forwards into the future, but, as the explanatory clause which follows (from before, etc.) clearly shows, in that of backwards into the past". The thought is looking backwards from the time they commenced rebuilding the temple - "before a stone was laid upon a stone in the temple of the Lord."

2. The expression "this day" refers to the day the foundation of the temple was laid, and the word "upward" should be rendered "onward". S. R. Driver states that "'this day' refers to the day on which the prophet is speaking, the 24th of the ninth month (Chisleu [Zech 7.1])", and that the phrase "and upward" means "'and *onwards*' (1 Sam 16.13; 30.25; and in the formula, 'from twenty years old *and upward*,' i.e. *and onwards*, Num 1.3, and often)". The thought is that of looking onward

from the day in which the foundation was laid to the commencement of the rebuilding of the temple.

For further comments on these two views see S. R. Driver in *The Century Bible* at pages 164-166. Most commentators take the first view. Whichever is accepted the period in view is the same: the period of the Jews' neglect of the temple.

The expression "before a stone was laid upon a stone" refers to the recent rebuilding upon the foundation laid some sixteen years before. They were to ponder earnestly that period and the punishment of Jehovah because of their disobedience. This is evident from vv.16-17 where they are reminded that their expectations in past days had not been realised. The phrase "Since those days were" is a difficult one in the context. It is left out in Helen Spurrell's translation and given as "through all that time" in the RV. This rendering is accepted by many commentators. The Hebrew word used in the statement (DAY - 1767) means, as a noun or adverb, enough (Ex 36.5; Jer 49.9), or sufficient (Ex 36.7; Is 40.16), but it is used chiefly with a preposition (Strong's Concordance) and could be rendered, "Since such things were", "In those days", or "Through those days". It is generally accepted that the reference is to those days when Jehovah placed a curse on their harvests. In that period everything seemed to be cursed. When one came to a heap of sheaves expecting to have twenty measures of grain, after threshing it only yielded ten, half the expected amount. This was because God had withheld His blessing. The word *"measures"* is not found in the Hebrew text, but is supplied in the Septuagint by the equivalent Greek word. Jewish scholars such as Rashi, Redak, and Kimchi supply the Hebrew word (SᵉAH - 5429). Redak states, "From you being in this situation - that you would come to the heap of wheat that was fit to contain twenty *seahs* and it contained only ten - you could easily recognise that this (situation) was caused by a curse sent by God" (see Rabbi A. J. Rosenberg). A seah was a third of an ephah (Newberry Bible - Table of Measures, Weights, and Coins). The particular measure is not really important in itself because the emphasis is upon the proportion of their expectation that they received. That the heap (AREMA – 6194) was a heap of sheaves is evident from Ruth 3.7 and Nehemiah 13.15 where the Hebrew word is translated "sheaves".

They experienced the same loss at the pressing of the grapes. The word for "pressfat" (YEQEB - 3342) comes from a root meaning "to excavate; *a trough"* (Strong's Concordance), and mainly appears as "winepress" (Num 18.27; Is 5.2). Here the vat or trough into which the juice of the pressed grapes flowed is in view. S. R. Driver explains that, "The 'wine-vat' was the receptacle in which the juice, trodden out by the feet of men in the 'wine-press' was collected. Both were commonly cavities hewn out in the rock (cp. Is 5.2) at different levels, the upper one, the *gath* or the wine-press, having the larger superficial area, the lower one, the *yeqeb* or wine-vat, the greater depth; the juice expressed in the *gath* flowed down into the *yeqeb* through a connecting channel. Many remains of ancient wine-presses and wine-vats have been found in Palestine". When the Jews went to the wine-vat they found far less wine than they expected.

The word "vessel" is not in the original Hebrew text. However, Jewish scholars, along with christian commentators, have inserted the Hebrew word PURA (6333) or the English "press-measures". Although PURAH is translated "winepress" in Isaiah 63.3 it refers to a measure. Instead of the fifty measures of wine they expected from the grapes they only obtained twenty which was 40% of what they anticipated.

The reason for such small yields from both the threshing floor and the wine-vat is given in v.17. Jehovah had not only denied them His blessing, but had also smitten their crops with blasting, mildew and hail. This was His judicial hand upon them similar to that described in Amos 4.9. Blasting has reference to the scorching wind that withered and burned the growing corn (cp. Gen 41.23,27). This hot wind came from the Arabian desert and was able to destroy the grain in a day. Mildew refers to a blight which turns the ears of corn to a pale yellow which yields no grain. This discolouring is implied in its Hebrew word (YERAQON - 3420) which means paleness. In Jeremiah 30.6 it is used to describe the "paleness" of men in distress and fear. Blasting would naturally follow drought whereas mildew would naturally follow excessive rain. Both of these are mentioned under the curses for disobedience (Deut 28.22). Whereas blasting and mildew refer to the grain, the hail may only refer to the damage it caused to the vines (Ps 78.47). However all three are related to everything the people had cultivated with much effort and toil. In spite of God's discipline over a long period of scanty harvests, the people did not repent and turn to Jehovah. The chastisement of God is intended to bring back His people to Himself. However, here it was totally ineffective because the people had not seen Jehovah's hand in discipline in the calamities that overtook them. Thus they were not conscious of His chastisement and saw no need for repentance or a change of heart. They should have recognised His hand upon them from the teaching of the books of Moses, but they were indifferent to the law and therefore blind to their true condition. Therefore they continued in their neglect of Jehovah's dwelling place. Thus they needed a fresh word from Jehovah through His messenger Haggai. It was that word of challenge, reminder and instruction that produced a change of heart in the people and resulted in the commencement of the rebuilding Jehovah's House. The word of God is "quick, and powerful, and sharper than any twoedged sword, piercing even to the dividing asunder of soul and spirit, and of the joints and marrow, and is a discerner of the thoughts and intents of the heart" (Heb 4.12).

The promised blessing (vv.18-19)

In these verses there is a double call to take to heart what Haggai had proclaimed. The first seems to be related to the future and the second to the past. This is intended to contrast the promised blessing in coming days with the disastrous past days. There are difficulties in these verses, but they are removed when the last part of v.18 and the main part of v.19 are taken as parenthetical. In this way the verses are divided into two parts: "Consider now from this day and upward, from the four and twentieth day of the ninth month… from this day will I bless you", which looks forward to future days, and the remainder of the verses which looks back to the past.

After the prophet's appeal in vv.15-17 to consider the past period, during which the blessing of Jehovah had been withheld, the people were called upon to consider what was before them. There is an obvious break with the past in the opening statement of v.18. This is evident from the repetition of "from" and the date mentioned in the second clause. Some take the expression "the four and twentieth day of the ninth month" as referring to the day the foundation of the temple was laid, in light of the statement immediately following it. However, the word "even" is not in the Hebrew text, and besides this the date stated here would clash with Ezra 3.8-10 which clearly states that the foundation of the temple was laid in the second month of the second year of Cyrus' reign. The date mentioned here can only be the day when Haggai delivered this message from Jehovah to the Jewish remnant (v.10).

The Hebrew word for "upward" (MAAL - 4605) is the same as in v.15 which is generally translated in this way or as "above" (Amos 2.9). However it is also rendered "forward" (1 Sam 16.13; 30.25) and that is the sense of the word here in contrast to v.15 - "from this day and forwards". This is how it is translated by Helen Spurrell. "This day" commences a new era. In order that the promised blessing in v.19 might be a powerful contrast to the stress and difficulties of the period mentioned in vv.15-17, the prophet repeats the appeal of v.15 but extends the period to include the past three months in which they had continued to work in rebuilding the temple. This is clear from the opening question of v.19: "Is the seed yet in the barn?". For the past three months the people had engaged in the work of rebuilding the temple, but it seemed that their problems had not ceased. These months fell in the period after the last harvest which would have been poor because of their unfaithfulness. They were also in the period of the sowing of a fresh harvest. The prophet is drawing attention to their present situation because of their past neglect. Therefore, their answer to Haggai's question could only be, "No", because the small yield of the past harvest had been used up to meet their daily needs and in the sowing which had already taken place for the future harvest.

They had repented for their past unfaithfulness, there had been a change of heart, and they had hearkened to the message of Jehovah by commencing the work of rebuilding His House. After a long period of apathy and spiritual failure, the remnant had turned to Jehovah and become busy in His work instead of in their own things. However, they had continued to experience want and hardship and they were in danger of being disheartened because no change had taken place in their situation. There was no seed in the barn and the fruit trees had been stripped by the hail before they had commenced the rebuilding. The present crop was not ready, the vine, fig, pomegranate and olive trees had not yet produced fruit. What would the coming harvest be like? Would it be a repetition of past harvests? Ah, no, Jehovah is gracious, for His promise comes: "from this day I will bless you". Jehovah, who had brought calamity to them in chastising them in order to bring them to repentance and a change of heart, now promises to withdraw His hand of discipline and replace it with His blessing. Since their disobedience and indifference to His House was now removed He was able to deal with them in grace. As stated previously, "this day" is the day the prophet proclaimed this message as in v.18. From now on the improvement in the harvests would become evident. Haggai predicts an abundant harvest in view of their obedience and Jehovah's promise (Lev 26.3-4), although there was no sign of it as yet.

The promise came at a critical time (November/December), which was the time of the early rain. The coming of this rain was vital for the harvest and the production of the fruit. The promised blessing of Jehovah ensured the coming of rain so that the fields and fruit trees would produce abundantly and thus they would experience fruitful seasons (Deut 28.8). Although there was no outward evidence of this promise they could depend upon its fulfilment. The promise given was intended to remove the anxiety and perplexity of the Jews. They could rest assured knowing that what Jehovah promised He carried out. It is a comfort also to Christians to know that God's promises are sure and that they will be fulfilled.

This section illustrates the principle stated in 1 Samuel 2.30: "them that honour me I will honour, and they that despise me shall be lightly esteemed". Believers are to honour the Lord in their lives, serving Him "acceptably with reverence and godly fear" (Heb 12.28). Christians should be engaged continually in that which the Lord has called them to do. This involves the expending of energy right on to the end - "And let us not be weary in well doing: for in due season we shall reap, if we faint not" (Gal 6.9). There is to be no neglect or laziness in our living for God. So often there is lethargy in divine things and yet plenty of activity in temporal and material things. In light of eternity one does well to challenge one's heart and become more determined to carry out the will of God. Departure from the word of God and apathy in the work of God leads to barrenness of soul. However, restoration to the Lord and obedience to His word results in renewed enjoyment of His blessing.

Verses 20-23: A Message of Vision and Victory

The chapter concludes with this last message which was given on the same day as the previous communication containing the promise of Jehovah's blessing. The reason this message was not included in the previous one was because it was addressed personally to Zerubbabel, the appointed governor and recognised leader of the returned remnant. He was the uncrowned son of David. Although the message relates completely to future events it was intended to encourage Zerubbabel and then the people through him. The end times are in view and the promise of vv.6-9 is enlarged with further details. It predicts the manifestation of the omnipotence of Jehovah in the shaking of the heavens and the earth as well as the overthrow of the throne of the kingdoms of the world (vv.21-22) and the preservation of the Davidic monarchy as represented in Zerubbabel. He is singled out as the representative of the coming Messiah who, as the signet ring, will not only reign over Israel, but also over all nations. The promised exaltation of the nation of Israel under the Messiah, its glorious King, would provide strength for the rebuilding of the temple (v.23). In this message we note the divine plan (v.21), the divine purpose (v.22), and the divine promise (v.23).

The opening expression of v.20, "And again", indicates that the prophet Haggai proclaimed this message on the same day as the previous one, since the Hebrew word for "again" (SHENI - 8145) means second and is generally translated in this way. The change from "by Haggai" in the previous messages to "unto Haggai" here could be because the message is for Zerubbabel alone instead of to the whole company. He is addressed, as the people's civic leader, and not Joshua, their religious leader. He was their governor, and their security and welfare depended on him. Although he is addressed as the representative of the throne of David, the prophetic content looks far beyond his time to the coming of Christ the Messiah.

The omnipotence of Jehovah (vv.21-22)

One notes the activity of Jehovah in these verses: "I will shake" (v.21); "I will overthrow" (v.22); and "I will destroy" (v.22). These expressions manifest His omnipotence and His ability to carry through His purpose. The expression "I will shake the heavens and the earth" looks back to v.6 and, as there, refers to catastrophic upheavals in nature prior to the manifestation of Christ. It is introductory to the following expression, "I will overthrow the throne of kingdoms" (v.22). This is a development of "I will shake all nations" in v.7. There are three views taken of this expression because the word "throne" is in the singular.

1. It refers to the throne of the Antichrist who for a little while will have global power, having received the kingdom from the ten kings (Rev 17.17).

2. It refers to the power of the heathen nations.

3. The singular is used distributively, i.e. to mean every throne of the kingdoms.

Most commentators take the third alternative which corresponds with the plural word "kingdoms". Whichever view is taken, the Gentile nations, opposed to God, are in focus.

Not only will Jehovah overthrow the thrones of the nations, He will also destroy their strength. The strength of the nations lies in their military power portrayed here as chariots and cavalry. The event described is terrible and affects the whole world, and it can only refer to the second advent of the Lord Jesus Christ when He will set up His Kingdom. It is referred to by Luke: "And there shall be signs in the sun, and in the moon, and in the stars; and upon the earth distress of nations, with perplexity; the sea and the waves roaring; Men's hearts failing them for fear, and for looking after those things which are coming on the earth: for the powers of heaven shall be shaken. And then shall they see the Son of man coming in a cloud with power and great glory" (Lk 21.25-27). In that day Satan will use special means of deception to gather together a vast army at Armageddon (Rev 16.13-16), called the valley of Megiddo (2 Chr 35.22), the valley of Jehoshaphat (Joel 3.2, 12), and the valley of Megiddon (Zech 12.11). This will be in keeping with the divine plan as predicted in Zechariah 14.2: "I will gather all nations against Jerusalem to battle". Satan is but an instrument in Jehovah's hand. The nations are gathered together to eradicate God's people and to oppose the claims of the rightful King (Ps 2.6). When Jerusalem is surrounded and the city taken, "the houses rifled, and the women ravished; and half of the city shall go forth into captivity, and the residue of the people shall not be cut off from the city. Then shall the Lord go forth, and fight against those nations, as when he fought in the day of battle" (Zech 14.2-3). When Israel's extermination seems inevitable then shall their Messiah, the Lord Jesus Christ, be manifested in all His glory, grandeur, and greatness riding on a white horse to execute judgment upon the Gentile nations and the apostate of Israel. He will come as earth's rightful King, the King of kings and Lord of lords. He will come to wrest power from the Antichrist, from his satanic master, and from those who corrupted the earth (Rev 19.11-21). Then will Psalm 2.9 be fulfilled: "Thou shalt break them with a rod of iron; thou shalt dash them in pieces like a potter's vessel", and Habakkuk 3.12: "Thou didst march through the land in indignation, thou didst thresh the heathen in anger" (cp. Dan 2.34-35,44; 7.11-14).

During that time the riders shall be brought down, "every one by the sword of his brother". Then Zechariah 14.13 will be fulfilled: "And it shall come to pass in that day, that a great tumult from the Lord shall be among them; and they shall lay hold every one on the hand of his neighbour, and his hand shall rise up against the hand of his neighbour" (cp. Ezek 38.21). However the final overthrow of the vast army will be accomplished by the Lord Himself. The Jews of that day will suffer much, but the closing verse of this prophecy will provide assurance for them as to Israel's salvation as well as encouragement for God's people in Haggai's day.

The faithfulness of God (v.23)

The opening expression, "In that day", indicates that the message continues to refer to a future day when the events of vv.21-22 will take place, i.e. when the heathen nations shall be overthrown. The message of assurance and of Jehovah's faithfulness extends to another remnant in a coming day. As in vv.6-9 the title "the Lord of hosts" is used in relation to these prophetic events. It indicates His sovereignty, and emphasises that the events, which are all under His control, will fulfil His divine purpose. The expression "will I take" is intended to introduce an act that is important (cp. Deut 4.20). It does not, in itself, imply being personally taken under Jehovah's protection, although it is contained in His action. Zerubbabel must not be taken personally here since the events predicted would not take place in his lifetime. He must be regarded as either representative of the people, Israel, or as a type of the Messiah. Both might be intended although the second is more likely in view. Most Gentile, as well as some Jewish, commentators accept that the Messiah is referred to. However, in applying it to Israel one notes that the title "my servant" is used of Israel: "But thou, Israel, art my servant" (Is 41.8; 44.21; 49.3). Also, as the signet was considered precious so Israel was to Jehovah: "Since thou wast precious in my sight" (Is 43.4). Israel has been kept "as the apple of his eye" (Deut 32.10; Zech 2.8). Israel has also been chosen: "the Lord thy God hath chosen thee to be a special people unto himself" (Deut 7.6; Is 44.1). Jehovah has committed Himself to Israel's ultimate blessing and He will keep His promise.

Although this application to Israel can be made, the prophecy is primarily Messianic, i.e. it refers to the Lord Jesus Christ. He is God's signet and He is the executor of God's judgment upon the earth. He will administer the purposes of God when He comes back to reign. The term "my servant" belongs to Him in a special and unique way: "Behold my servant, whom I uphold; mine elect, in whom my soul delighteth…He shall not fail nor be discouraged, till he hath set judgment in the earth: and the isles shall wait for his law" (Is 42.1-4). He alone is the Perfect Servant who brought infinite pleasure and glory to God in His devoted service on earth: "I have glorified thee on the earth: I have finished the work which thou gavest me to do" (Jn 17.4). He alone could say, "I do always those things that please him" (Jn 8.29), and of Him alone could be said, "He hath done all things well" (Mk 7.37).

The expression "the son of Shealtiel" is intended to draw attention to the royal line of David from which the Messiah will come. Zerubbabel was in that line, as was David, and is mentioned in both genealogies of the Lord Jesus Christ (Mt 1.12; Lk 3.27). As the prince of Judah (Ezra 1.8), Zerubbabel (Sheshbazzar) represented the royal line and, as stated, is a type of the Messiah. The statement "will make thee a signet" refers to a place of honour and authority. The signet was an important possession which was constantly in view. The word (HOTAM - 2368) means to seal and is translated so in the Song of Solomon 8.6: "Set me as a seal upon thine heart, as a seal upon thine arm". It was not always a ring (Jer 22.24), but could be an engraved stone (Ex 28.11,21,36). Thus it could be hung by a chain from the neck or arm. It was viewed as special and of great value, and spoke of the king's authority.

The implication here is that the Messiah is precious to God (1 Pet 2.4,6) and as a signet in His hand will imprint His majesty upon the world. All honour and authority will belong to the Lord Jesus Christ. The reason why He will be made the signet is given in the closing expression - "for I have chosen thee, saith the Lord of hosts". The Lord Jesus Christ, the Messiah, is God's chosen One (Mt 12.18; 1 Pet 2.4). God has already chosen His King who will sit on His holy hill of Zion (Ps 2.6). This is envisaged when "the seventh angel sounded; and there were great voices in heaven, saying, The kingdoms of this world are become the kingdoms of our Lord, and of his Christ; and he shall reign for ever and ever" (Rev 11.15). Then the Lord Jesus Christ will sit upon the throne of His glory (Mt 25.31), as a priest upon His throne (Zech 6.13), and He shall reign in righteousness (Is 32.1). Then the message of the angel to Mary will be fully fulfilled: "He shall be great, and shall be called the Son of the Highest: and the Lord God shall give unto him the throne of his father David: And he shall reign over the house of Jacob for ever; and of his kingdom there shall be no end" (Lk 1.32-33).

One can do no better than to close with the words of F. A. Tatford: "Thus Haggai completed his ministry. It lasted only three months and twenty-four days and during that time he uttered only five short messages. But his words aroused a lethargic nation and converted a slothful people into zealous servants of God. Unknown, without genealogy or personal history, he passed off the stage, his ministry accomplished and the Divine purpose through him achieved...Within a few months, the restoration temple was completed and its dedication took place amidst general rejoicing (Ezra 6.15,16). The adversary may seek to hinder and obstruct, but the omnipotent God is on our side. 'Therefore, my beloved brethren, be ye stedfast, unmoveable, always abounding in the work of the Lord, forasmuch as ye know that your labour is not in vain in the Lord' (1 Cor 15.58)". The prophecy begins with rebuke and ends with blessing.

APPENDIX

THE TEMPLE

The word "temple" is used in the Scriptures of the dwelling-place of God. It is used of a literal building and also in a figurative or spiritual way. The temple in the land of Israel replaced the tabernacle in the wilderness. The tabernacle was for the wilderness when God condescended to dwell in the midst of His people on their journey to the promised land. It is viewed as a type of the dwelling place of God amidst His redeemed people today as they move through this wilderness scene on their way home to Glory: "I will dwell in them, and walk in them; and I will be their God, and they shall be my people" (2 Cor 6.16). The temple was for the promised land and is linked with the established kingdom as well as looking on to the Messianic Kingdom. It speaks of the seat of divine rule as well as the place of approach to God. The first mention of God dwelling among His people is immediately after the exodus (Ex 15.17).

LITERAL

Solomon's Temple

After David came to the throne and Jehovah had given him rest from his enemies, he had a desire to build a permanent dwelling-place for Jehovah: "Lo, I dwell in an house of cedars, but the ark of the covenant of the Lord remaineth under curtains" (1 Chr 17.1). However, Jehovah revealed to David that he would not build the house, but that his son, Solomon, would do so (2 Sam 7.1-17; 1 Kings 8.17-20). It seems that David chose the place where the temple was to be built: "Then David said, This is the house of the Lord God, and this is the altar of the burnt offering for Israel" (1 Chr 22.1). It is not recorded that there was a direct word from Jehovah, but rather that David had spiritual perception of Jehovah's holiness and pardoning grace being displayed there (2 Chr 3.1). Although David was forbidden to build the temple he provided abundantly for its construction (1 Chr 22.3-6,14) and gave the pattern for the House, which he had received by the Spirit, to Solomon (1 Chr 28. 11-19). It was built on Mount Moriah where Isaac was placed on the altar and which was the place where the sword of judgment was stayed (1 Chr 21.27). The temple took seven years and six months to build (2 Chr 3.2 with 1 Kings 6.38) and when completed was glorious, being overlaid with gold (1 Kings 6.21-22). It was sixty cubits long, twenty cubits wide, and thirty cubits high (27 x 9 x 13.5 metres) the holy place being forty cubits by twenty cubits (18 x 9 metres) and the holy of holies a cube of twenty cubits (9 metres) in length, breadth, and height. Against the wall of the temple were built chambers at three levels. Full details of the temple can be found in 1 Kings 6 and 2 Chronicles 3. Because of Judah's transgression, 426 years after the completion of Solomon's temple the Babylonians carried away the vessels and treasures of the House of the Lord and plundered and burnt the temple (586 BC; cp. 2 Kings 25.8-17; 2 Chr 36.14-21).

Zerubbabel's Temple

After Judah had completed the seventy years of captivity, Cyrus, the king of Persia, made it possible for a remnant of the Jews who were still in captivity to go back to Jerusalem. They returned under Zerubbabel in order to rebuild the temple (Ezra 1.1-4). Cyrus not only authorised the rebuilding of the temple, he restored the golden and silver vessels of the House of God taken away by Nebuchadnezzar, and also stated that the foundation should be strongly laid (Ezra 6.3). That foundation was laid in the second month of the second year of Cyrus' reign (Ezra 3.8-10). However, it was sixteen years later, in the sixth month of the second year of Darius' reign, that the Jews began, in earnest, to rebuild the temple. God used the ministry of the prophets Haggai and Zechariah to stimulate and encourage the Jews in that work. There are not many particulars given of it other than that recorded in the decree of Cyrus which stated that the height was to be "threescore cubits, and the breadth thereof threescore cubits; With three rows of great stones, and a row of new timber" (Ezra 6.3-4). There are no dimensions given of the holy place or the holy of holies. It seems that there were chambers as in Solomon's temple: "Then Ezra rose up from before the house of God, and went into the chamber of Johanan the son of Eliashib" (Ezra 10.6); "And I came to Jerusalem, and understood of the evil that Eliashib did for Tobiah, in preparing him a chamber in the courts of the house of God...Then I commanded, and they cleansed the chambers" (Neh 13.7-9).

While the foundation was laid in 536 BC, the temple was not completed until 516 BC. Although this temple was pillaged a number of times, the main desecration was carried out by Antiochus Epiphanes who not only plundered it, but polluted it by setting up an idol in the court near the altar in 170 BC. The sacrifices were discontinued for some time, but restored by Judas Maccabeus.

Herod's Temple

While built by him, the Jews never recognised this temple as Herod's, but referred to it as the second temple, i.e. Zerubbabel's. The Idumean king, Herod the Great, decided to rebuild and beautify the temple of Zerubbabel. He intended it to be a glorious edifice in the hope of gaining the Jews' loyalty to himself. It seems to have been built over the existing structure so as not to hinder the temple service. According to Josephus it was different from and larger than Solomon's temple. He added a court of the Gentiles and a court of the women, both of which are not mentioned in Scripture. This temple was built over a period of forty-six years (Jn 2.20) and on a magnificent scale. It was in existence when the Lord Jesus Christ was on earth. His disciples considered the grandeur of the temple and exclaimed, "Master, see what manner of stones and what buildings are here!" (Mk 13.1). It is also stated that, "some spake of the temple, how it was adorned with goodly stones and gifts" (Lk 21.5).

Under the inspiration of the Holy Spirit two Greek words are used in the New Testament when referring to the temple. These must be distinguished. The Greek word *hieron* (*2411*: from *hieros, 2413*, meaning sacred) is used of the whole temple including the courts and buildings. The Greek word *naos* (*3485*: from *naio* meaning to dwell) refers to the inner part, the holy place and the holy of holies or most holy place. It was only into the external courts that the Lord Jesus entered. He could not enter the inner temple because He was from the tribe of Judah and not from Levi. "For it is evident that our Lord sprang out of Juda; of which tribe Moses spake nothing concerning priesthood" (Heb 7.14). "For Christ is not entered into the holy places made with hands, which are figures of the true" (Heb 9.24). The priests entered into the holy place to trim and light the lamps, to burn incense on the golden altar, and to arrange the shewbread on the table. The destruction of this temple was prophesied by the Lord: "And Jesus said unto them, See ye not all these things? verily I say unto you, There shall not be left here one stone upon another, that shall not be thrown down" (Mt 24.2). This prophecy was fulfilled in AD 70 when the Romans, under Titus, completely destroyed the temple.

Antichrist's Temple

There is no temple in Jerusalem today. The Mosque of Omar or the Dome of the Rock stands and has stood on the firm foundation of the former temples for centuries. However, the word of God makes it clear that there will be a temple there in Jerusalem before the manifestation of the Lord Jesus Christ in all His majesty and glory. When that temple will be erected we are not told, but it seems inevitable that it will take place after the Jews have returned to the land in unbelief and before the middle of Daniel's seventieth week. The temple and temple worship will be in place before the rise of the Antichrist to a place of power. This is evident from Daniel 9.27: "And he shall confirm the covenant with many for one week: and in the midst of the week he shall cause the sacrifice and the oblation to cease". The week here is a week of years. "And arms shall stand on his part, and they shall pollute the sanctuary of strength, and shall take away the daily sacrifice, and they shall place the abomination that maketh desolate" (Dan 11.31). This takes place in the middle of Daniel's seventieth week at the commencement of the Antichrist's three and a half years' reign and is referred to by the Lord: "When ye therefore shall see the abomination of desolation, spoken of by Daniel the prophet, stand in the holy place, (whoso readeth, let him understand:) Then let them which be in Judæa flee into the mountains" (Mt 24.15-16). Paul refers to this temple in relation to the man of sin, "Who opposeth and exalteth himself above all that is called God, or that is worshipped; so that he as God sitteth in the temple of God, showing himself that he is God" (2 Thess 2.4). John also refers to the same temple: "And there was given me a reed like unto a rod: and the angel stood, saying, Rise, and measure the temple of God, and the altar, and them that worship therein…and the holy city shall they tread under foot forty and two months" (Rev 11.1-2). This temple will be destroyed to make way for the millennial temple just before, or at, the second advent of Christ. There may be a reference to this destruction in Psalm 74.1-8.

The Millennial Temple

In the Millennium there will be a temple erected which will be the centre of worship, not only for Israel, but also for the Gentile nations, "for mine house shall be called an house of prayer for all people" (Is 56.7), "and all nations shall flow unto it" (Is 2.2). The description of this temple is given in the closing chapters of Ezekiel. It will be built in the middle of the land devoted to the Lord, a holy portion for the priests, which "shall be for the sanctuary five hundred in length, with five hundred in breadth, square round about" (Ezek 45.1-4). There will be five courts.

1. The large outer area will be enclosed with a wall 500 reeds by 500 reeds, surrounding the temple and other buildings, and seems to be for the Gentile nations (Ezek 42.15-20).

2. In the centre of this large area will be another square 500 cubits by 500 cubits, called the utter (outer) court which will be for the Israelites (Ezek 44.19). These measurements are not stated, but are obtained from the main dimensions given in the description.

3. Within the outer court is the inner court which will be a square of 300 cubits. Some have called it the court of the Priests and others the court of the Levites.

4. Within the inner court will be the court of the temple which will be 100 cubits square upon which the temple will be built (Ezek 41.13-15). Only the priests will be allowed access into this.

5. The court of the altar will also be 100 cubits square (Ezek 40.47) with the altar of burnt offering in the midst. The altar is in the centre of the separate place, east of the temple (Ezek 41.14). It occupies, not only the centre place of the courts, but also the central position of the whole temple area. Every point of approach converges upon this special and sacred place. It certainly suggests that the cross will be paramount in that day of glory as it will be eternally.

There is little stated of the materials used in the construction of the temple itself. The glory of God, which left Solomon's temple and the nation of Israel (Ezek 10.18-19; 11.22-23), will return in that coming day and fill the millennial temple. Then the latter glory of the House of God will exceed all that has gone before, for the Lord Himself will be its glory.

The Temple which is in Heaven

There is another temple mentioned in the book of Revelation: "And the temple of God was opened in heaven, and there was seen in his temple the ark of his testament: and there were lightnings, and voices, and thunderings, and an earthquake, and great hail" (Rev 11.19). We are not told much about this temple and no details are given of it. The opening of the temple and manifestation of the ark are related to what is mentioned in the rest of the verse and the judgments that follow. It indicates that the judgments upon the earth are the outcome of the holiness of God. This temple is filled with the glory of God (Rev 15.8) and the voice of God out of the temple commands seven angels, "Go your ways, and pour out the vials of the wrath of God upon the earth" (Rev 16.1; cp. also v.17). These are the final judgments of "the great and the terrible day of the Lord" (Joel 2.31). The expression "the temple which is in heaven" (Rev 14.17), indicates that there is also a temple on earth at Jerusalem at that time.

SPIRITUAL or FIGURATIVE

The Lord's Body
In answer to the Jews' request for a sign, the Lord answered, "Destroy this temple, and in three days I will raise it up" (Jn 2.19). The Jews did not understand that the Lord was not referring to the literal temple at Jerusalem, but to His body, and thus to His death and resurrection: "But he spake of the temple of his body" (Jn 2.21). The Greek word translated "temple" in this latter verse is *naos*, denoting the sanctuary (the holy place and the holy of holies). The body of the Lord was the temple in which God alone dwelt: "God was manifest in the flesh" (1 Tim 3.16); "And the word was made flesh, and dwelt among us, (and we beheld his glory, the glory as of the only begotten of the Father,) full of grace and truth" (Jn 1.14). The glory mentioned is not the glory of His humanity, but the glory of deity. The glory worthy of, and suitable to, the Only Begotten fresh from alongside the Father. It was such glory that belonged to Him exclusively, the glory of the Everlasting Word shining through the veil of His humanity. One has stated that this temple was Deity in Manhood. It was the Sanctuary in which all the fulness of the Godhead dwelt (Col 2.9).

The Christian's Body
The purity of the Christian's life is essential, and thus the Apostle Paul draws the attention of the Corinthian believers to the sacredness of the body: "What? know ye not that your body is the temple of the Holy Ghost which is in you, which ye have of God, and ye are not your own?" (1 Cor 6.19). The Greek word translated "temple" here is again *naos* indicating that the body of the saint is the inner shrine of the Holy Spirit. It is the dwelling place of the Spirit in fulfilment of the promise, "And I will pray the Father, and he shall give you another Comforter, that he might abide with you for ever; Even the Spirit of truth; whom the world cannot receive, because it seeth him not, neither knoweth him: for he dwelleth with you,

and shall be in you" (Jn 14.16-17). The gracious Spirit of God takes up residence in the believer's body the moment that person trusts the Lord Jesus Christ, so that the body might be used for the pleasure and glory of God. The Christian must keep this truth in mind and regulate his/her life accordingly. How can the saint think of using that which is the dwelling place of the Spirit for any vile purpose? In addition to this, believers are not their own for they have been bought with a price, the precious blood of the Lord Jesus Christ. Christians have no right to use their bodies as they please or desire since these bodies are not only the sanctuary of the Spirit, but also belong to God and should be used for His glory. The context of 1 Corinthians 6.19-20 indicates that the Christian's estimate of fornication, and other unclean actions, is to be completely opposite and opposed to the estimate of the world.

The Local Church

Believers gathered to the name of the Lord Jesus Christ in a locality are declared to be the temple of God in that locality: "Know ye not that ye are the temple of God, and that the Spirit of God dwelleth in you?" (1 Cor 3.16). Again the Greek word *naos* is used showing that the local assembly is the sanctuary of God. The statement "the Spirit of God dwelleth in you" is a reference to the deity of the Spirit and indicates His glorious presidency in the assembly. He should control and guide the functions of the assembly which is set apart as a place that is sacred and should be characterised by holiness. It is intended to be a place where the beauty of godly character is seen. Therefore the manner of life of those who comprise that sacred place must be suitable to God's presence. This figure is used again by Paul in his second letter: "for ye are the temple of the living God; as God hath said, I will dwell in them, and walk in them" (2 Cor 6.16). In the first epistle the believers are warned against defiling the sanctuary. This can be done by allowing false teaching or by strife and division. In the second epistle the warning is against the unequal yoke, uniting with unbelievers, in the context of those who were idolaters. The activities and spiritual condition of the saints have a bearing upon the assembly, God's sanctuary. God is in the midst of His people, which is a glorious and yet solemn fact, and the measure of one's enjoyment of that fact depends upon the measure of one's separation: "Wherefore come out from them, and be ye separate, saith the Lord, and touch not the unclean thing; and I will receive you" (2 Cor 6.17).

The Dispensational Church

The Church in its completeness, comprising every believer from Pentecost to the Rapture, is called a temple: "In whom all the building fitly framed together groweth unto an holy temple in the Lord" (Eph 2.21). Paul in that chapter is referring to the oneness of all believers, believing Jews and believing Gentiles. They are joined together to form the holy temple. The "temple" here is again *naos,* the sanctuary. It is clear from the expression "groweth unto an holy temple" that at present this temple is in the process of being constructed but will be completed in God's time, prior to the Rapture. It is a spiritual house and believers are viewed as living stones (1 Pet 2.5) - living because of the life they have received from Christ, each one possessing eternal life.

The temple is spiritual in contrast with the ceremonial and the natural. It is a building not made with hands, not material or temporal but eternal. "Howbeit the most High dwelleth not in temples made with hands" (Acts 7.48; Acts 17.24). The Lord Jesus Himself is the chief corner stone (Eph 2.20; 1 Pet 2.6). Therefore, the whole building takes its character from Him. In Christ all the building is fitly framed together. The Church is to be the dwelling place of God, a living sanctuary, manifesting the glory of God. It is a "holy temple" set apart for God and will be the centre of worship and praise. Being "an holy temple in the Lord" indicates that it is under the authority of the Lord and that He will be the leader of the praise of His people (Ps 22.22; Heb 2.12). He will lead the saints as they unite in praise and do so with delight. He is also the source of its holiness for the saints are holy through union with Him.

ZECHARIAH

J. J. Stubbs

CONTENTS

Page

INTRODUCTION

The Man Who Wrote the Book

We know very little of Zechariah's background. He was a young man when he commenced his prophetic ministry (2.4) and was probably born during the captivity in Babylon. He returned to the land of Israel in the first caravan of exiles from Babylon in 536 BC. Nehemiah 12.4,16 mentions Iddo the grandfather and Zechariah the grandson, and they are said to have returned from Babylon in company with Zerubbabel and Joshua. Berechiah the father may have died when Zechariah was young. He became the next representative of the family after the grandfather Iddo, whom he followed in the priestly office under the high priest Jehoiakim, and he was called, as was frequently the case under such circumstances, "the son of Iddo" (Ezra 5.1; 6.14).

The name Zechariah was a common one in the Old Testament, for there are at least twenty-seven men referred to who bore the name! Zechariah means, "He whom Jehovah remembers", or "Jehovah remembers". His name was an encouraging reminder to the people that God will never forget His promises to Israel, but will yet bring about their restoration to Himself. We learn from Nehemiah 12.4 and Ezra 5.1 that Zechariah belonged to a priestly family as did also Jeremiah, Ezekiel, and Ezra. Clearly he was familiar with priestly things as the following references will show: 3.1-10; 6.9-15; 9.8,15; 14.16, 20-21. Thus his name was very fitting and his background was equally appropriate for God to take him up to give challenge and encouragement to the people. He does give a short profile of his ancestry at the beginning of his prophecy and simply identifies himself as "Zechariah, the son of Berechiah, the son of Iddo" (1.1).

It is impossible to determine how long his prophetic ministry lasted. Some think that this Zechariah is the very one that our Lord spoke of in Matthew 23.35 as being slain by the Jews between the temple and the altar. There He refers to Zacharias the son of Barachias, but in the Chronicles account he is called the "son of Jehoiada" (2 Chr 24.20-21). However, as H. A. Ironside says, "In that case we have to suppose either a Berechiah in the genealogy of Jehoiada, or else a copyist's error in transcribing the Greek text. In the absence of proof to the contrary, it seems safer to assume that Zacharias the son of Barachias is none other than the prophet…The Jews have a tradition that he perished in the manner described. J. N. Darby, in his 'Irrationalism of Infidelity', says that 'the Jewish Targum states that Zechariah the son of Iddo, a prophet and priest was slain in the sanctuary'. As the rabbis could have no possible reason for seeking to confirm the words of the Lord Jesus, it would seem as though their testimony was conclusive". It would be most interesting if the Zechariah the Lord mentions is indeed the writer of this prophecy, but we cannot be certain. It is thought that he died at an advanced age and was buried near to the prophet Haggai, with whom he had associated in his prophetic work.

The Time the Book was Written

Zechariah began his prophetic ministry about 520 years before Christ came and continued prophesying for just over two years at least (1.1 with 7.1). Zechariah began to prophesy two months later than his contemporary Haggai. Each of the prophets Haggai, Zechariah, and Malachi lived and ministered at the time that the Jews were returning to Israel from seventy years of captivity in Babylon. The books of Ezra, Nehemiah, and Esther all refer to the same time period. Babylon had given way to the advance of Persia. Cyrus the king of Persia, being favourable to the Jews, in one of his first acts as supreme monarch in Western Asia issued a proclamation which gave permission to the Jews to return to Jerusalem and build the temple (Ezra 1.1-4). They had first begun to build, but this was hindered until the reign of Darius. In the sixth month of the second year of his reign Haggai the prophet prophesied. Zechariah ministered in the eighth month of that same year. There were three stages of movement back to Jerusalem. The first under Zerubbabel took place about 536 BC (see Ezra 2). The second took place between fifty and sixty years later with Ezra the scribe to the fore (see Ezra 7). Some ten years later, in a third movement in 466 BC, Nehemiah, on hearing of the conditions of things in Jerusalem, was exercised to return there to build up again the walls of the city.

The Reason Why it was Written

Zechariah was raised up by God to minister encouragement to the remnant that had returned from Babylon and to inspire them to continue with the rebuilding of the temple. He was also used of God to give them hope as to His purpose for them to destroy all their enemies and to set up a Kingdom over which their Messiah would rule universally. There was every reason for the returned remnant to feel despondent, not only because of the difficulty of the task in hand with opposition to face, but the glowing prophecies, for example, of the former prophets Isaiah and Jeremiah had not yet taken place. Zechariah's ministry was to show these Jews that God had not forgotten His promises; though they might be deferred meantime. Even a cursory reading of the book should reveal that the over-riding message of Zechariah is that the prophet is concerned to encourage the downcast and pessimistic remnant. While Haggai concentrated on the need for the remnant to finish the building of the temple, Zechariah had a much wider view. He saw Israel in the context of the world, and looked by the Spirit of God to the end times with some outstanding prophecies. The prophet's eye is on the present difficult task confronting them; his heart anticipates the great prophetical day to come when God will keep His covenant to them and bring them glory, and his hands meanwhile are prepared to work with them in the building of the temple (Ezra 5.1-2). It is plain to see from this latter reference that Zechariah was no dreamer or mystic, as some may conclude from his visions in the first section of his prophecy, but that he was a very practical man burdened about the conditions in which the Jews were at this time. By his prophetic messages and by his very presence among them he, under God, was doing all that he could to lift up the hearts of the remnant.

The Contents of the Book

The prophet Zechariah ministered with Haggai as they encouraged the Jewish remnant to rebuild the temple. Haggai is more concerned about the temple, while Zechariah is more occupied with the city of Jerusalem. In fact it is mentioned more than forty times in his prophecy. The key text in this connection is, "I am jealous for Jerusalem and for Zion with a great jealousy" (1.14). Although Zechariah has no more than fourteen chapters, he compares very favourably with the longer prophecy of Isaiah. It would be true to say that he is more comprehensive than any other of the Minor Prophets. While Isaiah refers to the coming glory he says little of the kingdoms at the end time, and while Daniel, for instance, sees the kingdoms, he says little of the coming glory of the Messiah. Zechariah, however, sees both and gives much detail concerning these two themes. In Zechariah's fourteen chapters and two hundred and eleven verses, he sums up and condenses most of what the former prophets had written. It is interesting to note that he speaks of the two advents of Christ. He predicts the first coming in grace (9.9) and also His second coming in glory (14.1-4). In the course of this commentary the precise details of Zechariah's description of these events will be noted. It is also worth mentioning that he alone of the Minor Prophets refers to Satan (3.1). Outside of Daniel he is the only other prophet who alludes to Alexander the Great (9.1-8). He is the only prophet who specifically mentions that Christ will be a priest in the Millennium (6.13). He is the only Minor Prophet who gives great detail concerning Armageddon (12.1-4; 14.1-3, 12-15). These are interesting points and show how valuable the contribution of Zechariah is in the revelation of Old Testament prophecy.

One pervading and glorious person is dominant in all Zechariah's prophecies. The clear cut figure of the Messiah - Saviour and Priest - is seen throughout. For this very reason the book of Zechariah is important, instructive, and so valuable to the believer today. Zechariah presents the many glories of the Messiah in relation to the city of Jerusalem, the people of God, the temple and the coming Kingdom. The prophecies concerning Israel's Messiah are remarkable as to the extent of their coverage, for he touches upon the whole history of Christ from His appearance to Israel and His wonderful public ministry in their midst to His future coming to the earth to deliver the nation from their enemies. We are much indebted to this young priest-prophet for the scope of his prophecies concerning the Lord Jesus Christ. Zechariah has more references to the Person and work of the Messiah than all the other of the Minor Prophets put together. To get some idea of this, consider the following twelve references to Christ in the book and note how much they take in of the Lord and His work in connection with the nation of Israel. They are set out here in their chronological order.

1. His public ministry (11.4-14).
2. His entry in Jerusalem on the ass (9.9).
3. His valuation by the people and rejection by them (11.12-13).
4. His crucifixion (13.7).
5. His smiting by God (13.7).
6. His coming again (14.1-3).
7. His standing on the Mount of Olives (14.4-5).
8. His recognition by Israel (12.10).
9. His destruction of the enemies (12.3 & 9).
10. His building of the temple at the start of the Millennium (6.12).
11. His Royal Priesthood in the Kingdom (6.13).
12. His reign over the earth in the Millennium (14.9).

It should be pointed out that the triumphal entry of the Lord into Jerusalem (9.9), the price at which He was valued (the price of an ox or a slave in the east), and the use to which the money was applied (11.12-13), with the piercing of His holy side (12.10) are Messianic predictions fulfilled to the letter. How clear it is from all these references that the book of Zechariah fills a position of remarkable importance in the development of Messianic prophecy.

Zechariah in the New Testament
The prophecy of Zechariah is referred to directly or indirectly on at least five occasions in the New Testament. These references illustrate the familiarity of New Testament writers with the book, and show that they regarded Zechariah's writings as having great Christological significance and prophetical and spiritual import. Three of the passages cited are specific prophecies regarding the Lord Jesus. Two of them clearly were in the minds of the writers and are at the background of what they write.
    1. Matthew 21.4-5 and John 12.14-15 cite Zechariah 9.9 as being fulfilled in the Lord's entering the city of Jerusalem on the ass.
    2. Matthew 26.31 – "smite the shepherd and the sheep shall be scattered" - shows how Christ's rejection, death, and the scattering of the disciples fulfilled Zechariah 13.7. The beginnings of this prophecy were fulfilled when "they all forsook him, and fled" (Mk 14.50). It was a sample, on a small scale, of that greater dispersion of the Jewish nation which took place later. This New Testament reference is all the more significant and valuable because it is good to notice that the Lord Jesus Himself quotes the prophecy of Zechariah.
    3. John 19.37 - "They shall look on him whom they pierced" – is a citation of Zechariah 12.10, and shows that the prophecy had a partial fulfillment

at Calvary. The context of Zechariah 12 looks on to the time of the revelation of Christ to Israel.

4. The two olive trees in Zechariah 4 are in the mind of the Apostle John as he writes concerning the two witnesses in Revelation 11 particularly at v.4.

5. The Apostle Paul in Ephesians 4.25 exhorts the Christians in Ephesus to "speak every man truth with his neighbour". In these words he is quoting from the Septuagint translation of Zechariah 8.16.

Thus Matthew, John, and Paul each refer to Zechariah's writings. From this we see the relevance of the book and its importance to the development of truth in the New Testament.

OUTLINE OF THE BOOK

In chapters 1-6 we have prophecies during the building of the temple. In chapters 7-14 we have prophecies after the building of the temple. There are two great subjects in the two sections of the book. In chapters 1-6 we have the nation and the temple. In chapters 7-14 we have the Messiah and the Kingdom.

In general we have two main divisions in the book.

1. The future blessing of Judah and Jerusalem, with judgment upon the Gentile oppressors of Jehovah's people, closing with the introduction of Messiah's millennial reign as King and Priest upon His throne – presented in a series of visions (chapters 1-6).

2. The moral condition of the people; the relation of the Gentiles to Israel in the future days, with their full and final destruction; a remnant spared and the latter day glory – Jerusalem being the centre (chapters 7-14).

There appears to be a clear structure to the book of Zechariah, for it begins with eight visions – chapters 1-6. It continues with the questions of the remnant as to whether they should still keep four fasts commenced in Babylon – chapters 7-8. It ends with two great prophecies concerning Christ and Israel's glorious future – chapters 9-14. Thus we have eight visions, four fasts, and two prophecies. We might put this outline in another way.

The Foes of Israel – will they yet be conquered? This is answered in chapters 1-6.

The Fasts of Israel - should they still be observed? This is answered in chapters 7-8.

The Future of Israel – does the nation have any hope for the future? This is answered in chapters 9-14.

A brief summary of each of Zechariah's fourteen chapters should be of interest.

Chapter 1 – Jehovah's jealously for Zion, His return in mercy to Jerusalem, and the overthrow of Gentile enemies who have scattered Israel.

Chapter 2 - The future establishment of Jerusalem as a secure city with Jehovah in the midst.

Chapter 3 – The cleansing and pardon of Israel as seen in the taking away of Joshua's filthy garments.

Chapter 4 – The testimony of Israel restored as God's light-bearer in the world.

Chapter 5 – The law of God will again be effective in Israel, and Babylon in the future is seen as the seat of commerce on earth where it will be judged.

Chapter 6 – The nations are the subject of divine judgment, paving the way for Christ the builder of the temple and the bearer of the glory.

Chapter 7 – The returned remnant called to exercise practical righteousness.

Chapter 8 – The people's future return to Zion and the latter day glory and blessing of Jerusalem.

Chapter 9 – The historical fulfillment from Alexander's overthrow of Persia until Christ.

Chapter 10 – The nation of Israel gathered as God's people and strengthened by and for Jehovah.

Chapter 11 – The Messiah rejected by the nation, but the Antichrist accepted.

Chapter 12 – The Destruction of Gentile powers at Armageddon, Israel converted, and mourning in the presence of her crucified Messiah.

Chapter 13 - The cleansing of the people, the mass of the nation cut off, and a remnant number delivered.

Chapter 14 – The arrival of the Lord on the Mount of Olives to crush the nations gathered against Jerusalem, resulting in the reign of Christ in the millennial Kingdom.

ZECHARIAH 1

Verses 1-6: The Prologue to the Book

This preface to the prophecy of Zechariah 1 opens with a call from God to His people to turn to Him and to beware lest they follow their fathers in their backsliding and disobedience. In these opening verses we are reminded seven times that the word is the Lord's. The prophet assures the people that the divine word can never pass away, and that punishment must overtake sin. To follow in the footsteps of their predecessors, who utterly scorned the voice of God through the prophets, was the sure and certain pathway to the discipline of God. The book, then, commences with a solemn warning. It is a call to repentance. There could be no blessing for the nation unless they turned to Him. Recalling the past enforces this appeal.

It is most interesting to compare this prologue to the book with the conclusion of the first main division in Zechariah. In 6.9-15 the first major section of Zechariah ends with a message from Jehovah. There it is a word about the future, but here in the opening of the book it is a warning from the past. There we have a priest in Joshua (symbolically) becoming a king, for Joshua is crowned, a picture, as we will see, of Christ the coming Priest-King. Here we have in Zechariah a priest becoming a prophet. There the condition for future blessing in the nation rests on the obedience of the nation. Here the condition of present blessing for the nation rests on repentance. There in the conclusion to the visions of chs.1-6 we have the significance of three names: Heldai, Tobijah, and Jedaiah. Here, too, in the preface to these visions we have the significance of three names: Zechariah, Berechiah, and Iddo. This comparison between that which introduces these visions and that which concludes them demonstrates a rather striking and significant structure. The lover of the inspired Scriptures will delight to see that there is a pattern and plan to this great book of Zechariah. We now consider this message of warning.

The foundation of the temple had been laid during the reign of Cyrus, but had been interrupted until the reign of Darius. When he ascended the throne things began to change in the favour of God's people. Darius appears to have been a gracious and generous ruler, and especially favourable to the Jews. Thus God began to over-rule for the good of His people, and used even Darius to further His purpose. Encouraged by this, the people were roused up by the ministry of Zechariah to continue with the work of the building of Zerubbabel's temple. Though a young man, Zechariah was God's instrument, fitted by Him, and combining the compassion of the priesthood with the authority of the prophet. As called and chosen by God, he was ideally suited to influence the people for blessing in building the temple. To a large extent the people owed much to Zechariah as they exerted themselves to carry out the completion of that work (Ezra 6.14). Who can fully measure the importance of ministry and its effect upon the people of God? Today, ministry has a most important place. Without it God's people would have no guidance or even incentive to continue in God's work, especially in times of difficulty being faced in the testimony today.

The timing of the message (v.1a)

It is helpful to notice the date of this first word from God through Zechariah and to compare it with that of the older prophet Haggai. Zechariah's first message was two months after Haggai's first message to the people and a week or two after Haggai's second message about coming glory for the nation of Israel. What is to be learned from this? Was it fitting that such a solemn warning to the remnant not to bring the same punishment on themselves by repeating the same evils as their fathers had should follow Haggai's encouraging message of hope? It is surely most fitting! Before ever Israel could be restored and enjoy the great blessing God had in store for them, they would need to be in a right condition and in a right relationship with God. This book explains that the time will come when the nation will repent and obey God. They will yet be the nation that God intended them to be, but their glorious future will come about through God dealing with them to produce their repentance, which will result in the way being paved for their national greatness again, under the reign of their Messiah. It is the same for the believer today. No blessings from God or right relationships with Him can possibly be enjoyed unless the heart is in a right condition and sin has been confessed and judged in the presence of God.

The date given, "In the eighth month, in the second year of Darius", when Zechariah commenced his prophecy, shows that the times of the Gentiles had begun. God had sent His people into captivity in Babylon. No longer was His throne in Jerusalem, but Gentile power had taken over. The nation of Israel had failed. The kingdom of God in their hands had miserably been lost. Soon, as seen in the metallic image of Daniel 2, the empire of Babylon would be succeeded by that of Medo-Persia, then by the third kingdom of Greece and finally by the Roman Empire. Gentile dominion will continue into the period of the Tribulation following the Rapture of the Church and will culminate in the final phase of Gentile powers in the ten-kingdom confederacy. It is important to note this, because it is very significant that, as in Haggai, so in Zechariah - both begin with the times of the Gentiles and end with prophecies concerning the time when the times of the Gentiles will suddenly cease with the Lord's second advent in glory to the earth (see Zech 14.4-16).

It may well be helpful to set out a chronology of the prophecies uttered by the prophets Haggai and Zechariah. It reveals an interesting structure and shows, too, how they were united in their ministry.

Sixth month	Haggai 1.2-11: Feasting when they ought to have been fasting. Haggai 1.12-15: Relaxing when they ought to have been building.
Seventh month	Haggai 2.1-9: The glories of the past, present and future temples. "I will fill this house with glory" (v.7).
Eighth month	Zechariah 1.1-6: Discipline, judgment through failure to obey. Admonition to return.
Ninth month	Haggai 2.10-23: Discipline, judgment through failure to obey. Assurance of blessing.
Eleventh month	Zechariah 1.7-17: Glories of God's purpose for His House. "I will be the glory in the midst of her" (2.5).

SILENCE FOR TWO YEARS (see 7.1).

| *Ninth month* | Zechariah 7 & 8: Fasting, but they will be feasting. Remorse, but they shall rejoice. |

From the dates when each of these prophets gave their messages, one can see how the older and younger prophets worked together to challenge the people and to encourage them. The correspondence between messages one and six, two and five, and three and four are obvious and show how these men of God complemented each other in their ministry. At the same time, each had a definite and separate message for the people. Haggai emphasizes the House of God; Zechariah emphasizes the God of the House. Haggai in his ministry is simple and plain; Zechariah is profound and mystical. Haggai directs his message more to the conscience that the people might be rebuked; Zechariah directs his message more to the heart that he might encourage the people. Haggai is occupied more with the present; Zechariah is occupied more with the future. God takes up and fits His servants and sends them at the right time and with the right message.

The teaching of the names (v.1b)
In the first verse of Zechariah, there is a significant message in the meanings of the three names. Zechariah's name means "remembered of the Lord"; his father's name means "Jehovah will bless"; while his grandfather's name means "timely", or "the appointed time". By putting these together we have a very reassuring line of truth, not only for Israel, but also for the people of God today. What is the combined message of these names and how may they be applied? Linking them together gives, "The Lord will remember His people to bless them at the right time". Is not this a most comforting message for God's people? The book of Zechariah goes on to bring out the meaning of these names and how God in a future day will remember His people to bless them at the appointed time. Take for instance, the last three chapters of the book. Chapter 12

shows how God will once again open His eyes upon the people (v.4). He will not forget them or His promise to them in His word. Chapter 13 shows how He will bless them when the fountain for sin and uncleanness will be opened for them (v.1). He will bless them on the ground of the work of Calvary. In chapter 14, the great concluding chapter, He will come to deliver His people in the Person of the Messiah when the Mount of Olives will open and cleave in two. How timely His arrival will be for Israel! The nation, seen in the remnant of that day, will be sorely tempted to think that Jehovah has forgotten and forsaken them, but God will keep His promise at the appointed time. The believer, too, must in every trial and crisis hold on by faith to the truth of God's remembrance. It is good to read that when Noah was in the ark, and while the flood rose and bore up the ark, that "God remembered Noah" (Gen 8.1). The faith of Noah may have been tested. We do not know whether he was tempted to feel that God had forgotten him, but if he did he need not have feared. God will ever remember us with a view to blessing us in His own good time. It is our part to wait and trust and not despair. His timing is always right.

The title of the Lord (v.2)
The Lord of hosts is mentioned five times in these opening verses. It is a title found here with great force and meaning. The prophets of the returned remnant from Babylon used it very frequently. It is a remarkable fact that the title occurs more often in the prophecies of Haggai and Zechariah than in all the rest of the word of God. It is used forty-eight times alone in the first eight chapters of Zechariah! Why is this the case? The answer is that the people to whom Zechariah ministered were in great weakness. They were much discouraged. Their past had been one of disobedience. They were in a very low condition and doubtless had succumbed to the hopelessness of the task before them. What then is the significance of this title in the context here? It should be plain to see that the title has very much to do with the desperate need of the people in Zechariah's day. Yes, they faced a great task in building the second temple. Yes, they had much to discourage them. True, their recent history furnished no example or incentive to them to go on in dependence on God. However, if they knew anything about this title of their God they would surely know well enough that all the resources they needed were in Jehovah of hosts. He is in control no matter how great the crisis. He has the charge of heavenly hosts, and He has the power to meet the need and bless His people. The first time the title is found in Scripture is in 1 Samuel 1.3, and Hannah uses it also in v.11 of that passage. That godly lady had a burden about giving birth to a man-child for the good of the nation. She prayed about this one child to the God who had power in every sphere and had a numberless throng of angels to do His bidding. Could He not answer the prayer of Hannah and grant her one request? Of course He could, as He also, in the last occurrence of the title in James 5.4, could meet the need

of the poor and despised workers whose wages had been kept back from them. Their cries had entered into the ears of "the Lord of sabaoth". God has not changed and our need can be met too. The returned remnant needed the reassurance that their God had not changed. All was at His disposal and they could rely on His strength and sufficiency to aid them in their task.

What had the Lord of hosts to say to His people? It is rather arresting to see how very abruptly and solemnly this word of the Lord commences: "The Lord hath been sore displeased with your fathers". It was one thing for the nations to displease God (v.15), but quite another for God's own people to do so! What a beginning to the book! Zechariah immediately tells the people what they really knew from their history. Had their fathers obeyed God, that history would have been so very different, but, as a consequence of their sins, God had punished His people and sent them into captivity in Babylon. Hence the weak condition of the people as Zechariah ministers to them. They sorely needed the ministry of this prophet. What a contrast there is between his first message here in ch.1 and his last in ch.14. The final word of Zechariah is a prophecy of God's holiness seen everywhere in the future land of Israel. How such blessed and ideal conditions will be brought about for Israel by God's dealings with them is the great subject of this book.

The turning of the people (vv.3-6)

Three times the word "turn" is used here. God longs to bless His people, but only if they repent and turn to Him. "Therefore say thou unto them, Thus saith the Lord of hosts; Turn ye unto me, saith the Lord of hosts, and I will turn unto you, saith the Lord of hosts." The Lord waits to welcome His people. This is an important truth, but to have the Lord turn to us there must first be a turning to the Lord. This is the condition of blessing. The ground or reason why the people addressed by Zechariah were to turn, has been given in v.2: God's anger with their fathers for their evil ways. The Lord cannot turn to His people if they are unrepentant and disobedient. If anything is to be accomplished for God, our relationship with Him must first be put right. Note the urgency of this message. It is turn "now".

In vv.5-6 the prophet refers to the history of the nation. It makes sad reading. This word from the Lord shows us that, as the people of God then, so now with past matters. It is not only sins and departure in our day, but the sins of the past that sound a warning voice to us. Looking at history in relation to God's dealings with our fathers is not always a bright picture. It was certainly not so with Israel. Their fathers had displeased God (v.2), they had disobeyed God (v.4), and they had been disciplined by God (v.6). Israel were bidden by the prophet to look at their history, to be solemnly warned by it and to be challenged to take out of it any lesson that might furnish fresh strength for their present duty. Zechariah's word here should have spoken to the remnant to cause them to avoid the mistakes of their fathers and to make them a wiser and better people by seeking to obey God. How greatly needed was such a word, for how could they hope to know the approval and help of God in the building of the temple if they were in a wrong condition.

In these verses the references to the prophets and the word of God must be noticed. The questions in v.5 reminded the people so vividly that the fathers and the prophets had long since gone, but the word of God was still with them. It is a reminder of the words of Isaiah 40.8, cited by Peter in the New Testament (1 Pet 1.25): "The word of our God shall stand forever". The human instruments God had used to warn and demand repentance from their fathers had ceased. Their voices had long since become silent, but the divine word had been solemnly fulfilled, for the threat of punishment for their sins had overtaken their fathers and seventy years of tragic captivity in Babylon had had to be endured. After this calamity had visited them, and their fathers had returned to God and acknowledged that He had been just in so dealing with them. Sadly, their turning to God in confessing their evil ways had come too late and they had had to experience the shame of their captivity. They had lost their dignity, identity, and potentiality as a nation.

From this solemn opening message in Zechariah we learn not to disregard God's dealings with His people in the past, but to profit by them. Israel's history left little to boast in. There was need for them to live in the present for God. We may learn, too, the principle of reaping set forth in Galatians 6.7: "Be not deceived; God is not mocked: for whatsoever a man soweth, that shall he also reap". Finally, there is the importance of repentance, without which there can be no recovery. Until the people are repentant the great blessings promised to them in the visions that follow can never be fulfilled in the life of the nation.

The Visions of Chapters 1.7 – 6.8

About three months after Zechariah gave God's word of warning to the people, he is given in one single night a series of eight visions probably succeeding each other one by one fairly rapidly. These visions are followed by a symbolic transaction in the crowning of Joshua (6.9-15). The visions take up the major part of the first division of the book and very sharply contrast in their character with the rest of the book. These early chapters are mainly apocalyptic and contain different symbols of great import for Zechariah and for Israel, whereas chs.9-14 are prophetic in character and contain specific predictions concerning Israel's future blessing in the millennial Kingdom. The two sections so differ in their nature and style that some commentaries have tried to advance the idea that a writer distinct from Zechariah must be credited with the later chapters. There is no evidence whatsoever for this two author view. There may well be a time difference between the dated chs.7 & 8 and the undated prophecies of chs.9-14, but in all the manuscripts of the book which have been preserved, there is no space between chs. 8 & 9, or anything to suggest a break. The believer may be assured that Zechariah is one book from one author with one great theme, namely the future restoration and blessing of the nation of Israel.

Looking at these visions in a general way it is helpful to note that visions one to three have to do mainly with the building of the temple, visions four and five have to do mainly with Joshua and Zerubbabel, and visions six to eight have to do mainly with the spiritual transformation of the people. In the last three of these visions God is dealing with the sin of the individual (5.1-4), the sin of the nation (5.5-11), and the sin of the world (6.1-8). The visions begin and end with the sovereignty of God over the earth. In the first vision the horses are interpreted as "These are they whom the Lord sent to walk to and fro through the earth". In the eighth and last vision the four horses are interpreted as "The four spirits of the heavens, which go forth from standing before the Lord of all the earth". In these visions too there are some delightful and interesting presentations of Christ that should not be missed. He is seen in a variety of aspects in connection with His earthly people Israel, and believers may glean lessons of great comfort and blessing from these views of the Saviour.

Generally speaking, the standard pattern of the visions is that Zechariah first describes what he sees, then he asks questions as to the meaning, and finally the interpreting angel gives the explanation. The visions are given to Zechariah, it would appear, in one single night. This may well picture the dark history and condition of the nation of Israel. They had recently returned from a gloomy period of seventy years captivity and needed encouraging. The divine design in these visions is to encourage the remnant with messages of hope concerning the salvation and glory to come. One may view therefore the eight visions as a step-by-step divine answer to the problems and questions that concerned the people in their weak condition and their need. Looking at them in this way shows us their great purpose and furnishes, too, the believer of this present age of grace with practical lessons of comfort and assurance.

In connection with four of the visions Zechariah lifts up his eyes (1.18; 2.1; 5.1; 6.1), and in the case of the vision of the lampstand the angel awakens him (4.1). This is the only time this happens in all the visions and one needs, when considering that vision, to enquire why this is so. Zechariah, in order to see these visions and to be given their meaning, had to have his eyes open. He had to be alert, otherwise none of these communications would have been given him. It does not appear that he receives these revelations from God in a dream, but rather he is in an ecstatic condition as brought about by the Spirit of God which enabled his mental and spiritual powers to be fully attentive and responsive to the divine promptings. In this way he was in a good condition to receive all these wonderful messages with their symbolic pictures of much spiritual import.

The date when the visions were all given may be also suggestive. The day upon which these revelations of divine purpose were made known to Zechariah was the twenty-fourth day of the eleventh month, namely the month Sebat and in the second year of Darius. Sebat runs from the new moon in February to the new moon in March. The term is Chaldean and means "a shoot", or the month when trees begin to shoot. This was precisely five months after the building of the second temple had been recommenced (Hag 1.15). This is an interesting fact, and the idea of the new moon may well suggest that these visions tell of Israel, who will yet have their new moon experience when they will be restored and blessed and spring into life as a nation and bring forth fruit to God.

Verses 7-11: The First Vision. The Divine Presence – the Man among the Myrtle Trees
Question: "Is the Lord still with us?"

In these verses we have first the vision from God in vv.7-11 and then the message from God based upon the vision in vv.12-17. In this first vision Zechariah sees a man riding on a red horse among the myrtle trees. Four matters need to be considered in this vision.

> The rider of the red horse – Who is he?
> The myrtle trees – What do they symbolize?
> The location of the trees – What is the significance of their being in the bottom of the valley?
> The reference to the red, speckled and white horses – What do these represent in the vision?

The rider on the red horse
The small group of people, having listened to the ministry of Haggai and returned to Jerusalem to rebuild the temple, would feel greatly their weakness, and probably were impatient to establish themselves once again in a city that had been devastated and ruined. It is very likely that they wondered if the promise of God through Haggai would be fulfilled. Now back in Jerusalem, their anxious question would be, "Is the Lord still with us as His people, and can we count upon Him for His help, for we have been so long in Babylon?". In the vision of the man on the red horse God answered their doubts by assuring them He was with them. Thus the picture of the man on the red horse standing among the myrtle trees is that of the Lord standing vigil, as it were, sympathizing with His people, and ready to act for His people. The Lord Jesus, represented as riding upon a horse, may perhaps denote swiftness in the working out of the will of God providentially in seeking to help His people. At the Lord's second advent, John depicts Him as the militant word of God coming to deliver His people (Rev 19.15). Then how swiftly He will work for the blessing of Israel. The vision should have had a very reassuring message for the remnant!

We must, however, enquire as to who this rider is. Comparing v.8 with v.11 gives a clear clue as to his identity. In v.11 there is mention of the angel of Jehovah. One or two commentaries have tried to show that the man on the red horse cannot be identified with the angel of Jehovah, but the argument is weak and unconvincing. When comparing v.8 with v.11 the conclusion should be inevitable. Both are referred to as standing among the myrtle trees. The man on the red horse and the angel are quite clearly one and the same. Here in this vision is the Pre-incarnate Christ. He is presented as being with and standing for His earthly people. The man is ready-mounted, prepared to intervene in their behalf. That the man is a divine person is plain from his being also called the Angel of Jehovah (to be distinguished from the interpreting angel). This is the description applied to the Angel who represents Jehovah and is distinguished from the ranks of lower angelic beings. This being will be seen again in the third vision in 3.1. In other references in the Old Testament to this Angel He speaks and acts for Jehovah and has attributes that only belong to deity. In Genesis 16.7-14 note that Hagar called the Angel of Jehovah, "God" (v.13). In Exodus 3 after it is said, "The angel of the Lord (Jehovah) appeared" (v.2), the writer goes on to say in reference to the same person, "When the Lord (Jehovah) saw…" (v.4)! In Exodus 23.20-23 Israel are warned to beware of Him and to obey Him. He has the power to pardon sins and He it is that will lead them into the land. Surely this Angel must be a divine being. In Judges 6.12-14 and 17-24 the Angel of Jehovah came to Gideon and accepted Gideon's sacrifice! Finally in Isaiah 63.9 there is an interesting reference to the Angel of His presence, who had ever been present with Israel in their coming out of Egypt and in their journeys through the wilderness. Then in v.10 Isaiah speaks about the people grieving His Holy Spirit! The conclusion is again obvious for the Holy Spirit belongs to the holy Trinity and He is Christ's Spirit. Putting all these passages together there is no doubt that the Angel of Jehovah is marked by deity and, while the time had not come in Zechariah's day for the Lord's entering into manhood, He is seen in this vision as a man watching over His people Israel. It is an evidence of the vital doctrine of the pre-existence of Christ and shows us His willingness to presence Himself with His people and His readiness to act in power for them.

The believer may glean much comfort from this vision. The Lord who had been with His people in leading them out of Egypt and through the wilderness and was with the little remnant in Jerusalem is the same today. He has not changed. All power belongs to Him. His wonderful promise is, "I will be with you always". How blessed to know that "The Lord is at hand" (Phil 4.5). We can therefore count upon His presence and know the reality of His interest in us. It is helpful to notice that the rider on the red horse is presented as standing in the forefront with the other riders and their horses behind him. This shows that the Lord Jesus is pre-eminent and is in control of these heavenly forces. They are guided by Him and do His bidding. He is the pre-eminent Leader working behind the scenes on behalf of His people. How true it is that He moves behind the scenes and moves the scenes He is behind. This is a great reassuring fact for believers to understand and enjoy.

The myrtle trees

The man, we read, "stood among the myrtle trees". One may naturally enquire, "Why among the myrtle trees?". Is there some significance or symbolism about this tree? Do these myrtle trees have anything to teach the people, especially in their circumstances at that time? The myrtle is an evergreen and is a modest tree of unassuming appearance with no majestic branches or brilliant flowers as some other trees have. Yet it is a beautiful tree and possesses qualities of perennial freshness and is covered here and there with delicate white flowers that emit a pleasant fragrance. The myrtle tree no doubt speaks of the nation of Israel. The myrtle is not like the stately cedar or the upright palm tree, but is a lowly and fragrant tree, and in the vision represents Israel in their present condition as returned from Babylon, after God brought them through much humiliation and shame.

With this reference, the myrtle tree is mentioned in four passages of Scripture. All the references are associated with the divine promise and speak of the fact that God will fulfil His promise to Israel and bring them into future blessing. It is noticed by Nehemiah as one of the trees which supplied branches for the construction of booths at the Feast of Tabernacles (Neh 8.15). This particular feast typically sets forth the joy of Israel in the millennial Kingdom. The prophet Isaiah used the tree to indicate the great changes that will be brought about in the land of Israel. In Isaiah's glowing predictions of future prosperity he assures the people of Israel that seven trees will be planted in the wilderness and among them is the myrtle (Is 41.19). God will by His hand provide much for His people in the way of refreshment and comfort. This will only be fulfilled for the nation in the coming day of Christ's millennial reign. Isaiah again, speaking of that blessed epoch, contrasts the ugly thorns of the brier with the purity of the myrtle and says, "Instead of the thorn shall come up the fir tree, and instead of the brier shall come up the myrtle tree: and it shall be to the Lord for a name, for an everlasting sign that shall not be cut off" (Is 55.13). "What God will bring about in the blessedness of the millennial Kingdom will have a twofold effect: it will tell forth His glory and will be a constant reminder to His people of His attributes and actings of grace and power" (W. E. Vine, *Isaiah*). So from these Scriptures one may with confidence conclude that this tree stands connected with God's promises to Israel. In the vision of Zechariah 1 it has no doubt a near fulfilment in what God would accomplish for the remnant in Jerusalem, but it also has a more distant fulfilment when God again will move for His people and restore them in ideal conditions. Both these aspects should have had a most uplifting effect upon the small group of God's people. The divine purpose in this vision was that this message of encouragement should be conveyed to them.

The shade of the valley

In the vision Zechariah sees a grove of myrtle trees in a dell. They are presented as being "in the bottom". The picture is that of a deep valley. A valley with an abundance of myrtle trees may well have existed in the neighbourhood of Jerusalem and have been well known to its inhabitants. The location suggests the low, weak and depressed condition in which the land and the people were at that time. It is a condition that remains with the nation up until the present. It is a condition that will not change until God deals with them again. God brought His people out of the valley of captivity in Babylon and sent His servants to exhort and encourage them. He worked and over-ruled for His people so that they might return and establish His temple. Alas, subsequent to this history, His people sank into sin and unbelief and today they are in a low and degraded state again. God, to humble and teach them, will bring them through the valley of the time of the Tribulation. There is an interesting and wonderful prophecy in Hosea 2.15 where the prophet declares that God will give the nation "the valley of Achor (meaning "trouble") for a door of hope: and she shall sing there, as in the days of her youth, and as in the day when she came up out of the land of Egypt". What trouble, even the time of Jacob's trouble, the nation will pass through, but through that most awful period God will be with them to preserve, humble and prepare them for the peace and joy of the Messiah's millennial reign. A myrtle grove in a valley must be a beautiful sight and this may signify that although they are in the deepest degradation, yet His people are precious to Him. Hence He is with them, in their very midst and identified with them in their suffering and affliction. In the next chapter of Zechariah God describes Israel as the "apple of his eye" (v.8) and therefore especially dear to Him. Because of this God will begin to work for His people.

The coloured horses

There seems to be an emphasis more on the mission of these horses than on their colours. In Revelation 6 there is an explanation given of the meaning of the different coloured horses referred to there, but not in this passage. Yet the fact that the different colours of the horses are mentioned may indicate a symbolic meaning. The horse on which the man is riding is of a special colour – red. If "red" suggests the colour of blood then it may picture the mission of the rider to execute judgment and vengeance on the nations that have suppressed and trodden down God's people (cp. Is 63.1-6). While the vision certainly has its near fulfilment in the assurance God was giving the remnant of His presence, at the same time the vision is a prophecy that has not yet been fulfilled. It really looks on to the time when the Lord Jesus Himself will deal with all Israel's enemies. This will

take place at His second advent, when at the crisis of Armageddon He will
swiftly destroy the armies gathering against Jerusalem (see Rev 19.11-21).
The "speckled" or "bay" horse is of that kind in which the background
is mixed with white. This may suggest other means that the Lord will
use to accomplish victory over their foes. The Lord's conquest will not
be wrought by the sword alone, but the two beasts, for example, will
be taken and cast into the lake of fire alive. On the other hand, the
mixed colour of the horse could suggest that the Lord's dealings with
the enemies will be mixed in character by mercy as well as judgment.
In conquering the enemy He will have mercy on Israel, and the prayer
of v.12 as to the longing for mercy upon Jerusalem will be wonderfully
answered. The white horse may best be interpreted by reference to
Revelation 19.11 where it is the symbol of victory and power. The white
horse is probably placed last in the vision because it speaks of the Lord's
ultimate victory. It ushers in the final consummation and reign of Christ,
ending not only the Tribulation period but also the period of Gentile
dominion.

The times of the Gentiles had already begun at this stage of Israel's
history, but this message announces that these times will come swiftly to
an end and governmental power will be given back to Israel. The horses
and their riders positioned behind the man on the red horse appear to
present a picture of angelic agencies and powers, who, under the control
of the man on the red horse, do His bidding and report conditions in the
nations to Him. This vision of these angelic beings, with several other
references of a similar nature, does give an interesting insight into the
sphere and function of angels. Certainly the word "angel" is not found in
the details of this vision itself, but there can be no doubt that the horses
with their riders set forth God's providential dealings with the earth
through the ministry of heavenly messengers. Zechariah asks the
interpreting angel the question, "What are these?", and is told, "I will shew
thee what these things be". Then it is the man on the red horse who answers
the question: "These are they whom the Lord hath sent to walk to and fro
through the earth" (v.10). Then it is most interesting to note that it is the
Angel of Jehovah whom the messengers address and in such a way that
indicates they are reporting to Him conditions on the earth. For they say,
"We have walked to and fro through the earth, and, behold, all the earth
sitteth still, and is at rest" (v.11). The expression "the earth" speaks of the
Gentile nations enjoying undisturbed conditions of prosperity during that
period. At the time of the vision then there was no indication from the
report of these angelic riders that the prophecy, for example, of Haggai
2.6-7 as to the shaking of the nations was about to take place. That prophecy
to the remnant looks on to a future fulfilment when all the kingdoms of
this world opposed to Israel's interests will be overthrown. In the future,
in the latter part of the Tribulation period, all will seem at rest under the
despotic reign of the Antichrist, but God will break up this false peace in

the Gentile world and bring sudden destruction upon the nation's enemies (1 Thess 5.2-3).

What may we learn from vv.9-11 ? The passage does throw some light on an interesting aspect of angelic ministry and supplies a picture of the Lord Jesus as the Revealer of truth and the Enlightener. First we should carefully observe that it is the Angel of the Lord that answers Zechariah and not the interpreting angel. In understanding the mind of God as revealed in His word it is good to get help direct from the Lord Himself. Human help through gifted men may be valuable and should not be despised (1 Tim 5.17), but all light and truth ultimately comes from Christ and still does so in this age of grace through His Holy Spirit. It is always better to get light on truth directly from the Lord, for when we receive it from Him and make it our own it tends to be more highly appreciated and a greater blessing to the soul. Yet of course it is not the only way to learn, for the Lord Jesus has given teachers for the edification of the Church. It is also true that a believer can make truth his own by understanding Scripture through the helpful ministry of such gifted men. It is a wholesome habit for the Christian to ask questions as Zechariah does, and it is especially good for a young believer to do so. Zechariah, we believe, was a young man at the time of these visions and clearly he had his difficulties as to their significance. The meaning of the visions under the direction of the Lord is made plain to Him. It is quite true that in all the visions that follow it is the interpreting angel who leads and explains things to Zechariah, but this must have been allowed of the Lord and the angel only speaks and shows to Zechariah that which would have been in reality the voice of God to him. The fact that it is the Angel of Jehovah who is to the fore in this first vision shows the importance of knowing that Christ has an interest in happenings on earth, and reveals what will take place in future days too through the prophecies contained in the visions.

The Lord Jesus is not only the Revealer of light and knowledge, but He is the Controller of heavenly forces. Angels not only do His bidding, but are seen here reporting to Him conditions among the Gentile nations. Angels will have a ministry in the future to Israel as they did in the past history of the nation. They now have a ministry in relation to the church. It must not be overlooked, however, that they have a ministry in relation to the nations of the world. This is seen very clearly in the book of Revelation. Daniel 10.10-13 should also be looked at carefully with regard to this. There an angel had appeared to Daniel to encourage him, but had been hindered by the prince of the kingdom of Persia. Had it not been for the intervention and assistance of Michael, one of the chief princes, that message would not have got through to Daniel. The prince of the kingdom of Persia is an evil angel opposing the purpose of God. Without expanding the details of that chapter we refer to it to illustrate the reality and existence of what takes place behind the scenes with respect to national powers. Angels are by no means redundant servants even today. It certainly gives confidence in the heart to know that God is in control and uses these created beings to accomplish His own ends, no matter what takes place on earth or indeed for that matter in the land of Israel.

Verses 12-17: The Message Applied from the Vision
In these verses we have the message based on the vision. It is a message that anticipates some of the prophetic statements of the rest of the book, which will be commented upon. It is also a message that contains another view of Christ. He has been seen as the Sentinel of mercy and the Leader of heavenly forces, but here in v.12 the Lord Jesus is shown as the Intercessor pleading for His people. It is a most interesting aspect of Christ. It may appear strange to think of Him praying for Israel in His pre-incarnate state, but we may regard the picture of the Lord here as the Lover of His people Israel and setting forth what He is doing even now. It is wonderful to think that the prayers of Christ will be answered. To think of Israel's future restoration and blessing as an answer to His prayer only adds force to the truth revealed in Scripture, that the nation will be regathered and be what God ever intended them to be. Chapters 12-14 of Zechariah surely show how, in a miraculous and powerful way, the prayers of Christ for His earthly people will be answered.

It has been suggested that the Angel of Jehovah here could be Michael the archangel, but this would make the Angel of Jehovah in this verse to be lower in dignity and rank than the Angel of Jehovah in v.11 and would introduce a third person into the vision. Given that it is the same designation – the Angel of Jehovah as in v.11 – it would be rather confusing to see a separate and distinct being here. The idea of an angel praying would present an aspect of angelic ministry which Scripture does not support, for angels, unlike men, do not need to pray. They worship and serve God, yes, but do not seek His face to request blessing or guidance. It is enough that God commands them in their functions in service.

There are three points to note in this prayer. The way He addresses God, for whom He prays, and the knowledge the Pleader had as to how long they had been in captivity in Babylon. He addresses in the plea the "Lord of hosts". The significance of this title has already been commented upon. It is so fitting that it is used here, for the title shows us that the One who controls all and has mighty ranks of heavenly messengers at His disposal is well able to answer this prayer, no matter how dismal and distressing the circumstances appear to be. The world may be opposed to the little nation of Israel and though they have yet to pass through so many terrible things the Lord of hosts will work for them and answer their cries and subdue every foe. Now notice that He prays for mercy upon Jerusalem and the cities of Judah. The Lord of hosts in His mercy will answer this prayer. Jerusalem and all Judah, which had been the objects of divine displeasure, will at last be the objects of divine favour. Further prophecies in Zechariah reveal how this will be fulfilled (see 2.4-5 ; 8.3-6). It is good to learn from this that the Lord Jesus intercedes for His people when they need it most. His intercessory ministry is always prevailing, for it was answered immediately in v.13 with comforting words to the angel who was commissioned to communicate with Zechariah. Our Lord's intercession for His people today is never in vain. It is very uplifting to the soul to know He is presently engaged in this ministry for us His people. Here, however, the Lord Jesus longs over His earthly people Israel. His love for the nation, though He was rejected by them and crucified, has not changed. His attitude toward them remains the same. The cry "how long" will be echoed in the hearts and on the lips of the remnant during Tribulation days, as they eagerly await His return to set up His Kingdom. He who is now the Lover of the nation will assuredly be their Liberator in a coming great day.

This compassionate and earnest intercessor knew exactly how long the people had been in captivity – "these threescore and ten years". For seventy long years of captivity the people had suffered the loss of national honour and independence, but there was One who understood their need, saw them in their shame, and measured the exact time of their being away from Jerusalem and the land. The Angel of Jehovah in the vision here is the very same as the One of whom Isaiah spoke: "In all their affliction he was afflicted, and the angel of his presence saved them: in his love and in his pity he redeemed them; and he bare them, and carried them all the days of old" (63.9). Lovely words these! He had been with them throughout their wilderness wanderings. Even in the seventy years when God's indignation was upon them the Pleader here had never forsaken them. Though His people Israel will yet have to pass through the terrible furnace of the Tribulation, this great Intercessor will continue to pray for them. He was their Saviour in the forty years in the wilderness, He was their Sympathizer in their seventy years captivity, He was their Mediator in the three and a half years of His ministry among them (compare the parable of the fig tree in Luke 13.6-9 and the Lord pictured as the dresser pleading with the owner of the fruitless tree to "let it alone this year"). He will yet be their Deliverer after the seven years of the Tribulation. Finally, praise God He will reign over them as their Messiah for one thousand years. All these periods through the history of Israel show clearly the passionate and loving interest the Lord Jesus has in the nation of Israel. They will yet be His people and be blessed by Him. If the Lord knew with divine accuracy the time of their captivity, how comforting it must be for the believer to know that the Lord Jesus cares so much for us that should we pass through trial He not only measures the intensity of it but also its very length.

Sovereign love appoints the measure and the number of our pains,
And is pleased when we find pleasure in the suffering He ordains.

God's answer (v.13)

In this verse the Lord answers the interpreting angel with good words and comforting words. It might be wondered why it is that God does not answer the Angel of Jehovah, but it is not impossible that the answer may have first been given to the Angel of Jehovah and then through His instrumentality to the interpreting angel (see C. H. H. Wright). The reason why the message is communicated to Zechariah indirectly appears to be that, unlike the previous part of the vision where the prophet asks a question and learns the meaning by observing and listening to a conversation, the importance of this message is such the angel speaks so that it might so take hold of him that he might preach the "good words and comfortable words" to the people. These good and comfortable words are seen in the rest of the message in vv.14-17. They relate to the establishment of the temple and the city, and look on to the future blessing of the nation. Jehovah will be good to His ancient people, for they will yet exclaim with wonder and joy, "How great is his goodness" (9.17), and He will yet comfort them by giving them prosperity and flourishing cities (v.17).

God's attitude (v.14)

What a message Zechariah is to preach. It is a message of hope in every way. It announces the very words of Jehovah to them: "I am jealous for Jerusalem and for Zion with a great jealousy". Here we have the divine passion not only for the people, but also the city where God had in the past been pleased to place His name. More than once in the Old Testament we find God's jealousy for His people. He will have no competitor for Israel's affections, but here it is God's love for Jerusalem itself. It had been taken by Nebuchadnezzar, had been under Babylonian control for so long, and in Zechariah's time was part of the Persian Empire. God yearns over it. His passion for the city had not changed after the seventy years had run their course. He wanted it for Himself. The prophecy of Zechariah shows how God will own it. When this comes to pass it will then be called "a city of truth" (8.3). As a practical thought it is interesting that in the New Testament the Apostle Paul speaks of his jealousy for the Corinthian assembly: "I am jealous over you with godly jealousy" (2 Cor 11.2). This jealousy Paul had for them reflected God's jealousy for the assembly. It is the only jealousy permitted – a jealousy of divine interest in the saints. The assembly belongs to God and as a chaste virgin espoused to Christ must be faithful and pure for Him. All in it should ask, "Am I pleasing to Him, and the things that I do and where I go, will they conform to my betrothal to Christ?". It is sad when an assembly, like Israel, disobeys God and comes under the control of the world or of men. God wants the assembly for Himself.

God's anger (v.15)

God's displeasure with the nations that are at ease may be contrasted with His sore displeasure with His people in v.2. Perhaps their being at ease is not the idea of being at ease itself, but being at ease when they ought not to be, i.e. being at ease in their sin. The displeasure of God with His people in the past was clearly only temporary. God had used Babylon as His instrument to chasten His people, but now the empire of Babylon had passed away and would be no more. The instrument had been cast aside, but Babylon and other nations had gone beyond what God had intended in causing Israel to suffer unjustly and unnecessarily. For this God would punish them, but at the same time show mercy to His people. The poor Jew has been the subject of much cruelty and persecution by the nations, and Jerusalem, God's beloved city, has been the scene of many atrocities and devastation. It cannot be long now, however, to the time when the mission of the horses will be completed in executing vengeance on the proud Gentile powers. The nations' treatment of God's earthly people the Jews will not be forgotten and God will take vengeance on them. Gentile powers now are at ease, feeling secure, and continue to afflict Israel, but soon the whole situation will be changed, for the nations will be sore afflicted by the divine judgments, and God's chosen people will rest in perfect safety under the reign of their Messiah. A very similar principle is seen in 2 Thessalonians 1.6-9 where Paul encourages the suffering Thessalonians, that though they have trouble from unbelieving men and the world has rest, when Christ comes at His second advent it will be the world's turn to have trouble and they, with all believers, will have rest! No wonder he can say, "To you who are troubled rest with us, when the Lord Jesus shall be revealed from heaven with His mighty angels".

God's arrival (v.16)

Here we have God's reassuring word to the remnant that He will return to the city, His House will be built, and Jerusalem will be established. A line will be stretched forth over Jerusalem so that the city will be built according to the divine plan in a restored condition. The foundation of the temple had been laid and the work needed to continue. The city itself required much toil, but under God this would all be accomplished. This no doubt had a partial fulfilment then, but it also looks on to a time when a new temple will be built in the Millennium. This temple, according to Ezekiel 40-48, will be built in the renewed and enlarged land. The city of the future will be greatly extended. The word "mercies" is to be noted, for being in the plural it indicates that God, in His dealings with His people, will not only perform for them one act of mercy, but will repeat His mercies toward the nation. He has shown mercy to them in the past and He will do so in the future. What joy and blessing for Israel when God returns to the city and dwells in the new sanctuary. This glorious time is alluded to later in Zechariah when God says, "I am returned unto Zion, and will dwell in the midst of Jerusalem" (8.3).

God's assurance (v.17)

The first vision is concluded with a divine assurance of what God will yet do for Israel. The entire land will be changed and enlarged and benefit from God's restored relationship with His people. This future blessing will be seen in three areas: the cities, Zion, and Jerusalem. God calls the cities of the new land, "My cities". It is not only that His people will then belong to Him, but the land itself and every city in it. While other lands and cities will share in the prosperity and peace of the Millennium, none of them will be able to claim that they are God's possession. God will so delight in His people and in His land that He will then be able to say of every city in it, "They are mine". What a day that will be for Israel when all the inhabitants of every city will live in the consciousness of the knowledge of this great fact. God says, "My cities…shall yet be spread abroad", or "overflow" (PUTS – 6327). The meaning of the word is often given as "scatter". How interesting that the scattered people will have spreading cities! The people of Israel who will populate Immanuel's land of the future will be greatly increased as a nation. Not only will Israel then be prosperous and pre-eminent as a people, but also their houses will be filled with happy citizens who will enjoy in their homes an abundance of provision. God's mercy to them will overflow with much blessing. No longer will God be angry with them, but will comfort them and will show to a wondering world in that day that His original choice of Jerusalem has not changed. The purpose of God with regard to Jerusalem will be fulfilled. Three times the Spirit of God in Zechariah gives us this statement of truth (see also 2.12; 3.2). One word from God should be enough to assure man that this will be so, but God repeats it, as if to show that although conditions and circumstances in Jerusalem when the remnant returned seemed contrary to it, yet His word will come to pass.

Looking carefully through this first vision one may conclude that at best its details could only be partially fulfilled in the return from Babylon. The full extent of the vision must look on to the future time of the Millennium. This movement on the part of the Jews, sadly, would not produce permanent enjoyment of God's presence and comfort, for their subsequent history records how the people and the land sank into a terrible dark period of ruin and apostasy. Scripture predicts that Israel, and in particular the city of Jerusalem, will suffer much and be the seething pot of the nations, and will be trodden down of the Gentiles until the Lord Himself comes to deliver them. It must not be overlooked, however, that the vision does have a definite message for the remnant in Zechariah's day. Poor and despised though that little remnant were and their effort hardly, if at all, noticed by the world at large, yet in this message was contained much to encourage and everything to provide an incentive for them as they returned to build. Had they been occupied with their outward circumstances it could easily have dampened their spirits, but God revealed to this despised few all the great things He will yet do for the nation. They had therefore to see things as God saw them and on the strength of His word to press on. This is an important lesson for believers engaged in God's work today.

As we leave this important vision it is good to be reminded of the precious and so encouraging glimpses of Christ in it. He dwells with them and comforts and assures them in their weakness. He speaks to them and enlightens them in so doing. He works behind the scenes in order to bring them to the blessing of recovery. Finally, He prays for them that the promise of God for them might be fulfilled. He is then their Comforter, Enlightener, Intercessor, and Lover. These are aspects of Christ the believer today can and should enter into and enjoy.

Verses 18-21: The Second Vision. The Divine Power – the Four Horns and the Four Carpenters
Question: "What about our enemies, Lord?"
In this the briefest of the eight visions Zechariah sees four horns and four carpenters. The horns represent the Gentile powers that oppose Israel. These nations are the bitter opponents of Israel and seek to scatter them, but the four carpenters remove the horns. Israel had been taken into captivity by a cruel enemy and would have to face further Gentile antagonists in the future, but the concern of the little remnant which had returned from Babylon was how they would cope with and succeed in the building of the temple, in view of the almost certain and inevitable opposition of the enemy. This vision answers this concern, and God shows to Zechariah that He will deal with any such opposition. He is able to remove any power arrayed against them. This is the primary message of the vision and like the previous vision should have encouraged the remnant and given them much confidence in their effort.

It is significant to notice that this particular vision, following the message of blessing and comfort promised by God for His people, indicates that before this could be fulfilled there was the great need to deal with Israel's enemies. No matter how mighty a force confronting Israel or how weak the nation, God by His almighty power would not only defend them, but also scatter the foe. It is Christ Himself who will be the Smiter of the enemy for Israel. The vision had a timely relevance to the people whom Zechariah ministered to, but its message has an application far beyond the feeble remnant, and looks on to the end time, when the Lord as the stone cut out without hands will smash the Gentile armies as a potter's vessel (Dan 2.34).

In considering the details of the vision and the meaning of the horns and carpenters it is important to understand that the vision is a prophecy that yet awaits its fulfilment. Bearing this in mind will help in its interpretation. A vision, then, of four horns now draws the attention of Zechariah. This vision enlarges upon v.15 where God speaks of His displeasure with the nations that are at ease and His people who are oppressed and weak. God's displeasure and His reason for it are now disclosed in this second vision.

The meaning of the four horns

What is the significance of the picture of the horns and their number being four? Actually, three points here must be commented on, not only the horns themselves and their number, but to whom the horns belong, or whom they represent. It is not difficult to see in the horns a symbol of power (Amos 6.13). So often in the Old Testament horns speak of power. "Horn" is used in the plural, as the symbol of strength, in the apocalyptic visions: (1) on the head of the Lamb as symbolic of Christ (Rev 5.6); (2) on the heads of beasts as symbolic of national potentates (Rev 12.3; 13.1; 13.11; 17.3; 17.7; 17.12; 17.16 - cp. Dan 7.8; 8.9). This word is used metaphorically for strength in Deuteronomy 33.17. Horns are emblems of power, dominion, glory, and fierceness, as they are the chief means of attack and defence for the animals endowed with them (Dan 8.5,9; 1 Sam 2.1; 16.1,13; 1 Kings 1.39; 22.11; Josh 6.4,5; Ps 75.5,10; 132.17).The expression "horn of salvation," applied to Christ, means a salvation of strength, or a strong Saviour (Lk 1.69). Clearly, then, the horns in the vision speak of power, and power in the plural.

To whom do these horns belong? The powers here are most decidedly powers organized against Israel, therefore obviously they do not speak of divine power but the might of human or national powers opposed to God's people and intent on scattering them – "These are the horns which have scattered Judah, Israel, and Jerusalem". These horns represent the Gentile powers that would seek to exterminate Israel. It would be tempting to follow the line of some writers who see a connection here with the four empires in Daniel's metallic image – Babylon, Medo-Persia, Greece, and Rome (Dan 2). Israel as a nation has existed through these four empires and survived. While this view has much in it to make there appear to be a good link with this vision, one feels that there are several difficulties in such an interpretation. In the first place Medo-Persia removed Babylon and then Rome conquered Greece. Are we to say they were the carpenters? If so the carpenters are human and national powers and not divine, unless the view is taken that God used them as instruments. Then again, in point of fact it does say that these horns not only scattered Judah and Jerusalem, but also Israel, yet it was neither Babylon nor Medo-Persia, but the Assyrians who removed Israel. In the judgment of the writer it is better to see the carpenters as a symbol entirely of the sufficiency of divine power to remove those opposed to Israel. The four carpenters do appear to be quite distinct from the horns. In addition, in the vision the four carpenters are seen working together and the removal of the horns takes place at one and the same time and not at certain stages throughout Israel's history. It is a prophecy looking on to the end of the times of the Gentiles when the powers of this world will come against Israel and Jerusalem at the crisis of Armageddon. God, through Israel's Messiah, will suddenly and swiftly destroy the devil's armies assembled against them. It is Christ Himself who will accomplish this.

The number of the horns

While, as mentioned, some writers favour comparing the four horns to the four empires of Daniel 2, in the writer's view it is simpler and better to attach the usual biblical significance to the number four. Four in Scripture speaks of that which is universal. The number would remind us of the four cardinal points of the compass. One does not need to move outside the book of Zechariah to be helped in such an interpretation. Zechariah 2.6 speaks of "the four winds of the heaven". In the eighth vision the prophet sees four chariots which the interpreting angel explains as "the four spirits of the heavens" (6.5). With these references may be compared Daniel 7.2 and Revelation 7.1. Beyond the fact that the horns represent powers against Israel, the angel does not identify which powers are in view. One can only suggest therefore, bearing in mind the number four, that they stand for widespread national hatred of Israel. Down through their history the nation has suffered oppression, persecution and death, as witnessed last century in the terrible holocaust by Nazi Germany. The fact that God's earthly people have come through all this is evidence of a miracle of preservation and of the inspiration of Scripture, which predicts that there is yet a glorious future for them. If, however, this vision looks on to the end time, and we believe it does, then the word of God reveals that a great many national powers, including the Arab world, will join together to attack Israel. This confederacy of nations will hate Israel and, inspired by the devil and demons, will seek to destroy Israel from being a nation (see the whole of Psalm 83, and note Revelation 16.13-14; 19.17-21). The cry of this ungodly confederacy will be, "Come, and let us cut them off from being a nation" (Ps 83.4). The vision of the four horns and carpenters shows that not Israel, but these opposing powers, will be cut off and removed! In fighting against Israel the nations will be fighting against God, for Israel are His people. Herein lies the folly and the weakness of their bitter and hostile attitude. These powers will so afflict Israel and enjoy seeming initial success that the prophet adds, "So that no man did lift up his head" (v.21). God's people have many times in their history been depressed, downcast, and prostrate as a result of opposition from their enemies. This will be true on a much larger scale, when in the final phase of Gentile dominion the Devil's armies will move against Israel. Israel will then be very low and against the greatest military assemblage which the world has ever seen and Israel has ever faced. The sight, next, of the four carpenters reveals not only how God has dealt with past hostile powers against Israel, but will also deal a fatal and destructive blow to her future enemies.

The four carpenters

The four carpenters are God's answer to the four horns. Why does God use the image of carpenters, and why are there four? Then again, what is the work of these carpenters? The word for "carpenters" is "workman" or "smith" (HARASH – 2796). It really refers to skilled workers in wood, metal or stone. Whether one uses the AV "carpenters" or the RV "smiths" the meaning is clear enough. God uses them to remove or cast down the horns of the Gentiles. This is a great and encouraging word to the feeble builders, for it was important then, and for believers today, to see that for every horn there was an instrument to counteract it. The four carpenters, therefore, symbolize the instruments of divine omnipotence by which the Gentile powers would be overthrown. Normally speaking one thinks of carpenters or craftsmen accomplishing constructive work and not destructive work. The end in view in the purpose of God is the building up of God's people. It is good to remember that though the powers that scatter may be great, the power that will build up His people is greater. The work of the carpenters is explained in the vision as being to "fray" or "terrify" these powers and to cast them out or cast them down as the RV translates. It is only right to mention that some writers suggest that these four agents of God represent the four judgments of God found in Ezekiel 14.21 and Revelation 6.1-8, these being war, famine, wild animals, and pestilence. The opening of the different seals, however, in Revelation 6 will be a sequence of terrible judgments which God will bring upon the earth, but here, in the vision of the four carpenters, it is submitted that the removing of the four horns does not take place in succession, but is the sudden once for all destruction of the enemies of Israel. This part of the vision shows that, while Israel at the end time will not be able to lift up her head, God will intervene at last for His people and cause terror for their enemies and defeat them. It will be a fearful time when God does this. No-one can read Revelation 19.11-21, for example, without being stirred by the solemnity of the crisis of the second advent of Christ, when He suddenly arrives on the scene to intervene for Israel to deliver her from her enemies. What a shock the world will be given when He returns to earth and what terror will fill the hearts of the Gentile armies.

As an application for the time at which the prophecy was given it could be said that God took up and used four carpenters to help and encourage His people to go on in the building of the temple in spite of all that they feared from any possible threat to oppose them. These servants of God had a powerful effect for good among the people. Ezra 5.1-2 gives the names of four men, all of whom were with the remnant at that time. How could the feeble builders have prospered or even started the work without Haggai, Zechariah, Zerubbabel, and Jeshua (Joshua). Two of them were prophets, one was a governor, and the other was a priest. Ministry, rule, priesthood, and worship are all seen combined in these men. These functions were just what the people needed. They may have hardly been able to lift up their heads, to use the language of v.21, and been much cast down, but these four separate characters would help in the work of God at that time. They may not have removed every hindrance, but they would have certainly inspired the remnant to complete the work. In each of these men we may see pictured the Lord Jesus, the pre-eminent Carpenter. He is the Prophet, Priest, and Ruler for Israel. It is wonderful to think that He who once was Jesus the lowly carpenter from Nazareth will in a future day be Israel's Deliverer. One can stand on the heights of Nazareth, as the writer has done more than once, and see clearly in the distance the plain of Megiddo where the smashing of the Gentile armies by Christ will take place. The Carpenter of Nazareth will be the Conqueror of the foe. The enemies of Israel will be removed and cut off by the One whom Israel despised, rejected, and crucified. God says, "To him whom man despiseth, to him whom the nation abborreth, to a servant of rulers, Kings shall see and arise, princes also shall worship"(Is 49.7). The Maker and Ruler of the world and Israel's true Messiah in His first advent came to Israel and subjected Himself to human laws and the conditions of the land and people, when they were under bondage to the Romans. This is the same One who will rescue Israel in a coming day. When He will do it, why He will do it, and where He will do it are all most interesting questions. God's chosen people are precious to Him, and at the Lord's second advent He will fulfil the prophecies of Scripture and in the valley of Jehoshaphat will bring the campaign of Armageddon to a swift end by completely destroying the nations gathered there. "I will also gather all nations, and will bring them down into the valley of Jehoshaphat, and will plead with them there for my people and for my heritage Israel, whom they have scattered among the nations, and parted my land" (Joel 3.2).

What lessons may we learn from this vision? It teaches us the invincibility of Israel. None can attack God's people with impunity. No nation can ever be blessed that hates and goes against the nation of Israel. God is greater and mightier than all their foes. He has said, "No weapon that is formed against thee shall prosper; and every tongue that shall rise against thee in judgment thou shalt condemn. This is the heritage of the servants of the Lord, and their righteousness is of me, saith the Lord" (Is 54.17). There will never be a repetition for Israel of past troubles from nations. They will never fear any enemy again, for there will be no enemy. The remnant that had returned from Babylon was to take heart from the fact that the nation would never be swallowed up by the enemy.

The vision also illustrates the important teaching of Romans as to the eternal security of the believer. The children of God are too precious and important to God for Him to stand by and allow any power to defeat us. He who has chosen us will protect us. So much so that each believer can say with the Apostle Paul, "If God be for us, who can be against us?" (Rom 8.31). No power whatsoever can separate the believer from the love of God (Rom 8.38-39). Just as God's purpose will be fulfilled for His earthly people, so God's purpose cannot be thwarted for His heavenly people. This is a most reassuring truth in which to rejoice.

ZECHARIAH 2

The Third Vision. The Divine Protection – the Man with the Measuring Line

Question: "What about our city, Lord?"

Another vision captures the attention of Zechariah. He sees a man with a measuring line. This vision develops 1.16 where God says, "I am returned to Jerusalem with mercies…and a line shall be stretched forth upon Jerusalem". The great message of this vision is that Jerusalem will be restored. The concern of the remnant would be whether the city would be reconstructed to anything like it had been before. God assured them that the city would be rebuilt and expanded. While the vision applied to the immediate circumstances of God's people then, it is clear that the vision refers to the distant future, when with the presence of the Lord in their midst they will be a means of blessing to many nations. This chapter divides into two sections. The first, in vv.1-5, deals with the city as it was then and yet will be in the future. The second, in vv.6-13, concerns the people as they were then and yet will be in the future. Christ is seen in the first section as the Surveyor of the city and then in the next section as the Servant of Jehovah sent to deal with the nations who oppose His people. The main message of the vision is that God can and will protect His people. It should not be overlooked that the prophet speaks for God, addressing the present need of the remnant in the light of the future glories in store for the nation. In the same way, future events revealed in the New Testament pertaining to the Church and the believer should have a challenging and encouraging effect upon the child of God today.

Verses 1-5: The Man with the Measuring Line

In this vision we have little imagery compared to the previous two visions. The importance of the vision is seen in the actors in it. We have the surveyor of the city, the interpreting angel, another angel, and Zechariah himself, described in v.4 as "this young man". We do not know how old Zechariah was: whether he was a young man or merely designated as a "young man" in comparison with the more senior prophet Haggai. There certainly should be no doubt that the young man here referred to must be Zechariah himself. His ministry complemented the ministry of the older servant. Both were raised up together to prophesy to the Jews who had returned from Babylon (Ezra 5.1).

Zechariah sees a man with a measuring line and, as before, the vision puzzles him, so that he once again asks a question. Note that he addresses not the interpreting angel, but the man with the measuring line: "Whither goest thou?". The man answers, "To measure Jerusalem, to see what is the breadth thereof, and what is the length thereof". Who is this man? Can we fix his identity? Clearly he cannot be either the interpreting angel of v.3 or the other angel mentioned in the same verse. Who this man is cannot really be so mysterious. The first vision will help in the interpretation. The man on the red horse and the Angel of Jehovah have already been accepted as one and the same person, and a divine person at that! The only conclusion therefore that can be arrived at is that this man in the third vision must again be the Angel of Jehovah, for no other hint in the vision is provided as to his identity. In view of the fact that this vision, as do the two previous ones, looks on to the city in the time of the Millennium, one must give a Messianic application to the passage. The man with the measuring line is none other than Israel's Messiah, who assesses in perfection the condition of His earthly people, knows their need, and will meet it in His own glorious way.

One should not miss a practical lesson here. The Lord Jesus today is among His people and in many ways is still the Measurer of all things. He measures the motives of all who engage in His service. He measures the true and not the assumed condition of each assembly gathered in His name. This is solemnly seen in the Lord walking among the golden lampstands in Revelation 2 and 3. His assessment of the condition of each of the seven churches is perfect and therefore unerring. Just as here the Lord is seen measuring with a view to the expansion of the city, so the purpose of His scrutiny of the churches is in order that it might result in their spiritual expansion. The Lord, the day before His second purging of the temple, measured the goings on in the temple and what was being then allowed there. Mark 11.11 tells us that "He...looked round about upon all things". It is certainly a searching thought that the Lord Jesus still functions in this way today. Just as He measured the city then and found limitation and narrowness, so He comes to His people even now to assess their condition with a view to enlarging them spiritually. He may and often does find limitation, but He desires to enlarge our hearts, our thoughts and our lives so that we may spiritually prosper. His eye sees the need, His heart yearns to meet it, and His hand moves towards us to touch our lives in order to give expansion. One must never forget that He is looking on and observes everything. Nothing, absolutely nothing escapes His attention.

Christ here is measuring the city with a view to its expansion. The clear message is that the city of Jerusalem will be a larger and safer city to dwell in. This never came to pass during the time of building in the return from Babylon. It has never taken place since this prophecy. It awaits a yet future fulfilment. This is seen in that another angel meets the interpreting angel and is told to tell "this young man" (Zechariah), that "Jerusalem shall be inhabited as towns without walls" (v.4). It should be obvious that the city is seen in its millennial setting in vv.4 & 5. In the revival under Nehemiah the walls around the city had to be repaired, but here God informs the young priest-prophet of a time when no such defence will be needed. There will be no enemy in the Messiah's reign of peace. Israel during the Millennium will need to fear no enemy. Isaiah speaks of this wonderful time. Quoting the relevant passage in full shows Isaiah's agreement with

Zechariah in fulfilling what God will accomplish: "Look upon Zion, the city of our solemnities: thine eyes shall see Jerusalem a quiet habitation, a tabernacle that shall not be taken down; not one of the stakes thereof shall ever be removed, neither shall any of the cords thereof be broken. But there the glorious Lord will be unto us a place of broad rivers and streams; wherein shall go no galley with oars, neither shall gallant ship pass thereby" (Is 33.20-21). The galley mentioned there is not a merchant vessel, but a war vessel with a long shape, and propelled by oars. The description of the second ship, "gallant", is the same Hebrew word as for "glorious" previously (ADDIR - 117). The word "mighty" is appropriate in both places: a ship of war is again meant. It means that no "mighty vessel" will dare to pass where the "mighty Lord" stands as the defender of His people. What a day this will be after all the long centuries of Jerusalem being the scene of many a battle and the place where its inhabitants have been often filled with fear of attack and a terrible sense of insecurity. God will be its protection without and His presence will be within (v.5).

All this will take place when Israel have had removed from them the veil of judicial blindness and they will have been dealt with by God, bringing about their repentance and faith, in order that they may receive the Lord Jesus as their Messiah. During the period of the Millennium the city of Jerusalem will never again come under attack. The restored nation will then be dependent on God, who will never fail them. Walls, gates, and bars will have gone (cp. Ezek 38.10-11). God Himself will defend His people. The lovely conditions of Psalm 46.5, "God is in the midst of her; she shall not be moved", will then be fulfilled and the nation will be able to say, "The Lord of hosts is with us; the God of Jacob is our refuge. Selah" (v.11). What a difference the enjoyed presence of God makes for God's people. His presence is salvation and security. Believers and assemblies today should as fully depend upon the Lord alone as the nation of Israel will do when they are under the benevolent reign of their Messiah.

Verses 6-13: The Servant Sent of the Lord of Hosts

Verse 6 is a message to the Jews then in Babylon. The land of the north is seen in v.7 to be Babylon. They were told to flee from the land of the north. Babylon is to the east of Jerusalem and not to the north, but it seems to be called the land of the north because, in attacking Israel, Nebuchadnezzar had come by way of the north. Since that time Israel also has been scattered further north. Therefore, the north is especially mentioned in many prophecies concerning Israel's regathering. Yet in the verse the Lord speaks of His spreading Israel abroad as the four winds of heaven – in every direction away from their land. The larger number, however, have gone northward and great numbers remain there to this day. God says, "I have spread you abroad as the four winds of the heaven". It should be noticed that this is really a further means by which the people can escape Babylon. This is not to be understood in the sense of God scattering the Jews because of their sins. It is true that this is the present condition of the nation, but here it is spreading rather than scattering and points to the fact that God would use His people for blessing in the world of the Gentiles. The nation will yet be restored and greatly increased in number and will be spread abroad to all parts of the earth. So v.6 gives God's people in Babylon two motives as to why they should leave Babylon. Both motives are future – the judgment of Babylon and the spreading of His people worldwide.

Just a small remnant of the Jews had returned to Jerusalem, but a large number had evidently chosen to settle down in Babylon. The Medes and Persians had taken Babylon and there was liberty for God's people to return to their own land again, but many had probably become wealthy and settled there and found life satisfactory. Many others had become so used to Babylon and its ways that they were not prepared to leave. They had no interest in the little revival of interest among some of their fellow Jews to go back to Jerusalem and build. In v.7 they are told to "Deliver thyself". Both the RV and JND render the word "deliver" as "escape". This stronger and more urgent word suggests that Babylon was to be judged. Therefore, why build hopes, hold on to relationships, and settle down with contentment and ease in a place soon to be judged by God? God had sent them into captivity and they had had no choice but to go (Jer 39.9), but the way had opened up for them to return and it would have been the right thing to have done so, yet sadly only 42,360 had responded (Ezra 2.64). So the situation was that the city was considered as still dwelling or being settled down with the daughter of Babylon. The Jews were dwelling with the daughter of Babylon and had become happy there with a wrong association.

There are clear lessons here for the child of God. It is certainly easy for us not to respond to the call of God, for instance, to be separate from the world. How possible it is for a believer in the Lord Jesus Christ to be at ease in the world and make wealth the goal in life. God has called His people to "be separate". It is true that as believers we live in this world and work among unsaved people, and separation does not mean isolation or that no contact whatsoever is to be had with the world of the unsaved. But how often believers, instead of having an interest and exercise in the work of God, are not prepared to bestir themselves because of their lives being crowded with the pressure of business interests, or they are too happily content with life as it is in this world. As a result God's interests suffer and the things of God are left to the exercised few. The challenging word from God to us too is "come forth" and "escape". Let us not be entangled in the affairs of this life. Since the time is short it is not for the believer to be building his hopes in this world and to lose out in the things of God. As the Jew had the choice to go back to his country and build up the city of Jerusalem, so the believer should let the prospect of the heavenly city so thrill him as to stir his heart to be exercised in heavenly things and to build for eternity.

> It is not for me to be seeking my bliss,
> And building my hopes in a region like this;
> I look for a city, which hands have not piled;
> I pant for a country by sin undefiled.
>
> (H. F. Lyte).

While vv.6 & 7 specifically relate to the time of the vision, vv.8 & 9 look on prophetically to the time of future blessing for Israel when the Lord will deal with the enemies who have oppressed them. The word of God here will have particular force for them in a coming day, when God will complete His work in the nation after the manifestation in glory of the Lord Jesus. What should be especially noted in this passage is the repeated phrase "hath sent me" (vv.8,9,11). Without doubt the Messiah Himself is speaking and is referring to Himself as the Servant sent by Jehovah of Hosts. There is clear evidence of the identity of the Servant with Jehovah. It is one of a number of passages in the prophets where the deity of the coming Messiah is established. Israel's deliverer is truly man, but He is also a divine person. This the Jew to this day cannot see. A suffering Messiah they cannot understand and reject completely. A divine Messiah, one who is equal with Jehovah, they will not tolerate but would consider as a christian belief of the western world, yet this article of faith was first preached by Jews to Jews. Their estimate of Jesus the Nazarene has never changed from that of their forebears, when the Lord was in their midst. They still mockingly refer to the Saviour as "the hanged one" or "the transgressor". How sad this is, and what a despicable way to refer to the very person who is yet to be, in the future, their salvation as a nation. Isaiah predicts, "To him whom man despiseth, to him whom the nation abhorreth, to a servant of rulers, Kings shall see and arise, princes also shall worship, because of the Lord that is faithful" (Is 49.7). How amazing to think that the Messiah, God's Son, though the maker and ruler of the world, came in such lowliness in a way unexpected and undreamt of by the nation, and subjected Himself to human laws and the conditions at the time of His people, being under bondage to the power of the Romans. Throughout the whole of Jewish history no person has been more bitterly hated than the Christ who came to bless the Jewish nation.

One cannot fail to see, then, that we have in these verses the utterance of a divine being. Jehovah is speaking and yet, mystery of mysteries, here is Jehovah, yet sent by Jehovah. With the Lord's servants as men, there is the Sender and the sent, as is seen in Haggai 1.12, and of course one appreciates the difference between the sender and the sent. This must be a necessity between men as men and God as God. In this interesting passage it seems as if Jehovah is sending Himself. One may not be able to understand this, but it is a fact that can only be explained by appreciating that this is a Messianic passage. Short as the passage is, it is one of the most important in the Old Testament with regard to the majesty and mission of the Messiah in the future. Here then we have the precious truth of the equality between the Sender and the Sent. What belongs really and essentially to Jehovah in His attributes, is applied to the One who is sent. This is the message of the Gospel of John, where constantly the Lord Jesus is recorded as saying, "The Father hath sent me". In this fourth Gospel the doctrine of the Son's equality with the Father is fully supported and presented. A careful consideration, for example, of the Lord's teaching and claims in John 5.17-30 will readily confirm this.

When the Lord Jesus comes to deliver Israel they will then know in a most solemn way that Jehovah of Hosts has sent Him. What a discovery this will be and what a shock to them. It will be the very reversal of how they reacted to His first advent. They rejected the claim that He was the Sent One, but in the coming day of glory what a change in attitude there will be for they will then learn through their great deliverance that God has sent Him. Here then is another proof that these verses (vv.8-12) relate *not* to the first advent of Christ into the world, but to His second advent in power and glory. When He came the first time He was not recognized. The nation did not know He was their Messiah and had been sent by God. Paul wrote to the Corinthians that "the princes of this world…had they known it, they would not have crucified the Lord of glory" (1 Cor 2.8). In the deliverance of the nation from their enemies, and in the wonderful victory accomplished, three points should be noted as to when, why, and how this will be achieved.

When will He do it?

In vv.8-13 we have a summary of events that will happen when their Messiah returns to rid Israel of their enemies and bless them as a nation. The Lord Jesus, the speaker here, says, "After the glory hath he sent me unto the nations which spoiled you". The phrase "after the glory" should be carefully observed as it indicates when this wonderful deliverance will take place. Though the subject of much discussion, this section must and can only refer to the second advent of Christ, when He comes to restore the nation and set up His Kingdom. It is after the Lord Jesus is manifested in glory that He will come to fulfil the prophecies of centuries, to deal a fatal blow to the haters of Israel. Zechariah 14 in the Old Testament and Revelation 19.11-21 in the New Testament, support this view. This cannot be a reference to the first phase of the second coming when the Rapture of the Church will take place, for then the Lord Jesus will not descend to the air to deal with Israel and to conquer their enemies. The Rapture will be for the blessing of the Church, but the second phase of the Lord's return will be to smash the Gentile foes of Israel. It is very important to see the difference. Paul in 2 Thessalonians 2, for example, speaks of the Rapture in v.1 as, "our gathering together unto him", but in v.8 he speaks of the second advent when Christ will come to the earth to destroy the lawless one by "the brightness of his coming". It is only when the Messiah comes in His glory that these things will take place. The nation cannot be saved, and there can be no salvation for the Gentile nations, until the Lord Himself comes to the earth.

Why will He do it?

"He that toucheth you toucheth the apple of his eye." This shows how precious the nation of Israel is to Jehovah. The illustration could not be more explicit and picturesque. The apple of the eye is the pupil of the eye, through which all rays of light pass to the retina. It is a tender and most sensitive part of the body. "God has sent Him to the heathen, namely, because they have plundered His people, and have thereby touched the apple of His eye...the apple of the eye (lit., the gate, the opening in which the eye is placed, or more probably the pupil of the eye...as being the object most carefully preserved), is a figure used to denote the dearest possession or good, and in this sense is applied to the nation of Israel as early as Deuteronomy 32.10" (Keil & Delitzsch). In the Deuteronomy passage the figure is used to give the reason why God cared for them and preserved them as a nation in the wilderness. Here it is the reason why He will remove their enemies in the future. In Proverbs 7.2 the same symbol is used for the need of watching over with care God's law or commandments. They are to be treasured and regarded as of great value. In Psalm 17.8 the Psalmist prays, "Keep me as the apple of the eye". "No part of the body is more precious, more tender, and more carefully guarded than the eye; and of the eye, no portion more peculiarly to be protected than the central apple, the pupil, or as the Hebrew calls it, 'the daughter of the eye'. The all-wise Creator has placed the eye in a well-protected position; it stands surrounded by projecting bones like Jerusalem encircled by mountains. Moreover, its great Author has surrounded it with many tunics of inward covering, besides the hedge of the eyebrows, the curtain of the eyelids, and the fence of the eyelashes; and, in addition to this, he has given to every man so high a value for his eyes, and so quick an apprehension of danger, that no member of the body is more faithfully cared for than the organ of sight" (C. H. Spurgeon, *Treasury of David*).

The thought, then, of the apple of the eye, is that of preciousness and extreme value. Here is the secret, surely, of Israel's survival as a nation throughout history. Though the nation is still away from God and has been so for over two millennia yet God has preserved His earthly people and will yet preserve them through the terrible times of the Tribulation period. Why, it may be asked, is this the case? Why has God been so longsuffering with them, and why has He so often intervened for their deliverance? The answer must be that God has chosen this people as His nation and loves them to the extent that they are very valuable to Him. What the apple of the eye is to the body, the nation is to God. Such an interesting figure as "the apple of his eye" reveals the love of Jehovah for His earthly people. It is about the most expressive emblem God uses in the Scripture for setting forth what His people are to Him. Other figures illustrating how dear Israel is to God are that they are like precious and rare "jewels" (Mal 3.17), and that they are like chickens for whom the parent hen has tenderness and so cherishes them as to hide them under its wings to protect from evil and danger (Mt 23.37). Such is the way God regards His people. They are precious to Him and any enemy that touches and hurts His people touches and hurts God too. They are in reality fighting against Him. God's eye is ever upon His covenant people on earth and because they are precious to Him He will never allow them to be destroyed. God will display to the world in the future how He regards His people.

While it is wonderful that Israel stands in this relationship to God, it is good to remember that believers of this church age are far more precious to God than Israel. From New Testament teaching we see what the Church is to God and to Christ. To God the church is as a pearl of great price. Believers who form the Church are His peculiar people (the word means a thing essentially one's own and therefore precious and dear). The Church is to Christ what Israel never was nor will be - "the Bride" (Eph 5.25-27; Rev 19.7-8). The nearness to God enjoyed by believers now is a spiritual nearness which is much more blessed and close than the national nearness Israel had in the past (contrast the "made nigh" of Ephesians 2.13 with "them that were nigh" of v.17). The believer should rejoice in these greater blessings and in the knowledge that he is part of something that is unique and therefore infinitely more precious than Israel, even in their future status when restored.

How will He do it?

Just a wave of the hand from the Lord will accomplish this mighty deliverance. The God that only needs to touch the land with His finger and it melts (Amos 9.5) will suddenly intervene for His people. The mighty forces of the devil in the crisis battle of Armageddon will be overcome and smashed with divine ease. It will only take a look and a word from the all powerful and conquering Messiah and the brightness of His coming, to consume the wicked one who will head these armies. The speaker in v.9 is undoubtedly the Messiah. It is He who will shake His hand upon the Gentiles who have opposed His people. The reversal of things for Israel, being no longer the servants of the Gentiles but their conquerors and masters, will be all brought about with wonderful ease. Will it indeed only take a wave of Messiah's hand and the whole thing will be done? Yes, for the great fact is that Israel's Messiah is God and nothing is too hard for Him. Isaiah speaks of the nations as a drop of a bucket. They are counted as nothing and less than nothing (Is 40.15,17). The world and its many nations may dwarf us, but they do not dwarf God. The world, teeming with its active and bustling millions, no more affects God than the chirping and hopping of a grasshopper in the summer affects us. "They shall be a spoil to their servants" indicates that "they become...booty to the Israelites, who had previously been obliged to serve them" (Keil & Delitzsch). A great change is in store for Israel. Instead of being the servants of the nations, the nations will serve them. Isaiah expands on this when he predicts, "Strangers shall be joined with them, and they shall cleave to the house of Jacob...the house of Israel shall possess them in the land of the Lord for servants and handmaids: and they shall take them captives, whose captives they were; and they shall rule over their oppressors" (Is 14.1-2). This is a remarkable prophecy and a great contrast to Israel's condition when God sent Moses to deliver them. Then they were captives in Egypt. They had been captives in Babylon when Zechariah was raised up to minister to them and throughout the centuries they have served the Gentile powers.

The future blessing of Israel shared by many nations (vv.10-13)

In the closing verses of this chapter Israel is seen in relation to the Messiah, the land and the world.

Israel and the Messiah (v.10)

It is no surprise that the daughter of Zion is told to sing and rejoice, for the same Lord of hosts who will have accomplished the great victory over their enemies will come and dwell in the midst of her and take the place of central importance and pre-eminence. For the long depressed, troubled, and suffering people this will cause the greatest rejoicing. The wilderness era with its tabernacle began with God dwelling in the midst of His people. God has ever desired to be in the midst of His redeemed people, but sadly the nation failed and God's presence in the Shekinah glory was withdrawn from them. Now here in this prophecy the Messiah twice declares, "I will dwell in the midst of thee". Thus the Messiah, the Lord Jesus Christ, will be in the midst of Israel. He will not merely visit them, but will be among them. God had dwelt in the tabernacle and the temple of Solomon, but this is different. What a great and wonderful cause for Israel to sing. The nation has had nothing to sing about for centuries. The song they sang on the other side of the Red Sea after God delivered them from the Egyptians soon died out and gave place to groans and cries of discontent. The day is coming, however, when they will sing again. Hosea prophesies that God will give them "the valley of Achor for a door of hope: and she shall sing there, as in the days of her youth" (Hos 2.15). The song of redemption in Exodus 15 was never repeated, but it will be revived again. The song of Moses will be sung when Israel is delivered and restored (see Rev 15.3). The idea of the word "Sing" in v.10 is to shout aloud with joy. So Israel will have great joy after the seven-year period of sorrows in the Tribulation (Mt 24.8).

Israel and the world (v.11)

"And many nations shall be joined to the Lord in that day, and shall be my people" (v.11). In the Millennium Israel's status will be reversed. Now they serve Gentile powers and they are still downtrodden and hated as a nation, but Christ their Messiah will then be the Governor among the nations. The one who was rejected and crucified and was accounted "a worm and no man" will then be exalted to the highest place on earth. He will not only control Israel, but He will control the nations of the world. He will judge between the nations (Is 2.4). Ethiopia and Egypt, for example, will come then into blessing (see Ps 68.31; Is 19.21-25). A privilege that was once peculiar to Israel will be enjoyed by Gentile nations. God will own them as His people and will receive worship from them. Israel will still retain the great distinction of having the presence of Jehovah again in their midst. This will be the great reason why people from the various nations at that time will be attracted to the Jew and desire to join them. Chapter 8.20-23 enlarges on this great reversal of Israel's position in the world.

Thus Israel's future deliverance and blessing will lead to the conversion of many Gentiles from various nations. God will own Gentile people as His people. The Gentiles in the millennial Kingdom will owe much to the Jew in that day. They will see that God is with them. Such will be the greatness of the Jew that Gentiles will be attracted to them and desire to join themselves to Jehovah who has so blessed the nation. Not only will the city of Jerusalem then be protected, but the Jew will prosper. When God's presence is with His people and they are spiritually prospering, those who are really seeking God will be attracted to them. The widespread blessing to the nations in the future will be really the result of the Lord Jesus dwelling in the midst of Israel. There is certainly a lesson here. When the presence of the Lord is being enjoyed in reality by assemblies there should be an extension of blessing in the evangelical sense, leading to the conversion of others. This does provoke the question, "Are the Lord's people in the assemblies today so enjoying the presence of God and going on for Him that they attract others to gather with them and listen to the Christian message?". It may be a simple point, but it is also good to remark that at that time it will not be a case of Gentiles merely joining the Jews, but rather joining Jehovah. God Himself among His people will be the great attraction. So it should be with the Lord's people today. A believer was asked sometime ago, "Why are so few people from the world joining the church?". The reply was, "Because so many people from the church are joining the world"! One would love to think that this was not true of assemblies gathered to the name of the Lord Jesus Christ, but, alas, in some cases it is.

It might be helpful to add a comment as to how it will be that there will be Gentiles from different nations populating the millennial Kingdom. It should be pointed out that many Gentiles, after the Rapture of the Church and during the Tribulation period, will believe the gospel of the Kingdom preached by the faithful Jewish remnant (Mt 24.14). Those saved Gentiles are described as sheep by the Lord in Matthew 25.32-40. The Lord says He will "separate them one from another, as a shepherd divideth his sheep from the goats". The pronoun "them" is masculine and refers, not to the nations, but to the people from the various nations. It must never be thought that a saved nation will go into the millennial Kingdom, but people belonging to the different nations will be saved and will inherit the Kingdom. Some nations that exist now will, it would appear, have sufficient people left after the tribulation to be able to continue nationally into the millennial Kingdom. The people from the nations that will have survived the Tribulation horrors and will have responded to the gospel of the Kingdom, are called "strong nations" in Zechariah 8.22.

The final statement of v.11 repeats what Messiah says in v.9, "Thou shalt know that the Lord of hosts hath sent me unto thee". The phrase "unto thee" is added here to the same formula as in v.9. This seems to indicate a difference between the knowing of v.9 and the knowing of v.11. The knowledge of v.9 is more a general knowledge. They will know in a general way as a result of the punishment inflicted by the Messiah on her foes. After this she will know experientially and specifically the particular sending of Messiah unto her. To have a general knowledge is one thing, but an experiential knowledge is quite another matter. Israel will have both. So, for Christians, we may know who the Lord is and what He has done for us, but it is much better to have, by the Lord's presence and blessing with us, an experimental conviction that the Lord is truly the Sent One and is all that He claims to be. Once again notice that Jehovah here says, "I will dwell", and then that Jehovah of Hosts sent Him. So the truth leaps again out of the page to us that Jehovah the Sender and Jehovah the Sent must be one.

Israel and the land (v.12)

"And the Lord shall inherit Judah his portion in the holy land." Although God will bless the Gentiles and call them His people, this does not mean that the nation of Israel will lose their distinctive place as God's earthly people. They will not need to fear that this will happen, for God has never given up Israel and His covenant with Abraham and Jacob will not be forgotten. They are His inheritance and His portion. The word "portion" (HELEQ - 2506), the equivalent of the Greek *akeldama* (184), can mean both possession and territory (TWOT at 669a). The nation will be His and the land will be His. The description of the land as "the holy land" here is interesting. It is the only time in Scripture that it is called by this phrase. After Israel entered into Canaan the land became corrupted and was marked by conflict. The land of Israel at the present time is far from holy. It is a land troubled with fear, insecurity, and subject to the danger of terrorist attack. Sin is in this land as in any other. Many Jews in it are far from happy with the present situation of the land, but in the glorious time of the millennial reign of Christ it will be "holy", for it will be "Immanuel's land". God will be there. His holy sanctuary – the millennial temple - will be there. The city of Jerusalem will then be truly the "holy city" (Is 52.1) and God's holy standards will be its basis and governing influence. The glory of God and of Christ will be displayed everywhere (Is 40.5).

The land of Israel in the future will be greatly enlarged. The land as it was known in the time of the Lord Jesus was only some 140 miles in length by about 40 miles in breadth – somewhat smaller than Scotland. The new land in the time of the millennial Kingdom has been calculated to be over twice the size of the United Kingdom and Ireland, covering an area some 300,000 square miles, with Jerusalem as its centre. God will have chosen Jerusalem again as His city. It will be the great religious metropolis of the Millennium. The city, which throughout its history has been a hotbed of violence and bloodshed, and will yet have to suffer far worse, will then be truly God's city. It will be the city of truth from whence will go forth the word of the Lord (Is 2.3). Judah then will be His chosen portion and Jerusalem His chosen centre. Judah is the royal tribe from which our Lord Jesus Christ came, and its name means praise. How fitting this is, for God will receive praise from His redeemed people Israel. Jerusalem means the foundation of peace. Tragically, throughout history Jerusalem has never fulfilled its name, but has been a place troubled periodically by wars. In the time of the Millennium it will be wonderfully true to its name, for the peace introduced by the Lord Jesus will be founded on righteousness. Righteousness will become the character of the city. Then Isaiah 32.17 will be fulfilled: "The work of righteousness shall be peace".

In the final verse of this vision there is a solemn appeal to the Gentile nations and perhaps the unbelieving Jews are included. The nations who have prided themselves in their powers and have been bitter opponents of Israel are to be silent, for the time is coming when God who has been silent so as not to intervene for Israel will then break His long silence and arouse Himself as if out of sleep, to deal with the enemies of Israel and bring about the fulfilment of this prophecy. There are no delays with God, but at the appointed time He will move. This dealing in judgment will take place at the coming of the Messiah. "His holy habitation" is God's dwelling place in heaven and from here in the Person of the Messiah He will descend to accomplish a wonderful intervention for Israel. What a solemn word this is to the nations, for God will step in to calm the turbulent waters of the worldwide conflict and trouble. To witness this will be an awesome and fearful thing, and there will be no doubt among the nations that it is God alone who can and will have accomplished this. Psalm 46.10 will be the word for all in this fearful time: "Be still, and know that I am God". Man will learn then as never before how frail, puny, and mortal he is. All rebellion will be put down, for He who brought calm to the stormy sea will put an end to the stormy conditions at the height of the campaign of Armageddon and bring in universal peace.

ZECHARIAH 3

The Fourth Vision. The Divine Pardon – the Cleansing of Joshua

Question: "What about our defilement, Lord; we have been in Babylon so long?"

In this vision we have the cleansing, clothing, and crowning of Joshua the high priest. This sets forth the cleansing of the priesthood, but as Joshua is the high priest of Israel he represents the nation. The vision is prophetic of the ultimate cleansing of the nation. Israel will be pardoned and a power for God during the reign of Christ in the Millennium. If Israel are to be over the Gentiles and restored, as the previous visions show, how can they possibly be fitted for this because of their sin and defilement? The fourth vision here answers this problem. The land of Israel might be called "the holy land" in 2.12, but before this can ever be realised the nation's sin before God has to be taken away.

Clearly Joshua represents the nation, but in the vision there is also a picture of gospel truth. The vision is remarkable and most interesting in the fact that the plan of God's salvation for a sinner is wonderfully illustrated in one man. In the Old Testament may be found statements, incidents, parables, and types which picture the way of God's salvation, but the vision of Joshua is unique in this, that in no other person of the Old Testament do we have such a near, complete picture of the way of salvation than in what happens to Joshua in this vision. The vision is also interesting in that it is the only place in the Minor Prophets where Satan is mentioned, and in view of this it has some valuable points to teach with regard to Satan and his activity against the believer. Another feature to point out about this fourth vision is that, unlike the previous three and the following four, it is the only time Zechariah does not ask a question. This may be regarded as a simple point, but it is good to notice these differences and to ask the reason why. In this case Zechariah did not need to ask a question, for, in the first place, he did not need to be told who Joshua was, for Joshua was a familiar figure among the people. Secondly, the angel does not need to explain such an obvious meaning of the transaction in the vision, for it pictures all too clearly God in grace pardoning the sin of the people. The great message of the vision is that God is able to cleanse the sin of His people and fit them for His service. It is interesting, too, to see in the chapter that Jehovah does three things. He rebukes Satan (v.2); He restores the priesthood (v.5); and He removes the iniquity of the land (v.9).

The chapter is in two sections. The first, in vv.1-7, deals with the cleansing of the high priest. The second, in vv.8-10, deals with the cleansing of the land - note particularly v.9. Then again, in vv.1-5 Joshua may be seen as a picture of the sinner and how he is pardoned. In vv.6-7 the same Joshua is seen as a picture of a saint and how he should walk. There is a nice balance too in the chapter, showing the difference between position and condition, or the need and importance to maintain a consistency between these two.

Thus we have the cleansing of Joshua and his acceptance before God (v.4), and then the need for Joshua to walk in obedience in God's ways (v.7).

Verses 1-7: The Cleansing of the Nation
In considering the vision it is important to note the actors and the part each has in it. First there is Joshua the high priest (v.1a), then the angel of the Lord (v.1b). Next is seen Satan (v.1c), and finally there is Zechariah himself. Joshua is standing before the Lord, the angel is intervening for Joshua, and Satan is accusing Joshua. Zechariah is not only observing all that happens, but also taking part in it. The one who shows Zechariah this vision is, we may assume without too much difficulty, the interpreting angel of the previous visions.

The first part of the vision may be profitably considered in four ways: What the Lord says – the rebuke to Satan (vv.1-2); What the Lord does – the removal of sin (vv.3-5); What the Lord expects – the requirement from saints (vv.6-7b); What the Lord will give – the reward for service (v.7c).

What the Lord says (vv.1-2)
Joshua is seen standing before the Lord. This refers no doubt to his priestly privilege and function. In his ministry he stood before Jehovah on behalf of His people and represented them. It was a great honour and responsibility for Israel's high priest to serve the people in this way. The idea of standing before Jehovah refers not merely to special occasions, but to the general service of the priest daily in the sanctuary. It indicates that Joshua officially stood before God representing the people and praying for them. Satan, too, was standing beside Joshua, seeking to accuse him. It is so interesting to see throughout the whole action that Joshua remains passive. He does not speak or do anything. The Lord Himself does the speaking and the acting. There is a clear gospel lesson here, for when it comes to the experience of salvation the sinner cannot speak for himself or depend upon anything he has done. When the sinner is cleansed from sin he realizes that he cannot say anything or do anything, for it is what the Lord says and does that is essential to rest on. It is by the Lord's pure grace alone that He is able to save the sinner. Since, however, Joshua does represent Israel in the vision, the nation, too, in the future will discover that it is solely divine grace that will remove their guilt.

To interpret this vision it is important to see that Joshua is not to be seen here merely as an individual or in his capacity as Israel's high priest. Rather, the details of the chapter apply to him as he represents the nation. Thus in the removal of his filthy garments is pictured the taking away of the iniquity of the nation. This is clearly proven in the fact that it is God who chooses Jerusalem and not Joshua (v.2), and it is not the iniquity so much of Joshua which is removed, but of the land (v.9). Accordingly, in the vision of the cleansing of Joshua is seen the cleansing of the nation which will be delivered from any thought of trying to do works of righteousness to be acceptable to God. On the Day of Atonement, for example, the injunction is given by God: "And ye shall do no work in that same day: for it is a day of atonement, to make an atonement for you before the Lord your God" (Lev 23.28). So Israel, when the Day of Atonement is fulfilled, will know the blessing of divine pardon without works through the death of Christ. The well-known old hymn could have its second line changed to be equally true of the nation:

> Nothing either great or small;
> Nothing, Israel, no;
> Jesus did it, did it all,
> Long, long ago.

It will be helpful to answer several questions with regard to the reference to Satan here. Why should he appear when Joshua is interceding for the people before God, and why is he seen at the right hand of Joshua? There is no doubt that Satan is a powerful foe and the reference to the right hand in Scripture often suggests the place of power. No believer is any match for this powerful being. Satan is seen here as the accuser and in this capacity he endeavours to insinuate that Joshua is not worthy to represent the people as their high priest because of his personal defilement. It is doubtful whether the scene should be regarded as judicial, for Satan is present not as a judicial accuser, but as an enemy ready to oppose Joshua's efforts for the good of the people, and to hinder his interests with the Angel of the Lord. It seems best then to view the reference to Satan standing at the right hand, not as a formal accuser in a trial, but as a hinderer to Joshua's ministry for the people. The Angel of Jehovah too, it should be noted, is not represented as sitting on a throne of judgment, but standing by (v.5). There is no thought of any judicial procedure in the vision. It seems better therefore to understand that Joshua is interceding for the people in his official role as high priest in the presence of the Angel of Jehovah.

In the Tribulation to come, Satan is seen as the accuser of the brethren (Rev 12.10). It is interesting to note that the brethren there are the Jewish brethren. This links us with the vision in Zechariah 3 and shows again the fact that Satan seeks to argue that the nation is far from holy and is defiled, and therefore to question how their sacrifices to God and the service they engage in could be acceptable to Him. In spite of any sin in the priesthood it must continue to function for the nation and the nation, too, must continue to exist and be yet glorious. In Joshua, God was about to establish the priesthood again and this being the case Satan, the accuser, sought to object to God that the sins of the priesthood rendered the priests unworthy and unfit to have the honour of serving Him. Satan's design was that God would take note of their sins and disqualify them from functioning. If Satan had been successful in this opposition, God would have had to abandon

His choice of Jerusalem and not continue His work of bringing back His people out of captivity. His whole purpose for the nation and its future would have collapsed. This could not be, for divine choice and purpose must be fulfilled. Hence, before Satan could begin to utter one word in his charge against Israel, the Angel of Jehovah speaks: "The Lord rebuke thee, O Satan; even the Lord that hath chosen Jerusalem rebuke thee: is this not a brand plucked out of the fire?". Notice that the word "rebuke" is repeated for emphasis and shows the certainty with which Satan's attempts against Jerusalem and Israel would be defeated.

The Angel of Jehovah gives two reasons as the grounds of the priest's and the nation's complete pardon. The first is God's electing love in His choice of Jerusalem (cp. Rom 9.16 & 11.5), and the second is the fact that He had delivered Joshua and others from the fire. Nothing could possibly change God's choice, or influence Him to place His people back in Babylon, for who would think of putting the brand back in the fire! God cannot go back on His word or revoke His electing choice. Neither, having so recently brought His people out of captivity, is He going to put them back to suffer captivity again in a place where the nation had very nearly been brought to destruction. This would have been the case had it not been for the working of God through an exercised remnant to cause the return. No; His people had been snatched, as it were, from the fire. The fire in the passage primarily must refer to the seventy-year period in Babylon viewed as a furnace from which the people had been delivered. Fire is a symbol of punishment, and here it is a reference to Israel's being punished for her sins throughout the seventy years.

It is interesting to notice that the Angel of Jehovah does not engage in any long argument with Satan and that Satan has nothing to say in reply to the angel's words. In the rest of the passage we hear no more of him. Every accusation against God's people is swept away and his challenge as to Joshua's right to serve as high priest is answered. He is silenced by this one wonderful and perfect truth – God's choice. If the matter had rested with Jerusalem or the nation, then Israel would have had to be condemned, but Jehovah had pardoned them. How this could be will be seen later in the chapter by the introduction of the Lord Jesus as the Servant, the Branch. It is in His Person and in His work at Calvary that the nation will be accepted.

The believer today may apply the lessons here. Satan seeks to challenge our right to serve God and may point to our unworthiness. He would seek to oppose the very purpose of God for us and in us. In addition, as the Accuser he works to undermine the work of God in the believer and to unsettle faith in even sowing doubts as to one's salvation, but the vision will go on to show and to teach that God alone pardons the sinner and does the work of justifying. It is He who cleanses and clothes the sinner. It is His word that declares, "I have caused thine iniquity to pass from thee". The Saviour's work at Calvary gives the acceptance, and the word of God gives the assurance. So much so that the believer can say with Paul, "Who shall lay anything to the charge of God's elect? It is God that justifieth" (Rom 8.33). Not even Satan the Accuser can mar God's work of justification. So the believer can sing:

> I hear the accuser roar
> Of ills that I have done;
> I know them well, and thousands more,
> Jehovah findeth none.
>
>   (S. W. Gandy).

Touching the reference to Satan, it might be good to mention that he has access to God's presence respecting the believer (cp. Lk 22.31). This is seen in the book of Job and in Revelation 12. There is no reason to believe that, in this age of grace, Satan's going into God's presence is not permitted. It would appear that he is still allowed to enter there today and in fact is not cast out of the heavens until midway through the Tribulation period, from which moment his operations will be in the sphere of the earth. There is certainly some mystery associated with this and we are not able to understand all that is involved, but the indications in Scripture that he does enter betimes into God's presence are clear. Another point to be noted, by way of practical application, is that it is only when Joshua drew near to God that we hear of the adversary. Perhaps Satan is never more active in his accusations and oppositions than when we are praying in the presence of God. The poet may say, "The devil trembles when he sees the weakest saint upon his knees", but prayer in reality is a conflict and when engaged in, God's help and power can be given to overcome the Evil One in his opposition to the work of God.

The name Satan (7854) means "the adversary". "In a paronomasia the inspired writer declares that Satan was there to satanize him – the accuser to accuse" (F. A. Tatford). Even in the different choices of description for the Evil One in Scripture there is significance. When Mark in his Gospel records the wilderness temptation of the Lord Jesus, he does not speak of the tempter coming to Him or the devil, terms used by Matthew in his account, but he uses the word "Satan", simply and significantly, because Satan is the great accuser and is against God's work and would oppose it in the Son of God. It ever needs to be remembered that in all true work for God, Satan will seek in some way to oppose and the believer engaged in it must always be alert and especially pray for divine help. It is solemnly interesting to note that the terms "slanderers" (1 Tim 3.11), and "false accusers" (2 Tim 3.3 and Titus 2.3) are the very same word as is used for Satan as the "accuser". It is the translation of the word *diabolos* (*1228*). Sadly, it must be recognized that the believer can do Satan's work for him. Let us make sure we are not used as a tool of Satan by making false accusations. One more point is worth noting, for the way in which mention is made in Zechariah 3 of Satan makes clear that he is a real person. This is no reference to a mere influence of evil unconnected with a person. Right from the beginning, before man fell and also before the captivity in Babylon, Scripture makes reference to an evil being who is bitterly opposed to the mighty God of eternity and against His purpose and work.

What the Lord does (vv.3-5)

The next part of the vision brings before us the scene of the cleansing, clothing, and crowning of Joshua. The filthy garments with which Joshua is clothed, the removal of these garments, their being replaced with other garments, and the mitre set upon his head, all picture great spiritual truth, illustrating not only what God would do for His earthly people Israel, but also what He can do for the sinner, cleansing him by the blood of Christ. Joshua and his men are "Men (to be) wondered at" (v.8), or, as J. N. Darby puts in a footnote in his so useful translation, "Men to be observed as signs or types". Joshua therefore is a type here of the nation, and a picture too of the sinner in his need to be cleansed from sin. Later in the book, in a different setting, Joshua is seen as a type of the Messiah (6.9-13). Does it seem a contradiction that in one passage Joshua is seen as a type of Israel and in another of the Messiah? There is no contradiction in this, if it is remembered that the Holy Spirit is the author of the word of God. Each context is dealing with a different matter, the one what the Lord will do for Israel and the other what the Lord will be to Israel – their king. Joshua here is seen as a mere man. Though he may hold the honourable office of high priesthood, yet he has defilement. He is not some despicable man, who has erred grievously, but nevertheless he is a sinner, and in order to be fitted for his privileged service he needs his defilement removed. No one can draw near to God and serve Him acceptably without being cleansed from sin. This lesson should not be missed. Hence the filthy garments had to be removed (v.3).

In v.4 the Angel of Jehovah directs the angels near to Joshua: "Take away the filthy garments from him". This is only a picture, and yet, as so often the case, there is a contrast with what happens today when a soul is cleansed from sin. We see that the Lord used His heavenly servants to do this. No such process takes place in this gospel age. Angels may rejoice in the salvation of souls and view with wonder what God does in grace for fallen man, but they do not assist God in the removal of the sins of a sinner. God Himself does all on the basis of Christ's death. God may use unnamed men as instruments to accomplish the awakening and conviction of a sinner, but it must always be remembered that the work of saving souls is altogether His. What words of grace then follow to Joshua: "Behold, I have caused thine iniquity to pass from thee, and I will clothe thee with change of raiment". The filthy garments with which Joshua was clothed are not, of course, his priestly garments. Normally, in standing before God in his official position as high priest, he would be clad in the ceremonial garments, but the change of raiment placed upon him here are festal garments. There may be a link here with the high priestly garments for glory and beauty (Ex 28.2,40; 29.4-5). What an exchange from filthy garments to festal garments; the rags of sinful defilement removed and the robes of privileged priestly service put on! Is this not a picture of what God in wonderful grace has done for the believer? To remove the iniquity of Joshua is not enough for God, for He has a further great purpose in mind. He not only pardons the sinner, but also fits the same pardoned one for His service. It will be so in the future for the cleansed nation of Israel. Not only will they be delivered and pardoned, but also God will set them up as a priestly nation in blessing the Gentiles. Isaiah predicts that when God restores the nation His original purpose for them will be realised, for he says concerning them, "Ye shall be named the Priests of the Lord: men shall call you the Ministers of our God" (Is 61.6). What a pre-eminent and privileged position Israel will have, but this will only take place after God has made them righteous (Is 26.2; 60.21). For the believer, the guilt of sin is removed and in its place God gives the great blessing and honour of serving in priestly capacity in the assembly, in order "to offer up spiritual sacrifices, acceptable to God by Jesus Christ" (1 Pet 2.5). The purifying of the soul in the previous chapter of 1 Peter answers to the cleansing and clothing of Joshua (1 Pet 1.22). Every believer should keep before him what God has done in grace and should seek to serve the Lord humbly, thankfully, and reverently in the light of this.

In v.5 Zechariah prays. So far he has been an observer of the transaction in the vision, now he interjects with a request, "Let a 'fair mitre' be put upon his head". The people who had returned from Babylon to Jerusalem needed a further assurance. If Joshua represents the nation and the removal of his filthy garments signified the putting away of Israel's sin, the question would still remain, "What about the priesthood?". In the fair mitre put upon Joshua's head, God was showing to Zechariah that He was about to re-establish the priesthood in Joshua. It is quite understandable that Zechariah would have concern about the priesthood, belonging as he did to the priestly order. Hence his prayer shows he was no mere unaffected bystander in these visions, but had serious feelings and a great burden for the condition of the nation and the priesthood. The mitre might well be rendered "turban" and again possibly links with the high priest's mitre upon which was the golden plate with the words engraved, "HOLINESS TO THE LORD" (Ex 28.36; 39.30). Zechariah, therefore, in his concern for the priesthood would have been greatly comforted when the ministering spirits, in response to his request, placed the mitre upon the head of Joshua. "And this mitre, or turban, was the glory and complement of the high priest's sacred and symbolical attire – the portion of his dress in which he carried his office, so to speak, upon his forehead" (David Baron). The word "fair", better "pure", would contrast with the word "filthy" by which the garments of Joshua are described. The mitre here (TSANIPH – 6797) "...is not a turban, such as might be worn by anybody, but the headdress of princely persons and kings (Job 29.14; Is 62.3), and is synonymous with mitsnepheth, the technical word for the tiara prescribed for the high priest in the law (Exodus and Leviticus), as we may see from Ezekiel 21.26, where the regal diadem, which is called *tsâniph* in Isaiah 62.3, is spoken of under the name of *mitsnepheth*" (Keil & Delitzsch). Thus, spiritually speaking, God confers upon the believer royal dignity and fits him for the royal priesthood. As a practical thought and lesson, one may note that a turban for the head is specifically mentioned. In applying the picture of Joshua setting forth the sinner cleansed and clothed, it is good to know that when Christ is trusted, the attitude of the mind is completely changed. The thinking of the believer is adjusted. The mind of the believer should be kept pure and clean. Yet Joshua in the passage, as already indicated, primarily represents Israel. Israel, too, will have their thinking changed incredibly and radically; so much so that Isaiah 53.4-5 shows that their thoughts as to the Lord Jesus will undergo a miracle of change. Zechariah himself prophetically bears witness to the transformation in the thoughts of the nation (see 12.10-14). God will change their minds as to their rejected Messiah.

During the whole transaction we read that the "angel of the Lord stood by". The Lord stood by throughout all that was happening. There is no reason to doubt that the Angel of the Lord is to be identified with the Angel of the Lord in the first vision and is in fact the same person seen as the man with the measuring line in the third vision. Here is a divine person present with Joshua all the time that Satan was accusing. The standing by of the Lord Jesus indicates His interest and concern in all that was happening. How good it is to know that the Lord Jesus is always present and near when the sinner is pardoned. All the time that Satan was watching Joshua the Lord was watching Satan. His challenge, claiming Joshua was unfit to serve God, was completely unsuccessful. This is proved in the scene of God removing the defilement of Joshua and fitting him for His service. How good it is to know that the Lord Jesus is with and for His people and will never forsake them.

What the Lord expects (vv.6-7b)

The first part of the vision concludes with a solemn adjuration from the Angel of Jehovah: "And the angel of Jehovah protested unto Joshua, saying…". The word "protested" (UD – 5749) means variously to solemnly testify, warn, or charge. The word is used by Solomon to Shimei: "Did I not make thee to swear by the Lord, and protested unto thee…" (1 Kings 2.42). In that passage and here, it stresses the solemnity of the charge about to be given. The words of the Lord to Joshua emphasize the importance of right behaviour and the need for faithfulness in his service as the high priest. If Joshua has been seen representatively of Israel in the earlier verses, here it is a word to Joshua personally. Note again the nice yet important balance between position and condition. Both are pictured in Joshua. He is the forgiven man first of all, but now he is required to be the faithful man. It is one thing, then, for the believer to be positionally in Christ cleansed and pardoned, but another matter to walk so as to please God. The lesson should be clear. Those who have been cleansed by the Lord and made fit for His service must seek to live to obey God.

There are two matters, then, that God required Joshua to attend to. The first was to walk in His ways and the second to keep His charge. The promised blessings in v.7c are connected with and conditional upon obedience. God's promises to Israel in the Old Testament are seen as conditional upon their obedience - "If thou wilt walk in my ways". God has His own ways for His people to walk in. His ways are His laws. "Blessed are (they)…who walk in the law of the Lord" (Ps 119.1). What does it mean for the believer to walk in God's ways? It suggests first the abandonment of one's own ways, and, second, entrance into God's ways. Walking in them indicates that we are on them. Third, it implies progress in the things of God. How good it is when the believer understands that to be pardoned is a wonderful blessing to enjoy, but also to walk in the path of obedience is a joy for God to behold. Nothing pleases God more than when His children walk in His ways, but it is a very sad matter when a soul knows forgiveness of sins from God and does not feel a debt of loyalty and faithfulness to God for what He has wrought by His sovereign grace.

The second condition of blessing announced is, "If thou wilt keep my charge". Keeping God's charge refers to the ordinances of the Lord – the ceremonial and ritualistic service, or in general to the faithfulness of the priests in their daily duties. The Lord will always reward faithfulness. In the New Testament this principle is announced to the disciples by the Lord Himself: "Ye are they which have continued with me in my temptations. And I appoint unto you a kingdom, as my Father hath appointed unto me" (Lk 22.28-29). There the blessing of privileged nearness to Christ and administrative position in the coming Kingdom is promised. The future position of a believer in the Kingdom will reflect how faithful to Christ that believer has been in life. This is a solemn and searching truth that should influence for good the walk and work of all who serve the Lord.

What the Lord gives (v.7c)

God will reward the faithful priests with a threefold blessing. The preceding conditions being observed, Joshua and those with him, representing the restored priesthood, would have the great honour and privilege of administering justice in God's House, of taking charge of God's courts, of leading the people in God's worship and service (see Ps 27.4; 84.10; 134), and of free entry among the angels into the presence of God - "I will give thee places to walk among these that stand by". The angels have an appointed place of honour and dignity in being close to God's throne (cp. 4.14; 6.5; Lk 1.19; Mt 18.10). While these words are addressed to Joshua, one cannot remove from him the office in which he served. God, in establishing again the office of the priesthood, would, if Joshua were faithful, perpetuate the office for the nation. All three blessings mentioned here would be the privilege of the priests. No doubt these things in their fulness really look on to Israel's future and will not be fulfilled until they are restored, but what exactly is meant by, "I will give thee places to walk among…"? Some find these words difficult to interpret. F. A. Tatford understands the promise to mean "…admission to the immediate presence of God…the access promised to the earthly people of God is, however already the privilege and experience of the heavenly people of today". On the other hand, David Baron believes the Hebrew would allow the following paraphrase: " 'If thou wilt walk in My ways and keep My charge, thou shalt not only have the honour of judging My house and keeping My courts, but when thy work on earth is done thou shalt be transplanted to a higher service in heaven, and have 'places to walk' among these pure angelic beings who stand by Me, hearkening unto the voice of My word' (Ps 103.20-21)". This latter idea does not really suit the context, in which there seems to be no hint of a promise of reward in the after life as a result of resurrection (as Baron and others suggest), but rather that the reward is in this life. It seems better to take the view that this is a promise that will be fulfilled in Israel in the future period of the Millennium. If this is what it means, then restored Israel will have the blessing of free access into the presence of God, but even then they will need the mediation of the Messiah to function for them as High Priest, leading them into the presence of God. That this will be a blessing for the nation is true, but it is difficult to conceive that Israel then will have quite the same privilege as the saints of this dispensation. The believer now has the blessed privilege of nearness to God and the experience of drawing into the immediate presence of God. Being where angels are is one thing, but being able to approach God in worship and prayer now brings the believer into a closer relationship and nearness to God's throne than even that which angels enjoy. The lesson must not be forgotten, however, that in the future there will be a reward for obedience. God may give unmerited forgiveness and cleansing, as seen in His grace to Joshua, but He does not give unmerited reward for faithfulness. Hence the message to Joshua and Israel, and indeed by application to the believer today, is to seek to be faithful to God in view of a coming glorious day. The word "if" twice mentioned in v.7 should solemnly show that such a reward depends on the condition being fulfilled.

Verses 8-10: The Cleansing of the Land

In the first section of the chapter Joshua alone is addressed, but in the second it is Joshua and the priests. They are viewed as typical men (v.8). The reason for the inclusion of the priests in the address by the Angel of Jehovah may be that Joshua and the priests being delivered out of Babylon is typical of a greater deliverance that the nation will enjoy in the future.

The first section dealt with the removal of the iniquity of Israel represented in Joshua, the second deals with how the iniquity of the land will be removed. The second section links closely with the first by showing prophetically how it will be possible for the nation to be cleansed – it will be brought about by Jehovah's Servant the Branch, the Lord Jesus Christ, Israel's Messiah.

Israel and the Messiah (vv.8-9)

In these verses we have wonderful teaching concerning the Person of Christ. As Israel's Messiah He is presented in three ways: as the Servant, the Shoot, and the Stone upon which are seven eyes. All of these figures illustrate wonderful truth setting forth that Christ will bring new life to Israel and will complete for them God's great work of blessing them as a nation. In these final verses of this vision we have what God will do by His power and grace. Notice the three statements by God: "I will bring forth"; "I will engrave the graving thereof"; and "I will remove the iniquity of that land in one day". The emphasis is on all what God will do and alone can do for His people and no other.

The Servant – Christ the future of the nation

"Behold, I will bring forth my servant." It is so good to see the Lord Jesus brought in here. Notice the reference to the Servant is introduced by the word "Behold". It points to the greatness and the importance of the subject. It is essentially the same word twice used by Isaiah the prophet in the preface to the first and last of his four servant songs (42.1 & 52.13). The link with the previous passage is clear. All the blessings God has in store for the nation of Israel will be realized through and dependent upon Christ. Joshua and the priests were "men of sign" ("men wondered at"), anticipating a new Israel pardoned and restored by God and brought to what God intended them to be at the beginning - a nation of priests! Only the Lord Jesus Christ could make this possible, and He will in a most wonderful way. He is the great source of the nation's entire future blessing.

What is to be learned from the Servant character of Christ and why is it mentioned here? A link with the prophecy of Isaiah has already been mentioned in connection with the Lord as the Servant, where the description is the characteristic title of Messiah. Isaiah the prophet especially depicts the Lord Jesus as the Servant. For example, in the so-called four Servant Songs in chs. 42,49,50 and 53, Isaiah shows what will be the future mission and work of the Messiah as the Servant of Jehovah. Christ will be the new Moses, who will effect a new and greater exodus for Israel than that which they experienced in coming out of Egypt. In ch.42 Isaiah shows that the Servant will declare new things and enable Israel to "sing unto the Lord a new song" (vv.9-10). In ch.49 he shows that the Servant is conscious that He has been raised up to be God's Servant, in order "to bring Jacob again to him" (v.5), that is, to bring about their restoration. In ch.50 he shows that Israel's enemies are the Servant's enemies and all opposition to the nation in the future will come to naught, for "they all shall wax old as a garment; the moth shall eat them up" (v.9). Finally, in ch.53 he shows that it is through the sacrificial suffering of the Messiah-Servant that Israel will be pardoned. Thus Israel will realize that Christ's death is the basis of their future blessing. Isaiah's ministry concerning the Servant helps us to understand that Israel's hope of a glorious future is dependent upon Jehovah's Servant, the Lord Jesus Christ. God's purpose to bless and restore the nation will be accomplished. God Himself will work to bring Christ in for the blessing of His earthly people in their great hour of need. God says, "I will bring forth my servant the BRANCH". God is determined to display Christ as the fruitful branch. Nothing will stop God from this purpose.

The Shoot – Christ the fruit of the nation

The figure of the branch, or sprout (TSEMACH – 6780) suggests the picture of that which springs up or grows. This symbol of the Messiah is used in four other passages. He is the beautiful Branch of Isaiah 4.2, the "righteous Branch" of Jeremiah 23.5, He is "the Branch of righteousness" in Jeremiah 33.15, and "the man whose name is The BRANCH" in Zechariah 6.12. Another Hebrew word, NETSER (5342), used only four times in the Old Testament, is once very clearly used in a Messianic sense in Isaiah 11.1, where the prophet speaks of the Lord Jesus Christ as a Branch out of the root of the stem of Jesse. The title "The Branch" links with the royal line of David. It speaks of Christ the Messiah, a tender branch from the almost extinct royal line of David, for when the Lord was born at Bethlehem the royal house and line of King David was almost finished. It was certainly at a very low ebb. The trunk of the old tree of the house of David had become decayed and the nation, when the Lord was born, was dead religiously, politically, and nationally and yet, how wonderful, from the roots of this same tree our Lord sprang forth. He was like a slender little twig shooting out from this tree. The Messiah as the Shoot or Sprout points to the revival of the nation, so that Israel will be for God a fruitful nation again. The Servant, the Branch, will make this possible for them. Under Him they will prosper. The Lord Jesus as the Branch will also be a source of blessing and fruitfulness to the whole world in the time of the Millennium. The picture is not that of the stately cedar tree or of the upright palm tree, but rather that of a shoot, small and insignificant to begin with, but growing and developing gradually and eventually into a great tree. Such was the birth and life of the Lord Jesus. Born in the outside place, laid in Bethlehem's manger, living in the despised place of Nazareth, unwanted and rejected in His ministry, He was finally crucified in humiliation on a cross. Yet this same blessed One was destined to reign supreme in the world and to become King of kings and Lord of lords.

See, lying on His mother's breast,
An Infant weak and small.
Ah! Who would guess that this is He
That offers life to all.

Christ is both the root and the fruit of David (Rev 22.16). He is not only David's son, but also David's Lord! He will make the land of Israel fruitful, for the desert will blossom like the rose and He will cause Israel to be a fruitful nation in the Millennium.

There is a fourfold mention of the Lord as the "Branch" in the Old Testament that is so interesting and enjoyable and links so well, as many have appreciated, with the four records of Christ in the New Testament. In Jeremiah 23.5 He is the King, as in Matthew. Here He is the Servant, as in Mark. In Zechariah 6.12 He is Man, as in Luke. In Isaiah 4.2 He is Jehovah, as in John. All these references make for a profitable study for the believer. It should be noted that in these passages concerning the Lord Jesus as the Branch or shoot one can see the vital facts of the deity and manhood of the Saviour clearly indicated. In Isaiah 4.2 He is not only the Branch of Jehovah, but the fruit of the land. His origin is heavenly and His birth and life and death are in the arena of earth.

The Stone – Christ the foundation of the nation
Another most interesting symbol of the Messiah is found in v.9. Again the commanding word "behold" is used by God to Joshua twice in the verse: "For behold the stone that I have laid before Joshua; upon one stone shall be seven eyes: behold, I will engrave the graving thereof, saith the Lord of hosts". The "beholds" here are just as important as the "Behold the Lamb of God" of John 1.29. Thus again the importance of these prophecies concerning Christ is stressed. The stone Joshua sees probably was of considerable size and importance and it is not impossible that it may have been the foundation stone of the second temple. The stone here without doubt is a type of the Messiah to come. In both the Old Testament and the New Testament Christ is presented under such a symbol. Isaiah says, "Behold, I lay in Zion for a foundation a stone, a tried stone, a precious corner stone, a sure foundation" (28.16). Matthew records the words of Christ when He spoke of Himself as the stone which the builders have rejected and which will become the head of the corner (Mt 21.42). Peter, too, writes of the Lord Jesus as the rejected stone towards Israel and the stumbling stone towards the unbeliever (1 Pet 2.6-8). In the past He was the rejected stone to Israel. In the present He is the foundation stone upon which the Church is built (Mt 16.18). In the future He will not only be the foundation stone of Israel's blessing, but He will be the crushing stone that will crush the hostile Gentile powers of the world as seen in the great image of Daniel 2. In the next vision, in Zechariah 4, mention is made of the headstone, which is the final stone to complete the temple.

Christ will complete the great work of Israel's blessing in their restoration.

In the vision seven eyes are upon the stone. Are the eyes actually on the stone itself or are they looking upon the stone? Does it indicate Jehovah's interest in it, or are we to regard the eyes as linking with Revelation 5.6 and therefore speaking of the perfection of the intelligence of Christ? Both are possible interpretations. It seems more fitting, however, in this Messianic millennial context, to regard the eyes as engraved on the stone itself. The picture would then depict the Lord Jesus as the One who has perfect wisdom to rule justly and rightly in the millennial age. Isaiah 11.2 supports this view. The first nine verses of that passage clearly set out, prophetically, millennial conditions. The sevenfold power of the Spirit will rest upon Christ. Not, of course, seven different spirits, but rather portraying the sevenfold perfection of the Spirit in intelligence and power, which will mark the Lord Jesus in the millennial age. He will be perfectly fitted to rule and judge in maintaining perfect peace for one thousand years. Christ will have every quality of discernment, wisdom, and knowledge in exercising government in the world to come.

Before leaving the image of the stone, it is interesting to point out the wonderful contrast between the idea of the shoot and the stone. Is it not amazing to think that the tiny shoot will finally become the great stone? God makes sure that, lest it be thought that from the figure of the lowly sprout the Kingdom of the Messiah will be weak and insignificant, the figure is changed to that of a stone which speaks of strength and power. In the vision the supremacy, solidarity and singularity of the stone is seen. Notice it is one stone! There is no other stone to be compared to this. There never has been nor ever will be any other stone like it. It is a stone of miraculous origin, "cut out of the mountain without hands" (Dan 2.45). It is a "living stone" (1 Pet 2.4), and a "chief corner stone" (1 Pet 2.6). How wonderful it is, then, to see in this prophetic message a threefold reference to the Lord Jesus. It is He alone who will give Israel a future; it is He alone who will make them fruitful; it is He alone who will be the foundation of all their blessings as a nation. The believer too, today, has no future apart from Christ, no fruit is possible in the life apart from Christ, and He is the foundation upon which the believer's security rests.

God then says, "I will remove the iniquity of that land in one day". The order here is significant. There can be no blessing for Israel and cleansing from their sin until the Messiah comes. Any question of Israel's iniquity being dealt with and removed cannot be possible apart from Christ. This is why there is the reference to the Saviour as the Servant and Stone. It will be because of the Messiah and His work at Calvary that there will be divine pardon for Israel. An interesting question is to what the reference to "one day" refers. Does it mean that there will be a speedy end to God's work of grace in the nation and that things will move rapidly at the end times and especially when Christ comes at the second advent? The day in the final verse of the vision refers to the period of the Millennium. The phrase "that day" in the prophecies of the Old Testament very often refers to God's final dealings with Israel, but could the "one day" here speak of the day of Calvary? Is it not true that by Christ's once-for-all sacrifice on that day, Israel will be cleansed from their sins? This is the only way that God could remove the iniquity of the land of Israel. "The day on which the great result of atonement was completed for Israel was on 'the day of Golgotha', when the iniquity of the land was removed by that full, perfect, and sufficient sacrifice, offered by Christ on the cross" (C. H. H. Wright). One may also understand that the "one day" could refer to the day in the future when Israel will nationally repent and their sins will be removed on the ground of Christ's atonement. In Israel's religious yearly calendar the great and critical Day of Atonement was the day their sins were cleansed for one more year. The true fulfilment of the Day of Atonement, however, took place at Calvary, but the eyes of Israel will not be opened to this truth until Christ Himself appears to them. Thus in this one verse we have one stone, the Person of the Lord Jesus, and there never will be another like Him; and we have one day, referring to the work of Christ on the day of Calvary, and there never will be another work like it. These two references to Christ's Person and work are stupendous and should never cease to cause wonder in the heart of the believer today.

Israel and the Millennium (v.10)

What a delightful picture we have in the last verse of the vision. It is a scene that depicts a beautiful condition of millennial blessing. So far we have had the prophecy of the Lord's coming, when God will bring Christ to the nation and what will happen when He comes in removing the iniquity of the land, but now we have the great result of this seen in the peaceful conditions of the millennial age. "In that day, saith the Lord of hosts, shall ye call every man his neighbour under the vine and under the fig tree." The happy and prosperous conditions described are the blessed results of the nation having been pardoned and now under the righteous and peaceful reign of Christ. The joy and gladness will be so great that each true Israelite will want to share with others the blessings experienced and so will invite friends to join them under their own vine and fig tree. An interesting piece of information regarding a Jewish custom practised after the conclusion of the Day of Atonement is given by C. H. H. Wright and others: "We are told in the Talmud (Yoma, 7,4) that when, on the great Day of Atonement, the high priest had performed the various duties of that solemn day, he was escorted home in a festive manner, and was accustomed to give a festal entertainment to his friends. The maidens and youths of the people went forth to their gardens and vineyards with songs and dances; social entertainment took place on all sides, and universal gladness closed the festal of that solemn day". In citing this F. A. Tatford well comments, "If that was true after the temporary work of atonement of that earlier age, how great will be the joy when God removes His people's defilement and reconciles them to Himself".

A similar description of ideal peaceful conditions is used in connection with the reign of Solomon: "And Judah and Israel dwelt safely, every man under his vine and under his fig tree, from Dan even to Beer-sheba, all the days of Solomon" (1 Kings 4.25). The widespread tranquillity of Solomon's kingdom only faintly pictures the far greater secure and peaceful conditions of the Kingdom in the Millennium. This wonderful time envisaged here should be read along with Micah 4.1-4 where the prophet speaks of some of the characteristics of the millennial Kingdom and uses the same language as Zechariah 3.10: "They shall sit every man under his vine and under his fig tree; and none shall make them afraid". When a Jew desired to express the idea of rest, joy, and safety, he did so by using the picture of every man sitting "under the vine and under the fig tree" – a scene of quiet, refreshment and gladness. These two trees are typical of Israel. Israel had been planted as a vine in the vineyard (Is 5.7), but was desolated because of disobedience. The fig tree is a symbol of Israel restored after the captivity, a fig tree planted in the vineyard, but which the Lord when here found to be unfruitful (Lk 13.6). Both these passages speak of the failure and ruin of the nation, but the Lord Jesus will bring its sad history to an end by restoring it and giving it permanent, peaceful and prosperous conditions.

How great it is that the believer now enjoys peace with God and complete eternal security as a result of Christ's sacrificial death. So much so that we can say with Paul the apostle, "We also rejoice in God through our Lord Jesus Christ, through whom we have now received the reconciliation" (Rom 5.11, RV). Has not the Christian far greater cause to have joy and gladness in view of the vast blessings Christ has secured by His death, and should not times of social fellowship be also enjoyed among Christians, sharing with each other the experience of spiritual blessings brought from God through Christ?

ZECHARIAH 4

The Fifth Vision. The Divine Privilege – the Lampstand

Question: "Will the nation, Lord, be a testimony for Thee again?"

In this vision God speaks to the remnant who would be concerned, with some degree of exercise, about the testimony of the nation. They had lost their power and potential for God as a people. Having been seventy years in captivity in Babylon they were now spiritually weakened. Would they ever be restored to such an extent that they would once again be a power and a light for God to the Gentiles? God, through the prophet, gives encouragement to them. The message of the vision is that, yes, under God the remnant will still have a testimony to be maintained through the Spirit. The nation can and, prophetically, will be a light bearer again and God will enable them to be effective in their witness. The key verse very decidedly in this chapter is v.6, where God says, "Not by might, nor by power, but by my spirit, saith the Lord of hosts". This statement contains the very essence of the message of this vision. The heartening message is that God can empower His people for Himself. There is a clear and significant order in the fourth and fifth visions, which should be commented on, as it suggests a very practical lesson for God's people today. The cleansing of Joshua in the previous vision comes before the vision here of the lampstand. This surely shows to us that God will bless, use, and give power only to those who have been cleansed. The nation in the future will experience the cleansing power of the work of Christ at Calvary and then God will take them up to be His light bearer to the Gentiles. The reader should take note of this order: cleansing first and then power. No believer can really be used as God intends if the prerequisite of cleansing in the life has not been attended to.

The chapter is divided up into two main sections. In vv.1-5 we have the vision itself. There are two constituent parts to the vision. First, Zechariah sees a lampstand and then he sees two olive trees standing on either side of the bowl. In vv.6-14 we have the explanation of the vision and its message. Here God answers the question of the perplexed prophet, who is baffled as to the meaning of what he sees. It is at the end of this section that God interprets the picture of the two olive trees.

In this vision Zechariah's interest is stirred up and increased and he returns to asking questions as he did in visions one to three. Unlike the previous occasions, he actually asks three times about the meaning of the two olive trees (v.4; vv.11-12). As a result, God answers him and enlightens him. God will reward spiritual interest in divine things. One might just ask, Does the reader have a real and earnest interest in the things of God? Does he long to understand the mind of God and to know the gracious help of God in the interpretation of Scripture? How can there be spiritual growth and understanding if there is no real interest first of all in the soul? Asking the Lord questions makes us dependent more on Him to reveal

His truth. God will ever guide His child and respond to an earnest desire to know.

Verses 1-5: The Details of the Vision

In the first verse Zechariah is awakened as a man is wakened out of sleep. The interpreting angel arouses him. It is likely that the first four visions had exhausted him. It must be remembered that these visions were given to Zechariah during the night time. Their very nature, and all the mystical details, may well have affected him both physically and mentally. It is important to point out that one must not conclude from this that Zechariah had been dreaming. Possibly he was not asleep, as we know it, but was in a state of trauma, overwhelmed by the previous four visions that had come to him in quick succession one after another. God would have the prophet to be alert. How possible it is for the believer to be spiritually asleep, or so much influenced by the things all around and even the lawful duties of daily life, that one can become inattentive to the things of God. The angel asked Zechariah, "What seest thou?". Am I a seeing believer? Zechariah had to be aroused and to have his eyes open to behold the lampstand and the two olive trees. It was very important for the young prophet to see the symbols clearly if he was to understand their message to himself and the remnant. No divine illumination will come to any believer without their first being spiritually awake and looking carefully at what God is pleased to reveal from His word.

What did Zechariah see? He saw a lampstand with seven lamps and seven pipes to the seven lamps. He also saw two olive trees, one placed on each side of the lampstand, which itself is central to the vision. In these apocalyptic visions, so full of figures and symbols, the lampstand is plainly an emblem of something, but of what? The specific function of a lampstand is to give light. It is therefore a picture of light and testimony. It signifies that the nation of Israel will yet be God's light bearer. They will, in God's great purpose, function as His witness throughout the millennial reign of Christ. Several passages in Isaiah support this view (Is 42.6; 43.10-12; 49.6; 60.1-3).

It will be helpful in the interpretation of the lampstand if we do not confuse it with the lampstand in the tabernacle in the book of Exodus. Some have seen a link with the tabernacle vessel and consider that the one in Zechariah 4 is a figurative representation of the seven-branched golden lampstand in the tabernacle and that therefore it must speak of the Messiah. First of all, the lampstand in the vision here differs in appearance from the one in Exodus. It has three points of difference. The vessel Zechariah saw has a bowl, seven pipes, and two olive trees. These the lampstand in the tabernacle did not have. There are no priests seen with this lampstand. It needs no trimming or dressing. The lampstand in the tabernacle was humanly supplied and maintained, but this one, as the passage goes on to show, needs no human agency to keep its light burning, for the Spirit of God will empower the nation in the future. Again, the lampstand in the tabernacle stood in the sanctuary and lit up that holy place. It did not stand in the court or outside in the wilderness, yet the lampstand in the vision is not located in the sanctuary, but rather is seen outside. Its appearance, place, and function fittingly speak of the nation of Israel. One must not conclude, however, that Israel's Messiah is not to be seen in the vision, for He it is who will sustain and maintain, by His Spirit, the testimony of the nation in a day to come. Since the vision must have had an immediate fulfilment, it is very likely that the two olive trees refer to Joshua and Zerubbabel. At the time Zechariah was writing his prophecy, God had raised up these two men to arouse and encourage the testimony in Israel. Joshua the high priest represented the religious ministry in Israel. Zerubbabel represented the civil authority in Israel. So in these two men we have what answered to the two olive trees then. In both of these men we see combined priesthood and rule. These men both foreshadow the coming Messiah of Israel who in the future day will be a king-priest, for in ch.6 Zechariah prophesies of Christ who will sit as a priest upon His throne. Thus the Lord Jesus, who is the true Messiah, will be perfectly fitted to sustain Israel's witness throughout the Millennium. Apart from Him they will be nothing, but by His Spirit Christ will give power to the nation. A constant flow of oil as it were, will come down from Christ to His people. What a power for God the nation will be throughout the Millennium. The secret and source of their power will be their Messiah and Saviour.

There will be no lack in the supply of spiritual power to enable the nation to continue to be God's witness in that time. It is really no different today. God has His witnesses today. The Lord Jesus said to His disciples before He ascended to heaven, "Ye shall be witnesses unto me" (Acts 1.8). There are over fifty references to the Holy Spirit in Acts. We certainly see that the work of God prospered and progressed not by might and power or by any human means and methods, but by the Spirit. In the record of Acts, Luke shows how the Lord Jesus, by His Spirit, empowered His servants to do what would have been impossible otherwise during the early apostolic period. If the glorified Head in heaven had not been working in and through the apostles and others by His Spirit, the Christian message would never have triumphed as it did. The Lord Jesus, as the risen Head of His Church, can and does supply the power needed through His Spirit to maintain the testimony of the present day. It is needful, however, to remember that spiritual power can only flow through and be experienced by spiritual persons. It is not enough to know about the Spirit and to even understand that this is the Spirit's day, but the great need is to have a life yielded to the Spirit so that He may be able to use us in the work of God.

The lighted lampstand represents Israel as a nation. It is a fitting symbol, showing that they will be Jehovah's chosen witness to give spiritual light to the world in the coming millennial age. After Israel has been restored they will have this great privilege. This is one of the reasons why God will take the nation up again. That the image of a lampstand, chosen by the Holy Spirit to represent Israel, is so apt and suitable may be seen in the fact that even today the symbol of the lampstand is used by the Jewish people to stand for their state and uniqueness as a nation in the eyes of God. It is interesting, for example, that the official seal for the state of Israel was unveiled on 10th February, 1949. It consists of a seven-branched menorah (lampstand/candelabra) with an olive branch on either side. Opposite the entrance to the Israeli Knesset (parliament) stands a great menorah with branches that are sixteen feet high and thirteen feet wide (5m x 4m). This particular menorah is decorated with figures highlighting Israel's history and engraved with the Scripture, "Not by might, nor by power, but by my Spirit saith the Lord of hosts". The menorah, olive branches, and inscription, are symbols of the rebirth of the state of Israel – a graphic reminder and witness to God's power and promise to preserve the Jewish people. The inspiration for both Israel's seal and the inscription on the giant menorah was taken from Zechariah's fifth vision here in ch.4. The same symbols that inspired modern-day Israel were first used centuries earlier to inspire Zerubbabel and the remnant to finish the construction of the temple.

While the appearance of the lampstand with its seven lamps is considered by some to be the counterpart of the one in the tabernacle, this one was unusual in that each lamp was supplied with oil by seven pipes running from a bowl, or reservoir, situated at the top of the lampstand's central shaft. Forty-nine pipes, it appears, fed this lampstand. If this is correct then each branch of the olive trees had seven pipes attached to it. (The reader should be aware that there are several other views of the actual structure of the vessel, but the lessons from it ought to be clear.) It was well supplied with an abundance of oil to keep the lampstand burning brightly. Thus, with this lampstand there is no suggestion of a periodic replenishment, as in the case of the lampstand in the tabernacle. The olive trees, the bowl, and the pipes combine to indicate a continuous flow of the Spirit. The significance of this in its application to the remnant in Zechariah's day will be commented on in the explanation.

Zechariah was curious about the two olive trees and asked the interpreting angel, "What are these, my lord" (v.4). The angel answered the question with a question: "Knowest thou not what these be?". Zechariah responded, "No, my lord" (v.5). The angel's question indicates that Zechariah, who was a priest as well as a prophet, should have understood what he saw. The question is not really answered until the end of the chapter. Zechariah has to wait for the meaning of the two olive trees. It is good to have a real interest and the desire to understand the Scriptures, but sometimes in the Lord's dealings with us in revealing His truth much patience is required.

Verses 6-14: The Meaning of the Vision

In these verses we have the application and explanation of the vision to the remnant that were seeking to build again the temple, and restore the testimony of the nation for God. How was this to be done? There were many difficulties and the task was overwhelming. The message to them was that divine resources were readily available for them. Weak the remnant might have been, but God was able to meet the need by supplying the strength. They were not to despair, God was for them. The message of the vision for the people was most encouraging. The Spirit of God Himself would enable them. His power would energize them in deeds to be accomplished (v.6), in difficulties to overcome (v.7), in duties to be completed (vv.8-9), and in discouragements to be experienced (v.10).

In deeds to be accomplished (v.6)

Now we have the angel's message from God. It is a message of vital importance, not only for Zerubbabel but for believers in every age and sphere. If it is treated with indifference it will be very much detrimental to the work of the Lord. Zerubbabel and the remnant needed to be reminded of it and so does the believer engaged in God's work today. Zerubbabel represented what was known of the power of government as it was among the Jews at that time, but he is told, "Not by might, nor by power, but by my spirit, saith the Lord of hosts". The lesson for Zerubbabel, and for the believer too, is very clear. It is needful, vital, and searching – that work for God can only be accomplished by the power of the Spirit of God. If the task of rebuilding the temple was to be successful, it could not be done by any human strength, wisdom, organization, or even military force; God's Spirit alone would accomplish the task and not Israel. How true it is that it is not better methods that are needed in the Lord's work, but rather better men, men who are filled with the Holy Spirit. The two words "might" and "power" are interesting. The first is HAYIL (2428), and is used fifty-six times in the Old Testament for "army". The second is KOAH (3581), and it is used fifty-eight times in the Old Testament for "strength" (human strength). So, if any deeds for God are to be accomplished they cannot be done either by military power or human strength.

There is a great need in the work of the Lord today among assemblies, and weakness abounds. There is a power shortage in the work of the gospel, in seeing souls saved, and assemblies added to. There is a great lack in ministry, which should be in the power of the Spirit, producing results for the glory of God in the lives of the saints. Some are loath to admit it; others can see it and mourn over it. Some sadly seem blind to the spiritual poverty of the testimony. What is to be done about such conditions and how can the work of God really prosper? Many have tried new methods and practices in an attempt somehow to bolster up their weak condition. Some of these methods may be appealing to the flesh and for a while may attract, but such things only serve to mask our terrible lack of spiritual power. The only answer to the great need that exists is much communion with God in prayer, obedience to His word, and reliance upon the Spirit's ability. Those who serve God today should not depend on human organization, wisdom, oratory, or worldly methods, but on the power of the Spirit alone. In preaching and teaching the word, how easy to rely on brain power. In seeking to carry on the Lord's work how easy, too, to rely on past power enjoyed, when what is sorely needed is a fresh experience of the present available power of the Spirit. This power, of course, can only be realised in the measure in which God's servant is yielded to the Spirit of God in his life and is in a condition suited to be used by God. The Spirit of God will only take up a clean vessel to further God's work.

In difficulties to overcome (v. 7)

God assured Zerubbabel, who had laid the foundation of the second temple sixteen years earlier, that he would complete the work. The overwhelming and insurmountable difficulties in completing the construction could only be overcome by the power of God's Spirit. A finished temple would provide Zerubbabel and the returned remnant with clear evidence of the fact that God's Spirit alone had accomplished the work. The angel then revealed to Zerubbabel that he would face obstacles and opposition. Notice the words, "Who art thou, O great mountain?". The word "who" is used to personify the expression "great mountain", which is a metaphor of the opposition that would confront Zerubbabel. The great mountain of obstacles refers to the opposition of the Gentiles. This was a real problem to the remnant. When Zerubbabel started to rebuild the temple after the remnant had returned to Jerusalem, he immediately faced what seemed to be insurmountable hindrances. Gentiles living in the land tried to stop the temple reconstruction (Ezra 4). They did so in three ways. First, they wanted to help with the task, but were rejected because they did not follow the God of Israel. Making an ungodly alliance with these people would have diverted the Jews and weakened their resolve to finish the project. Then those Gentiles tried to discourage and intimidate the workers by hiring counsellors to frustrate the construction. Finally, those opposing the work wrote letters of complaint to king Artaxerxes, petitioning him to shut down the project. Nevertheless, this seeming mountain of opposition would be levelled by the Lord. The book of Zechariah describes how, at the time of the second advent of Christ, God will remove a mountain and make it a plain. In the land of Israel at present, physically and geographically there are many difficulties in the way of Old Testament prophecy being fulfilled. If the land of Israel is to be enlarged and the great millennial temple is to be built, then God will have to remove the Mount of Olives and make changes to render this possible. How this will be done and what will happen will be dealt with in ch.14.

The second part of the text refers to the headstone: "He shall bring forth the headstone thereof with shoutings, crying Grace, Grace unto it".

The headstone or capstone of the temple indicates its completion. It is not "the headstone of the corner", but "the stone of the top". It is the finishing, or gable stone, brought from the place where it is cut and prepared, to be set in its proper place in the building. The Lord Jesus is not only the foundation of the temple in the future, but He is also the full completion of it. There would be much joy, no doubt, when the remnant would bring forth the topstone and complete the second temple. There will be greater joy when the final temple in the Millennium will be completed. Shouts accompanied the laying of Zerubbabel's temple (Ezra 3.11-13). Shouts of acclamation, "Grace, Grace unto it," will be heard when it is finished. The temple erected by Zerubbabel is but a faint shadow of a glorious day to come when all Israel shall be saved. The repetition in the words "Grace, Grace" emphasize how that from beginning to end all that God will accomplish for Israel will be due alone to His grace. When things begin to move to bring about Israel's repentance and recovery, it will be God who will cause the Spirit of grace to be poured upon them (12.10). Grace will be predominantly seen. Believers today are privileged to know in advance the grace of God. As we consider what has been accomplished by Christ in His cross-work and the wonderful blessings experienced as a result of this, grace draws forth praise and rejoicing from the redeemed soul.

In duties to be completed (vv.8-9)
Any duty taken up for God can only be completed by the power of the Spirit. The message here is clear: the servant who relies on the Spirit will find the needed grace and help to complete the task. By the Spirit's power Zerubbabel would not only commence the work, but also complete it. "The hands of Zerubbabel have laid the foundation of this house; his hands shall also finish it." Considerable time had elapsed since the laying of the foundation of the temple and the time of this prophecy. The temple was yet a long way from being completed, but God says clearly that Zerubbabel would finish it. Is there not a lesson here? How good and necessary it is, not only to commence a work for God, but by His help to finish it. Sadly there have been servants who have begun well, but then, perhaps because of the difficulties and demands of the work, have given up and put down the task given them by the Lord. May what the Lord said to the church of Sardis never be true of those who serve the Lord today: "I have not found thy works perfect (complete) before God" (Rev 3.2). Each servant needs much grace and help from the Lord to be consistent and to complete the task given. More than ever today there is great need to be "steadfast, unmoveable, always abounding in the work of the Lord" (1 Cor 15.58). If we are assured that it is indeed the work of the Lord, meeting with His approval and for His glory, then it deserves our faithfulness.

Notice that when Zerubbabel and his helpers would complete the work of the temple, it would be a confirmation to all the Jews of the fact that he had been called to it and that his ministry was of God: "and thou shalt know that the Lord of hosts hath sent me unto you". Such a statement had been mentioned twice in the third vision at 2.9 & 11. There it is a clear reference to the Messiah. Can we not make an application here to the Messiah? It might be asked, "Who is this who is sent?". While in the first place it refers to Zerubbabel, there is no reason why we should lose sight of the typical character of this prophecy as looking on to the future temple in Jerusalem during the Millennium, which will at the right time be built and completed by Israel's Messiah. When the Lord returns to Israel, restores the nation, and builds their temple, they will certainly know that Jehovah has sent Him to them. One thing is sure, that when Israel begins to build their new temple under the instructions of the Lord Jesus, they will finish it. The foundation will be laid and the whole edifice, big as it will be, will be finished. There will be no suggestion then that what the Lord commences to do, He will not complete. God and the Lord Jesus always, without fail, finish what they start (cp. Phil 1.6; Heb 12.2).

In discouragements to be experienced (v.10)

The message of this verse is that whatever discouragements there may be in the work of God, the Spirit of God will help to overcome them. The phrase "day of small things" is often misunderstood on at least two counts. First, in the context it is only a day of small things in the estimate of men and not of God, for note that we read in the verse of the eyes of the Lord, which suggest His providence and intelligence. The eyes of the Lord are upon the plummet in the hand of Zerubbabel. Therefore, the work that Zerubbabel had commenced on the House of the Lord (the temple), God will ensure is brought to completion (v.9). Then, second, the day of small things is really but the start of great and important things on earth in so far as God is concerned, for His eyes rested upon the little lump of stone or lead in the hand of Zerubbabel, to which is attached the string for checking the building, and this was truly setting in motion what to God was something that would work out grander and bigger. The words "They shall rejoice, and shall see the plummet in the hand of Zerubbabel" are not easy to interpret. Do they refer to the remnant, or to God Himself? If they refer to the seven eyes of Jehovah, then the message is that the God who beheld the work as it progressed, would take pleasure in its completion. While, then, there were those who despised such a work, God took pleasure in it. What a contrast this is to those who considered it a day of small things! If this is the meaning, it shows the importance of seeing things as God sees them. In any work engaged in for God it is good to ask, "What is the character, need, and importance of the work in God's sight, and does it bring joy to Him?". To the dispirited and despondent remnant in Zerubbabel's day, what seemed a day of small things was really a time of great importance. As one has written, "These beginnings may seem small, but this restoration to the land will eventually result in the birth of the Messiah with all the blessings attendant to that event" (G. Coleman Luck).

If we are viewing conditions with our own eyes then all may appear a day of small things, but if we see things "as the eyes of the Lord" we will appreciate that God has the desire to bring before our hearts the great things of His purposes. The remnant that returned with Zerubbabel were in danger of forgetting this. They were obviously cast down with the hugeness of the task and with the overwhelming odds which were against them. It was to such that the question of Jehovah was directed: "For who hath despised the day of small things?". Already God had revealed, for their comfort, that He would deal with the mountain of difficulties and make them a plain (v.7). It is all too possible, even in the midst of the weakness of assembly testimony and the great indifference to the preaching of the gospel, that we try to reassure our hearts by persuading ourselves it is a day of small things and we cannot expect matters to be much better. However, the real need is to see that however small our work may appear to be, it is God's work and could lead on to greater things if He so wills it. We must not be given to talk about a day of small things unless we first understand exactly what is meant by the expression in the context of Zechariah 4. The practical teaching of the chapter is clear enough. The remnant under Zerubbabel were viewing things through their own eyes and not from the divine standpoint. Consequently, to them it seemed to be a day of small things, but looking at what was happening from Zechariah's ministry, it was God who attached great importance to the event.

There is a sense in which the present church age, whatever difficult periods it may have, could not really be described as a day of small things. God is doing things on a large scale today. The Holy Spirit is still working in the world. God is still taking out of the nations a people for His name (Acts 15.14), and the blessings, too, are far greater than in any previous age. On the other hand, we have to remember that God often occupies Himself with what may be little in the eyes of men. Often God's work commences in a small and insignificant way. We may think, for example, of the tiny handful of disciples on the day of Pentecost. Who would ever have thought that they would eventually conquer the mighty Roman Empire with the gospel? It has been estimated that there were about 4,000,000 Jews in Palestine at that time. How small the 120 must have felt in comparison to them. Again, think of Paul and Silas in Acts 16 taking the gospel for the first time to Europe. The work in Philippi began so quietly and insignificantly with only a small company of pious Jewish women. The vast stream of Christianity in Europe, which has flowed on for centuries, can be traced back to the little gathering by the river side. Would any have imagined it would have increased in volume and depth like Ezekiel's river (Ezek 47)? We must not despise any work for God that may seem small, or be cast down if there are difficulties. If God has given us a work to do we must look to Him and carry on until He shows us otherwise. The believer must look at the potential of any work for God. We must realise that even our little efforts, with all their difficulties, are connected with God's great and large purposes. If the believer is tempted to feel it is a day of small things, let him remember how and in what way it was so in Zerubbabel's time and see in the question of 4.10 a tender rebuke from God to His people.

In the light of this most encouraging passage (vv.4-10) Zerubbabel and His fellow-workers could take heart, and all who serve God today may take heart too, and, if tempted to quit the work God has given, remember the message of this vision and consider the assurances God gives to His workers. The God we serve is the God who provides power (vv.1-6). He is the God who removes obstacles (v.7), and He is the God who gives promises (vv.8-9), so He can be trusted even when there is opposition. The temple project may have been delayed for some years, but eventually God helped the remnant to finish it.

The meaning of the two olive trees (vv.11-14)

In this last section of the chapter we have the answer to the questions of Zechariah concerning the two olive trees. While the vision of the lampstand itself had been explained, the symbolism of the two olive trees still concerned the prophet. In these verses the question of Zechariah is answered more specifically and it becomes now evident that the reference to the two olive trees looks beyond Joshua and Zerubbabel and awaits a future fulfilment. It is interesting to note that Zechariah, when he asks a second time the same question concerning the trees, is more precise in describing them as "olive branches". Thus the first question is left unanswered and Zechariah needs to ask again, "What be these two olive branches?". Why does he need to ask again, and why in response to the second question does the interpreting angel say, "Knowest thou not what these be"? One can only conclude that the presence of the olive trees is important to complete the picture, and that it is left to this further revelation from God to explain the function of the olive trees or branches, as well as to describe who they represent; the "two anointed ones" ("sons of oil", JND; RV). It would be true to say that Zechariah, as a priest in Israel, ought to have known at the very least that the olive tree does speak of Israel, for the nation is compared to a "green olive tree, fair, and of goodly fruit" (Jer 11.16). Could he not have understood that the two trees signified the two leaders whom God was then using for the restoration of the civil and religious ministry in the nation? The words "Knowest thou not what these be?" almost seem like a rebuke.

It is rather striking that it becomes clear in these further details of the olive trees that, as mentioned previously, they are spoken of now as "olive branches". This means, to be true to the picture, that not all the branches on the trees were fruit bearing, but that each tree had one fruitful branch from which the oil was derived. Yet, if the picture of the trees with the seven pipes to each branch is correct, why are there only two fruitful branches? This fact is not commented on by the angel nor given a figurative application. In the absence of an explanation as to this point, it would be unwise to make any positive suggestion as to why this is so in the vision. The only point one can make is that if the two olive trees picture in the first place two persons and these two persons foreshadow the Messiah, then like every type and picture of Christ, they fall short. It is so true to say that Christ, Israel's Messiah, in the future will have no deficiency about His person anywhere. He will be an All Fruitful Branch to the nation.

The two anointed ones, or sons of oil, show that these men will be Spirit anointed. Both priests and kings in Israel were anointed with oil when inducted into their office. This anointing was poured upon the head and symbolized that God would endow them with His Spirit. These two olive trees here look on to a future fulfilment when God, midway through the Tribulation, will raise up in the land of Israel two witnesses. A clue to this interpretation is the fact stated that they "stand by the Lord of the whole earth". During the Tribulation time the Antichrist, who is called "the man of the earth" in Psalm 10.18, will be the devil's superman at that time, but God owns the earth. It is His by right of creation. This the devil seeks to dispute, but God will show He is the Lord of the earth. It belongs to Him, and His Son alone will yet have universal sway in it. Before the Messiah comes to the earth, God will have two men, described as witnesses in Revelation 11.1-12. These two witnesses are distinctly described as the "two olive trees, and the two candlesticks standing before the God of the earth" (v.4). The link back with the prophecy of Zechariah should be noted. Notice, too, that the title of God as "The God of the earth" in Revelation parallels "the Lord of the whole earth" in Zechariah 4. The difference to be especially observed is the fact that not only are the two witnesses the olive trees of Zechariah 4, but they are referred to also as the two candlesticks or lamps in Revelation 11.4. In our passage in Zechariah the olive trees are quite distinct from the lampstand. Since the nation is seen as the lampstand in Zechariah 4, it must be pointed out again that the nation will not be God's witness or light bearer until the Millennium. God will not leave Himself without witness even in the terrible days of the Tribulation. So it is quite understandable that the two men are also described as lamps. They are God's witnesses at a time when Israel will have sunk very low in their failure and will have accepted the false Messiah. In addition, there is only one lamp in the vision of Zechariah 4, but here there are two lights for God, though it should be pointed out that their ministry, mission, and power are one. They stand as one and in unity together they will be faithful unto death.

This is not the place to give an exposition of Revelation 11, but a few remarks may be helpful. In the writer's view these two witnesses are not Moses and Elijah or Enoch brought down from heaven by God, but rather men living in that period whom God will use. No doubt they will have the characteristics of these great men of Israel's past history. It is very evident that they will be persons of great authority and sanctity. John does not say anything about their history or background, but it is good to see that Christ is the speaker in Revelation 11. He calls them "MY" witnesses. This gives special solemnity to the words He utters and the events He describes. It is clear from v.6 of Revelation 11 that divine power will maintain the testimony of these servants of God, just as, to a greater degree, the same power later will maintain Israel's witness. Their testimony will be a short (1,260 days), spiritual, supernatural, and suffering testimony, for the Beast, the Antichrist will kill them. Then the passage states that the "Spirit of life" will enter into them, and to the wonder of the world they will be raised from the dead and taken up to heaven. The mention of the Spirit indicates the source of their power. It is He who will enable them to serve so faithfully and courageously and it is He who will raise them up. Thus we have another link with Zechariah 4, for the olive trees speak of spiritual power and this power the Spirit of God will give. Zechariah 4.11-14, then, will have its future fulfilment in the two witnesses, and later in the Millennium the Lord Jesus as the Messiah will fulfil what is prefigured in the two men used by God in Zechariah's day.

This vision of the lampstand has a great message of encouragement for all who serve God today, and the lessons from it are salutary and most needful. Servants need the power of the Lord to serve. They must not consider as unimportant any small beginnings when God is in them. They should have the confidence of faith to believe that whatever the difficulties, God will keep to His programme and fulfil it. Last and by no means least, if service for God is to be effective then there is the great need to stand by the Lord of the whole earth and to live consciously in His presence.

ZECHARIAH 5

The Sixth Vision. The Divine Precepts – the Flying Roll
Question: "Lord, will Thy law be again effective among us?"

Verses 1-4: The Flying Roll

The three visions that follow, the fifth, sixth and seventh show God dealing with sin and judging it. In the vision of the flying roll God deals with the sin of the individual in Israel. In the seventh vision – that of the ephah - He deals with the sin of the nation, while in the eighth and last - the four horses and chariots - He deals with the sin of the nations in the world that oppose Israel. The first five visions of Zechariah emphasised God's grace in bringing blessing to His people, a glorious future of victory over their enemies, and the restoration of the nation and the enlarging of Jerusalem. This was intended to greatly encourage the Jewish remnant who had returned from Babylon. The visions that follow, however, are entirely of a different character, for instead of speaking of blessing they refer to wickedness that must be removed. The visions are visions of judgment and not of blessing. If Israel were to enjoy the blessing spoken of in the previous visions then they had to be purged from two kinds of wickedness. Not all "which are of Israel" will have part in Israel's future blessing (Rom 9.6). It has already been seen that God will deal in grace in cleansing the nation from their sin (ch.3), but the visions of this chapter show that He will also deal in holiness with His people's perversity. He will deal with them in righteous judgment, so that the coming millennial Kingdom will be established with sin purged from the land of Israel. These two visions deal with the matter of individual and national wickedness in Israel. In considering the first vision in the chapter concerning the flying roll we will look at it in relation to its significance, swiftness, size, sides, and severity.

Its significance

Zechariah looks up and sees a large flying roll, or scroll. Following the good example of Zechariah we will ask some questions relative to this vision. The first question must be why it is that Zechariah sees a roll. What is pictured by a roll in the Scriptures of truth? In some cases a roll contained the words of men such as the one that had written in it the decree of Cyrus which gave the Jews permission to return to Jerusalem to rebuild the temple (Ezra 6.2). Quite often in the Old Testament a roll contained the word of God. Jeremiah 36.2 for example reads, "Take thee a roll of a book, and write therein". Again, in Isaiah 8.1 the prophet writes, "Moreover the Lord said unto me, Take thee a great roll, and write in it". Ezekiel also is bidden to eat a roll that he had seen in a hand sent to him. This roll was written within and without, and Ezekiel was commanded by God to "Speak with my words unto them" (i.e. "the house of Israel") (Ezek 2.9-3.4). From these references one can conclude without any difficulty that the roll Zechariah saw is a clear picture of the word of God. The vision answers the remnant's concern about God's law. They would be anxious to know if God's law would be effective again and if His word would still have relevance for them in their present situation. The vision then greatly emphasizes the importance and application of the word of God to the lives of the remnant. Divine principles and standards were still to have force and application to the people. The roll was obviously open otherwise Zechariah could not have seen what was written on it. One thing to note about the word of God is its openness and absolute honesty as to sin and how it condemns it in the life of a believer. There is no duplicity in the word of God and nothing concealed and hidden in it as far as God's standards are concerned. In this it is a sharp contrast to the next vision of the woman hidden in the midst of the ephah. With man very often evil is hidden and there is that which may be devious and deceiving, but God's word is open and can be relied on.

Before Israel can enjoy the future blessings of millennial glory, the word of God must be allowed to be effective in the life of the nation. It must be obeyed and its searching character submitted to, so that it produces repentance and change. The interpreting angel tells Zechariah that the scroll represents "the curse that goeth forth over the face of the whole earth" (v.3). This accords with the fact that the law condemns every infraction against it and pronounces a curse against all who disobey it (Deut 22.14-26). The whole land of Israel had been characterised and indeed contaminated by the disobedience of the people to God's law. Those who remained in their sinful condition of rebellion would suffer the solemn judgment of this curse. The curse was a message of retribution addressed to Israel and destined to fall upon all who broke the commandments. Thus this solemn vision reveals that the word of God containing His law will cut off in punishment all who disobey it.

Its swiftness
What Zechariah saw was a huge unrolled scroll flying swiftly through the air with God's law inscribed on either side. This flying scroll may also be likened to a bird of prey hovering over its quarry ready to devour it. "It flies viewless and resistless, poising like a falcon over her prey, breathing a ruin the most dire and desolating…" (Thomas V. Moore). The thought of its flying speaks solemnly of the swiftness with which God's punishment will fall upon the transgressors. The scroll picturing the word of God reminds us of Hebrews 4.12: "For the word of God is living and operative, and sharper than any two-edged sword"(JND). "The figure of the flying roll therefore conveys the active power of God's word. You cannot play around with it. If you don't believe the word of God it condemns you. The word of God cannot be disobeyed with impunity, precisely *because it is the word of God*. It carries the very character of God Himself. Zechariah

chapter 4 tells us that 'the eyes of the Lord…run to and fro through the whole earth'. None can hide from his gaze and none can hide from His Word" (John Riddle, *Studies in Zechariah*, Believer's Magazine). How very true this is, and how often the power of God's word is felt keenly in the soul and pricks the conscience. God's word finds us out and often indeed finds us wanting. It is penetrating and makes its demands upon us. It insists that God cannot tolerate individual sin, and that all corruption must be put away whether, as here in these verses, it be stealing or swearing falsely, or any other sin committed against man or God.

Its size

Why was this flying roll so big? Is there any significance in its size? It was like a long banner flying through the sky. Clearly it was not a roll wrapped round a stick or that needed to be unwound to be opened and read as the custom was when the Scriptures were read in the synagogues. This the Lord Jesus did at Nazareth when reading from Isaiah 61. This roll was big, unrolled, and could be easily seen as it flew and moved to turn over to reveal what was on its other side. Its so solemn warning message was therefore openly declared to all. There was no way Zechariah could miss it or not see what was written on both sides of the roll. The word of God is clear and plain, especially in its message of condemnation upon sin. One has only to read Psalm 19.7-11 to find a summary of the integrity, honesty and power of the word of God, and its effectiveness and usefulness in the life of those who fear God and His word.

The measurement of the roll is doubtless also significant. It is twenty cubits by ten cubits (about 9m x 4.5m). This is interesting because it is exactly the measurement of the holy place in the tabernacle and also the size of the porch of Solomon's temple. Can one conclude that no significance is to be attached to this detail given here by the Holy Spirit? Without stretching a point it is submitted that there is an important and searching lesson in this. Just as the lampstand of the previous vision causes one immediately to think of the Mosaic lampstand in the holy place, so this flying roll connects itself with the holy place itself in the tabernacle. The fact too that the roll was written on both sides with the two tables of the law takes the reader back in thought to Exodus 32.15. It is good to see these links in Scripture and to ponder their meaning and message. The size then of the roll is the measure of the sanctuary. The fact that it has the same dimensions as the holy place emphasises that the measure in which the judgments of the roll will be carried out will be according to the measure of the holy place. While it is true that with this measure all sinners will be measured, it must not be overlooked that the primary reference has to do with the land of Israel. Thus the measure of judgment will not be according to man's standard, but according to the measure of the sanctuary. "Klieforth seems to have assigned the true reason for the roll having the dimensions of the sanctuary, and hence 'the curse' commences first at the House of

God (cp. Ezek 9.6; and 1 Pet 4.17). Men are not to be judged as to sin by their own measures or weighed in their own false balances. The measure of the sanctuary is that by which actions are to be weighed (1 Sam 2.3)" (C. H. H. Wright).

A practical lesson here should be applied to assemblies today. All judgment within it must be according to God's standard and not man's idea. The word of God must control everything in the assembly if its testimony is to be effective. The great ruin of the testimony down the ages has been the intrusion of man's ways and man's intellect into the things of God. God's word is openly displaced. The sin of Christendom has been to set aside the plain teaching of the word of God and to replace it with methods and traditions that are entirely humanly devised. Yet assemblies too are not immune from adopting practices which have no authority from Scripture. In this vision of the divine principles all should make sure that personally and collectively they are governed by the word of God. The remnant who had returned to Jerusalem were right to be concerned about God's law and should have seen from this vision that God's word was still to be the standard now that they were in a new phase of Israel's history. Their fresh circumstances demanded that they revered the word of God. If they manifested this spirit God would bless them.

Its sides

In v.3 it is specified that the roll was written on both sides – "On this side" and "on that side - that is on the front and back. The important thing to notice here is what was written on it. On each side of the roll the law of God is written. God chooses two of the prohibitions from the Ten Commandments to represent the whole of the law. Thus the curse will fall on "every one that stealeth" and "every one that sweareth". Theft is found in the second table of the law in the eighth commandment. It concerns responsibility manward. On the other side of the roll is "swearing falsely by God's name". This is the third commandment of the first table and relates to responsibility to God. Thus "the central commandment from each of the two tables of the Decalogue are selected as illustrative of the whole plainly implying that the breach of the one commandment constituted a breaking of the whole and rendered the individual a transgressor" (F. A. Tatford). God's curse will fall upon both thief and perjurer. Those who break these commandments will be rooted out or removed from Israel. Both then will be judged by the curse, the one according to the one side of the scroll, the other according to the other side. Sin against man and sin against God will be punished. The Lord Jesus summed up the ten commandments in Luke 10.27: "Thou shalt love the Lord thy God with all thy heart, and with all thy soul, and with all thy strength, and with all mind; and thy neighbour as thyself".

Whatever sin is committed against others has the element of stealing in it, and any sin committed against God will always have falsehood in it. Of course for sinners (those who are not saved) who have not judged these roots of evil in their hearts they will not escape the curse of the judgment of God, but will be cut off. Hence it is true that the curse "goeth forth over the face of the whole earth", but in the context it needs to be stressed again that God's people are particularly in view. The land of Israel had been contaminated by disobedience to God's law. So, if the remnant were to prosper in the rebuilding of the temple, honesty of action and purity of speech must mark them. In Malachi 3.8 (cp. Neh 13.10) theft is the charge the prophet makes as he accuses the people of sacrilege. They were guilty of robbing God. Malachi complains strongly of this. The Jews "robbed God" by neglecting to give to Him for the building of the temple, whilst they built their own houses (Hag 1.4), thus forswearing their obligations to Him. Believers too can rob God by applying to their own selfish purpose that which belongs to God.

Its severity

Verse 4 makes solemn reading and should be read soberly for it shows the effects of the flying roll. God's curse is seen moving among the households of Israel seeking to find and apprehend offenders. When either the thief or he that sweareth is found they will be punished swiftly and severely. The thief may enter into other people's houses, but the curse will enter his own house, not coming just for a brief visit, but remaining to destroy to its very foundation. The destruction of its timber and stones is symbolic of the destruction of all the personal interests and possessions of the unbeliever in Israel. It should be made clear that this is not a picture of man's final punishment in the lake of fire, but rather the Lord cleansing out of His Kingdom all things that offend. This judgment will be carried out on earth. Of course, later at the end of the Millennium these same unbelievers will have to be summoned to the Great White Throne to be judged there according to their works. Notice the certainty of this judgment: God says, "I will bring it forth" – there is no way of stopping it. Notice the scrutiny of the judgment: "it shall enter into the house…" - there is no exception! Notice the permanency of the judgment: "it shall remain in the midst of his house" - there is no end! Notice finally the intensity of the judgment: "…shall consume it with the timber thereof and stones thereof" – there is no escape! How solemn all this is. While the context here has to do with Israel, no believer can assume that, because we are not under law but under grace, the believer may therefore do as he pleases. This should not be and cannot be according to the teaching of Scripture. More than one Scripture makes clear that dishonesty, impurity, and indeed any sin committed by a believer will not be tolerated by God and must be dealt with in judgment if not confessed and put away. 1 Corinthians 11.27-31, Galatians 6.7-8, and Colossians 3.25 should be seriously pondered by every Christian as these passages show that believers who sin will suffer God's dealings with them and loss at the Judgment Seat of Christ. It may be good to add, however, that while sowing and reaping is a Scriptural principle and that grace is not an excuse for licence, yet God in His grace may choose to work to save us from the full consequences of sin. If this were not so, no believer would survive very long. As an Old Testament example David and Bathsheba illustrate just this point. Both, according to the law, should have been put to death. This did not happen. They did suffer for their sin, but grace allowed that judgment to be mitigated.

The judgment seems comparable to that of Leviticus 14 in connection with the removal of leprosy from the house. When the priest was to deal with the disease of leprosy – a type of sin in the Old Testament – similar language is used to that of Zechariah 5.4: "Behold, if the plague be spread in the house, it is a fretting leprosy in the house: it is unclean. And he shall break down the house, the stones of it, and the timber thereof, and all the mortar of the house; and he shall carry them forth out of the city into an unclean place" (Lev 14.44-45). So it is here, for every vestige of sinners and of sin shall be carried away. The contaminative element God will totally eradicate. This must be so if the testimony of Israel seen in the previous vision is to be fulfilled. God will punish those who take away from His word and He will punish those who add to His word. If the testimony of any assembly is to be effective then sin must be purged and put away by believers who are in these assemblies.

In concluding the consideration of the vision of the flying roll, the lesson from it must be emphasised and not forgotten that God will judge all persistent evil committed by the returning remnant. No Israelite in Zechariah's day could hide their sin or escape God's retribution, and the same applies to believers today. Sin, whether in the individual or in the family, will bring ruin and devastation.

The Seventh Vision. The Divine Prophecy – the Ephah
Question: "Lord, will the evil habits learned in Babylon be cast away?"

Verses 5-11: The Ephah
This is the only one of the eight visions where the interpreting angel bids Zechariah to lift up his eyes and identify an object. Previously he had done this without being directed to do so. Some consider the vision to be the most perplexing of all Zechariah's night visions. Because he was not able to identify what he saw, Zechariah answered, "What is it?". The interpreting angel told him, "This is an ephah…". In the previous vision of vv.1-4 Zechariah learned that God would deal with sinning individuals and remove them from the land. This vision goes a step further and pictures God removing all wickedness from the land and in particular, we believe, the snare of commerce and materialism that had taken over the people after being in Babylon. Some commentaries regard the ephah as setting forth the removal of wickedness in a general way and not as representative

of commerce. The ephah must obviously represent something, but what? Just as in the previous visions the imagery seen by Zechariah is symbolic of prophetic realities, so here, it is submitted, the ephah is symbolic of the principle of trade and commerce. This should be honest (Ezek 45.10), but sadly so often in Israel it was commonly perverted by greed (Amos 8.5).

The ephah was a large Hebrew dry measure, similar to the bushel in the western world. The ephah Zechariah saw was a basket or container that held an ephah of grain or flour. Here it is a symbol of commerce. Israel had learned the arts of commerce while in Babylon and have ever since beaten the Gentiles in this work, but much of it among God's people had become corrupt. In order to understand this vision, the question must be asked, "What did the Jews bring to their land from Babylon when they returned after their captivity?". The answer is - commercialism. They had been an agricultural people before they went to Babylon, but many of the Jews born in Babylon had become people of the city and successful merchants. So, in this vision we will see that it is the spirit of competitive commercialism that is represented by the woman in the ephah, for both the ephah and the talent are measures of commodities. Commerce had become the new principle with which the Jews had become imbibed in Babylon. Many of the Jews, then, in the returned remnant from Babylon had become infected with the spirit of Babylon and the virus caught during their time in Babylon has never been eradicated from them. It will not be, until the Lord restores them and they are set in millennial conditions, for then Jerusalem will not be a commercial centre, but a religious centre.

The continuing progress of commerce (v.6)
The interpreting angel in answer to Zechariah's question replies, "This is an ephah that goeth forth". The words, "goeth forth", which are repeated, picture commerce like a mighty army marching swiftly forward. It speaks prophetically of the rise and reign of commerce in the end times. Commerce will have universal sway, for we read, "This is their resemblance through all the earth". This indicates that the people resembled an ephah. The description, too, is all-embracing and takes in all the land of Israel and the whole world. Before the Lord returns to the earth in glory and power the Jews in the time of the Tribulation for the most part will be given over to and obsessed with the spirit of materialism. Commerce and materialism as we know it is everywhere today. Sadly even many Christians can be and are influenced and motivated by it. In what must be now the last days, commerce is the big thing. It is not for religious purposes that men lay cables, build better ships, faster planes, bigger airports and highways, make treaties, invent, scheme, and strive. All is done in the interests of commerce and material ends. Today almost everyone in the civilized world is caught up with commerce in one way or another. It is hard to avoid it in today's world. Believers need to make sure that the spirit of Babylon is not in the heart.

What, then, is the spirit of Babylon? The spirit of Babylon seeks not heaven, is content with worldly success, emphasises the social over the spiritual, and in the extreme is rampant materialism, costly luxuries, the noise of music, and utter godlessness. In the commercial Babylon in Revelation 18 it is materialism, merchandise, money, music, merriment, and magnificence. All these and more are seen now, but in the Tribulation they will be very much the order of the day, causing multitudes of people to be so gripped by these things that they will forget God and live for time and self. Therefore, the one great reigning power will be commerce. It is gaining ascendancy now. It is "going forth". Have we been affected by it, or have we by God's help overcome the snare of materialism? The Bible is really the tale of two cities – Babylon and the New Jerusalem. Which city are we really building for? As this vision concerns the nation of Israel it is interesting, but not surprising to point out that many Jews will be in Babylon during the three and a half years of the Antichrist's reign. This is why there is the call from God in Revelation 18.4, "Come out of her, my people". Some of God's people in that day - Jews - will have lingered in association with this Mecca of society. In Isaiah 11.11 there is an interesting reference predicting that in the future "the Lord shall set his hand again the second time to recover the remnant of his people, which shall be left". Among the eight areas from which God will recover them, Shinar (Babylon) is mentioned! God will not have His people of that day mixed up with or controlled by the commercial principle.

The corrupting principle of commerce (vv. 7-8)
Zechariah then sees a talent of lead. A talent among the Hebrews was their largest commercial weight. It was a circular plate of lead weighing around 1cwt (50.5 kilos) - the measure of quantity. It is a symbol, as already suggested, of merchandise. Commerce at the end time will be corrupt. This vision is a prophecy of how God will remove this evil from His people. Just as the Lord by His grace took away the filthy garments of Joshua in ch.3, signifying the taking away of the uncleanness of Israel, so here He carries away the ephah, signifying He will take away from His people the wickedness of corrupt dealing. It is important to point out of course that there is nothing wrong with honest trading and all Christians involved in business and trade should certainly, in being concerned about their testimony, see to it that in all their dealings they are honest, just, and dependable. Here, however, it is the nation of Israel having been tainted by corrupt dealing.

The woman in the vision is pictured as being hidden in the ephah. She is viewed as preparing to spring up from her imprisonment, but she is not permitted to rise. There is restriction on the woman. It is true that God restrains wickedness from being fully developed in the world. This idea is seen in the teaching of Paul in 2 Thessalonians 2.6-9, where in his description of the Antichrist or lawless one he says, "And then shall that

Wicked be revealed", implying that Antichrist had been previously in existence, though unseen. So with this woman, for she had been in existence in the ephah all along, but it was not until the lead cover was lifted that she was seen. This weight of lead on the mouth of the ephah is keeping the woman down and corresponds with Paul's statement, "And now ye know what withholdeth that he might be revealed in his time". There will be a supernatural power which will hold back the Antichrist until the appointed time. This may be compared with the heavy plate which keeps down the woman. The same is really also true of commerce. This type of wickedness is not seen destroyed, but limited. It will be dealt with when its character comes out fully. Its destruction is not mentioned in this vision. One needs to go to Revelation 18 to find a prophecy of this. A woman in Scripture is often seen to be a picture of a corrupt religious system as seen in Matthew 13.33, Revelation 2.20, and chs.17 & 18 where we have the harlot – religious Babylon. She is to be distinguished from the two women in Zechariah 5.9 who are seen coming out of the ephah, though it seems clear that these women further the interests of the woman in v.7. If this is the case, then the fact that she "sitteth in the midst of the ephah" suggests that she is resting and settled there, as Israel were in the past in their idolatry and will be in the future in commerce. In fact, from Revelation 18 the whole world is seen to be controlled and influenced by commerce. There is a lesson here, for how easy it is for the believer to be tranquil under sin as if we were at home in it and to be at ease, too, in this materialistic world. The very thought ought to fill us with holy fear and give each believer the strong desire not to be so influenced by materialism as to find himself settled in it and conditioned by it. How true to a large extent this is of the Jew in the present, but it will be much more so in Tribulation days. The word to the remnant in Zechariah's time is a must for the believer in this day and age. The believer, too, needs to guard against the desire for gain.

Is it not to be admitted that even now everything around us indicates that the time is approaching when the prophecy of this vision will be fulfilled? The woman, it can be said, is in the ephah, but not yet manifest. All the elements in this vision are rapidly increasing in view of the final development. Wickedness is manifesting itself with startling force. Many forms of sin and crime have existed in the past, but so often were hidden and carried on in secret. Now wickedness has no shame. The moral consciousness of so many people today has to a large extent ceased to be troubled. The media present vice in such a familiar way that with most it hardly causes even a shrug of the shoulder. The terrible desire for instant gain is seen in gambling, whether through the lottery, football pools, or on the race course. It is not confined now to Monte Carlo or Las Vegas. It is carried on openly in many places, even on the Stock Exchanges and places of business. This is by no means an exaggeration. Bad as it is now it will be far worse during the Tribulation. Materialism will be the order of the day. Everything will revolve around it. All these things will not be allowed to come to a head until the Rapture of the Church has taken place and the Antichrist is manifested. How important for the Christian to be alert to the solemn message in the woman in the ephah.

The controlling power of commerce (v.9)

God wants to show to His people in this part of the vision that He will take away commerce from Israel and put it down in its place. There are three points to remark on in this verse: the women supporting the ephah; the influences advancing the ephah; and the exaltation of the ephah. Why are two women seen carrying the ephah? It would be easy to suggest, as some do, that the reason is because of the woman inside and that two women are used because two are required to carry such a large and heavy object. This may suffice as a literal and physical answer, but it is better to view them as symbolic of God's instruments to accomplish His purpose in removing commerce back to its place. The women may be a picture of civil and ecclesiastical authority. Both will be dominated by the ephah and will become supporters of its rule. These will unite as sponsors and protectors of the system. Concerning the women it is said that "the wind was in their wings; for they had wings like the wings of a stork: and they lifted up the ephah between the earth and the heaven".

One cannot agree with Eugene H. Merril who interprets the wind as referring to the Spirit of God and says, "The same spirit that empowered Zerubbabel in temple building (4.6) was now at work transporting wickedness to her destination". In the present writer's view it is better and more fitting to see the wind as picturing demonic and satanic forces propelling the ephah forward. God will, in His sovereign purpose, allow such sinister influences to be His instruments to control commerce. It is solemn to note in Revelation 18.2 that the Babylon of the future will be "the habitation of devils (demons)…and a cage of every unclean and hateful bird". That demons will be active in Israel during the period of the Tribulation appears to be borne out in Zechariah 13.2 where God says, "I will cause the (false) prophets and the unclean spirit to pass out of the land" (compare this reference with Revelation 9.20; 13.4 & 15; Matthew 12.43-45). There will be a Master-mind behind the monetary system of the world of the future.

The fact that the wings are like the wings of a stork is also significant. In the first place the storks, for the Israelite, were unclean birds, according to Leviticus 11.19 and Deuteronomy 14.18. The image is therefore solemnly apt because of the unclean spirits which will be behind the advancement of commerce. The wings of a stork are very large. They are strong, motherly birds which are capable of carrying loads a long distance in flight. They will give a motherly attention to their task. Some have pointed out that the word "stork" (HASIDA – 2624) can mean "faithful one". The stork-like women will be allowed of God to faithfully stick to their purpose in taking the ephah to the God-appointed terminus.

Zechariah sees the women lifting up the ephah between earth and heaven. He sees the ephah flying through the air swiftly to its destination. The word "heaven" (SHAMAYIM – 8064) in "from earth to heaven" seems to have the idea of being "lofty", coming from a root having that meaning. It points to the exaltation of commerce during the Tribulation. It will be the big thing around which life will revolve. It will indeed dictate the habits and conduct of the world. Men under the reign of the Antichrist will believe that all the differences between peoples and nations will have at last been solved, not through politics or religion, but through trade. The so-called "mighty dollar" today will be as nothing compared to these days when commerce will hold sway.

The centralising point of commerce (vv.10-11)

The concern of Zechariah now is the destination of the ephah. The angel answers, "To build it an house in the land of Shinar". The reference to the land of Shinar is, of course to Babylonia (see Gen 10.10; 11.2; Is 11.11). In the plain of the land of Shinar men of the world in those early times first attempted to unite in rebellion against God and to form a universal confederacy. From this and several other passages in the word of God one may conclude that there will be a future centre of commerce that will attract men to it. If the reader carefully considers Isaiah 13 and Revelation 18 he ought to discover that what is said here about the building of a base or centre for commerce must be accepted as literal, and just as literal as the building of the temple in the next chapter (6.13). Today there is an increasing tendency for everything to concentrate around the interests of commerce. Commerce now is away from its base, but when it returns to where it began its house will be built. Man's great earthly centre will be commercial, but God's will be religious. God will allow commerce to develop and centralize in Babylon. As there was a city Babylon built in the beginning in Genesis 11, so there will be a city of Babylon built in the end times. What happened in Genesis is going to happen again.

Some do not see a future literal Babylon in Scripture. One of the main arguments used against the literal interpretation is that the predictions concerning the destruction of Babylon in Isaiah and Jeremiah have already been fulfilled in past history. H. A. Ironside, for example, is typical of this stance when he writes, "Both Jeremiah and Isaiah make clear, in my judgment, that Babylon has fallen to rise no more. It has been literally burned with fire and utterly destroyed, and God Himself has solemnly declared that for that wicked city there shall be no healing nor revival".

Is this view sustainable? A brief look at the context of Isaiah 13 should help. It concerns "The burden of Babylon" (v.1). While it is true that there may have been a partial fulfilment of the prophecy it is submitted that much in the chapter yet remains to be fulfilled with regard to the city of

Babylon. One principal question which needs to be answered and which will make clear that the doom of Babylon is yet to be fulfilled is, "When will its destruction take place?". In answer to this, the prophecy follows on from Isaiah 12 where the day of Israel's salvation is predicted. By connecting this with Jeremiah 50.17-20 it will be seen that until Babylon is destroyed Israel's salvation as a nation cannot take place. Its destruction will take place, says Isaiah, in the Day of the Lord (Is 13.9). We are not yet in the period of the Day of the Lord. This is yet future. In v.10 Isaiah speaks of changes which occur in the heavens. This links with Matthew 24.29 and takes place between the end of the Tribulation and the second advent of Christ.

In v.20 of Isaiah 13 such will be the complete overthrow and desolation of the future Babylon that Isaiah says, "It shall never be inhabited", yet Babylon was still there in the Apostle Peter's day (1 Pet 5.13). Certainly it had lost all its former glory, but a city called Hillah was built in AD1100 largely of material salvaged from the ruins of Babylon, contrary to Jeremiah 51.26 where we read, "And they shall not take of thee a stone for a corner, nor a stone for a foundation; but thou shalt be desolate forever, saith the Lord". The ruins of ancient Babylon have been also used to build other cities. The city of Hillah in Iraq existed on the site of suburbs of ancient Babylon and in 1890 had 10,000 inhabitants. According to the latest information it is a city with about 540,000 inhabitants (2005 estimate), lying on the Al Hillah stream, the eastern branch of the Euphrates river about 70 miles (110 km) south of Baghdad. It is a port and the main cereal market of the Middle East Euphrates area. We mention these interesting facts because it goes a long way to show that the utter desolation spoken of in Isaiah 13.20-22 has not yet come to pass. The future great city of Babylon will be the seat of Satan during the Tribulation, but will be destroyed by a sudden cataclysm in much the same way as Sodom was. History tells us that the ancient Babylon was never destroyed like that, but in 541 BC it was captured by Cyrus, who quietly and quickly took it over. There was no destruction of the city. All these points should put it beyond doubt that the complete destruction of Babylon in the land of Shinar is yet to be fulfilled. The home of commerce in Babylon is yet to be built, but built it will be. When it is set up men will think the centre permanent, but God will intervene as He did in the days of Genesis 11 and He will destroy it.

In leaving Zechariah 5 and the visions of the flying role and ephah, what is the message for the believer today? The flying roll speaks of the word of God controlling the life of the believer. It should ever be hidden in the heart to keep us from sin and to live that life which is free from all dishonesty and falsehood. The ephah speaks of the need for each believer to be marked by godly contentment and not be overcome by the snare of materialism. No believer can serve both God and mammon. The aim of each believer should not be to seek to grab all he can out of this world, but to find all his satisfaction in Christ, ever realizing that the things of this world, like the ephah, will all be carried away one day. How striking and telling are the six times repeated words in connection with all that Babylon will enjoy in its music, merriment, luxuries and delicacies – "NO MORE" (Rev 18.14, 21-23). All that the modern world of that day has to offer will suddenly be gone forever!

ZECHARIAH 6

The Eighth Vision. The Divine Providence – the Four Chariots
Question: "Lord, are there any protective forces for us?"

Verses 1-8: The Four Chariots

This vision is the last of the series of visions given to Zechariah. The long and eventful night for him was about to end. It is good to see the vision in its setting and its links with the previous visions, and also in its clear connection with what follows in vv.9-15. The vision links with the first vision, for the images are similar to those described in 1.7-17, but some of the details are significantly different. The focus of attention here is on the horses and chariots rather than the riders, and their ministry is that of accomplishing God's purpose. In the first vision there were many horses and riders, but here there are only four chariots, each with their horses and no riders. In the first vision horses are seen standing in a valley among the myrtle trees. There it is Israel in weakness and humiliation. In the eighth vision horses are seen emerging from between two mountains made of brass. Here it is Israel being defended by God and exalted over their enemies. The series of visions began with angels patrolling the earth and reporting back to God. The same is seen here in v.7. This vision is really the answer to the prayer of the pre-incarnate Christ in 1.12, "O Lord of hosts, how long…?". This vision, then, shows how the problem of the first vision will be resolved. The vision links, as already indicated (but important to recall here), with the previous two in the following manner. In 5.1-4 God is seen removing the sin of the individual. In 5.5-11 He is seen removing the sin of Israel nationally. In 6.1-8 He is dealing with the sin of the nations. Then again, it is good to note that in its placing here it comes before the symbolic transaction of the crowning of Joshua the high priest in vv.9-15, and indicates that the judgments seen in this vision will pave the way for the crowning of Christ in His Kingdom.

The message of the vision is that God has not ceased to carry out His government in the world and He will yet judge Israel's enemies. It shows that there is a working of God in His government and providence which goes on during the time of the Gentile kingdoms. There is something going on all the time which is hidden from the eyes of men, but which is providentially causing things to work out for the furtherance of the plan of the Lord of all the earth. In the vision we shall consider the four chariots, the four horses, the four winds, and the two mountains. The symbols used are all most intriguing and invite close consideration. What is the meaning of the horses and the significance of their colours? What do the two mountains of brass represent? What or who are the four winds? Such questions are interesting and thought provoking, for God in these things most surely has something important to teach the remnant of Zechariah's time, and also the believer today.

The four chariots (v.1)

For the last time during this night season Zechariah lifted up his eyes and now beheld in this vision four chariots. The four chariots with their horses represented the "four spirits" from God, that is, four angels assigned to different parts of the world to do God's bidding (v.5; cp. Heb 1.14). "The chariots of God are twenty thousand, even thousands of angels" (Ps 68.17). The presence of chariots suggests warfare and this implies judgment. "For, behold, the Lord will come with fire, and with his chariots like a whirlwind, to render [bring down] his anger with fury, and his rebuke with flames of fire" (Is 66.15). Chariots were among the most formidable of ancient military engines and were also used on great state occasions. They came to be symbolic of authority and of resistless might, as may be seen in Psalm 68.17, Isaiah 66.15, Habakkuk 3.8, and Haggai 2.22. They represent the invisible mighty agencies sent forth by God to accomplish His purpose. In Psalm 104.3-4 we read, "Who maketh the clouds his chariot: who walketh upon the wings of the wind: Who maketh His angels spirits".

The chariots are obviously war chariots. Some commentators consider that the fact that there are four represents the four world empires mentioned in the prophecy of the image in Daniel 2. Is this a correct view? The writer of this commentary believes that the four kingdoms in Daniel are not presented here, for two reasons at least. First, it is plain from the context of this vision that the four chariots are described as the four spirits (winds) of heaven in v.5. Second, the four geographical notations in no way conform to the four kingdoms of Daniel 2. These chariots rather represent the different agents of God's providence that He will yet use toward the nations that have been the inveterate enemies of His people. The fact that the chariots are four in number points symbolically to God's universal judgment, just as we saw in the vision of the four horns and carpenters in 1.18-20. The same idea again was seen in the four winds of the heaven in 2.6.

The two mountains of brass (v.2)

Zechariah sees the chariots coming out from between two mountains of brass. What is the meaning of these mountains, and why brass? Some think the mountains are Mount Zion and the Mount of Olives, between which lay the valley of Jehoshaphat. These two mountains certainly figure much in Israel's history and both will be important in Israel's future. Some believe the colour bronze was due to the rising sun. This results in the interpretation that the first vision takes place in the evening and the last at the rising of the sun. While the scene that follows the visions in vv.9-15 may well be a morning one, this interpretation seems somewhat far fetched. A third suggestion is that they are the two parts of the Mount of Olives which will be divided when the Messiah returns to the earth. This is rather an ingenious proposition, for this is exactly what the prophet tells us will happen when the Lord comes to the earth (14.1-4), but again this idea overlooks the fact that the cleaving in two of the Mount of Olives will occur, as mentioned, at the second advent of Christ, whereas the vision here of the four chariots of judgment rather points in its setting and significance to the judgments which will take place leading up to the second advent.

On balance it is much better in the context, and in line with the contents of all the eight visions, to see the mountains and the brass as figures representing truths in relation to God and His purposes providentially in the world. The mountains seem to stand for God's high and immoveable purpose in government and judgment. He is the great God of judgment and puny man cannot interfere with or alter God's purposes in judgment. This will be true in the Tribulation period leading up to the Lord's coming to the earth. Nothing man can do can stop God moving in judgment with men and nations. That the two mountains are made of brass shows they are symbolic. There are no mountains of brass in Israel or anywhere else in the word of God. Quite often brass in Scripture speaks of judgment. The brazen altar in the tabernacle and the temple was made of wood covered with bronze. They were the places where sin was judged when the sacrifices were burned. The serpent that Moses put on the pole was made of bronze (Num 21.9). When the Lord Jesus appeared to John and was about to judge the churches, His feet were likened to bronze "as if they burned in a furnace" (Rev 1.15). The fact that there are *two* mountains, would emphasize that God's judgments will not only be great and stable, but also perfectly just. Deuteronomy 19.15 shows that "two" speaks of adequate testimony. This to God was a most important principle in judging matters.

The four winds (vv.4-5)

These four winds, or spirits, represent angels. Hebrews 1.14 teaches that angels are spirit beings – "Are they not all ministering spirits". The four spirits, then, are angelic beings from heaven, ministers of God appointed by the Lord of all the earth to implement judgment on the nations opposing Israel before the Lord returns to the earth. If it is asked, "How is this judgment executed?", the answer is that the judgment of God will be administered by the power of God's angels. There are examples of this in incidents of the Old Testament (see 2 Kings 19.35 and 2 Chronicles 18.18-21), and the book of Revelation is full of the power of angelic agency in bringing divine judgment in varying degree and character upon the world and nations in it (Rev 7.1; 9.14-15; 15.1; 16.1-17).

The subject of angels and their activities for God was brought into prominence in recent history by remarkable stories told by soldiers who declared that they saw heavenly guardians during the memorable retreat at the battle of Mons. An army corporal in 1916 gave his testimony before a large audience in Preston. His testimony was as follows. "It is an absolute fact that the angels came to the assistance of the British forces at a critical period of the Mons retreat on 25th August, 1914, and I cannot understand how people in this country can laugh at the testimony of so many eye-witnesses and say they were dreaming. There was no time for dreaming in that awful retreat. We were outnumbered by nine to one, and when we thought all was lost and were preparing to make the last stand, God intervened in a miraculous way. The Germans were coming to close quarters when suddenly a light appeared in the sky, small at first, but gradually it became brighter and brighter, and then there seemed to be something in the light which we could not at first discern. But God removed the scales from our eyes, and I saw with my own eyes three angels...There was no fighting then. We stood spellbound...I saw it all myself, and I ask you to believe me. There are others who will tell you the same, and I am certain as that I am standing here today that the angels came in answer to prayer to save us...I am convinced that the British army would have otherwise been annihilated...Many men who saw the apparition have been converted as a result". This is interesting, but as Christians it is easy to receive such testimonies with a measure of reserve. We must, however, not be absolutely incredulous, as if there were no such beings as angels, for they are mentioned in Scripture over 300 times and often have intervened visibly for the deliverance and protection of men and in the execution of judgment and punishment.

Angels are powerful beings, for only one angel was sent by God to slay 185,000 of the Assyrians (2 Kings 19.35). They are God's servants who obey His command (Ps 103.20). God may use them in blessing or in judgment or punishment as seen, for example, in Acts 12.7 & 23. While we read of angels in the Old Testament and learn from the book of Revelation that they have a future mission, they certainly are not redundant beings in this age of grace. Angels fly at the behest of God (Is 6.2), they engage in the battles of God (Rev 12.7), they enjoy the presence of God (Mt 18.10), and they serve the purpose of God. Angels are real and wonderful beings, for in their ministry there is a marked economy both of words and of the display of power. Their words are always few and directly to the purpose, and as for the power they exercise it is always ample, but never more than ample. They never indulge in the slightest self-display, and in their obedience they never go beyond the limits of their commission. They never add to or diminish the message they carry. They have no preferences in their service. No errand is beneath them. Whatever it is, it is for them an honour to serve their Lord. They consider not the nature of the command, but its author. One may learn much from them as to how to carry out God's service today. Humility, obedience, reverence, and diligence are their characteristics.

In 6.5 they stand before the Lord of all the earth, indicating they are ever and always ready to serve God and do His will. The passage already cited in Revelation 9.14-15 shows this too: "...And the four angels were loosed, which were prepared for an hour, and a day, and a month, and a year". There is surely a lesson here for those who would seek to serve God today. How good to be found in God's presence and ready to do His bidding. It is instructive to note the description of God here in Zechariah. He is, "the Lord of all the earth". God is not only the owner of the heavens, for he is often seen in Zechariah as "the Lord of hosts", but He is also the Sovereign owner of the earth (Ps 24.1). Men may dispute this, and Israel's enemies will move against them regardless of this, but God will arise to defend His people and through angelic agency remove the opposing powers to restore His people and set up Christ's Kingdom.

The horses (vv.6-8)

In the interpretation of the horses it is to be noticed that the red horses which are seen pulling the first chariot are not mentioned again in the vision. This is a difficulty that is not easy to explain, but see Baron and our later comments on v.7. It is assumed by some that four horses were attached to each chariot, but this is not stated. We will consider the horses in three ways.

The definition of their meaning

Horses fill up the picture in this vision and denote swiftness and strength in executing God's judgments in the lands to which they are sent. Horses are often used as symbols of swiftness (Jer 4.13), strength (Job 39.19), and sure-footedness (Is 63.13). One of the most graphic and detailed descriptions of a horse in all literature is found in Job 39.19-25. In prophecy, horses also play an important role, as in Joel 2.4-5 and Revelation 6.1-8 where four horses of different colours are associated with different tragedies. Military victories such as those of Genghis Khan or Alexander the Great would have been impossible without horses. When the exodus occurred, Pharaoh's army was equipped with horses and chariots (Ex 14-15). Herodotus reported the use of horses by the Persians in their postal system 3,000 years ago. The horse was used for war by Syrians (1 Kings 20.20), the Philistines (2 Sam 1.6), the Medes and Persians (Jer 50.42), and the Romans (Acts 23.23,32).

The differences in their mission

The different colours of the horses in each chariot must be of significance. Some writers do not attach much, if any, meaning to the colours of the horses and consider that no importance is to be placed on this, but rather on the fact that they were hitched to chariots of war, ready for immediate action to bring God's judgment upon the world. It seems strange that the Spirit of God should take the trouble to mention the colours specifically if they had no symbolic meaning whatsoever. If the horses' colours are significant, then Revelation 6.1-8 can assist us. In connection with the first four seals there, horses are mentioned. The different coloured horses in that passage symbolize varying types of judgment to fall upon the earth. Each of the first four seals set forth successive judgments: the success of the false Christ, the slaughtering of men, the scarcity of food, and the scaling down of world population. So far as the colours of the horses in Zechariah's vision are concerned, they must have the same meaning here as they do in the first vision (1.8). The red horses symbolize war and bloodshed; the black horses, famine; and the white horses victory and triumph as seen in the conquests of the Antichrist in Revelation 6.2, while the speckled or "grisled" point to pestilence and other fatal plagues. There are no dappled horses in the vision John had, but they could well symbolize plagues. During the Day of the Lord God will use wars, famines, plagues, and death to punish the nations of the earth.

The directions of their movement
    The second, third and fourth war chariots mentioned in vv.2 & 3 are now referred to again and their destinations are specified. The black horses are sent to the north country, and the white go after them. North of Jerusalem is the direction from which most of Israel's enemy invaders descended on the Promised Land (i.e. Babylon: see Jer 1.14; 4.6; 6.22; and Ezek 1.4). The grisled are sent to the south country, while the bay or strong go forth walking to and fro through the earth. Because of the geographical situation of Israel, all her enemies came against her from the north or from the south. The Mediterranean Sea on the west and the Arabian Desert on the east would have made it very difficult for any major foreign force to invade Israel from these directions. At the time of Zechariah the north country was Babylon and the south country Egypt. These had been Israel's enemies, but the complete fulfilment of this vision looks on to a future day.
    The vision is really concerned with the end time, when from the north Israel's most terrible enemy will come. Israel will face their great northern foe, the Assyrian, or the king of the north (Is 10.12; Dan 11.15). Assyria was Israel's ancient and most bitter enemy. They, headed by their leader, will rise up against them again in the last days, but that king will be dealt with and destroyed by the Lord Jesus. How significant then is the reference to the north country when one considers that the vision is dealing prophetically with the time of the end, when the invasion from the north will take place. Since, according to the AV, the white horses follow the black, this would indicate how, in the punitive judgment upon the northern foe, victory will be gained. (It is fair to say that some think that the reference to the white horses should be rendered, "…went forth to the land which is behind them", i.e. to the west.) Daniel 11.40-43 reveals that in this period Israel will also be invaded by Egypt – the king of the south.
    In v.7 the bay, or strong horses, are seen patrolling the earth. These horses are given divine permission to go forth over the earth – "Get you hence, walk to and fro through the earth. So they walked to and fro through

the earth". This is obviously not just the land of Israel here, but the whole world. Angelic beings will patrol the world, ever watchful that other hostile nations do not harm Israel. The judgments of God here are world wide. We have mentioned previously that the red horses in the first chariot are not mentioned again in the passage when God begins to take action in judgment, but Tatford and others suggest that they may be identical to the bay or strong horses in this verse. If this is the case then it would solve an apparent problem in the passage, but this suggestion is by no means fully satisfactory. The red horses must have a service to do for God in these times of judgment. They could just be waiting for God's bidding.

The final word of the vision in v.8 contains this message from God to Zechariah: "Behold, these that go toward the north country have quieted my spirit in the north country". The horses that had gone out to the north had appeased God's wrath there. This in measure had been fulfilled in that under His sovereign control Persia had been allowed to take over Babylon. In Zechariah's time Babylon had fallen to the Persians twenty years earlier in 539 BC, and in their case God alone could say that His anger was satisfied. While God's judgment had already visited Babylon, it must be understood that in the fulfilment of this vision His spirit will be quieted there in the end time, when Babylon and all enemies from the north, including the king of the north, will be judged. Thus the prophecy looks on to a future day of the Lord's judgments, towards the end of the Great Tribulation, when He will punish the last enemies to face Israel. Only when this happens will God's spirit be appeased and find perfect rest. In the first vision it was said, "The earth sitteth still, and is at rest" (1.11), but in this last vision the earth is a scene of judgment and much unrest as God begins to intervene in the affairs of the nations of the world for the blessing of His people. How interesting then and reassuring to the remnant that this vision returns to the message of the first, showing that the prayer of the pre-incarnate Christ for Israel (1.12) will then be fulfilled. Then, at last, God will turn in mercy to His people and restore them to Himself.

In summarizing the important message of the vision, it sets forth the solemn subject of God's judgment upon the nations of the earth. In the four spirits of v.5 is seen the scope of the judgments – they are universal. In the colours of the horses (vv.2-3) is seen the character of the different judgments. In the four chariots (v.1) is seen the agents God uses to carry out these judgments – the angels. In the fact that God's judgments are the subject of this final vision is seen the necessity of them, in order to clear the way for the return of the Messiah and the establishing of His Kingdom.

Zechariah's vision assures us that God is in absolute control of the future and will deal in judgment with the Gentile nations during the Tribulation. True, as the Apostle Peter says, God is longsuffering (2 Pet 3.9), but there comes a time when the nations fill up the measure of their sins (Gen 15.16), and then God's judgment must certainly fall. The remnant are taught in this vision that where the fiercest opposition abounds, even there God will have His agents to triumph in dealing with it. Zechariah and the little remnant are clearly told in this that God does have protective forces working behind the scenes for His people, and they have every reason not to despair, but to have hope in God and wait on Him, for in the end He will not fail them.

Verses 9-15: A Symbolic Transaction – the Crowning of Joshua

The series of night visions now comes to a fitting end with the crowning of Joshua the high priest. The placing of this ceremony after the visions is instructive. It forms a kind of climax to the eight visions and teaches that immediately after God overcomes the Gentile world powers (seen pictured in the horse-drawn chariots) the Messiah will be manifested in His glory to set up His Kingdom (typified in the crowning of Joshua). Wherever one looks in the prophetic Scriptures this is the usual order of events in God's future programme. See for example Revelation 19.19-21, and 20.4-6, where we have the second advent of Christ first to destroy the Gentile armies and then to set up the Kingdom which will follow this. It is important to understand clearly that the scene here is not a vision, but an action that takes place which has great prophetic significance.

This new section is introduced, in a way that is usual in the prophets, by the statement: "And the word of the Lord came unto me, saying…". Zechariah is charged by the Lord to meet three men who had come as a deputation from Babylon with silver and gold for the making of a crown. Zechariah is bidden to take the gift from the men and with it make a crown for Joshua. With this crown he is personally to engage in a symbolic act by placing the crown on the head of Joshua. The whole transaction was to have great meaning. Whether Zechariah himself understood that his action had a prophetic bearing is not clear, but he must have wondered and considered it strange. There are few actual incidents recorded in Zechariah, but this scene presents one of the great prophecies of Israel's Messiah. It is perhaps one of the most valuable we have in the Old Testament. The scene, so interesting and full of meaning, will be considered simply under three headings: a commandment - vv.9-11; a coronation - vv.12-13; a commemoration - vv.14-15.

A commandment (vv.9-11)

The night during which Zechariah saw his visions has now ended and the morning has dawned. The day mentioned in v.10 is probably the same as that of 1.7. What a suitable end to the night visions this crowning of Joshua is. The message of the visions has been clear that God will not only deal with the sin of Israel, but also with the evil of the nations and will destroy all the enemies of Israel. This will happen when Christ returns to the earth to be God's recognized and ideal King. It will be like a new dawn for Israel after their long night of suffering. It will be the morning of the Kingdom and will bring new hope and blessings to Israel.

The book of Zechariah commenced with a significant introduction in 1.1-6, and attention was drawn there to the meaning of three names mentioned in that section. Here in 6.9-15 the first major division of Zechariah concludes also with three names. As in ch.1 the names had spiritual import, so likewise is this true of the names of the three men who had come up to Jerusalem from Babylon with their offering. Zechariah was to find these men in the house of Josiah. There God commanded him to meet them, to take from them the precious silver and gold, and with it to make an elaborate crown. Who these men were, where they had come from, the time when they arrived at Jerusalem, and the gift they brought with them are all of interest, but the significance of their names has a particular message in this prophecy.

Heldai, the first of the three, means strong and speaks of the wonderful strength God will give to His people in a coming day when He will act supernaturally for them. They will not be able by their own might to overcome their foes nor deliver themselves from their greatest ever crisis that will befall them. Thus we read in the first message of the first oracle of chs.9-11 that God says, "I will strengthen the house of Judah", and again, "I will strengthen them in the Lord" (10.6,12). The second name, Tobijah, means goodness of God, and speaks of the wonderful fact that God will show great goodness to Israel even though they do not deserve it. This links with the second message in 9.17, for after all that their Messiah will have miraculously done for them, looking back they will be able to exclaim with joy, "For how great is his goodness, and how great is his beauty". The third man named is Jedaiah and his name means God knows. This thought is well illustrated in the third message. One only has to read carefully through ch.11 to see the perfect knowledge of God in anticipating in such detail events in the life of the Lord Jesus, especially in the rejection of the Lord and His being sold for thirty pieces of silver (11.12). How precise are the particulars even to the exact amount, and how perfectly God knew all that would happen in advance. Truly God knows. This is the one great matter that impresses the reader of a book like Zechariah. It reveals so wonderfully that because God knows all He therefore controls every situation and allows things to develop for His glory. We too can know God's strength in every aspect of life. We can rejoice in experiencing the Lord's goodness, and can be assured that He knows all. Every detail of the life of a believer is known to Him. These thoughts of God and what He can be to us should be so reassuring to every saint.

The gift of silver and gold brought by these men was probably intended to be used as an offering to God in connection with the building of the temple. Did this present a problem to these respected Jews, for money from Jews in Babylon was supposed to be used for the completion of the temple? Zechariah no doubt would explain to them that God had

commanded him to take the gift in order to make the crown for the head
of Joshua. Unusual as it was, the men complied with the request and gave
Zechariah the material. The word for crown is in the plural in the AV, but
we are not to think that Zechariah made two crowns, one of silver and one
of gold. No one wears two crowns on the head. The verb in v.14 is in the
singular, so the crown was to be a composite one. The word for "crowns"
(ATAROTH – 5850) "denotes here one single splendid crown, consisting
of several gold and silver twists wound together, or rising one above
another, as in Job 31.36, and just as in Revelation 19.12 Christ is said to
wear, not many separate diadems, but a crown consisting of several diadems
twisted together, as the insignia of His regal dignity" (Keil & Delitzsch).
Thus the command was given to place the crown on the head of Joshua.
By this act God was showing that in the coming day Christ His Son will be
crowned and will be both a Priest and a King. Though now believers "Crown
Him Lord of all", He is not yet King, but those who love Him can take their
gifts, like the woman's box of spikenard and pour it upon the head of
Christ. Just as the gifts of silver and gold were brought from Babylon to be
made into a crown for the head of Joshua, so the believer can, as it were,
take every gift he possesses to put it as a crown on the head of Christ.
Such gifts may come out of the earth and sometimes the offering may be
lowly, but they are truly consecrated and transfigured when they touch
Him.

A coronation (vv. 12-13)

When Joshua is crowned Zechariah is directed to address a prophetic
message to him. These two verses are full of Christ. Once again the Lord
Jesus is seen as the Branch, and then five things are stated of this view of
Him in these verses. First, as the Branch He will branch or shoot out;
second, as the Messiah He will build the temple; third He will bear or
carry the glory; fourth He shall sit and rule on his throne; and fifth He
shall be a priest on His throne. In summary, our Lord as the Branch is seen
prophetically in three ways. He is the Builder of the temple, the Bearer of
the glory and the Bringer of peace.

The man whose name is The BRANCH

Suddenly the Lord speaks to Zechariah to give to him what in fact is a
momentous prophetic word to Joshua the priest: "Behold the man whose
name is The BRANCH; and he shall grow up out of his place". The words
must have amazed Joshua and caused him to question who it was of whom
the Lord spoke. There is no possibility that the words addressed to Joshua
could apply to him. There is nothing in the passage to indicate whether
he understood that the words were referring to the Messiah to come. On
the other hand there is no way that the well known Messianic description,
the Branch, could refer to Joshua. All the passages in which it is found
speak of the dignity, greatness and the deity of the person of Israel's

Messiah. It is clearly a unique utterance. So important is it here that God Himself emphasizes it by repeating the statement that Messiah will build the temple. Its importance is also seen in the word "Behold" which is often used by the prophets to fix attention on something of great importance. Once again we have the Lord Jesus as the Branch (see 3.8). This time He is the *man* whose name is the Branch. Emphasis here is upon the manhood of the Lord Jesus. In 3.8 it was upon His servant character. It is of interest to note the fourfold description of the Lord as the Branch in Scripture and to see that each title corresponds to the presentation of Christ in the four Gospels. In Jeremiah 23.5, as the Branch He is the royal King; in Matthew he is seen as the righteous King. In Zechariah 3.8 He is the Branch the Servant; Mark's Gospel shows the Messiah as the perfect Servant of Jehovah. Here in the present passage He is "the man whose name is The BRANCH"; Luke presents the Messiah as true man. Finally, in Is 4.2 He is the Branch of the Lord; this description of Him corresponds with John's Gospel where He is seen as the Son of God.

Of the Lord as the Branch it is said, "He shall grow up out of his place". This would better read: "shoot forth from under him". This means that the Messiah would shoot up from His humble place of origin. It is true when He first came He was "as a tender plant" (Is 53.2), but this prophecy indicates that He will shoot upward and that He will branch out as a quickly growing plant until He is elevated and exalted to great heights. The words in the AV "grow up out of his place" do not, it would seem, refer to Bethlehem or Nazareth, but they mean that He shall grow up by His own power, without man's aid, in His conception and birth. He shall grow from below upwards, from lowliness to eminence. The idea seems to be that Christ's glory is growing, but not yet manifested as a *full grown tree.* "He shall not openly descend from heaven, in visible glory and greatness, but shall slowly grow up out of the earth, in lowly humiliation. This was true of him as a man, for He was the humble carpenter's son for thirty years, and grew slowly in the shade of Nazareth" (T. V. Moore). Now notice three precious aspects of prophetic truth concerning Messiah's person.

The builder of the temple
Twice over the prophecy repeats the mission and work of the Messiah. The statement at the beginning of v.13, "Even he shall build the temple of the Lord", is very emphatic, as is the pronoun "he". There can be no doubt that this temple will be built. When is this temple going to be built and what is it? It cannot, as some think, refer to the second temple of Zerubbabel which he had already commenced, for back at 4.9 it was predicted that he would finish it. It clearly must refer to another temple which the Messiah Himself will build. Some interpret the words to refer to the Church. It is true that our Lord is the builder of the Church. He said Himself, "I will build my church" (Mt 16.18), but this temple in Zechariah 6 is "the temple of Jehovah"(the word "Lord" is literally Jehovah) and this title of God that

has to do with His relationship with Israel cannot be applied to the spiritual structure of the Church. Moreover, the immediate context contains a prophecy, not of something which will take place in this present church age, but rather of the millennial age. The prophecy is looking on to the future and to a time beyond the day of grace. It is clearly the time of Messiah's rule. This temple will be built and Christ will reign when Israel has been restored and has obeyed God (v.15).

If then the temple here is not the second temple or the spiritual temple of the church, it can only refer to a literal and material temple that will be built in the Millennium. Will such a temple exist during the Millennium? The answer is a definite "Yes", for Ezekiel the prophet, in the last nine chapters of his prophecy, speaks of a literal temple that will be located right in the midst of the land of Israel during the reign of Christ. From Ezekiel it will be found that the future temple will be a very large structure. It will be built under the supervision of the Messiah. Unlike the tabernacle of old or Solomon's temple, it will not be adorned with silver or gold, but made of simple material of stone and wood. One reason for this is that God will not allow anything in this temple to detract from the glory of the Lord Jesus. It will be an impressive object lesson to Israel and the nations of the holiness of God. There will be no high priest in it. There will be no ark in the holiest of all. There will be no veil. The Lord Jesus will fulfil the need of Israel in that day and His glory will be manifest everywhere. Outside of the book of Ezekiel this future temple is spoken of three times. Here in Zechariah 6 we have its divine builder. In Isaiah 60.7 we have its divine beauty: "I will glorify the house of my glory", or "beautify my beautiful house" (RV margin), and in Haggai 2.9 we have its divine blessing: "In this place will I give peace, saith the Lord of hosts". One must not miss a practical application. Every local assembly gathering in the name of the Lord Jesus should be a place of beauty with Christ alone having pre-eminence. Nothing should detract from this. The blessing, too, of peace within the assembly should be enjoyed. This blessing will only be realised so long as Christ has His place of authority among His people.

The bearer of the glory

Zechariah is told that the One who will build the future temple will also "bear the glory". It might also be rendered that He will "carry" or "wear" the glory. Thus it might be read, "He will wear the glory" (Helen Spurrel), as if all like a magnificent garment will gloriously adorn Him. He will bear all the glory, for intrinsically and mediatorially He will be able. The word can mean to lift, bear up, carry, and take (NASA - 5375). The idea of bearing is similar to what is said of Eliakim who is a picture of the Messiah in Isaiah 22.24. He was to have "all the glory of his father's house" hung upon him.

What is the meaning in 6.13 of "glory"? Glory here is the thought of regal majesty, or, better still, of divine splendour. While the word is used often in the Old Testament for the special glory of God, it has also the thought of kingly glory. In at least two passages it implies especially this (see Jeremiah 22.18 & Daniel 11.21 – translated "honour"). It is used of the glory or majesty to be laid on the ideal king in Psalm 21.5, "Honour [glory] and majesty hast thou laid upon him". Orthodox Jews apply this to their expected Messiah. It is interesting that earlier in the same Psalm it is said, "Thou settest a crown of pure gold on his head" (v.3). This links well with the passage here where the crown is placed on the head of Joshua. In the Psalm it is what God does, and in the future day God Himself will see to it that His Son will be crowned with the kingly crown, so that He will reign over Israel and the whole world. In the next Psalm (Psalm 22) we have the suffering of the Messiah, but how good to note the same Psalm goes on to say, "For the kingdom is the Lord's: and he is the governor among the nations" (v.28). How incredible to think that He who earlier in the Psalm could refer to Himself as "a worm, and no man" (v.6), is yet to be exalted as the worldwide ruler! The Apostle Peter says that the Lord Jesus at Calvary "bare our sins in his own body on the tree" (1 Pet 2.24). During the hours of darkness, in holy suffering He bore the burden of sins, but when He returns to earth again He will bear the weight of glory upon Himself. What a great difference!

The Messiah who will bear the insignia of His kingly glory upon His person "shall sit and rule upon His throne; and he shall be a priest upon his throne". Zechariah was from a priestly family and would well know that no Levitical priest ever wore a kingly crown of gold (except for the golden plate fastened to the mitre of the high priest), or could fill the role of kingship in Israel. They were two separate offices and neither a king nor a priest could fill their role unless born into the priestly or kingly family in Israel, and one man could not combine both functions because of their tribal connections. No priest in Jewish history ever served as king, and the one king, Uzziah, who tried to become a priest, was punished by the Lord (2 Chr 26). Only in the Messiah will God unite both the throne and the altar. Thus the Messiah will combine in Himself the two offices of kingship and priesthood and this will perfectly fit Him to reign in the Millennium. Had Zechariah been charged to place the crown on the head of Zerubbabel he might not have been too surprised. Then again, by crowning Joshua God was not seeking to put Zerubbabel out of his role as a ruler. Zerubbabel, it must be remembered, was a governor, but not from the kingly tribe of Judah. We do not read that the elders were present or that Zerubbabel himself witnessed this, yet such was the importance of the occasion it is very probable that they were there. There is no record of how Zerubbabel reacted to this procedure. It is hardly likely that he was offended by it, thinking the crown should have been upon his head. It surely would have been enough that God commanded it.

The bringer of peace
The last part of v.13 has caused not a little difficulty with some. The

question to be asked is to what the statement "and the counsel of peace shall be between them both" refers? Is the clause saying that the counsel of peace shall be between two persons, Jehovah, mentioned in the verse, and then the Messiah? Is this some plan of peace being worked out between Jehovah and Christ? Such an interpretation is not clear and seems a strange thought to introduce. The "both" must refer to the two offices of king and priest in the person of the coming Messiah. The double character combined for the first time in Christ will be so perfect and ideal that He will be able to bring about peace to Israel and to the world. In a way this is faintly foreshadowed in both Zerubbabel and Joshua, who, by joining together their offices, had been able to be a blessing to the remnant who had returned to build. If then their combined efforts had been such a help to Israel, what might the Lord Jesus Christ be able to accomplish for His people in the future when these two great offices will be exercised by Him. Messiah's counsel will produce peace for Israel. "The counsel of peace" implies that this is the plan for the divine ordering of the Kingdom: for this very reason the Messiah is described as "Counseller" (Is 9.6). Peace will then be possible for the nation, because in His priestly capacity Christ will have expiated the sin of Israel and by His kingly function He will root out sin in the Millennium and judge it immediately. Christ's mediatorial priesthood purchases peace, and His kingly rule maintains it. What a great blessing then the Messiah is going to be to Israel and the nations. How great He is in His person. How wonderful will be His work. How ideally His offices will function. Though the passage shows here what Christ will yet be to Israel, surely the believer looking at such a prophecy can only be profoundly grateful to know this One as Saviour and to rejoice in the perfect peace which He has brought to the soul through His atoning sacrifice. In the light of such a detailed prophecy of what Christ will be and what He will do in the future, one can only respond in worship and praise to God.

A commemoration (vv.14-15)

In the scene thus far the material, the making, and the message of the crown have been considered. Now concerning the crown it is further mentioned that it is to be "for a memorial". The crown must have been on the head of Joshua just for a brief period, for Zechariah would then take it from Joshua's head and would give him back his priestly mitre. This had to be the case, because the act was only a symbolic one. When the procedure was over all would understand that the crown did not personally belong to Joshua. The prophetic message to the remnant and to all who read this incident is very clear - that the regal crown belonged by right to the Messiah to come. He will have it permanently, for His Kingdom is an everlasting Kingdom. God will fulfil this symbolic act. The crown was to be taken and deposited in the temple as a memorial to the three exiles from the captivity and to the son of Zephaniah. The messengers who had brought the material for the crown and the one who had graciously received these men under his roof, were honoured by the crown being placed in the temple. While this is true, the crown would chiefly be a memorial to the coronation of Joshua to remind the people of the Messiah, who, in the transaction, had been foretold as the anti-typical King-Priest yet to come. The word "Hen" in the passage is not another name for Josiah, but is really an appellative signifying favour or kindness and points to the favour Josiah had shown to the messengers. The memorial of the silver and gold being laid up for these men, shows that every offering for Christ and even the very courtesy extended to those who in any way serve Him, will never be forgotten in the coming Kingdom.

In the closing verse of the chapter it is so interesting to see that Gentiles shall come from afar to build in the temple. "They that are far off" must not be regarded as being other Israelites living in far off foreign lands, but rather Gentiles. Like the Jewish delegation from Babylon, righteous Gentiles who have been saved (by believing the gospel of the Kingdom and entering into the millennial age) will bring their offerings to Jerusalem. These the Messiah will use for the construction of the millennial temple. Thus the men mentioned earlier in vv.10 & 14 were typical of Gentiles who will come in the last days to help build the Lord's House. According to Isaiah 60.5,11, and 61.6 many nations will bring their wealth to Jerusalem. When this takes place the world will know that God has sent the Messiah to bless the nation of Israel. This temple, then, will be built under the direction of the Messiah Himself. It shows the grace of God in allowing Gentiles to participate in it. All this will come to pass says God, "if ye will diligently obey the voice of the Lord your God". How can this be, for is not the millennial reign of Christ and the building of the temple all part of the sovereign plan of God for Israel? Yes it is, but at first sight this promise seems to be conditional. It may be looked at in two ways. First, only those individuals in Israel in a coming day who believe and obey God will share in the blessings of the millennial Kingdom. Second, it cannot be said that the unbelief of the Jews will set aside God's purpose as to Messiah's coming, but that Messiah appearing in glory as the King-Priest will not take place until they turn to Him in repentance and obedience.

The visions have ended and the symbolic transaction following them has been enacted and Oh! what a vivid panorama of God's programme for Israel has been set forth. God's great plan for removing evil from Israel and overcoming their enemies will climax in the King-Priest sitting on the throne of David, ruling over not only Israel but the whole world. He will fulfil all the prophetic pictures and promises revealed in the first six chapters of Zechariah. What a message to the remnant, but what a message also to the nation today if only they would believe that Jesus of Nazareth is the Messiah and accept the clear teaching in Zechariah in the visions and the coronation of Joshua.

ZECHARIAH 7

Problems and Answers

Chapter 7 is very closely connected with the following one. In these chapters a new method of communication is introduced, for the interpreting angel departs and God Himself speaks directly to the prophet. Chapters 7 & 8 therefore commence a new section in the book of Zechariah and form its central division. The chapters go together and bear on the problem as to whether the people should continue keeping fasts that commemorated certain times of national tragedy. Since the remnant had returned to Jerusalem, naturally they wondered whether it was still necessary and consistent to continue the observance of fasts which commemorated the destruction of the sanctuary and the state, now that this was in course of being reconstructed and the national life restored. The Jews while in exile had instituted four fasts to commemorate various tragic events connected with the destruction of Jerusalem in 586 BC. The two chapters are easily divided into four sections, each one of which opens with formulae similar to: "The word of the Lord of hosts came unto me, saying…". This Spirit-constructed division contains a fourfold message to the people. In ch.7 God answers the questions negatively rebuking the people, while in ch.8 He answers them positively, reassuring them with some wonderful prophetic promises. The seventh chapter urges them to be obedient by calling their attention to disobedience seen in the failure of their fathers. The eighth chapter continues to urge this obedience in the light of future prosperity and the promise of wonderful blessings to come. In this chapter will be found a request (vv.1-3); a reply (vv.4-7); and a rebuke (vv.8-14).

Verse 1-3: The Enquiry from Bethel
The date

The visions of the first six chapters had taken place during the eighth month of the second year of the reign of Darius (1.1). Two years later in the fourth year of the reign of Darius we have the question asked in v.3. The word of the Lord came to Zechariah two years after the building of the temple was started again and two years before it was finished. God spoke to Zechariah at a time when the building of the temple must have been well advanced. The month "Chisleu" which means torpidity, describes the state in which nature was in November, answering to this month. The meaning of the month is certainly a contrast to the people, for they were by no means lazy or stagnant. Haggai the prophet earlier had rebuked them for their complacency and indifference (Hag 1.2-4), but, acting upon his ministry, they had been stirred up and, far from being lazy, with some exercise and effort they had come back to Jerusalem. God grant that as believers we may not be torpid as to the needs and demands of spiritual work. While the original word for "house of God" in v.2 is "Bethel", the temple was never actually called this in Scripture. The RV reading of the text makes sense: "Now they of Beth-el had sent Sharezer…". Scholars of the Hebrew text say this is a better translation, and simply means that the people of the city of Bethel sent a delegation made up of the men mentioned by name and other men who are not identified to enquire primarily concerning the fast commemorating the destruction of Solomon's temple.

The deputation

The embassy from Bethel was composed of two leaders who were representatives of the exiles from Babylon. Their names are heathen in character, being Babylonian. This may suggest that they were born in Babylon during the captivity. Many Jews in Babylon were given Babylonian names. The prophet Daniel for example was given the Babylonian name of Belteshazzar. Daniel, though given a heathen name, never forgot his loyalty to God and to His word. He was never so immersed in heathen life in the city of Babylon that he became defiled or lost his separation. These men sent from Bethel had possibly returned from Babylon with other returnees. How they had lived in Babylon is not revealed. They may have lived separated lives and been true to God. They at least should be credited with a true concern for the situation. They were to ask the prophets and priests, "Should I weep in the fifth month, separating myself, as I have done these so many years?". The personal pronoun "I" of course is corporate and not individual. The whole community is in view. In coming to Jerusalem with their problem they went to the right source – the priests and prophets. Both offices in Israel were required by God to give guidance. They were to communicate the word of the Lord to the people. So this was a commendable action on their part. How good and necessary it is that when believers have spiritual problems they should go to those who will give light from the word of God. Custom, expediency, and even changed circumstances are not to be relied upon, but the word of the Lord is. It is possible that the statement "as I have done these so many years" may indicate that they had a true desire to stop keeping the fast of the fifth month. A particular custom may well have been practised for many years, and Christians can get so accustomed to the tradition and conditioned by it that it is easy never to ask, "Is this practice or this way of doing things according to Scripture?".

The desire

These men had come to Jerusalem "to pray before the Lord", or "to entreat the favour of the Lord" (literally "to stroke the face of"!). The latter idea suggests that they would seek to do this by offering sacrifices on the altar which had already been built about eighteen years before. The men came from Bethel about ten miles north of Jerusalem. They had come to the capital to ask how they should worship the Lord. Bethel in Israel's history had been long associated with apostate worship (1 Kings 12.29-33; 2 Kings 10.29; Jer 48.13; Amos 3.14; 4.4; 7.13). From 1 Kings 12 one may see that Bethel was one of the two centres where Jeroboam set up his idolatrous practices when he separated the ten tribes from Judah and Benjamin. The Assyrians took the ten tribes into captivity before the temple was destroyed (2 Kings 17.6). Now it is good to see men from this very place not only mourning the destruction of the temple, but sufficiently interested and exercised to be drawn back to Judah and to the true centre of worship that God Himself had established in Jerusalem. It is obvious that God's House in Jerusalem meant so much to them that they mourned over its destruction and were very happy to see many of their brethren seeking to rebuild it. This was a good exercise indeed and one that many believers would do well to emulate. The question is how much are we exercised about the House of God and the state of things generally in the testimony? Are traditions from the past still to be perpetuated? Are they to influence believers and assemblies today? If they are good and scripturally authenticated traditions there is nothing to fear, but sadly some traditions are adopted without any divine sanction. Now that times have changed should any traditions be changed and who has authority to change them? All these questions are challenging, but each believer and each assembly should see from the word of God the difference between truth and tradition. How easy to carry on practices and use methods even in assembly life that are nothing more than tradition and custom. It is far better to search the Scriptures to make sure that every practice adopted has divine approval.

The difficulty

The delegation was concerned about the fasts that had been kept for some years during the captivity. These fasts had been self–imposed by the nation. They never originated in the mind of God. The only fast demanded by God under the Law of Moses was on the holy Day of Atonement which was on the tenth day of the seventh month. The people would have known that the exile in Babylon would last for seventy years (Jer 25.11-12) and sixty-eight of these years had passed already. How natural then for them to think that fasting over the destruction of the temple in the fifth month might now be inappropriate since they had been able to rebuild the temple and restore the service of worship to God. God answers directly the question as to these fasts in 8.19. There He shows that they will yet be turned into feasts. Here the people needed first of all to be rebuked for their inconsistent behaviour in connection with the keeping of these fasts and reminded also of the need to be obedient to the word of God. It will be helpful at this stage in the commentary to list them:

1. The fast of the tenth month – The siege of Jerusalem - 8.18-19
2. The fast of the fourth month – The capture of the city – 2 Kings 15

3. The fast of the fifth month – The destruction of the city – 2 Kings 25.8ff

4. The fast of the seventh month – The murder of Gedaliah – 2 Kings 25.25.

Concerning fasts it might be well to consider the question of fasting for Christians today. In the first place, nowhere in the New Testament are believers commanded to fast either in a collective way or as individuals. This does not mean that no believer has the liberty to engage in fasting. They did so in the church at Antioch (Acts 13.3). There may be times when a believer thinks it fitting to discipline himself in order to help him to be more devoted to the Lord in some spiritual exercise. To forgo eating or refusing legitimate pursuits in daily life may help one believer, but not necessarily another. Because one believer fasts it would be wrong to press this practice on other believers and make it binding for them. The Lord Jesus taught that if fasting was engaged in, it should be done without any outward show (Mt 6.16-18). An important point which must be remembered is that whether it is national, church, or personal, fasting has no virtue in itself.

Verses 4-7: The First Message – The Need for Reality in their Observances

This first answer takes on a more negative character and presents three main questions which are rhetorical. The answers to these questions being in the negative shows the wisdom of obeying God rather than adhering to self-imposed and man-made observances which are mainly for man's honour and not for God's. The question of whether to continue these fasts was obviously important to the people in Bethel, but to God what was more important was the attitude and conduct revealed by the people. It was one thing to be concerned about the futility of continuing the outward observances of the fasts, it was another to be living so as to please God and to be marked by reality. It is reality in the life and service of the believer that God is looking for. It does not please Him when a believer professes outwardly more than his heart feels and has reached, or carries on in external observances without having genuineness of the soul.

Was the fast in the mind of God? (v.5)

Notice that this word is addressed not merely to the citizens of Bethel, but to all the people of the land and to the priests. The word of the Lord of hosts was very embracive. None were exempt from it. This shows how widespread the problem of mere outward ritual and ceremony was, without obedience to God. God had to ask as to the feasts of the fifth and seventh months, "Did ye at all fast unto me, even to me?".

How sad that the question these men put showed they were more anxious about a ceremony than they were about moral obedience. Even if the fasts had been commenced with proper motives, they certainly did not continue that way. Clearly they had degenerated into mere formal, religious, and selfish observances. The serious problem was that the fasts did not originate in the mind of God. Israel in captivity had never a "Thus saith the Lord" for adopting these practices. The lesson here for all is this, that if believers are considering adopting a practice or some new form of service in the assembly, it is essential, however well-intentioned and convenient it may be, to make sure that the word of God backs it up.

Was it for the glory of God? (v.6)

Now we have especially the object before the people in keeping the fasts. They did it for their own ends. God was really saying to them, "It was yourselves you regarded throughout". They were not exercised about the cause of these national tragedies. These terrible setbacks had not driven them into the presence of God in humiliation of soul or repentance. They made the fasts, as many do today in religious observances, an end meritorious in itself, not a means to God's glory. Had these tragedies led to them confessing their sin and growing in holiness in the fear of God? Sadly it had not produced any such good spiritual results for the nation in its relationship to God. These are solemn and searching words: "Did not ye eat for yourselves, and drink for yourselves?". They expose the motives which lie at the root of all that is done professedly for God. It is either God or self that each believer lives for in all that is done every moment in life. This is all the more true in relation to spiritual activity in assembly life. There is no middle ground here. The life of a believer may easily be glossed over, but the question still remains: "Is it for God or for self?". This important matter must be applied to every believer engaged in some aspect of service in the assembly. Paul could say to the Corinthians, "Whether therefore ye eat, or drink, or whatsoever ye do, do all to the glory of God" (1 Cor 10.31). While in that passage the context has to do with eating things offered to idols, the principle is most important, for no believer should ask what will be most agreeable or best suited to the interests of self, but rather what will best promote God's glory.

Was it approved by the word of God? (v.7)

God is asking here whether these fasts were at His request. In one sense it was a matter of perfect indifference to God whether they fasted or not. What was well-pleasing to Him was not some pharisaic abstinence from eating or drinking, but the observance of the word of God and living by it. Had they in the first place obeyed the word of God from the past prophets they would never have had occasion for these fasts. Their city and temple would never have been destroyed. The prophets referred to had lived before the captivity when the land of Israel and its cities were full of inhabitants and prosperous (Is 58.3-9), but their disobedience had changed all that. An example of outward conformity in that which is not according to the Word of God is seen in the observance of Lent, but, sadly, when it is over many often return to their old ways of folly, pleasure and sin. What spiritual change has it wrought in their souls? A true believer may fare no better, for how possible it is to even be spiritually unaffected by attendances at gatherings which have been commanded by the Lord. The Feasts of Jehovah which God ordained had degenerated when our Lord was here into the "feasts of the Jews". May God help each one of us who has the privilege of keeping the ordinance of the Lord's Supper to make sure that the motive is pure and the life suitably conditioned in obedience to the Lord's command.

The ordinance of the Lord's Supper is the only commemoration Christians are commanded corporately to keep. Lent and religious festivals practised by many are without divine decree and are a combination of Judaism and paganism which have been copied in Christendom. How one needs to understand that going outwardly through the motions of the Breaking of Bread does not necessarily constitute a true remembrance of the Lord if it is done unworthily and not in reality. It is easier to insist on outward observances than to humble oneself before God and to obey His commandments. Joel in his prophecy could appeal to the people of his day: "Rend your heart, and not your garments" (Joel 2.13). Rending the garments externally is easier than rending the heart inwardly. Man is more partial to the externals because by nature he is not spiritual, but natural. The inward is more difficult than the outward and it requires much thought and diligence, and man cares not to submit to the word of God. Many crowd the outer courts of religious ceremonies and observances, but shun the holy place of repentance, confession of sin, and faith. The great need for Israel then and for the believer today is reality in all things to do with the life Godward.

One must not leave this first message without applying yet again its so searching teaching. In vv.1-3 may be seen that which was right and commendable in that the men sent from Bethel went fittingly to the right place and persons to seek an answer to their question. They went to the House of God and to the priests and prophets. How good for the believer when seeking guidance to seek the Lord's face in prayer and to consult, for example, with godly leaders among the saints. In vv.4-7 may be seen that which is wrong and not to be commended. In this section God rebukes the people for keeping observances that are merely external ritual without the spirit being right. The Jews had fasted and had mourned in the fifth and seventh months for seventy years. To them this may have been correct as to the form, but in spirit the service was wrong, hence the reproof contained in the word from God.

Verses 8-14: The Second Answer – The Need for Respect in their Relationships

The word of the Lord of hosts came a second time to Zechariah. This section begins with, "Thus speaketh the Lord of hosts", implying that the precepts addressed to their forefathers before the captivity and repeated here were the requirements of Jehovah still. If the fasts adopted had been honestly for God this would have been shown in the way they behaved to others. God is concerned about the relationships of His people and the attitude they display to one another; hence the term "brother" used twice in vv.9 & 10. Zechariah had referred to the voice of the former prophets in v.7. He does so again in v.12. This message then contains a summary of the teaching of these past prophets. The moral and spiritual features that they demanded from the people in their day are now applied by Zechariah to his own generation. One may learn from this the value of teaching from the past. If it has come from God then it is still adaptable and applicable to future generations. Israel should have profited from their past history, especially the teaching of the prophets. They should have readily seen that the reason for their present weak state of things was due to their failure to obey the voice of the prophets.

What did the Lord require? (vv.9-10)

The moral laws imposed upon their fathers were still of primary importance. Spiritual features were what God was expecting from His people. There must be right relationships among believers. "It is probable that the root of all departure, and consequent loss of blessing, could be traced to the weakening and giving up of those links of love which normally bind the brethren together" (C. A. Coates). How true this is and how sensitive believers should be to endeavour to see to it that right and happy relationships are maintained among the saints. Notice how practical the teaching is, and that Zechariah condenses it into four terse and pointed exhortations. Those who practised the things spoken against here only showed that they did not have a proper spiritual relationship with God and that if such behaviour continued there remained the very real peril of suffering retribution from God. How could their relationships one with another be right if their relationship with God was not right? This principle was taught by the Lord Jesus in Matthew 5.23-24. Zechariah was not giving the people a new message. It was woven into the warp and woof of the Law of Moses and the prophets for centuries had clearly given the same moral demands from God (see Is 56.1; Micah 6.8). Notice how in the third message Zechariah returns to the theme of the importance of moral principles (8.16-17).

The need for impartiality

"Execute true judgment" – This, to quote C. H. H. Wright, means "Judgment agreeing with truth in all things, without any respect of persons or partiality". Often God through the law and the prophets demands that His people be free from injustice to their fellow men (Ex 22.21; Lev 19.15-18; Jer 7.5-7). God desires righteous dealings. By not exercising right judgment in their dealings with their brethren they showed a wrong attitude to them. By so doing they were only proving that their relationship with God was not right. This is a searching fact, for this should cause the believer, too, to make sure that the attitude to God is right. If it is, then the attitude to one's fellow believers will be right also. There must be fair dealing among the saints, and judgments passed upon believers must be impartial and based upon the righteous principles of the word of God. This moral principle should mark all believers, especially in their dealings with unbelievers in business and work.

The need for mercy
"Shew mercy and compassions every man to his brother" - the two words "mercy" and "compassions" indicate different aspects of kindness. The first word implies kindness and love in general, the second is kindness displayed in the form of compassion and sympathy towards those who may be afflicted and distressed. What a lack even among the saints today of love and kindness. These have been shown to us by God. He has moved in wonderful love and kindness to us in grace and He expects to see in His children these same characteristics manifest in the life towards others. Believers who are right with God will never be slow to express these lovely features. What a help to harmony and right conditions in an assembly if God is obeyed in this way. The Lord Jesus pronounced a woe upon the Scribes and Pharisees and said, "…hypocrites! for ye pay tithe of mint and anise and cummin, and have omitted the weightier matters of the law, judgment, mercy, and faith: these ye ought to have done, and not to leave the other undone" (Mt 23.23). Things had not changed in Israel when the Lord was here. The Lord utterly condemned their disregard for the moral principles of the law.

The need for sympathy
"Oppress not the widow, nor the fatherless, the stranger, nor the poor" – unscrupulous people can be cruel and can take advantage of a widow's lack of knowledge in business matters. Even apart from a commercial aspect, widows are to be treated with tender consideration and respect, for God is the God of the widow. Luke in his Gospel gives five references to widows. Luke's is the Gospel that shows the lovely compassion of Christ. He delights to show us Christ's concern and sympathy for the widow. In 1 Timothy 5.3-16 we have teaching on the attitude of an assembly to different kinds of widows. Thus the New Testament does not fall behind the law, but even goes further than this, for in Galatians 6.10 Paul exhorts that the believer is to do good to all. The fatherless, the stranger, and the poor are all vulnerable to those who would oppress them. What practical teaching we have in James 1.27: "Pure religion and undefiled before God and the Father is this, To visit the fatherless and widows in their affliction". This is practical Christianity and needs to be seen more among believers.

The need for piety

These concise and comprehensive utterances from God to His people climax in the requirement that if God's people are godly then they certainly will never imagine evil in their hearts towards their brethren. It is the lack of piety in the life that can cause what begins as evil thoughts in the heart against our brethren to come out in cruel action. What was the good of observing fasts if this kind of behaviour was going on among them? It made it all a farce. What a need there was for morality in their conduct. Yet morality is certainly not piety, but piety which does not act in morality is a delusion. It mocks God and insults man. Piety will manifest itself in morality. Both are needed and the prophet emphasises to the remnant this unchanging exhortation from God. Today this message is needed more than ever, for what a great and sad lack there is of impartiality in judgment, mercy to others, sympathy for the needy, and piety in the life. God's principles never change. It is implied in these moral requirements of vv. 9 & 10 that because past generations of the people had not displayed these things judgment from God inevitably overtook them.

How did the people react? (vv.11-12)

Sadly, these verses show that while God's principles never change (vv.9-10) His people do! Notice the steps by which God's people reached the state of an adamant heart. First they refused to hearken – their soul was contrary to God. Next they pulled away the shoulder. The picture here is taken from a beast which refuses to bear the yoke (see Neh 9.29; Hos 4.16). It is like the sulking boy that shakes off the hand laid in remonstrance on his shoulder. One may compare with this the idea of giving the cold shoulder to someone (cp. Jer 7.24). Finally they "stopped their ears" lest they should hear God's voice. No wonder the state of their hearts as "an adamant stone" was reached. The word "adamant" was used for engravings on which nothing could be graven by any other instrument. Some render it, "to make the heart diamond", that is, as hard as diamond. The picture here is that of a stony heart that is not susceptible to spiritual impressions from the word of God spoken to it. What a sad state this is and, alas, the believer too may not be immune from it. It is so important to make sure we have a heart that is open to the word of the Lord in order to obey it. These varied expressions graphically reveal the terrible spiritual condition into which the people had descended. They had become persistent in their stubborn disobedience. If the heart is not right there will be no disposition to hear God's voice. God's people must have a yielded heart open to God otherwise there will be no desire to hear His word. God's people in Zechariah's day were reminded of the value and vindication of ministry by the Spirit through the prophets. References to the Spirit of God in the Minor Prophets are few, but there are three mentions in Zechariah of the Holy Spirit and each has to do with the nation of Israel. In 4.6 it is the Spirit and the testimony of Israel. In 12.10 it is the Spirit and the conversion of Israel. Here it is the Spirit and the word of God to Israel. In spite of the fact that the Spirit Himself had spoken to them through their prophets, Israel had repeatedly disobeyed God. Tragically, Zechariah has to tell them that the consequence of all this is, "therefore came a great wrath from the Lord of hosts". No wonder this had happened and seventy years of captivity had had to be endured. To institute four fasts because of the tragedies that occurred in Jerusalem, *and yet not repent because of the sins that caused these tragedies,* was to miss the whole purpose of God's discipline.

What were the results? (vv.13-14)

Now as a consequence we have the law of righteous retribution. What was the outcome of such persistent disobedience? Three things Israel would suffer. They would experience the loss of any response from God to their cries; they would be scattered among many strange nations; and their land that God purposed to give them would be utterly desolate. Since their forefathers had refused to listen to the Spirit of God when He spoke to them through the prophets (cp. Neh 9.20; 2 Pet 1.21), God would refuse to listen to them when they cried to Him in their distress because of their sins. What serious words then are these: "as he cried, and they would not hear; so they cried, and I would not hear, saith the Lord of hosts". We sin and reject God's word at our peril. As they pushed away the yoke of obedience, God laid on them the yoke of oppression. How this illustrates that "God is not mocked: for whatsoever a man soweth, that shall he also reap" (Gal 6.7). God had scattered them among many nations as if a windstorm had suddenly blown them out of the land of Canaan. They did not want God and His word, so he put them among many people that did not know God. They had to learn what it was to be away from God with all His kindness, compassion, and faithfulness. Israel have still not learned this, and God will have to humble them and teach them in the Tribulation they will yet have to suffer.

Following their captivity in Babylon "the land was desolate after them, that no man passed through nor returned". The desolation of what was once a pleasant land was due to the sin of the people of Israel. Bombs, weapons and tanks may and have caused lands to be desolate, but there is nothing more ruinous to a country than sin. While the Jews were in captivity no travellers passed through the land. This was to be a solemn sign to them of God's righteous government. The land lay in ruins all this time. Whenever the Jewish people are out of the land it becomes desolate, but in these days after centuries many Jews have returned. The land of Israel has already begun to bloom again and it is still quite a tourist attraction. True, because of recent troubles in the Middle East and the conflict between Israel and the Palestinians, tourism has suffered in Israel, but even now at the time of writing tourism in Israel is picking up again. In a glorious day to come when the Messiah returns to bless Israel the land will be fertile and fruitful in a way it has not been before. It will be truly "the pleasant land" (or the land of desire and delight). God in His mercy and providence watched over even the "desolate" land, and during the time of the seventy years of captivity Israel's enemies were never allowed to possess it. God reserved it for them and is still watching over it and them until the time comes when His prophetic word will be fulfilled when Immanuel's land shall be permanently theirs. He is preserving the land and He is preserving them for it.

The first two messages in ch.7 may have been negative and the question of the Bethel delegates not answered specifically, but it is plain to see that God through the prophet gets to the core of the problem which was that outward religious form and service was useless and empty unless it was accompanied by a spirit of obedience and confession of sin. It is far easier to have a religion of mere habit instead of a religion of the heart. May the challenge of these two messages not be lost upon believers of the present day. God help all believers in our Lord Jesus to examine their motives in serving God and to be marked by that reality of heart exercise which is pleasing to God. When this is done right relations among the saints will surely be enjoyed.

ZECHARIAH 8

Problems and Answers (continued)

Verses 1-17: The Third Message – The Need for Righteousness in Their Dealings

In this chapter we have the second half of the Lord's answer to the question concerning the last days. It is a very positive and direct answer. If in ch.7 Zechariah urged them to obedience by the failure and fate of their fathers, in this chapter he presses it upon them by promises of great blessing and future prosperity. The chapter is divided into two sections - vv.1-7, and vv.18-23 - each commencing with one of the last two of the four messages from God. As previously noticed, each section commences with the formula, "The word of the Lord of hosts came to me saying...". Chapter 8 not only contains two major messages from God, but it also gives ten wonderful minor messages of promises of future blessing for Israel. It is a decalogue of divine promises that make up the two major messages. Seven of these promises are found in the third message and the remaining three are found in the fourth message. "Thus saith the Lord" introduces each of them: vv.2,3,4-5,6,7-8,9-13,14-18,19,20-22,23. The enquiry from the deputation provided God with an opportunity to confirm His promises to the remnant of His people in order that He might lift their minds away from their present difficulties and give them a more objective outlook on their spiritual, moral, and national life. These promises set forth seven wonderful changes that will be brought about by God in the Israel of the future. The chapter may be very profitably looked at in this light.

The third message here and also the fourth and last reveal great prophecies of the restoration of Israel and speak of conditions of peace and blessing that have never yet been experienced by the nation. It is important to make this clear and to prove that the predictions given remain to be fulfilled in the future. Four points from the messages in the chapter should put this beyond any doubt. First, the lovely picture depicted in vv.4-5 of the old and young dwelling in complete safety in Jerusalem has never yet been fully realised. Nothing in the history of the city has fulfilled this. Second, in v.7 God has not yet saved His people from the east and the west. The national salvation of Israel is yet future. Third, in v.13 the nation has not yet been a blessing to the Gentiles. It is true that according to Galatians 3.14 & 16 Christ is "the seed" through whom the blessing of Abraham comes to the Gentiles (and of course He has come), but there is still further blessing to come through the nation when it is restored (Rom 11.12 & 15). Fourth (v.23), we have not yet witnessed people from the nations longing to share the privileges of the Jew and to have fellowship with them. There is still a widespread bitterness and hatred toward the Jew, but in a future day God is going to turn things around completely and the Jew will be esteemed.

The whole chapter presents Israel's eventual restoration and full participation in millennial blessing. The restoration of the people in Zechariah's time did not come anywhere near to the blessings prophesied here. The return of the remnant to the land was only a little picture and precursor of much greater blessings to come for the nation. One unique and interesting feature of this chapter is the repetition of the title "The Lord of hosts". In the book of Zechariah the title occurs 53 times, yet in this one chapter it is found no less than 18 times! In the first six verses alone it occurs 6 times. Perhaps no other passage in the Old Testament focuses such attention on this title. Zechariah's emphasis is significant because, while the predictions may seem far too wonderful to the remnant and beyond all human power to accomplish, it will come to pass through the infinite resources at the disposal of the Almighty One who is the Lord of hosts.

The chapter brings before us seven wonderful changes that will take place in the experience of the nation. These we will consider, together with other details in this most interesting chapter. They are as follows:

> 1. Return instead of departure (vv.1-3)
> 2. Peace instead of war (vv.4-5)
> 3. Salvation instead of scattering (vv.7-8)
> 4. Fruitfulness instead of barrenness (vv.9-12)
> 5. Blessing instead of cursing (vv.13-17)
> 6. Feasts instead of fasts (vv.18-19)
> 7. Dignity instead of hostility (vv.20-23).

Return instead of departure (vv.1-3)

Here God reveals that He is very jealous for the love of His people. "I was jealous for Zion with great jealousy." He would not tolerate any rival for the affections of His people. Such divine jealousy had been also revealed in the first vision in 1.14 and this loving jealousy still burned within Him. God is a jealous God (Ex 20.5) and in this character has a great interest in His people in seeking to maintain their interests, defend their cause, and safeguard their uniqueness as a nation. He desires the allegiance of His people. Jealous for Zion, and full of the fury of His wrath towards those who hate her, such is the way in which these promises of future blessing are introduced. The perfect tenses are used here, prophetically, of that which God had resolved to do and was now about to accomplish. Thus God speaks as if what He purposes has already been fulfilled. So certain are these promises of being fulfilled that God is determined Himself to accomplish them. Jerusalem is to be called, "a city of truth", and "the holy mountain". These promises have never yet in any sense been realized, and are still future. Ezekiel the prophet had seen the glory depart from the temple (Ezek 10.4,18; 11.23). Zechariah now announces that it will return in the person of Israel's Messiah, the Lord Jesus Christ. The Lord declares that He will return to Zion and dwell there and when He does what a change there will be, for the people will call Jerusalem "a city of truth" and they will refer to the temple mount as "the holy mountain". The city of Jerusalem has never acquired this character since the time of their captivity, for, though not defiled by gross idolatry as in the times before the captivity, it has ever been defiled by other moral abominations as much as it was before. God loves His people, God is a God of truth, and He is also holy in His character. This is seen in v.3, for what God is, the city of Jerusalem will be. His character will be reflected in the city. God has always intended that Jerusalem should be a place of truth and holiness. It will be this in the Millennium. In the days of the Tribulation it will be called, "Sodom and Egypt" (Rev 11.8), for morally and politically it will then be characterized by immorality and worldliness. What an awful picture of the conditions that will then prevail within its walls and how far removed from what God desires for it. Jerusalem then will be far worse than ever it has been in its past history. Thank God all this will be changed when the Lord Jesus returns to His people. These vast changes will take place because God loves Israel. This is the one great cause that will bring about such wonderful blessings for the nation. God says, "I am returned", "I...will dwell". Are these expressions, so clear and emphatic, to be spiritualized? Some may attempt to interpret them as meaning the spread of the gospel or as blessings for the Church, but this cannot be, for the words must be accepted literally.

God is still a jealous God today and yearns for the allegiance and affections of His children. He desires His assemblies to be marked by truth and the holiness of His presence.

Peace instead of war (vv.4-5)

"Thus saith the Lord of hosts; There shall yet old men and old women dwell in the streets of Jerusalem, and every man with his staff in his hand for very age. And the streets of the city shall be full of boys and girls playing in the streets thereof." Could any human paint a more graphic and beautiful picture of contentment, confidence, and peace than this? There are three enjoyed blessings here: peace in the city, prolonging of life, and the playfulness of children. The old and the young are those who suffer most in times of war. When Jerusalem was taken and destroyed, both of these groups had suffered much (Lam 2.21). The time referred to here is when war shall have ceased, for the nations shall not "learn war any more" (Is 2.4; Micah 4.3). This is certainly not true of Jerusalem in the present. This does not mean that the intermediate ages are excluded. How terrible that the last two world wars have swept away millions of young men and caused devastating, tragic, and unnecessary loss to many families. In the one thousand year reign of Christ there will be universal peace as well as a greatly extended life expectancy (Is 65.20). Neither Jerusalem nor any other city in any country let alone Israel will have to endure war and conflict.

What happy and blessed days to live in. So God describes a city so safe and friendly that the elderly can sit in the streets and talk leisurely, and the children can play in the streets and not be in danger. In today's man-made cities, the elderly and the children are not safe in the streets or anywhere else! Thousands of children in the UK alone are aborted before they have a chance to be born, and when the elderly are no longer useful euthanasia is promoted as a means to end their lives. But all of that will change when the Lord Jesus returns and righteousness reigns.

One must note here God's interest in the old and young. God even takes cognizance of little children playing together in a street. Mighty and Eternal God as He is, He is not oblivious to the needs of children and to their innocent pastimes and games. What a beautiful scene in the Lord's own life when children were taken up in His arms and He blessed them (Mk 10.13-16). What an experience. Would they ever forget it? God has care for the old too. It must, for example, delight Him when the old and the young are seen together gathering to listen to His word. While assemblies may have their separate meetings for Sunday school and children's meetings and God has blessed these, how it must please Him when all are found together. Believers should take time and effort to show a practical interest in both the old and the young. How often they are neglected. Brethren, too, should encourage times when all can be together listening to His word. God's word, when taught rightly and simply with a love for God's people, can only be a great blessing to all ages.

Are these conditions some kind of dream? Would it be considered impossible for them ever to take place? God anticipates any possible doubts in the minds of the remnant and thus He says, "If it be marvellous in the eyes of the remnant of this people in these days, should it also be marvellous in mine eyes? saith the Lord of hosts" (v.6). The remnant having returned from captivity would have seen the city desolate and the walls and houses ruined. It must have been hard for them to believe what God was promising the nation. It seemed incredible to accept in their present situation. They were measuring God's power by their own, and like Israel in the past had "limited the Holy One of Israel" (Ps 78.41). If God had spoken to them this should have been enough, but how often believers too have narrow and limited thoughts of God. The word "marvellous" (PALA – 6381) is better rendered "difficult", i.e. beyond one's power to understand, or too difficult to do. It is very interesting to notice in this verse that God's rhetorical question is bracketed on each side with the words, "saith the Lord of hosts". What an assurance of God's authority and power. As the Lord of hosts He will be able to accomplish the deliverance He has promised. If the word here is connected with a building of a city, it is also helpful to see that the same word in the Old Testament occurs in two other passages in connection with the birth of a child and the buying of a field. In Genesis 18.14, "Is any thing too hard for the Lord?", it is used in connection with the birth of a child, Isaac. In Jeremiah 32.17 & 27, it is used in connection with the buying of a field. Both these occurences of the word have to do with that which is impossible to man. The birth of Isaac was miraculous and took place in spite of the fact that Sarah naturally and physically was beyond the possibility of child bearing. Abraham, "being not weak in faith…considered not his own body now dead, when he was about an hundred years old, neither yet the deadness of Sara's womb" (Rom 4.19), and had faith in God to believe the impossible. In the buying of the field of Anathoth Jeremiah was willing to obey God and purchase a field that was an apparently valueless piece of land. This was to be evidence of his faith, not only in God's predictions through him, but in God's faithfulness. With the enemy at the gate of Jerusalem and the city about to fall, real estate would have been valueless. To buy a field then would have been considered a foolish act in the eyes of men, but it was God's way of showing to Jeremiah that what He promised would take place, "For thus saith the Lord of hosts, the God of Israel; Houses and fields and vineyards shall be possessed again in this land" (Jer 32.15). These are two good illustrations of the word. God wants faith from His people and not doubt.

Salvation instead of scattering (vv. 7-8)

God says, "I will save my people from the east country, and from the west country". This is the future national salvation of Israel. The prophecy clearly points to a literal future fulfilment and was not realized in the remnant returning from Babylon. The exiles who had come from Babylon to the land came only from the east, but here God promises that He will bring His people back to live in Jerusalem and the land from both the east and from the west. From far flung distant places God will restore His people. It will be another great exodus. In fact it will be much greater than the exodus from Egypt. Jeremiah speaks of this: "Therefore, behold, the days come, saith the Lord, that it shall no more be said, The Lord liveth that brought up the children of Israel out of the land of Egypt; But, The Lord liveth, that brought up the children of Israel from the land of the north, and from all the lands whither he had driven them: and I will bring them again into their land that I gave unto their fathers" (Jer 16.14-15; see also Jer 23.7-8). Again, such a prophecy cannot possibly refer to the bringing up of God's people from Babylon, for this bringing up and bringing back to the land is much greater. The Lord Jesus said in His Olivet discourse that "He shall send his angels with a great sound of a trumpet, and they shall gather together his elect from the four winds, from one end of heaven to the other" (Mt 24.31).

Israel has been scattered worldwide, but will be delivered and restored by God. In the lands to the west of Israel many Jews are found. It will be a great ingathering, for the so-called ten lost tribes will be gathered too and the nation will be reunited. Amos 9.15 compares Israel's restoration to a planting. God will plant them in the land and they will never be uprooted again from it. The nation will not only be restored in the national sense, but they will be back in a spiritual relationship with God. This will be a covenant relationship, for God promises, "I will be their God, in truth and righteousness". God will have dealt with the nation in righteousness, so much so that they will then be a "righteous nation" (Is 26.2). They will never apostatize as a nation again. Their restoration will be permanent.

Fruitfulness instead of barrenness (vv.9-12)

Zechariah introduces the sixth of the decalogue of promises in this chapter by saying, "Thus saith the Lord of hosts; Let your hands be strong, ye that hear in these days these words by the mouth of the prophets". They are told to be encouraged. God did not want His people to be despondent, but to have courage. The remnant greatly needed encouragement in their work of rebuilding. "Every part of the truth revealed was meant to fit them better for the task then in hand. So Zechariah exhorts them to be strong for the work before them and for the days ahead. In the fourth year of Darius (7.1) the people were in the midst of their work of rebuilding and needed encouragement. The words of the prophets Haggai and Zechariah were directed toward this very objective; therefore the people do well to heed them" (C. L. Feinberg). The exhortation to be strong is a much needed word for the believer too. It is interesting to note that the word "be strong" is found in three significant connections in Scripture. In Joshua it has to do with divine territory to possess. In this passage it relates to a divine temple to be built. In the New Testament in 2 Timothy 2.1 it is linked with divine truth to be preserved - "Be strong in the grace that is in Christ Jesus". That exhortation of Paul to Timothy shows us that the believer in this dispensation has a greater reason not to be discouraged, because he has a never failing provision and supply of grace from the exalted Christ. Israel under Joshua in going in to possess the land, and the remnant under Zerubbabel in building the temple, had not available to them that which believers can enjoy today – "the grace that is in Christ Jesus". Every believer involved in the work of the Lord today and in the assembly should, in seeking to preserve the truth of God, draw upon this grace and experience the reality of it in the life. Without it one may soon falter and give up.

Verses 10-12 refer to the condition of things among the people prior to the recommencement of the work of building the temple. In these verses, by making a contrast between the present times and the former ones, the reason is given as to why they should have courage. Before the time when the building of the temple was resumed agricultural pursuits did not repay the labours of either man or beast (cp. Hag 1.6, 9-11; 2.16-19). As the people went about their daily tasks there was no safety from without and no real rest within, for they were confronted by their enemies and there was no peace with their neighbours. So much was uncertain and unsafe, but now all this was to change. Since the building of the temple had recommenced God says, "But now I will not be unto the residue of this people as in the former days, saith the Lord of hosts. For the seed shall be prosperous; the vine shall give her fruit, and the ground shall give her increase" (vv.11-12). The seed mentioned here as being prosperous is the vine. It is, in the Hebrew, "the seed of peace" (2233 & 7965). The reason for this is because the vine can flourish in times of peace, but not when the land is laid waste by war. God's message to the remnant is that He will bless and reward their obedience to Him and give them fruitfulness and increase instead of the barrenness that they had known. Instead of the people experiencing God's chastening by withholding the dew (a great miss and calamity in a dry country like Israel where it can rain very seldom), God will give them the dew and the rain. There is no doubt that these material blessings so much needed were promised there and then to the remnant for their obedience in building His temple, but again, beyond this, the promises of God here look on to a future fulfilment when in the peace of the Millennium God will give abundant increase and fruitfulness in the land of Israel. How refreshed and beautiful the land of Israel will be in the Millennium. God says through Isaiah, "The desert shall...blossom as the rose" (Is 35.1). From Deuteronomy 27 & 28 and Leviticus 26 we see that God's covenant with Israel declared that He would punish them physically and materially if they disobeyed Him, but bless them if they obeyed Him. In the New Testament no such covenant is made with Christians, for the inheritance and blessings enjoyed today are spiritual and eternal. A believer may be rich, but this is no evidence that they are specially loved by God. A believer may be poor, but this is no evidence that God has forsaken them. There is no doubt that God will reward spiritually, either in this life or the next, believers who render obedience to Him.

Blessing instead of cursing (vv.13-17)

God promises to bless His people instead of cursing them. Notice that both Judah and Israel (the ten tribes) are mentioned, indicating that the long standing division in the kingdom and between the tribes will cease, and God says, "So will I save you, and ye shall be a blessing". This, too, shows that the prophecy has not yet had its full accomplishment, for Israel has never yet been restored, though individuals of the house of Israel returned with Judah. Thus it is not just that restoration will take place, but reunion too. How wonderful this will be. The cursing and blessing mentioned here points to the fact that they will no longer be the object of cursing by the nations, but will be an object of blessing to them. The Jews shall yet be a source of blessing to the Gentile nations (Micah 5.7; Zeph 3.20). Israel for centuries have been cursed and hated and opposed by many Gentile nations, but all this is going to change. In the light of this they are exhorted to "Fear not, but let your hands be strong". God, who had punished the people in the past for their sins, is now willing to do well for them if they are obedient. In the light of this promise of blessing and hope, God, for the second time in these verses, says, "Fear not" (vv.13,15). What was it that could remove this fear from their heart and make them strong to serve and build? Surely the answer is the word of God. By the opened ear to the word of God, the listening ear and the humble and contrite heart, they would experience the strengthening power of the word of God and as a result of this blessing would be theirs. Is it not the same for the believer today? As one faces the demands and difficulties of the Lord's work, believers too must take heart to this word from God: "Fear not".

In vv.16 & 17 God reveals again His standard of holiness for His people (cp. 7.9-10). He requires moral conditions among them. These verses stand closely connected with the promises of vv.13-15, and all the promises too of the passage. Instead of cursing them He will bless them and instead of punishing them as He had done in the past He will save them. These great promises were intended by God to be a motive to urge the remnant to holiness in their lives - "These are the things that ye shall do". Four conditions are mentioned here: truthfulness of speech, rectitude of conduct, benevolence of feeling, and abhorrence of falsehood. God expected, too, that what He was going to do should characterize the remnant. Thus if Jerusalem was to be a city of truth (v.3), they were to speak truth. If the city was yet to be a place of peace (vv.4 & 5), then they were to execute the judgment of truth and peace in their gates. The gates were the places where justice was to be administered in righteousness so that peace would be the result. If Jerusalem was to be the "holy mountain" (v.3), then they were to be a holy people, not imagining evil in their hearts against their neighbour. If God was going to remove the sin of perjury from them as a nation (5.3), then they ought to love no false oath. The character of God in holiness, truth, and righteousness will be reflected in the restored nation. These characteristics God desired to see being reproduced in the remnant. The Apostle Paul quotes from 8.16 in writing to the Ephesian Christians: "Wherefore putting away lying, speak every man truth with his neighbour: for we are members one of another" (Eph 4.25). Thus the principles urged upon the people in Zechariah's day are applied in the New Testament and put in christian dress, as it were. In the context of the citation by Paul, the believer has an added powerful reason to avoid lying and unrighteousness. He has the indwelling Holy Spirit, and clearly telling lies and acting unrighteously grieves Him. Hence Paul exhorts, "Grieve not the holy Spirit of God, whereby ye are sealed unto the day of redemption" (Eph 4.30).

In leaving this third section one can clearly see a very important threefold message addressed by Zechariah to the remnant. God demanded faith instead of doubt (v.6). God demanded courage instead of despondency (vv.9 & 13). God demanded holiness instead of disobedience (vv.16 & 17). The same threefold message is greatly needed by believers today.

Verses 18-23: The Fourth Message – The Need for Rejoicing in Their Blessings

In this fourth and final message God answers more directly the matters raised by the deputation from Bethel. The remaining three promises are found in this fourth communication. Note again that these promises are prefaced by, "Thus saith the Lord of hosts". The second and third promises explain the contents of the first more clearly. The first, in v.19, is God's promised seasons of joy in Zion. The second, in vv.20-21 is God's promise of extended attractiveness to Zion. The third, in v.23, is God's promise of a destined centre of blessing in Zion. These last six verses reveal that still more wonderful changes for Israel will take place in the future when God begins to work again for His people. Perhaps the deputation was thinking that God would say, "Abandon these fasts now that you are back in the land". They probably would have been content enough with this and seen the sense of ceasing their man-made fasts, but it must have been completely unexpected to be told in this message that greater things would yet take the place of these fasts. Two more great transformations are to be enjoyed by Israel in a coming day, thus completing the cycle of seven national blessings announced in this chapter.

Feasts instead of fasts (vv.18-19)

The fasts of the fourth, fifth, seventh and tenth months are all to be turned into days of rejoicing (notice that to the two fasts mentioned previously in 7.5 two more are added). For Israel, fasts without Christ are to become feasts with Him. The Lord Jesus was asked by the disciples of the Pharisees and of John the Baptist why His own disciples did not fast while they did. In reply the Saviour says, "Can the children of the bridechamber fast, while the bridegroom is with them? as long as they have the bridegroom with them, they cannot fast. But the days will come, when the bridegroom shall be taken away from them, and then shall they fast in those days" (Mk 2.19-20). Israel is without Christ today. Not until Israel turns to Christ and accepts Him as their Messiah will they have joy and blessing as a nation. The Lord will give to Israel in the future such a fulness of salvation nationally that they will only have to rejoice in the blessings that God's grace will bestow upon them. These blessings will not depend upon the goodness of Israel, but will be the result of the gracious promises of God. The Lord could say to His disciples, "Your sorrow shall be turned into joy" (Jn 16.20), and the presence of the Lord with Paul and Silas turned even the dungeon at Philippi into a very heaven, causing them to sing with joy to God. How much more, then, shall it be with Israel in a coming day. All this will come to pass, says God, when they "love the truth and peace". Israel when restored will love the truth and peace. There is however a practical lesson here for the remnant, for by being told of these wonderful blessings *they* ought, in the light of them, to love truth and peace. The believer in Christ, too, being told in the word of God of many wonderful eternal blessings to come, should all the more seek to love the truth and peace. God's prophecies of the believer's future joys should lead to an intense desire to know more of the truth and should promote love and harmony among the saints.

The feasts are called "cheerful feasts". The prophecy of Scripture is clear that in the Millennium Israel again will keep the Feasts of Jehovah. Ezekiel reveals that the Feast of the Passover and the Feast of Tabernacles will be kept during the course of the millennial reign of Christ (Ezek 45.21-25). It is interesting to note that the Feasts of Firstfruits, Weeks, Trumpets, and Atonement are not mentioned in Ezekiel's prophecy! Why should this be? There is no wave sheaf in connection with the Feast of Firstfruits because Christ has already risen. There is no Day of Pentecost because the church age will have already run its course and the pouring out of the Spirit will already be known by Israel. There will be no blowing of trumpets because the gathering of Israel will have already taken place. There will be no goat of the sin offering on the Day of Atonement because the true fulfilment of the type was when Christ died at Calvary. The first and last of the seven Feasts of Jehovah will be kept throughout the Millennium. By keeping the Passover Israel will not be allowed to forget the redemptive work of Christ on the cross, for this is the reason for their being so blessed in that day. One significant feature of the millennial Passover is that no longer will a lamb for a house be slain, but a bullock will be sacrificed (Ezek 45.24). Why this difference in the animal? It may suggest that Israel's appreciation of Christ will reach a high level in the Millennium. Knowing Christ in the way that they will then, there is no wonder they will have such joy as a nation. The last great concluding Feast of Tabernacles is the most joyous of all the feasts. It was timed to follow the gathering of the fruit of the land (i.e. the vintage harvest) and prophetically foreshadows Israel's millennial joy and blessing. God said to Israel with regard to the observance of this feast, "Thou shalt rejoice in thy feast" (Deut 16.14). It was therefore intended to be a time of great joy to the Jews. Their true and lasting joy will be realized when the Messiah returns, converts the nation, and takes them into the Millennium. The closing chapter of Zechariah shows how this feast will be celebrated by Jews and Gentiles. The description of the feasts replacing the fasts as "cheerful feasts" is therefore most apt in view of the joys that will be theirs during the Millennium.

Dignity instead of hostility (vv.20-23)

In the remaining four verses, what a blessed position of privilege and supremacy is anticipated for the Jew. What a contrast it is to the sad history of Israel and even to their present status as a nation. The Jew has been hated and downtrodden for centuries. They have been persecuted and put to death in their millions. Very few among the nations have had any desire to be associated with them and yet here God says that many from the nations will long to be with them. The whole picture will be reversed.

Now they suffer hostility, but then under Christ with God's presence among them, they will experience a dignity and a religious, political, and national predominance. Every one will desire to follow them. This promise must have even surprised the few and weak Jews who were at that time building the temple of Jerusalem. Israel will have a great testimony when the Messiah returns to them and reigns over them. People from many cities will go to Jerusalem. The reference to "people" here must mean the tribes of Israel and not the Gentile nations mentioned in v.22. They will eagerly join together with other Jews and make their way to Jerusalem to seek God's favour and blessing in prayer. The response at the end of v.21, "I will go also", may indicate the readiness of the other inhabitants of each city to go too. There will be such a zeal and desire to seek God and worship Him. This eagerness therefore will affect other nations, so much so that we read, "Yea, many people and strong nations shall come to seek the Lord of hosts in Jerusalem" (v.22). "Let us go speedily" implies that there will be a great revival movement and indicates the reality with which they will entreat the favour and grace of the Lord. What an influence Israel will have then over all the earth. Israel evangelically will be a great blessing to Gentiles in many nations and will travel the world speaking of the Messiah and the true God.

In the final verse of the passage God says, "In those days it shall come to pass, that ten men shall take hold out of all languages of the nations, even shall take hold of the skirt of him that is a Jew, saying, We will go with you: for we have heard that God is with you". The attitude of the nations towards the Jew will change from scorn to esteem. They will desire to share in the privileges of the Jew. The phrase "Out of all languages of the nations" makes clear that Zechariah is not just referring to the nations that surround little Israel, but he is including the distant nations of the world. That which will draw them to the Jew and to visit Jerusalem will be the glorious fact, realized at last, that God will be present with His people. It is this that will make the Jew and the city attractive. The book of Ezekiel has a wonderful and majestic ending, for in the last verse of his prophecy he says, "And the name of the city from that day shall be, the Lord is there (Jehovah Shammah)". What a fitting conclusion to that book. Just to think that the city from which the glory had departed, the city which so often through history has been the subject of God's judgments, the city through which the Lord Jesus once walked, the city by which He was rejected, and the city outside of whose gate He was crucified, that same city will be made the centre of the Saviour's rule and glory. The news that God is greatly blessing the Jew will stir the nations up and cause them to desire fellowship with them so as to share in these blessings.

The ten men taking hold of the skirt of a Jew needs to be commented on. The number ten is not to be taken literally, but is used indefinitely to express a large number (see the same usage in Leviticus 26.26, Numbers 14.22, and Amos 6.9). The taking hold of the skirt of a Jew is not a direct reference to the Messiah as the person is termed here simply as "a Jew". It is true when the Messiah was in Israel that in His ministry among them He wore the ribband of blue upon the hem of His garment – the distinctive mark of the Jew. The woman with the issue of blood touched the heavenly blue on the border of His garment and was instantly healed. Here, however, it is a Jewish man who no doubt will be dressed distinctively as a Jew and in common with all Jewish men at that time will be enjoying distinctive blessings. The idea of "taking hold" is so that a Jew might be detained and appealed to that others might go with him. This is really an amazing prophecy when one considers that today there is increasing Anti-Semitism. Satan is busier than ever seeking to hinder God's programme for Israel. The converted Jew in the Millennium will be able to speak the words of Moses to Hobab, "Come thou with us, and we will do thee good" (Num 10.29). What a day that will be!

Though v.23 has not yet been fulfilled, needless to say these happy conditions will surely take place according to the word of God. Israel will be so much in happy relationship with God and with one another that it will lead to worldwide blessing. There is a lesson from this that must be mentioned. If assemblies and individual believers in them are anxious to see blessing in the salvation of souls, then it is vital that right relations with God and with one another be enjoyed. The reality of the presence of God in the assembly would act as a magnet for exercised souls to be among us (1 Cor 14.25). When conditions are such that the presence of God is enjoyed there can only be blessing not just for saints in assemblies, but for the unconverted too.

ZECHARIAH 9
The Second Division of Zechariah – Two Prophecies and Their Significance

Chapters 9-14

These chapters contemplate Israel under three different rules. Chapters 9 & 10 refer to the period of rule by Greece; chapter 11 refers to rule by Rome; chapters 12 to 14 refer to the future when the nation will be under the domination of the coming Antichrist in the days of the Tribulation period. In chapters 9 to 11 the rejection of the King is in view. In chapters 12 to 14 the return of the King is in view. Chapters 9 to 11 are mainly concerned with the first advent of Christ. Chapters 12 to 14 are mainly concerned with the second advent of Christ. These undated prophecies could well have been written some considerable time after the previous part of the book. The character and style of this second division of the prophecy is in many ways quite different from the preceding eight chapters and this has led some commentators to believe that it cannot be the work of Zechariah. There is no reason to doubt the authenticity of this section of Zechariah. If one examines closely and critically the two parts of the book it becomes clear that there is no real ground whatever for such a view. They form two parts of one whole which are closely bound together by inseparable links, showing how the promises of the earlier section will be brought about by God. That the ascription of the book in the Jewish canon is wholly to Zechariah also confirms this view. The whole book is the inspired writing of the prophet whose name it bears.

The aim of the prophecies

Chapters 9 to 14 of Zechariah form the second of the two parts of the book. They consist of two undated oracles concerning the Messiah and the future blessing of Israel (see 9.1 & 12.1). The first oracle contains three chapters – 9 to 11, and the second oracle contains three chapters – 12 to 14. These two oracles or "burdens" fix attention on the two advents of Christ – His first coming in grace and His second coming in glory. The word "burden" in the headings at 9.1 & 12.1 indicates that the two portions have the common character of a threatening prophecy burdened with wrath against the guilty. They speak in the main of judgments to fall upon the enemies of Israel and God's dealings with His people in order to restore them. The chapters expand and develop the eschatological content of the visions in chapters 1 to 8. The second section of Zechariah contains perhaps some of the most remarkable prophecies of the Messiah anywhere in Scripture. There is a tremendous concentration of truth concerning the Messiah, so detailed, so graphic, and so accurate. In these very rich chapters one pervading Person is much to the fore, it is the Messiah, the coming Saviour and King of Israel. He is presented as the Saving King (ch.9), the Strengthening Advocate (ch.10), the Shepherd Lover (ch.11), the Mighty Warrior (ch.12), the Suffering Saviour (ch.13), and the Coming Deliverer (ch.14). The aim then of these prophecies is to highlight the person of the Messiah.

The accuracy of the prophecies

In considering these passages one cannot but be impressed by the accuracy of prophecy concerning the Lord Jesus Christ. Look, for example, at 9.9, 11.12, and 12.10 and note how these prophecies regarding the procession of the Lord into the city of Jerusalem, the price at which He was valued when betrayed, and the piercing of His side at the cross were each literally and dramatically fulfilled. Could there be any doubt that the other great prophecy concerning the parting of the Mount of Olives at His second advent will also be fulfilled (14.4)? Again, at the very beginning of the first oracle one meets with a great example of the accuracy of Scripture prediction in its foretelling, 200 years before the events took place, the conquests of Alexander the Great. What confidence in the infallible word of God this should give the believer. It can truly be said that prophecy is history pre-written and Zechariah and others wrote some of that history. The Bible can be rightly called "a prophetic book". Bible prophecy is really a miracle in words showing the perfect knowledge of God as to the future. If God declares what is to happen there is nothing more certain than that it will be exactly fulfilled as He said. He is the God who declares "the end from the beginning" (Is 46.10). Attempts here and elsewhere have been made to claim that the statements must have been written after the events. This approach simply demonstrates a lack of appreciation of the glory of God in His omniscience.

The application of the prophecies

What about the application of these great prophetic utterances? While there are no direct words spoken to the remnant as there are in chs.7 & 8, it must not be forgotten that Zechariah is ministering to the remnant, many of whom were despondent. These glowing predictions of things to come for the nation were surely intended by him to encourage them in their present circumstances and to spur them on in the work of building the temple. It is unthinkable that Zechariah spoke these prophecies to no one in particular. No, these oracles would have their message of hope to Zechariah's compatriots and from them lessons should have been drawn of the need to believe God and wait on Him. The prophecies are amazing and thrilling statements that had everything in them to inspire Zechariah and his brethren. The believer today may glean much profit and uplift from these closing chapters. They may chiefly concern Israel and what will happen in the Tribulation and the Millennium, but it is important to be reminded that "All Scripture…is profitable". How true it is "that not all Scripture is about us, but all Scripture is for us"! What the Lord Jesus then will be to and for Israel in the future, He desires to be to us spiritually now. Such applications will be touched upon as this commentary continues.

Chapter 9: The Saving King of Israel

This most interesting chapter may be conveniently divided into three sections. Verses 1-8 deal with the campaigns and conquests of Alexander the Great in 333 BC. Verses 9-11 speak about the coming of the Messiah and His entry into Jerusalem in AD 33 and look on also to His millennial reign. Verses 12-17 take in mainly the conflicts of the Maccabean period in 175 to 63 BC and in particular when the Jews rebelled against the tyranny of Antiochus Epiphanes, but look on also beyond that to the restoration of Israel. It is significant to note that in the chapter we have three battles and three victories: the battles and victories of Alexander, the victory of the Messiah, and the victory of the Jews through the Maccabees. First the chapter shows how God used Alexander as His instrument to punish Gentile cities. (It is appreciated that some commentators do not see the first section of ch.9 as referring to the Greek conqueror, but the details given seem so precise and fitting to the campaigns of Alexander that the present writer has no doubt that Alexander's march and victories are in view.) Then it also shows how God would use Israel as His instrument to subdue Gentile enemies, for Judah will be His bow and Ephraim His arrow (v.13). Looking at these three sections we will consider them in the following way: vv.1-8 - The *Advances* of Alexander the Great; vv.9-11 - The *Advents* of the Messiah in grace and glory; vv.12-17 - The *Adversaries* of the Jews.

Verses 1-8: The Advances of Alexander the Great

These verses describe the march of Alexander the Great and his army through the area north and east of Palestine. It is interesting to note how the chapter begins and ends. It commences with the eyes of men (v.1), or as some read, "Jehovah has His eyes upon men…" (cp. JND; LXX etc.), and concludes with the eyes of God in v.8. Zechariah traces the course of Alexander's conquests, beginning at Damascus and extending along the Mediterranean coast to Philistine cities (vv.2-7), and concludes with God's concern for the safety of the Jewish people amidst the conquests of Alexander (v.8). This first section contains two prophecies that were dramatically fulfilled over 300 years before Christ came. Verses 2-4 refer to the fall of Tyre and v.8 refers to God protecting Jerusalem from the advance of Alexander. Zechariah is not alone in his prophecy concerning Alexander, for Daniel pictures him as a he-goat in his victory over the Medo-Persian Empire (Dan 8.5-9) and describes him as the "mighty king" (11.3) who invaded Persia and destroyed that empire, died early, and whose kingdom was divided into four parts. None of his family succeeded to his authority, nor did any of the generals who divided the empire rule with his supreme power, and in due time the whole Grecian empire was "plucked up" and passed to "others besides these" generals, that is, to the Romans. The prophetic details concerning Alexander given in the passage are graphic, fascinating and most interesting and show what a wonderful book the

Bible is. Zechariah traces the course and campaign of Alexander in the following way: his conquest over Syria (v.1); his conquest of Phoenicia (vv.2-4); his conquest of Philistia (vv.5-7); God's protection of His people from Alexander (v.8). All the cities mentioned in the passage are representative cities. Damascus and Hamath represent Syria; Tyre and Zidon (Sidon) represent Phoenicia; Ashkelon, Gaza, Ekron, and Ashdod represent Philistia or the Philistines.

Before going through this remarkable section it is of interest at this point to give a little historical sketch of Alexander. His name was Alexander III of Macedonia, though he has become better known as Alexander the Great. He single–handedly changed the entire nature of the ancient world in a little more than ten years. Born in the northern Greek kingdom of Macedonia in 356 BC to Philip II and his formidable wife Olympias, Alexander was educated by the philosopher Aristotle. Following his father's assassination in 336 BC, he inherited a powerful yet volatile kingdom, which he had to secure – along with the rest of the Greek city states – before he could set out to conquer the massive Persian Empire in revenge for Persia's earlier attempts to conquer Greece.

Against overwhelming odds, he led his army to victories across the Persian territories of Asia Minor, Syria, and Egypt without incurring a single defeat. With his greatest victory at the battle of Gaugamela in 331 BC, in what is now northern Iraq, the young king of Macedonia, leader of the Greeks, Overlord of Asia Minor, and Pharaoh of Egypt also became Great King of Persia at the age of 25. Over the next eight years, in his capacity as king, commander, politician, scholar, and explorer, Alexander led his army a further 11,000 miles, founding over 70 cities and creating an empire that stretched across three continents and covered some two million square miles. The entire area from Greece to the west, north to the Danube, south into Egypt, and as far east as the Indian Punjab, was linked together in a vast international network of trade and commerce. This was united by a common language and culture, whilst the king himself adopted foreign customs in order to rule his millions of ethnically diverse subjects. He died in 323 BC at the early age of 32. Although Alexander's empire was torn apart in the power struggles of his successors, his mythical status rapidly reached epic proportions and inspired individuals as diverse as Julius Caesar, Cleopatra, Louis XIV, and Napoleon.

His conquest of Syria (v.1)

The land of Hadrach mentioned here seems to be a symbolical name used by Zechariah to represent the second great world-power of the book of Daniel, the Medo-Persian Empire. The cities mentioned were within the land of Hadrach and belonged to that Empire. These are Damascus and Hamath. Zechariah announces a severe judgment upon them, and to accomplish this God used Alexander to inflict it. How solemn to think that God can use heathen men and a powerful and brilliant person like Alexander as an instrument in His hand to bring about His purposes.

Alexander and his armies fell with all their force upon these Syrian towns. In attacking Syria Alexander really wanted to capture Damascus. It soon fell to him, and Hamath, which bordered on Damascus, suffered the same fate. One can imagine the devastating and dispiriting effect these conquests would have had on other nearby nations such as Israel, Phoenicia, and Philistia. The great success of Alexander must have filled them with fear. But then Zechariah says, "When the eyes of man, as of all the tribes of Israel, shall be toward the Lord". If this translation is correct it could mean that as Israel and other nations looked upon Alexander and his success they would see God at work in and through him to inflict punishment upon a people and city like Damascus that had been bitter opponents of His people. Several have rendered it otherwise, including Helen Spurrel in her translation: "Surely the eye of Jehovah is upon man, yea over all the tribes of Israel". This then would mean that the Lord is not only watching over His people Israel, who at that time were surrounded by the might of this world-power, but also watching over the men – their foes – who were bent on destroying Israel. He had His eyes upon both and was controlling everything. If this is the meaning, and in our view it seems to fit in well with the context of God controlling the movements of Alexander, then it is good to take from this the most reassuring thought that God is ordering all the arrangements of men in this world and all the counsels of its rulers for the good of His people. Nothing can happen or be done without Him, and whatever takes place His care for His people remains constant.

It is to be noted that Damascus was not to be destroyed, but God's judgment was to permanently dwell there. This is indicated in the words, "the rest thereof". Damascus has figured in history long since Alexander conquered it and remains today. Apparently Damascus has been occupied continuously for a longer period of time than any other city in the world and can claim to be the world's oldest city. Damascus became a captive state of first the Assyrians, then the Babylonians, Persians, Greeks, Ptolemies, and Seleucids. Finally, Rome gained control under Pompey in 64 BC. Jews began to migrate to Damascus and establish synagogues there. Thus Saul went to Damascus to determine if any Christians were attached to the synagogues there so that he might persecute them (Acts 9). The Damascus Road became the site of Saul's conversion experience and Damascus the place of his introduction to the church. He had to escape from Damascus in a basket to begin his ministry (2 Cor 11.32-33). The Arabs captured it in AD 636 and made it a capital city for the Moslem world, which it continues to be.

His conquest of Phoenicia (vv.2-4)

Alexander defeated the Persians in 333 BC at the Battle of Issus, and then turned to conquer the leading cities of Tyre and Sidon in Phoenicia.

These cities were located on the coastal plain between the mountains of Lebanon and the Mediterranean Sea. Tyre and Sidon were ancient cities, having been founded long before the Israelites entered the land of Canaan. Extra-biblical sources first mention Sidon before 2000 BC and Tyre just after 2000 BC. While Sidon seems to have been the more dominant of the two cities during the early part of their histories, Tyre assumed this role in the latter times. Both were known for their maritime exploits and as centres of trade. In these verses we have a succinct and exact outline of an historical event, namely the capture by Alexander of the city of Tyre. The details are precise and true as to what happened to Tyre. Either this prophecy, as others in Zechariah, was a literary fraud written after the events, or else it was what it purports to be, a divine prophecy. Faith happily accepts the latter.

Tyre was noted for its wisdom (see Ezek 28.3,4,5,12,17). The wisdom of its inhabitants is seen in building a stronghold. They put their confidence in the city's great physical fortification which had been built for her protection. They constructed a wall 150 feet high around the city, which stood on an island just offshore. The Assyrians in the past had for five years tried to overcome it. Later Nebuchadnezzar laid siege against it for thirteen years, but it remained untaken and unconquered. Although Alexander had no navy, in seven months he built a causeway from the mainland out to the island bastion and took and destroyed the city. He thus with brilliant thinking and determination accomplished what Nebuchadnezzar could not do in thirteen years. In so doing, this Scripture was literally fulfilled without Alexander having the least idea that he was fulfilling Hebrew prophecy, nor probably knowing a word of the prediction. How wonderful is God's word and how good for the believer to look back in history and see how the prophetic word of God never fails.

The rest of the prophecy concerning Tyre describes her great wealth which had been amassed through commerce. This is further emphasized and underscored by the similes: "heaped up silver as the dust, and fine gold as the mire of the streets". Such was Tyre's proverbial wealth, but her abundance and boast in her strength could not save her from destruction. This is announced in v.4: "Behold, the Lord will cast her out, and he will smite her power in the sea; and she shall be devoured with fire". Any parts of the city which did not go down into the sea would be consumed by fire. No matter how secure or wealthy people make themselves, God will bring it to nothing. The true security and wealth of the believer lies in dependent faith in the Living God. It is interesting to note that Zechariah is not the only prophet who pronounced the doom of Tyre, for Ezekiel too foretold its destruction as given in 26.1-14 of his prophecy. His language is just as remarkable as Zechariah's regarding exactly what would happen to Tyre, as for example, "And they shall destroy the walls of Tyrus, and break down her towers: I will also scrape her dust from her, and make her like the top of a rock" (v.4). Zechariah says, "The Lord will cast her out". God had ordained in His purposes to destroy these places and used Alexander to this end.

His conquest of Philistia (vv.5-7)

The taking of Tyre would have spread fear and consternation among the nations which were next in Alexander's path of destruction. Hearing of his approach to Tyre they must have had high hopes that it would again withstand another attempt by an enemy to capture her and that Alexander's progress would be hindered in his advance southward through Philistia to Egypt. It would have been very alarming for Philistia and Israel when hearing the tidings that Tyre had fallen. Ekron especially, being the northernmost of the four cities mentioned, would be afraid. Thus we read, "Ashkelon shall see it, and fear; Gaza also shall see it, and be very sorrowful, and Ekron; for her expectation shall be ashamed". They would reason that if a city like Tyre with its virtually impregnable defence had been overcome, what hope had they with far smaller defences. God would destroy these cities and populate Ashdod with a "bastard" (or an alien people of a mixed race). The cities were destroyed and its citizens slain or made slaves. After his victories Alexander often populated the cities with people of a mixed race. The only historical record outside of Scripture of Alexander's conquering of the four Philistine cities is that of Gaza. It states that after the city fell to him he had their king tied to a chariot wheel and dragged through the streets of the city until he perished. This cruel action was intended by Alexander to be a lesson to other cities that he was a force to be reckoned with and would not tolerate resistance.

God declares that He will "cut off the pride of the Philistines". As Alexander swept through the south this is just what happened. The pride of the Philistines was humbled. The loss of their political independence, their national distinction, and their religious temples was a terrible rebuke to their pride. She was an arrogant nation and God was going to change her by breaking down her pride. The next thing we learn that God was going to do is stated in v.7. He was going to remove two things from their mouths: the blood of idolatrous sacrifices, and the polluted or ceremonially unclean food. Their repulsive rituals would be judged. All this and no doubt other heathen practices were part of their pagan worship. The Holman Bible Dictionary describes the Philistines as "One of the rival groups the Israelites encountered as they settled the land of Canaan. References to the Philistines appear in the Old Testament as well as other ancient Near Eastern writings. *Philistine* refers to a group of people who occupied and gave their name to the southwest part of Palestine. Ancient Egyptian records from the time of Merneptah and Ramses III referred to them as the 'prst'. Ancient Assyrian records include references to the Philistines in the terms *Philisti* and *Palastu*". Yet here is a wonder; God's judgment would be mixed with mercy, for He would preserve a remnant of them for Himself - "But he that remaineth, even he, shall be for our God, and he shall be as a

governor in Judah, and Ekron as a Jebusite". This is where the verse
becomes prophetic of the future. The plain meaning is that a remnant of
Philistines will be preserved and go into the millennial Kingdom of Christ.
Just as after David conquered Jerusalem, the Jebusites, the original native
inhabitants of the city, were spared and were merged into Judah, so some
Philistines will have a place with Israel in the Millennium. This is rather
remarkable because it is well known to students of Scripture that the
Philistines have always been the enemies of Israel.

God's protection of His people (v.8)

"I will encamp about mine house because of the army, because of him
that passeth by, and because of him that returneth." This promise was
partially and very remarkably fulfilled when Alexander marched into Egypt
and overran the area. The house referred to may either be the land of
Israel or the temple. "Jeddua the high priest at the time heard that
Alexander was coming. He was terrified and ordered his people to join
him in prayer and sacrifice to God. Appearing to him in a dream God told
him to take courage and decorate the city with wreathes. The people were
to clothe themselves with white and the priests with the robes of their
order. They were then to march out of the gates to meet the Macedonians,
for they would not be harmed. Jeddua on awaking rejoiced and announced
this revelation to all. When he learned that Alexander was not far from the
city, he went out in procession with the people. When they met, Alexander
prostrated himself before the high priest and greeted him. His officers
wondered if he had suddenly become insane. Then all the Jews together
greeted Alexander with one voice and surrounded him. Alexander was
escorted into Jerusalem by the high priest and his attendants. He went up
into the temple, where he sacrificed to God according to the high priest's
directions. And when the book of Daniel was shown to him, which
predicted that one of the Greeks would destroy the Persian Empire, he
thought himself to be the one so designated" (Josephus, *Antiquities of
the Jews*, Book 11). Alexander not only spared Jerusalem and the temple,
but showed the Jews many favours. If the Jewish historian is correct in his
facts, and there is no reason to doubt the incident, then the terms of
Zechariah's prophecy were met by what took place. Thus providentially
God cared for His people and protected them from the armies of Alexander.

The prophecy however, has never yet been completely fulfilled for God
adds, "No oppressor shall pass through them any more". Here in the middle
of the verse we have a great leap in time from the amazing event of God
defending His people against Alexander to the time when Jerusalem and
Israel will never again be overrun by oppressors. This must look on to the
second advent of Christ when the army of the king of the North at the
time of the end will come against Israel. When the last oppressor of God's
people has been overcome, this prophecy will then have its final fulfilment.
In this one verse again we have an example of a near fulfilment and a more

distant fulfilment of prophecy. The passage ends with the comforting words, "For now have I seen with mine eyes". Just as God had seen the affliction of His people long ago in Egypt (Ex 3.7) and had moved to intervene, so He saw the danger of His people when Alexander advanced and will see the greater danger of His people in the end time. How true is Psalm 121.4: "Behold, he that keepeth Israel shall neither slumber nor sleep". Today we live in very critical times when so many nations are indifferent to little Israel and some nations too are very opposed to her. Even the USA, at one time pro Israel, is not as forthcoming in their support as they once were. As believers we should pray for the peace of Jerusalem and yet rest assured that God will always protect His earthly people and, according to the prophetic word, will deliver and preserve them for His glory.

Before leaving this section one might ask, "Why has Zechariah written all this concerning Alexander and why does it come in just before the wonderful prophecy of the first advent of Christ?". The answer is that Alexander changed world history, and by spreading Greek culture and the Greek language he unified the world, and under God, without realising it, prepared the way for the coming of the Saviour into the world. When the Romans took over, they found an empire already there for them. Greek was the language of literature, and the New Testament was written in the common Greek language of the people of that day. In many ways it was an ideal time for the Lord to come into the world, and after His death, resurrection, and ascension to heaven the common language greatly facilitated the spread of the gospel over the then known world.

Verses 9-11: The Advents of the Messiah in Grace and Glory
The coming of the King (v.9)

At v.9, from contemplating the coming of the conqueror Alexander, Zechariah makes a sudden transition to the coming of the far greater Conqueror and King, the Lord Jesus Christ. It is through the coming of this great and mighty One that God will camp about His House, deliver His people, and bring to pass that blessed and wonderful time when "no oppressor shall pass through them anymore". The portrait here of the King and His salvation concerns the first advent of Christ as He came in grace to the nation of Israel. It is perhaps one of the greatest and most remarkable of all the prophecies in the Old Testament. The event of the Lord entering Jerusalem riding on the ass is so important that each of the four Gospels in the New Testament record it. Our Lord rode into Jerusalem to present His claims as the true King of Israel. This is often referred to as the Lord's triumphal entry into Jerusalem on that first Palm Sunday. He was commencing His last week on earth which would culminate in His crucifixion. Some brief comments on the way that Matthew and John use this great prediction should be profitable. Matthew makes clear that the scene he portrays of the entering into the city was a literal fulfilment of this prophecy, for he says, "All this was done, that it might be fulfilled which was spoken by the prophet saying…" (21.4). In Matthew's use of the passage, as also in John 12.15, there is no reference to the word "rejoice". How could the nation rejoice when they rejected their own King? There can be no joy to Israel until the Lord returns to them and they accept Him as the Messiah. How sad that the nation was so blind, and that as a result no salvation could be enjoyed by them. In John's use of the passage it is to be noted that there is no mention of the Lord's character as being "lowly". This is because John in his Gospel is occupied with the glory of the Son.

The whole verse touching the Messiah King deserves some attention. Four aspects of the Lord's person as the King are presented by Zechariah and every one of these show God's ideal King and very sharply contrast with Alexander the ambitious and powerful king. The coming of Alexander the Great in the main caused much fear among the people he approached, but the coming of the Messiah could only cause great joy. Hence this prophecy is prefaced with these words to the nation, "Rejoice greatly". What joy the nation lost through their rejection of their Messiah.

His character

"Behold thy King cometh cometh unto thee: he is just." Here we are introduced to a king in contrast to the one who has been the subject of vv.1-8. God calls Him, "*thy* King". In Psalm 2.6 He is "*my* king", says God. In Isaiah 32.1 the prophet says that He is "*a* king" who will reign in righteousness. In Revelation 17.14 the Apostle John says simply, He is "King of kings". The pronoun "thy" in the passage here is interesting and significant making clear that the Lord Jesus was Israel's very own King. He was sent by God to be such. He was the greatest King Israel could have had. Unlike the wicked and cruel Herods He would have delivered, blessed and protected them. The first great reason why Israel should rejoice is because of the coming of this King. Here is a King unlike other kings who in every sense is "just", not merely in His dealings, but in His very character. This is the characteristic of the ideal King, and the Lord Jesus fills to perfection David's words, "He that ruleth over men must be just" (2 Sam 23.3; cp. Ps 72.1-3 and Is 9.7). The righteous character of the Lord's life on earth was beyond the slightest doubt and it is interesting to see in Matthew, the Gospel of the King, that he alone in recording our Lord's trial mentions the threefold testimony to the Lord's character. First from Judas the betrayer who said, "I have sinned in that I have betrayed the innocent blood". Then from Pilate's wife, "Have thou nothing to do with that just man". Finally Pilate himself, "I am innocent of the blood of this just person" (Mt 27.4,19,24). There was no King like Him before or since, and there never will be. What a contrast to Alexander. Far from just he was a sinner. Though his men loved him and he inspired their devotion, he could be cruel and merciless. Does the lovely character of Christ and what He has done for us inspire our love and devotion?

His blessing

"Having salvation" - what blessing the Lord had for His people, but alas they were blind to who He was and to the great deliverance He had come to give them. After the incident of entering the city on the colt Luke records that He wept over the city and said, "If thou hadst known, even thou, at least in this thy day, the things which belong unto thy peace! but now they are hid from thine eyes" (Lk 19.42). While one may read into this "salvation" that which delivers from sin's penalty, i.e. the salvation of the soul, it is better to interpret the word in the context as specifically relating to the salvation of Israel. Thank God for the salvation of every sinner through faith in Christ and His sacrifice, but here Zechariah speaks of a wonderful deliverance that Christ came to give the nation from their enemies. The opportunity to experience this they missed, but the next verse goes on to show that after the second advent of Christ this will certainly be achieved – "all Israel shall be saved" (Rom 11.26). Needless to say when Alexander rose up and marched through many lands his purpose was to destroy and not save.

His disposition

Here is a unique King indeed, for He is lowly. This is not what the nation might have expected in a King. Few, if any, kings even in Israel's past history can truly be described as "lowly". This disposition was not appreciated by the nation of Israel when the Lord of glory moved among them. Instead they despised and rejected Him and one may well wonder at this, when their own Scriptures foretold that this would be true of the coming Messiah. His lowliness is seen demonstrated in His riding an ass. Usually a king would ride a horse, for the horse is the symbol of strength and victory. This will be true of the Lord when He returns to the earth in majesty and power, for He is depicted by the seer in Revelation 19.11-16 seated on a white horse, but the ass is a symbol here of lowliness. In spite of this amazing prophecy the nation did not recognize such a quality in Him and even the Pharisees openly resisted Him (Lk 19.39). God's King and Israel's stood one day and said, "I am meek and lowly in heart" (Mt 11.29). How delightful this is and how good and reassuring to see that His lowly character is the very thing that should draw the believer to Himself to take His yoke upon them and learn of Him. Thus we have both the experience of Christ to enjoy and the example of Christ to emulate. From what is known of Alexander in history he certainly was not lowly, but proud and ambitious, yet he died at a young age without permanently enjoying the fruits of his world-wide conquests. Through humility and lowliness Christ was exalted to the throne of God and because of this God will reward Him with universal rule. Alexander by contrast, after all his successes in his lust for power and world-wide dominion, died with his plans unfulfilled. If we were to press the meaning and usage of the word "lowly" it means to be bowed down, to suffer, or to be afflicted. The word embraces the whole of the lowly and suffering condition so detailed in Isaiah 53. It indicates how lowly He became even in His suffering on the cross.

His control

The fourth feature of the King here is that He would ride upon an ass and upon a colt the foal of an ass. Normally our blessed Lord walked from place to place in His public ministry. What a picture this is of the Messiah sitting upon an ass, and not only an ass but upon a colt, a young animal unbroken and untrained: "…and upon a colt, the foal of an ass". The second part of the phrase more precisely defines the kind of ass upon which the Messiah would ride and shows again how accurate Zechariah's language is. Both Mark and Luke tell us that it had never been ridden before. In spite of this the animal was submissive to Christ. "The inexperienced colt may not have had strength to bear the burden and certainly had no knowledge of the way to Jerusalem. He who had called it would supply all needed energy and He knew every step of the dusty road which led up to the city of God" (H. St John, *An Analysis of the Gospel of Mark*). The ass, in being controlled by Christ, was a picture message to Israel showing that the nation should have immediately recognized Him and been willing to be under the authority of the lowly Son of Man. In the ancient east rulers commonly rode asses if they came in peace, but in warfare they rode on horses (Judg 5.10; 10.4). Horses would have been present and used in our Lord's day, but it seems that since Solomon's day (he multiplied horses) no king is mentioned as sitting upon an ass. At the very least the Lord riding the ass shows that in Him there was an absence of pomp and worldly display. The Lord Jesus, then, rides not on the noble horse, but on the humble donkey. Still thinking of the contrast between the two kings Alexander and Christ, Alexander rode a mighty steed and riding it proudly led a great army from one victory to another, but the Lord rode a lowly donkey and came in humility. There are touching contrasts between how the Lord entered the city and how six days later He came out of it to be crucified. As He entered the city they took off garments and laid them in His path, but when taken out of the city they stripped Him of His garments. When He entered the city they laid down palm leaves as He approached, but at Calvary they put a crown of thorns upon His head. As He entered the city He was carried on an ass, but as He left it He carried His own cross. Entering the city they cried, "Hosanna", and praised Him, but as He left it they said, "Away with him", and thus pained Him. There is much here to feed and move the soul and cause the heart to well up in praise for such a Saviour.

The Lord's entry into Jerusalem on the ass was typical of His whole life of humility and lowliness and may also be regarded as a symbolic act or rehearsal of what will happen on a much larger scale at His return to the earth and the city of Jerusalem. In John 12 there seems to be a Spirit-constructed dispensational picture, for after resurrection and reunion seen in Lazarus restored to his sisters in Bethany, there is the supper in the house, then the Lord as King entering into the city, and thirdly the coming of Gentiles to see and worship Christ. What a suggestive picture of that which will follow the resurrection of the church – the marriage supper, the second advent, and then the universal acknowledgment of Christ's Kingship.

It might well be asked, what has Zechariah 9.9 to do with the people in Zechariah's day? It must have had a message for the little remnant. Is this not why the great prophecy is announced to the daughter of Zion and Jerusalem? This word "daughter" must be a reference to the remnant. Should they not have taken great comfort from the prophecy? Their expected Messiah would surely come to deliver, and the character in which He is presented was exactly suited to the remnant in their weakness and need. Then again one may think of the remnant in the Lord's day, for the Lord here is presented in such a way that only the remnant with spiritual discernment and with knowledge of the Scriptures would recognize Him. One practical lesson we may draw from this is simply to ask why it was that the Lord needed the colt. His direction to the two disciples sent to fetch the animal was that if they were asked, "Why do ye this?", they were to reply, "The Lord hath need of him" (Mk 11.3). Did the Lord need to be seated on the animal merely that He might be elevated and therefore easily seen by all? No. He needed the colt so that He might fulfil His own word and further His purposes. The Lord needs each individual believer. Many believers consider themselves of no use to the Lord and feel too that they are just a tiny dot among many millions in this world, but we all need to understand that the Lord has a need and place for us and how wonderful it is to be used by Him even in some small and unassuming way to further His work.

The condition of the Kingdom (v.10)

In this verse the prophet passes over the church dispensation and goes on to speak of the second advent in glory of Christ. Without the use that the New Testament makes of v.9 one might easily get the impression that Zechariah speaks of one coming and not two, but this passage is one of the great instances of long gaps in God's prophetic programme. What is the cause of this gap? Sadly it is there because of the rejection of the Messiah predicted in ch.11. So between v.9 and v.10 the entire age of the church fits in. There are other examples of such time gaps in prophecy such as Isaiah 9.6-7 and Isaiah 61.2. Verse 9 here announces what the Messiah will do and what will be the consequences of His second advent. He will bring to an end four things.

The division of the Kingdom will end

The verse gives a second reason why the remnant can rejoice, not only for the salvation the Messiah will bring, but for the establishment of His

Kingdom. When the Messiah begins to reign there will no longer be a need for tools of warfare, for the chariot from Ephraim and the horse from Jerusalem and the battle bow shall be cut off. Weapons of warfare will either be removed or converted into peaceful purposes. The mention of Ephraim and Jerusalem here denotes the ten tribes and Judah and Benjamin. Under the reign of the Messiah the two kingdoms will be united once more and the division which took place in the time of Rehoboam and Jeroboam will be healed (1 Kings 12). This is seen in the prophecy of Ezekiel in ch.37 concerning the two sticks, one representing Ephraim and the other Judah coming together as one. Thus there will be a full restoration of Israel. The long standing differences and conflicts between Ephraim and Judah and the weapons used when engaging in battle with one another will all come to an end. There is quite a contrast between v.9 and v.10, not only because they refer to the two separate advents of Christ, but because the lowly one of v.9 becomes the mighty victorious one of v.10. What a difference too between the mention of the ass in v.9 and the mention of the horse, the more powerful beast, in v.10.

The distress of the Tribulation will end
"He shall speak peace unto the heathen", that is He will speak authoritatively, so as to bring all the conflicts of the nations to an end. The Millennium will be characterized by universal peace. For seven years at least, prior to Christ's Kingdom, there will be unrest and disquiet among the nations and a struggle for supremacy between them. The second half of the Tribulation will be the beginning of sorrows for Israel and there will be worldwide trouble culminating in the campaign of Armageddon. What a relief it will be for Israel and all the nations after this period of distress. There will be times of refreshing for them from the presence of the Lord (Acts 3.19).

The dictatorship of the Antichrist will end
"His dominion shall be from sea even to sea, and from the river even to the ends of the earth." The two seas mentioned here are most likely the Red Sea and the Mediterranean. The river is the Euphrates. Jerusalem and the land of Israel will then be extended to the limits promised to Abraham, and will be the centre of the Messiah-King's future dominion, from whence it will be extended to the remotest parts of the earth (Ps 72.8; Micah 7.12; Is 7.20). The ambition of the Antichrist will be to have universal sway. He will accept what the true Messiah refused from the Devil in the temptation in the wilderness. He took the Lord up to a high mountain and showed Him all the kingdoms of the world and the glory of them, and said, "All these things will I give thee, if thou wilt fall down and worship me" (Mt 4.8-9). The Antichrist will accept the glory of the kingdoms, but it will be short-lived. He will reign supreme for three and a half years, but his world-wide dictatorship will be brought to a sudden and solemn end when the

Lord appears in glory and power. One look and word from the Messiah will paralyse the Devil's superman and his armies and they will be destroyed (2 Thess 2.8; Rev 19.19-21). The Lord Jesus is the true Heir to the kingdoms of this world. In Psalm 2.8 the Messiah is addressed by God: "Ask of me, and I shall give thee the heathen (nations) for thine inheritance". The time to ask and receive these nations so that they all may be in subjection to Christ is not now, nor in the Tribulation, but when He comes to conquer and set up His Kingdom. Thus the fear and distress among the nations caused by the Antichrist will be over.

The mention of the River Euphrates is interesting. It is one of the four rivers referred to in Genesis 2. It is the future boundary of the Promised Land, and figures much in the prophecies of things to come. The Euphrates was known as "the great river" (Gen 15.18; Josh 1.4) or "the river" (Num 22.5) to the Hebrews. It formed the northern boundary of the land promised by Jehovah to Israel (Gen 15.18; Deut 1.7). The Euphrates is mentioned in the book of Revelation as the place where angels were bound (9.14) and where the sixth vial was poured out (16.12).

The dispersion of the Jews will end

"As for thee also, by the blood of thy covenant I have sent forth thy prisoners out of the pit wherein is no water." Here in v.11 Jerusalem is addressed with these words and they indicate that in addition to cutting off the weapons of warfare and extending the dominion of the Messiah to the ends of the earth, God will also deliver His exiled people from their foreign captivity. They are pictured here as in "a pit wherein is no water". Dungeons were often pits without water, and miry at the bottom. Jeremiah sank down in one when imprisoned (Jer 38.6). The image of the pit portrays the misery that the Jews have been in for centuries. They had been in the pit of Babylonian captivity, but in the end times they will find themselves in a far deeper and more wretched pit, yet God will deliver them. These foreign Jewish exiles from all parts of the world will all be delivered by the blood of the covenant which must mean according to the covenant vouchsafed at Sinai and ratified by the blood of sacrifices (Ex 24.8; Heb 9.18-20). In virtue of this blood by which Israel has been received into covenant with God, they will be delivered from all bondage and strife. God will gather His people from all parts of the earth. Scattered and dispersed all over the world as they are, God will bring about the miracle of their restoration to Himself and the land. Of course it must not be forgotten that the blood of Christ shed at Calvary will bring blessing to the nation of Israel in the future. The sacrifices at Sinai that established the covenant only had virtue in prefiguring the sacrifice of Calvary.

Verses 12-17: The Adversaries of the Jews

This last section mainly takes in the period of struggle for independence

by the Jew in the land in the time of the Maccabees. This period commenced
with efforts on their part to oppose and resist Antiochus Epiphanes. He
sought to impose idolatrous Greek worship upon the Jews. The struggles
of this period, however, are only a foreshadowing of the troublesome times
ahead for the Jew and of the coming of Christ when He will intervene for
their deliverance from a far greater enemy. The appeal in v.12 for the
prisoners of hope to look to the "strong hold" is a beautiful reference to
the Messiah. He will be Israel's Stronghold. The opposite of a pit is a
stronghold or place cut off, that is, a fortified place. Israel will find security
in their Messiah. He will not disappoint them or surrender them to their
enemies. In the earlier verses Tyre was mentioned as a stronghold. They
assumed that fortifying their city as they did rendered it impregnable to
their enemies, but what they thought was impossible was not so in the
eyes of Alexander, and eventually it fell to him. This stronghold will never
give way or fall to the enemy. Israel will find a safe refuge in Christ. The
description of the people as "prisoners of hope" is interesting and
significant, for it implies that Israel possess a wonderful hope of deliverance.
God said to them through Jeremiah, "There is hope in thine end…that
thy children shall come again to their own border" (Jer 31.17). In the days
of the Tribulation and the Antichrist and when at the height of Armageddon
Israel is being attacked, their hope will seem lost (Ezek 37.11), but their
Messiah will come to deliver and their hope for the nation will then be
revitalised and their joy will be full. How comforting are these words for
Israel: "I will render double unto thee". This refers to their full restoration.
It is God's promise that He would give Israel double of all He had allowed
their enemies to take from them. When will this happen? The appeal here
is to "Turn you to the strong hold". Only when the nation turns to Christ
and places their trust in Him will they be delivered. The "today" mentioned
here must be the day when Christ returns with salvation for His people
and speaks peace to them.

Messiah their Leader (vv.13-14)

There is no doubt that these verses had an initial and partial fulfilment
when, in the time of the Maccabbees in the second century BC, the Jews
overthrew the Greeks. It was a bitter, violent and murderous conflict which
finally brought victory to the Jews. They were inspired and strengthened
in these battles which they were fighting in the belief that it was God's
cause and that He was with them. It was His battle and He would give
them victory. They were fighting for their independence. Against
overwhelming odds God gave them strength to win these battles and
secure for themselves freedom from the cruel yoke of Antiochus
Epiphanes. Thus God indicates here that the Jews once again, before
their Messiah comes, will possess military power. This has been the
case in more recent times when in the remarkable Six Day War they
overcame Egypt. Israel today in a military sense possess much skill and

genius, but in the coming great conflict it will be the Messiah who helps them to victory and not any modern weapons or military skill on their part.

These verses are full of figurative language. "I have bent Judah for me, filled the bow with Ephraim." Jehovah is pictured as a warrior gaining the victory for His people. Judah is the drawn bow, Ephraim the arrow, and Zion the sword in the hand of Jehovah. Both Zion and Greece are addressed here and God speaks of His people under the imagery of the sword of a mighty man. The nation under the hand of God will be like the sword wielded in the hand of a powerful warrior – "irresistible and invincible", to use the words of T. V. Moore. Again there is little doubt that such prophetic words refer to the handful of Jews who finally overcame their Greek enemies. The Jews fought and won like heroes. It is remarkable that God should address the "sons [of] Greece" here, for it must be remembered that at the time that Zechariah wrote this the Greeks were little known beyond their own land and were far from being a world power. It is another example of the wonder of prophecy and shows how much was revealed to this young priest-prophet. That the Greek power should be referred to here is natural and understandable, for after Alexander's death it was Greece that succeeded him in worldwide dominion.

"The Lord shall be seen over them." Three more graphic images are used by the Spirit in this verse to describe the powerful and swift way the Messiah will deal with the enemy. He will lead His people to victory. He will visibly take His place as Commander of His armies. He will be over them like a banner or standard. As in the beginning of Israel's history Jehovah vanquished Pharaoh and the flower of his trained army, so again in and through the Messiah He will miraculously deliver His people. His arrows will shoot forth swiftly like lightning, not missing their mark. He will blow the trumpet to advance, and its sounds will be like claps of thunder and the noise of a whirlwind storm coming from the south. Messiah will come to deliver His people riding the stormy winds. In all His fury as a mighty warrior He will go forth, and just as storms from the south can cause much fear so the enemies of Israel and the Messiah will be filled with dread at His advance. Storms and whirlwinds are often used in the Old Testament as solemn pictures of divine wrath. The prophets, for example, used the storm-wind as a figure for judgment (Is 5.28; Jer 4.13; Hos 8.7; Amos 1.14; Zech 7.14).

Messiah their Protector (v.15)

"The Lord of hosts shall defend them." The Messiah will not only fight for His people, but He will be a shield to them as well, covering them against the weapons of their enemies. Hence they are able to destroy their foes, and like the devouring lions to eat their flesh and drink their blood. It is an awful picture, but that this lies at the root of the word "devour" is made clear from the imagery that Balaam uses of

Israel in Numbers 23.24. Zechariah may well have had Balaam's words in mind: "Behold, the people shall rise up as a great lion, and lift up himself as a young lion: he shall not lie down until he eat of the prey and drink the blood of the slain". Thus under the Messiah Israel will unsparingly devour her enemies. "Subdue with sling stones" might be better rendered "tread down with sling stones". It is not the idea of subduing with sling stones as David did with Goliath using such a simple weapon, but rather that Israel will tread under their feet the stones the enemy hurls at them. It is an image of how the nation will completely crush their foe. The last picture in the verse is that Israel will be like men making a noise as though drunk with wine – in this case the blood of their enemies. They will be filled with blood as were the bowls in which the priests caught the blood of the animals that were slain. As the corners of the altar were sprinkled with the blood, so Israel will be sprinkled with the blood of their enemies. Their Messiah too is depicted in Revelation 19.13 as being clothed with a vesture dipped in blood – not His own blood, but the blood of His and Israel's enemies. How graphic the imagery and yet how horrible and fearful it is. The arrival of the Lord to deal with Israel's foes will be sudden and the sight of Him will strike fear in the hearts of the armies opposing Israel.

Messiah their Saviour (v.16)

The imagery changes here from bloodshed and war to that of the shepherd with his flock. "The Lord their God shall save them in that day as the flock of his people." The Lord Jesus is seen here in two aspects. He is both Saviour and Shepherd to Israel. The Lord will not only give His people victory, but afterwards safe and lasting peace. Because Israel is His people He will tend them as a shepherd tends His flock. If it be asked, "Why will He do this?", it is because He regards His people like precious and costly stones – "stones of a crown, lifted up as an ensign upon his land", or, as the RV, "lifted on high over his land". The Lord Jesus their Messiah will by His grace give Israel honour and dignity. They will be like stones lifted up and placed upon His crown. The Lord will demonstrate to the world how precious His earthly people are. They will indeed be lifted up or lifted on high. There is quite a contrast here with the sling stones of the previous verse. There Israel's enemies are viewed as worthless sling stones to be trodden under foot. Here His people are compared to stones of the crown (Is 62.3; Mal 3.17), lifted up as an ensign that all may flock to them (Is 11.10-12). The words "lifted up" show what the grace of God will do for them in lifting them out of the long degradation and ruin they have experienced. It contrasts beautifully with the picture of the pit in v.11. Messiah will lift Israel out of the deep pit of the Tribulation and give them the highest possible glory. Israel will be the envy of the world and, like precious jewels, they will sparkle upon the land. What great things are in store for this nation, but all this will take place because the Messiah will have come as their Saviour at His second advent and then He will shepherd His people like a flock of sheep for one thousand years. Believers can rejoice in the knowledge that they are like precious stones. Each saint has been lifted up and exalted so high that they have been made to sit with Christ in heavenly places. One day the Church too will shine for God and be like a mirror reflecting the beauty of the Lord Jesus Christ.

Consummate praise (v.17)

"How great is his goodness, and how great is his beauty." It is true that the nation in future will recognize and appreciate as never before God's gracious ways with them in granting them deliverance and blessing, but it is better to understand these words of exclamation as coming from the prophet Zechariah himself. It seems that as he contemplates all the wonderful things that God will do for Israel in the future he bursts forth with praise to God. This then is his response to the prophecies of future blessing for the nation. It lets one see that Zechariah was not without feeling and soul interest in the prophecies from God that he announced. Even as the believer today reads such wonderful prophecies it should produce a similar response of praise to God. The question is, to whom do the words "goodness" and "beauty" refer - to God or to the Messiah? Some have drawn attention to the fact that the word "beauty" here is never used of God in the Old Testament, whereas the word "goodness" is (see Ps 31.19). "Beauty" is applied to the Messiah in more than one Old Testament passage (see Ps 45.2,3; Is 33.17; 53.2). In the previous verse, however, "his people" and "his land" clearly refer to Jehovah, so that it is perhaps safe in the context to think here that Jehovah is in view, and that He, through the Messiah, will display His goodness and beauty to His people. Israel too will reflect the goodness and beauty of Jehovah as jewels reflect the light. As our eyes are directed to the Lord's goodness and beauty, we also in some measure can reflect this in our own character.

Once Israel has recognized the goodness and beauty in their Messiah and given Him His place, material prosperity and abundance will follow. What a delightful description of millennial blessing is next given, for the young men will flourish through abundance of grain, the maidens through new wine. Whatever the extent of agricultural fruitfulness there may have been in the period following the Jewish victory over Antiochus Epiphanes, these conditions of blessing in the land await their complete fulfilment in the Millennium. The land of Israel then will be most fruitful, but the language here is poetic of spiritual benefits too. Young men who may have been involved in conflict during the Tribulation period will prosper as never before. Young women too whose hopes for marriage will have been reduced because of mortality among the men

who may have been fighting in the battles of that time, will be supplied
with the new wine of new-found spiritual joy in the great change in all
their circumstances.

> Now on the place of slaughter
> Are cots and sheepfolds seen,
> And rows of vines and fields of wheat
> And apple orchards green.

ZECHARIAH 10

The Strengthening Advocate of His People

The first verse of this chapter may be looked upon as a beautiful conclusion to the preceding chapter, for it commences with the blessing upon nature the Messiah will bring. The last verse of the previous chapter concluded with the prosperous and fruitful conditions marked by the abundance of corn and wine. These figures refer to the many temporal blessings Israel will enjoy in the Millennium, but no doubt they picture the spiritual blessings also that the nation will receive from their Messiah. Chapter 10 continues this in the opening verse with its reference to the latter rain. The key word in the passage is "strengthen", for twice over Jehovah declares He will strengthen His people (vv.6 & 12). The thought that God will empower His people at last to overcome their enemies is seen in the word "mighty" also occurring twice. Note that in v.5 Judah shall be "as mighty men", and Ephraim too "shall be like a mighty man" (v.7). The Messiah when He comes will give to both Judah and Ephraim superhuman strength. When God gives strength to His people, they become victorious. The sheep becomes a war horse (v.3). The feeblest person can be a hero like David (12.8) when one goes in the strength of the Lord.

The chapter is in two sections. Verses 1-6 deal with Judah and their future blessing. Verses 7-12 concern Ephraim and their restoration. It is good to see that Ephraim will receive the same salvation as Judah, and the chapter is divided in this manner to show this more clearly. One thing to note in this chapter is the fact that both Judah and Ephraim are mentioned as well as Joseph in v.6. Both Joseph and Ephraim refer to the ten tribes of Israel. There may have been a hint previously in Zechariah of blessing for the ten tribes (see 9.10), but here in this passage it is very much emphasized. How good to know then that Israel will not only be restored, but also reunited as a nation. The prophecy divides very conveniently into two sections. The first shows Israel as sheep without a shepherd needing the care of the Shepherd. In the second Israel is seen as seed sown in other countries, yet being brought back to the land in response to the Lord's calling. In the first they are seen pictured as horses battling against the enemy. In the second they are pictured as heroes overcoming the enemy. It is interesting to note that the first section begins with a call to prayer and ends with the prayer-answering God. The second section begins with Ephraim possessed of all power to conquer and it ends with the source of their power, Jehovah Himself.

Verses 1-6: Israel Without the Shepherd Scattered

The first message here is a call to prayer and it comes in immediately after the promise of 9.17. The corn and wine cannot grow without rain, so the prophet says, "Ask" for it. The Lord will give it if they, under a sense of their great need, will ask. What will be the result of such earnest prayers? The Lord will make clouds charged with lightning and give showers, not merely drops of rain, and "to every one grass in the field". "Grass" is a generic term that includes all vegetatious food supplies for both men and cattle. Spiritually it also includes the supply of every need for the soul. God's promise of rain, though sure, does not mean that His people are not to pray. It might be said, "Why pray for rain in the time of the latter rain, is it not to come anyway in its natural course?". This may be so, but it is good to look to God in prayer and He delights to hear His children cry to Him. Israel were not dependent on the laws of nature, and neither are we; such dependence must be upon the living God who is behind these laws controlling them. So Israel was not to desire rain through depending either upon any magical or natural process, but to look to the Lord alone. The former rain in Israel was around October and was needed to bring on the seed sown. The latter rain fell in March or April and was needed to ripen the grain. Spiritually speaking, Israel had as a nation their former rain of blessing in Acts 2 on the Day of Pentecost when many Jews were saved. In Acts 3 the promise of further blessing of times of refreshing from the presence of the Lord could have been theirs if they had repented. One may note then the omission of all reference to the early rain, but for Israel the time spiritually of the early rain had forever passed away for, as mentioned, God had already given the first rain on the Day of Pentecost. The latter rain of blessing, when the full harvest of the nation's conversion will be gathered in by God, is still to be earnestly longed for and prayed for. Israel will enjoy their time of latter rain when they accept the Messiah and are restored by Him.

Zechariah now directs attention to that which hitherto had been the hindrance to these blessings, namely idolatry (v.2). So, from depending on God in prayer Zechariah now turns to those who were trusting in idols. The word for "idols" here is TERAPHIM (8655). It is the word used for a family or household idol or shrine (see Gen 31.19; Judg 17.5; 18.14; 1 Sam 15.23; Hos 3.4). Such household and secret gods were used by many Israelites to predict the future. Divining with these idols was a complete delusion and resulted in lies. Like fortune tellers of today they gave the people a false hope, were in contrast to the one and only true God, and could give no comfort to the people. They led the people astray and the diviners saw deceiving visions and dreams. As a result it is no wonder that those who trusted these idols wandered like sheep without a shepherd and had experienced unnecessary trouble and affliction. "Trouble" (ANA – 6031) here indicates being browbeaten or humbled through life. Sadly Israel's trouble still exists today and worse is to come. Many years before, God had warned Israel not to look to the abomination of divination for help (Deut 18.10-12).

The Lord Jesus regarded the Jews in His day as sheep without a shepherd.

He is the only Shepherd and believers must trust in Him for the issues of life. Sadly, some believers have not been free from an unhealthy curiosity to find out what the future holds for them and have dabbled in the occult and magic arts, seeking some guidance for the future. The modern day equivalent to the teraphim of Zechariah's time is the upsurge and rise of magic and spiritism. The believer must avoid this and have no fellowship with the unfruitful works of darkness. The child of God should consult the word of God and pray to God for guidance in the pathway of life and not rely on Satan's deceptions. Consulting a palmist, for instance, to tell one's future may seem tempting and harmless to some, but it is wrong. The palmist may say, "Show me your hand and I will tell you your times", but thank God the Psalmist says, "My times are in thy hand" (Ps 31.15). The believer should be content to leave them there.

Next, God's anger is aroused against the false shepherds (v.3). These shepherds are a reference no doubt to the leaders of the people, their rulers, princes, and priests. Note that in the verse we have what their leaders should have been – "shepherds", and we have what they really were – "goats". The leaders were guilty of leading astray the often ignorant and unsuspecting sheep. God actually calls them "he-goats" (ATTUD - 6260), for this is their true character. They were headstrong, wanton, and cruel. Therefore the wrath of the Lord fell upon them and they were "punished" or "visited upon". The Lord, however, will take pity on His flock and visit them. God's care for Israel is not just limited to delivering them from the oppression of bad shepherds, for He will make His people Judah (Israel), like the war horse ready groomed, noble, and strong for battle. He will empower them to the extent that His sheep marked by weakness would become like a strong horse. When Israel in their weakness submit to the Lord He will make them victorious in battle. If their leaders have failed in showing care for them, the Lord Himself promises to care for His people. Believers too may feel the very weakest of the weak, but if we place ourselves in the hand of God we shall soon see what God can do for us. Our weakness is God's best workshop. The believer must allow God to work in and through him.

In v.4 we have some lovely glimpses of Israel's coming Messiah. Some might wonder as to why a reference to the Messiah is found here. The immediately preceding context has mentioned that because of the sins of v.2 Israel has had to do without a Shepherd King. God will supply that great lack and provide the Lord Jesus for Israel. So the help that the nation so much needs will come from the Lord Jesus. Thus Zechariah presents four strongly marked features of the Lord's conquest of the enemy, His restoration of Israel, and His establishment of divine rule as God's millennial King. He is described as a cornerstone, a tent peg, a battle bow, and the sovereign. These four features speak of what Christ will be to Israel. Judah will be independent of any foreign aid for the Lord will be everything to them. The Lord Jesus is seen here in different aspects for the blessing of

Israel. Note that four times it is repeated that Christ will come forth from Judah. While it is true that "Judah" speaks of Israel, yet Judah is the royal tribe, so Christ is presented as coming out of Judah, the royal tribe. Our Lord Jesus, says Hebrews 7.14, "sprang out of Juda". The prophecy here is full of the Messiah and reveals that He will fulfil every need of Israel in a future day. There is no doubt that the verse is speaking of Christ and that all four titles or descriptions are Messianic. All the pictures used set forth the strong, stable, and reliable character of the Messianic rule.

Christ the Stability of His people

The cornerstone is that on which the whole building stands. The word was used for the bond of union between two walls. A cornerstone was the boulder laid at the corner of a building where two walls met. It was the principle stone of a foundation, giving a structure stability and strength. In the New Testament the Apostle Paul identifies the Lord Jesus as the chief cornerstone (Eph 2.20). Throughout the word of God Christ is seen as the stone of stumbling (Is 8.14), the smitten stone (1 Cor 10.4), the smiting stone at His second advent to destroy the foe (Dan 2.34-35), and a rejected stone that will become the chief cornerstone (Ps 118.22-23; Mt 21.42). The Lord Jesus then is the cornerstone of God's edifice. It is lovely to see that Isaiah 28.16 speaks of Him as "a precious corner stone". Peter in his first epistle clearly shows that this refers to the Lord Jesus (1 Pet 2.6). Just as the cornerstone is the reference point for the whole building, so all receives its character from Him. He is the One who will provide stability and lasting security for Israel in contrast to the insecurity of the condition described in v.2.

Christ the Support of His people

The Messiah will be like a nail or tent peg (YATED – 3489 – implying firmness and security) in that He will hold the Kingdom firmly in place. The word was also used to describe a peg or nail inside the tent or home of the Israelites upon which were hung beautiful things which adorned their dwellings. It was therefore used not merely for a tent peg, but for a nail on the inner walls of houses on which to hang utensils. The idea of upholding things seems to be the main meaning of the word in the context. This thought is very expressive as one thinks of Israel's Messiah, for all Israel's burden will hang upon Christ. Just as the nail bore the load, so will Christ bear Israel's burdens. Terrible burdens will sorely afflict Israel in the Tribulation and in the crisis of Armageddon, but the Lord Jesus will swiftly remove them and the nation, realizing that their future hangs on Christ, will turn to Him for support. In addition the figure of the nail may also suggest that Christ will bear a weight of glory in the future day that no mere mortal could bear. Upon Him will rest the hopes of Israel and the glory of the millennial reign. In Isaiah the "the nail" or "peg" is used of the Lord Jesus in a passage which is clearly Messianic, for in 22.23 of his prophecy he speaks of Christ as a "nail in a sure place". There Eliakim is chosen to be entrusted with the government of Israel and to take up the responsibility of rule over God's people. He is a type and picture of Christ, but like all types there is an imperfection, for Eliakim's rule would not be permanent. The time would come when he would "be removed, and be cut down, and fail" (v.25), but not so with the Lord Jesus, for when He takes up the burden of rule He will never fail and never die. His government will be permanent and His Kingdom everlasting.

Christ the Sufficiency of His people
Here is another symbol of Christ. The battle bow symbolizes strength for conquest. It is an expressive figure for military power. The Messiah is the great Conqueror and Avenger of His and His people's enemies (Rev 19.11-16). As the bow releases the arrows effectively to defeat the power of the enemy, so the Lord's arrows will unerringly find their mark. This reminds us of Psalm 45.5: "Thine arrows are sharp in the heart of the king's enemies". The Lord Jesus will accomplish great victories. At His second advent He will come as the great Warrior King, He will be "the Lord mighty in battle", and be welcomed as He enters the war-torn city of Jerusalem fresh from His conquest of the enemy. He then will be acclaimed as the King of glory and the Lord of hosts (Ps 24.8-10).

Christ the Sovereign of His people
The last description, "Out of him (Judah) every oppressor together", is not as easy to interpret as the three preceding figures have been. Some, like M. F. Unger and C. L. Feinberg, do not think there is a reference to the person of the Messiah here. They regard it to mean that the Lord will remove every oppressor from Israel. The word "together" for them signifies more than one person. This interpretation points more to the results of the Messiah's rule and power in dealing with all oppressors, every one of them together. In this sense the last part of the verse would have to be interpreted as saying, "From the house of Judah would also go forth (depart) every oppressing ruler". This will certainly be true of the activity of the Messiah in the coming day, but the present writer believes the description is true of the Messiah and fits in both with the preceding titles used of the Lord Jesus and the context. It seems better to understand from this picture that it indicates that Christ will be invested with all authority and sovereignty. The description is still a title of the Messiah seen not so much in relation to Israel, but rather relative to their, and of course His, enemies. The word rendered "oppressor" in the AV is not necessarily to be understood in a bad sense. Its idea seems to be that of a despotic ruler or "exactor" (Is 60.17). In the context here it is one who exacts tribute from those nations who are made tributary to Judah. When Christ rules in the Millennium, nations will be under His authority and pay Him the tribute of worship and submission. He will be God's King and

combine in His person every kind of ideal rule. He will have under Him subordinate rulers or princes (Is 32.1). Perhaps the word "together" indicates the unity of these rulers in subjection to the Lord Jesus. Interestingly, Helen Spurrell in her translation from the original Hebrew renders the last expression as, "From Him proceedeth every governor together".

In the light of these precious pictures of Christ, the believer of the present age of grace can say that the cornerstone of His earthly people is now the chief cornerstone of the church. The tent peg of Israel is now our surety and upon Him we cast all our burdens. The battle bow is the Captain of our salvation and will help us to be "more than conquerors". The One who will have all authority in the coming day and to whom will be paid the tribute of praise and obedience is the One who exacts and deserves now from His people all devotion and praise.

Next God says, "And they shall be as mighty men, which tread down their enemies in the mire of the streets". God will make the house of Judah like heroes to tread down their enemies as the mire. They are Jehovah's war horse and as mire is trodden down, so will they tread down their foes (cp. Micah 7.10; 2 Sam 22.43). The city of Jerusalem has been trodden under foot of the Gentiles for many centuries. It will be so in the Tribulation, but all will change dramatically when the Lord comes to deliver His people. Then it will be the turn of the might of Gentile armies to be trodden under foot by Israel. Because the Lord will be with His people they will enjoy supernatural help. The infantry will overcome the cavalry! "The riders on horses shall be confounded." Though riding imposing war horses they will be put to shame. The chief strength of Asiatic rulers was in their cavalry (see Dan 11.40). Facing overwhelming odds in the battle they will win the conflict by God's help. Such will be the wonderful courage of Israel under their Messiah that their enemies, even the very flower of their army, the cavalry, will stand stunned and shocked at it, and this will take all strength from them. Jehovah will do with them what He did with Pharaoh and His army and utterly destroy them. Though this prophecy may have had a partial fulfilment in the victories of the Jews under Judas Maccabeus over the Seleucids, it really looks on to the crisis of Armageddon, at the height of which the Lord Jesus will descend in judgment. There is a lesson here for the believer to allow the Lord to fight for us in the spiritual conflicts of life, especially against evil principalities and powers in heavenly places. The believer can only overcome, not in his own strength, but in the power of His might.

In the final verse of the first section of ch.10 God says that He will strengthen the house of Judah and save the house of Joseph. The mention of Judah and Joseph includes the whole of the ten tribes. This indicates that the fulfilment is yet to take place in the future, for Judah alone, with a few Israelites from other tribes, returned from Babylon. E. Dennett has the following interesting and helpful comments on Judah and Joseph. "The exactitude of the expressions used will scarcely fail to strike the intelligent reader. Thus, I will 'strengthen' the house of Judah, and I will 'save' the house of Joseph, and 'bring them again', etc. Judah would already be in the land before the appearing of their Messiah, and being delivered, He would 'strengthen' them. The house of Joseph, Ephraim, i.e. the ten tribes, will still be scattered among the nations, and undiscovered, in spite of modern pretensions, until after the return of Christ to Zion, and hence the terms employed in our passage". This will be fulfilled under Christ at His second advent. "I will bring them again in order that I may place them in their own land". This is the plain meaning of this verse. Three great things will happen for the blessing of Israel. They will be restored, as seen in Judah; they will be reunited, as seen in the saving of the house of Joseph; and they will be reinstated in their own land. How is it that all this will take place for Israel? They certainly do not deserve it after many centuries of rejecting God's word, of disobedience and apostasy, but Zechariah traces all that will happen to Israel to the one great source of all these blessings - the wonderful mercy of God. God says, "I have mercy upon them". All the blessings each believer enjoys can also be traced back to the very same mercies of God. So wonderful and thorough will be their national salvation that all the past sad history of failure and calamity will be as though they had never been, for when God again deals with them in His mercy and grace it will be as though He had never "cast them off". Israel will be so filled with joy and the glory of their restoration and victory that their past troubles will be put out of their minds.

We have seen that the section begins with a call to pray and here it ends with God who hearkens to prayer. This is so interesting and encouraging, for it shows that behind the restoration of the nation in a future day will be the exercise and burden in prayer of a remnant who will cry to God for His mercy and intervention. True, God's sovereign purpose for Israel is fixed and He will be faithful to his covenant with the nation, but it is good to see that prayer will play its part. The restoration of the nation will be God's answer to the cries of His people. In these verses we have the one clear and direct reference to the ten tribes in Zechariah. These ten tribes will also share with Israel in the blessings of the millennial Kingdom. These tribes may have been lost and hidden for hundreds of years, but God knows where they are and will have mercy upon them as well as upon Judah. So it is doubly interesting to see that prayer here is in connection, too, with these supposed lost tribes. God will accomplish the miracle of bringing them back to the land and thus in a wonderful way answer prayer. What an incentive and encouragement this is even for believers not to forget to pray for Israel. This is one great reason why this portion of Scripture ends with the promise, "I will hear them". So the reference to God answering His people's cries is very much related to the context wherein we are told of God's blessing in fully restoring the nation. Israel will be at home at last, and as they look back they will with joy know that the Lord is the hearer of prayer and that He has heard their prayers. The long centuries of prayer will have not been in vain. It will be the same for the believer, for when at home with the Lord in heaven what joy and assurance will fill the heart to know that prayer was so worth it after all.

Verses 7-12: Israel with the Shepherd Gathered
In this second half of the chapter God is seen calling His sheep back to His land from the many countries where they have been scattered. The Lord will gather His people again (vv.7-9). This gathering will be like a second exodus, for they will pass through not a liquid sea, but a sea of affliction before they can return to the Lord (vv.10-12). It is most interesting that in this section God compares the future deliverance of Israel to their past deliverance. The comparison with Israel's beginnings with God historically is at least twofold, for first Zechariah refers to the promise of their increase (v.8). This recalls their increase in spite of affliction and suffering in Egypt. Second, Zechariah shows that Israel will enjoy a greater deliverance in the future than they did when they came through the Red Sea (vv.10-11). In vv.7-9 the nation is seen as seed sown in many lands. This is a result of God's government in dealing with them because of their sins. In vv.10-12, however, they are seen as sheep being gathered again. This will be the result of God's dealings in grace with them in spite of their sins. In vv.1-6 it was noted that the section began with the need for prayer and ended with God hearing the prayers of His people. Touching the structure of this second section it begins with Ephraim being like a mighty man endued with power and ends with Jehovah who will be the source of their strength in the coming day: "I will strengthen them in the Lord" (v.12).

The seed sown (vv.7-9)
In considering vv.7-9 it is nice to note that Israel will enjoy their three blessings. They will rejoice in their liberty; they will be regathered to their land; and they will remember their Lord. In describing what God will do for His people Zechariah uses the following three metaphors.

Strengthened like heroes
How good to see from the mention of Ephraim that they will obtain the salvation of Jehovah just like Judah. They are compared to a mighty man or hero who has won a great victory over a superior foe. Ephraim stands for the northern kingdom of Israel. Their captivity has been much longer than that of Judah. At the time that Zechariah prophesied Ephraim was still in exile, though as we have previously mentioned a very small number of them had returned to Jerusalem with the children of Judah. Looking at the circumstances of this time in relation to Ephraim, all looked outwardly bleak and hopeless and any idea of their restoration and God making them mighty heroes seemed so far removed from the weakness of their situation then. Does this mean that all confidence in God's promises for Ephraim is

unfounded? No, this cannot be. God will accomplish the impossible and fulfil His prophetic word through His prophets. "Ephraim…shall rejoice as through wine." They will fight joyfully in the battle like a hero strengthened with wine. It will not be a short-lived restoration, for it will be permanent and lasting, so much so that the prophet declares that "their children shall see it, and be glad". If vv.1-6 have shown that Israel's restoration will not be partial, but full, this section shows that it will not be passing, but permanent. No wonder the verse ends with, "Their heart shall rejoice in the Lord". What is said of Ephraim here will certainly be true of Judah. The rest of the passage must be understood as including the whole nation of Israel and not just Ephraim.

Shepherded like sheep
    Two things are stated here. Israel will be gathered, and being gathered in the land they will increase as a people. The metaphor used here is most interesting: "I will hiss for them" (8319). This is said to come from those in charge of bees making a noise to induce the bees to settle down in a desired locality. The use of this illustration is seen in Isaiah 7.18, but the word was also used for a shepherd whistling or making a shrill noise with a pipe to gather together his dispersed flock. Deborah in her song uses it in this sense: "Why did you tarry among the sheepfolds, to hear the piping for the flocks?" (Judg 5.16, RSV). The latter figure is, we believe, more suited to the context here where God is seen calling and enticing His people back to Himself and the land. What a lovely and blessed picture this is, for it illustrates God's care for His people and how He desires to have them together so that gathering them He might bring them home and protect them. Canaan, Immanuel's land, is Israel's true home. Israel will respond to this call. The reason this will happen is because God says, "For I have redeemed them", that is in His electing purposes for the nation. Prophetically speaking their national redemption was yet future, but on the ground of the covenant God had made with His people they would surely be delivered.
    Then it is said, "And they shall increase as they have increased". Here reference is made to the increase of God's people in Egypt. The more they were afflicted the more they multiplied. The Egyptians sought to take measures to prevent Israel's increase in their land, but God used the suffering they inflicted upon His people to cause them to multiply (Ex 1.10 & 12). Israel will yet have to endure suffering in the Tribulation, which will far outstrip the sore affliction suffered in Egypt, but, as the passage goes on to show, God will bring them through it all. After the terrible suffering Israel will undergo in the time of the sorrows to come, they will so much increase that even in the greatly extended borders of Israel it will be difficult to find a place for them – "And place shall not be found for them" (v.10). How often God allows suffering and opposition to be experienced by His people in order to bring about His own purpose. It

was so in the early days of the Church in the book of Acts. The early believers, too, suffered much persecution and intense opposition, but in spite of this, notice the expressions Luke uses of the development of the testimony in those days and trace in the book how increase comes in after a time of crisis (Acts 6.7; 9.31; 16.5; 19.20). One may take heart from this to realize that in spite of what man does and how bitter and cruel he is in his persecution of the Lord's people, God will complete His purpose and be glorified in the end.

Sown like seed

"I will sow them among the people." An agricultural analogy is used here. As seed is scattered and buried in the soil, so God's earthly people have been sown like seed and buried among the nations. The word that is used here for "sow" is not used in the Old Testament for scattering seed, but for sowing in a field that has been prepared to receive seed. Just as seed is sown in the soil and increases, so by God sowing the Jews among many nations they will grow and increase. This has been the case throughout history. How significant that the nation is likened to seed sown. While it is true in one aspect that God has scattered them because of their disobedience and this is His judgment upon them, yet in divine sovereign purpose He has sown them in many lands in order that He might reap them one day. Just as a man may sow seed in the soil with a view to reaping fruit, so God has sown His people with the great purpose in view that He might see the nation spring to life and power. They may seem now buried in the soil of the Gentile nations and their growth in the world may pass unnoticed, but God will bring forth a nation with beauty and fruitfulness for His glory. God is working still today behind the scenes with the nation and they are being prepared for their glorious future. Let it be remembered that the functions of the sower end with the sowing. Those of the reaper begin with the harvest. All that lies between is left to God and the mysterious laws of growth and co-operation between the soil, rain, and sunshine. All is dependent on God. So as far as the Jew is concerned today, all may seem so unpromising and unlikely, yet God is working and the blessing of the nation is dependent on Him. He will bring it to pass.

God's people will remember Him in all the countries where they have been scattered. Comment has already been made on the significance of the name of Zechariah – 'Remembered of Jehovah'. God will remember His covenant and promise and in faithfulness to these He will yet bless the nation of Israel. Here, however, it is the Jews in the distant countries of the Gentiles who will remember Jehovah. So, though in far off lands, the people will not forget the Lord their God. Many of the Jews will not only survive in these lands, but will begin a movement back to the homeland. This happened to some extent when Israel became an independent nation in 1948, but what Zechariah predicts here is on a much larger scale. It is the world-wide regathering of His people. It is interesting to see that though

Israel had been restored to the land after their exile in Babylon, yet Zechariah still anticipates in these verses the prospect of a restored and unified nation. Again, the prophetic nature of the passage written by Zechariah after the date of the return from exile should be noted. One cannot interpret this merely spiritually or infer from the prediction that it is only a temporary blessing for Israel to be back in the land. On the contrary, this is a clear prophecy of Israel's full and permanent restoration to the land. "They shall live with their children, and turn again." The words "they shall live" could either be understood as "they will still be alive", or "they will come alive". In keeping with the thought of the "seed", the seed of course appears to die when it is sown, but then when it germinates and grows into a plant it appears to come alive as if from the dead. The Apostle Paul uses the same illustration of the seed sown in the earth to prove the fact of resurrection (1 Cor 15.36-44). Israel is now nationally dead, and, apostate, but God will bring them back as it were from the dead and, to use the imagery of the prophet Ezekiel, the dry bones shall live (Ezek 37.3-6). The fact that it adds, "they shall live *with their children*", proves again that Israel's restoration will not be a passing phase, but an enduring reality. The permanent character of their national blessing further repeats what the prophet had said in v.7, "their children shall see it", thus emphasizing this great prophetic truth.

The second exodus (vv.10-12)

In this final section Zechariah compares what God will do for Israel in the future with what He did for them in their past deliverance from Egypt. The former deliverance had been glorious, but the future deliverance will be even more so. Four places are mentioned in v.10: two countries - Egypt and Assyria, and two areas in the land of Israel - Gilead and Lebanon. Why the mention of Egypt and Assyria? Egypt was the first of Israel's oppressors, and Assyria was the last and, with its Gentile successors, has continued thus to the present time. Assyria of course was the power that took the ten tribes into captivity. God says, "I will bring them again", that is He will bring the nation back to their own land. It is interesting to note that Zechariah confirms here what had been predicted by the former great prophet Isaiah concerning the restoration back to the land of Israel. In 11.11-16 of his prophecy, Assyria and Egypt head the list of countries from which God will gather His people. Here, only Egypt and Assyria are mentioned, but are very likely used by the prophet as representative of the many places from which God will call His people: Egypt in the south and Assyria in the north. The Jew has been scattered in many lands, but from every place in the far flung countries of the earth God will gather them. God will bring them into the land of Gilead and Lebanon. The whole of the new land of Israel is described here by these two boundaries of Gilead and Lebanon, the eastern being Gilead beyond Jordan and the northern being Lebanon. They will be brought into Gilead with its rich pasture land and Lebanon with its mighty forests. Thus God will give His people the whole territory and greatly extend its borders. The promise to Abraham and His covenant with David as to the land will be fulfilled (Gen 15.18; 2 Sam 7.16). "And place shall not be found for them." The numbers of God's people restored and back in the land will be so great that it will be difficult to find room for them (see also Isaiah 49.19). What a contrast this is to how desolate the land was and how few Jews were in it when the remnant returned to Jerusalem from Babylon. In the present land of Israel with many Jewish immigrants still seeking to enter into it to live there, the Israeli government is hard pressed to find places for them. Immanuel's land of the future, even with its greatly extended borders, will be populated with a multitude of Jews that will be far greater than ever seen in its previous history.

Zechariah now refers to what happened in Israel's past to illustrate what God will do for His people in the future. Just as He did of old in causing the Red Sea to cease to be an obstacle, so God by His power will make a way through every hindrance to bring about a greater deliverance for His people. It is interesting that after this great miraculous event at the beginning of the nation's history it is referred to some twenty times throughout the rest of Scripture. It had its important lessons for God's people, reminding them of His power and also of His care for them. Just as God opened up a path for them through the sea and overthrew Pharaoh and His army, so God will remove every difficulty that stands in the way of His people's restoration by overcoming the armies gathered against them and cleaving in two the Mount of Olives. "And he shall pass through the sea with affliction, and shall smite the waves in the sea", or "And he shall afflict the sea". This has been found difficult to translate, but the general sense is clear that, "Under the symbol of an exodus from Egypt and from under its power, and a march through a sea and river such as occurred in the days of the first triumphal march of Israel, the great truth is set forth, that amid all trials and afflictions the covenant people would be delivered by the protecting hand of God" (C. H. H. Wright). "The deeps of the river (or, The depths of the Nile, RV) shall dry up". The River Nile stands for Egypt, but the reference to the Nile is not used in a literal sense, but rather in a metaphorical sense to indicate that nothing will prevent God's purpose for His people. Israel passed over the River Jordan dry shod. He will remove all impediments. "The pride of Assyria shall be brought down, and the sceptre of Egypt shall depart away." The tyranny of Asshur is characterized by pride and haughtiness (see Isaiah 10.5-16) and that of Egypt by its sceptre and its taskmasters. These will both cease. No tyranny or governmental power shall ever enslave God's people again. Whatever among the nations of the world there may be of the old tyranny of Assyria or the iron rod of Egypt in Israel's way will be removed by God's power and His people shall pass on and enter with joy and glory into their own land. How wonderful all this is and how clear the prophecy is, for God is able to remove all obstacles in the way of His purposes. This is a good thing to remember even for the believer today.

Not only will God restore Israel to the land, but the last verse of the passage shows that they will be strengthened in the Lord and will walk up and down in His name. God has declared that He will strengthen Judah (v.6). Now the same thing is said, but including Ephraim. The restored nation will have as their source of strength Jehovah Himself. He will never fail His people. Remember He is the God who can turn weak and helpless sheep into all-conquering and powerful war horses! The phrase "walk up and down" suggests liberty and freedom and contemplates a people enjoying fellowship with God in the land. Long ago God had bidden Abraham to walk up and down the land (Gen 13.17), the very land that God had promised to His people. Here are His descendants walking in this same land at peace and in the will of God. We have Israel here, spiritually speaking, experiencing the refreshing showers of the latter rain long promised to them. So the chapter began with an appeal to pray for the latter rain, it continued with an encouraging reminder that God hears (v.6), and now here at the end we see how that which was prayed for and which was according to God's will has been wonderfully answered by Him. From a practical point of view this should be an encouragement to all believers to continue in believing prayer and in dependence upon God for spiritual blessings in the knowledge that God hears and in His own time and for His own glory He will answer.

These two blessings of being strengthened in the Lord and walking in His name link well with truth in both Philippians and Colossians. Paul says, "I can do all things through Christ which strengtheneth me (or keeps on pouring into me His strength)" (Phil 4.13). Then he exhorts the Colossians, "Whatsoever ye do in word or deed, do all in the name of the Lord Jesus" (Col 3.17). Oh that each believer would enjoy Paul's experience and be so consecrated to the Lord as to do all in His name.

One thought more on this last verse should be remarked upon and it is a testimony to the deity of Christ. It is Jehovah who speaks here. Look at the verse again: "And I (i.e. Jehovah) will strengthen them in the Lord; and they shall walk up and down in his name saith the Lord (Jehovah)". There are clearly two distinct persons here, the speaker is Jehovah and the person and name ("his name") referred to must be the Messiah! Already in Zechariah we have seen that Christ is Jehovah. The Jews to this day despise and hate the name of our Lord Jesus Christ, but there is coming a day when they will rejoice in it, and all that they do will be in His name and for His glory. How much evidence there is in Zechariah's prophecy of the divinity of our blessed Lord.

ZECHARIAH 11

The Shepherd Lover of the Flock

The chapter now before us concerns the rejection of the true Shepherd of Israel – our Lord Jesus Christ, Israel's Messianic King. The previous two chapters have been occupied mainly with blessing and peace for the nation, but in contrast this chapter contemplates scenes of sin and punishment. It concludes the first burden of prophecy in chs.9-11 and prophetically deals with the suffering of Israel because of their rejection of Christ. The chapter shows that the rejection of Christ not only brought defeat and devastation to Israel by the Roman armies in AD 70, but ultimately will result in their acceptance in a coming day of the Antichrist who will be dealt with in judgment by God. It is a dark chapter – the darkest yet in Zechariah concerning the nation and the two periods of terrible suffering they would yet have to pass through at the time that Zechariah prophesied. In vv.1-3 we have a picture of the punishment of Israel. In vv.4-14 we have a picture of the rejection of Christ. In vv.15-17 we have a picture of the false shepherd. The chapter is interesting in that it speaks of three kinds of shepherds. In vv.1-3 Zechariah refers to wailing shepherds. In vv.4-14 he gives much detail of the worthy or good shepherd. Finally, in vv.15-17 a worthless shepherd is portrayed. Zechariah solemnly yet clearly predicts that the sorry tale of Israel's suffering was not fully realized in their rejection of the true Shepherd, but will greatly increase in the events leading up to the second advent of Christ. Looking at the threefold division of the chapter one may see how extensive and embracive it is, not only in its details concerning the Lord Jesus in the middle section, but in the three periods of time prophetically envisaged. Thus in vv.1-3 the period of AD 70 is referred to when we believe Israel was punished by God. Verses 4-14 move back in time thirty-eight years from AD 70 to give the reason for the judgment in vv.1-3. Then vv.15-17 anticipate the time of the Tribulation when the Antichrist will be accepted by the nation. The chapter begins with God punishing Israel and ends with Him punishing them again in giving them the Antichrist – the false shepherd.

Verses 1-3: The Godless Shepherds – The Religious Leaders

The chapter begins with graphic poetic language announcing doom to the nation. Zechariah pictures a violent storm from the north bursting through the Lebanon range. The lightning splits the tallest cedars, the tempest roars through the forest, the cypresses and oaks crashing and falling before it. The wild beasts are terrified and can find no cover and the shepherds view with consternation the desolated track of the storm. Israel can offer no resistance to this impending storm of judgment, and so v.1 reads, "Open thy doors, O Lebanon, that the fire may devour thy cedars". The fire is a reference to an invading army coming into Israel and Jerusalem.

This army will destroy the strong oaks and rich pasture lands of Bashan north-east of Lebanon and the thick forest lining the Jordan River in the south. Some view the little poem as forming a conclusion to the previous chapter, but it is better in the context to see that it is really an introduction to the following section and gives, as already suggested, God's judgment upon the nation due to their rejection of their Messiah. The references to Lebanon, Bashan, and Jordan seem to favour this approach. Some commentators regard the first three verses of this chapter as entirely figurative. Others take the language to be understood literally, but there is nothing in the passage to suggest that the mention of Lebanon, cedars, fir trees, oaks, and young lions may not be taken both literally and figuratively. They apply to the land and everything naturally connected with it. They may also be considered as symbolic representations of the state and its rulers. The judgment predicted here covers the people, the land, and the temple. All suffered as a consequence of the destruction caused by the Roman invasion of the first century.

Lebanon was famous for its cedar trees, but these will be consumed. According to the Talmud, the Jewish rabbis identified Lebanon here with the second temple "Which was built with cedars from Lebanon, towering aloft on a strong summit – the spiritual glory and eminence of Jerusalem, as Lebanon was of the whole country" (Baron). 1 Kings 6.15-18 and 2 Chronicles 2.8-9 may support such an interpretation of "Lebanon". The royal palace in Jerusalem was definitely referred to as Lebanon in Jeremiah 22.23. There are those who may consider such a meaning put on Lebanon as somewhat fanciful, but God's judgment upon the nation would also include the temple. There is no doubt that the language in these opening verses refers to a very severe, merited, and inclusive judgment which will visit the nation. The cedars may well refer to the highest and noblest in the land, and the fir trees may represent the common people who will mourn the loss of their leaders. With the destruction by Titus the hopes and pride of the nation were also lost. The oaks of Bashan come next in order. Bashan was famous for its oak forests (Is 2.13; Ezek 27.6). They are called upon to howl, for they fall down under the same march of death. They will all fall with the great cedar forest of Lebanon. Because of this devastation of all that is natural, civil, and ecclesiastical, there is a howling of "the shepherds", or Jewish rulers, because their glory is spoiled – their wealth and magnificence, as well as that of their temple. The young lions or princes are so described because of their tyranny. They are depicted as roaring because "the pride of Jordan", its thickly wooded banks, the lair of lions, is spoiled. Thus all that is lofty and powerful and glorious in nature and in the state are represented as in despair and utter ruin under the mighty hand of the Roman power. While commentators disagree as to the reason for and the time of this awful judgment, the following passage would make clear that the reason is Israel's rejection of the true Shepherd. As to the time of it, it is most interesting to see from the New Testament that after Israel's religious leaders rejected Christ He said, "Behold, your house is left unto you desolate" (Mt 23.38). On the Mount of Olives our Lord predicted the destruction of the temple so graphically and minutely: "Seest thou these great buildings? there shall not be left one stone upon another, that shall not be thrown down" (Mk 13.1-2), and again, "For the days shall come upon thee, that thine enemies shall cast a trench about thee, and compass thee round, and keep thee in on every side, And shall lay thee even with the ground, and thy children within thee; and they shall not leave in thee one stone upon another; because thou knewest not the time of thy visitation" (Lk 19.43-44).

Thus both the prophecy of 11.1-3 and that of the Lord were actually fulfilled when Titus invaded Judea and destroyed the city and Herod's temple. This happened thirty-eight years after the crucifixion of Christ. The following information is of interest in connection with 11.1-3. The Jewish zealots, reacting in opposition to Caligula's campaign, began a revolt against Rome, a revolt which led to Roman legionary soldiers from Syria destroying the food stocks of the Zealots and the local Jewish population. The inhabitants of the city of Jerusalem died in great numbers from starvation (Lk 21.20-23). The Roman general Titus, who later became Caesar, encircled the city, and began the siege of Jerusalem in April of AD 70. He posted his 10th legion on the Mount of Olives, directly east of and overlooking the Temple Mount. The 12th and 15th legions were stationed on Mount Scopus, further to the east and commanding all ways to Jerusalem from east to north. On 10th August that year (the 9th of Av in Jewish calendar reckoning), the very day when the King of Babylon burned the temple in 586 BC, the temple was burned again. Titus took the city and put it to the torch, burning the temple, leaving not one stone upon another. Thus, Jerusalem was totally destroyed as the Lord Jesus had predicted. The judgment of 11.1-3 describes a terrible desolate and devastating state. After the city was taken by Titus conditions were really desperate. Jerusalem and Judea were left in ruins, most of the people were either killed or being held in captivity, or had become refugees fleeing to remote lands. All that remained in Israel was the defiant little garrison on top of the mount at Masada, a fortress complex to the west of the Dead Sea, which was built by Herod the Great. Thus when the temple was destroyed in AD 70 the period of the second exile began. All this shows the wonder and precision of prophecy, but how very solemn and tragic to think that the Jews not only suffered then, but have suffered as a people for centuries and will yet face worse sufferings because of rejecting their Messiah. The details of Christ's rejection are given prophetically in the next section, vv.4-14.

Verses 4-14: The Good Shepherd – The Lord Jesus

In many ways this is an amazing passage in Zechariah. Its portrayal of the ministry, valuation, and rejection of the Messiah and the consequent loss to the nation should be all too obvious to the reader who loves the

Lord Jesus and knows the historical details of the New Testament regarding events in the Lord's life. Reading through the section one can only conclude that it gives the particulars of the Lord's ministry to the nation of Israel when He was here. It anticipates with such startling clarity how the nation would respond to the arrival in their midst of their Messiah. It is such an intriguing section. For example, what are the two staves of v.7? Who are the three shepherds, and when was the one month of v.8? Why the particular amount of thirty pieces of silver in v.12? M. F. Unger sets out well the reason for this passage coming in as it does here. "The decimating judgment of God sweeping down from the north on Palestine, so graphically depicted in vv.1-3, is now explained with regard to its cause. Underlying it is a crime which represents unbelief and crystallized wickedness of such colossal proportions that the fiery judgment which prefaces the description of it is made a divine necessity".

These verses concerning the Messiah may be conveniently divided into two subsections: one gives the purpose of Messiah's ministry to Israel (vv.4-7), and the other the price at which He was valued by the nation (vv.8-14).

The purpose of Messiah's ministry (vv.4-7)

In v.4 we have the commission to Zechariah to "Feed the flock of the slaughter", and in vv.5 & 6 we have the very sad state of things in the land of Israel when the Lord was here. In v.7 Zechariah obeys the charge given to him by God, takes the two staves of "Beauty" and "Bands", and begins to act out symbolically before the people this message from God that tells them exactly what would happen to the nation by rejecting the true Shepherd. Some may regard what Zechariah was commanded to do as a very strange procedure indeed, but we must not fall into the trap of entertaining the notion that all this took place in a vision and that it was all just an inward spiritual experience of Zechariah. There is nothing whatsoever in the passage to hint at this. Zechariah was asked to enact a parable before the people. This was really nothing unusual for a Hebrew prophet to do, for Jeremiah and Ezekiel before him had been required to do the same. Zechariah is to do an impersonation act, but who is it that He was to impersonate? It was no other than Jehovah Himself – the Messiah.

God says, "Feed the flock of the slaughter". What a tragic and terrible description of God's chosen nation! It occurs again in v.7. It is very sadly a description that fits the poor nation of Israel so well. In it is summed up the fateful history of the Jews down to this day, and it will be even more true of them in days to come. The description is explained in the next verse (v.5), for many of them are slain and many taken for slaves. At least part of this was fulfilled in AD 70 and the period that followed. Zechariah here is to care for a flock doomed to slaughter. The word for "feed" (RA'A – 7462) implies more than just tending to the flock, it includes also protecting, watching, guiding, and healing. This the Lord Jesus desired to do for the nation, but alas the nation did not want this lovely Shepherd.

Zechariah's reference to Jehovah as "My God" must not be overlooked, for here is his personal relationship with God. He knew God, spoke for God, and acted for Him. What a contrast this was, not only as regards many of the Jews in Zechariah's time, but even in relation to the Jews in the land in the Lord's days on earth. The nation did not know God and what is worse the professed leaders of the people did not know God. They read the Scriptures, but they missed the One whom they predicted and did not accept His claims and sought to put Him to death. It is the most tragic thing in all history.

Dreadful misery is described in v.5. Cruelty, impiety, and an avaricious spirit are the three things to note in v.5. The verse probably refers to two parties – "Whose possessors slay them and hold themselves not guilty". These were the Roman oppressors, the instruments of God's righteous judgment. Then we have, "they that sell them say, Blessed be the Lord; for I am rich: and their own shepherds pity them not". These were the leaders of the nation at the time the Lord was here. The great Shepherd of the sheep desired to "feed the flock" and preserve them from the "slaughter", but had at last to exclaim sadly, "I would, but ye would not". The Lord Jesus was hindered in this purpose by their rulers – the Scribes, Pharisees, Herodians, chief priests, and officers all combined. These so-called shepherds had only their own advantage in view. It is stated that they "pity them not". These men by their avaricious rapacity had virtually sold their country to the Romans and at last filled up the cup of their iniquity by selling the Messiah for thirty pieces of silver. These are the shepherds that are represented here as saying, "I am rich", and at the same time, like the Pharisee in the temple, lifted up their eyes to heaven, and in deepest hypocrisy exclaimed, "Blessed be the Lord". How strikingly Zechariah the prophet in these words pictures the actual scenes of our Lord's own day! No pen save that of an inspired one could have drawn the picture so perfectly. What confidence again this should give the believer in the wonder and authority of the Holy Scriptures. Not only did they "sell" the sheep, but at last they sold their Shepherd. There was only one true Shepherd in their midst and that was the Lord Jesus Christ.

In v.6 we have the announcement of coming judgment on the land and the people of Israel on account of the rejection of the Messiah. It was tragic enough that the leaders had no compassion for the people, but it was infinitely more tragic for the Lord Himself to declare that He would no more have compassion on them. Jehovah gives them up to internal feuds – "I will deliver the men everyone into his neighbour's hand". It is a well-known fact of history that at the time of the invasion of Jerusalem by the Romans the turbulent and factious Jews expelled and slew one another by turns. There were many divisions among the Jews, so much so there was fighting and bloodshed daily. This spirit among them prevailed to such an extent that it hastened the downfall of the city. God says He will deliver the men also "into the hand of his king". There does not appear to be any doubt from the context that the king mentioned is the Roman emperor. Later from the Gospel records even the Jews acknowledged, "We have no king but Caesar" (Jn 19.15). The Jews renounced their own King whom God had sent to them. Thus when they said, "We have no king, but Caesar", God took them at their word, and delivered them up into the hand of the king they had deliberately chosen. The king whom they had chosen "shall smite the land". These words are literally, "Shall dash to pieces their land". This was exactly fulfilled at the destruction of Jerusalem by Titus. At last the king they had chosen entered the city and all it contained fell into his hands, and out of this terrible ruin and carnage God did not deliver them.

Zechariah begins to act upon the commission given him in v.4 and says, "I will feed the flock of slaughter, even you, O poor of the flock". This goes a long way to understanding that Zechariah did act out the part of a shepherd and by doing what he did he was anticipating the life and ministry of the Messiah Himself. He gave special attention to the poor of the flock. This reminds us of the Lord Jesus who ministered to the little remnant in Israel. This remnant is in view, we believe, in the reference to the poor of the flock. The prophet took two staves, one called "Beauty" or "graciousness" and the other "Bands" or "union". The shepherd in the east carried a rod or stout club hewn from a tree to beat off wild beasts attacking the sheep, and a crooked staff for retrieving the sheep from difficult places (compare the rod and staff of Psalm 23.4). This suggests the divine purpose in the mission of the Lord to Israel. He is described as the "minister of the circumcision for the truth of God, to confirm the promises made unto the fathers" (Rom 15.8). The Lord as the true Shepherd Messiah desired to beautify and bind together the nation. If they had accepted Him this would have been the blessed result of His ministry. He would have given them grace and unity as a nation. Instead they lost all dignity and strength nationally. There is a lesson here for every assembly, for if assemblies are to be beautified and kept in unity they need to enjoy and respond to the shepherd ministry of the Saviour. He must have the pre-eminent place and be depended on. When this is the case the assembly will truly be in a healthy condition and be a place of beauty and unity. "And I will feed the flock." Zechariah was obedient to the charge given him and in spite of knowing that the coming Messiah would be rejected still kept to the terms of the commission. The Lord when here knew that the nation would reject Him, and yet He faithfully went on feeding the flock, especially the poor of the flock.

The price by which he was valued (vv.8-14)

In these verses the Lord's ministry to Israel is enlarged upon and most interesting details are given by Zechariah of the experience of the Messiah when in the midst of Israel. If this great passage is linked with the Gospel of Matthew one can readily see that what Zechariah writes anticipates how the Lord's ministry is presented in that Gospel. There are four ways by which one may enjoy these links with Matthew and thus profit from a comparison between Zechariah 11 and the later chapters of the first New Testament Gospel.

The cutting off of three shepherds in one month (v.8)

The Lord having taken up His ministry to Israel as He does in the earlier chapters of Matthew, He cuts off the shepherds. This one may see in Matthew 22 where the Lord has to deal with three religious heads of the people. The three shepherds are the Pharisees, Herodians, and the Sadducees. They are all mentioned in Matthew 22. Many suggestions have been made as to who these shepherds are and whether we are to think here of a literal month or of a short period of time, but, keeping it in context concerning the Messiah and linking the whole passage down to v.14 with the later chapters of Matthew, one is able to see that the verse at the very least illustrates the Lord as the true Shepherd dealing with three groups of leaders of the people and authoritatively, by His teaching, cutting them off. The words "cut off" do not mean to destroy or put to death, but rather to disavow (M. F. Unger). In Matthew 22 the Lord is seen disowning and renouncing the teaching of the three false shepherds. The "one month" may refer to the period of time just before the leaders of the nation crucified the Lord Jesus which resulted in sealing the doom of the nation.

He disowns them and breaks His staff of Beauty (vv.9-10)

In v.9 we have divine rejection. This was remarkably fulfilled in AD 70. "Then said I, I will not feed you." Continuing in his role as a shepherd, Zechariah abandoned his sheep. This is something totally out of character for a shepherd. The words that follow in the verse show that God gave Israel over to the punishment predicted for it: "Let what is dying die…Let those that are left eat each other's flesh". This solemn prophecy was literally fulfilled during the tragic and awful Roman siege in AD 70 (cp. Deut 28.54-57). Many Jews died and others suffered greatly. Many, too, of the Jews resorted to cannibalism in the siege and they evidently will do so again in the Tribulation. The following from the Jewish historian Josephus makes tragic reading. "Throughout the city people were dying of hunger in large numbers, and enduring unspeakable sufferings. In every house the merest hint of food sparked violence, and close relatives fell to blows, snatching from one another the pitiful supports of life. No respect was paid even to the dying; the ruffians [anti-Roman zealots] searched them, in case they were concealing food somewhere in their clothes, or just pretending to be near death. Gaping with hunger, like mad dogs, lawless gangs went staggering and reeling through the streets, battering upon the doors like drunkards, and so bewildered that they broke into the same house two or three times in an hour. Need drove the starving to gnaw at anything. Refuse which even animals would reject was collected and turned into food. In the end they were eating belts and shoes, and the leather stripped off their shields. Tufts of withered grass were devoured, and sold in little bundles for four drachmas". What dreadful conditions, and how tragic that the Jews should be reduced to this and to suffer such unparalleled extremities. The rejection of their Messiah resulted in this, and sadly there is more painful suffering for the Jew in the future until they are humbled and prepared for the Lord Jesus to reveal Himself to them.

"And I took my staff, even Beauty, and cut it asunder." This symbolized God breaking the covenant which He had made with the peoples. The covenant here is not the unconditional covenants made with Abraham and David, but the Mosaic covenant made with Israel, which alas they had already broken. Zechariah breaks the staff of Beauty, picturing God removing His protective grace from the nation and paving the way for destruction from their enemies. The word "people" (which is actually in the plural), is the same as in Genesis 49.10. The unreadiness of Israel to accept their Messiah made it impossible for Him to gather Gentile nations and thus fulfil the prophecy of Genesis 49.10. The link with Matthew 23 should now be clear, for the sorrowful words of the Messiah in that chapter touch the heart: "O Jerusalem, Jerusalem…how often would I have gathered thy children together, even as a hen gathereth her chickens under her wings, and ye would not! Behold, your house is left unto you desolate" (vv.37-38). In line with Zechariah's symbolic enactment, the Lord breaks the staff of Beauty in two and leaves the apostate nation to its own fate.

The poor of the flock and the word of the Lord (v.11)
The poor of the flock, having watched Zechariah break his staff, realized it was the word of the Lord. The poor of the flock in the context were the little remnant referred to in v.7 as the afflicted of God's flock. The more distant application of this reference must speak of those Jews who did not wait for Christ's second advent in power and glory, but recognized and accepted Him at His first coming. Of these it was true that they "waited upon me" and "knew". After the Lord says, "Your house is left unto you desolate", we find Him leaving the temple area and sitting upon the Mount of Olives, teaching the disciples and giving them the word of the Lord, prophetically touching future events: the destruction of the temple, the Tribulation suffering for Israel, His second advent in glory, the restoration of Israel, and the judgment of the living nations. This is a word of the Lord indeed! Thus we have a third link with Matthew 24 and 25 in which the Lord's Olivet discourse is recorded. The disciples, as the poor of the flock, waited upon the Lord Jesus as He taught them, and they knew that what they were listening to was the word of the Lord and would all be fulfilled. Although the little remnant of the disciples had much to learn, they discerned what the nation did not. They believed in the authority of Christ and that He was the Messiah. They discerned especially that the word of God was active in God giving up Israel as a nation to the awful consequences

of their rejection of Christ. Most of the nation when the Lord was here were callous and undiscerning. They had no idea that God was in control of things and that He was working out everything to fulfil His own word. "The anticipated accomplishment of the prediction, symbolized in the prophetic parable, is believed both by a faithful few who saw Zechariah enact this object lesson in his day, and by the faithful few who saw the historical fulfilment of the prediction toward the end of our Lord's earthly ministry (cp. Mt 23.1-39)" (M. F. Unger).

How good it is to wait upon the Lord. When we do so no time or breath is lost. The believer today who loves the word of the Lord can see that some of it has already been fulfilled, and has complete confidence that these prophecies yet unfulfilled of God's word will also be fulfilled literally. It is only when the heart is willing that the believer can begin to perceive the word of the Lord and the message being conveyed through His servant.

The betrayal and rejection of the Lord (vv. 12-13)

Verses 12-13 anticipate the scenes of the Lord's betrayal, rejection and death as portrayed in Matthew 26 and 27. "If ye think good, give me my price; and if not, forbear." This is the appeal of the Good Shepherd to the whole flock. It was an appeal made for the space of the three and a half years of His wonderful ministry among them. It was His last appeal to the nation to declare itself as to the value they placed upon Him and His ministry. In effect, as He moved among them and gave them such memorable teaching, He was saying, "What do you think of Me?". What was the price He was asking for? It was the price of loyalty, obedience, love, and the listening ear. This was what the Good Shepherd was looking for in Israel. How good to see that this price the poor of the flock had paid Him. He now asks the nation to declare itself.

What was their answer? "They weighed for my price thirty pieces of silver." How tragic that this was the nation's deliberate estimate of their true Messiah who had come to bless and deliver them (Acts 3.26). They not only refused to give Him the due He was worthy of, but they added insult to injury by giving for Him the price of a slave that had been killed (Ex 21.32). By paying such a price they made it clear to Him that they did not estimate His services higher than the labour of a purchased slave. A freeman was rated twice that sum. Jehovah commands the prophet to throw the miserable sum to the potter. "Cast it unto the potter" was a proverbial expression for contemptuous treatment. This is what Jehovah thought of the estimate the nation placed upon the services of the Messiah He had sent among them. Jehovah regarded the price they paid as paid to Himself, and this after all His work on behalf of the nation. Little wonder God treated the nation with contempt and punished them. It is not out of place here to ask each believer, how much value we place upon the Saviour. Do we give Him the price of our complete obedience and devotion? He still says today to each believing heart, "Give me my price". Are we prepared to give Him the price He is asking for?

It is wonderful how accurately this prophecy of the thirty pieces of silver was fulfilled by Judas in his betrayal of the Lord Jesus. "I...cast them to the potter in the house of the Lord." The thirty pieces of silver were thrown down in the temple, the very place where Judas cast them. They are said to be cast to the potter, because it is to him they were appointed by the Lord ultimately to go. God, whose secret operations and sovereign power extend over all men, had so arranged this matter that Judas threw down the money in the temple to bring it before the face of God as blood-money and to call down the judgment of God on the nation. The high priest, by purchasing the potter's field for this money, which received the name of "The field of blood, unto this day" (Mt 27.8), thus perpetuated the memorial of their sin against their Messiah. So the statement of Zechariah that he took the thirty pieces of silver and "cast them to the potter in the house of the Lord" was in this way literally fulfilled. Messiah in the person of Zechariah says, "I took, I threw". Matthew says, "They took, they gave them" (see Mt 27.6-7). The reason for this is that the act of Judas and the Jews together was the Lord's appointment (see Mt 27.10 & Acts 2.23). Thus remarkably in all its minutest details the wonderful prophecy of Zechariah was fulfilled.

Matthew in quoting the prophecy says, "Then was fulfilled that which was spoken by Jeremy the prophet saying, And they took the thirty pieces of silver, the price of him that was valued, whom they of the children of Israel did value; And gave them for the potter's field, as the Lord appointed me" (Mt 27.9-10). These words, however, are Zechariah's and not Jeremiah's. Some have concluded that this is a slip of memory on the part of Matthew, but a belief in the inspiration of Holy Scripture must cancel this idea out. It has been suggested that in Jeremiah 18 & 19 we have similar symbolic actions to that recorded in Zechariah and that Jeremiah was the original author from whom Zechariah derived the groundwork of the prophecy. Matthew therefore refers the prophecy to the original author. Another explanation for the apparent discrepancy is that the Jews to whom Matthew writes regarded Jeremiah as a leading or representative prophet and in this light Matthew cited Jeremiah and not Zechariah. Either way there is no contradiction. "The fulfilment, however, of the prophecy actually recorded by the evangelist was in itself most remarkable. The slight differences in the minor details do not in the least detract from its peculiar significance. The thirty pieces of silver paid to Judas by the chief priests and elders of the Jews were in reality the price at which those representatives of the Jewish nation valued the services of our blessed Lord. By fixing that as the price for His person they manifested how much they despised Him and His work. No prophet, as in the prophetic picture, but the traitor Judas it was who received that despicable sum" (C. H. H. Wright).

The story has been told of Mr H. St John standing in the private chapel of Keble College, Oxford, contemplating Holman Hunt's masterpiece, *The Light of the World*. Suddenly, the silence was broken by a crowd of tourists led by a guide, a man with a particularly strident voice. After a hasty explanation of the painting, he announced, "The original of this picture was sold for £5,000". Without a moment's hesitation Mr St John stepped forward and said very quietly, "Ladies and gentlemen, may I say that the true Original of this picture was sold for thirty pieces of silver!" After a brief silence, the crowd of people passed out of the chapel without another word. How solemnly true it is that there is more than one way to sell the Saviour. Thousands of believers today sell Him for a much smaller sum than thirty pieces of silver. We can sell Him for the sake of some passing gratification. We can sell Him in some hour of temptation. We can sell Him even when conscience whispers, "No, it will dishonour your Lord". We can sell Him in shrinking from the path of reproach for Him, and in a host of others ways. We cannot trust our own hearts, but look to the One who has done so much for us.

> Thirty pieces of silver
> For the Lord of life they gave;
> Thirty pieces of silver –
> Only the price of a slave!
> But this was the priestly value
> Of the Holy One of God;
> They weighed it out in the temple,
> The price of the Saviour's blood.
>
> Thirty pieces of silver
> Laid in Iscariot's hand;
> Thirty pieces of silver,
> And the aid of an arméd band,
> Like a lamb that is led to the slaughter,
> Brought the humbled Son of God
> At midnight from the garden
> Where His sweat had been like blood.
>
> "Thirty pieces of silver"
> Burns on the traitor's brain;
> "Thirty pieces of silver!
> Oh! it is hellish gain!"
> "I have sinned and betrayed the guiltless!"
> He cried with a fevered breath,
> And he threw them down in the temple,
> And rushed to a madman's death.

Thirty pieces of silver
Lay in the House of God;
Thirty pieces of silver,
But oh, 'twas the price of blood!
And so for a place to bury
The strangers in, they gave
The price of their own Messiah,
Who lay in a borrowed grave.
(William Blane).

The breaking of Bands (v.14)

The whole prophetic drama enacted by Zechariah concludes in v.14 with the final act which symbolizes the complete rejection of the nation. Thus there now follows the breaking of the second staff (Bands) which signifies the breaking of the unity of Judah and Israel – that is the whole nation. Their relationship to God had been severed by the cutting of the staff Beauty; their relationship with one another now suffers. Messiah's last link with Israel was broken by its own tragic sin of rejecting Him. There will be no more feeding from Him now, for all hope for them was gone because He was rejected. In rejecting Christ the nation was left in a worse state of discord and misery. The last paragraph of the chapter reveals even more serious consequences of the rejection. Historically speaking, the divided state of the nation is seen in that just before the destruction of Jerusalem in AD 70 the Jews broke up into parties that were very hostile to one another. This state of affairs accelerated their destruction by the Romans. Between the breaking of Beauty and Bands some space of time is hinted at and this may indicate that the Lord Jesus, when here, was reluctant to give up His people, but patiently waited in grace for their repentance and recognition of Him; alas this was not to be. Thus the Lord did not restore their unity. It is no exaggeration to say that the rejection by Israel of Christ was catastrophic for them as a people, and yet even the destruction of their city and their dispersion among the nations is not to be permanent, for this very prophecy of Zechariah contains clear promises of Israel's future deliverance.

One cannot refrain from saying that if Christ is not given His place among believers in assembly fellowship, there will be no unity. So there is a word of caution here to make sure that Christ in His beauty is the centre of the thoughts and endeavours of the saints. Christ must be enjoyed and kept before every believer, for if not there is the very real danger of the staff Bands being broken and assembly unity and strength being lost.

Verses 15-17: The Greedy Shepherd – The Antichrist

Zechariah in this third section of the chapter moves into the circumstances of the Tribulation when Israel will fall into the hands of a cruel ruler who will make havoc of them for his own advantage. The raising up of the Antichrist will be a judgment from God upon Israel for their rejection of Christ. The features of the Antichrist here recall Samuel's prediction concerning Saul in 1 Samuel 8. The key expression there mentioned six times is "he will take". He treated the flock of God in much the same way as the Antichrist will treat Israel in the future. Saul used the people over whom he reigned for his own ends and so will the Antichrist to a greater degree. Saul, the man of the people's choice, was given to the people because they had rejected Samuel, or rather the Lord in Samuel. So God in judgment upon His people at the end time, will raise up the Antichrist because of their rejection of His Son.

Israel did not value or accept the Lord Jesus, but they will readily accept the false shepherd and put their trust in him. In speaking of the false messiah the Lord Jesus referred to him as follows: "Another shall come in his own name, him ye will receive" (Jn 5.43). Did they not in their own history prefer Barabbas to their Messiah, and did this not show their willingness to accept a bad person in place of a good one? As Zechariah had been bidden to impersonate the Messiah he is now asked by Jehovah to act out the part of the bad shepherd – "Take unto thee yet the instruments of a foolish shepherd". Notice this false shepherd is called "a foolish shepherd". The word "foolish" means "worthless" and has the idea of being morally deficient (see Prov 1.7). In the Old Testament the word is synonymous with ungodliness and sin (Ps 14.1). The shepherd is described in other portions as "that man of sin" (2 Thess 2.3), "the lawless one" (2 Thess 2.8, RV), "the beast" (Rev 11.7), "the man of the earth" (Ps 10.18), the "little horn" (Dan 7.8), "the prince that shall come" (Dan 9.26), and the wilful king (Dan 11.36). All these names and more concerning this monster of a man are very revealing. Since Israel would not have the good shepherd they shall have the bad one. In his new role Zechariah represented one who will completely fail to do for the people all that the Lord Jesus could have done for them. What exactly the instruments of this false shepherd are is not revealed. If they are the same as those of a good shepherd then they will not be used to help and bless the nation of Israel. Instead of being good to Israel he will be selfish, cruel, and power seeking, and will let them down in the end. He will miserably afflict the flock, the people of Israel.

In this rather sombre pen picture of this cruel individual to come, Zechariah shows that he will be deficient in three important functions.

He will lack in watchfulness (v.16a)

God says, "I will raise up a shepherd in the land". This of course must signify the land of Israel. From this one may conclude that the Antichrist will be a Jew or one descended from Israel. It is hard to conceive that the Jewish people will accept a person as their messiah if he is not a Jew. There are four things the false messiah will not do for the people and these are the very opposite of what the Lord Jesus would have done for them. Leaving out the words "not", "neither", and "nor" gives a positive presentation of the character of a good shepherd. These four functions show the foolish shepherd to be lacking in watchful care for the flock. He will not visit those that are cut off, he will not seek the young one, he will not heal that which is broken, and he will not feed that which stands still. This proud and cruel character will fail to do what a true shepherd would do for the sheep.

A true shepherd in an assembly today will care for those sheep that have been isolated from the flock of God and have grown spiritually cold and weak. He will tend to the lambs of the flock, especially those who have just been born again. He will seek to heal that which is broken or "wounded" (JND). There are many wounded sheep among believers and they need to be spiritually healed. A true shepherd will also feed the strong or sound, appreciating that even they need spiritual sustenance and succour lest they begin to be spiritually unhealthy. Jehovah, Israel's God, will do these things for His people in a day to come (see Ezek 34.12-16). Let each exercised saint pray earnestly that God will raise up such shepherds within assemblies, for the need for such men is very great.

The false shepherd will not care for Israel in spite of promising them his protection. They will find him to be callous, selfish, openly unconcerned and, worst of all, cruel.

He will lack in tenderness (v.16b)

The person of the Antichrist has been described in negative terms, but the prophetic picture continues with a positive and terrible description of a wicked side to this false Christ. He will have no tenderness whatsoever in his heart for God's people, but will be marked by incredible greed in eating the fattest and best of the sheep. In speech he will have wonderful oratory. In character he will be charismatic. In status he will exercise universal sway and demand world-wide worship, but these will hide a deadly and destructive cruel streak within him, which he will use with terrible force against God's people Israel. Instead of feeding the sheep, he will feed on them – preying on the unwary. So cruel will this bad shepherd be that he is pictured as tearing off the hoofs of the sheep, apparently as M. F. Unger suggests, "in avaricious search for the last edible morsel". Pretending to be devoted to protecting Israel and seeking their welfare he will deceive them, and when he is in a place of prominence, in the middle of Daniel's seventieth week, he will break the covenant he made with Israel and turn against them. He will bring upon Israel the severest tribulations ever experienced by this race. Israel will have put their confidence in him, but instead of giving them protection he will persecute them. Psalm 55.21 depicts the appealing character of the Antichrist, but shows at the same time his wicked designs against Israel: "The words of his mouth were smoother than butter, but war was in his heart: his words were softer than oil, yet were they drawn swords". How different the foolish shepherd will be from the Lord Jesus Christ. Of the shepherd character of Christ we read, "He shall feed his flock like a shepherd: he shall gather the lambs with his arm, and carry them in his bosom, and shall gently lead those that are with young" (Is 40.11). What a beautiful description of the true shepherd! The sheep of the flock today more than ever need much gentle and tender care.

He will lack in faithfulness (v.17)

This same sinister figure is now called "the worthless shepherd" (JND) because of his diabolical deeds such as forsaking the flock, in contrast to the Lord Jesus Christ the Good Shepherd (Jn 10.11-13). The foolish shepherd will forsake the nation in the hour of its greatest need, but thank God for the great reassuring thought that the Lord Jesus will never leave His flock nor forsake the least of His own – "I will never leave thee, nor forsake thee" (Heb 13.5) is His promise. Being "worthless" the false shepherd is only fit to be cast out. The solemn woe of God will fall upon him in devastating punishment, for the word of God reveals that he will be cast alive with the false prophet into the lake of fire (Rev 19.20).

Although God will place Israel under the worthless shepherd, and by this His plan is to discipline His people severely for their rejection of Christ, yet in this last verse Zechariah prophesies that whatever boastful prominence and hellish power the worthless shepherd will have, it will all be short-lived and come suddenly and solemnly to an end. "The sword shall be upon his arm, and upon his right eye: his arm shall be clean dried up, and his right eye shall be utterly darkened." Is Zechariah here giving exact prophetic details again as He has done with the betrayal of the Lord and also His procession on the ass into Jerusalem? From Revelation 13.3, accepting that the first beast is the Antichrist, one can plainly see that the foolish shepherd will be wounded, but will recover from what will appear to be a deadly wound. Hence the entire world will wonder after the beast. The reason, however, why the sword of judgment is upon the arm and eye, is to show how completely the worthless shepherd will be punished. His arm that should have protected them and his eye that should have watched over them will be rendered useless. The arm of his power will be paralyzed and the eye of his intelligence will be nullified. The Lord Jesus, the true shepherd, will destroy him (2 Thess 2.8) and thus make him incapable of hurting others or defending himself. He who had exercised the power of the evil one will be completely powerless to resist the Messiah.

Thus the first oracle or burden, predicting the first advent and rejection of the Messiah, is concluded. It began in ch.9.1 with judgment upon Gentile nations and ends with God's judgment upon Israel in putting them under the despotic reign of the Antichrist. How great God is, how solemn are

His ways, and how sure His sovereign purpose is for this world and Israel. All will be fulfilled according to His plan, for what has been shown in this first prophetic burden will pave the way for the second advent and acceptance of the true Messiah as seen in the second burden in chs. 12-14.

ZECHARIAH 12

Chapters 12-14 – The Second Prophecy

   The prophecies found in this second burden mainly relate to the return of the King. The section is concerned with events that have yet to take place. All is prophetic and relates to things that even now are still future, except for the reference to the death of Christ in 13.7. Reading through these chapters one can readily see that the book of Zechariah well merits being described as "the apocalypse of the Old Testament", for it deals with a series of events that begins with the Tribulation, and climaxes with the crisis in the battle of Armageddon, the deliverance of Israel from their enemies, their conversion, and the great sequel of the Lord's second advent in glory and His millennial reign. These three remaining chapters of Zechariah thus form one prophecy in which is depicted the awful struggle Israel will have to face to stay alive as a nation. If the first burden in chs.9-11 has shown the anointed King rejected, this second burden shows the rejected King enthroned. There are some most interesting links between these closing three chapters of Zechariah. It is particularly significant to see the way the Lord Jesus is presented in each chapter. In ch.12 He is the Smiting Warrior against the enemy; in ch.13 He is the Suffering Saviour of Calvary; and in ch.14 He is the Sovereign Controller of the world. In each chapter, too, one rejoices to note clear evidence of the deity of Christ, showing that He is Jehovah. In 12.10 He says, "They shall look upon me whom they have pierced". The speaker is Jehovah, as is clear from vv.1,9, & 10. In 13.7 the Lord Jesus is "the man that is my fellow". In 14.4 "his feet shall stand in that day upon the mount of Olives". Compare that statement with pronouncement of v.5 where Zechariah says that "the Lord my God shall come" - what clear testimony to the deity of Israel's Messiah. Then again, in each of these chapters of the second burden notice that there are things which are opened. In 12.4 we have the opened eyes of Jehovah; in 13.1 it is the opened fountain; and in 14.4 it is the opened mountain. Chapter 12, then, is divine protection of Israel. Chapter 13 is divine purification of Israel. Chapter 14 is divine power for Israel.
   In seeking to expound each chapter as it appears in this book, it is helpful to note that this second burden of Zechariah is actually in two sections. The first, in 12.1-13.6, concerns the gathering of the nations against Israel, the victory of Israel and their conversion. The second, in 13.7-14.21, concerns the crisis in the Day of the Lord, the second advent and the subsequent reign of Christ in the Millennium. These three chapters, as do the previous three of the first burden, treat of the war between the nations and Israel. It is also most interesting to note that the second burden commences with a reference to the power of God as Creator. Is this not a fitting introduction to the closing three chapters of Zechariah? God is not only the Creator in the past; He is the Sustainer of creation in the present.

If He by His almighty power controls the functions and movements in creation, then He is able to fulfil what He has prophesied and promised. Indeed, the fourteenth chapter, for example, shows how the Creator God will intervene in His creation and cause physical changes and miraculous transformations, so much so that the Mount of Olives will cleave in two. Thus nothing in His creation will hinder the carrying out of His word. This certainly gives confidence to the believer as he reads about this great divine programme.

Chapter 12: The Smiter of the Enemy
A brief survey of the chapter shows:

In vv.1-4: How the conflict with Judah and Jerusalem will result in the destruction of nations gathered against her.

In vv.5-9: How Jehovah will endow the rulers of Judah and the inhabitants of Jerusalem with superhuman strength to gain victory over all their foes.

In vv.10-14: How Jehovah will pour upon Israel the Spirit of grace and supplications, so that they will bitterly repent of having crucified their Messiah.

The passage, however, can be profitably considered in its twofold division, the first in vv.1-9 presenting Israel's protection, and the second in vv.10-14 presenting Israel's penitence. In the first section the Lord Jesus is seen in His David character as a man of war winning the battle. In the next section the Lord Jesus can be seen in His Joseph character winning His brethren – His second advent will produce repentance in Israel as Joseph's revelation of himself did to his brethren (Gen 45). Since it already has been seen that Zechariah's prophecy gives ample evidence that Christ is Jehovah, there are some lovely and yet solemn glimpses of Christ in the varied aspects of His character and work for the nation. He is the Sustainer of creation in v.1; He is the Smiter of the foe in vv.2-4; He is the Strengthener of Judah in vv.5-9; He is the Sender of the Spirit in v.10a; and, finally, He is the Sufferer of Calvary in vv.10b-14.

Verses 1-9: The Protection of Israel
Messiah the Sustainer of creation (v.1)
We have already remarked how suggestive and significant it is that Zechariah begins the second burden of his prophecy with the power of the Creator. The burden of Jehovah concerning Israel stands by the side of the burden of Jehovah concerning Hadrach (9.1), the seat of the great world power. It is called a "burden", or weighty prophecy, filled with destruction for Israel's foes. The phrase may also refer to Israel's distresses that precede their deliverance. It should be pointed out that this heading, "The burden of the word of the Lord", is not confined to this chapter, but relates to the whole prophecy, from the commencement of this chapter to the close of the book. The reference to the creation of the world and of God forming the spirit of man within him is in order that this may remove

from the mind all doubts as to the fulfilment of the wonderful things He is about to do for Israel. The words in this verse are not to be referred to the creation of the world once for all, as in Genesis 1, but they refer to the upholding of the world as a work of the continuous providence of God. What a great introduction to this second burden of chs.12-14! There are similar prefaces in other passages (see Is 42.5 and 65.17-18). In the light of Colossians 1.16 and Hebrews 1.2 the Lord Jesus is the Creator and Preserver of all creation. This ought to dispel any doubt or unbelief concerning the predictions of these closing chapters. The Lord is incomparable in His majesty, power, and sovereign control. The One who cares for the world in its vastness and complexity is the same One who will accomplish His own word and manifest in a wonderful way His care for His earthly people. What an encouragement this is also for believers today. The enemy may come in like a flood and all may seem wrong, but He is in control and His glory in the end will be displayed.

Messiah the Smiter of the foe (vv.2-4)

These verses speak of the siege of Jerusalem and can be read with Zechariah 14.1-3 and Revelation 19.19-21. There have been many sieges of Jerusalem throughout its long history, but the one described here is the last and the most terrible of all. One must point out that the authority of this prophecy is divine, for it comes from God. It is the word of the Lord (v.1). Its scene is Jerusalem (vv.2,10 & 11). Its setting is in the period of the Day of the Lord. Notice the phrase, "In that day". This is used frequently in both Zechariah and Isaiah. It is found sixteen times in the last three chapters of Zechariah alone (six times in ch.12), showing that prophetically it refers to the Day of the Lord, a time of God's wrath and blessing that will extend from the beginning of the Tribulation to the end of the one thousand year reign of Christ.

The severity of God's judgments at this time is solemnly pictured in the two images of a "cup of trembling (reeling)" and a "burdensome stone". It is interesting to note that the word "make" is found twice in vv.2 & 3. God by His power will do this. The word is in keeping with the reference to the Creator in v.1. The one who is the Maker of the heavens and earth will prepare a bowl of reeling and a burdensome stone for the nations who will be gathered against Jerusalem in this pivotal crisis event during the Day of the Lord. He who by His omnipotence brought the world into being and by His omniscience still sustains it will find no difficulty in gathering the nations together against Israel. These two figures of what Israel will yet be to their enemies are vivid and solemn. As "a cup of trembling" or "reeling" they will render their enemies powerless. The word "cup" (or bowl) is used of the basin in which the blood of the Paschal lamb was caught (Ex 12.22), and of the bowls used in the temple service (1 Kings 7.50). It is a symbol of the judgment of God (cp. Ps 75.8). The nations may be eager to drink down its contents, but the draught proves to be far other than they anticipated and they will stagger back confused.

As "a burdensome stone" they will break, injure and crush the enemy. The nations which in that day will seek to crush God's people will be crushed by them. All these national powers joined together against Israel will think the tiny nation easy prey and will be confident of success against her, but they will find Israel as a heavy stone hard to move or heave away. The stone will cut in pieces anyone who tries to attack her.

Thus the victory over the enemies of Israel is compared to a man who drinks more than he can hold and so staggers and falls, or like a man who tries to remove a stone heavier than he can lift and in the process is hurt by it. Both of these shall Jerusalem be to the nations that fight against her in that day. Such shall she be "though all the people (nations) of the earth be gathered together against it". This ungodly confederacy against the Jews shall be all but universal. The anti-Semitism which has long been a terrible threat and worry to Israel, and is gaining in power today, will reach a satanically inspired climax in this siege. The Jews, who when the Lord was here fell on the "Rock of offence", their Messiah, and were broken, will find that the same Rock will fall upon the nations who burden themselves with it in this siege of Jerusalem, and it shall grind them to powder (Mt 21.44).

In v.4, as the battle against Jerusalem progresses, the Lord will cause confusion, panic, and dismay among the enemy, so much so that everything will grind to a halt. The "horse" and "rider" are terms denoting military might and speak of the whole machinery of the armies of Armageddon brought together against little Israel. God, however, in His majesty and power will execute divine wrath upon Israel's enemies. He will throw them into confusion. We can compare this with what He did for Israel at the deliverance of His people in the Red Sea. There the "horse "and the "rider" were thrown into the sea (Ex 15.1). The three punishments of the enemy here, namely astonishment, madness, and blindness, are the three plagues with which rebellious Israel were threatened (Deut 28.28). What a change for Israel in that day! It is now their enemies' turn to suffer these things. While He will smite every horse with blindness, Jehovah will open His eyes upon Judah for its protection. The opening of the eyes of Jehovah suggests that His eyes, as it were, have been shut, as having no regard for the nation, but now He awakens for her help and deliverance. This is only imagery of course, for God "neither slumbers nor sleeps". He cannot forget His promises to His people and He will not forsake them in the hour of their greatest danger yet.

Messiah the Strengthener of Judah (vv.5-9)

God will cause confusion and tumult among the enemy in order to prevent any possibility of them injuring His people. He will take away the power of the enemy, but will empower and strengthen Judah to resist and conquer the foe. Against their enemies they will be invincible and will experience a supernatural victory from the Lord. The inhabitants of Jerusalem will have turned to the Lord for their strength, for they will recognize that "the Lord of hosts" alone is able to strengthen and sustain them in the conflict. The leaders of the surrounding area of Judea will greatly value the example of the inhabitants of the city in drawing their strength from the Lord. The leaders of Judah are mentioned as the leaders of the people in war, and what they say is the conviction of the whole country. That they "say in their heart" shows a deep conviction.

Judah and Jerusalem are distinguished here as the country and the metropolis. The repulse of the foe by the metropolis will assure the Jews of the country that the same divine aid shall save them. Both the leaders and the citizens together will know the strengthening power of the Lord. They will realize that power and triumph comes from the Lord. He alone will be the source of all that they will need in the crisis. Psalm 46.5 speaks of the very same period and declares of the city at that time: "God is in the midst of her; she shall not be moved: God shall help her, and that right early". From ch.11 we learn that the city that rejected Christ and the city that will have accepted the Antichrist will have become, when Messiah arrives for their deliverance, the city owned of God with its inhabitants blessed by God. Strength for the believer, too, is in the same Lord of Hosts. God has not changed. He is still Jehovah of Hosts with mighty armies at His disposal. How wonderful to know that the God who will intervene for His people in the future and who will perform great wonders for them, is the God and Father of each believer today. God's power is for us, God's power is in us, and God's power can work through us, so that we need not despair. Paul's prayer for the Ephesians was that they might know "what is the exceeding greatness of his power to usward who believe, according to the working of his mighty power, Which he wrought in Christ, when he raised him from the dead, and set him at his own right hand in the heavenly places" (1.19-20). What an incredible statement it is that the very same divine power demonstrated in the resurrection of Christ is available for the believer! Divine power that has also seated Christ in heaven has delivered the believer from a state of spiritual death and communicated life (Eph 2.1). The power that will work for Israel in the future will be wonderful indeed, but in the spiritual sense the necessary strength for the christian conflict is wonderful too and very real. Oh to experience it in reality!

In v.6 Zechariah uses two similes to describe how easily and quickly they will overcome the power of the vast armies that will come against them in that day. They will be "like an hearth of fire (a firepan or firepot) among the wood". They will be "like a torch of fire in a sheaf" (or a torch among sheaves of grain). The whole confederacy, led by the Antichrist, shall be as easily and completely consumed as a woodpile ignited by a firepot of hot coals, or a pile of bound sheaves set alight by a fiery torch.

The imagery is very graphic, for swiftly and quickly from every side will the attackers of Jerusalem be destroyed. Throughout the battle the inhabitants will not flee, but will remain in their own place, even in Jerusalem. Notice that the city is mentioned twice here at the end of the verse. Why is it repeated? Is it not to fix attention on the land itself and to show again the literal character of the prophecy? It is as if the Holy Spirit had foreseen the modern error of some commentators in spiritualising the words of many prophecies and applying them to the Church. Therefore the expression is repeated, "even in Jerusalem". This is another instance where we see the literal character of Zechariah's prophecies. One may, and should, see spiritual lessons in the literal predictions, but the literal interpretation must never be lost sight of.

In vv.7 & 8 the theme of the protection and the deliverance of Judah is continued. The country districts will be delivered first and then the defended city of Jerusalem. The rural areas will be helped first because of their vulnerability, but all Judah shall share equally in the miraculous deliverance. "The Lord also shall save the tents of Judah first, that the glory of the house of David and the glory of the inhabitants of Jerusalem do not magnify themselves against Judah." How interesting this is and how it shows the way in which God works. The way God will work when intervening for His people in that day is in order that they will realize that the deliverance they will experience is entirely of Himself and not by any human skill or military power on their part.

The tents of Judah form quite a contrast to the buildings of the capital and probably also point to their defenceless condition. Thus the "tents of Judah" emphasizes the weak position of Judah, exposed outside the city walls to the danger of the wrath of the enemy. It will be a time of much fear among the people. The whole land of Israel will flow with blood at this time (Rev 14.20) and two thirds of its inhabitants will have been cut off (Zech 13.8), but Jehovah's exceeding great mercy will be shown to the weak first. Here is an important spiritual truth, for the law of God's Kingdom is that He chooses "the weak things of the world" to bring to nought the mighty (1 Cor 1.27). Another principle of God's ways is also illustrated, for the Apostle Paul said to the Corinthians, "But he that glorieth, let him glory in the Lord" (2 Cor 10.17; cp. Jer 9.23-24). Judah will glory in the Lord in the day of their deliverance. God's work with His people is never to cause jealousy, but to keep all humble and delighted in Him. To save Jerusalem and the royal house of David first would create pride and haughtiness on the one hand, and envy and jealousy on the other. This would soon hinder all God's work and create disorder and upset among His people. Thus, although God's deliverance of His people will be miraculous and His punishment of the enemy will be sudden and solemn, it will be marked by order so that His cause will prosper and His people will be blessed. God's ways of working may be unexpected, or He may bless others first and not us, but His ways must be bowed to and accepted, and above all He must be the basis and source of our glorying. How often the human heart seeks self glory, but if we are to prosper and know the Lord's help we must keep lowly before Him.

In v.8, although the surrounding country of Judah is saved first, yet shall the city be specially defended by the Lord against the foe (cp. Is 31.4-5). Those who are weak are to become like David, the bravest hero of Israel (1 Sam 17.34-36; 2 Sam 7.8-10). The feeble are designated, in the Hebrew word KASHAL (3782), as the stumbling ones – those who cannot stand firmly on their feet (see 1 Sam 2.4). These are to become like David. David was the great champion of Israel in the valley of Elah, but Israel's Messiah, our Lord Jesus Christ, is greater than David. David seemed invincible in battle and gained many victories, but the Lord Jesus will be a mighty man of war and will wonderfully deliver His people from the mighty Goliath of the largest armies ever assembled in the field of conflict against Israel. David became famous in Israel as a mighty warrior, but the Lord Jesus, as a result of His mighty triumph over Israel's foes, will become universally acclaimed. The strong ones are designated as the "house", that is the household or family of David. They are to become like Elohim God, yea, like "the angel of the Lord before them". This is the Angel of Jehovah – a divine Person, even the pre-incarnate Christ who went before His people through the Red Sea and the desert and smote the Egyptians and all the enemies of Israel (Ex 23.20; 32.34). The Lord Jesus as their Messiah will not only supernaturally deliver them and be with them, but will go before them as their Leader. As David was to the Jew the highest type of strength on earth, so the Angel of Jehovah may be viewed as the highest type of strength and glory in heaven. How true it is that when as believers in the Lord Jesus we are weak, then are we strong, because His strength is made perfect in weakness (2 Cor 12.9).

"And it shall come to pass in that day, that I will seek to destroy all the nations that come against Jerusalem" (v.9). The word "seek" (BAQASH – 1245) needs to be rightly understood. It certainly does not cast doubt on God's power to destroy the enemies of His people; neither does it question the outcome of His purpose. No, it means that Jehovah will give all His undivided attention and will set Himself, with determined earnestness, to seek out and destroy any nation that dares to attack Jerusalem. Israel's deliverance will not be a temporary deliverance from their foes, but a complete and permanent one.

Verses 10-14: The Penitence of Israel

This last part of Zechariah 12 shows the wonderful power and grace of the Lord Jesus Christ in dealing with Israel after many centuries of rejecting Him. Just as vv.1-9 refer to David the warrior king, so vv.10-14 recall the story of Joseph in the way that he dealt with his brethren when their circumstances virtually forced them into his presence (Gen 42-45). His brethren, after all the tests they were put through by Joseph, were brought to recognize their guilt and repent of their sin, and were restored to Joseph. So it will be in God's purpose for Israel. They will be brought through the terrible trial of the Tribulation to recognize at the Messiah's second advent their national guilt and they will repent and enjoy national conversion. Zechariah 12.10-14 is a wonderful passage. His description of the conversion of Israel is vivid, clear and touching. On the theme of Israel's conversion it can hardly be matched in all other Old Testament prophecies.

Messiah the Sender of the Holy Spirit (v.10a)

The section extending from 12.10 to 13.9 deals with Israel's complete deliverance from sin. If 12.1-9 predicts the physical and literal deliverance of Israel, these verses now describe the spiritual deliverance of Israel. The nation will not only be delivered, but they will be restored in a repentant and pardoned condition. Thus we read, "I will pour upon the house of David, and upon the inhabitants of Jerusalem, the spirit of grace and of supplications". In v.10 Israel's repentance for their sin and their resulting conversion is created by the Holy Spirit, caused by a look to Christ, and compared to the mourning for an only son and firstborn. There will be a great outpouring of the Holy Spirit upon the nation. There should not be any doubt that the term "the spirit of grace" refers to the Holy Spirit of God. It does not refer to a disposition of grace which will bring about Israel's repentance, but to the Holy Spirit, in all His powerful workings, convicting the nation of their sin in rejecting Christ, opening their eyes to recognize Him, and producing in them real repentance for having crucified their Messiah. In this passage and at the beginning of ch.13 one may see a good illustration of the elements of true conversion: the convicting work of the Spirit; the production of repentance; the bringing about of cleansing from sin (13.1); the resultant holiness of life (13.2). In all true conversion to God these things will be seen. Reader, is this your history? The title of the Spirit here is delightful and significant, "The spirit of grace". The title occurs again in Hebrews 10.29. There too it is in connection with Jews to whom the epistle is addressed. When God begins to work again with the nation of Israel it will be entirely a work of grace. The nation certainly does not deserve any blessing from God, owing to their centuries of failure and sin and in particular the crucifying of Christ.

It should be noted that the first person pronoun is used, "I will pour". The "I" refers to the Creator of the universe (v.1) who will pour out the Spirit of grace upon Israel. There is an interesting link here with John's Gospel. It commences by presenting Christ as the Creator (1.3), and then later in the same Gospel, John records the Saviour's words concerning His promise to send the Holy Spirit (16.7). Thus, as in this Zechariah passage, the Lord Jesus is both the Creator of the world and the Sender of the Spirit. In John, of course, the sending of the Spirit has to do with the Church; in Zechariah's prophecy it relates to the nation of Israel, but it is further evidence of the deity of Christ. It is the Spirit of God who bestows the grace of God upon men. This then is a movement of God. It is God who takes the initiative towards Israel. When God begins to move to bless Israel a wonderful change will take place in the nation. The word "pour" indicates an abundance of refreshment, just like water poured on thirsty ground. When this happens Israel will enjoy "times of refreshing…from the presence of the Lord" (Acts 3.19). Not only so, but the Spirit will produce supplication. There will be a great spirit of prayer to God. It will be the prayer of repentance. Thus it is plain to see that here the gift of the Holy Spirit is an exceptional one, because the effect of the Holy Spirit thus poured out will produce a work of grace within their hearts which will lead to deep repentance. The same effects will be seen in every true case of conversion to God.

Messiah the Sufferer of Calvary (vv. 10b-14)

The second part of v. 10 refers to the suffering Messiah – "they shall look upon me whom they have pierced, and they shall mourn for him". The "they" in the verse clearly refers to the nation of Israel as the immediate context shows; the house of David refers to the princely family and Jerusalem the capital is regarded as the representative of the whole nation. Jewish scholars have stumbled over this verse and even some christian scholars have found it difficult to interpret. Who is the speaker here? Can it be that the "*me*" and the "*him*" refer to deity? If so how can it be that God is pierced? Then again, must the piercing be understood as literal or figurative? These questions can be answered and all apparent difficulty can be resolved when it is seen that this great prophecy refers to the Lord Jesus Christ. He is Israel's Messiah and it is He throughout this chapter who is the speaker, hence the occurrence of the first person pronoun over and over again in the chapter (vv.2,4,6,9 & 10). The first part of the statement contains the words of Jehovah-Messiah; in the second part Zechariah is the speaker – he is speaking of Him. The "me" gives clear evidence of the deity of the Messiah and the "him" gives more than a hint of the distinct personality of the Messiah. The Apostle John, in his narrative of the crucifixion, cites Zechariah 12.10 in connection with the last act of indignity done to our blessed Lord on the cross by the Roman soldier, who with a spear pierced the side of the Lord. John is the only Evangelist who mentions this incident. This helps us to see that the piercing is literal (wherever the word "pierced" occurs in the Old Testament it can only mean the piercing of the body, as for example in 13.3 of this book) and that in John's estimate Zechariah 12.10 definitely refers to the Lord Jesus. Not only does the action of the Roman soldier correspond to this verse, but it is a partial fulfilment of it. While some apply the piercing to all the suffering of Christ, the use of the word and the reference to it in John 19.37 surely points to the literal spear which was thrust into the side of the Lord. It was done to make sure that the Lord was dead, but with no idea on the soldier's part that this was mentioned in Old Testament prophecy. The Apostle John mentions the piercing of the Lord again in Revelation 1.7, where he says that "every eye shall see him, and they also which pierced him". Gentiles and the Jew will see Him at His second advent. Not only will Israel mourn at the sight of Him, reminding them of what they did to Him, but "all kindreds of the earth shall wail because of him". This is another proof that the prophecy of Zechariah 12.10 has not yet been fulfilled.

At the second advent of the Messiah the veil over the heart of the nation will be taken away and their eyes will be open to receive and accept the Lord Jesus as the true Messiah. Then they will sing the song of repentance found in Isaiah 53. Israel will have then what answers to the Day of Atonement. The description of the repentance of the nation is really the fulfilment of the Day of Atonement concerning which Leviticus 23.26-32 speaks. Three times it is mentioned that Israel were to afflict their souls and do no servile work. If any one did not afflict their souls or did any work on that day, he was cut off in death. This looks forward in prophetic type to the time of the manifestation of Christ to Israel, when the sight of the One whom they pierced will draw forth their true contrition and profound repentance. Israel will then cease from depending on their own works and have an appreciation of the atoning work of the Messiah on the cross.

The word for "look" (NABAT – 5027) is not a mere passing glance, but it is a look of faith and trust. The idea is not "looking upon", but rather "looking to". It is the same word as is used in Numbers 21.9 of the Israelites who looked to the serpent on the pole. Yet the sight is not only a look of faith, for in the Hebrew the word is also used of bodily sight as well as spiritual. They will behold the returning Saviour on the Mount of Olives with their *bodily eyes*. "They shall look upon me whom they have pierced, and they shall mourn for him." What a moment of revelation this will be for the nation. The promise to Israel is, "Thine eyes shall see the king in his beauty" (Is 33.17). "Thine" – what grace to Israel. "Eyes" – what reality, for this will be no spiritual vision. "Shall" – what a promise, for it will surely come to pass. "See" - what a sight for them. It will be no mere passing glance. "The king in his beauty" - what a Person. He will be seen in all His glory. Thomas, who was not present when the risen Lord appeared unto His disciples, is a good illustration of Israel, for like Israel in unbelief he says, "Except I shall see…I will not believe" (Jn 20.25). When, however, the wonderful moment arrives when the Messiah is manifested to them, they will behold the wound marks of Calvary, an evidence of His love for them and will exclaim, "My Lord and my God" (compare the similar language of the nation in that day in Isaiah 25.9). In the remaining part of the tenth verse the Spirit of God touchingly and graphically describes the effects upon the nation of the sight of the Lord. Looking upon Him whom they pierced will produce a spirit of deep repentance. Their mourning is compared to that of mourning for an "only son" and is likened to being in bitterness for the loss of a firstborn. Perhaps the references to an only son and the firstborn make one think of the Lord Jesus as God's unique Son who was given by God in His matchless grace for the suffering, not only of our sins, but of Israel's too. The Lord Jesus is also the firstborn of all creation, given the place of dignity by God but insulted and despised by the Jew. How different it will be when the nation is converted and when they discover who He is. How real, intense and deep their repentance will be. What is all this mourning for? It is because they have crucified their Messiah. Their eyes will be open then to what they did to Him and who He is.

In the last four verses of this most amazing paragraph of prophecy, we have described in detail how thorough and intense the mourning of the Jew in that day will be. It will be private, public, and national (it will affect the whole land). It is the greatest instance of public mourning recorded in the annals of the Old Testament. In v.11 the mourning is compared to the mourning of Hadadrimmon in the valley of Megiddon. The mourning at Hadadrimmon is the greatest recorded in Jewish history; it was there the good king Josiah was slain in battle with Pharaoh-Necho. The death of this most pious of all the kings of Judah was bitterly bewailed by all the people, especially by the righteous members of the nation. It was so bitter that not only did Jeremiah compose an elegy on his death, but other singers bewailed him in dirges. This was placed in a collection of elegiac songs and preserved in Israel till long after the captivity (2 Chr 35.25). Zechariah, then, compares the lamentation for putting Messiah to death to this great national mourning.

All the families and households of the nation, not the men only, but the women too, will mourn. This widespread mourning and contrition for their sin will affect the royal line (David) and the priestly line (Levi). The family of the house of Nathan does not refer to the prophet Nathan, but a younger son of David from whom Zerubbabel was descended (see Luke 3.27-31 and 2 Samuel 5.14). Both David and Nathan represent the highest and the lowest of the royal line. Levi and Shimei, not the one who cursed David, but one of the priestly line (see Numbers 3.18), represent the highest and lowest of the priestly order. Thus there are four families mentioned, two of them from the royal line under David and Nathan, and two from the priestly line under Levi and Shimei. Then in the last verse we have "All the families that remain", which may refer to those who are left from the fiery ordeal through which they have passed and in which two thirds of the nation fell (13.8-9). The mention of these names is interesting and remarkable, for a point has been raised by some that would make a literal fulfilment of this prophecy in the future impossible in their eyes. It is the fact that for such a prophecy to be fulfilled, it would be necessary for some kind of revelation with respect to the genealogies of the Jews which have long been lost to be given. A miracle would be required to trace the families of David and Nathan. The simple answer to this argument against the literal and future interpretation is that the Omniscient God of Eternity will not only know where the so-called ten lost tribes are, but He does know and will know in the future who the descendents of David and Nathan are. Nothing is hidden from Him. Today by DNA analysis even men can trace genealogies; how much more the Lord. For God to fulfil His prophetic word many miracles will have to take place, but take place they will. Thus the names of the families here must be accepted as literal.

Nothing like this has ever been experienced in the nation. There is a faint picture of it in Luke 23.48 where Luke, describing the effect of the suffering and death of Christ upon those who witnessed it, records that the people who beheld the sight "smote their breasts, and returned". They were moved no doubt and filled to some degree with a sense of remorse, but we do not read that they repented. How different it will be when Israel beholds the Saviour! The enormity of their guilt in crucifying their Messiah, when it dawns upon them, will fill the Jews who are left after the Tribulation with remorse and deep sorrow. It will be so intense that it will cut them to the heart. Some have taught that this mourning was fulfilled on the Day of Pentecost, when as a result of the outpouring of the Holy Spirit there was an outburst of sorrow on the part of the Jews, but this cannot be, for the sorrow and contrition in these verses are a direct result of the sight of the glorified Christ – "they shall look upon me whom they have pierced". It is true that many Jews since Pentecost have wept with penitential sorrow for the sin which caused the death of their Messiah, but never has there been national sorrow to the extent and intensity described in these verses in Zechariah 12. No, the Jews who repented on the Day of Pentecost in response to Peter's address cannot fulfil the terms of this prophecy.

The expression "that day" in v.11 must be interpreted in the same way and applied to the same time as its occurrences in vv.3,4,6,8 & 9, namely to the end time, or to the time when the Lord returns to the earth.

In concluding this chapter we must not miss a practical lesson from what the Spirit of God says concerning this sorrow, for five times it is mentioned that the wives will mourn "apart". This is not a reference to the Jewish custom of wives living in a separate part of the house, or that they had to worship separately. It points rather to the fact, as C. L. Feinberg says, that "the mourning will be so intense as to transcend even the closest ties of earth, those between husband and wife". Such retirement and seclusion are always very needful for the deepening of personal piety and true humility. When there is contrition for sin and personal desire to be right with God it is good when the husband and wife in the family get privately before God. Husbands and wives should share many things in life and do things together for the Lord. Spiritual exercise should never be one sided and left to one partner alone in marriage, but in the matter of our own souls being in the right condition and in developing personal devotion to the Lord, there need to be times when the husband and wife get separately alone with God.

ZECHARIAH 13

The Suffering Saviour of Calvary

Zechariah 13 is directly connected with the prediction in ch.12, for the repentance of Israel will draw from God a wonderful response in grace and He will cleanse and restore the nation. The link between chs.12 and 13 is very close. In the first place we have the spiritual and logical outcome of the repentance described in ch.12. The order is both moral and chronological, for, following the penitent condition of ch.12, the nation is not only brought to recognize their Messiah, but they will enjoy from God an ample provision of cleansing. Thus in the first verse we have the fountain opened for sin. The people will be cleansed, and from v.2 we learn that the land itself will be cleansed. Thus in ch.13 Zechariah continues the theme of the conversion of Israel. It begins with "In that day", and refers to the same period mentioned six times in the previous chapter - "the goal of prophetic vision in relation to the nation, the great 'day' of Israel's national atonement – when the iniquity of the land shall be removed in one day, and when a whole nation shall, as it were, 'be born at once'" (David Baron).

It is both interesting and instructive to see that in the chapter we have two aspects or figures of the death of Christ. In v.1 the figure of a fountain is used to show the fulness of cleansing provided by Christ for Israel in His death at Calvary. In v.7 the figure of a sword is used to picture the judgment of God that the Saviour experienced at Calvary in order for Israel to have a future of blessing. Thus we have the need of cleansing for Israel and then the cost to the Saviour to make this possible. It is important again to see through the chapter the periods of time referred to, for this greatly helps in the interpretation of each section of the passage. In vv.1 & 2 we have the millennial period. In vv.3-6 we have the Tribulation period. In v.7 we have the time of Christ's death at Calvary. In vv.8 & 9 we have the sifting of the remnant during the second half of the seven year Tribulation period.

Verses 1-2: The Fountain

The fountain opened is a picture of the future application of the death of Christ to Israel. The fountain will not be opened for the first time to Israel, for thank God it has long been opened by Christ at Calvary, but the eyes of Israel will be opened to see it. Like Hagar in the desert (Gen 21.19), they remain in ignorance of the blessed resources so near to them. But now the Holy Spirit poured upon them opens their eyes. The God who bestowed the Spirit of grace will also provide the blessed means of cleansing from the defilement of sin. The figure of a fountain is so well chosen and most expressive. It is not the figure of a cistern or a well, but a fountain, suggesting fulness, freshness, and freeness. It speaks of the perennial freshness of the sacrifice of Christ to deal with the guilt of sin. The metaphor is very strong, speaking of a fountain in which the guilty can wash and be clean. The blessing of cleansing from sin ever continues to flow from the death of Christ. As far as Israel is concerned it is not just that their guilt will be removed, but that they will continue to be kept as a righteous nation by the death of Christ. The Hebrew word "opened" (PATACH – 6605) has a continuing force. This fountain is ever flowing. It is not like the laver which stood between the altar and the Tabernacle that needed to be constantly replenished with water. No, the wonderful effect of Christ's sacrifice will continue to bless the lives of the revived nation of Israel from the moment of their conversion onwards.

What kind of cleansing is in view here? We love the words of Cowper's hymn, "There is a fountain filled with blood", but the fountain here is not a fountain of blood, but of water! The blood of Christ has judicial cleansing in view, but the thought of water has rather moral cleansing in view. Thus the death of Christ for Israel will not only remove their guilt, it will deal with their state and touch their character, to purge away their unclean habits. It is true to say, however, that all the blessings of Israel will result from the blood of Christ. The figure of the fountain is taken partly from the water used for the purification of the Levites on the day of their consecration, and is called in the Hebrew "sin-water", or "water of absolution" (Num 8.7), and partly from the sprinkling-water prepared from the ashes of the red heifer for purification from the defilement of death, which is called water of uncleanness (Num 19.9). Both justification and sanctification flow from the blood of Christ. Judicial guilt and moral impurity are both removed by it. The mention of the removal of defilement here recalls the vision back in ch.3 of the high priest Joshua clothed with filthy garments. The filthy garments being removed corresponds to the water whereby the filth of sin is cleansed away. In the light of this verse one may ask the reader, "Do you know the blessedness of this opened fountain, by the putting away of all your sin?".

The word "sin" in the Hebrew here means a missing of the mark or way. Sadly, how long Israel have missed their way and how long would they continue to miss it were it not for the grace of God which will work in the nation. Apart from God's grace and the atoning work of Christ they would miss their way for ever. The same is true for each believer were it not for God's grace. There is potential in the work of Christ at Calvary to meet the need not only of Israel, but of the whole world. The sacrifice of Calvary was accomplished once for all when the Saviour suffered for sin on the cross, but it is made effective and experimental personally the moment the sinner's eyes are opened and he looks to Christ by faith.

Before leaving this verse it is good to see illustrated that the blessing of the death of Christ is for all time – it will pardon Israel in the future and continually fit them for God. It is for all men, for it is for the house of David and the inhabitants of Jerusalem - indicating national and individual sin, but also referring to the royal line, the rulers of the nation and the ordinary citizen of Jerusalem. It is for all sin – the terms "sin" and "uncleanness" denote not only the guilt of sin as such, but all its defilement. How full, complete, and efficacious the atoning work of Christ is.

From v.2 we see that before the Kingdom is established all apostasy and idolatry in Israel will be over. Evil spirits and false prophets will be removed. Messiah is the speaker and He says, "I will cut off the names of idols out of the land, and they shall no more be remembered". Verse 2 may be viewed as the fruits of the repentance in 12.11-14. Israel's conversion to God having taken place, God will demand that His people be holy and the land also be holy and free from that which is abominable to Jehovah. The cleansing in v.1 is an internal and spiritual one, but the cleansing here is an external one. The people and the land are outwardly to be seen as holy. The authority, power, and influence of idols will be removed. It will be a thorough and permanent cleansing of the land from all idols, for they shall no more be remembered. Israel throughout its history was troubled with idolatry. This sin was a constant snare to the nation. In the Tribulation, Israel again will indulge in idolatry and this will be a serious problem to them in their apostate condition. There will, for example, be idolatry associated with the Beast and the false prophet of Revelation 13, but these evil men and the idolatry they introduce will be cut off to clear the way for the Kingdom. There is a necessary lesson here that shows the importance of a genuine repentance. A genuine repentance will always manifest itself in holiness of life. For anyone to claim to be converted and yet show no evidence of a transformation in the life is a terrible anomaly. The word of the Apostle John to all in the family of God is, "Little children, keep yourselves from idols" (1 Jn 5.21). This is a last command. It is a decisive command and an embracive command that takes in every believer.

False prophets with all their deception will no longer lead God's people astray. The New Testament indicates that false prophets will be present in the Tribulation to trouble Israel again (see Mt 24.4-5,11,23-24; Rev 13.11-18; 19.20), but they too will be cleared from the land. Many false prophets in the history of Israel prophesied out of their own hearts, and then declared it to be the word of the Lord. Foolishly, Israel listened to these prophets and believed their deceptive words. It was this that was one of the great causes of their ruin as a nation. The land mentioned here is the land of Israel, though it has to be said that the whole world will be rid of that which God cannot tolerate and which will be inconsistent with His Kingdom.

The unclean spirit is next mentioned. The unclean spirits – demons which inspired the false prophets and confused, deceived and controlled the Jew, will also be removed. One cannot fail to see a contrast here with this reference to evil spirits and the mention of the Spirit of grace and His work in the previous chapter. The spirit of uncleanness is the very opposite of the Spirit of grace. The Spirit of God reveals the holiness of God and would make God's people holy, whereas the spirit of uncleanness would seek to defile God's people. Today more than ever there is so much impurity, indecency, and sexual licentiousness that one can only conclude that unclean spirits are at work. If this is the case now it will be far worse during the Tribulation, and Israel in particular will not be free from such demonic influences. May each believer now seek to know more of the sanctifying influence of the Holy Spirit in the life. It is significant that this is the only reference to "unclean spirits" in the Old Testament. In the New Testament we find a number of references to these emissaries of Satan. The Gospel of Mark mentions unclean spirits more than the other Gospels, for they were agents of Satan seeking to hinder the work of the Perfect Servant. Revelation 20.1-3 prophetically informs us that Satan will be confined to the abyss (the prison house of evil spirits) for the whole course of the one thousand year reign of Christ. The reference here to the removing of unclean spirits out of the land is also the only Scripture that gives us any indication that demons also will share the same fate as Satan, in being imprisoned throughout the Kingdom age. Thus this will be one of the great features of the Millennium and one of the reasons why there will be such universal peace.

Verses 3-6: The False

In the process of the Lord cleansing the land from idolatry and false prophets it is anticipated that a false prophet could possibly appear to do deceptive work in the nation. If such should be the case and he refuses to heed God's warning to stop his prophesying then his parents, as commanded in the Law of Moses, are to put him to death (Deut 13.6-11; 18.20) and will say to him, "Thou shalt not live; for thou speakest lies in the name of the Lord". The law commanded parents to put to death their evil sons by stoning, but in the Day of the Lord these sons will be stabbed to death. The word is "thrust him through". This is the same Hebrew word (DAQAR - 1856) used for "pierced" in 12.10 where the Messiah says that "they shall look upon me whom they have pierced". The measure of punishment inflicted by the parents is extreme to say the least, but the Tribulation will be extreme and evil of every kind will be rampant everywhere. This illustrates how serious in the sight of God are idolatry and false prophecy, so much so that love for God's honour and obedience to God's truth will in that day supersede the tenderest ties, even those of parents. We have already seen in 12.12-14 that husbands and wives are to get before God in repentance individually. Now, from the same faithful remnant, parents may be called upon to be faithful to God in their families. Today in this age of grace it would be very wrong and indeed a sin for a christian parent to slay a son if he was involved in evil and being used of Satan. Much prayer, counsel and love must be shown, but christian parents are expected to be faithful to God and His word no matter how their children behave. Not a few parents have lost much ground in compromising Scriptural principles because of their children's sinful conduct. God and His word must ever come first even in the family, however hard it is.

Not only will Israel in that day no longer tolerate any false prophet in their midst, but the prophets themselves will be ashamed of their calling, and because of the danger of death will be quick to deny involvement in such evil practices (v.4). The hairy garments of the ancient prophets will no longer be worn. These were in keeping with their frugal lifestyle and their solemn utterances. This was the kind of garment Elijah and John the Baptist wore (1 Kings 19.13; 2 Kings 1.8; Mt 3.4), but to avoid death the false prophet will discard this garment he wore to deceive the people and to cover up his activities. He will seek to pass himself off as a common slave who was bought when young and taught to farm by his master. When interrogated by those zealous to defend the law he will cry out in fear, "I am no prophet, I am a farm servant, a slave". This claim will be a falsehood, but will be said from the terrible dread of being suspected of being a false prophet. The reply to this false statement the man has made is, "If you have not pretended to be a prophet, what are these wounds in your hands?". He will answer, "Those with which I was wounded in the house of my friends". Thus he is at once detected and convicted of a falsehood. The incident brings before us quite vividly how false prophets will be treated in that day and how thoroughly they will be banished from the land.

Because of the mention of the wounds in v.6 many assume that the verse must refer to Christ's wounds, but the words in the context of the passage should not be seen as referring to Christ. The section in which they are set in vv.3-6 has to do with the false prophets of a future day, when God, just before the Lord returns to the earth, will begin to cleanse the land of Israel of false prophets and unclean spirits (v.2). These prophets will deceive by wearing hairy garments - a visible sign of a prophet - but these are removed to try to hide the fact that they were false prophets. They will protest that they were no prophets at all. Such will be the suspicion against them that they will be asked, "What are these wounds?". Those who are found out will experience strong feeling against them and will run the risk of being put to death. There are several reasons for not interpreting 13.6 as being a reference to the Messiah. In the first place the false prophet in that day will strongly protest and say he is no prophet (v.5). The Lord Jesus could never say, "I am no prophet". There is no way this could be true of Christ, for when the Lord was here He never denied that He was a prophet. Second, He could not say, "I have been a slave from my youth", for the Lord was never the slave of any man on earth. Third, our Lord was not wounded in the house of His friends, but in the house of His enemies and by the Roman executioners who had no relationship with Him. Tragically the Jews were no friends of Christ – they hated Him. Some render "wounds in thine hands" as "wounds between the hands". Whether this is a correct translation or not, the wounds in the context appear to be self-inflicted, such as was common among pagans of the ancient East, who in their religious frenzy made incisions on the body to please the gods or to induce them to give them favours. Fourth, the Lord Jesus was never questioned by the people of the world concerning His wounds after His resurrection. He only appeared to His own after His resurrection. Fifth, our Lord Jesus was a carpenter and not a farmer. In addition, the sequence of events given in the context of vv.1-6 does not agree with the time of the Lord's suffering on the cross. The context points to a false prophet and not to our Lord Jesus who at Calvary was wounded for our transgressions. To understand the reference to the wounds it is better to connect v.6 with the previous passage in vv.3-5, rather than with the following verse which clearly refers to the Messiah's suffering on the cross.

Verse 7: The Flock

In vv.7-9 we have a short history of Israel – the smiting endured by the Saviour at Calvary, the scattering of Israel as a consequence of crucifying Christ, and the sifting of the remnant in the days of the Tribulation. The prophetic message in the whole of this interesting verse is briefly this: the Shepherd would be smitten on account of the people, who would in consequence be scattered, but Jehovah would remember in mercy a little remnant of the flock, namely the poor in spirit, the humble ones who are little in their own eyes and give ear to the word of God. The section embraces the time from the rejection and crucifixion until the time when the millennial Kingdom will begin.

If vv.5-6 cannot refer to the Lord Jesus, then clearly v.7 can only refer to Him. The Lord cited this significant prophecy as referring to Himself in Matthew 26.31. Thus we have His authority for interpreting the verse in a Messianic sense. If there be any connection between vv.3-6 and v.7 it is one of contrast, for the wounds mentioned in v.6 are self-inflicted by the false prophet, but the sufferings of the shepherd in v.7 were not self-inflicted. The focus, then, shifts in v.7 from the wounds of the suffering false prophets to the sufferings of the true Shepherd who was smitten for His people's sins. There is a difference with 12.10 where the putting to death of Christ is seen to be the guilty act of the Jewish nation, whereas here it is described as an act of God (see, for example, both aspects in Acts 2.23 and 4.27-28). In this verse Zechariah returns to the theme of the Shepherd mentioned in ch.11. With regard to the Messiah, the verse is perhaps the most significant and remarkable in all the Old Testament Scriptures. Here, in one verse of prophecy, we have clear witness both to the death and the deity of the Messiah.

The sword

"Awake, O sword, against my shepherd, and against the man that is my fellow, saith the Lord of hosts." There are two great points of interest here - God's command, and God's companion. In this verse we have an instance in Scripture of a figure of speech called anthropomorphism - a direct address to an impersonal object as if it were a person. Thus Jehovah calls upon the sword to arouse itself as if it had been asleep, to administer judgment upon His shepherd. It is not a literal sword like the literal spear of 12.10 that pierced the side of the Saviour, but it is viewed here as the instrument of death and punishment. It is the sword of divine justice. The sword falling upon the shepherd implies a violent end. The sword is used in Romans 13.4 to indicate the highest judicial power and there clearly represents death. Here it is the atoning death of the Messiah for Israel. One can understand God striking down the foolish shepherd in ch.11, but what a mystery here, for of all the shepherds God has raised up to Israel there has been none like this one. The one dealing with the shepherd in this way is clearly God and with this agrees the word "smite" which in Hebrew is in the masculine gender. This then is not man's wrath being inflicted upon Israel's Messiah, but God's righteous wrath being poured out on Him who bore our sins in His own body on the tree. The fact that God commands the sword indicates that it was God's purpose that the Saviour was smitten. What a solemn wonder this is. Shall the sword fall upon Babylon as punishment for its sinful practices where Israel was in captivity for seventy years? Shall it fall upon guilty Israel, for do not they deserve it? Though Babylon, Israel, and we deserve God's judgment, yet mystery of mysteries this, that the sword of God's awful and just punishment for Israel's and our sins fell upon this lovely Shepherd. We think of the touching lines of Anne Ross Cousin:

> Jehovah bade His sword awake;
> O Christ, it woke 'gainst Thee!
> Thy blood the flaming blade must slake,
> Thy heart its sheath must be;
> All for my sake my peace to make,
> Now sleeps that sword for me.

The mystery deepens, for having considered God's command to the sword we now behold the one who is described as God's companion upon whom it fell. He is not only God's shepherd, He is "the man that is my fellow". There are several Old Testament words for "man". The word used here is GEBER (1397) which means strong man. The Lord Jesus is seen here in His true manhood. He is the perfect man. While here in the days of His flesh He was a dependent man moving in absolute trust in His God, yet the word the Spirit of God uses here indicates He was the strong man, in the sense in which He was strong in character, strong in His moral excellence, strong in His devotion to do God's will, and certainly strong to undertake the great sin question and deal with it to God's satisfaction.

He is the man who is God's fellow. Here we have clear Old Testament evidence of the deity of Christ. The description, "my fellow", is rather a rare word in the Old Testament and only occurs outside of Zechariah in the book of Leviticus. It is from a primitive root meaning to associate (AMIT -5997) and occurs eleven times in the following passages in Leviticus, being usually rendered in the AV as "neighbour", or "another" (6.2; 18.20; 19.11,15,17; 24.19; 25.14,15,17). The Lord Jesus is God's Associate, nearest Kinsman, Friend and Confidant, in that God and He share the same interests and have fellowship in the same great purpose in salvation and redemption, but even more than this, the word implies they share the same nature. The use of the word in Leviticus does not seem to imply similarity of office or position, but rather nearness of relation or kindred. Christ is equal with God, so much so He could say in public ministry to the Jews, "I and my Father are one" (Jn 10.30), not merely one in purpose and mission, but one in essence. He was "set up from everlasting, from the beginning, or ever the earth was" (Prov 8.23). As God's Shepherd He was the One provided by His love to bear the sins of the people and to put them away forever. As God's Fellow we see what it cost God to give up His only Son, His co-equal, to the cross and the suffering of punishment for sin which was not His own. As a revelation of truth from an Old Testament point of view the inscrutable and eternal deity of the Messiah could not be stated in clearer and stronger language. In the description, "the man that is my fellow", we see manhood and deity in one Person. One wonders whether Zechariah himself understood the import of this designation of the Messiah. The words may have been an enigma to him, but the prophet was writing by the inspiration of the Spirit of God. Now with the advantage of New Testament revelation in this age of grace, we know that when the Lord Jesus came into holy and sinless manhood there was indeed a Man who could be called "God's fellow". Do not overlook the fact that the Speaker who describes the Messiah is God – hence the phrase "saith the Lord of hosts". This makes all the more important and valuable the truth contained in this verse.

The shepherd
The verse goes on to say, "…smite the shepherd". There is no doubt that the shepherd here is none other than the Good Shepherd who gave His life for the sheep (Jn 10). He has already been described as "my shepherd" by Jehovah. It is true that when God took up Cyrus the king of Persia to be His instrument on behalf of His people He called him, "my shepherd" (Is 44.28). Cyrus, however, was a mere mortal man and, while it may have been an honour to be used by God, he could do no more than fulfil God's purpose at the time. He certainly could not be God's substitute for Israel's sins. Already in ch.11 we have seen the Lord Jesus presented as the Shepherd rejected by the nation of Israel. In that passage He is contrasted with the foolish shepherd whom God will raise up to discipline His people. There it is interesting to note that the worthless shepherd was to be struck with a sword and wounded, but here in 13.7 it is the Good Shepherd who is smitten by God's sword of just punishment for the sin of

Israel. In ch.13 we now see the contrast between the Lord Jesus and the false prophets of the Tribulation. They will have wounded themselves in their frenzy, but here our Lord's wounds are by God inflicted. God's leaders among His people and the kings over His people were intended by Him to have shepherd hearts and care for His people, but most of them miserably failed in this. The Lord Jesus is the true shepherd of His people, whether of Israel or the Church. He will not fail Israel in the future. Indeed He never failed Israel in the past, especially at Calvary. He never fails His people today. God calls Him in a special unique sense, "my shepherd", but the believer also can say with the Psalmist, "The Lord is my shepherd".

"Smite the shepherd", says God. God is not seen here smiting a foe that merits punishment or smiting a mere mortal, poor and frail man who deserves His judgment for sin, but smiting His Shepherd. He is the greatest Shepherd ever! At Calvary God smote the Shepherd who has all the beautiful qualities of shepherd character. How moving and touching this is. God had sent His Shepherd to Israel, but they did not recognize or want Him. Oh the tragedy of the rejection and crucifixion by Israel of the One who longed to be and could have been their Shepherd. As a consequence of this we shall see in the remainder of this great verse how the nation has suffered to this day.

The sheep

"And the sheep shall be scattered: and I will turn mine hands upon the little ones." "The flock scattered" is not the early church, but the Jewish nation, for they are viewed in 11.1-14 as "the flock of slaughter". The deserting of the Lord by the disciples was not a final fulfilment of this prophecy (Mt 26.31). What the disciples did in the hour of our Lord's greatest need prefigured the terrible scattering of the Jews. It was a sample on a small scale of that great dispersion of the Jews which took place after the crucifixion of Christ and intensified under Titus, when they were destroyed or scattered into all lands. In a number of Scriptures the nation of Israel is viewed as sheep or a flock of sheep (see Ps 78.52, 70-72; 79.13; 80.1). When their true Shepherd Messiah was here they were seen by Him as sheep without a shepherd and this has been their state ever since their rejection of Christ. "The sheep shall be scattered", but though scattered they are still the Lord's sheep and only await their being gathered together again by Him (Is 11.11).

"And I will turn mine hand upon the little ones." Commentaries on Zechariah are divided as to the interpretation here. Are these words to be understood in a good sense or a bad sense? Does it mean that God will have mercy on the remnant of His people, or does it mean that He will cause them to experience His punishment? M. F. Unger, for instance, gives his reasons why the words are not to be interpreted in a good sense and takes the "little ones" to be "the lowly persecuted followers of the Saviour (both Jewish and Gentile believers) who were despised and accounted as insignificant by their Jewish and pagan non-believing contemporaries". In his view the phrase "the little ones" has no idea in it of being pitied or protected by God. On the other hand, C. L. Feinberg comments, "God in grace promises that His hand would be turned upon the little ones, a designation of tender affection. The Lord will intervene on their behalf; that is, for the sake of the poor of the flock, the remnant. The Lord will watch over His own". Those described here are the same as the "poor of the flock" in ch.11, the faithful Jewish remnant. Turning the hand upon the little ones may mean either "over the little ones" or "upon the little ones". Often the term is used in the Old Testament in the sense of judgment. This point is to be admitted, but the immediate context here seems to favour God's hand being over them for their protection. God's hand has indeed fallen in judgment upon, and will yet fall more heavily upon, the nation that rejected Christ, but He will preserve a remnant for Himself in the nation, just as He had a remnant that recognized the Lord as the Messiah and sought to follow Him when He was here. It is true that the Lord protected His own, and especially the new believers who had trusted Christ in the early days after Pentecost, but this prophecy looks on to the time of the Tribulation when the Lord will have ready for Himself a remnant among the Jews who will be waiting for their Messiah. It is interesting to note that Helen Spurrell in her translation from the original Hebrew renders the last sentence of v.7 as: "Yet I will restore my help upon the little flock". The last two verses in the chapter explain the reference to "the little ones".

Verses 8-9: The Furnace

Prophetically speaking there is a mighty leap forward in time between v.7 and v.8. In v.7 the event of the cross is in view, but here Zechariah passes on to the end time. These verses relate to the final sifting of Israel, to bring to light a remnant just before the Lord comes to the earth. They show that Israel will yet have to face the greatest holocaust of their history during the time of the Great Tribulation for God says, "And it shall come to pass, that in all the land, saith the Lord, two parts therein shall be cut off and die; but the third shall be left therein". God's judgment will fall upon the land and two thirds of the Jewish population will perish during the Tribulation. How will this come about? Satan will seek to destroy Israel (Rev 12.1-17). The second beast, the false prophet, will kill any Jews that fail to obey the Antichrist (Rev 13.15). Many also, of course, will die in the last siege of Jerusalem in the crisis of Armageddon (Zech 14.1-3). The fact that a remnant will survive shows that in the time of this judgment upon the land, God will yet have mercy. We believe that these survivors are those of 12.10-14 who will look to the Lord in repentance and faith. They will form a nucleus of Jews who will go into the millennial Kingdom of Christ. They are also, we suggest, "the little ones" of v.7. Their faith will be sorely tested, for God will chasten them in preparation for the return of the Messiah.

The Lord, then, will refine the surviving one-third in the furnace of suffering and persecution: "And I will bring the third part through the fire, and will refine them as silver is refined, and will try them as gold is tried" (v.9). The illustration used by Zechariah reminds us of the value God puts on His people Israel: they are like gold and silver that need to be refined in the furnace of affliction. The process of refining metals, especially precious metals such as silver and gold, is sometimes used in Old Testament Scripture as a picture of the nation's spiritual purification (cp. Is 1.25 & Mal 3.3). In this verse the remnant of Israel is compared to the small quantity of pure metal which is left after smelting and refining. After two thirds of the nation has been cut off, the remaining third will be further reduced by being purified in the fire. Israel had experienced the furnace in Egypt. Bitter was that experience, but God was weaning them from Egypt and preparing them to come out (Deut 4.20). Their seventy years of captivity, too, in Babylon is also likened to a furnace experience (Is 48.10), but the time of the Great Tribulation will be their most trying "furnace experience" yet. The goldsmith refines the gold or silver so that the dross may be removed, and that is what the Tribulation in the last days will accomplish for Israel. The true believing remnant will be spared, while the rest will be rejected and perish. In Ezekiel 20.34-38 we have another interesting passage which refers to the remnant, but there God is dealing with the people scattered among the nations, refining them before He brings them into the land for blessing, whereas in Zechariah 13.9 we learn what God will do to those who are left in the land during the last days of the Tribulation.

If the reference to the "third part" is taken to be literal, then the following information, up-to-date at the time of writing, is interesting and makes one realize that a very great number of the nation will perish in the time of the end. On its 59th Independence Day, April 24, 2007, the population of the State of Israel stood at approximately 7,150,000 inhabitants – compared to 806,000 residents who lived in Israel in 1948, according to the Central Bureau of Statistics data. Of the total population, 5,415,000 are Jews (76%) while 1,425,000 (20%) are Arabs. 310,000 people (4%) were classified as "others," mostly non-Jewish immigrants from the former Soviet Union or those whose Jewish status is still undetermined by the Interior Ministry. Six million Jews died in the Holocaust under Hitler at the time of World War II, but this cutting off of Jews in the Tribulation will take place not in European countries, but in the land of Israel. Based on the number of the Jewish population, this means that if the judgment were taking place now 3,610,000 (two thirds of the total), would be cut off in death! This gives us some idea of how devastating and extensive the judgment in the land will be as far as the Jews are concerned. Some commentators do not take the "third part" literally. C. L. Feinberg, for instance, writes, "Mathematical exactness is not in view here, we know, because the remnant is spoken of in Isaiah 6.13 as a tenth". M. F. Unger thinks "the third part will likely be the 144,000 of the Tribes of Israel sealed in Revelation 7.1-8, and 14.1-5". In the Jewish war and the siege of Jerusalem in AD 67 to 70, 1,500,000 Jews died by the sword, famine, or disease, but by the end of the Tribulation far more will have perished. In spite of all the terrible suffering Israel will go through, and the sinister and determined purpose of the Arab world and others to cut Israel off from being a nation, God will never allow the nation to be destroyed.

When God's great end for the nation has been reached and the remnant refined and ready, then the blessings of the New Covenant between God and Israel will be enjoyed. The last part of v.9 clearly refers to the future, for Israel at present are not in covenant relationship with God. The words in the verse reveal what God will do and say and what Israel will do and say: "They shall call on my name, and I will hear them: I will say, it is my people: and they shall say, The Lord is my God". The remnant will call on God in their distress and affliction. This links with 12.10 where we read of the Spirit of grace and of supplication being poured upon them. They will cry to God and He will answer and bring them as a repentant and righteous remnant out of the Tribulation. He will acknowledge them as His people. The remnant will respond and say of the Messiah, "The Lord is my God". Having recognized Him the remnant, like Thomas, will worship Him. What a day that will be!

If the remnant will need this refining then each believer, too, at times needs it. Spiritually speaking, the Lord sometimes allows us to pass through a furnace of affliction in order that the dross may be removed from our lives and that we may call upon Him. The Apostle Peter speaks of faith being "tried by fire" (1 Pet 1.7; cp. 4.12). The Lord still presides over the crucible and blows aside the flame to see if the dross be gone. He would refine and purify us and remove the defilement, the unbelief, and the selfishness from our lives. The Lord draws near and puts the gold into the furnace and it seems He greatly increases the heat of the furnace, but all is well, for the Lord is there all the time watching by the side of our furnace. His eye is upon every flash of fire in order to bring us to realize even more than would otherwise be the case that He is our God and we are His people.

ZECHARIAH 14

The Sovereign Controller of the World

This closing chapter of Zechariah is a great conclusion to the book and justifies the description – "The Grand Finale". In it we have the most momentous event yet to take place on planet earth – the second advent in power and glory of the Messiah. This is a wonderful chapter, one of the greatest in the Old Testament Scriptures. Its imagery, detail, and authority can hardly be matched in all the prophetic sections of the Old Testament. In it is presented the glory of the Lord Jesus as Israel's Messiah, and God is exalted as the God of Israel who will be worshipped by all the earth. The time setting in the beginning of the chapter (vv.1-4) is exactly the same as in 12.1-4. Zechariah presents vividly the crisis point of the campaign of Armageddon when there will take place the last invasion of Jerusalem by the ungodly confederacy drawn from the nations of the earth. Once again it is important, and in this chapter especially so, to be clear as to what periods of time are referred to in the prophecy. Establishing this as we touch the sections will again greatly help in the interpretation. Thus in vv.1-3 the last days of the Tribulation are in view. In vv.12-15 Zechariah returns to this theme. In vv.4-11 and vv.16-21 the second advent and the Millennium are referred to. This demonstrates that Zechariah does not always present events in a chronological order.

It is good to note that Zechariah begins his book and ends it in relation to Christ. In ch.1 the Lord is seen standing among the myrtle trees in the valley. He is seen interceding for His people. In the last chapter the Lord is seen standing again, but this time on a mountain. He is depicted as intervening for His people's deliverance. In the one we have His sympathy and consideration for them. In the other we have His supremacy on behalf of them. The valley in ch.1 speaks of the lowly condition in which His people were then set. In this chapter we see the Lord in His power and glory bringing about the exaltation of the nation. What a vast difference then between ch.1 and ch.14! How wonderfully God will bring in, through the Lord Jesus Christ, a great transformation of His people. This is really what the prophecy of Zechariah is all about – how God will bring a lowly, despised, and persecuted people to be yet pre-eminent as a nation and distinct in a unique way nationally in its relationship to God. This very chapter begins with a persecuted nation whom the enemy will seek to exterminate. It ends with a priestly nation having conquered all foes and holy unto God. Although, then, the chapter begins so darkly and tragically, it ends so beautifully and triumphantly.

There are six different sections in the chapter each of which has much to tell us concerning the details of events in the last days. The sections, full of interest and instruction, may be summarized as follows. In vv.1-3 what a force the devil will have against Israel as vast armies gather to take Jerusalem. In vv.4-7 what a fright the world will have when Christ returns to the earth. In vv.8-11 what a future Israel will have when the Lord reigns over them. In vv.12-15 what a fate the enemies will have when punished by God. In vv.16-19 what a feast of joy Israel and the nations will celebrate in the Millennium. In vv.20-21 what a finish God's purpose will have when Israel becomes the holy nation.

Verses 1-3: The Crisis of Armageddon

The opening section of this great prophecy, then, takes us back in point of time to the beginning of ch.12. Verses 1-3 form a very suitable introduction showing the desperate and drastic situation in the city of Jerusalem at the time of the end. It shows the overwhelming need of deliverance and the, humanly speaking, hopeless and pitiable plight of the nation. There is only one person who can meet this need and answer the cries of the remnant caught up in the midst of the worst climactic event in the history of Jerusalem. This person will need to be omnipotent and divine. He will be no other than our Lord Jesus Christ - Israel's Messiah. He will burst on the scene suddenly and in great power and glory to deliver the city and His people. Thus vv.1-3 portray an event which will immediately precede the sudden appearance of the Messiah.

Zechariah here describes very graphically the attack against Jerusalem by the nations of the earth. Some have tried to link this with the siege against the city in 586 BC by Nebuchadnezzar and even the invasion against the city by Titus in AD 70. These two invasions could not possibly fulfil the prediction of Zechariah. The siege here is altogether different and the one great point which provides the clue as to when this event will take place lies at the very head of the chapter, for Zechariah says, "Behold, the day of the Lord cometh, and thy spoil shall be divided in the midst of thee". This "day of the Lord" is Jehovah's special day. It is a day which belongs to Him, when He will quickly bring to fruition His purposes for Israel. It refers to the intervention of Jehovah in the affairs on earth. Wherever the term is used it generally has to do with the period of Tribulation or the events just prior to the second advent. It is that day when He shall vindicate His justice by punishing the wicked and saving His elect people (see Mal 4.1-5; Joel 3.2, 11-16). The words used by Zechariah emphasize the certainty of its arrival.

We consider it necessary, touching the prophetic term "The Day of the Lord" that the believer should be clear as to the character and scope of this period. In order to do this we give a summary of the teaching of the word of God concerning it. It is mentioned about thirty times in the Old Testament (eg. Is 13.6,9; Joel 1.15; Zeph 1.14-15). It is spoken of in the New Testament in three places - 1 Thessalonians 5.2; 2 Thessalonians 2.2, RV; and 2 Peter 3.10. It is to be distinguished from the Lord's day (Rev 1.10), the Day of Christ (Phil 1.10) which is related to God's heavenly people and their entering into the fulness of their blessings in Christ, and the Day of God (2 Pet 3.12), which has the eternal state in view, when all God's purposes will be finally completed. Some time after the Rapture of the Church the Day of the Lord will commence. It does not necessarily follow that as soon as the Rapture has taken place and the Restrainer is removed (2 Thess 2.7) that then the Wicked One will immediately be revealed, but rather that the way will then be clear for the development of evil, as the Day of the Lord commences, when God initiates His judgments on earth after the Day of Grace expires. From the Old Testament Scriptures in particular we learn that the Day of the Lord will be one of gloom, darkness, and trouble for Israel as a nation (see Amos 5.18-20).

In Matthew 24.4-28 the Saviour refers to the period of the Day of the Lord. If there is any doubt as to this we need only consult Joel 2.2 and Matthew 24.21 and it will be readily agreed that it is not possible to have two periods which can be described as a unique and unrepeatable time of trouble. Therefore the two passages must refer to the same time, i.e. the Day of the Lord. As Christians we should be very thankful to God that we shall not have to pass through the awful days of the Tribulation. As Paul teaches in 1 Thessalonians 5.4: "But ye, brethren, are not in darkness that that day should overtake you as a thief". It will greatly help if it is appreciated that the Day of the Lord is a comprehensive term, a period on earth that includes the Tribulation, the darkening of the sun and moon (Joel 2.10), the second advent of Christ, and continues past the millennial Kingdom, for 2 Peter 3 indicates it will end at the dissolution of the heavens. At this point note carefully Matthew 24.29, "*Immediately* after the tribulation of those days", and Acts 2.20, "*Before* that great and notable day of the Lord". It is by putting these Scriptures together that we learn what will take place throughout the course of the Day of the Lord: the Tribulation; the darkening of the sun and moon, etc.; the great and notable Day of the Lord, when Christ will personally appear; this in turn will be followed by the millennial Kingdom when Christ will reign over the earth. Therefore, in between the end of the Tribulation period and the personal intervention of Christ with His saints, there will be the disturbances in the heavenly constellations.

The believer should carefully distinguish between "The Day of the Lord" and "The great and notable day of the Lord". The former has Israel especially in view, whereas the latter has to do with Israel's enemies. "The great and notable day of the Lord" is a critical point in "The Day of the Lord", a pivotal event. It refers to the manifestation of Christ on earth to destroy Israel's foes. This is what is referred to here in Zechariah 14.1-8. There are times in Scripture when "The Day of the Lord" has the same meaning as "The great and notable day of the Lord". This will be clear from the context (see Zech 14.1; Is 2.11-12). Isaiah in ch.2 twice says, "The Lord alone shall be exalted in that day" (vv.11 & 17). It cannot be correct to claim that the Lord alone is exalted at the time when the Beast and the False Prophet hold sway over the minds and hearts of men. Therefore "the day of the

Lord" in such passages refers to its climax, and this is more precisely called "the great and notable day of the Lord".

The sequence of events during this day which particularly belongs to the Lord is: the nations gathered by God to attack Jerusalem (v.2a); the city of Jerusalem taken and ransacked (v.2b); the booty of the city divided up inside its walls (v.1b); the Lord interposing for His people (v.3).

What is described in the first three verses of the chapter is the battle of Armageddon, or rather a final battle fought when the campaign of Armageddon reaches a crisis point at Jerusalem. Scripture predicts that a battle will be fought in the Megiddo valley, located close to the centre of the land of Israel. The writer has stood more than once looking down on this valley. It is quite a breathtaking sight. Napoleon Bonaparte is said to have stated with deep emotion after his first sight of this great plain, "This is the ideal battleground for all the armies of the world". In making this statement he may not have known that prophecy had already preceded him, that it will indeed be the world's greatest battleground. Zechariah, we believe, speaks of the invasion of Jerusalem by nations led by the Antichrist. By comparing this passage in Zechariah with Revelation 19.11-21 it should be clear that both Zechariah and the Apostle John are speaking of the same event. It is generally held by students of prophecy that vv.1-3 of Zechariah 14 refer to the gathering of nations against Jerusalem which is described in Psalm 2, Joel 3, Ezekiel 38 & 39, and Revelation 16 & 19. It is certainly clear that the nations here attack Jerusalem just before the appearance of the Messiah (vv.4-5) and the deliverance of the city takes place at the moment of His triumphant arrival.

There are three reasons at least for this great crisis conflict of Armageddon. The first is a divine reason, for it is God who will gather these nations to fulfil His purpose to provide an occasion for the destruction of Israel's enemies. This is the Day of Jehovah and stands in contrast to "man's day" (1 Cor 4.3, JND). This latter period is the present time, when God allows man to have his own way and continue in his defiance and pride. Man's pride and ambition will reach its most wicked height in the Great Tribulation and culminate in terrible defiance of God and determination to destroy His people. Then God will intervene to destroy these enemies. The second is a satanic reason, for we read in Revelation 16.14 of demons who will be allowed by God to gather the ungodly confederacy against Israel. They will "go forth unto the kings of the earth and of the whole world, to gather them to the battle of that great day of God Almighty". What can possibly induce the nations of the world to concentrate their forces in the valley of Megiddo and then to push on against Jerusalem? The answer to this question is the devastating power of the lying, froglike spirits that go forth from Satan in an attempt to prevent the establishment of the Kingdom of Christ on earth. The third one may be called a human reason, for those in league with the king of the North will seek to wrest from the Antichrist his world-wide leadership and annihilate Israel. However, in this the darkest hour in Israel's history all will be under the sovereign control of the God of all the earth.

The initial stages of the conflict will see the success of the armies of the enemies of Israel. But it will not end in triumph for them. The enemy will capture the city, plunder the houses, and rape the women. Half of its Jewish population will depart as slaves, but the other half will remain. The horrors of what will happen then will be indescribable, for the armies will be cruel and barbarous. No city has, so many times in its history, been besieged as Jerusalem. Here in its last siege will be the worst it will have experienced. The city will suffer such a defeat and destruction that the enemy will exult in their success and will feel certain of total victory. As a result, they will be so complacent that they will be in no hurry as they divide among themselves the spoils. Just when Jerusalem seems doomed for final destruction and the Jewish people destined for exile, the Lord will move in divine intervention, for Zechariah declares, "Then shall the Lord go forth, and fight against those nations, as when he fought in the day of battle" (v.3). The phrase "go forth" expresses the idea of a king going forth to do battle with an enemy. It pictures the Lord Jesus as a Warrior suddenly and swiftly bursting on the scene in order to come to Israel's aid to defeat its enemies. How fearful will be this appearance of the Lord. Suddenly He will be seen in the clouds and the brightness, or effulgence, of His glory will light up the whole world. He will come attired in battle array. He will come in righteousness to deal with these armies. Zechariah goes on to say that the Lord will fight "as when he fought in the day of battle". This shows that the Lord has done this previously, as in the case of the Red Sea deliverance in Exodus 14 and other occasions, for "the day of battle" is any occasion when Jehovah has miraculously intervened for the deliverance of His people.

It is most interesting to note that there are three great battles in the course of Israel's history. In the battle against the gods of Egypt God parted the Red Sea in two and delivered His people. This ended their suffering in Egypt. In the battle against Satan at Calvary God parted the veil in two in the temple and thus ended the system of their religion. In the battle against Israel's enemies in the future God will part in two the Mount of Olives and thus bring to an end the Times of the Gentiles and the Tribulation.

Verses 4-7: The Coming of the Messiah

In these verses that now follow it is most important to see that Zechariah is not speaking with poetic language, or merely giving imagery. Neither is this some kind of spiritual vision. Here we have specific prophecy that must be taken literally. By no system of interpretation can it be spiritualized or explained away. To do so is to fly in the face of plain language and to ignore the precise details which are such a feature in Zechariah's book. The geographical description of the Mount of Olives given, the physical upheaval that will result from the Messiah's arrival, as well as the vivid and graphic style and the fleeing of the remnant through the escape route of the valley opened up, all combine to make clear that the only right interpretation the passage deserves is a literal one. The context throughout the chapter supports this view and should make every honest reader feel that this vivid drama will surely be enacted on our earth and in the sight of all men. Zechariah here gives us one of the most wonderful prophecies of the Old Testament. The same prophet who gave precise details as to the first advent in grace of the Lord Jesus in ch.9 now gives us precise details of the second advent in glory of the Saviour. It will be an earth - shattering and transforming event. It will be a universally known event. It will be a supernatural, terrifying event for the world, and it will be a timely delivering event for the remnant.

The location of Messiah's advent (v.4a)

"And his feet shall stand in that day upon the mount of Olives, which is before Jerusalem on the east." It is interesting to note that this is the only place in the Old Testament where this name for the mountain is found. The blessed, holy, and nail-pierced feet of the Lord Jesus literally will come to rest on the Mount of Olives as He descends suddenly and majestically to the earth. What a moment this will be and how solemn and awesome will be the sight. His feet are the feet of Jehovah. This is the inescapable conclusion from the context, as v.3 should make clear. Here is a mighty Warrior-King who is both man and God! The fact that His feet are said to "stand", i.e. rest upon or come into contact with, proves that Messiah's return to the earth will be a bodily and personal coming. Is it not fitting and so suitable that the Lord will come to this mountain? The Mount of Olives must have been sacred in the memories of the disciples. It is both wonderful and touching to think that the place of His tears and agony will one day be the place of His triumph and glory.

The Mount of Olives is separated from the Eastern Hill (the Temple Mount and the City of David) by the Kidron Valley, and has always been an important feature in Jerusalem's landscape. From the 3rd millennium BC until the present, this 2,900 foot (895 metre) hill has served as one of the main burial grounds for the city. The two-mile long ridge has three summits, each of which has a tower built on it. The Mount of Olives is first mentioned (as "mount Olivet") in connection with David's flight from Jerusalem as a result of the rebellion of Absalom (2 Sam 15.30), and is only specifically referred to once again in the Old Testament, in this passage. It is, however, frequently alluded to (1 Kings 11.7; 2 Kings 23.13; Neh 8.15; Ezek 11.23). It is mentioned in the New Testament (Mt 21.1; 26.30, etc.). The road from Jerusalem to Bethany runs over the mount, as it did in Biblical times. It was on this mount that the Lord stood when He wept over Jerusalem. The Lord Jesus is said to have spent a good deal of time on the mount, teaching and prophesying to His disciples (Mt 24-25), including the Olivet discourse, returning after each day to rest (Lk 21.37), and also coming there on the night of His betrayal (Mt 26.30).

There is no doubt whatsoever about the mountain's situation, for Zechariah is very explicit saying that it is "before Jerusalem on the east". Why should Zechariah give this specific detail? Perhaps the answer to this is because Ezekiel earlier had prophesied that the glory of the Lord, which had departed from this mountain, would return again to the mountain: "The glory of the God of Israel came from the way of the east" (Ezek 43.2). The "glory of the Lord" is, we believe, not only a symbol of the presence of Jehovah, but of the Messiah Himself. The glory had been seen slowly retreating from the city and the sanctuary. The last glimpse given of it by Ezekiel is when it stands upon "the mountain which is on the east side of the city" (Ezek 11.23). From thence it is implied it ascends to heaven. The glory that had slowly been withdrawn because of the sin of the people will suddenly return when Israel is cleansed and restored (Ezek 36-39). So the Lord Jesus ascended back to heaven from the Mount of Olives because of the sin of His people in rejecting Him, but He will suddenly return to the very same mountain to deal with the enemies of Israel and the sins of His people. This is the message of the angel to the disciples who had witnessed His bodily going up into heaven: "This same Jesus, which is taken up from you into heaven, shall so come in like manner as ye have seen him go into heaven" (Acts 1.11). Thus, from this we conclude that as He had ascended to heaven from Olivet personally and visibly in His glorified manhood, so He will return to the very same place visibly and personally in His glorified manhood.

The effects of Messiah's advent (vv.4b-5a)

Zechariah continues by telling us that the Mount of Olives will split in two. The splitting of the mountain is the effect of an earthquake under the footsteps of Jehovah-Messiah, before whom the earth trembles (Ex 19.18; Judg 5.5; Ps 68.8; Nah 1.5) and the object is to make a great valley, a way of escape for the besieged people. Half of the divided mountain will be forced northward and half southward, and "a very great valley" will be made to run between. Into this valley the half of the people in the city will flee, as a way of escape. The next verse (v.5) says, "And ye shall flee to the valley of the mountains; for the valley of the mountains shall reach unto Azal". The split, then, will create a massive valley running eastward to Azal. Azal's location is not known today, but it will mark the end of the newly-formed valley. This future earthquake will be so severe and catastrophic that it is compared to a time some two hundred years earlier when people "fled from before the earthquake in the days of Uzziah king of Judah". There is no Old Testament record of this earthquake, but it must have been a memorable and tragic event because it is also mentioned in Amos 1.1. When Jehovah went forth to battle as recorded in Exodus 14 and fought for Israel, His people then passed through a valley between mountains of water. In this battle they will escape through a valley between mountains of rock. Thus when the Lord comes to the earth a great convulsion will break the surface of the earth. An earthquake took place when the Lord died at Calvary in humiliation and shame. An earthquake will take place when He comes in majesty and glory!

The manner of Messiah's advent (v.5b)

At the end of v.5 Zechariah makes a sudden interjection in the prophecy. The change of personal pronoun is striking and his addressing Jehovah directly most significant – "The Lord my God shall come, and all the saints with thee". Notice that Zechariah expresses his relationship to Jehovah-Messiah, "My God", and his personal faith in Him, "The Lord my God shall come". He is confident that the Messiah will indeed come and fulfil the prophecies of Scripture. One cannot fail to see, in this interjection in the midst of his prophecy, the wonder and excitement of Zechariah as he thinks of this glorious manifestation of the Messiah. Already we have seen in his book that Zechariah's feelings had been moved and his prophecies affected him much (see 4.1 & 8.21). He was certainly no mere bystander in these prophecies. He did not receive these communications without being touched and moved by them. So it is here. It seems he cannot contain himself and the wonder of this momentous event causes him to address the Lord personally. If the young priest-prophet was thus overjoyed by the prospect of this event, should not the believer also wonder and be thrilled at this amazing prophecy? Each believer should be able, in the light of such prophecies, to exclaim with Zechariah, "My God". Israel's coming Messiah is our God too, and even by this revelation of truth our faith in Him should increase.

"All the saints with thee." How clearly again this verse teaches us that Jesus is Jehovah. When the Lord comes at His second advent there will accompany Him all "the holy ones" (JND). This will be the manner of His return. In the first phase of the Lord's second coming at the Rapture when He descends to the air for His Church, He will come unaccompanied, for Paul declares, "The Lord himself shall descend" (1 Thess 4.16). At His second advent, as announced here by Zechariah, He will have His holy ones to accompany Him. Who are these "holy ones"? A reference to angels may be included here, for the Angels of His strength (or power) will accompany Him in His manifestation (2 Thess 1.7), but it is more probable, when we compare this with Jude vv.14-15 and Revelation 19.14, that Zechariah is referring to redeemed humanity. At least three groups of saints will return in their glorified bodies with the Messiah: Old Testament saints (Jude vv.14-15), Church saints (Rev 19.8), and the saints in the Tribulation who will have been martyred for their faith (Rev 20.4). It is interesting to note that Zechariah 14.4-5, Jude vv.14-15, and Revelation 19.14 all speak of the same event and each writer predicts that the Lord will be attended by saints. This shows the harmony and agreement of Scripture touching this event. In the Revelation passage the saints are referred to as "armies" who will form a train or retinue behind the Lord as they descend with Him seated on white horses, the symbols of power and victory. One can hardly imagine or take in what it will be like to come forth with the Lord at this moment and not only share in His glory, but witness all the solemn and great things that will result upon His sudden return to earth. Truly it is a great thing to be saved and to have the blessing of association with Christ. Let us be very thankful for this.

In vv. 6 & 7 we have statements which some commentators find obscure and somewhat difficult to interpret. We must bear in mind that this is a unique day in the history of man, but what will assist us to understand what is in view is that when Zechariah uses again the phrase "In that day" he is describing the extended period of the Day of the Lord. It is not a day of twenty-four hours, but a dispensational period. Here especially it is the end of the Day of the Lord and what will take place just before the Lord descends to the Mount of Olives. "And it shall come to pass in that day, that the light shall not be clear, or dark." We understand this to mean that in that day the luminaries will dwindle (lit. congeal) and there will be a reduction of light on the earth. This time will be characterized by the absence of light, because the luminaries of the heavens will be congealed to give forth no brilliance. Other prophets beside Zechariah speak of the same cosmic phenomena of this period (see Is 13.9-10; Joel 2.31; Amos 5.18). The Lord Jesus and the Apostle John in the New Testament speak of the same supernatural occurrences (Mt 24.29-30; Rev 6.12-14). It would appear that sandwiched in between the end of the Tribulation and the second advent will be this brief period of disturbances in the heavenly constellations. This will take place on a day known alone to Jehovah (cp. Mt 24.36; Acts 1.7). The fearful situation will be such that it shall neither be day or night – not an admixture of both, nor a kind of twilight, but the natural sources of light will be withdrawn. It will not be night because of the brilliant light of the glory of the Lord as He descends.

"At evening time it shall be light" (v.7). Israel's long evening of centuries of failure will be over. The evening of their suffering in the Tribulation will suddenly come to an end with the dazzling and glorious appearing of Christ. What will happen just before the Messiah comes suddenly to earth? God will switch off the great lights He created, the sun and moon. The stars, too, shall fall from heaven and then suddenly from the dark backdrop of the skies the Lord will appear, with no need for a spotlight to be focused on Him for "at evening time it shall be light". The Lord will be seen in all the brilliant blaze of His glory. What fear will grip the hearts of earth's inhabitants and what terror will paralyze the vast armies of the nations gathered against Jerusalem when they see Him. Is all this to be taken literally? Will God in fact cause the sun and moon to change and to be interrupted in their functions? Yes indeed! For this is God's programme. Did not God cause that the sun should not shine at Calvary and was there not darkness over the land for three hours? What God did then He will do again on a much larger scale when Messiah comes to Israel's relief.

Verses 8-11: the Coronation of the King

In this section we now return to the theme of the Millennium and some of the wonderful and miraculous physical changes which will have taken place just prior to the commencement of the millennial Kingdom. One cannot help but be impressed by the contrast between the city under siege in vv.1-3 and the city as described in v.11. What a difference! The Messiah of Israel will make this difference.

The revitalizing river (v.8)

"And it shall be in that day, that living waters shall go out from Jerusalem." The changes to the topography of the land of Israel will bring about great changes in the water situation within the city and outside it. God will create a new river which will bring with it the blessings of healing and life. It needs to be stressed that this will be a literal river just as the coming of the Messiah in this passage is literal, though at the same time it is a symbol of life and blessing for Israel. One will look in vain in maps of the world to find this great river, for it does not yet exist. Ezekiel 47.1-12, Joel 3.18, and Psalm 46.1-4 speak of this mighty river that will flow in the new land of Israel. The river is described under the figure "living waters" because it illustrates the water as a living thing flowing quickly and sparkling in its constant movement and changing course.

Unlike the rivers of earth it will not have its origin in some range of hills or mountains, but according to Ezekiel the prophet the river will flow from the new sanctuary in Jerusalem. It will begin as a small stream in the temple and again, unlike the rivers of the earth, this radiant stream has no tributaries. From its own deep fountain it will draw its increase until within a few paces from its origin it has become a resistless flood – "waters to swim in". It will proceed by way of the altar and flow through the city. When the river has passed through the city, it immediately overleaps the battlements and plunges into the depths of the Jordan valley – between 3,000 to 4,000 feet of sheer descent, in order to reach the Asphalt Lake (the Dead Sea). No life can now exist in those waters; no vegetation can flourish on its banks. Probably there is not a more forlorn place anywhere, but "every thing shall live whither the river cometh". At the touch of its bright and healing waters the lake will be turned into a fresh water lake wherein there will be a multitude of fish. So much so, Ezekiel informs us, that fisherman will fish in it (Ezek 47.10). This wonderful river is a holy river and will be universally acknowledged as such, and it is a clean and pure river; thus it stands in contrast with many rivers today. It is a river that will never dry up and a river, too, which will exist in eternity.

Zechariah continues by saying that half of the river will go towards the former sea and the other half towards the hinder sea. Thus it will become two rivers. The former sea is recognized as the Mediterranean Sea and the hinder sea as the Dead Sea. We have seen that a very great valley will form when Christ returns and the Mount of Olives cleaves in two. This great valley will form the bed of the living waters after the remnant have fled the city and will flow west to the Mediterranean and east to the Dead Sea. Its entire length will be from some point on the Mediterranean coast, through Jerusalem to the Dead Sea, thus making Jerusalem a seaport. The river will make the whole new land of Israel most fertile and prosperous. The entire land east and west will be watered and the Messiah Himself will guarantee the perennial supplies of living water. The water will flow all year round, even in the summer, when most streams in Israel dry up. This phenomenon illustrates the fact that the city of Jerusalem in the Millennium will be a great centre from which God's blessing flows to all the nations of the world.

The rule of the Messiah (v.9)

Here we pass from the literal and physical changes of the land to the higher spiritual blessing, that Jehovah will be King over all the earth and His name alone will be mentioned and revered. This will be the glorious consequence of Israel being again recognized by God as His own people. He will not only be King over Israel, but over all the nations. God's King is the Lord Jesus Christ (see Psalm 2.6-8), and it is wonderful as well as so significant to see that Scripture here calls Him "Jehovah". He is God's ideal King. He will be Israel's true King and He will be the world's righteous King, for righteousness is what the world needs. There may be subsidiary kings in the world in the millennial age, as Isaiah 52.15 seems to indicate, and there certainly will be princes ruling (Is 32.1), but when the Lord rules all these will be under Him, for He is the King of the kings and Lord of the lords (Rev 19.16).

When the Lord in His ministry claimed, "I and my Father are one" (Jn 10.30), the Jews rejected this, but one day their eyes will be opened to see that in Christ "dwelleth all the fulness of the Godhead bodily" (Col 2.9), for "in that day shall there be one Lord, and his name one". We need to make it clear that this does not mean that Jehovah in the future time of the Millennium will be something He has not always been in Himself and in His essence in the past and present. It means He will be manifested as such to be the matchless and incomparable One. The Lord Jesus Christ's name will be universally adored and revered. Israel at that time will come to see that the God of Abraham, Isaac, and Jacob has been revealed and will continue to be revealed in the person of the Lord Jesus Christ. The phrase "in that day shall there be one Lord, and his name one" describes the Lord's universal rule and reign. He will be recognized as the one and only sovereign Lord. The Hebrew word for "one" here is EHAD (259), which speaks of a unique oneness possessed only by Jehovah. Thus in the Millennium, Jehovah will be universally accepted, worshipped, and served as the only unique, solitary God in the universe. Remember, this is the

Lord Jesus Christ! There will be no doubt then as to whom all men should believe and worship. We must not forget that by the start of the Kingdom age every idol will have been purged from the nation and every god set aside. The religions of Islam, and Buddhism, for example, which are now practised over much of the face of the earth, will be no more. No one will dispute His righteous rule in that day (though some in the course of the Kingdom age will grow discontented with it as we will see later in the chapter). In that day only one will must be recognized - the will of God through the Lord Jesus. This will be the secret of peace. It is true that Satan will be imprisoned in the abyss for the Lord's thousand year reign, but with the Lord's will universally obeyed peace will continue. Is this not the secret of peace in an assembly? Where there is more than one will there can be no peace. If there is to be unity and peace among the saints it can only be achieved and maintained by each believer seeking with exercise to do the will of God and not man's will in the assembly.

The reconstruction of the land (v.10)

In this verse the prophet predicts that the whole land will be levelled and lowered. He gives in brief what other prophets have touched on in some detail. Isaiah, for example, says, "The mountain of the Lord's house shall be established in the top of the mountains, and shall be exalted above the hills" (Is 2.2). Later in his prophecy he speaks of the changes God will make in the land and this shows the harmony of prophecy and in particular the agreement between both Isaiah and Zechariah: "Every valley shall be exalted, and every mountain and hill shall be made low: and the crooked shall be made straight, and the rough places plain: And the glory of the Lord shall be revealed" (Is 40.4-5). How good and reassuring it is to see the unity of the prophetic teaching of Holy Scripture and in particular the harmony between Isaiah and Zechariah. Isaiah's language must not be taken as poetic or merely expressing moral thoughts. What he predicts will literally take place as Zechariah himself makes clear. What is the purpose of these geographical changes? It is that Jerusalem may be left standing conspicuous and prominent.

Now there are mountains around Jerusalem (Ps 125.2), but when the millennial age will have begun these will be reduced to a plain and be no more, and Jerusalem will be pushed up and elevated. "All the land shall be turned as a plain from Geba to Rimmon south of Jerusalem." The surrounding hilly districts will be made like a plain, literally like the Arabah. "The Arabah is the geographical name of the deep rift that extends from the Sea of Galilee and the Jordan valley through the Dead Sea and on to the Gulf of Aqaba. It is remarkable that it is the deepest depression on the surface of the earth" (M. F. Unger). Thus Zechariah compares the levelling of the land to Arabah to illustrate its vastness and depth. Twice in his writings Josephus speaks of Arabah as the great plain (Wars, 8.2; Antiquities, 7.1). The cities of Geba and Rimmon represent approximately the northern and southern boundaries of the part of Israel given to Judah. "It", that is Jerusalem, "shall be lifted up" (JND), the hills all around it having been lowered (Micah 4.1). Moreover, it shall be "inhabited in her place", that is, Jerusalem shall dwell on its ancient site and the city will be restored and rebuilt (Jer 31.38) and is to be completely recovered from all the suffered ruin through its history brought upon it by conquest and plunder.

In the Millennium Jerusalem will be the capital of the world. It will not be London in the UK, Washington in the USA, or Paris in France. It is wonderful to think that Jerusalem, which has figured in history so long, will yet not only recover its old prosperity and its old dimensions, but far exceed these due to the effect of the earthquake when the Lord comes to the earth. What a beautiful sight the land will be then and what a beautiful sight the city will be. No matter from what direction people approach they will easily see Jerusalem towering above any other city that may then be in the land. There is a reference, we believe, to the lifting up of the city at this very time in Psalm 48.2, "Beautiful in elevation, the joy of the whole earth, is mount Zion, on the sides of the north, the city of the great King" (RV). Apart from its prominence in that day, what is it that will make the city so attractive and beautiful? Will it not be because of the Lord Jesus Christ? His presence will characterize it and something of His beauty will be seen everywhere in it. One reason why the new temple within will only be made up of wood and stone (see Ezekiel 40-42) and not with costly materials such as silver and gold, is that God will not allow anything in that day to detract from the splendour and glory of Christ. As a practical thought in this connection, it needs to be appreciated that God's assembly, spiritually speaking, should be marked by elevation and be as a city upon a hill that cannot be hid. Nothing about the testimony of an assembly should detract from Christ's glory, for He should have all the pre-eminence.

Zechariah continues with precision to detail the extent of the change which will take place in the city and its environs, for he says, "From Benjamin's gate unto the place of the first gate, unto the corner gate, and from the tower of Hananeel unto the king's winepresses". These locations can be identified. Benjamin's gate in the north wall, through which the road to Benjamin and thence to Ephraim ran, was no doubt the same as Ephraim's gate (Neh 8.16). Then we have the first gate to the corner gate. These two definitions seem to define the extent, both eastward and westward from Benjamin's gate, which, as we have said, stood near the centre of the north wall. The first gate is taken to be the same as the gate of the old city (Neh 3.6; 12.39) and its place, at the north-eastern corner of the city. The corner gate would then be in the west. Finally Zechariah says, "And from the tower of Hananeel to the king's winepresses". This will be the extent of the city from north to south, just as the other was from east to west. The tower of Hananeel (Jer 31.38; Neh 3.1) stood at the north-east corner of the city, and the king's winepresses were in the king's gardens at the south side of the city (Neh 3.15). Again the reader should not fail to

see with what exactness and carefulness the word of God here through
Zechariah describes and maps out just how extensive the change is going
to be. Such detailed descriptions cannot be otherwise than literal and
should cause us to realize that only the inspired word of God could possibly
give us such fine details.

The repopulation of the city (v.11)

"And men shall dwell in it." This statement, we suggest, is in contrast to
the Jews going out of it as slaves and fugitives (v.2). What a blessing it will
then be to be a citizen of the Messiah's Millennial Metropolis. It will be a
delight and joy to be there and to be without any fear whatsoever. It will
be a holy city, a protected city, and peaceful city. Jerusalem even today, in
spite of all its past distresses and ravages, is quite an intriguing and
remarkable city to visit and see, but what will the same city be like when
the Lord has worked for its reformation? "And there shall be no more utter
destruction; but Jerusalem shall be safely inhabited." The word here is
literally, "no more curse" (HEREM – 2764 – see RV), for then the curse
upon man and the earth shall have been lifted. If sin should rear its head it
will be immediately judged and punished. Temporal blessings and spiritual
prosperity will move in harmony together throughout the Millennium.
The same Lord that will return and make Jerusalem a delivered city just as
the enemies will be rejoicing in their success, is the same Lord who will,
by His wonderful power, make the city a delightsome city. How fascinating,
and even exciting, these prophecies are. How the believer today should
rejoice in these wonderful God-breathed predictions of truth.

Verses 12-15: The Confusion of the Enemy

In this section Zechariah goes back to the conflict of vv.1-4 (often
prophecy goes back to a previous event in Scripture). Thus, chronologically,
these verses describe for us what will follow v.3 when the Lord suddenly
appears on the scene. We have details here of how the Lord will deal with
these enemies of Israel. The enemies will be destroyed by the Lord and
will suffer indescribable and painful agonies. Note three things: the plague,
the panic, and the prowess. God will use these three instruments to
accomplish His fearful vengeance on the enemy. He will send,
supernaturally, a plague, He will cause panic to overtake the attackers, and
He will use the remnant and empower them to engage in the fight against
the enemy, thus completing their total destruction.

The plague (vv.12 & 15)

Zechariah here gives more detail concerning the destruction of the
enemies besieging Jerusalem. The armies will be destroyed even while
they stand on their feet. The description of the effect of the plague is
terrible in the extreme and nothing quite like it has been experienced in
warfare before, unless one compares it with what happened when atomic

bombs were dropped on Hiroshima and Nagasaki in Japan, in 1945. However, it is not nuclear warfare which will be the means of such terrible suffering, for the victory will be achieved by the power of God alone. The consuming of the enemy here is not the result of any humanly devised scientific invention. It is clear then from the passage that the plague comes from God - "This shall be the plague wherewith the Lord will smite all the people...". The foes of Israel will be destroyed by a living death, the rotting of the body while still alive. How horrible this will be. There will be the corruption of death together with an awful sense of their sin in seeking to overthrow God's people and city. Such will be the character of the plague that those who suffer it and those who witness it will be compelled to own that it is the hand of God in judgment. In order to convey the utter destructive effects of the plague, Zechariah describes the different parts of the body that will endure its stroke. In the first place it will result in inflicting upon them a putrefying body. Satan will use these men to invade the land of Israel and Jerusalem, but they will be smitten by God. Then there is added the rotting of the eyes. These will be the eyes of soldiers who will have looked upon the nakedness and vulnerability of Jerusalem, thinking victory is assured. Finally, we have the rotting of the tongue. Why is the tongue singled out? The two different parts of the body mentioned doubtless have a solemn significance. The tongue is the member with which this satanically inspired army will blaspheme God and His earthly people. God's just punishment will be meted out upon them.

From v.15 we see that the animal kingdom also will suffer, just as they did when the curse was pronounced upon man, the earth, and the beast after the Fall (cp. Josh 7.24). Thus the same plague by which men will be destroyed will also affect the animals. We may compare this with God's command to Saul to destroy completely not only Amalek, but also their animals (1 Sam 15.3). Everything connected with those who rebel against God and seek to destroy His people will suffer the same judgment. Some of these animals destroyed, like the horse and the camel, will mean that they cannot be used by any of the enemy to escape.

The panic (v.13)

To the plague there is added a panic, or consternation, through which Israel's enemies are thrown into confusion, so that they turn their weapons against one another. An example of this, and to which the description given by Zechariah probably refers, is found in the reign of Jehoshaphat (see 2 Chr 20.23). The grasp of the other's hand is a hostile one, the object being to seize him, and having lifted his hand, to strike him dead. As God confounded the enemies of Israel in the past, so will He do again, but this time on a much larger scale. Psalm 83 refers to the same time as Zechariah 14.13. There the ungodly confederacy of nations against Israel is in view and the prayer of Asaph is, "Let them be confounded and troubled for ever; yea, let them be put to shame, and perish: That men may know that thou, whose name alone is JEHOVAH, art the most high over all the earth" (vv.17-18). Asaph's prayer will be answered *"in that day"* (that is, the time of the crisis of Armageddon).This will take place, it would seem, outside Jerusalem and means that thus far Israel will not have fought in the battle, for the Lord alone will have taken the initiative for His people.

The prowess (v.14)

Superhuman strength will be given to the saved remnant of Judah to complete the great victory over the enemy, and "Judah also shall fight at Jerusalem". This refers, we believe, to the Jewish remnant that initially escaped the invasion of Jerusalem through the valley opened by God (vv.4-5), and will return to Jerusalem to overcome the invaders who survive God's judgment during the campaign and crisis of Armageddon. The wonderful power granted to the remnant has already been mentioned by Zechariah in 12.5. God will not only smite the enemy miraculously with plagues and confusion, but He will allow the remnant actually to take part in the conflict. What a joy and blessing it will be for them just to know that God will graciously give them a part in the battle and use them for the display of His majesty and glory. The remnant will seize as booty all the costly possessions of this heathen army, and so visit them with ample retribution for the plundering of Jerusalem referred to in v.2 (cp. Ezek 39.10-17). Thus the spoils of the war will be enormous. We have a picture of this victory at the end time in connection with King Jehoshaphat (2 Chr 20), when a great multitude came against him consisting of Moab, Ammon, Syria, and Mount Seir. With confidence in God, the king and his people went to battle. On that occasion God spread confusion in the ranks of the enemy and fighting against each other they were slain. Israel did not have to fight at all. The spoil was so great that it took Israel three days to gather it. We may learn from Zechariah 14.14 that, when in the christian conflict we move with confidence in God, He will empower us and use us so that we are conquerors through our Lord Jesus Christ.

If one compares Revelation 19.11-21 with Zechariah 14.12-15, which details the methods by which the enemy will be punished, the question might be asked whether both passages refer to the same event and if so why there is no mention in Revelation 19 of the plague. Certainly the impression one may get from a perusal of John's prophetic vision is that the Lord alone will deal with the enemy. It is stated in v.21 of John's prophecy that the "remnant were slain with the sword of him that sat upon the horse". Yet in Revelation 19 there are clear links with Zechariah 14. Both speak of the sudden appearance of the Lord and both refer to saints who will accompany Him. Then again, in Zechariah 14.1-3 and Revelation 19.11-21 we surely have the immediate effects of the Lord's second advent upon the enemy. Zechariah and John may both be referring to the enemies of Israel who will have taken Jerusalem and will be there when the Lord comes. These armies in Jerusalem will be dealt with by the

Lord. From Zechariah 14.12, however, we read of a plague smiting the enemy. This could refer to the enemies outside Jerusalem and still approaching the city. Revelation 19 also, for instance, does not refer to any confusion among the enemy as in the Zechariah passage. Thus it is submitted that there is a first phase in the conflict, when the tide of war will go against the people of Jerusalem (Zech 14.2), but then there is a second and final phase when Israel, seen in the remnant, will, by the help of God, win this further stage in the battle. Most of those who will rally to chase and conquer the enemy will come from the surrounding country. They will come to the aid of the city against the common foe. There is no mention in Zechariah 14 of the Beast and the false prophet. To appreciate prophecy one must put together the whole picture from various Scripture passages that present the same incident. It would only be right to say that some students of prophecy see Zechariah 14 as the conflict against the Assyrian, or the king of the north, and consider this person to be the last enemy that Israel will face. Therefore, in their view the events described in Zechariah 14 are subsequent to those in Revelation 19.

Verses 16-19: The Chastisement of the Wayward
   The section we enter here gives details of the Kingdom age and the worship that will take place in it in connection with the Feast of Tabernacles. Thus, from war in the land of Israel (vv.12-15) we are glad to pass on to worship in the Millennium. Two subjects are considered in the passage – reverence for Christ in the Millennium, and rebellion of men in the Millennium.

Reverence for Christ in the Millennium (v.16)
   Gentiles who will live in the millennial Kingdom will be required by God to attend the Feast of Tabernacles in Jerusalem to worship the Lord. Why is it that Gentiles need to keep this feast and why is it that this feast in particular will be observed throughout the Millennium? These are interesting questions in the light of this revealing section of Zechariah's prophecy. The Gentiles will go up to worship in Jerusalem because, first of all, God will command them to do so, secondly because it will provide them with the opportunity to praise God for the fruitful harvest He has provided, and lastly, by their celebrating this feast they will express their submission to the Lord as the only true God of the universe. God will overcome all the foes of His people. Many He will destroy, others He will bring into willing subjection. Those then who are "left of all the nations" are people who will be converted to God, for no person not born again will enter into the Kingdom age. What an amazing turnaround this is. They who had been enemies against God and Israel are now saved and obedient to Him! These saved Gentiles are the sheep mentioned by the Lord Jesus in Matthew 25.31-46, in connection with the judgment of the living nations, who will have survived the Great Tribulation. These sheep are placed on

the right hand of the Lord – the place of honour. This judgment will take place after the return of the Lord to the earth and before the setting up of the Kingdom. It will take place in the valley of Jehoshaphat between the Eastern Wall of the Temple Mount and the Mount of Olives (Joel 3.2 & 12).

It is clear from what the Lord says in His Olivet discourse that the sheep are saved Gentiles from the nations who will inherit "the kingdom prepared for (them) from the foundation of the world" (Mt 25.34). The saved Gentiles at that time will consist of those who have given evidence of their regenerated nature by their kind and sympathetic treatment of the Jewish remnant during the Tribulation. These will not have been involved in the ungodly confederacy of nations against Israel. But from v.16 of Zechariah 14 we have another party of saved Gentiles who will have submitted to Christ and in mercy been spared by Him to enter with those whom the Lord describes as "sheep" into the Millennium. These redeemed Gentiles will make an annual pilgrimage to the world's capital in Jerusalem, in order to pray and worship the "King, the Lord of hosts". Notice this title again in Zechariah – "the Lord of hosts". This is literally "the Lord of armies". The title in the context here emphasizes the all-sufficiency of Jehovah to accomplish all He has decreed. It is wonderful to think that in the Millennium there will be no need of a United Nations. A nation then will not need to maintain an army, for universal peace will be enjoyed. Each nation will still preserve its identity and each nation will worship the Lord as Sovereign King over all the earth. The worship accorded the Lord Jesus will be universal, willing, and an expression of love and obedience to Him. The Lord Jesus will be acknowledged as the only true God.

It is interesting to learn that this feast and the Feast of the Passover will be the only two feasts that the Jews will take up again in the Millennium. Ezekiel 45.21-25 proves this fact. In the Kingdom age there will be no wave sheaf presented, for Christ has risen. There will be no Feast of Weeks, for the Church age will have run its course. There will be no Blowing of Trumpets, for the gathering of Israel will have taken place and there will be no Day of Atonement, for the sin of Israel will have been pardoned and cleansed. The Passover speaks of redemption, so, in keeping this feast, Israel will not be allowed to forget Christ's death and the shedding of His blood to redeem them. There will be certain changes in these feasts. For example, we read of a bullock to be offered in the millennial Feast of Passover and we read in Zechariah 14 of Gentiles keeping the Feast of Tabernacles. No Gentiles are mentioned as being involved in the Passover. A lamb was offered on the Day of Passover, but the bullock in the millennial Feast shows that when Israel are restored their appreciation of Messiah's person and grace will have reached a high level in the nation.

Why then is the Feast of Tabernacles singled out to be kept not only by Jews, but Gentiles also? It is because what is pictured typically in it will then be fulfilled. It was the most joyous of all Israel's feasts and was the last feast after the harvest of grain and wine was gathered in at the year's end, so that it was a feast of celebration. The Feast of Tabernacles is the most appropriate feast to keep, because prophetically it points on to the joy of the millennial reign of Christ. When the Millennium has begun, all the other feasts will have been fulfilled by their antitypes. Now at last in the Kingdom age this feast too will have found its antitype. The feast will be commemorative of the sojourn of the Jews, not merely for the forty years in the wilderness, but for over two thousand years of being dispersed among the nations. It was kept on their return from the Babylonian dispersion (Neh 8.14-17). It was the feast on which the Lord Jesus gave the invitation to come to the living waters of salvation (Jn 7.2 & 37).

Rebellion of men in the Millennium (vv.17-19)

In this section there is more than a hint that, wonderful as the millennial reign will be, there will nevertheless begin to be seen a rebellious and disobedient spirit against God's commands and the reign of the Person of Christ. Thus we read that God will require that all the families of the earth go up to Jerusalem annually to worship the Lord, but if any refuse to do so God will chasten them by withholding rain. Rain denotes the favour of God generally. Without rain the fruits of the land will not flourish. Scarcity of food, famine, pestilence, and all privations are the consequence of having no rain, and are especially felt in the East. The meaning, then, is clear in that those families that do not go up to worship the Lord will be chastened by Him with the withdrawal of necessary material blessings and they will suffer temporal calamities. It should be clear that we are not to read into this that God will be expecting every individual from each nation to go up, for this would really be a physical impossibility. Rather, each nation will be required to send representatives to Jerusalem on the occasion of the celebration of the Feast of Tabernacles.

Several of the Psalms provide an indication that many in the Millennium will render to the Lord a "feigned obedience" (see for example Psalm 66.3, AV margin). Outwardly they will appear to be willing to submit to Him, but they will merely be putting up with the righteous iron rule of Christ. If a proof of this was needed then it will be found in the final rebellion against God and Christ in Revelation 20.7-10. All born in the period of the Millennium will be born with a sinful nature and will need to be saved. Sadly, many will not trust Christ and when Satan is released from his confinement in the abyss he will not have learned his lesson, but will again go out to deceive men and gather around him a force of unsaved and ungodly men to oppose Christ. It is just incredible to think that men who will have enjoyed the great benefits of the reign of Christ will so quickly, being deceived, rally to Satan's sinister cause. In the Millennium men will have a last test from God and this test will show man to be depraved and sinful. Even living in the ideal conditions of the Kingdom age man will not improve. There is a lesson for the believer here. How possible it is to show outward attachment and devotion to Christ even to other believers and yet be discontented in our hearts and not happy in our show of apparent obedience. Again, we are thankful that in the present age of grace we are under no threat of judgment or curse by not attending the meetings of the saints. If we were there would be no absentees from the assembly gatherings!

It is interesting to observe that Egypt is singled out as an example that if they go not up to Jerusalem, God will smite them with the plague. This is not necessarily the same plague with which God will smite His enemies (v.12), but perhaps the awful idea of a plague used to threaten Egypt, or any other nation that goes not to Jerusalem, would remind all in that day of the terrible plagues of Egypt. In connection with Egypt there is no threat of rain being divinely withheld from them, for such a threat would have no force, since Egypt as a nation depended on the Nile's overflow and not on the rain. Indeed, Egypt would probably despise such a judgment, but God has other judgments, for "there shall be the plague". Thus none shall escape, nor despise the great goodness of God. "This shall be the punishment (margin "sin") of Egypt", that is, it shall be the punishment for their sin (Num 32.23). One interesting point to mention is that according to Isaiah 19 Egypt will exist as a nation in the Millennium. From this we may conclude that there will be enough from Egypt spared at the end of the Tribulation to go into the Kingdom. Scripture predicts they will have blessing as a nation in the future. One reason for this may be due to the fact that Egypt sheltered the Lord Jesus in the days of Herod's murderous attempts to destroy Him. God will not forget this.

Verses 20-21: The Consecration of the Nation

What a tremendous finish to the book of Zechariah is now reached. It began in ch.1 with God appealing to a disobedient people to turn to Him. It now ends with God's great purpose for Israel completed in that true holiness and worship will characterize His people in the Millennium. Israel will at last be "a holy nation". Zechariah now dwells on the marvellous change in Jerusalem, for the impress of holiness and consecration to God will be stamped upon everything in the nation in that wonderful day. Holiness will not only mark their persons, but their possessions. The earthly capital of Jerusalem in the Millennium shall then fully answer to its name, "The holy city". All distinctions, such as profane and holy, will cease. Holiness will be universal. It will embrace the affairs of common life. It will embrace all domestic concerns. It will embrace everything of a religious character.

Holiness in public life

"There shall be upon the bells of the horses, HOLINESS UNTO THE LORD." The bells were metal plates hanging from the necks of horses and camels as ornaments, and which tinkled by striking each other. Is there a hint here that the very bells of the horses will tinkle His praises? Horses have been mentioned previously in Zechariah. Here it is good to note that no longer will horses be used in warfare, but they will be consecrated to the Lord in His service. There is nothing like holiness in the life to bring praise to God. "HOLINESS TO THE LORD" was graven upon the mitre of the high priest, reminding him and Israel of their call to holiness. The engraving will make clear to all that every item will be fit for Kingdom use. Everything used in the Kingdom administration will be considered holy unto the Lord. In the public affairs of the Kingdom all will be consecrated to the Lord. This section signifies that the most external things in that day, and things having no connection whatever with worship, will be as holy as those objects were which had been dedicated to the service of the Lord by special consecration.

Holiness in religious life

"The pots in the Lord's house shall be like the bowls before the altar." The "pots" in the sanctuary which were used for boiling the sacrificial flesh, were regarded as being much less holy than the "bowls" in which the blood of the sacrificial animals was received, and out of which it was sprinkled or poured on the altar. In the Millennium these pots will be just as holy as the bowls.

Holiness in private life

Thus there will be no distinction between secular and spiritual life, for all will be consecrated to the Lord. This should be true in the life of the believer today. Christians cannot do what they like in the secular or public sphere and then expect to be consecrated to the Lord in the spiritual scene of the assembly. No, we must understand that everything in the life of the believer really belongs to Christ. Practical sanctification should mark the character and every sphere of life the believer touches. The very presence and rule of the Messiah in that day will demand that not only His temple, but also His people, land, and possessions must be holy.

Zechariah's final word regarding Israel's future blessing is, "There shall be no more the Canaanite in the house of the Lord of hosts". What a note to end Zechariah's great prophetic book! The idea of the Canaanite in the Old Testament signified a person who was profane, ungodly and unclean. While it is true that no such person will serve in the millennial temple, we believe the reference to the Canaanite in this closing sentence indicates much more than the banishment of the literal Canaanite. In Hosea 12.7 (AV margin) the word, "Canaan" is used of the nation of Israel. To call Israel "Canaan" or "merchant" shows what Israel had become. They had copied the Canaanites in trading and had become a commercial people instead of a religious people set apart to God and many of them were indulging in dishonest business practices. The Hebrew word (KᵉNAAN – 3667) can also mean "merchant" or "trader". In early history, the Canaanites or Phoenicians were the then great merchant-people, in the same way as astrologers were called Chaldeans. Thus the statement might equally well be rendered, "There shall be no more a trafficker in the house of the Lord of hosts". Throughout Israel's history the Lord's House, the temple, had often been desecrated with the spirit of commerce, and sadly in our Lord's day it was no better; so much so He had to rebuke the people by saying, "Make not my father's house an house of merchandise" (Jn 2.16). There were men who were taking advantage of the Jewish religion to further their own business interests. The temple in the future will be free from such defilement, for the House of the Lord will be "an house of prayer for all people" (Is 56.7; Mk 11.17) – a place of spiritual exercise and not commercial gain. The Ephah (corrupt commerce) in the vision of ch.5 will have been already removed prior to the setting up of the Kingdom. Let the lesson be learned here that the Lord Jesus must be honoured in all the relationships of God's people and this includes business. Business life must not be allowed to interfere with the service of the House of God.

Conclusion

In summing up Zechariah 14 we recall the meaning of Zechariah's name – Jehovah remembers. The whole book, and especially this closing chapter, shows in a most blessed and comforting way that God has not forgotten Jerusalem, nor has He forgotten the nation of Israel. Chapter 1 may begin by showing God's people in the valley of despair with a city to build, but at the close of this final chapter our prophet shows us a restored people living in a secure city that has been lifted up to be the millennial metropolis of the world. This is what God will accomplish for the Jewish people. The chapter anticipates that in the Millennium there will be universal homage to Christ, universal happiness for the world, and universal holiness in all spheres. At the end of our study of Zechariah we can only say, "WHAT A GLORIOUS CONSUMMATION TO THE BOOK"!

MALACHI

P. Harding

CONTENTS

INTRODUCTION
The Position of the Book

Malachi is the last of the prophetic books and the final book of the Old Testament. The Old Testament opens with a man in a garden, free from sin, and in happy fellowship with God. It closes with man in his sin, fallen, and far from God. How important it is to remind one's heart that the only place of safety is in the will of God. Malachi acts as a bridge between the Old and New Testaments. It looks forward to the coming of both John the Baptist (3.1; Mk 1.2) and the Lord Himself (3.1; 4.2). The general conditions of an outward form of godliness with no reality seen in Malachi are also seen in the Gospels. The faithful remnant who feared the Lord in Malachi 3.16-18 is a reminder of the faithful remnant in the opening chapters of Matthew and Luke. The fear of the Lord is the beginning of knowledge and wisdom (Prov 1.7; 9.10) and should characterise every child of God. It is to hate evil (Prov 8.13), and is a fountain of life (Prov 14.27; 19.23).

After Malachi, God paused in His communications to men, in the form of divinely inspired Scripture, until we come to the angel's message to Zechariah concerning the birth of John (Lk 1.11-17). For 400 years after Malachi there was no further divine revelation - God was silent. This period is referred to as the Intertestamental Period, and the concluding chapter of this volume gives a brief review of this interlude.

The Period of the Book

Malachi is one of the post-captivity books of which there are six - Ezra, Nehemiah, Esther, Haggai, Zechariah, and Malachi although some would exclude Esther. Nehemiah is the last historical book of the Old Testament, whereas Malachi is the last prophetic book. It is evident from the prophecy itself that Malachi prophesied after the captivity, while Judah was a Persian province (1.8 - "thy governor"), after the rebuilding of the temple (1.10; 3.1-10) and the restoring of public worship (1.6-14). Thus Malachi must have been written after Haggai and Zechariah and after the events of the first six chapters of Ezra.

There is a close link between Nehemiah and Malachi, for the conditions rectified by Nehemiah (Neh 13) are the very conditions that Malachi condemns. It seems that just as Haggai and Zechariah supported Joshua and Zerubbabel in the building of the temple, so Malachi supported Ezra and Nehemiah in their reforms. The fact that Nehemiah was supported by prophets is implied in Nehemiah 6.7. It has been noted that "The second Temple was completed in 516 BC", that "The Book of Nehemiah opens in the twentieth year of Artaxerxes, 445 BC", and that, "in 432, he visited Jerusalem again (Neh 13.4-31)" (S. R. Driver). The close similarity between the abuses that Nehemiah found on his return and those which Malachi attacked indicate that this prophecy must have been written after Nehemiah's second visit to Jerusalem (432 BC), or in the period of his absence from Jerusalem. However, the fact that Nehemiah finds the abuses prevalent on his return to Jerusalem implies that Malachi did not commence his prophetic ministry until after Nehemiah's return. Thus a date of 420 BC has been suggested. Most agree that the period of Malachi was between 450 and 400 BC although some place the book as far back as 540 BC which is most unlikely.

The People of the Book
    The ministry of Malachi is addressed to the remnant that had returned out of Babylon under Zerubbabel and Joshua as recorded in the books of Ezra and Nehemiah. That remnant had returned conscious of the love of God (Jer 29.10-14 - God had fulfilled His promise), concerned for the honour of His name (Neh 1.9,11; 9.5), with a compelling desire to rebuild the House of God (Ezra 1), and with a conviction as to the claims of God (Ezra 3). When we come to Malachi, that remnant which was once marked by devotion and determination, self-sacrifice and spiritual exercise had fallen into moral and spiritual decay. Declension and departure had set in and thus Malachi's ministry is directed to those characterised by a lack of devotion to God, with a feeble grasp of the honour of His name, little zeal for the House of God, and a failure to meet the claims of God. They were marked by irreverence, unfaithfulness, formalism, immorality, dishonesty, and materialism. There is a close link between the remnant when they first returned from Babylon and the assembly at Philadelphia (Rev 3.7-13), and between the remnant in Malachi's day and the assembly at Laodicea (Rev 3.14-22). Today assemblies claim to be gathered to the Lord's name and to keep His word, yet one is driven to the conclusion that much in assemblies corresponds to conditions in Malachi and Laodicea. Half-heartedness in light of the truth committed to believers is surely repulsive to God. The kind of ministry that Malachi gives is the only remedy for such dreadful conditions.
    Within this remnant there was a further faithful remnant which was encouraged by Malachi, who not only reminded them of the certainty of the coming of the Lord, but also informed them that they were listed in God's book of remembrance and that they made up His jewels (3.16-18).

The Prophet of the Book
    Nothing is known of Malachi beyond that which can be gathered from the book itself. His lineage, his birth place, and the time of his prophecy are not mentioned. Since this is the case, it is disputed whether the name is of an actual person or an official name given to the writer. It has been claimed that "The Chaldee paraphrase identifies him with Ezra wrongly, as Ezra is never called a prophet but a scribe, and Malachi never a scribe but a prophet" (Jamieson, Fausset & Brown). C. F. Keil states, "The circumstance that the heading does not contain any further personal description, whether the name of his father or the place of his birth, is not more striking in our book than in the writings of Obadiah and Habakkuk, which also contain

only the name of the prophet in the heading, without any further personal descriptions". Jewish tradition states that Malachi, along with Haggai and Zechariah, was a member of the Great Synagogue. He seems to come upon the scene suddenly, like Elijah, and is the last messenger of God until John the Baptist. He delivers his message and reproves the people, and then no more is recorded of him. It seems, from a comparison of the prophet's condemnation of the people's sin with Nehemiah's reforms, that Malachi was contemporary with Nehemiah (compare 2.8 with Neh 13.15,19; 2.10 with Neh 13.23-27; 3.7-12 with Neh 13.10). His name means "My Messenger" or "Jehovah's Messenger". Since the priests and their service are prominent in the prophecy some have suggested that he himself was a priest.

Malachi was aware of the conditions - eleven times the words "ye say" occur in his message. However the Lord always had an answer for the people (note the use of the word "but" in the book).

Malachi gave clear instruction - the expression "saith the Lord" appears twenty-five times. The only remedy for the conditions described in the book was for the people of God to take heed to the voice of God in the messages from God. This is the only remedy for us today.

Malachi was involved in his ministry, for he knew the wrongdoing of the people, he felt the weight of the ministry and he unfolded the truth and wealth of God. Thus the book states Malachi's identity (My Messenger), his understanding of the prevailing conditions, and the ministry he gives.

The Purpose of the Book
The historical purpose

The purpose of Malachi's message was to bring about spiritual revival in his day and to rectify moral and spiritual departure from the divine revelation. With stern vigour he reproved the nation for its departure from the truth of Jehovah yet, in yearning tenderness, he appealed to the people for repentance and a return to the Lord. Malachi rebuked the proud and bigoted self-righteousness of the many who claimed the favour of God which they had really forfeited by their unbelief and neglect of the law, yet he encouraged those who feared the Lord.

The prophetic purpose

This was three-fold – to indicate that a time of mercy, in the coming of the Forerunner, will precede the day of God's wrath (3.1); to warn the people of God that the Lord, as the Refiner, will come to purge away all dross (3.2-3); and to remind them that the Lord will come as the Sun of righteousness in judgment and yet with healing in His wings (4.1-3). Such prophecy was intended to be a warning to the people in general because of their disobedience and departure from the divine revelation, but it was also intended to be an encouragement to those who feared the Lord.

The practical purpose
Again, this had three facets – to unfold the unchanging character of God and His claims upon His people; to emphasise the authority of the divine revelation (the word of God) committed to His people; and to indicate abiding principles which should affect the lives of the people of God in every age and generation.

This type of ministry, in any day of declension and departure, is not palatable to those who disobey or set aside the word of God. Neither is it easy to give, and thus, for Malachi, it was called "the burden of the word of the Lord" (1.1).

The Particulars of the Book
It is likely that the contents of the book were delivered orally by Malachi over a period of time. The main object of the prophecy was to condemn the practices of the majority of the people of God, including the priests. These practices were inconsistent with the teaching of the law and had apparently increased during Nehemiah's absence from Jerusalem. The prophecy was intended to support and strengthen Nehemiah in his reforms on his return to Jerusalem. The book indicates that a spirit of indifference and carelessness prevailed. Malachi directly addressed the sins which were prevalent among the people, thus showing the inconsistency of their claim to be the people of God. The moral and spiritual conditions of his day are those of Christendom today where there is an outward form and profession, but no reality. He adopts the form of stating the truth, followed by the anticipated objection, and finally replies by reiterating and substantiating the truth already stated. Thus, instead of the rhetorical development of a subject used by some of the prophets, Malachi uses a dialectic form by means of question and answer. An outstanding feature of the prophecy is the eight occasions where the charge of Jehovah is challenged: as to the love of Jehovah (1.2); the despising of Jehovah's name (1.6); the pollution of Jehovah by their sacrifices (1.7); their unfaithfulness in marriage (2.14); their wearying of Jehovah (2.17); their departure from the ordinances of Jehovah (3.7); their robbing of Jehovah (3.8); and their speaking against Jehovah (3.13). Over and over, Jehovah, whom they outwardly professed to serve, charged them with departure in heart, and on each occasion they dared to contradict the charge by asking for proof, which only emphasised the seriousness of their wayward condition. F. C. Cook states, "To every charge a rejoinder is made, which is put into the mouth of the accused in an interrogative form, and supplies the prophet with an occasion of enforcing and explaining his rebukes to the conviction of the hearers".

Although he stresses the importance of maintaining the purity of public worship or ceremony and the distinctive character of the nation, Malachi also demands a spirit of reverence and faithfulness to God. C. F. Keil points out that "Throughout the whole book we meet with the spirit which developed itself among the Jews after the captivity, and assumed the concrete forms of Phariseeism and Saduceeism. The outward or grosser kind of idolatry had been rendered thoroughly distasteful to the people by the sufferings of exile; and its place was taken by the more refined idolatry of dead-work righteousness, and trust in the outward fulfilment of the letter of divine commandments, without any deeper confession of sin, or penitential humiliation under the word and will of God". Unlike Zechariah, who announces that the coming of Jehovah to His temple will be a time of rejoicing and comfort (Zech 2.10-12; 8.3), Malachi announces that His coming to the temple will be a time of purging and judgment (3.1-3). The reason seems to be that in the time of Malachi conditions in Judah had deteriorated and become more serious after the temple had been rebuilt.

The prophet commences by charging the people with slighting and spurning the love of Jehovah (1.2-5). He then proves that the priests insulted the honour and dignity of Jehovah's name by their contempt and profanity in offering flawed sacrifices, and in their unholy service (1.6-2.9). He charges the people with disregarding their national calling because of their mixed marriages, and with defiling the holiness of the Lord by their treachery and immorality in divorcing their Israelitish wives (2.10-17). He proclaims the coming of Jehovah as a just Judge to purify the nation and punish the wicked (3.1-7). He faces them with robbing God and with declaring that it was not beneficial to serve Jehovah since the righteous had no advantage over the wicked (3.8-15). He closes the prophecy by encouraging those who feared the Lord and by unfolding the promise of future blessing (3.16-4.6).

Thus Malachi points out their inconsistencies and their irreverence towards God; he rebukes the priests for their unholy practices, and reminds them of the holiness of God and of His claims set out in His word, which they had forgotten; he condemns the practice of divorce, the withholding of their tithes, their tolerance of evil men; and he reminds them that the faithful remnant would shine forth as the sun. It is to be noted that the prophecy begins with the love of God and ends with avoiding of the curse of God.

OUTLINE OF THE BOOK

Introduction (1.1)

The Love of Jehovah's Heart (1.2-5)
    A. The proclamation of Jehovah's love (1.2)
    B. The proof of Jehovah's love (1.2-5)

The Majesty and Dignity of Jehovah's Name (1.6-2.9)
    A. The exposure of the priests' condition (1.6-14)
        1. Irreverent (1.6)

2. Indifferent (1.7-8)
3. Covetous (1.9-11)
4. Discourteous (1.12)
5. Wearied (1.13)
6. Hypocritical (1.14)
B. The exercise of priestly service (2.1-9)
   1. The commandment (2.1-4)
     a) The responsibility of the priests (2.1-2)
     b) The result of disobedience (2.2-4)
   2. The covenant (2.5-7)
   3. The charge (2.8-9)

The Weariness of Jehovah's Spirit (2.10-17)

A. The wickedness of Judah (2.10-13)
B. The witness of Jehovah (2.14-17)
   1. The covenant of marriage (2.14)
   2. The creation of God (2.15)
   3. God's hatred of divorce (2.16)
   4. The corruption of the truth (2.17)

The Immutability of Jehovah's Ways (3.1-15)

A. The purifying power of Jehovah's presence (3.1-6)
   1. The coming of Jehovah (3.1)
   2. The purifying presence of Jehovah (3.2-4)
   3. The judgment of Jehovah (3.5-6)
B. The priority of Jehovah's claims (3.7-12)
   1. The charge against Judah (3.7-9)
   2. The promise of Jehovah (3.10-11)
   3. The response of the nations (3.12)
C. The perversity of Judah (3.13-15)
   1. Their words (3.13)
   2. Their work and walk (3.14)
   3. Their ways (3.15)

The Righteousness of Jehovah's Recompense (3.16-4.6)

A. The faithful remnant (3.16-18)
   1. Their fear (3.16)
   2. Their fellowship (3.16)
   3. Their recompense (3.17-18)
B. The fulfilment of Jehovah's purpose (4.1-3)
C. The final exhortation (4.4)
D. The future restoration (4.5-6).

MALACHI 1

The deterioration in the spiritual life of the remnant which had returned from the Babylon captivity is unfolded by the prophet Malachi. They were unresponsive to the love of Jehovah. Although He had displayed His love for them they had refused to acknowledge it and so had withheld the honour and reverence which were His due (vv.2-5). Not only did they lack reverence for the Lord, they actually despised His name by their flawed sacrifices (vv.6-14). They were ignorant of the magnitude of their departure from the word of Jehovah. They were lacking in spiritual discernment and thus, when their departure was pointed out, they saw no harm in it. Their attitude to the claims of the Lord is highlighted by the repetition of the word "Wherein".

Verse 1: Introduction

The expression "The burden of the word of the Lord" indicates that the prophecy was from Jehovah and also the seriousness of it. "Burden" (MASSA - 4853) generally signifies a burden or weight although some have taken a figurative meaning of utterance or oracle. It is never used before announcements of joy or deliverance, but is used of a weight to be carried (2 Kings 5.17). When used in prophetic passages it proclaims heavy judgment upon wickedness (Is 15.1) and the solemn consequences of departure from God (Hab 1.1). Here it indicates that the prophecy unfolds the dreadful departure of the returned remnant from the word of Jehovah and the consequences of this departure. It also indicates that the message was, in general, one of rebuke rather than of encouragement. The prophet felt the weight of responsibility in being the messenger of Jehovah to make known to the people such a message. His ministry was not palatable and was not easy to give, but it was necessary for the people.

Sometimes it would be far easier today for those who teach the Scriptures to give the saints what is palatable rather than to be faithful. However, faithful men with a burdened spirit are often compelled to give what is needful and challenging in order to stem the tide of declension and to produce, in the saints, something for God. The purpose of all ministry should be to develop Christlike character in the people of God. It is important for those who minister the word of God to feel the weight of divine truth in their own souls first and then faithfully to convey that truth to the saints.

The expression "to Israel" or, as some translate, "against Israel" indicates that the returned remnant represents the whole of the nation. It could be that there were individuals from each of the ten tribes among those of the kingdom of Judah that returned from the Babylonian captivity. It is clear from both Ezra 1.3; 2.2 and Nehemiah 1.6; 2.10 that the returned remnant were viewed as Israel as a whole. After the division of Israel in the reign of Rehoboam it seems that the kingdom of Judah became a representative of the whole nation for there were still some of Israel that remained in the cities of Judah (1 Kings 12.17; 2 Chr 10.17). It is also significant that the priests and Levites in the territory of the kingdom of Israel left for Judah and Jerusalem, and those out of the tribes who set their hearts to seek the Lord came to Jerusalem to sacrifice (2 Chr 11.13-16). Also, on occasions the princes of Judah were called princes of Israel (2 Chr 12.6; 21.4) and both Jehoshaphat and Ahaz, kings of Judah, were called king of Israel (2 Chr 21.2; 28.19; also cp. 2 Chr 12.1; 24.5-6,16).

Verses 2-5: The Love of Jehovah's Heart
This last book of the Old Testament commences with the wonderful theme of Jehovah's love for His people. It reiterates the persistence of His love in spite of Israel's departure from Him and His word. The love of God is unchanging and is not dependent upon the state of His people. It is significant that Jehovah declares His love for them before He rebukes them for their sinful ways and departure. This opening section is both an introduction and the foundation of the rest of the prophecy. Everything that follows must be viewed in the light of the love of Jehovah. The love that He had shown to Israel should have been the motive and example for their attitude and activity toward Him. In this section the ministry is general in character and is addressed to all Israel. The emphasis here is upon the love of Jehovah's heart. They had slighted the love of the Lord. They had spurned His love by their challenge, "Wherein hast thou loved us?" (v.2). His love was unmistakable, and there was a time when they had responded to that love (Jer 2.1-4), but now things were different. Has this no voice for believers today? Has the love of Christians waned? Are they slighting His love by the way that they live? Is this true of assemblies today? Have they left their first love (Rev 2.4)?

The proclamation of Jehovah's love (v.2)
Many take the reference to Jacob and Esau as indicating their posterity and, in the light of vv.3-4, this seems to be the case. However, there is also a historical reference to the book of Genesis where one sees God moving out from Himself in ways characterised by absolute sovereignty in His choice of the nation of Israel. The Lord loved Israel and was faithful to His covenant with the people of Israel, not because of what they were, but in spite of what they were - "The Lord did not set his love upon you, nor choose you, because ye were more in number than any people; for ye were the fewest of all people: But because the Lord loved you...Know therefore that the Lord thy God, he is God, the faithful God" (Deut 7.7-9). Is this not true of believers today? Christians must remember that God loved them before they loved Him and the Lord Jesus gave Himself for them to make them His own - "Herein is love, not that we loved God, but that he loved us, and sent his Son to be the propitiation for our sins" (1 Jn 4.10); "We love him, because he first loved us" (1 Jn 4.19). The love of God

is not capricious or arbitrary and does not set aside man's responsibility to Him.

How wonderful is this measureless love for unworthy Jacob. The compassion and tenderness of Jehovah were seen in the declaration of His love and were intended to touch the hearts of His people. The love of Jehovah here is shown in the contrast between the devastation of Edom and Israel's ultimate blessing. How incredible that such love should be challenged - "Wherein hast thou loved us?". The immeasurable love of Jehovah was unchanging despite Israel's waywardness, and thus their disdainful challenge stands in stark contrast to His compassionate love. This demonstrated the true condition of the people and revealed their lack of love for Him. In fact their insensibility to that love and their failure to respond to it was the root of their own wickedness and rebellious spirit.

Was their scepticism the result of their own reasoning? Human reasoning has no place in living for God. The word of God alone must direct and control the life of the child of God. Were they looking for material prosperity and worldly glory as a proof of His love? Having had prosperity taken from them, were they implying that they now had no evidence of Jehovah's love for them? They had forgotten what He had done for them, and were living for self and material things. There is a danger of believers today being so taken up with the things of this life that they forget all that God has done for them and fail to respond to His love for them. It is easy for saints to lose an appreciation of the love of Christ by living for self and then question His love when things go wrong. God's love is often least acknowledged where it is most manifested.

Were God's people thinking of their past greatness and their present insignificance and thus questioning the reality of Jehovah's love? Had they forgotten that their circumstances now were the result of their departure and infidelity for which Jehovah had chastised them? Instead of attributing their sufferings to the correct cause, sin in general or their own sin in particular, men accuse Jehovah of indifference and lack of love. Israel should have known that the chastening of the Lord was in itself a proof of His love for them - "My son, despise not the chastening of the Lord; neither be weary of his correction: For whom the Lord loveth he correcteth" (Prov 3.11-12; Heb 12.5-6; cp. Job 5.17-18). One must not imply that the afflictions and trials of life are evidence that God does not love. Christians are not to despise the chastening of the Lord but are to endure it, for it is to their profit that they might be partakers of His holiness and that it might yield the peaceable fruit of righteousness (Heb 12.5-11). Believers often question the love of God because of adverse circumstances, trials, and adversity. It is good to remind one's self that nothing can separate the Christian from the love of Christ (Rom 8.35-39) or annul His promise, "I will never leave thee, not forsake thee" (Heb 13.5). The love of Christ should be the driving force in every Christian's life - "For the love of Christ constraineth us; because we thus judge, that if one died for all, then were all dead: And that he died for all, that they which live should not henceforth live unto themselves, but unto him which died for them, and rose again" (2 Cor 5.14-15).

The proof of Jehovah's love (vv.2-5)

In answer to their ungodly and impudent question Jehovah, with amazing patience, repeats the fact of His love for Jacob in contrast to His hatred of Esau. Thus the love of Jacob is set against the hatred of Esau. Some commentators have taken the word "hated" (SANE - 8130) as being relative, i.e. not loving in the same degree (see F. C. Cook and Jamieson, Fausset & Brown). However, generally it is used as being opposite in meaning to the word translated "love", indicating a loathing or detesting, and this is how it is used here. God waited until Esau and his descendants showed what they were before making the statement, "I hated Esau". It is important to note that the statement quoted in Romans 9.13 is taken from here and not the book of Genesis. There is no thought here of rejection before birth for that is never taught in the Scriptures. The absolute sovereignty of God is never employed in this way. The first book of the Old Testament unfolds the sovereign choice of Jacob as to the nation of Israel while the last book unfolds the hatred of Jehovah towards Esau and the nation that springs from him. The underlying cause of Esau's enmity against Jacob was his profanity, shown in his despising of the birthright. He sold his birthright to gratify self and for passing pleasure (Gen 25.29-34). One must remember that the flesh always gratifies self. This enmity was carried through to his posterity and was manifested in Edom's refusal to give Israel passage through its border (Num 20.14-21). It was continuous (Ezek 35.5) and expressed in anger, violence, and rejoicing over Israel's calamities (Ps 137.7; Amos 1.11). The primary reference here is to the posterity of Jacob and Esau. S. R. Driver writes that "The reference is to Jacob and Esau, not as individuals, but as representatives of the nations descended from them; in fact, it is the nations whom the prophet has really in his mind (cp. Amos 1.11 and Obadiah v.10 where the nation Edom, is called Israel's brother, and Obadiah v.6 where Esau stands for Edom, just as Jacob often in poetry stands for Israel)". One notes the change from "Esau" to "Edom" in v.4, and this in turn identifies with Esau's request for the red pottage. Its use is really an expression of Esau's character as well as a reference to his posterity. He was so completely identified with the flesh (self) that it becomes his name - materialistic, profane, rebellious. In the opposition of Edom to Israel one sees a picture of the opposition of the flesh to spiritual progress - "For the flesh lusteth against the Spirit, and the Spirit against the flesh" (Gal 5.17). Thus believers experience conflict within and should be aware that the flesh will grasp every opportunity to hinder spiritual development. Christians must not make any "provision for the flesh, to fulfil the lusts thereof" (Rom 13.14). They are no longer debtors to live after the flesh (Rom 8.12), but have been brought into liberty. However, one must not use that liberty for an occasion to the flesh (Gal 5.13). The flesh will always rebel against the purpose of God and has no place in the things of God.

The expression "his mountains and his heritage" refers to Mount Seir and the surrounding territory given to Esau for an inheritance (Deut 2.4-5; Josh 24.4). "Waste" (SHᵉMAMA - 8077) means desolation, and indicates a land uninhabited rather than a land uninhabitable. It is disputed as to when this desolation took place. According to C. L. Feinberg, "Some understand the reference to be to the conquest of Edom by the Nabateans; others, the wars between the Persians and Egypt; and still others, the desolation by the Babylonians. The Chaldeans had invaded their country five years after the destruction of Jerusalem in 586 BC". However, the context would suggest that the reference is to the invading armies of Nebuchadnezzar in the same period as when Judah was taken into captivity (cp. Jer 25.9,21).

The phrase "We are impoverished" indicates that the land of Edom (Idumea) was still desolate in Malachi's day in contrast to the land of Israel. Thus the contrast between the statements "I loved Jacob" and "I hated Esau" is emphasised by the restoration of Israel (represented by the remnant) to its land and the continued desolation of Idumea. Even the rebuilding of the temple in Jerusalem, under the protection of Jehovah, was an evidence of His love for them. The prophet's appeal to this disaster for Edom as a proof of Jehovah's love was intended to produce a response in the hearts of His people. The emptying of the land of the Edomites was to make it a place for the dragons (or jackals). The Septuagint translates "dragons of the wilderness" as "dwellings of the wilderness". However, the word rendered "dragons" (TANNAH - 8568) does not contain the idea of a dwelling place. Strong in his concordance states that the word is probably the feminine of the Hebrew word TAN (8565) and adds, "a female jackal". Whatever be the meaning of the word TANNAH, it is clear that the land of Edom had become the dwelling place of some wild animal which is identified here by Malachi as an indication of Jehovah's hatred of Esau.

The statement "we will return and build the desolate places" implies the insolence of the Edomites and their determination to establish themselves again in rebellion against God, and in opposition to Israel. The title "the Lord of hosts" is a Jehovah title (Jehovah Sabaoth) which first occurs in 1 Samuel 1.3 and is found over 200 times in the Old Testament. It is found 24 times in this short prophecy and indicates Jehovah's majesty and glory as the Sovereign over all the hosts of heaven and earth. As the Sovereign over all He has righteously determined that Edom will never recover its former glory. Edom may seek to rebuild the ruined places, but He would tear down what they succeeded to build. C. F. Keil states, "The threat in v.4, that if Edom attempts to rebuild its ruins, the Lord will again destroy that which is built, is equivalent to a declaration that Edom will never recover its former prosperity and power". The expression "They shall build" indicates that Edom, in its pride, did return to build again the desolate places, returning to its profanity and wickedness. However, the apellation "The people against whom the Lord hath indignation for ever" envisages the complete and perpetual desolation of Edom because of the intense anger of Jehovah.

The word "border" (G^eBUL - 1366) has the thought of territory here and in v.5. The land of Edom would be called the territory of wickedness, indicating that the desolation was because of its wickedness. The complete fulfilment of these verses, as well as those of Jeremiah 49.7-22; Amos 1.11-12; and Obadiah, belongs to a future day when Israel's glorious King will appear (Is 34; 63.1-6). God will deal with Edom in a coming day when He will use Israel as His instrument of judgment (Is 11.13-14; Ezek 25.12-14). Thus Israel will see the ineffectual attempts of Edom to recover. In this judgment one can see the solemn principle: "...as thou has done, it shall be done unto thee: thy reward shall return upon thine own head" (Obad v.15). Does not this remind one of "whatsoever a man soweth, that shall he also reap" (Gal 6.7)? The establishing of Israel in their land will make her the centre from which the glory of God will radiate throughout the earth.

The greatness of Jehovah will be manifested in His acts of grace and power. There is a wonderful future for Israel. In the light of this glorious prospect well might one ponder how Israel could have slighted the love of Jehovah and acted in complete disregard of His claims. The coldness of their hearts was the reason for this. Christians too can be guilty of coldness of heart toward God in spite of His unmistakable love for them and the glorious future that awaits them. May each believer challenge his/her heart in regard to these solemn things.

Verses 1.6-2.9: The Majesty and Dignity of Jehovah's Name

In this second section Malachi's ministry is addressed to the priestly family, but it also applies to the whole nation. The emphasis is on the dignity of Jehovah's name, reference to which occurs repeatedly in the section. They had insulted the majesty and dignity of His name yet asked, "Wherein have we despised thy name?" (v.6). The priests who had the privilege of entering into the sanctuary should have known the majesty of His name and the reverential fear of which He was worthy. However, they had such low thoughts of the Lord and His dwelling place that anything was suitable to bring to Him. Is this not a challenge for today? Is there not a lack of reverence and are there not low thoughts in regard to the place where God dwells, the local assembly - "Know ye not that ye are the temple of God, and that the Spirit of God dwelleth in you?" (1 Cor 3.16)? What appreciation is there in us of the majesty of His name and of the reverential fear of which He is worthy?

The priests were responsible for the moral and spiritual life of the nation. There is a historical reference here to Exodus 32 and the distinctive blessing pronounced upon the tribe of Levi (2.4-6) because of their obedience (Deut 10.8-9). In Malachi 2 the prophet reminds these priests of the covenant of Jehovah originally made with Levi. In this covenant they were given the blessings of life and peace, the enjoyment of which gave them a place in the sanctuary and priestly dignity. The clear teaching of the New Testament is that every believer in Christ is a priest to God because of the value of the work of redemption wrought by the Lord Jesus Christ for us upon the cross, and the Holy Spirit's work of regeneration in us. "Levi" means "Joined" and reminds us of our union with Christ - joined (1 Cor 6.17) with the risen, ascended, glorified Christ in the new creation where we have been brought into perfect harmony with all that God is in the infinite holiness of His Person (cp. 2 Cor 5.17). Joined to Christ, we have the blessings of life and peace, and priestly dignity to move in the sanctuary. However, the message to the priests here reveals the possibility of being priests in title and office, yet not being priestly in character and activity. Here the priests, who entered the sanctuary, should have known the majesty of His name and the reverence and honour of which He was worthy, yet their thoughts of Him were so low that they considered anything would do for Jehovah. Have we lost an appreciation of the holiness of God and of the greatness and grandeur of His Person?

The exposure of the priests' condition (vv.6-14)

How did Israel respond to the love of Jehovah? The rebuke to the priests because of their dishonour and irreverence for Jehovah in the blemished and inferior sacrifices they offered revealed Israel's response. These verses show the awful condition to which these priests had sunk. Instead of meeting their responsibility they were marked by moral and spiritual degradation. They were irreverent (v.6), indifferent (vv.7-8), covetous (vv.9-11), discourteous (v.12), wearied (v.13), and hypocritical (v.14).

Irreverent (v.6)

The priests were those who had been chosen to stand before Jehovah, offer sacrifices to Him, and instruct the people. They were to conduct themselves as those who moved in the presence of Jehovah and only an appreciation of their relationship to Him would safeguard them from becoming casual in His presence and service. The priests had been consecrated to the service of Jehovah and were responsible before Him for the condition of His people. In fact their condition would be reflected in the people. This solemn principle is evident in Paul's exhortation to the Ephesian elders: "Take heed therefore unto yourselves, and to all the flock" (Acts 20.28). What a solemn responsibility rests upon the shoulders of those who take the lead amongst the people of God. How important it is for them to conduct themselves in keeping with the claims and character of God.

The prophet turns from Jehovah's love for them to their relationship with Him. He commences with two principles of relationship to which Israel could not object. These two principles should have governed the attitude of both the priests and the people of Israel. What was applicable to the one was applicable to the other, and the response of the priests would be the response of the people. The relationship of a son to a father and that of a servant to a master are simply stated as truths that no one would question. Both these relationships are used of Jehovah and Israel and would be admitted without contradiction. In the song of Moses Jehovah is called the Father of Israel: "Is not he thy father that hath bought thee? hath he not made thee, and established thee?" (Deut 32.6), and earlier Israel is called His son: "Israel is my son, even my firstborn" (Ex 4.22). The prophets also mention this relationship, and thus Isaiah states, "Thou, O Lord, art our father, our redeemer" (Is 63.16), and Jeremiah pens the words of Jehovah, "For I am a father to Israel, and Ephraim is my firstborn" (Jer 31.9). As the Lord God of Israel (Lk 1.68) He was their Sovereign Master and they were His servants: "For unto me the children of Israel are servants; they are my servants whom I brought forth out of the land of Egypt: I am the Lord your God" (Lev 25.55 – the last phrase occurring frequently in the Old Testament). Since He is a Father, the honour a son owes his father was due to Him, and since He is a Lord (or Master), the fear the servant owes to his master was also due to Him. The two questions addressed to the priests in v.6 clearly indicate that Jehovah had not received the honour and reverential fear that belonged to Him. The solemnity and seriousness of these questions are evident by the title Lord of hosts. There was a complete lack of devotion and obedience on their part. Christians today must challenge themselves as to their attitude of heart to God who is their Father and Lord.

The idea in the word "honour" (KABOD – 3519) is that of deserving respect and obedience. It means to highly esteem and is manifested in practical allegiance and willing obedience. It goes beyond lip service, demanding a character and conduct in keeping with the character of God (cp. Is 29.13). Are Christians today guilty of honouring God with their lips and yet marked by disobedience to His word and carelessness in the things of God? The Christian's appreciation of God is reflected in loyalty to Him and in the measure of unhesitating obedience to His word. It is so easy to claim to love God and yet display an indifference to His word. Where there is a genuine love for the Lord it will be displayed in one's life: "If a man love me, he will keep my words" (Jn 14.23; cp. 2 Jn v.6).

"Fear" (MORA – 4172) has the thought here of reverential fear. It is the controlling motive which prevents the servant from displeasing the master. However, the priests had forgotten the greatness of Jehovah and that He was their Sovereign Lord and Master, and so failed to reverence Him. Thus they became lax and careless. Are believers today guilty of familiarity and carelessness in their approach to God? Have they forgotten the greatness and holiness of His Person - "holy and reverend is his name" (Ps 111.9)?

Casualness is altogether out of place in His presence and in His service. Reverential fear for God shrinks from anything that would dishonour Him, and will cause Christians to be careful that they act in keeping with the character of God. It will result in a constant watchfulness in what they do, say, and think. This fear is not a terror of God, but a fear of displeasing or dishonouring or misrepresenting Him. Believers are to enthrone Christ as Lord in their hearts as the One to whom they owe fidelity, loyalty and devotion (1 Pet 3.15). Where there is reverence for God there will be holiness of life and faithfulness to His word (cp. Prov 8.13; 15.33).

The application is made forcibly to the priests who ought to have been leaders in holiness, devotion, and obedience. However, instead of being leaders in piety and submission to Jehovah they were foremost in despising His name. David West explains that "The reason for Israel's condition was to be found in the declension of those who should have been their spiritual leaders. They had failed to teach the character and claims of God and this was largely the reason for the deplorable condition of the nation". Their carelessness and irreverence were really a despising of the majesty and dignity of His name. Christians must remember that their actions and attitude are indicative of their appreciation, or lack of appreciation, of the greatness and glory of God. The word "despise" (BAZA - 959) means to despise, disdain, or hold in contempt. Not only were these priests dishonouring the name of Jehovah, but they seemed to be ignorant of that fact. They were unaware of the gravity of their behaviour and thus they ask, "Wherein have we despised thy name?". With declension comes a lack of spiritual perception and sensitivity to the claims of God. How easy it is to maintain an outward form without realising that there has been a loss of spiritual perception and power.

Indifferent (vv. 7-8)

Verse 7 is not an answer to the priests' question in v.6, but rather an explanation of the charge made against them. The proof that these priests despised the Lord's name was in the kind of sacrifices they offered. Contempt for Jehovah's appointed sacrifices implied contempt for Him. The word "bread" is used to describe the offerings as food of God (Lev 3.11; 21.6). The gravity of the priests' sin was in the laxity and neglect of their duties in the rebuilt temple. "Polluted" (GAAL - 1351) refers here to ceremonial defilement, and so the expression "polluted bread" alludes to blemished sacrifices (Deut 15.21). They had no respect for the word of Jehovah because, despite the clear teaching of Leviticus 22.22 and other passages, they thought anything would do for Him. They were indifferent to the claims of Jehovah so they had low thoughts of Him, and thus they replaced His word with their own ideas and opinions. Is there not a danger of introducing the ideas of men into the gatherings of the Lord's people, thus setting aside the teaching of the Holy Scriptures? Is there not a philosophy of casualness and lightness in the things of God today? One can allow the spirit of indifference which is in the world to affect one's spiritual exercises. What is brought to God must be in keeping with His word and suited to the greatness of His Person. As one moves in the sanctuary of the presence of God one must do so with reverence and with an appreciation of His glorious Person.

Again the priests are prepared to challenge Jehovah by asking, "Wherein have we polluted thee?". They had lost all sense of what was acceptable to Jehovah. Were these priests seeking to justify themselves in implying that whatever was offered to Jehovah did not really affect Him? They saw no evil in what they were doing. However, what was offered on the altar was a reflection of their estimation of Jehovah and their attitude to Him. Their lack of appreciation and insensibility were borne out by the phrase "In that ye say, The table of the Lord is contemptible". This expression and v.8 give the answer to their haughty questions. The word "contemptible" is translated "despise" and "despised" in v.6. In this passage the altar and the table of the Lord are the same - it is called the altar as a place of sacrifice and it is called the table of the Lord as a place where He receives satisfaction. Although the priests may not have used these actual words, they are clearly indicated by their contempt in placing little or no value on what was for Jehovah. They treated the altar as common in spite of its being designated most holy (Ex 29.37; 40.10). Their disobedience to the word of Jehovah declared their contempt for Him. How solemn to know that to undervalue the things of God and deliberately disobey His word is showing contempt for Him. Well might the saints today challenge their hearts about these things.

The kind of offerings mentioned in v.8 could well be indicative of the condition of the priests and the people of Israel.

The blind. They had no spiritual perception because they were not illuminated by the word of Jehovah. There was no appreciation of the majesty and greatness of Jehovah and no insight into the truth of Jehovah. What about Christians? Is there a lack of spiritual perception today? Are believers lacking in their appreciation of the greatness and grandeur of God? Have saints failed to allow the word of God to illuminate their minds. Is there a lack of understanding of the word of God?

The lame. They were unbalanced in their perception because of being spiritually blind to the truth of God and thus being uneven in their walk. There was no uprightness or honesty in their lives. They were living contrary to their position as priests. Is this not a challenge to believers today? So many who claim to belong to Christ live contrary to the teaching of the word of God.

The sick. There was no spiritual health and no vigour in the things of Jehovah. How easy it is for saints today to be apathetic in the things of God. Lack of diligence in the truth of God results in an unhealthy spiritual condition. One needs the wholesome instruction of the word of God for spiritual health and strength.

The repetition of the expression "is it not evil", which has been rendered "it is no evil" (eg. ASV, RV), seems to be an irony, i.e. there is no evil or harm in your opinion, it is quite good enough for such a purpose. Their conscience had become so dulled that they were no longer governed by the word of Jehovah. Thus they saw no wrong in violating the teaching of Holy Scripture. How true this is in the day in which we live! Moral standards are lowered, even by believers, to conform to those of the world. Divine principles are ignored and violated. Service for God is carried out in unscriptural ways. The three kinds of sacrifices mentioned here are a violation of Deuteronomy 15.21 (cp. Lev 22.20; Deut 17.1).

They would not dare to offer to their governor what they had the boldness to offer to Jehovah. This indicated that they had more consideration for their human governor than their Divine Sovereign. If their human governor would not accept such offerings how would Jehovah, their God, Lord over all, accept them? Malachi is referring here to the sacrifices, not only of the priests, but also those sacrifices of the people offered by the priests to their Lord God which would have been rejected by their human ruler. It has been stated that the expression "will he be pleased with thee" should be rendered "will he be pleased with it", referring to the offering rather than the offerer. The word for "be pleased with" (RASA - 7521) is the same as that translated "accept" in vv.10 and 13 and has the thought of being favourably received. In the light of this and the following expression, "accept thy person", it seems that the offering is in view here. The inevitable answer to Malachi's question was, "No". The prophet was saying that what they knew would not be acceptable, or even respectful, to their governor they were offering to Jehovah.

One knows how to apply this. One would never be half-hearted in one's own things, in one's business or secular life, yet very often there is half-heartedness in spiritual things. Formal or half-hearted service or worship is disrespectful to God. He demands, and is worthy of, our best. "Accept" (NASA - 5375) has the idea of "lift up thy face", which is a Hebrew figure for receiving favourably, or regarding with favour. Again the answer to the question was, "No". How can one expect the Lord to regard one with favour if there is but formal or half-hearted service or worship? How do Christians measure up to the solemn challenge of these verses?

Covetous (vv.9-11)

They had no love for the sanctuary and no appreciation of the dignity of being engaged in the service of Jehovah. There are two ways of looking at the opening of v.9, "And now, I pray you, beseech God that he will be gracious unto us".

1. As a note of irony. You offer sacrifices, intercede for the people, and proclaim the priestly blessing, but what value is there in such activity in light of your disrespectful behaviour? How can you beseech God? Do you

think that God would take heed of your petition to be gracious because of your polluted and flawed sacrifices offered to Him?

2. As a rebuke or challenge exposing the condition of the priests. The fact that their governor would not receive such offerings (v.8) leads to the conclusion here that God would not hear the petitions of the priests for Him to be gracious to the people. This conclusion is high-lighted by the challenge to supplicate the face of God for compassion towards the nation.

The implication that their petition would be ignored is in the question, "Will he regard your person?". One notes that the prophet changes from the name Jehovah (the Lord) to the name El (God) which is singular and indicates that He is the mighty One. This is to strengthen the contrast with their governor. You would not treat your governor in this way; how then do you expect God, the Judge of all the earth, to favour you? The fact that the Lord of hosts (Jehovah Sabaoth) asks the question further emphasises the contrast. There does not seem to be here an appeal to the priests to repent and to cry to God for pardon that some suggest is in the passage. Rather, the emphasis seems to be on the contrast between their governor and God. If the governor would not receive their worthless offerings graciously, how could they, having offered flawed sacrifices, expect a gracious answer to their prayers from God. The priests, who ought to have instructed the people in right ways, had acted disgracefully and offered contemptible sacrifices. How could they be suitable channels of blessing or worthy intercessors? Their ministry had become merely an outward form with no benefit to the people. How important it is to appreciate that one's personal condition before God is reflected in one's service for Him. There is a tendency among many saints to think that serving God is the most vital thing in the christian life. Service is important, but the most important thing is holiness and personal enjoyment of communion with God. Only when the life is right before God will service for Him be acceptable to Him and bring Him pleasure and glory.

The expression "by your means" is literally "from your hands", indicating that such reprehensible offerings proceeded from the priests. It was more the sin of the priests than the sin of the people. Although there is no appeal to the priests to repent they needed to do so and to seek the face of God for forgiveness. Failure to do so would mean they would continue to be disregarded. God would not show favour to anyone on their account if they continued as they were, disregarding His name. Their prayers could never avail while they continued to offer such sacrifices. Malachi placed the blame wholly upon their shoulders. Christians need to remember that sin in the life of the believer breaks the enjoyment of communion with God and this affects their service for Him – "If I regard iniquity in my heart, the Lord will not hear me" (Ps 66.18). How good to know that "If we confess our sins, he is faithful and just to forgive us our sins, and to cleanse us from all unrighteousness" (1 Jn 1.9).

The meaning of v.10 is disputed. C. L. Feinberg points out that "There are those who believe that the priests were so greedy and covetous that they demanded a price for the smallest exertion, even of the closing of doors. Others think the priests were so lazy and careless that they might not close the Temple doors at the right time. The best explanation is that, since the worship was outward and insincere, God would rather it ceased (see Is 1.11-15.) It is better to have no sacrifices, than vain ones. The Lord had no pleasure in priests or sacrifices". The suggestion that the priests were so lazy that they might not close the doors at the right time is most unlikely and does not suit the context. The RV renders the opening part of the verse as: "Oh that there were one among you that would shut the doors, that ye might not kindle fire on mine altar in vain". The doors mentioned would be the doors into the inner court where the altar of burnt offering was. This rendering suggests that Jehovah was expressing that it would be far better to close the doors on the priests so that their empty ritual and contemptible sacrifices might cease. The wish is expressed ironically in keeping with the previous verse. The RV expression "in vain" implies being without any use or object indicating that Jehovah had no pleasure in either the priests or the sacrifices offered. Jamieson, Fausset & Brown states, "Better no sacrifices than vain ones (Is 1.11-15). It was the duty of some of the priests to stand at the doors of the court of the altar of burnt offerings, and to have excluded blemished victims". Although most commentators accept the RV rendering and its implications, which seem to be in keeping with the context, there is no need to set aside the AV translation. The Hebrew word translated "vain" in the RV and "nought" in the AV (HINNAM – 2600) means for nothing or, as another has put it, gratis. This is just as suitable to the AV translation which continues the exposure of the priests. The opening statement would then be a rebuke of the contempt, negligence, and covetousness of the priests. As H. A. Ironside explains, "Covetousness was the root-sin that was leading them daily farther astray. The priests would not so much as shut the temple doors save for wages, nor kindle the altar-fire except for gain. True love for Himself was lacking, and their holy office had been prostituted to a mere worldly profession, and used as a means of enrichment".

The statement "neither do ye kindle fire on mine altar for nought" reveals that they were materialistic and so covetous that even their privileged duties in the sanctuary were looked upon as a means of gain. Instead of appreciating the dignity and privilege bestowed upon them, and finding deep pleasure in priestly service for the glory of Jehovah, they were only concerned about their material benefit (cp. 1 Sam 2.13-16). How dreadful covetousness is and how solemn to see that materialism can even enter into activities that one would call spiritual. Surely one can draw attention to similar conditions that prevail today among those who claim to be children of God. Is it not true that materialism and worldliness are prominent features in many believers and that godliness and spiritual desires are little sought after? Even among those who claim to be gathered to the name of the Lord Jesus Christ the evil principles of covetousness, worldliness, and self-will have infiltrated. The carelessness and apathy of the world to the things of God have insidiously crept into the lives of many believers. One needs to take heed to the exhortations: "Watch ye, stand fast in the faith, quit you like men, be strong" (1 Cor 16.13), and "watch and be sober" (1 Thess 5.6). "But godliness with contentment is great gain. For we brought nothing into this world, and it is certain we can carry nothing out" (1 Tim 6.6-7). Jehovah found no pleasure in the priests and had no regard for their offerings because, in spite all their activities, there was nothing for Him. How sad to be engaged in service for God and yet produce nothing for Him, bring no pleasure to Him, and have no commendation from Him. Whatsoever a believer does should be done "heartily, as to the Lord, and not unto men" (Col 3.23) – "be ye steadfast, unmoveable, always abounding in the work of the Lord, forasmuch as ye know that your labour is not in vain in the Lord" (1 Cor 15.58). The believer's ambition should be to please God (2 Cor 5.9; 2 Tim 2.4).

The opening "For" of v.11 indicates the reason for Jehovah's rejection of the priests and their offerings in v.10. The reason is that His name will be magnified and He will receive pure offerings. The suggestion that Jehovah was then being honoured among the Gentiles by their heathen sacrifices in contrast to the dishonour brought to Him by Israel's sacrifices is untenable (see S. R. Driver; for contrast see also Keil & Delitzsch). It is evident from the verse that the future is in view in contrast to the covetousness and contempt of the priests and people of Malachi's day. C. L. Feinberg writes, "There is no reference here that God regards the worship of the heathen as pure worship of Him, nor that the prophet is speaking of conditions in Malachi's own day (for which some writers contend), but of the future time". There is a clear prediction here of the Gentiles exalting His name and worshipping God in a pure way that is acceptable to Him. Some suggest that this verse has in view the rejection of Israel and the bringing in of the Gentiles which is being fulfilled in this present day of grace. There may be a sense in which part of the verse is true today, but the whole verse is really prophetic, looking on to millennial times. It surely points forward to the future day when the Lord will be the object of universal praise and worship.

The phrase "from the rising of the sun even unto the going down of the same" indicates that Jehovah will be worshipped over all the earth. The prophetic Scriptures speak much of that coming day of the "restitution of all things" (Acts 3.21). In that day many nations will be joined to the Lord and shall be His people (Zech 2.11). His glory shall be declared among the nations (Is 66.19), and He will bring peace to the world and be exalted in the earth (Ps 46.9-11). The House of the Lord will be established and exalted in Jerusalem, and all nations will flow into it (Is 2.1-2; Micah 4.1-2). The name of Jehovah will be great among the Gentiles when they have

witnessed His awesome power and wondrous works as well as hearing of
His grace proclaimed by His people. Zephaniah 3.8-9 speaks of the
awesome judgment of God upon the nations and the resulting conversion
of a remnant among them (Rev 7.9-17; Mt 25.32-46). One is not minimizing
the effect of the message of the gospel proclaimed at that time. Having
learned of the righteousness of God through His judgment the saved
Gentiles will magnify His name and worship Him. Not only will they worship
Him, but they will serve Him with oneness of heart. Verse 11 looks on to
the Messianic Kingdom when the Lord Jesus Christ will reign supreme.
Then shall His name be honoured and His word obeyed throughout the
world and all nations will partake of His bounty. The expression "pure
offering" is taken by the Roman Catholic Church to justify the Mass. It is
based upon the word translated "offering" (MINHA - 4503) which is taken
to mean meal-offering and thus, they say, it is prophetic of the Mass or
Eucharistic offering. However MINHA is used in vv.10 and 13 of sacrifices
in general, including animal sacrifices, and must be viewed in that way in
this verse. Thus there is no basis upon which the doctrine of the Mass can
be justified. It has also been seen that this verse looks on to millennial
days and thus there can be no way to justify from this verse the practice of
the Mass. The mention of incense and a pure offering is to emphasise that
all will be in keeping with the character and claims of God in contrast to
the flawed sacrifices being offered by the priests of Malachi's day. Saints
today ought to consider the greatness of their God and appreciate the
privilege they have of magnifying the name of the Lord in their lives. They
should own His Lordship, not only in profession, but also practically in
their lives and continually offer the praise of their hearts and lips.

Discourteous (v.12)
    This verse is almost a repetition of v.7, but the rebuke here is to contrast
the attitude of the priests with the attitude of the nations when Jehovah
manifests His power and the greatness of His name. The Gentiles will act
in keeping with the character and claims of Jehovah, but these priests,
who claimed to be priests of Jehovah, were acting contrary to the dignity
that they claimed. They were insensitive to the greatness and holiness of
Jehovah. Instead of honouring His name they profaned it. "Profaned"
(HALAL – 2490) has the thought here of defilement by doing violence to
the law of Jehovah, i.e. bringing flawed animals to sacrifice on the altar of
burnt offering. The tense indicates that they were continually doing so. In
v.7 they offered polluted bread upon the altar, here it is the table (altar) of
Jehovah itself that is polluted. As in v.7 it is ceremonial pollution because
imperfect animals were sacrificed upon it. It is not that the priests were
literally saying, "The table of the Lord is polluted", but that they were
expressing it by their actions. The expression "the fruit thereof, even his
meat, is contemptible" also refers to the sacrifices offered. The Hebrew
word for "fruit" (NIB – 5108) only occurs elsewhere in Isaiah 57.19 and

means produce or income. Thus the produce of the table of Jehovah was the sacrifices offered upon it, which are also called food or bread (v.7). This can be looked at in two ways.

1. Their portion. Those parts of the sacrifices prescribed by God for them (Lev 6.16-18, 26-30; 7.6-7, 14-21) were despised. They treated with contempt their portion of the blemished sacrifices with no thought of the dishonour they were bringing to Jehovah. Did these priests consider that they deserved better than what they were offering to Him? Were they despising the means Jehovah had provided for their welfare and nourishment? How discourteous of priests to act in this way. This does not seem likely since the priests themselves accepted the blemished animals for sacrifices. If such animals were too bad for food in their estimation then they would not have accepted them. However, it is possible for believers to be marked by this kind of inconsistency. God has provided food in His word for the minds and hearts of the saints. That food is linked with the altar for it is His own blessed Son. God intends Christians to feed upon Christ as He is presented in the word of God. This food is for the spiritual well-being and nourishment of believers so that they might be spiritually healthy and spiritually strong, yet they can be guilty of treating that provision with contempt by worldly and materialistic ways.

2. God's portion. The priests considered the altar of the Lord to be common, not sacred in any way. They had no concern for the precepts of Jehovah and thus treated them with contempt. They considered that they could do just as they liked and so ignored what Jehovah had instituted. They were not prepared to offer the sacrifices in keeping with the Holy Scriptures, but brought flawed sacrifices which marred the holiness of the altar and dishonoured Him. How like the world today and, sadly, how like some who claim to be Christians. What are Christians bringing to God today? What are they prepared to lay upon the altar for God? Are all the people of God today prepared to place themselves upon the altar as living sacrifices for His pleasure and glory (Rom 12.1-2), or do many of them consider that anything will do for God? One must remember that the conduct of the believer should be in keeping with the word of God – "that ye henceforth walk not as other Gentiles walk, in the vanity of their mind" (Eph 4.17); "See then that ye walk circumspectly, not as fools, but as wise, Redeeming the time, because the days are evil" (Eph 5.15-16). It is inconsistent to claim to be a child of God and at the same time ignore the teaching of the word of God.

Wearied (v.13)
The priests added to their sin by complaining about the service of Jehovah. The word translated "Behold" (HINNEH – 2009) is an interjection that demands attention. Here it draws the mind to the dreadful attitude of the priests to their responsibilities in the service of Jehovah. Because they treated the altar as common and with contempt, their service became a

burden to them, whereas they should have willingly engaged in it, regarding it as a privilege to serve Jehovah. The phrase "what a weariness is it" implies that they considered it a drudgery to observe all the details of the law. Their whole service in regard to the sanctuary was wearisome to them because their hearts were not in it. Thus they sought to get it over quickly by not scrutinizing the animals and so offered the most worthless sacrifices. There was no sincerity in their service; it was no longer a privilege and a dignity to them but had become an intolerable burden and effort. This attitude is referred to in Isaiah 43.22-24 where Jehovah states that He had not wearied Israel with His demands, but that they had wearied Him with their iniquity. It is also referred to in Micah 6.3-5 where Jehovah challenges His people to testify wherein His service was a hardship in view of what He had done for them and in light of His righteousness.

"Ye have snuffed at it" is a term of discontent and contempt, a complaining by snivelling. The service of the temple, which ought to have been regarded as their highest privilege, had become wearisome to them and needless labour. It brought them no joy, though to serve Jehovah should have been their greatest delight. The zeal that characterized the remnant when they first returned from captivity was now absent. How easily one can become weary of the things of God and feel that spiritual activity has become burdensome. The freshness and joy of the things of God when first saved can wane unless the believer spends time in prayer and the reading of the word of God. When one becomes cold in heart spiritual things are replaced by worldliness and materialism, and gathering with the saints becomes a mere form. When one loses sight of the privilege and dignity of worship and serving God, such activities become merely a sense of duty and an effort. Christians need to appreciate constantly the dignity and honour God has bestowed upon them and they need to be continually in communion with God to prevent such a condition developing.

They first brought worthless animals to the altar to slaughter and then, knowing that they were flawed, they offered them as sacrificial gifts to Jehovah. Because the service of Jehovah had become such an effort they were prepared to offer any kind of sacrifice. In such a condition and with such an attitude they violated the Holy Scriptures and dishonoured Jehovah. Christians need to examine their condition and attitude as they engage in the things of God lest they bring dishonour upon Him. One cannot serve God in any old way. The believer's service must be in keeping with the character of God and according to the word of God. How solemn to engage in the work of God with a wrong attitude and in a wrong way thus dishonouring Him. They were weary of keeping the law, of examining the animals to see that there were no blemishes. They considered that it did not really matter and thus it was not necessary (cp. v.8). How wrong they were. The word "torn" (GAZAL – 1497) has the idea of stolen in Deuteronomy 28.31 and may indicate here the offering of what had been stolen which was hateful to Jehovah (Is 61.8). In worship, God expects the saints to come with their own appreciation, with what they have made their own, and not with another's appreciation. In giving, God expects believers to give what is rightfully theirs and not what belongs to another (cp. 2 Cor 8.12). The rebuke here closes with a rhetorical question similar to v.8, the inevitable answer being in the negative in keeping with v.10. All their offerings were unfit and unacceptable, and were therefore not reckoned to them. It is possible for Christians to be engaged in what they call worship and yet what they are engaged in is not acceptable to God. They cannot approach God any how or with any kind of attitude. One must appreciate that God is infinitely holy. It is possible for Christians to claim to be serving God and yet their labour not to be acknowledged by Him. Both worship and service must be in keeping with the character of God and according to His word.

Hypocritical (v.14)
   To the answer of "No" in the closing part of the previous verse there is added in this verse the curse upon all who offer sacrifices not in keeping with the law. This verse broadens out to all the people. "Deceiver" (NAKAL – 5230) is translated elsewhere as "conspired" (Gen 37.18), "beguiled" (Num 25.18) and "deal subtilly" (Ps 105.25). It occurs only in these passages. Here the idea is of the hypocrite, one who seeks to deceive men and who thinks he can deceive God. A similar thought is seen in Acts 5 where Ananias and Sapphira, desiring to appear devoted and sacrificial like Barnabas in the previous chapter, sought to deceive Peter as to their giving. One may be able to deceive men, but one cannot deceive God (cp. Jer 32.19). Some suggest that there are two classes in this verse (Keil & Delitzsch).
   1. A person who acted deceitfully by offering a female animal as a burnt offering for his vows contrary to the law (Lev 22.18-20), pretending he did not possess or could not obtain a male when there was one in his flock.
   2. A person who offered a female animal that had a blemish as a peace offering to accomplish his vow (Lev 22.21-23).
   Both cases could fit the context. However, the second case seems to be more in keeping with the passage. An Israelite was not duty bound to make a vow, but if he did so, he was to offer either a burnt or peace offering without blemish (Lev 22.18-24). The peace offering could be either a male or a female animal, but it had to be without blemish. A vow was intended to be an expression of zeal and devotion for God. It was no sin not to vow, but when a vow was made it was sacredly binding (Deut 23.21-23). Therefore a vow should not be made hastily (Eccl 5.4-5). Since a vow was to be an expression of devotion to God, the very best should be offered to Him. Although a female animal was permissible as the peace offering relative to a vow, a male without blemish was the most valuable. A female with a blemish was not acceptable and would be the worst kind of offering to bring. The thought here seems to be of a man who, having made a vow

and possessing a male without blemish in his flock, brings a blemished female as an offering to accomplish his vow. Instead of offering the best he brought the worst to Jehovah. How could Jehovah accept such a sham as satisfactory to Him? Such offerings were an insult to His majesty and greatness as stated in the following expression. There was an outward show of devotion to Jehovah, but it was hypocritical. There was no reality, no genuineness in it, and the person's true condition and attitude were manifested in his actions. How dreadful is this kind of deception – to make a show of devotion to God and keep back the best of one's life for self. Christians need to examine themselves for they can become masters of veneer covering over fleshly desires and worldly pursuits with an outward form of spirituality. Regarding these verses David West gives the challenge: "And what of the application to ourselves? We have been constituted 'an holy priesthood, to offer up spiritual sacrifices, acceptable to God by Jesus Christ' (1 Pet 2.5). Worship ought to be the highest expression of spiritual devotedness to God and whatever is devoted to God must not be polluted - He deserves the very best that we can bring. How sad if we find such spiritual sacrifices irksome!".

Although Jehovah was a great King they had forgotten His majesty and greatness and thus offered to Him what they would not have dared to offer to their earthly ruler. They would not have tried to deceive and cheat an earthly king or governor for fear of being found out and punished. They, who had witnessed the power and grace of Jehovah, dishonoured His name instead of showing Him reverence and obeying His word. The greatness and grandeur of His Person demanded the very best. The reason for the curse is given by reminding them of the greatness of Jehovah's majesty. Believers should appreciate the importance of acknowledging the greatness of God and of living accordingly.

The expression "my name is dreadful among the heathen" is intended as a reproach to His people who did not fear Him (v.6). If the heathen fear His name, how much more should His people reverence Him. The last part of this verse is really looking on to a future day and will have its complete fulfilment in the Millennium. The people in Malachi's day should have been living in light of that coming day. So Christians today should be living in view of that coming day of glory and in light of the Judgment Seat of Christ.

MALACHI 2

Verses 1.6-2.9: The Majesty and Dignity of Jehovah's Name (continued)

This chapter continues with Jehovah's rebuke of the priests that commenced in 1.6. Through the prophet, He shows that these priests were unworthy of the priesthood. Unless they took heed to Jehovah's rebuke He would send a curse upon them and they would be disgraced in the sight of the people (vv.1-9). The prophet then turns from the priests to those who violated the sacred marriage bond and married foreign women. He shows that divorce was an unnatural cruelty and an offence against the love and faithfulness of those bound to them - wives and children (vv.10-17).

The exercise of priestly service (vv.1-9)

It has already been noticed that this second section is addressed to the priestly family and is linked with book of Exodus. Their privilege was to enjoy communion with Jehovah, to exalt His name and to instruct the people in the things of Jehovah, all of which demands holiness. In these verses there is one of the clearest definitions of priestly dignity and privilege and yet one of the most solemn charges made against the priests. Here the prophet enlarges on the sinful condition of the priests in order to bring home to their consciences the consequences of their departure from the law of Jehovah. Although "ordained for men in things pertaining to God, that he may offer both gifts and sacrifices for sins" (Heb 5.1), they neglected their sacred duties and promoted themselves. The priests are rebuked because, although their part was to lead the people in keeping with the law and to reprove sin, they actually encouraged the people to violate the law thus leading them into sin. Their actions showed that they were unworthy of their calling and their ancestry. Thus the rebuke of the priests in ch.1 is followed here by the announcement of their punishment. If they refused to take heed to Jehovah's admonition and did not reverence His name Jehovah would send a curse upon them and they would be disgraced before all the people. This second part is divided into three - vv.1-4: The commandment; vv.5-7: The covenant; and vv.8-9: The charge.

The commandment (vv.1-4)

There are different views as to what "this commandment" in v.1 refers. Some think it refers either to the law concerning sacrifices acceptable and unacceptable to Jehovah, or a return to obedience to the law which seems to be intimated in the passage. S. R. Driver states, "The 'commandment,' or charge, is apparently the commandment to reform, implicit in vv. 2,3". Most commentators view it as referring to a decree or threat of punishment. C. F. Keil takes the view that "Verse 1 introduces the threat; this is called *mitsvah*, a command...The reference is to the threat of punishment which follows in vv.2 and 3, but which is only to be carried out in case the priests do not hear and lay to heart, namely, the warning which the Lord has addressed to them through Malachi (1.6-13), and sanctify His name by their service". Whichever view is taken, it is evident that the thrust of the passage is that the priests ought to be carrying out the law (Lev. 22.20; Deut 15.21; 17.1) bringing glory to the name of Jehovah.

(a) The responsibility of the priests (vv.1-2). The responsibility of the priests was to carry out the law in regard to the sacrifices offered, to teach the people the word of Jehovah, and to be an example to the people. There were clear directions given to the priests in the law with regard to their service for Jehovah and their service, on behalf of the people, to Jehovah. They had therefore a duty to carry out these instructions. They were responsible to hear the solemn threat, to lay it to heart and to give glory to His name by obedience to the word of God. The use of "lay it to heart" implies that these priests not only violated the law, but had no conscience in doing so. However, the voice of Jehovah to them was also the instructions given in the Law of Moses, and to these instructions they were to take heed, carrying them out for the glory of Jehovah. It is not enough for the Christian to hear the voice of God through the word of God or to listen to ministry. One must lay it to heart and give glory to His name by living it out in one's life. The responsibility of Israel was to bring glory to His name in their testimony for Him among the nations. This was only possible by complete obedience to the instructions given in the Holy Scriptures. The priests were responsible not only to carry out these instructions themselves but also to see that the people obeyed the word of Jehovah. The charge against the priests was that they had despised His name (1.6). They had little or no appreciation of Jehovah's name and thus attached no significance to the place in which He had set His name.

Today, that name is fully expressed in the Lord Jesus Christ and those who are gathered to His name have a responsibility to bring glory to that name in their collective testimony for God. Is there failure among those so gathered in accordance with God's word and thus a failure to bring glory to the Lord's name? To be gathered to the name of the Lord Jesus Christ surely means that He is the centre of attraction, that His Lordship is owned and that His word is paramount. It means being drawn to Him outside the camp (Heb 13.13) and finding sufficiency in Him. His name is the sum of all that He is and involves His claims as absolute Lord. All must be in keeping with the loveliness, majesty, dignity, and holiness of His name. His name is all important and of necessity excludes all other names. It is the believers' privilege to exalt His name. Each local assembly has a responsibility to bear a faithful and harmonious testimony to all the truth of God in the locality, by complete obedience to His word and thus bring glory to His name. Those so gathered need to hear, take heed and honour God by obedience. The word of God is not given merely to increase head knowledge but to affect the heart and govern the life. One learns from these verses the important lesson that obedience from the heart brings glory to God.

(b) The result of disobedience (vv.2-4). The result of disobedience was the hand of Jehovah upon them in governmental discipline (vv.2-3). This was in order that they might know they had violated the covenant which He had made with Levi (v.4). How important it is to learn that disobedience will not only rob one of the enjoyment of communion with God, but it will also bring upon one the hand of the Lord in chastisement.

The word "If" is not an "If" of doubt, but implies that Jehovah would be merciful to these priests should they take heed to His threat and turn from their evil ways, but, if not, His chastisement was certain. Should the priests continue in their sinful ways in spite of Jehovah's solemn warning, He would send the grievous curse upon them. In the Hebrew text "a curse" is definitive – "the curse" – and is thus emphatic, indicating that the curse of the law is in view (cp. Deut 27.15-26; 28.15-68). Jehovah speaks of the condition to which He would reduce them as retribution for their unfaithfulness. Instead of the blessing of the Lord being upon them the curse would be their portion. In continuing in their lawlessness and by offering unacceptable sacrifices they would be dishonouring Jehovah and His name. He would not allow their disobedience go unpunished. His hand would be upon them in chastisement. Believers today must appreciate that there is a price to be paid for disobeying the word of God. Those who do so come under the Father's government and His chastisement is for their spiritual benefit (1 Pet 1.17; cp. Heb 12.5-11). The expression, "I will curse your blessings", in v.2 has been viewed as either the blessings the priests enjoyed or the blessings they pronounced on the people. S. R. Driver states, "As Deuteronomy 28.2 - here more particularly of the privileges and advantages bestowed by Yaweh upon the priesthood"; C. F. Keil writes, "Blessings are obviously not the revenues of the priests...but the blessings pronounced by the priests upon the people by virtue of their office"; while C. L. Feinberg includes both in stating, "The blessings spoken of are not to be restricted to the revenues of the priests only, but must include all the benefits of God's gracious hand, those promised the people by the priests by virtue of their office". Since the passage deals mainly with the service of the priests it seems that the blessings they pronounced upon the people are in view. Thus those blessings Jehovah would not only make ineffective, but they would be actually turned into the opposite of what was intended, i.e. curses. The purposes of these disobedient priests would be thwarted. God's intention for the child of God is spiritual enrichment and the enjoyment of His presence in the sanctuary. However, disobedience results in the loss of the delight of communion with God and in spiritual poverty.

The curse had already taken effect, for Jehovah knew that they would not take heed to His warning. The idea here is that Jehovah had already cursed each particular blessing pronounced by these unfaithful priests. They were already experiencing the failure of their ministry as it brought no benefit to the people. In fact their unfaithfulness and disobedience resulted in the people's moral and spiritual departure. The spiritual condition of the leaders among God's people is generally reflected in the people. Spiritual elders will seek to maintain the truth of God in the assembly and strive to feed the saints so that they are spiritually healthy and wealthy. How sad when one's ministry is blighted by departure, and characterised by carnality. Not only does the individual suffer by disobedience but others suffer through their influence.

The phrase "ye do not lay it to heart" implies that there was no feeling of shame or regret with these priests. Despite the rebuke of the word of Jehovah through His servant Malachi, their hearts remained untouched. How sad that Christians can sit under faithful and challenging ministry and yet remain unmoved and unchanged in their lives. The priests had hardened their hearts and self-will ruled instead of the will of Jehovah. The most important thing in the life of the Christian should be the will of God. That is all that will matter at the Judgment Seat of Christ - how one has treated the will of God as unfolded in His word.

Verse 3 is the only place where the Hebrew GAAR (1605) is translated "corrupt". In Jeremiah 29.27 it is translated "reproved", and elsewhere it is always translated "rebuke", or "rebuked". "Behold" indicates the importance of what follows and calls upon the priests to take note, to consider. The expression "I will corrupt (rebuke) your seed" is viewed in three different ways.

1. That the word "seed" refers to the posterity of the priests. H. A. Ironside states, "Their seed should be rejected, and thus the family of Levi set aside from their appointed place of privilege, as has been the case ever since the rending of the veil, though only manifestly since Jerusalem's destruction by the Romans under Titus".

2. That the word "seed" should be rendered "arm". C. F. Keil is of the view that "...since the priests did not practice agriculture, it is impossible to see how rebuking the seed, i.e. causing a failure of the crops, could be a punishment peculiar to the priests. We must therefore...adopt [the rendering] 'the arm'... rebuking the arm, therefore, signifies the neutralizing of the official duties performed at the altar and in the sanctuary".

3. That the word "seed" refers to the harvest. Feinberg's opinion is that "He threatens to rebuke their seed. The word should not be translated 'arm' as parallel to 'faces' in the same verse. What is meant is the seed of their land, for since the priests were dependent on the increase of the harvest for their tithes, they would inevitably suffer if God cursed the seed".

The third view seems more acceptable, but whichever view is taken the main thrust seems to be that of fruitlessness. Their activity was fruitless because it did not have the divine approval. All their service was of no value because it was governed by self instead of by the word of Jehovah. There is the equivalent idea in Haggai 1.6 where there was barrenness, wantonness, emptiness, coldness, and poverty because the people were taken up with their own things at the expense of the things of Jehovah. The same principle is seen in 1 Corinthians 3.12 in the wood, hay, and stubble which are valueless, being unable to stand the test of the fire of divine scrutiny.

The phrase "spread dung upon your faces" is a figurative statement indicating that Jehovah would deliver over the priests to contempt and scorn. It is an expression of the greatest contempt cast upon a person. Because they had treated the Lord's service with contempt they would reap contempt. Since the Lord's work had become irksome instead of a privilege to them, their work would be scorned. They would reap what they had sown. The dung of animals sacrificed on feast days is in view. There may also be the suggestion that the dung of the sacrificial animals of the feast days, which should have been removed (Ex 29.14; Lev 16.27), had been left in the court and thus their feasts were as dung. The expression "your solemn feasts" is in contrast to "the feasts of the Lord", and "my feasts" in Leviticus 23.2. The feasts had ceased to honour Jehovah and were no longer in keeping with His word. They had become formal and meaningless. Their disrespect for Jehovah and His word and the retribution deserved is clearly indicated. It is a serious thing to consider the teaching of the word of Jehovah as meaningless. To set aside the principles unfolded in the Scriptures which should govern and guide one's life is folly. How sad when believers attend the various meetings of an assembly out of mere formality. The Lord would repay the contempt of the priests by giving them over to the greatest ignominy, i.e. they would be treated as dung, carried away and cast aside. They would be viewed as being unclean and unfit for His sanctuary and service. How solemn for a believer to lose the enjoyment of communion with God in the sanctuary. How solemn to be a vessel of dishonour not fit for the Master's use (cp. 2 Tim 2.20-21).

When such disgrace came upon the priests, then they would know that Jehovah had sent the commandment to them (v.1) and that the rebuke of the previous verses was indeed from Him. They would know by practical and bitter experience that Jehovah was holy and that He was acting in righteousness in keeping with His threat. It would have been far better for them to have learned something of His righteousness and holiness from His word and in the sanctuary than through His just retribution. It is far better for Christians today to learn the character and claims of God from His word and in communion with Him, than by experiencing His hand upon them in chastisement because of disobedience and waywardness. The priests would also know that His chastisement was in order that His covenant with Levi might remain firm and be maintained. Levi here stands for the tribe and particularly the priesthood. The covenant with Levi involved separation to the Lord, holiness, and faithfulness in Jehovah's service (Num 8.14-16; Deut 10.8-9; 33.8-9). Levi in his faithfulness in the crisis of the golden calf (Ex 32.25-29) is purposely introduced here in contrast to the unfaithfulness and disobedience of the priests of Malachi's day who ought to have been the most careful as to the law and Jehovah's glory. There may also be a reference to Levi's consecration on that occasion in contrast to the failure of Aaron who was himself of that tribe. The thought here is that Jehovah was indicating, by His warning and judgment, that the priests were not only to keep His law, but were to teach the people to do so that He might be glorified. God intends that saints today live in keeping with His character and His word for His pleasure and glory.

The covenant (vv.5-7)

The prophet here unfolds the nature of the covenant with Levi and contrasts the godly character and conduct of Levi with the character and censurable conduct of the ungodly priests of his day. Phinehas' faithfulness and zeal (Num 25.11) is contrasted with the priests' violation of the law. Although Phinehas is clearly referred to, one must include the faithfulness of the tribe of Levi at the event of the golden calf and the covenant Jehovah made with that tribe because of its fidelity (Deut 33.8-11).

The nature of the covenant was to grant and guarantee life and peace (cp. Num 25.10-13). The expression "for the fear wherewith he feared me" has been viewed in different ways. Rabbi A. J. Rosenberg, quoting Jewish commentaries, renders this part of the verse as: "that he accept them with fear, and so he did, and he feared Me", and quoting other authorities explains it as: "I gave him life and peace because of the fear with which he feared Me". However it has also been stated that "the Hebrew is, literally, 'My covenant was with him, life and peace (to be given him on My part), and I gave them to him: (and on his part) fear (i.e. reverence), and he did fear Me'...The former portion of the verse expresses the promise, and Jehovah's fulfilment of it; the latter, the condition, and Levi's steadfastness to it (Deut 33.8,9)" (Jamieson, Fausset & Brown). Although one favours the latter sense, whichever view is taken the stress is upon the contrast between the tribe of Levi in Moses' day (also that of Phinehas) and the priests in Malachi's day. "Life" here may include the continuation of the priesthood implied in the term "everlasting priesthood" in Numbers 25.13. The word "peace" (SHALOM - 7965) embraces all the blessings required for well-being and has the thought of unimpaired relationship with Jehovah. This twofold blessing is the basis of priestly service, for how can one worship or serve God without possessing life and without being at peace with God? Compare this with the statement in Colossians 3.4, "Christ, who is our life", indicating that the Christian possesses that life and so has the spiritual capacity to move in the presence of God and to enjoy communion with Him. Also in Ephesians 2.14 one reads, "For he is our peace", so that in Christ the Christian has been reconciled to God having been brought from the place of distance into the place of nearness (Eph 2.13). Thus saints are in harmony with all that God is and with all that He requires, and can enjoy His presence. The principles that ought to govern christian living lead to the enjoyment of communion with God which is the power of a victorious christian life. This is vital, fundamental.

If the priests had been in the enjoyment of life and peace they would have been characterised by reverence towards Jehovah and by obedience to His word. However they claimed the privileges of the covenant, yet neglected the conditions of it. They were implying that Jehovah was obligated to bless them in their service, but that they were free to act as they liked. In contrast, Levi reverenced Jehovah and acted accordingly. The priestly man lives in the sanctuary of the presence of God and the result is a reverential fear, an awe of God. Those who are near to God in priestly communion are those who have the greatest appreciation of His holiness. The enjoyment of communion with God inevitably produces holiness of life. The reference here is primarily to Phinehas who, with the javelin, stayed the plague abhorring the defilement that had entered the camp. Those who are near to God and have an appreciation of His holiness will not only be characterised by personal holiness but will also abhor defilement in any form and have a dread of grieving Him (cp. Eph 4.30).

"Afraid" (HATAT - 2865) means "to prostrate" (Strong's Concordance) and has the basic idea of "to be broken". Although in most passages it has the thought of terror, here the sense is that of awe and humility. H. Spurrell translated the phrase "afraid before my name" as "served with awe in My presence". The thought in the verse is that Phinehas' action expressed complete reverence and humility in appreciation of the Person and name of Jehovah. The priests had a responsibility to honour and exalt His name and thus, in the course of his message, the prophet mentions "my name" eight times. "My name" is the sum total of the revealed character of God - the full revelation to one's heart of all that is knowable of God including His claims. The enjoyment of communion with God will not only produce holiness of life, but will also lead to maintaining conditions of holiness in the place where God dwells in the midst of His people (Ps 93.5).

Verse 6 indicates that the fear of Jehovah in Levi displayed itself in the faithful and willing discharge of priestly duty. It gives a lovely description of true and faithful devotion to Jehovah and His word. The opening expression indicates that the truth contained in the law had not only been the basis of his life, but had also been the content of what he had taught the people. For the priestly man the word of God was law. It was the only guide and the only court of appeal. The word of God should be this to every child of God. His teaching was according to the proper oral character of the law and was given correctly and faithfully in contrast to the error of the priests addressed here, who led the people astray. Their teaching was for their own selfish ends instead of for the spiritual well-being of the people. One notes a similar contrast in the New Testament where the

Apostle Paul states, "…nor handling the word of God deceitfully; but by the manifestation of the truth commending ourselves to every man's conscience in the sight of God" (2 Cor 4.2). Many today try to use the word of God for their own ends by changing it into what is a lie (Rom 1.25). Such were the false teachers in Paul's day and such are false teachers today. In contrast, Paul would only make known the truth of God for the spiritual enrichment of the people of God. The same idea is found in 1 Thessalonians 2.3 where Paul gives a threefold negative description of the message he and his fellow labourers proclaimed.

1. "Not of deceit". It was not calculated to lead astray, but was the truth which would bring blessing. It was genuine, being the unadulterated word of God in contrast to the deceit of the false teachers.

2. "Nor of uncleanness". It was not gratifying the flesh. It was free from either lust for power or greed for gain. They were free from self-ambition, self-advancement and self-pleasing in contrast to the spirit of the world.

3. "Nor in guile". It was not using it as a cloak to cover over the motive. Their message was true, being the word of God; their motive was pure; and their conduct was blameless and transparent.

These features should characterise those who teach the saints today and, indeed, should characterise every child of God.

The first word translated "iniquity" (AWEL - 5766) comes from a primitive root (UL - 5765) meaning to distort, and thus to act unjustly, unrighteously, or to pervert. It implies conduct or speech which is not regulated by the truth but by selfishness and self-interest. Therefore the expression "iniquity was not found in his lips" indicates that he was not partial in his teaching and judgment, neither was he perverted by bribes to the dishonour of Jehovah. His teaching and judgment were not affected by men, but were in keeping with the word of Jehovah, which was in contrast to the perverted teaching and judgment of these priests. The leaders and teachers of the people of God, in every generation, should be just and transparent in the sight of God for His pleasure, "not as pleasing men, but God, which trieth our hearts" (1 Thess 2.4). Christians should strive to please God by faithfully and obediently serving Him who has entrusted them with His service. One should also appreciate that He will put to the test the motives and the methods of one's service.

The phrase "walked with me" denotes close fellowship and harmony with Jehovah. Walking with God and pleasing God go hand in hand (cp. Gen 5.22 with Heb 11.5). They involve surrendering one's will to the will of God. "Peace" here may indicate the tranquillity of reverent obedience to the word of Jehovah. "Equity" (MISHOR - 4334) literally means to go straight, or a level place, and has the idea here of rectitude of mind or uprightness, being free from hypocrisy. It could well be translated as "with justice" describing the way judgment is given. Because he was in the enjoyment of peace with Jehovah, and marked by uprightness, he was able to enjoy unbroken communion with Jehovah. Walking with God demands:

1. Harmony - "Can two walk together, except they be agreed?" (Amos 3.3). It involves an acceptance of His will and a readiness to tread the pathway marked out in His word.

2. Holiness - "As he which hath called you is holy, so be ye holy in all manner of conversation" (1 Pet 1.15). Holiness of life is essential in order to enjoy communion with God.

3. Humility - "He hath shewed thee, O man, what is good; and what doth the Lord require of thee, but to do justly, and to love mercy, and to walk humbly with thy God?" (Micah 6.8). The result of such a life and the faithful instruction given was that many were brought back from their sinful ways to right ways and to the fear of Jehovah.

The second word translated "iniquity" (AWON - 5771) here is a different word to that so rendered earlier in the verse. It is a collective noun and denotes both the deed and the consequences, thus it is also translated "punishment" (Gen 4.13). The closing expression of v.6, therefore, may also include the idea of turning many from the consequences of sin. Example and precept must go hand in hand when appealing to the people of God to live for Him. The perfect example is seen in the words, "...all that Jesus began both to do and teach" (Acts 1.1).

Jehovah's intended service for the priest in Israel is indicated in v.7. The priest is called "the messenger of the Lord of hosts" bringing instructions for the people. Thus his lips should uphold the knowledge of Jehovah and His will unfolded in the law. Therefore, he needed to read the law, earnestly and carefully, in dependence upon Jehovah, in order to convey it to the people accurately and faithfully. As Jehovah's messenger he was the appointed teacher of the Law of Moses to the nation. He was responsible to instruct the people in the law for they sought from him, as Jehovah's messenger, the will of Jehovah. What a solemn responsibility this was. Every man who takes the platform today, whether to preach the gospel or to minister the word of God, should be conscious of the solemn responsibility of clearly making known the truth of God. Leaders and teachers among Christians should be priestly men and they have the responsibility of conveying the mind of God to the saints. How vital for such men to get to know the word of God and to be diligent in the word of truth. One is exhorted to "Study to show thyself approved unto God, a workman that needeth not to be ashamed, rightly dividing the word of truth" (2 Tim 2.15). Is there not a requirement for wholesome, health-giving ministry, spiritual food that contains all the elements necessary to build and beautify christian character? There is a great need for priestly men who will spend time in the sanctuary with the word of God in order to obtain food for the people of God. There ought to be a desire on the part of the people of God for scriptural instruction and sound teaching, which is God's method of imparting truth to the saints. It is important for believers to listen to the teaching of the word of God so that they can walk in ways pleasing to Him.

The charge (vv.8-9)

The priests are charged with failure to measure up to the dignity bestowed upon them. It seems that they were unaware of their dreadful condition just like those in Laodicea. It has already been stated that the reason for Israel's condition was because of the departure of the priests, her spiritual leaders, from the word of the Lord. The spiritual condition of the people of God never rises above the spiritual level of their leaders. How important for elders in assemblies to maintain spirituality by constant communion with God and by applying the word of God to their lives.

There was a marked contrast between the Levi of Israel's early history and these priests of Malachi's day who had departed fundamentally from the way outlined in vv.5-7. "Departed" (SUR - 5493) has the thought of turning aside as translated in Deuteronomy 17.20 - "that he turn not aside from the commandment, to the right hand, or to the left" (cp. Deut 11.28; 31.20). The priests had reduced divine communication to religious ceremony with no real meaning. Their hands were full, but their hearts were cold because they had set aside the word of Jehovah and had introduced their own ideas. The setting aside of the divine revelation and the example of Levi, along with introducing their own ideas to the people, resulted in many departing from the law. They became a law unto themselves just like the people in the days of the judges - "every man did that which was right in his own eyes" (Judg 17.6; 21.25). Lawlessness is setting aside divine revelation for one's own ideas. How solemn to set aside the word of God and be a stumbling block to others. When Christians set aside the word of God, which is intended to guide and govern every department of their lives, they become a law unto themselves and their spiritual lives and testimonies are blighted. The principle of lawlessness is seen in independence, self-will and self-pleasing. Having turned away from the path of obedience themselves, the priests, through their disgraceful example and false teaching of the law, caused others to stumble. Their false teaching involved the idea that the law allowed things which were, in reality, sin. Thus they influenced others to violate the law as they were doing. How one lives and what one says always influences others, "For none of us liveth to himself" (Rom 14.7). Although every Christian lives under the gaze of the Lord and as His servant, the kind of life lived affects others. One must be careful not to cause another believer to stumble (Rom 14.13,21). One influences others for good or for bad by the kind of life one lives. The priests made void the covenant by setting aside the word and claims of Jehovah. They made the covenant of none effect, by not fulfilling its conditions and therefore forfeiting its promises (cp. Neh 13.29; Zech 11.10). They brought that which was defiled to the altar and thus corrupted the covenant of Levi by making it inoperative through their disobedience. The bringing of such sacrifices brought defilement both to the altar and the dwelling place of Jehovah. The consequences are unfolded in v.9. How careful one must be not to bring defilement into the things of God.

At the beginning of v.9 the words "I also" indicate that, in view of the priests' evil activity, Jehovah, on His part, would assert Himself and visit them with appropriate retribution. Because they had annulled the covenant by their wicked ways Jehovah removed from the priests what Levi enjoyed, i.e. life and peace. The words "have...made" are equivalent to "will assuredly make". Although the action of Jehovah was future, He was so resolved to carry it out that it is spoken of as being already done (cp. Gen 15.18; Judg 15.3). Since they had despised His name (1.6) and treated His service as contemptible (1.7,12) Jehovah would make them contemptible before the people. The word for "contemptible" is translated "despised" in 1.6 and has the idea of attributing little or no value, and "base"' (SHAPAL - 8217) indicates abasement. The priests' degradation in the eyes of the people was just retribution for the way they had exalted themselves above the law of Jehovah and for having respect to men rather than the truth. "Kept" (SHAMAR - 8104) has the basic idea of exercising great care over and paying careful attention to something. The thought here is that the priests were not only responsible for protecting the ways of Jehovah, but responsible for practising those ways themselves. This way, or manner of life, was set out in the law. Christians today are responsible, not only to know the word of God, but to live in keeping with that word. The priests here had failed on both counts and were being partial in the law, i.e. in the administration of the law. They were unrighteous in the interpretation of the law permitting to one what they refused to others (cp. Lev 19.15). The implication seems to be that they were open to bribery - "the priests thereof teach for hire" (Micah 3.11; cp. Ps 82.2). The concept would be that of exacting higher fees from some and being unjust in their legal decisions for monetary gain. False teachers in the Apostle Paul's day were similar to these priests who were "teaching things which they ought not, for filthy lucre's sake" (Tit 1.11). The love of money is a root of all evil and there is great danger in longing to be rich (1 Tim 6.9-10).

Verses 10-17: The Weariness of Jehovah's Spirit
The subject is now changed and a new one is introduced by the question, "Have we not all one father?". The ministry in this section is addressed to Judah and Jerusalem and the emphasis is upon the weariness of Jehovah's Spirit. There is a link between this section and Leviticus, the book of the sanctuary where holiness is demanded - "Judah hath profaned the holiness of the Lord" (v.11). The sin of Judah, in relation to His holiness, was that of immorality and divorce. Here is a development of what has gone before - slighting the love of God leads to lack of priestly character and activity, loss of priestly character leads to little or no appreciation of the holiness of God, little or no appreciation of the holiness of God leads to failure in testimony and laxity in personal morality. They had sorely tried the Lord's patience yet challenged Him with the question, "Wherein have we wearied him?" (v.17). In addition to the offences of the priests outlined in the last

section, the priests and the people are charged here with unholy marriages and unlawful divorces. These great social wrongs of divorcing their wives and marrying foreign women (cp. Neh 13.23-30) are rebuked by Malachi. They had acted treacherously, and this was an abomination to the Lord. They allowed the standards of the nations around to affect them, and had forgotten the holiness of the Lord. Are not these things true today? The casual and immoral conditions prevailing in the world tend to affect the people of God. Is there not a tendency to forget the holiness of the One who dwells in the midst of the assembly? Is it not true that in many instances His holy claims are ignored? There are things associated with some assemblies which rob them of their dignity and sanctity. How dreadful this must be to God. One needs a fresh appreciation of the holiness of God and of His holy demands - "For God hath not called us unto uncleanness, but unto holiness" (1 Thess 4.7); "let us cleanse ourselves from all filthiness of the flesh and spirit, perfecting holiness in the fear of God" (2 Cor 7.1). The section is divided in to two parts: the wickedness of Judah (vv.10-13), and the witness of Jehovah (vv.14-17).

The wickedness of Judah (vv.10-13)

The accusation against Judah was that they had profaned the holiness of Jehovah and married the daughter of a strange god. It is evident that they had put away their Jewish wives and had taken in their place women from the surrounding nations. S. R. Driver states, "The practice of divorce he declares to be an offence against the love and faithfulness which as children of one Father they all owe to one another, an unnatural cruelty towards those who have been long bound to them by the ties of affection, and a challenge to the Divine judgement".

The opening question of v.10 has been viewed in two different ways. It has been suggested that the words "Ye say" should be added before the question which would make Judah the speaker. The thought would then be that Judah was claiming that there was no difference between them and the nations around - we have come from the same stock, God has made us all of one blood. They were setting aside their distinctiveness and their separation from the nations so clearly taught in the law. This spirit was evident in Samuel's day when they desired a king to be like all the nations (1 Sam 8.5,20). To justify their actions they used human reasoning without recourse to the word of God. Is not this a voice to us today? Many assemblies have lost their distinctiveness because of the desire to be like the religious systems of men and have justified their actions by human reasoning. Many individual believers have lost their distinctive character and set aside the truth of separation as a result of human reasoning instead of being guided by the Holy Scriptures. They desire to be like the world in pursuits, ambition and outlook but not in destiny. It is easy and convenient to use human reasoning to justify many things which are contrary to the word of God.

However most commentators accept that the prophet himself is the speaker, which is more in keeping with the passage. Malachi adopts the same method as in the previous section, commencing with a general statement (1.6) from which the evil of their practice is developed. There are various opinions as to whom the expression "one father" refers. Matthew Poole suggests either Abraham or Jacob; H. A. Ironside writes that "They had all sprung from one common father, Abraham"; while C. F. Keil states, "The one father, whom all have, is neither Adam, the progenitor of all men, nor Abraham, the father of the Israelitish nation, but Jehovah, who calls Himself the Father of the nation in 1.6". That the reference is to Jehovah is established by the parallelism, where God is mentioned in the second question and also by various other Scriptures (Deut 32.6; Is 63.16). In keeping with the fact of Jehovah being the father of Israel the prophet used the singular name of El (God), the mighty One (cp. 1.9), their Creator. Both these rhetorical questions, with the inevitable answer, "Yes", emphasise the oneness of Israel in contrast to the heathen. They stress that Israel was in covenant relationship with Jehovah, as His peculiar people (Deut 14.2; 26.18), set apart to God, and separated from the heathen - "I am the Lord your God, which have separated you from other people" (Lev 20.24). They were linked by common ties to Jehovah and thus were knit together by a common relationship and blessings. This being so they ought to have been in harmony, treating each other in keeping with that relationship with Jehovah. Why then was that oneness being broken and the covenant violated? Malachi used the pronoun "we" being an Israelite, identifying himself with the people.

The verb "treacherously" (BAGAD - 898) means to deal unfaithfully or deceitfully. It is used to denote unfaithfulness in a variety of relationships including marriage. The thought here is of unfaithfulness to fellow Israelites by violating the covenant, putting away their wives and contracting marriage with foreign women, which marred the oneness of the nation. They were neither true to their relationship with Jehovah nor to their relationship with each other. Christians are bound together as members of the body of Christ and should be characterised by brotherly love (Rom 12.10; Heb 13.1), seeking the welfare of each other. This truth should be manifested in the local assembly by oneness and harmony (Acts 4.32; Phil 1.27; 2.2). However, when brotherly love is lacking, friction, bitterness and discord arise marring the testimony and often resulting in believers turning to the world. How sad when this takes place. Israel had been forbidden to intermarry with the surrounding nations - "Neither shalt thou make marriages with them" (Deut 7.3). This disregard for the covenant, which separated Israel from the heathen, threatened its distinctiveness and opened the door to idolatry (Ex 34.16; Deut 7.3-4). The reason for this rebuke, and the development of it, is given in v.11.

The charge of unfaithfulness is repeated in v.11 and applied to the whole nation. Its seriousness is stressed by the declaration that it was an abomination in Israel and Jerusalem. "Abomination" (TOEBA - 8441) means to act unfaithfully, hypocritically or deceitfully. It is used of idolatry (Deut 13.13-14; 18.9-12), and here it refers to transgressing the covenant by bringing heathen women, with their idolatry, into the nation (cp. Deut 17.2-5; Ezra 9.14). The name Israel is used here to contrast the holy calling of God with the unholy conduct of the people and Jerusalem, the place where God had set His name, is used to indicate that Jehovah was in their midst. Their actions were contrary to both Jehovah's calling and His presence. They had violated the covenant which separated them from the nations around (Ex 19.5) and had broken the law which forbade all marriages with the heathen in order to safeguard Israel from idolatry. The expression "the holiness of the Lord" is governed by the phrase "which he loved", and thus it cannot refer to the divine attribute of Jehovah. It is suggested that the reference is to the sanctuary (the temple), and the Newberry Bible gives "sanctuary" for the word "holiness" in its margin. Other suggestions have also been made, but it seems from the context that Israel, as a holy nation, is in view (Ex 19.6; Deut 7.6; 14.2). For further discussion of this point see Keil & Delitzsch; C. L. Feinberg; Jamieson, Fausset & Brown; and S. R. Driver).

The addition of "which he loved" looks back to 1.2 and accentuates the enormity of their guilt. The closing statement of v.11 indicates the defilement of union with idolatrous women, and points clearly to the reason for the charge made by Jehovah. The charge is related to both immorality and idolatry. Surely one can apply here the principle of the unequal yoke. The Apostle Paul warns believers of the unequal yoke - "Be ye not unequally yoked together with unbelievers" (2 Cor 6.14). A yoke is a very powerful influence and generally the greater influence is exerted by the unbeliever. 2 Corinthians 6.14-18 embraces every part of the Christian's life indicating that temptation can be experienced in a variety of ways - e.g. political, social, religious, business, and marriage yokes. Any unequal yoke is wrong for the believer. The matrimonial unequal yoke is the most serious since it binds a person for life. Death or the coming of the Lord Jesus Christ alone breaks the marriage bond.

The consequences of such sin are given in v.12. Jehovah is against all who commit such sin and will cut them off. The Hebrew word translated "cut off" (KARAT - 3772) conveys the idea of destruction or bringing to an end, and is used of the termination of one's life (Ex 31.14). This sin is so grave and detestable to Jehovah that He threatens to destroy all who are involved in it. The expression "the master and the scholar" is difficult to explain and consequently there is a difference of opinion as to its meaning. In Hebrew the word "master" (UR - 5782) means to awake, and the word "scholar" (ANA - 6030) means to answer, or to respond. Thus the expression has been taken to refer to the temple watchers, the priests and laymen and the teachers and the students. However, these would not suit the context since the sin referred to is not limited to any section of the nation.

The more probable explanation is given by S. R. Driver - "If correct, this will be (in the Hebrew) an alliterative proverbial expression (like 'him that is shut up, and him that is left at large in Israel', 1 Kings 21.21), meaning every one (i.e. here, every one belonging to him, every member of his family, Is 14.22)". Those in view would be the offending Israelites, the heathen women they had married, and any offspring of such a union. It is unlikely that the Jewish wives and children, put away by them, would be included in the judgment. The expression may well convey that judgment would be meted out without respect of persons. Jehovah would spare neither priests nor people but cut them off from the nation. The last expression of v.12 can mean that no offering for such a person would avail to avoid the judgment, that there would be no one to offer a sacrifice for him, or that any who offered a sacrifice for such an abominable person would also be cut off by Jehovah. The last is the most likely meaning.

Verse 13 deals with a second charge against Judah indicating that there was another aspect to their marriage to idolatrous women. It was not confined to intermarriage with the heathen, but involved the divorce of their Jewish wives in order that such marriages could take place. The word "again" (SHENI - 8145) has the idea of "second" here and is translated in this way many times in the Old Testament (Gen 1.8; 2 Kings 1.17; Nah 1.9). Having dealt with the transgression of union with foreign women, Jehovah, through the prophet, takes up the second transgression of divorce and places it alongside the first that He had already condemned in the previous verses. The seriousness of this sin is implied in the previous verses and its effect is stated here before it is actually named in the following verses. In so acting, Judah had covered the altar of Jehovah with tears and weeping. The tears, weeping, and crying out were those of the forsaken Jewish wives and children who were driven to bring their plight and grief to Jehovah. These men were callous with no thought for the pain and anguish they brought to their families for whom they were responsible. How solemn and sobering, and how sad. Such conditions are indicative of the day in which we live - "Without natural affection" (2 Tim 3.3). That expression is very embracive, signifying the lack of affection in family life, and indicates that such affection is self-centred without consideration of family ties. It implies heartlessness. Today marriage and its responsibilities are treated lightly. Separation and divorce are the order of the day, without a thought for the effect upon the family. Self becomes all important - self-pleasing and self-gratification a way of life. What pain and anguish is caused by the permissive society. But how solemn when believers act in this way. One can widen the principle and ask how concerned are believers for other saints? How sad when believers have no concern for the spiritual welfare of fellow believers. How solemn when believers cause other saints pain and anguish because they speak or act with no thought for others.

The word translated "tears" (DIMA - 1832) occurs mostly in the Psalms and the writings of Jeremiah. It generally conveys the thought of mourning or lamentation. It has been stated that "whereas tears are associated with the eyes, weeping is associated with the voice". Weeping is generally the expression of the strong inward emotion of distress. The combination here implies deep lamentation and distress. The expression "with crying out" either adds greater force to the lamentation and distress or refers to the petitions of the wives to Jehovah. The fact that the Hebrew word for "crying out" (ANAQA - 603) is also translated "groaning" (Ps 102.20) seems to imply that it is the result of the lamentation and distress caused through being forsaken. Oh the pain and anguish caused by these heartless men. No wonder Jehovah would not accept their sacrifices. Since He heeded the anguish and petitions of the broken-hearted wives, He would not accept the offerings of those who caused such pain and grief. Their worship could not be accepted because of their treatment of their wives and children, which showed their disrespect for the word of God. One cannot deliberately violate the word of God and yet genuinely worship Him. One can apply this principle generally. Believers who have no concern for others and deliberately cause pain and anguish to them by their words or actions cannot really enjoy the presence of God, worship Him, or expect His commendation.

The witness of Jehovah (vv.14-17)

One notes that in vv.10-13 Judah had allowed the standards of the nations around to affect them. They had forgotten the claims of the Holy One who dwelt in their midst, and they sought to justify their actions by their own reasoning. In this section Malachi condemns their sin of divorcing their Jewish wives. In no other book of the Old Testament is so much said concerning the evil of divorce. This section shows that it is a sin which violates the creatorial intentions of God. The Lord witnessed all that had taken place and all that was taking place, and expressed His hatred of their actions.

The covenant of marriage (v.14)

The question "Wherefore?" is an enquiry into the reason why Jehovah would not regard or accept their offerings. It implied that they were not prepared to acknowledge their guilt which indicated the true condition of their souls. It is solemn to note that one can be ignorant of one's sin and can even challenge the fact that acting contrary to the teaching of the word of God is wrong. The prophet's answer is plain and pointed, exposing the dreadfulness of their evil-doing in the sight of Jehovah. He was a witness of the marriage to the Jewish wife as He was to all actions (cp. Gen 31.50). That marriage took place before the face of Jehovah and He was witness of the transaction. One needs to remember that God is witness of all that is said and done, not only what is outward, but also what is inward - the motives and intent of the heart.

The expression "the wife of thy youth," implies one who was once beloved. C. F. Keil states, "With the expression 'wife of thy youth' the prophet appeals to the heart of the husband, pointing to the love of his youth with which the marriage had been entered into; and so also in the circumstantial clause, through which he brings to the light the faithless treatment of the wife in putting her away". It could also indicate the heartlessness of such an action - setting aside the years of companionship, sharing both the joys and sorrows of life, and the solemn marriage bond. "Treacherously" here refers to unfaithfulness in the marriage bond. The word translated "companion" (HABERET - 2278) only occurs here and means consort. It is a feminine noun, a synonym of wife, indicating a close relationship. It has the thought of one to whom a person is joined.

The expression "the wife of thy covenant" indicates that marriage is a solemn and binding transaction that is witnessed by God Himself. Despite their unfaithfulness to their Jewish wives with whom they had been joined in covenant relationship, God still looked upon their wives as their true partners. In spite of the fact that they had put them away and had joined themselves to Gentile women, God still called their Jewish wives "thy companion" and "the wife of thy covenant". The marriage bond remained. What solemn lessons are here. Marriage vows are not to be taken lightly for they are binding in the sight of God. Marriage is a solemn undertaking to be entered into soberly and seriously. Believers should consider it seriously and solemnly as well as spiritually and scripturally. It is never to be treated lightly or entered into without much prayer. Neither should courtship be entered into lightly. The pattern of the world should never be adopted by the believer, and flirtation is a dishonour to God and a slight upon the believer's testimony. When a believing couple agree to marry it should be because they have decided that this is the will of God for them. Seriously, soberly, and in communion with God they have assented to His will and pledged each to the other. Marriage in the mind of God is a union between one man and one woman which is binding for life. Physical union before marriage is sin - "Marriage is honourable in all, and the bed undefiled: but whoremongers (fornicators) and adulterers God will judge" (Heb 13.4). Before marriage there should be purity and after marriage fidelity.

The creation of God (v.15)

According to C. L. Feinberg, "Verse 15 is a strong argument against divorce, but at the same time is considered the most difficult verse in the whole book of Malachi. It has always been a problem to interpreters, Jewish and Christian...We can safely say at the outset that the first portion is as difficult as the latter portion of the verse is simple". An alternative rendering of the opening expression has been taken to introduce Abraham into the verse. F. C. Cook states, "And hath no one acted thus, who yet had a remnant of sense in him? And hath no one acted thus with regard to his wife, who had any sense in him? The Jews put this question to the prophet in

reference to Abraham and his treatment of Sarah in the matter of Hagar",
making the speaker Judah. C. F. Keil writes, "'No man, who has even a
remnant of reason, or of sense for right and wrong, has done', what ye are
doing, namely, faithlessly put away the wife of his youth. To this there is
appended the objection: 'And what did that one do?' which the prophet
adduces as a possible exception that may be taken to his statement, for
the purpose of refuting it", maintaining the prophet as the speaker, but
introducing a supposition to introduce Abraham into the passage. The
introduction of Abraham here would be suitable as he took an Egyptian
woman, but it does not suit the flow of the passage. The simplest way is to
take the opening expression as it is, continuing the subject of the evil of
divorce from v.14.

The prophet now introduces the original creative institution of marriage
by stating that God made one woman for one man and the two became
one flesh (Gen 2.24). God was not limited in creation and could have
made more than one wife for Adam, but He only made one. The statement
emphasized the divine intention of one man and one woman in the
marriage bond - "For this cause shall a man leave father and mother, and
shall cleave to his wife: and they twain shall be one flesh" (Mt 19.5; Mk
10.7). Malachi goes on to give the reason why God only made one wife for
Adam - "That he might seek a godly seed". This phrase has also been viewed
in a number of ways. However, the thought seems to be of purity in the
marriage union, a seed according to God's intention, born in chaste
wedlock. God's plan is unchanged. His intention is the product of a union
between one man and one woman who are joined in matrimony. In spite
of the difficulty in the passage it is clear that the thrust of the verse is that
God's plan is one man and one woman in a marriage bond which is for
life, and that He demands purity and fidelity in that relationship. In the
last instruction, "Therefore take heed to your spirit, and let none deal
treacherously against the wife of his youth", the prophet changes from
the second person plural to the third person singular to stress that what
has been stated applied to every man. In light of the divine institution of
marriage and its solemnity Malachi warns every man to take heed to control
his spirit and not to be unfaithful to the marriage bond. How needful for
this exhortation today when marriage is not only taken lightly, but
sometimes even ridiculed. Christians need to beware of the modern
tendencies of immoral cohabitation.

God's hatred of divorce (v.16)

The reason for the rebuke and warning in the previous verses is given
in this verse - Jehovah's hatred of divorce. The prophet now uses two
names of God - Jehovah, the Elohim (430) of Israel. Elohim is plural
indicating the triune God. It is not without significance that Elohim is the
first name of God used in the Holy Scriptures and is linked with creation
(Gen 1.1). It is used here to emphasize His hatred of the violation of His

creatorial plan and intention regarding one woman and one man joined together in matrimony. One is convinced that only death or the Lord's coming breaks the marriage bond, and that divorce and remarriage should have no place in the Christian's life. David West stresses that "It was clearly the original purpose of God that marriage should be permanently binding, thus Paul says 'the woman which hath an husband is bound by the law to her husband so long as he liveth' (Rom 7.2). The law made provision for divorce in particular circumstances (Deut 24.1-4), but the Lord Jesus Himself affirmed, 'For the hardness of your heart he (i.e. Moses), wrote you this precept' (Mk 10.5). He went on to say, 'Whosoever shall put away his wife, and marry another, committeth adultery against her. And if a woman shall put away her husband, and be married to another, she committeth adultery' (Mk 10.11-12)". God declares absolutely that He hates divorce. The statement is not inconsistent with Deuteronomy 24.1-4 for that passage cannot refer to unfaithfulness in the marriage bond as the penalty for such was death (Lev 20.10-12; Deut 22.22; cp. also Num 5.13-31). Furthermore, neither can it refer to unfaithfulness in the betrothal period, which was as binding as the marriage bond, the terms husband and wife being used (Deut 20.7; 22.23; cp. also Mt 1.18-20), since its penalty was also death. To insist that unfaithfulness in the marriage bond is in view is absurd since it would condone violating the teaching of Deuteronomy 22.

The word "uncleanness" (ERWA - 6172) in Deuteronomy 24.1 means nakedness and is mainly translated this way in the Old Testament (Lev 20.11, 17-21). Nakedness is forbidden outside proper sexual relationships (Lev 18.6-19). Thus Deuteronomy 24.1 refers to some sexual act found in the wife taken. Although the intention of Deuteronomy 24 was to insist on a bill of divorcement to safeguard the wife who was being put away, it is necessary, in light of other passages in the law, to point out that only two classes could be referred to.

1. The betrothed wife forced by another man in the field (Deut 22.25-27). In this case, because of the hardness of the husband's heart (Mt 19.8), he was allowed to put her away.

2. An enticed maid, not betrothed, whose father utterly refused to give her to the man involved (Ex 22.16-17; Deut 22.28-29). On discovering she was not a virgin, although her past act had been dealt with and she was faithful in the betrothal period, the man, because of his hardness of heart and unforgiving spirit, was allowed to divorce her.

In these two cases only would the wife be innocent and need the bill of divorcement for her protection. One can only repeat that Deuteronomy 24 does not sanction divorce in the marriage bond and it is in perfect harmony with the statement here in Malachi 2.16 - "For the Lord, the God of Israel, saith that he hateth putting away". The New Testament, in harmony with this, affirms that divorce and remarriage is contrary to the mind of God.

A second reason is introduced in the expression "for one covereth violence with his garment" which is emphasized by the use of the Jehovah title "the Lord of hosts" (Jehovah Sabaoth) indicating His sovereignty. The reference seems to be indicative of a man on taking a woman to be his wife covering her with his garment (Ruth 3.9; Ezek 16.8). It may well represent union with, and protection for, his wife. The expression is God's commentary on putting away and has been rendered, "violence covereth his garment". Instead of his garment indicating union it was stained with violence. Instead of it being a protection to his wife it represented unfaithfulness. The word translated "violence" (HAMAS - 2555) means wrong, or wickedness. Its root word (2554) is used of violating the law (Ezek 22.26; Zeph 3.4). The garment that should have protected fidelity in the marriage was used to cover over the violating of the law of God. This wickedness would cleave to him in his present condition. Since raiment in the Scriptures is often symbolic of one's condition (Zech 3.4; Rev 3.4) it could be indicative of his rebellious heart. Because of the solemnity of the subject Malachi repeats his warning to beware of a lustful spirit and of such unfaithfulness.

The corruption of the truth (v.17)

Some commentators take v.17 as commencing a new section in the book. It is undoubtedly linked with ch.3, but it really forms a transition to that chapter through the closing question, which is answered in 3.1. The people of Judah had wearied Jehovah with their empty ceremonial activities and their idle statements. They had drawn near with their offerings and professed allegiance with their lips, but all was false since their hearts were far from Him. Their continued ungodliness, in spite of their outward religious observances, had exhausted the patience of Jehovah and yet they either seemed to be unaware of their true condition or they were not prepared to accept the charge against them. Thus the prophet answers the question "Wherein have we wearied him?" by charging them that they had corrupted the truth by claiming Jehovah favoured the heathen and delighted in the evil doer. They had looked at the prosperity of the heathen and at their past suffering, concluding that Jehovah had favoured the wicked. They had forgotten the reason why they had been in captivity and Jehovah's goodness in their restoration to the land. They had forgotten the threats in the word of God for disobedience and departure from Him. "How the heart of man delights in the blessings and benefits he receives from the hand of God, even when he does not thank God for them. Israel, too, took these blessings for granted. She did not realize her continuance was conditioned upon faith and obedience. As a result her blessings were replaced by curses. And is it not so all too often in the lives of believers also?" (C. L. Feinberg).

They challenged the justice of God and asked, "Where is the God of judgment?". The answer is given in the opening verses of ch.3. Such a sceptical spirit revealed they were far from God in their unbelief and ripe for judgment.

MALACHI 3

The closing chapters of this book are more familiar than the first two chapters since parts of them are quoted in the New Testament. They contain prophecy regarding both the first and second advents of the Lord Jesus Christ. Very often in Old Testament passages these advents are joined together. In such instances one must take care in discerning which statements apply to the first and which to the second advent of Christ. The prophecy here is directed against the discontented and murmuring people who had lost their faith in the promises of God because Jehovah's expected coming in power and glory to deliver them had not taken place. Their expectancy turned into disbelief causing them to call into question the holiness and justice of God, and to repudiate His coming to judge the world. In answer to the challenge of the people, "Where is the God of judgment?" (2.17), the prophet, in these closing chapters, unfolds the true nature of His coming to Israel. Chapter 3 reveals that before His coming Jehovah will send a messenger to prepare the way for Him. His advent would not be to restore Israel temporarily to the position it once had, but to judge and remove wickedness from the nation, indicating His unchanging character and ways. Malachi substantiates this in the first section of the chapter (vv.1-15) then unfolds the character of a faithful remnant in Judah (vv.16-18).

The answer of Jehovah to their murmuring is addressed to the whole nation as having departed from the commandments and having defrauded God (vv.7-9). The judgment they wanted to see would fall upon those described in v.5. The only ones distinguished from those in v.5 are the righteous of vv.16-18. It is evident that the attitude expressed in 2.17 and 3.13-15 was not the feeling of the whole nation, although it was true of the vast majority. The small remnant of the righteous was passed over in the condemnation of the people. The mention of this faithful remnant then introduces the subject of God's righteous recompense which continues to the end of the prophecy. The coming of Jehovah in judgment will make clear the distinction between the wicked and the righteous. Those who feared the Lord were reminded that the Lord had a book of remembrance (a record) written and that their faithfulness would be richly recompensed. It is always worthwhile being faithful to God and to His word; this is as true today as ever.

Verses 1-15: The Immutability of Jehovah's Ways

In this section we have a ministry concerning cleansing and restoration, therefore this readily links with the book of Numbers. There we have the passage of Israel through the wilderness where, every step of the way, they were in danger of contacting defilement. God dwelt in their midst and His sanctuary, which was among them, demanded holiness. In Numbers 19 God made provision for His people that they might be cleansed and made fit for the sanctuary and His service. In the last section of Malachi 2 Judah sought to justify their actions by their human reasoning, bringing God down to their level as if He would compromise and make no difference between their actions and His righteous character. They called evil good and said God would compromise His honour and holiness to vindicate their ways. However, in this section God shows this was an impossibility, and He emphasises the immutability of His ways and the unchangeability of His character. The speaker is the Lord of hosts, a title which occurs seven times in the section. The opening verses deal with cleansing from defilement in order to make the priests and Judah suitable for communion with God and fit to offer to God what was acceptable to Him (vv.1-6). They had denied the sovereign claims of the Lord by withholding from Him the tithes and offerings yet asked, "Wherein have we robbed thee?" (vv.7-12). They had no desire to give to God what was His by right. They set aside His claims and used what belonged to God for themselves. Their lives were self-centred and materialistic with little thought for the claims of God. There is a danger of this attitude affecting believers today when often the claims of God are set aside. The spirit of this age, with its materialistic outlook and self-advancement, is affecting many of the saints. It is possible for believers to live as they like, do what they like, and say what they like without any recourse to the claims of God. How are Christians using the ability and possessions God has given to them?

The closing verses of this section reveal the perversity of the people of Judah and the charge they made against Jehovah of dealing unfairly with those who served Him (vv.13-15).

The purifying power of Jehovah's presence (vv.1-6)

The principles that had been working in their lives had caused conditions to develop that made the intervention of God in discipline necessary with a view to cleansing and moral adjustment. These conditions reached their lowest ebb when the people sought to justify themselves as right before God, having no sense of responsibility to the One who, because He is the God of judgment, must bring all to account - "When ye say, Every one that doeth evil is good in the sight of the Lord, and he delighteth in them" (2.17). The principle here is that of 1 Peter 4.17: "For the time is come that judgment must begin at the house of God". Believers today must appreciate that they are answerable to God and come under His discipline (Heb 12.5-11; 1 Pet 1.17). It is evident that these verses are prophetic in character. The two advents of the Lord appear as two mountain peaks in the distance with no indication of the valley between. So often in the Old Testament the two advents of Christ are seen as if they were one, with no indication of the period between them. This passage can be considered under three headings.

1. The coming of Jehovah (v.1)
2. The purifying presence of Jehovah (vv.2-4)
3. The judgment of Jehovah (vv.5-6).

The coming of Jehovah (v.1)

The first part of v.1 is quoted in the New Testament (Lk 7.27) as belonging to the first advent of the Lord Jesus Christ, referring to the ministry of John the Baptist, but the latter part is a clear reference to the second advent. The opening word "Behold" (HEN - 2005) is an interjection demanding attention. It emphasises the importance of what follows. It is used to emphasise that despite their unbelief Jehovah would keep His promise and fulfil His covenant with Israel. The opening statement is clearly linked with the earlier prophecy of Isaiah: "Prepare ye the way of the Lord" (Is 40.3). Both prophecies predict the coming of the forerunner of Messiah. Although it has been suggested that no particular person is in mind but rather a whole line of prophets leading up to His coming, most commentators accept that the reference is undoubtedly to John the Baptist (Mt 3.3; Mk 1.2-3; Lk 1.76; 3.4). The Lord Jesus Christ Himself confirmed that this prediction was fulfilled in John the Baptist: "For this is he, of whom it is written, Behold, I send my messenger before thy face, which shall prepare thy way before thee" (Mt 11.10). It seems clear from Matthew 11.7-15 that the ministry of John the Baptist met the requirements of Malachi 3.1.

The expression "I will send my messenger" has its fulfilment in John 1.6: "There was a man sent from God, whose name was John". In stating that this prediction was fulfilled in John the Baptist, the Lord Jesus Christ was indicating that He Himself was the Lord of hosts. Preparing the way has the thought of removing obstacles that prevent Jehovah's coming. This announcement implied that the nation, in its present condition, was not prepared for Jehovah's coming. Instead of doubting His promise they should have repented and turned to Him. Here that preparation refers to the removing of unbelief through the preaching of repentance and salvation. John came with a message to reach the conscience of the nation, a message that emphasised the need for moral and spiritual rectification.

That was the need in Malachi's day and it is also the need today. One can lift certain moral principles from Luke 3.5 (see also Is 40.3-4) and see the change in character that the message was intended to produce: "Every valley shall be filled" - a change from degradation and despondency to holiness and gladness; "every mountain and hill shall be brought low" - a change from pride and haughtiness to lowliness of mind and humility of life; "and the crooked shall be made straight" - a change from crookedness and iniquity to honesty and righteousness; "and the rough ways shall be made smooth" - a change from hardness and roughness to tenderness and gentleness. These changes should take place in the lives of the people of God so that fellowship with God can be enjoyed. One notes that the first three Gospels, in quoting from this passage in Malachi, change the first person "me" to the second person "thy/thee" and add the expression "before thy face" (Mt 11.10; Mk 1.2; Lk 7.27). It is suggested that in the Gospels the words are viewed as the Father speaking to the Son when sending Him into the world as the Messiah and Redeemer (F. C. Cook).

Another name for God is introduced in the expression "the Lord, whom ye seek". This name is Adon (113) which indicates that He is Sovereign Lord or Master of the world since He possesses all, and acts in His own time and way. In this book it only occurs here. The expression looks back to the question of 2.17 and there seems to be a note of irony in it. However it could also be viewed as the desire of the people for the promised deliverer of the nation. "Suddenly" (PITOM - 6597) does not indicate immediately, i.e. in Malachi's day, but unexpectedly. It is used ten times in the prophetic books and is generally connected with some disaster or judgment. One is reminded of the Lord coming as a thief in the night (1 Thess 5.2). The idea is of suddenness and unpreparedness. The indication here is that the coming of the Lord would be a combination of judgment and vindication. The declaration that the Lord would come suddenly was a challenge because of the prevailing conditions. One can apply this challenge to believers today. The imminent return of the Lord Jesus for His own should cause Christians to live in the light of that coming. It is suggested that the Lord's sudden coming to His temple had a partial fulfilment in Matthew 21.12-13 when the Lord Jesus purged the temple (cp. Mk 11.15-17; Lk 19.45-46), but the complete fulfilment awaits the second coming of the Lord Jesus to the earth.

Verses 2-6 unfold the character and consequences of His coming. Then He will come as the glorious King Priest to remove the ungodly and to dwell in the midst of His people (Ezek 37.26-28; 43.7; Zeph 3.15-17; Zech 6.13). The expression "the messenger of the covenant" is a synonym of "the Lord", and is used to indicate that His coming would be in keeping with the covenant. The word translated "messenger" (MALAK - 4397) is also translated "angel". In fact it is the main Hebrew word for "angel", and is more often so translated. C. F. Keil explains that, "The coming of the Lord to His temple is represented as a coming of the covenant angel, with reference to the fact that Jehovah had in the olden time revealed His glory in His Mal'akh in a manner perceptible to the senses". This Person went before Israel during the exodus from Egypt (Ex 14.19); delivered the law to Moses at Sinai (Acts 7.38); and led Israel through the wilderness (Ex 23.20-23; cp. Is 63.9). As noted, He is the Lord Himself, the pre-incarnate Christ of the Theophanies (appearances of God in human form) in the Old Testament. He is the greatest messenger of all. The covenant in view is not the new covenant of Jeremiah 31 (cp. Heb 9.15) but the covenant already in force (Ex 24.8; Lev 26.9-12) which included Jehovah dwelling in their midst. The expression "whom ye delight in" parallels "whom ye seek" and is also ironic in view of the ungodly condition of Judah. The last clause of v.1 emphasises the certainty of His coming.

The purifying presence of Jehovah (vv.2-4)

The Lord's coming will be a time of judgment and purification. However, here it is not in relation to the heathen, which is what the people of Judah desired, but in relation to the nation of Israel. The Messiah would come, not as they expected, but as the Searcher of hearts and lives to cleanse the nation from iniquity. The day will dawn when He will come in His majesty and glory to make Israel suitable for His presence. The ironic statements of v.1, "whom ye seek" and "whom ye delight in", are followed by the two rhetorical questions of v.2. These questions are to emphasise the solemnity of the Lord's coming, awaken the conscience, and stress the inevitable answer, "No one". "Abide" (KUL - 3557) means to contain, but here it has the idea of enduring the judgment of Jehovah (cp. Joel 2.11). None can endure the consuming presence of His holiness - "For the Lord thy God is a consuming fire, even a jealous God" (Deut 4.24; cp. 2 Thess 2.8; Heb 12.29). The ungodly, being the vast majority of the nation, are undoubtedly addressed here. The second question substantiates the first by implying that no one can stand against Jehovah or face the consequences of His coming as the Judge of all men (cp. Rev 6.16-17). The reason for the Lord's coming is given in the two expressions at the close of the verse. He comes as a refiner's fire to remove the corrupt elements in the nation. This indicates the awesome manifestation of the Lord Himself and the dreadfulness of the judgment meted out to the wicked. The same allegory is used in Zechariah 13.8-9 concerning the experience of the nation during the time of Jacob's trouble (Jer 30.7) which will remove the ungodly and gather in the faithful. From the divine side it will be Jehovah's refining process, purging the nation and bringing it back to Himself (Jer 30.11-14). The expression "fullers' soap" reinforces the idea of removing defilement. The word for "fullers'" (KABAS - 3526) is used of the washing of clothes which have become contaminated. It has the thought of making them clean and soft by treading, kneading, and beating them in cold water (TWOT). Thus the idea of affliction and judgment is continued in this figure. John the Baptist, the forerunner of the Messiah, predicts the same purging of the nation in a coming day - "Whose fan is in his hand, and he will throughly purge his floor" (Mt 3.12), and the same portrayal of judgment upon the wicked is evident in that address in Matthew 3 - "the axe is laid unto the root of the trees", and the mention of the baptism with fire (vv.10-11).

The image of refining is carried on in v.3, but the emphasis changes from the removal of the foreign elements to the purifying of the base material, i.e. gold and silver. In all probability this verse refers to what the faithful remnant will pass through in a coming day. The Lord is viewed as sitting with the crucible before Him watching the process taking place, controlling the intensity of the fire and the time of purifying. Jamieson, Fausset & Brown states, "The purifier sits before the crucible, fixing his eye on the metal, and taking care that the fire be not too hot, and keeping the metal in, only until he knows the dross to be completely removed by his seeing his own image reflected (Rom 8.29) in the glowing mass". Just as Israel will be purified in a coming day so believers today go through the fires of affliction and suffering for their faith to be strengthened. The trials of life that Christians experience are like a refiner's fire removing the impurities and purifying the life to make them more Christlike and pleasing to God. Christians should take encouragement from this. He allows these trials for the ultimate benefit of the saints (2 Cor 4.17) and tried faith is much more precious than gold (1 Pet 1.6-9). How good to remember the word: "When he hath tried me, I shall come forth as gold" (Job 23.10). Only those precious things (gold and silver) require refining indicating that Israel is precious to Jehovah. It has always been precious to Him since He chose it for Himself. There will be a limited time and intensity to the purging process. The end product of the fires of the Great Tribulation will be a nation (for the saved remnant will then constitute the entire nation) restored to a genuine relationship with Jehovah. The conversion of Israel and return to the land, with its Messiah King in their midst, will be for God's glory and bring delight to the nation (Ezek 37.21-28; Zeph 3.13-17). Christians have, by the grace of God, been brought into an even closer and more precious relationship with God. They have the bright prospect of the coming of their glorious Bridegroom (Jn 3.29; 14.1-3); they have the present indwelling of the Holy Spirit, the perfect Comforter (Jn 14.16-17); and they have God as their Father (Col 1.2,12). Because of this Christians should be joyful and delight in the Lord.

Israel as a whole will be purged, beginning with the sons of Levi, by which the priests are particularly intended. They are singled out because of the corruption prevalent in the priesthood. They ought to have been the spiritual leaders of the people, but their offerings were unacceptable because of their ungodly ways. Thus the priesthood needed to be cleansed from the sins described in 1.6-2.9. The Lord, as the refiner and purifier, will purge the priesthood, setting aside for Himself the sons of Zadok, who shall judge themselves and turn to Him (Ezek 48.11). One is reminded of 1 Peter 4.17: "For the time is come that judgment must begin at the house of God". When the dross is removed they will be in a suitable condition to offer what is pleasing to Jehovah. Believers today need to be in a right spiritual condition to render worship and service to God which will please Him. The result of the purifying presence of the Lord will be priests who offer to Him sacrifices in righteousness. The thought here is not of righteous sacrifices being offered, but rather of the moral character of the priests (as 2.6) who offer them. Since the moral character of the priest would be in keeping with the character of God, the sacrifices he offered would be in keeping with the word of God. Roman Catholicism takes this as a prophecy of the offering of the Eucharist. However, this, together with the following verse, refers to millennial days when the Lord has returned to the earth and has established His Kingdom in righteousness. Thus the claim that the offering in righteousness is prophetic of the Eucharist is false.

The introductory word "Then" in v.4 is a time note as to when the offerings of Israel will be acceptable to Jehovah. When the priests have been purified and are offering sacrifices in righteousness then the offerings of the whole nation will be pleasant to Him. In the context this is undoubtedly a reference to the reinstated sacrifices and offerings in millennial days (cp. Ezek 43-45). Whereas the sacrifices of Israel in the past looked on to that one, never to be repeated, great sacrifice at Calvary, the sacrifices during the Millennium will look back to that central event in the purpose of God. They could not be effective sacrifices, and so are like the Levitical sacrifices which could never take away sins (Heb 10.4). Only the sacrifice of the Lord Jesus upon the cross could put away sin (Heb 9.26) and His precious blood alone is the basis of redemption and cleansing from all sin (1 Pet 1.18-19; 1 Jn 1.7). Whereas the Levitical sacrifices were signposts pointing on to the one sacrifice for sins (Heb 10.4) the millennial sacrifices will be commemorative of that sacrifice. Just as Christians remember the Lord Jesus Christ and His work at Calvary at the Lord's Supper every Lord's day during this day of grace, so the sacrifices of the millennial days will be a memorial of that same Person and His work for redeemed Israel.

The expression "days of old" is indefinite referring to various periods such as the days of Moses, the reign of David, and part of Solomon's reign, as well as the reign of godly kings such as Hezekiah and Josiah. The last expression of the verse, "in former years", reinforces the previous clause. Since the word "former" (QADMONI - 6931) has the thought of ancient, the early years of Israel's sojourn in the wilderness may be in view (Jer 2.2). Whatever the period or periods referred to, the intention of the verse is not to imply that millennial days will be like the days of old, but to contrast those days with Malachi's day when the sacrifices were not pleasurable to Jehovah. They were not pleasurable, not only because of the sins of the people, but mainly on account of the corrupt priests who offered them. Similarly, by way of application, one can contrast the apostolic days (i.e. the days of old) with today and note the deterioration in spiritual things and the departure of assemblies from the principles of gathering as set out in the word of God. Believers today should be much before the Lord as to their position regarding faithfulness to His word.

The judgment of Jehovah (vv.5-6)

The refining by Jehovah in v.4 changes to judgment upon the wicked in v.5. This judgment is threatened against those who asked sarcastically, "Where is the God of judgment?" (2.17). To the evil ones Jehovah would draw near in judgment. "Judgment" (MISHPAT - 4941) has the thought here of exercising judgment in absolute justice, as it does in 2.17. The justice of Jehovah in carrying out this judgment is established by His swift witness to the violation of His just demands. One must not take the word "swift" to indicate that the judgment would take place in Malachi's day, but rather to emphasise the rapidity of the event in the day of Jehovah's coming (v.2). It is not only swift in giving evidence as a Witness to their wickedness, but also rapid as a Judge in carrying out the judgment. The thought seems to be that His coming would convict the wicked of their guilt as the punishment is meted out. It is different in this present day of grace when conviction of sin is intended to produce repentance and faith in the Lord Jesus Christ. However, believers must remember that they come under the government of God in their earthly lives. Having been accepted on the basis of grace and faith in Christ they have a great High Priest and Advocate, the Lord Jesus Christ, but are expected to live in keeping with their standing in Christ. Christians need to be watchful, prayerful, and self-judging in order to maintain purity of mind and holiness of life, for God their Father sees all and judges each work without respect of persons (1 Pet 1.17).

A catalogue of the wicked, who will come under the judgment of Jehovah, is now given, commencing with sorcerers, who practised witchcraft. This was forbidden (Deut 18.10-11) and the penalty for such was death (Ex 22.18). It existed in Ahab's reign having been brought in by Jezebel (2 Kings 9.22), and was also prevalent in the reign of Manasseh (2 Chr 33.6). In post-captivity days it was probably introduced into the nation by the idolatrous foreign women referred to in ch.2, and it continued even to New Testament days (Acts 8.11; 13.8). This will be characteristic of the period before the manifestation of Christ and of the coming antichristian confederacy (Mt 24.24; Rev 13.13-14; 16.13-14). Adulterers are included, in keeping with the condemnation of the law (Lev 20.10; Deut 22.22). It is suggested that this term has in view those living with foreign women having set aside their Jewish wives (2.10-16) (see C. L. Feinberg and Keil & Delitzsch). The false swearers, those who are false witnesses, are mentioned in the list for they too are condemned in the law (Ex 20.16; Lev 19.12) as also are the oppressors of the hireling, the widow, the fatherless, and the stranger (Ex 22.21-22; 23.9; Lev 19.13; Deut 24.14-15; 27.19). These last three are specific objects of Jehovah's care and He had made particular provisions for them (Deut 10.17-18; 14.28-29; 24.19-21). To oppress them was a violation of that care and provision. The closing expression "and fear not me" indicates the source from which the enumerated sins, and indeed all wickedness, flows.

The reason for the refining and the judgment in vv.2-5 is given in v.6: "For I am the Lord, I change not". The stress here is upon the name Jehovah, the covenant name of God to Israel (Ex 6.3), "He that always was, that always is, and that ever is to come" (Introduction to the Newberry Bible). The emphasis is upon the immutability of God, His unfailing faithfulness to His covenant with Israel. It indicates that God is unchangeable, totally reliable and a sure source of power, might, and security. He is immutable in His nature and thus unchangeable in His promises and dealings with men. This is a source of comfort and encouragement to believers, but a warning and a source of terror to unbelievers. Had it not been for the changeless character of Jehovah and His faithfulness to His word the sons of Jacob would have been destroyed. Some have taken the expression "sons of Jacob" as representative of the nation while others have viewed it as the faithful remnant in Israel (see C. L. Feinberg and Keil & Delitzsch). Whichever view is taken it is plain from Romans 11.29 that Israel's bright future depends upon the fact that the gifts and calling of God are unalterable. God is unfailingly faithful to His word and His promises, whether of blessing or of judgment. Christians have confidence from the word of God that they will never perish because of the finished work of Christ and that they are seen in Him without spot or stain. His preservation of them does not depend upon their faithfulness, but upon His unchanging faithfulness and love (Rom 8.31-39). However, they must realise that the unalterable character of God demands that He discipline them again and again for their waywardness, and that He must withhold blessings which He longs to bestow because their lives are contrary to His character and claims.

Since Jehovah is changeless in His character and in His purposes, and because Israel, as the people of God, is not to perish, He will remove the wicked of Israel in judgment (vv.2 & 5) and refine the rest (vv.3-4) to mould the nation in keeping with His plan. This is also seen in Jeremiah 5.18: "Nevertheless in those days, saith the Lord, I will not make a full end with you". God limits the severity of His judgment, and in so doing His justice and mercy are manifested. Even in his lamentation over the captivity and the destruction of Jerusalem, Jeremiah could exclaim, "It is of the Lord's mercies that we are not consumed, because his compassions fail not. They are new every morning: great is thy faithfulness" (Lam 3.22-23). The nation's future was secure because of Jehovah's unchanging purpose for Israel. They had been set apart to God (Deut 7.6-7; 14.2). They were chosen, in keeping with God's promise to Abraham, to be His people with an earthly inheritance (Gen 12.1; 13.15). The saints in this day of grace are also a chosen people, but to be a heavenly people with a heavenly inheritance (Eph 1.3-4; 1 Pet 1.3-4). Christians should rejoice because of God's unvarying character and His unchanging promises in Christ. In this passage one can see Jehovah's absolute hatred of sin and yet also His longsuffering love and mercy. Since God is infinitely holy, sin in every form, whether in His people or in unbelievers, must be dealt with. It is well to remember this solemn and sobering fact.

The priority of Jehovah's claims (vv.7-12)

Jehovah, having proclaimed that He would come in judgment, now gives the reason why He had kept His blessing from them. He was unchangeable in His faithfulness and goodness to them, but they had not changed in their waywardness which was evident in their defrauding of Jehovah in the matter of their tithes and offerings. In so doing they were setting aside His priority claim upon them, for the tithes and offerings were but an acknowledgement that they owed all to Jehovah.

The charge against Judah (vv.7-9)

Here we see the continual disobedience and backsliding of the people. This characterised Israel in general throughout their history. They had never kept the precepts and commandments in a completely scriptural way, but had often transgressed the law (Is 43.27; Ezek 2.3). The condition of the people in Malachi's day was no different from the days of their fathers which had brought upon them the captivity in Babylon. This emphasises the fact that nothing but the unchanging faithfulness and longsuffering of Jehovah had prevented them from being consumed (v.6). From the days of their fathers they had consistently deviated from the instruction given by Jehovah, but now in light of His coming He calls upon them genuinely to return unto Him. There would be no blessing from Jehovah unless they repented and responded to His appeal. He would return to them in blessing only if they returned to Him (Zech 1.3). They had returned to the land, but their condition was such that they needed to return to the Lord. It is possible to be in the right place but in the wrong condition. This is true today for one can be correct in being gathered to the Lord's name in a local assembly, but in a wrong state of heart before God. Believers should always seek to be in the right condition before God. This appeal, which was compassionate (since God longs to bless), was also intensely personal, for it was an appeal to return to Jehovah whom they had abandoned. It was not an appeal to return merely to correct teaching and practice, but to Jehovah Himself. Returning to Jehovah would result in accepting His word and living in keeping with it. This is a challenge to believers today. Coldness of heart and failure to carry out the word of God is indicative of backsliding. Christians need to bear in mind that such regression is gradual and begins in the believer's heart, in the secret-place, before it is manifested to fellow believers. One is, of course, thinking of genuine believers, not of the host of those who have merely professed but who have never been saved. Backsliding begins through the neglect of two things.

1. The neglect of communion with God, time spent in the presence of God. Prayer and communion are essential for maintaining a right condition of soul (Lk 18.1; 1 Thess 5.17). Time in the presence of God is necessary for the enjoyment of fellowship with God and the prevention of backsliding. It is when prayer degenerates into the saying of prayers that backsliding commences. One needs to be on guard to prevent prayer becoming a mere habit or sense of duty instead of the desire and joy of one's heart. Christians are exhorted to continue in prayer and watch in the same (Rom 12.12; Col 4.2).

2. The neglect of the word of God. To neglect the word of God is to set aside the only guide God has given to direct one's footsteps in the path He would have His people to tread (Ps 119.105). It is also necessary to apply the word of God to one's life in order to cleanse it from the defilement which results from living in an evil and corrupt world (Ps 119.9; Jn 17.17). The Psalmist could say, "Thy word have I hid in mine heart, that I might

not sin against thee" (Ps 119.11). How important it is to meditate on the word of God (Ps 1.2). The neglect of prayer and the reading of the word of God brings about coldness of heart, which, if it continues, will manifest itself in departure from the things of God. There will be failure in testimony, in standing for Christ, and the neglect of the gatherings of the Lord's people (Heb 10.25). It is necessary for believers to search their lives either to prevent backsliding taking place or to repent where it has already taken place, and return to the Lord (2 Cor 7.9-10; 2 Tim 2.25). Christians need to be in a right condition before they can appreciate and enjoy the rich blessings of God.

One notes the love of Jehovah's heart yearning over His people and granting them the opportunity to repent and return to Him. In spite of their long period of departure and disobedience He was willing to receive and bless them if they returned to Him. God is the same today, and in His love He yearns for the backslider to return to Him in penitence and longs for the sinner to repent and trust the Lord Jesus Christ. In spite of their condition the ungodly majority of Judah regarded themselves as righteous, and in self-righteousness they arrogantly asked, "Wherein shall we return?". They were satisfied with their lives and saw no need to turn from their sinful ways. All was well as far as they were concerned and as long as the outward ceremonial forms were carried out they saw no reason to change. Thus they had no intention of responding to Jehovah's appeal to repent and return to Him.

The answer to their question is given in the charge laid against the people of robbing Jehovah of what was rightfully His. They were doing what no one should attempt to do. The claim of Jehovah was set aside and they feasted upon what belonged to Him. This revealed one of the ways in which they had departed from Him and showed the righteousness of Jehovah's appeal to them to return as well as its necessity. The rhetorical question, "Will a man rob God?" (v.8), is intended to arrest the ungodly majority of the people and to emphasise the seriousness of their sinful condition. Was it possible that frail mortal man could rob the great and eternal God? The answer is immediately given, "Yet ye have robbed me". The word rendered "rob" and "robbed" (QABA - 6906) is only found elsewhere in Proverbs 22.23 where it is translated "spoil" and "spoiled". It is a primitive root meaning to cover and thus, figuratively, to defraud (Strong's Concordance). They were doing what seemed incredible for any of the people of God to do. This solemn charge should have been sufficient to justify the demand of Jehovah that they repent and return to Him. However, in their self-justifying spirit, and in amazing boldness, they challenged such a charge with the question, "Wherein have we robbed thee?". Such a spirit continued among the Jews and was evident in the day of the Lord's public ministry (Lk 10.29; 16.15). This attitude is not uncommon to man, being prevalent in the world today and, sad to say, also characterising some Christians. The answer to their self-righteous question was that they had defrauded Jehovah in tithes and offerings which were His absolute right. They had defrauded Jehovah by either reducing their tithes or withholding them altogether. The tithes belonged to Jehovah and were to be used in keeping with His word. The tithe (MAASER - 4643) was a tenth part, and its first occurrence is in Genesis 14.20. Tithes were either from the produce of the land (Lev 27.30) or from the herd or flock (Lev 27.32). There were different kinds of tithes.

1. Tithes given to the Levites (Num 18.24; Neh 10.37).

2. Tithes given by the Levites, out of the tithes they themselves received, to Aaron the priest, i.e. the priestly family (Num 18.28; Neh 10.38).

3. On coming into the land the tithe of all produce was to be taken to Jerusalem (Deut 12.17-18) or, if Jerusalem was too far away, it could be turned into money and on arrival at Jerusalem anything desired could be purchased to be eaten with the family, the servants, and any Levites there (Deut 14.22-27).

4. Every third year, the tithe was to be laid up within the gates for the Levites, the stranger, the fatherless, and the widow within those gates (Deut 14.28-29; 26.12).

The Hebrew word for "offerings" (TᵉRUMA - 8641) is only used here in the prophecy and has the thought of lifting up or taking off from a larger mass, and is used extensively of heave offerings. Nehemiah substantiates the fact that these tithes and offerings were not correctly given (Neh 13.10) and thus the charge of defrauding Jehovah was justified. Christians today can be guilty of robbing God. There is a tendency for believers to use their time and energy in selfish pursuits. They can also use their possessions to further their own cause instead of using them for God. Barrenness in the prayer and the breaking of bread meetings is robbing God. How does christian giving today measure up to that of the Macedonians, who first gave themselves to the Lord then, despite their great trial of affliction and deep poverty, gave willingly and liberally to meet the needs of others (2 Cor 8.1-5)? The Lord's priority claim is upon the saints, whom He has purchased (1 Cor 6.19-20), and also upon all that He has bestowed upon them. All christian giving should be as unto the Lord Himself and out of deep devotion to Him.

The consequences of their actions were already at work, for the curse of Jehovah was upon them because they had deliberately violated the law (v.9). In spite of the curse they continued in their sinful ways. They seemed to persist in their wicked course unaware of their true condition and indifferent to the condemnation of Jehovah. H. A. Ironside states, "It is a question which was the most solemn - their sinful course, or their calm indifference concerning it. Conscience seemed completely gone; and when a good conscience has been put away, anything can be indulged in with a degree of self-assurance that seems inexplicable". In the language of the New Testament, their conscience was "seared with a hot iron" (1 Tim 4.2). By constantly stifling the warnings of Jehovah their conscience no longer bothered them. Through their continual disobedience their conscience had become defiled (Tit 1.15). Christians should have a good conscience (1 Tim 1.5,19) which is directed by the divine revelation and judges all things by it. The conscience is good when there is no accusing voice within because the life is in keeping with the word of God. Believers today should seek "to have always a conscience void of offence toward God, and toward men" (Acts 24.16). In defrauding Jehovah the people were actually defrauding themselves by bringing the curse of barrenness upon the land (v.11). The people of God need to appreciate that being half-hearted in the things of the Lord is never beneficial. It never pays to be apathetic in the service of God or to compromise the truth of His word. It always pays to be faithful to the word of God and to willingly and whole-heartedly serve Him. This may not necessarily appear to be true now, but a coming day will prove it so. The last expression of v.9, "even this whole nation", indicates how far the ungodly nation was from Jehovah and stresses the enormity of its guilt. Such language also emphasises the need for repentance and recovery.

The promise of Jehovah (vv.10-11)

If the people would return to Jehovah and render to Him what was rightfully His, then He would pour out His abundant blessing, which He longed to bestow, upon them. He would fulfil His promise if they fulfilled their responsibility. If Christians would give the Lord the first place in their lives and render to God what is rightfully His then they would enjoy the rich blessing He longs to bestow upon them - "But seek ye first the kingdom of God, and his righteousness; and all these things shall be added unto you" (Mt 6.33). In these verses Jehovah is again giving the people opportunity to repent and return to Him. In the opening expression of v.10 Jehovah calls on them to bring all the tithes into the storehouse. The emphasis is upon the word "all" (KOL - 3605) meaning the whole (Strong's Concordance). They were to bring the whole tithe and not just a portion of it, for that would be defrauding Jehovah. In bringing the whole tithe into the storehouse they would be faithful to the law and would acknowledge the just claim of Jehovah upon them. There is a divine principle implied here which is applicable in every dispensation and in every generation - God opens the storehouse of His rich and abundant blessing to those of His people who are zealous in their devotion and obedience to Him. Believers today should challenge themselves as to this important principle. The storehouse here refers to the chambers built in the House of the Lord, also called treasuries, for the storing of the tithes (2 Chr 31.11-12; Neh 10.35-39; 12.44; 13.5, 12-13). Bringing the tithes to the house of the Lord was an acknowledgement both of Jehovah's goodness and of His claim upon them.

God has a similar claim on the people of God today and there are principles regarding giving set out by the Apostle Paul in 1 Corinthians 16 and 2 Corinthians 8-9. Although a special collection to meet the need of the saints at Jerusalem is in view in these chapters, Paul unfolds abiding principles for the guidance of the saints in every generation in regard to this subject. In 1 Corinthians 16.2 Christians are taught to give regularly - "the first day of the week" - week by week; individually - "let every one" - each one whatever their age or status; systematically - "lay by him in store" - setting aside God's portion to be used in keeping with His will; proportionately - "as God hath prospered him" - the more God bestows the more the believer is enabled to give. In 2 Corinthians 8 & 9 the instruction is to give spiritually - "first gave their own selves to the Lord" (8.5) - yielding one's self to the Lord and looking at things from His viewpoint; willingly - "a willing mind" (8.12); bountifully - "he which soweth bountifully" (9.6) - "The liberal soul shall be made fat: and he that watereth shall be watered also himself" (Prov 11.25); purposefully - "according as he purposeth in his heart" (9.7); and cheerfully - "God loveth a cheerful giver" (9.7) - counting it a joy to give.

The expression "that there may be meat in mine house" seems to refer to necessary provision to maintain the priests and Levites in their service for Jehovah (Num 18.24-28). This is confirmed by Nehemiah 13.10-14. The people were responsible for bringing in their tithes to meet the material needs of the priests and Levites who served Jehovah on their behalf and made known His word to them. This principle of maintenance is carried through to the New Testament (1 Cor 9.10-11, 13) showing that those who are taught in spiritual things have a responsibility to provide for the material needs of those who teach them (1 Cor 9.11; Gal 6.6) - "Even so hath the Lord ordained that they which preach the gospel should live of the gospel" (1 Cor 9.14). Jehovah, who is over all, challenged them to prove Him or put Him to the test as to whether He was still the righteous, holy, and faithful God. This they could only do by obedience in bringing all their tithes to Him. The result would be the opening of the windows of heaven, the emptying out of blessing. The imagery used here denotes an abundance of blessing bestowed upon them like the pouring of rain. The figure, taken in the light of v.11 where drought is implied, might well refer to the coming of rain which would change the parched and barren ground into a fertile land, producing harvest with undamaged fruit (2 Chr 31.10). They were to honour the Lord first, then He would abundantly bless them - "Honour the Lord with thy substance, and with the firstfruits of thine increase: So shall thy barns be filled with plenty, and thy presses shall burst out with new wine" (Prov 3.9-10). When believers today honour the Lord with their substance they are acknowledging that all they have is His to be used as He directs. So great is God's goodness that when saints so honour Him He sees that there is no lack with them, for He bestows upon them out of His abundance. Everything comes from God and yet He graciously receives from those He has redeemed. No matter how much one gives to God, He is no man's debtor.

Not only would Jehovah bless them for their obedience, but He would

also rebuke the devourer (v.11). The idea in the word "rebuke" (GA'AR -
1605) is that of restraining or holding back. Here it has the thought of
averting the intention of the devourer. The "devourer" seems to refer to
the locust which consumes voraciously all before it (2 Chr 7.13; Ps 105.34-
35). When the rain watered the thirsty fields and the harvest grew, Jehovah
promised to withhold the locust and any other blight from their harvest
which thus would prosper and nothing would hurt the fruit. "Destroy"
(SHAHAT - 7843) means to decay, or to ruin, and has the idea here of fruit
which perishes and drops off before it ripens. Thus Jehovah would protect
the fruit of their vines if they willingly brought their tithes into the
storehouse. There is a challenge for believers today in these verses. A charge
can be made against some Christians today of defrauding God with material
possessions. There can be a lack of exercise in regard to giving, forgetting
that all that has been bestowed is from God. Although believers today are
not under the law but under grace, surely one should not give to God less
than what was required under the law, but rather more in view of what He
has already abundantly imparted to them. Sadly some Christians forget
this responsibility and use their possessions in selfish pursuits. It is possible
not only to defraud God in material things, but also in the time and energy
given to His service and in spiritual things. One can also rob God through
lack of communion with Him in the secret place. The only way for the
believer today to be in the enjoyment of God's presence and blessing is by
keeping close to Him and obeying His word.

> But we never can prove
> The delights of His love,
> Until all on the altar we lay;
> For the favour He shows,
> And the joy He bestows,
> Are for them who will trust and obey.
>   (J. H. Sammis).

The response of the nations (v.12)
    Verse 12 will only have its fulfilment in a coming day, in the golden age
of the Millennium when the Lord Jesus Christ will sit upon the throne of
His glory (Mt 25.31) and establish the Kingdom in righteousness (Is 32.1).
Only then will God be fully acknowledged and all His claims be met. Then
Israel will enter into its promised inheritance and the land will be
characterised by holiness (Zech 14.20-21). Jehovah's blessing will be upon
them as the result of repentance and obedience. This refers to the future
repentant remnant which will wholeheartedly return to God. It will be the
nucleus of the new nation which will experience the abundant blessing of
Jehovah. Blessed both spiritually and materially with all that the heart
desires, all nations will then call them blessed. Then they will fully

experience the blessings of Deuteronomy 28.1-13, and then will be brought to fruition the prediction of Deuteronomy 33.28-29 (cp. Ps 72.16; 115.9-12; Zech 8.13). The pronoun "ye" in the closing expression is emphatic drawing attention to the pleasantness of the land. Then will be fulfilled Isaiah 62.4 where Hephzibah means "my delight is in her". The land will not only be a delight to God, but also to all nations. It is necessary to stress the importance of the principle that the enjoyment of the rich blessing of God depends upon devotion of heart and willing obedience to His word. This is true in every age. All that is due to the Lord is often withheld from Him by believers because of their selfish aims. His due should be rendered to Him and He will have pleasure in bestowing in return His rich blessing. However, low spiritual condition because of worldliness and materialism frequently hinders His blessing. Christians today should take heed to Jeremiah's exhortation: "Let us search and try our ways, and turn again to the Lord" (Lam 3.40). The Psalmist could say, "Search me, O God, and know my heart: try me, and know my thoughts: And see if there be any wicked way in me, and lead me in the way everlasting" (Ps 139.23-24).

> Search me, O God, my actions try,
> And let my life appear
> As seen by Thine all-searching eye:
> To mine my ways make clear.
>
> Search all my sense, and know my heart,
> Who only canst make known;
> And let the deep, the hidden part
> To me be fully shown.
>
> (F. Bottome).

The perversity of Judah (vv. 13-15)

For the nation of Judah the time of blessing had not yet come, nor has it yet, for they knew not the time of their visitation (Lk 19.44). After Jehovah had unfolded the reason for withholding His blessing, He further charged the people with wickedness in unjustly speaking against Him. They complained that their outward religious observances brought them no advantage. The same scepticism displayed throughout the prophecy by the mass of the nation is now seen in these verses. Here we have their impatient murmuring against Jehovah which only further demonstrated their backslidden and perverse condition. Thus these are the last words addressed by Malachi to the people, leaving them, in general, untouched by his ministry.

Their words (v. 13)

Their speech was stout, or strong, against Jehovah and contrary to His character and claims. He censures the attitude adopted by these murmurers which is characteristic of the ungodly - "all their hard speeches which ungodly sinners have spoken against him" (Jude v.15). Every word spoken, with apparent impunity, against God will come under His judgment - "But I say unto you, That every idle word that men shall speak, they shall give account thereof in the day of judgment" (Mt 12.36). Men may cast aside thoughts of the day of judgment, saying that death ends all, but they will have to give an account in a coming day before the Lord who will be seated on the Great White Throne (Rev 20.11-15). The people of Judah were unmoved by this censure and, in their conceit and the willing ignorance of their wicked hearts, challenged Jehovah, implying that the rebuke was unjustified - "What have we spoken so much against thee?". No appeal, censure, charge, or warning seemed to move them in the slightest degree from their self-righteous and arrogant ways. Jamieson, Fausset & Brown explains that, "The Hebrew expresses at once their assiduity and habit of speaking against God. The…form of the verb implies that these things were said, not directly to God, but of God, one to another (Ezek 33.20)" (see also Keil & Delitzsch). The subjects of their conversations against Jehovah, which often took place, are stated in v.14.

Their work and walk (v.14)

They considered that reverencing, serving, and obeying Jehovah were unprofitable and thus of no value. They were influenced by their circumstances and did not appreciate that their own waywardness was the cause of those circumstances. They foolishly measured things by the standard of material prosperity and murmuringly concluded that it was of no value to serve Jehovah because the righteous, which they assumed they were, had no advantage over the heathen. They agreed together that there was nothing to gain by serving God. Thus their service and manner of life were contrary to the claims of Jehovah. This sceptical spirit was attributed to the wicked centuries before - "What is the Almighty, that we should serve him? and what profit should we have, if we pray unto him?" (Job 21.15; cp. 22.17). Now, in Malachi's day, the professed people of God were saying the same things. However, their claim to have served God was false because their spirit was wrong. It was with a materialistic spirit that they performed their outward ceremonies. They carried out their observances, not out of love for Jehovah, but from a selfish looking for material prosperity. However, God looks at the motive, at the heart, and not at the outward appearance (1 Sam 16.7). It is important that believers today appreciate this solemn fact. At the Judgment Seat of Christ (2 Cor 5.10) the Lord will bring to light the counsels of the heart, the desires and motives which were the basis for the decisions and actions of believers during their life time here (1 Cor 4.5).

The claim by Judah's people to have kept the ordinance was flawed. There seems to be a play on the word for "kept" (SHAMAR - 8104) and its derivative word translated "ordinance" (MISHMERET - 4931). The verb

SHAMAR means to exercise great care over, or be diligent in, something, and the noun MISHMERET has the sense of an obligation or a service. MISHMERET also has the sense of something that is kept or preserved (TWOT). Their claim was that they had exercised great care over or been diligent in the service of Jehovah by their outward observances. In the light of the flawed sacrifices offered to Jehovah, and the tithes they withheld from Him, their claim was not only ludicrous but also both deceitful and arrogant. They also considered that their outward appearance was sufficient instead of genuine repentance and humiliation, so they put on sackcloth and ashes (cp. Est 4.1-4; Is 58.5; Mt 11.21) pretending to be penitent. However, their outward show of humiliation passed unheeded. They had either ignored or forgotten Isaiah's censure of such false behaviour (Is 58.3-7).

Their ways (v.15)
   When prosperity was withheld from them they charged Jehovah with being unjust and, reasoning among themselves, they came to the conclusion that the proud were happy and the rebellious were prosperous. Their reasoning was governed by outward appearance and prosperity, and thus was limited to transient things. Their ways were taken up with the pursuit of material things at the expense of spiritual. It is easy for believers today likewise to be taken up with the material and to think only of the passing things of life. Christians can often be swayed by outward appearance and forget that the enjoyment of fellowship with God outweighs material prosperity. One can measure profit by the standards of the world and forget that in this day of grace our blessings are spiritual and not material. As the people of God, believers should be living for eternity - "Lay not up for yourselves treasures upon earth...But lay up for yourselves treasures in heaven...For where your treasure is, there will your heart be also" (Mt 6.19-21; cp. Col 3.1-2). Saints need to learn the important lesson that they should live in the light of eternity and near to God who is unfailingly faithful.
   The words "call...happy" are translated from the same Hebrew word rendered "call...blessed" in v.12. Not satisfied with complaining over their leanness and lack of prosperity, because of their half-hearted worship and service for Jehovah, they pronounced that He had favoured the proud. Some take "the proud" as referring to the godless in Judah while others believe that it refers to the heathen nations (S. R. Driver; Keil & Delitzsch). Although both may be embraced, here it is more probable that the prosperous heathen nations are in view. The people of Judah reasoned that since they, who served Jehovah, were not prosperous and the heathen flourished then they must be the ones blessed by Him. Thus there was no value in keeping the law or obeying the voice of Jehovah through His prophets. H. A. Ironside states, "What they did not take into account was that they were part of a failed nation, and still reaping the sad fruit of their

fathers' evil sowing. So they were stumbled at the prosperity of the wicked, but did not, like Asaph, enter with unshod feet into the sanctuary, that they might understand the end of the enemies of the Lord (see Ps 73)". Although they themselves had departed from Jehovah and His word, and were thus unjust in their charge of Jehovah's partiality, the problem of the wicked prospering while the godly are afflicted has continued throughout human history. It is a problem that has perplexed every generation in every country of the world and it is because of sin. Christians today may ask, "Why does God allow His people to suffer and the ungodly to prosper?", and, "How long will God allow wickedness to prevail?". There seems to be no answer, but that does not mean that God is not capable of dealing with the situation. He is Sovereign and all is under His control, and believers must accept this fact. It is not for Christians to know the reason why, but to rest upon Him waiting patiently for the fulfilment of His purpose. As one views the prevailing godlessness today and the departure from the word of God, even among genuine believers, well might one cry to God, "Help, Lord; for the godly man ceaseth; for the faithful fail from among the children of men" (Ps 12.1).

The last two statements of v.15 are placed in relation to each other by the use of "yea" (GAM - 1571). It is used to stress the pronoun "they" indicating that not only do the wicked flourish, but when they tempt God they seem to escape His judgment. The word translated "tempt" is the same word as that rendered "prove" in v.10. The idea seems to be that they not only prosper, but when they challenge God His judgment does not fall upon them since they are often delivered from adversity. However, although God's judgment is delayed because of His longsuffering, it is not set aside. The day will dawn when the wicked will experience the judgment of God (4.1).

Verses 3.16-4.6: The Righteousness of Jehovah's Recompense

It is suggested that in this last section we have the result of Malachi's ministry among a remnant that responds to his message (3.16-18). This remnant looks forward to a coming day and is a representative of the nucleus of the new nation upon which the Sun of righteousness will yet shine (4.2). The judgment mentioned in the last section will make clear the distinction between the wicked and the righteous, bringing destruction to the former and salvation to the latter (4.1-3). The prophecy closes with a final exhortation to remember the Law of Moses (4.4), and with the announcement that Jehovah would send Elijah before the coming day of judgment to turn the hearts of the people back to Him (4.5-6). The emphasis in this section seems to be upon the righteousness of His recompense. Those who feared the Lord were reminded that the Lord had a book of remembrance (record) written, and that their faithfulness would be richly recompensed. It is always worth being faithful to God and to His word. Christians should never forget that the Judgment Seat of Christ is ahead for every believer. In every aspect of life saints need to remember the sentiment of the following:

> Only one life, yes only one;
> Soon will its fleeting hours be done.
> Then in "that day" the Lord to meet,
> And stand before His Judgment Seat.
> Only one life, 'twill soon be past,
> Only what's done for Christ will last.

The faithful remnant (vv.16-18)

While Judah, in general, were complaining and speaking against Jehovah to each other, there was a godly remnant whose conversation was opposite to the prevailing attitude. In the midst of spiritual departure, failure and corruption, that godly remnant drew together, strengthening themselves in the fear of Jehovah. In their conversation and conduct they were a stark contrast to the majority of the nation. Until this section one is unaware of any who sought to carry out the word of God, but now we are introduced to those who sought to be faithful. It is encouraging to know that there is always a remnant in every age seeking to honour the word of God for His glory and pleasure. Three things are mentioned regarding this remnant.

1. They feared Jehovah.
2. They enjoyed fellowship together.
3. They would be richly recompensed.

Their fear (v.16)

This remnant feared Jehovah; they lived in reverential awe of Him, seeking to walk in His ways. They feared Jehovah, and instead of despising His name they thought upon His name. They reverenced Him and this delivered them from the fear of men (Prov 29.25), giving them courage to bear the reproach of carrying out the will of Jehovah. It is only reverential fear of God that will give courage to believers today to obey the word of God. This remnant had a dread of dishonouring His name and they hated evil (Prov 8.13) and this gave them moral strength to be faithful to the word of God and the ministry of Malachi. Do believers today fear God? "The fear of the Lord is the beginning of wisdom" (Ps 111.10). Like those in Acts 9.31 Christians ought to walk in the fear of the Lord. The exhortation of Peter is that saints should pass the time of their sojourning here in fear. Those who call upon God as Father are exiles in this world and while on the journey home to heaven they ought to have a reverential fear that will cause them to be careful to act in keeping with the Father's character (1 Pet 1.17). The believer who fears God will have the spiritual resolve to carry out the word of God faithfully whatever the cost.

Their fellowship (v.16)

The word "Then" indicates both the contrast between the conversation of the ungodly majority and that of the godly remnant, and also shows that the conversation of the ungodly caused the coming together of the remnant to strengthen each other in their trust in Jehovah. Instead of their speech being stout against Jehovah (v.13) it was about the things of Jehovah. The very circumstances they found themselves in drove them closer together, uniting their hearts in holy fellowship. They did not succumb to the conditions around them, but separated themselves from those conditions, uniting their hearts in harmonious fellowship. Each one of them had an earnest desire for the things of Jehovah and this resulted in happy fellowship. Their faith was in Jehovah as the holy and righteous God who would, in His time, recompense both the wicked and the just, and they could rest upon Him because of who He was. This description of the conversation and conduct of the godly remnant was an indirect admonition to the people of Judah, for their attitude to Jehovah should have been the same. The lives of the godly remnant were a powerful example to the rest of Judah. Their fellowship was not with the people in general, but with those who were like-minded. It was a characteristic feature, a habitual practice, of their lives to commune with each other about the things of Jehovah. Is this true of believers today? What is the subject of their conversation? Are Christians eager to speak about Christ and spiritual things or is their conversation generally taken up with temporal and transient things? The Lord and spiritual things should be the normal subject of the saints' conversation rather than the exception. It is love for the Lord and the things of God, along with a desire to walk in His ways, that unites the hearts of believers.

"Hearkened" (QASHAB - 7181) has the idea of paying close attention to what was being said. When together, the godly spoke of Jehovah, His truth, and their faith in Him. Jehovah listened intently to them and found delight in them. The word "often" is not found in the Hebrew text, although the implication of continuity is there. The word translated "heard" (SHAMA - 8085) involves not only listening, but also a fitting response to what is said, and so a book of remembrance was written. The Hebrew for "remembrance" (ZIKKARON -2146) is used of an object or act which brings something to mind. Here it refers to a historical record and appears as "records" in Esther 6.1 where an identical Hebrew expression is used. There the king's "book of records" concerning past events, in which Mordecai's devoted service and faithfulness to the king was documented, is in view (Est 2.21-23; 6.2). In the days of the kings there were recorders of particular events of significance and of those who rendered special service to the king (1 Kings 4.3; 2 Kings 18.37; 2 Chr 34.8). God also had His book of records in which were inscribed the loyal and faithful conversations and conduct of the godly in the midst of departure from Him. The book of remembrance is not mentioned to indicate that God needed to be reminded of certain events, for He is omniscient and all is known to Him, but it is mentioned for the encouragement of the godly remnant. It also gave them assurance of a coming day of reward - the promise of God that He would remember their faithfulness and reverential fear of Him in the day of recompense. They would be honoured in public in the day of Jehovah's glorious Kingdom. There is also a coming day of reckoning and recompense for the saints of this present dispensation of grace - "for we shall all stand before the judgment seat of Christ...So then every one of us shall give account of himself to God" (Rom 14.10-12). In that day "we must all appear before the judgment seat of Christ; that every one may receive the things done in his body, according to that he hath done, whether it be good or bad" (2 Cor 5.10). In that verse, "appear" (*phaneroo - 5319*) means to be made manifest, and indicates that all will be revealed, nothing being hid - "For there is nothing covered, that shall not be revealed; neither hid, that shall not be known" (Lk 12.2). The motives and desires of the heart will be made known (1 Cor 4.5), and "Every man's work shall be made manifest: for the day shall declare it, because it shall be revealed by fire; and the fire shall try every man's work of what sort it is" (1 Cor 3.13). The why, how, and what of the Christian's life will be manifested in that day.

> Only one life, the still small voice
> Gently pleads for a better choice,
> Bidding us selfish aims to leave,
> And to God's holy will to cleave.
> Only one life, 'twill soon be past,
> Only what's done for Christ will last.

However, not only is there a record of the lives of the people of God, but also a record of the lives of all men. The Psalmist writes, "Thou hast set our iniquities before thee, our secret sins in the light of thy countenance" (Ps 90.8), and Job could claim, "Also now, behold, my witness is in heaven, and my record is on high" (Job 16.19). At the Great White Throne the books will be opened and the ungodly will be "judged out of those things which were written in the books, according to their works" (Rev 20.11-15).

Their recompense (vv.17-18)
The result of their faithfulness would be that the Lord of hosts would make them His own in a special sense. The opening expression is translated by Helen Spurrell: "And they shall be unto me a special treasure". They would be His own possession and under His protection. Since Jehovah had been precious to them, they would be precious to Him. They would be of special value to Him because of their response to His claims in the day of the nation's departure from Him. "Jewels" (SᵉGULLA - 5459) basically means a personal possession and is translated "peculiar" (Deut 14.2; 26.18),

"peculiar treasure" (Ex 19.5; Ps 135.4), and "special" (Deut 7.6). The honour and dignity of being Jehovah's special possession or treasure that Israel as a nation had forfeited, because of its departure and idolatry, is transferred to the loyal remnant who reverenced Him. The day referred to is the day of judgment, as indicated in the following expression, but is here viewed in relation to the righteous. The remnant, who had maintained their faithfulness to Jehovah, would be particularly remembered and spared in the day of judgment in contrast to the punishment meted out to the ungodly. Jehovah would show His love and care as a father does to his obedient and dutiful son (cp. Ps 103.13) in contrast to the punishment of a stubborn and rebellious son (Deut 21.18-21). The Lord always has his own in mind and will take steps to protect them in a day of trouble. As there was a faithful remnant at the close of the age of law so there will be godly believers at the close of this present day of grace when there is so much departure from God and His word. In the midst of this departure there are those today who, with purpose of heart, seek to maintain the truth of God which has been unfolded in the word of God. They will be richly recompensed at the Judgment Seat of Christ.

Verse 18 continues to look ahead to the day of judgment when the difference between the righteous and unrighteous will be made manifest. Commentators differ as to whether the pronoun "ye" refers to the godly remnant or the godless majority. C. F. Keil states, "In v.18 the prophet bids the murmurers consider what has been said concerning the righteous, by telling them that they will then see the difference between the righteous who serve God, and the wicked who do not serve Him, that is to say, will learn that it is always profitable to serve God". However, C. L. Feinberg is of the view that while "There are those who think the 'ye' refers to the wicked murmurers in Israel…it is better to see here a reference to the righteous" (see also S. R. Driver). Whichever view is taken the same fact is established, namely that there is a difference between the godly and the ungodly. The verb "return" (SHUB - 7725) is used here as a kind of auxiliary to the verb "discern" (TWOT), presupposing that the difference between the righteous and unrighteous was seen in past days and was made evident in past judgments (Ex 11.7; 32.26; Num 16). Both the righteous and the ungodly had plenty of evidence from the nation's history to know that Jehovah, in His righteousness, did not treat all alike. The coming day of judgment will make this abundantly clear in the salvation of the godly and the destruction of the wicked.

MALACHI 4

Verses 3.16-4.6: The Righteousness of Jehovah's Recompense (continued)

In the Hebrew Scriptures there is no ch.4 since they, and most manuscripts of the original text, place the six verses of this chapter directly after v.18 of ch.3 thus lengthening that chapter to twenty-four verses. Although many consider the break in the English Old Testament unnecessary and out of place, it does not disrupt the flow of thought. In fact ch.4 seems to be the conclusion of the book, summarising the judgment predicted, the authority of the Law of Moses, and the coming restoration of Israel. The solemnity and importance of these verses are evident in that they contain the final message of the Old Testament. After this book there is no record of divine revelation until the New Testament where the voice of John is heard calling upon Israel to repent, "for the kingdom of heaven is at hand" (Mt 3.2). This indicates that the condition of the nation was unchanged throughout the 400 years between the Old and New Testaments. These years, known as the Intertestamental Period are reviewed in the next chapter of this volume.

In these verses Malachi continues the theme of the prophecy by stating that Jehovah would fulfil His purpose in judgment (vv.1-3), giving his final exhortation to obey the law (v.4), and predicting a future restoration of Israel (vv.5-6).

The fulfilment of Jehovah's purpose (vv.1-3)

The opening word "For" introduces the reason for the closing verse of the previous chapter. Jehovah is going to discern between the godly and the wicked in judgment. As before, "behold" (HINNEH - 2009) is an interjection demanding attention - Look, consider! Here it focuses the mind on the coming day of judgment. The importance of that day is emphasised by repetition in v.1 - "the day cometh", and "the day that cometh". The reference is to the Day of the Lord (v.5) which is a prominent prophetic subject throughout the Old and New Testaments. This expression does not refer to a particular day of 24 hours but to a long period of time or programme of events which is yet future. Although on occasions this expression is used to refer to local events, it is generally prophetic in character. Sometimes the expressions "that day" (Joel 3.18; Zeph 1.15), and "the day" (Is 13.13; Ezek 30.18) are used of this period of time. The Day of the Lord will be both a time of judgment (Zeph 1.14-18) and a time of blessing (Zeph 3.14-17). 2 Thessalonians 2.2-3 indicates that that day cannot commence until the manifestation of the man of sin. It begins with judgment (Is 13.6-18) and includes the Great Tribulation (Mt 24.21-29), the manifestation of Christ and His triumph over His enemies (Zech 14.1-3; Rev 19.11-21), the restoration of Israel (Is 14.1-4; Ezek 37.12-14; Amos 9.11-15), all the events of the Millennium when Christ will be in the midst of Israel (Zeph 3.11-17), and the passing away of the heavens and the earth (2 Pet 3.10).

One must distinguish between the Day of the Lord and the Day of God (2 Pet 3.12), and between the Day of the Lord and the Day of Christ (Phil 1.10). The Day of God refers to the new heavens and the new earth where righteousness dwells - the eternal state (2 Pet 3.13). The Day of Christ (also called the Day of our Lord Jesus Christ - 1 Cor 1.8, the Day of the Lord Jesus - 2 Cor 1.14, and the Day of Jesus Christ - Phil 1.6) refers to the events during the Lord's presence with His own (the Church) between the Rapture and the Revelation. In these opening verses the prophet Malachi is referring to the commencement of the Day of the Lord when God comes out in judgment upon the world and the Lord Jesus Christ will be manifested in majesty and glory on His return to the earth. That day will be dark and dreadful with the judgments of God. The language seems to be abrupt indicating the certainty and solemnity of the coming judgment.

The expressions in v.1 are figurative of that divine judgment. "Shall burn as an oven (furnace)" draws attention to the intensity of the judgment. The proud, and those who work wickedness, rather than being admired (3.15) will be as chaff consumed by the fire of the wrath of God. The judgment of God is often likened to fire - "the whole land shall be devoured by the fire of his jealousy" (Zeph 1.18; cp. Is 5.24; 30.27; Jer 7.20). The idea here is of the threshing floor where the chaff is removed and gathered to be burned. The same imagery is used by John the Baptist - "Whose fan is in his hand, and he will throughly purge his floor, and gather his wheat into the garner; but he will burn up the chaff with unquenchable fire" (Mt 3.12). The Apostle Paul referred to the same event - "...the Lord Jesus shall be revealed from heaven with his mighty angels, In flaming fire taking vengeance on them that know not God, and that obey not the gospel of our Lord Jesus Christ" (2 Thess 1.7-8). The expression "neither root nor branch" is figurative of the total destruction of the wicked. Not annihilation as some erroneously teach, but the removal of the ungodly from the earth in the destruction of the body to await, in hell, the judgment at the Great White Throne. The Scriptures never teach the extermination of any person. The thought here is rather that of the ruination of well-being, the loss of all that is worth while. One must appreciate that the judgment referred to here is not limited to the nation of Israel, but includes the whole world. The coming judgment will be universal. The depravity and wickedness of man demands the wrath of God who is infinitely holy. His holiness will not tolerate continual rebellion and lawlessness; neither will God allow His purpose to be thwarted. The whole earth will experience His fiery indignation when those who oppose Him and fill the earth with iniquity will be removed in judgment.

Verse 2 deals with the consequences of that coming day for the righteous, in contrast to its effect upon the wicked. To the ungodly it will be as an oven consuming the stubble, but to the godly it will be as the warmth of the Sun of righteousness bringing healing. In that day of judgment, with its darkness and gloom, the Sun of righteousness will arise dispelling the darkness and bringing blessing to the distressed hearts of the faithful remnant. The expression "fear my name" looks back to those who reverenced the name of Jehovah in the midst of the godless mass who blasphemed His name and rebelled against Him (3.16; cp. Is 66.5). These are representative of the future faithful remnant (Is 10.21; Ezek 14.22). That future remnant will pass through the fire of persecution and affliction which will purify them and cause them to call upon God who will hear and answer them (cp. Is 51.1; Zech 13.8-9). There has been a loyal, believing remnant throughout the history of Israel - Joshua and Caleb (Num 14.6-9); the 7,000 of Elijah's day (1 Kings 19.18); and the returning remnant from Babylon (Neh 1.3; see also Is 1.9; Jer 15.11; 44.28).

The impressive and lovely title "the Sun of righteousness" is used here of Jehovah, Israel's Messiah, the Lord Jesus Christ (cp. Ps 84.11). It is used because He comes in righteousness to display His justice to both the godly and the wicked (cp. 2.17 - "Where is the God of judgment (justice)). To Israel He is "THE LORD OUR RIGHTEOUSNESS" (Jer 23.6), and when He comes He will accomplish a work of righteousness bringing peace to the world (Is 32.17).

The word "wings" refers to the beams or rays of the sun (Ps 139.9) which spread warmth and light over the earth. It is suggested that the rays are called wings because of the swiftness with which they distribute light. However, the thought here is that at His coming the Lord will heal the wounds which had been inflicted upon the righteous. Then the righteous will go forth, in freedom from every constraint and persecution, with joy skipping as calves. The idea seems to be of going forth, in freedom, from the confined places where they had been protected. S. R. Driver states, "They will come forth from their hiding-places, and 'break into life and energy, like young calves leaping from the dark pen into the early sunshine'", and C. F. Keil writes, "Then will they go forth...from the holes and caves, into which they had withdrawn during the night of suffering and where they had kept themselves concealed, and skip like stalled calves". Whereas Israel's hope is the appearance of the Sun of righteousness, the hope of the people of God today is the coming of the morning star (Rev 22.16; cp. 2 Pet 1.19). The morning star ushers in the dawn and the Sun of righteousness brings in the bright day of the Millennium. What a glorious day that will be for Israel, but what a wonderful day for the saints of this day of grace when the Lord fulfills His promise and comes to take them home to heaven (Jn 14.2-3; 1 Thess 4.16-17).

In v.3 Jehovah reverses things, for instead of the wicked persecuting the righteous, in that coming day they themselves will be trodden down. In v.2 healing is brought to the godly, but here in v.3 power is given to them. This verse is the answer to 3.15 for the prosperity of the wicked and the adversity of the righteous will be reversed. The word translated "tread

down" (ASAS - 6072) means to press or crush by treading. The heathen
will be trodden down by Israel (Ps 47.3; Micah 7.10), the lawless being
viewed as ashes continuing the figure of the fiery judgment of Jehovah
(v.1). As a result of that judgment they are as ashes on the ground which
are trodden down under the feet of the godly. The figure is intended to
indicate the final triumph of the righteous over the wicked and the ultimate
blessing of the godly in contrast to the destruction of the godless. It is
helpful to quote H. A. Ironside at this point. "It should be plain to all
thoughtful students of the word of God that this passage completely
nullifies the theory of a converted world at the coming of Christ. Where,
then, would be the wicked who are trodden down? The fact is that Scripture
knows nothing of this favourite system of modern divines. There will be
no Millennium till Christ appears, for He must first act in power for the
destruction of all who have refused to own His claims, thus purging the
scene for the establishment of His Kingdom."

The final exhortation (v.4)

This verse stands out with its present call in the midst of a description
of future events, yet it is not out of place. The book closes with this
exhortation in the light of coming events. It is a call to Israel to remember
the law given through Moses for all Israel. The passing of time had not
altered that oral teaching that was permanently enshrined in the Holy
Scriptures. There were still those who were faithful to God and sought to
maintain the truth of His word, although the majority of the nation had
set aside the Law of Moses. Thus the exhortation is in light of the coming
day of reckoning. One can apply this to present day Christians. The word
of God has not changed and the truth of God remains the same. What was
taught orally by the apostles has been permanently enshrined in the divinely
inspired Scriptures of the New Testament. The exhortation of Paul to
Timothy was, "And the things that thou hast heard of me among many
witnesses, the same commit thou to faithful men, who shall be able to
teach others also" (2 Tim 2.2). It was to be unchanged, unaltered, and
unadulterated. The apostle was drawing attention to the important,
inspired, instructive teaching of the Scriptures that builds and beautifies
christian character - that vital, valuable teaching that guides and guards
the child of God. The admonition "Remember ye the law of Moses" was a
reminder of the holiness of Jehovah and a challenge to the people of Judah
in light of their lawlessness. The law was the test by which their true
condition before Him was judged. Obedience to the law showed their
loyalty to Jehovah, and disobedience indicated their departure from Him.
Obedience to the word of God is the test in every age and generation. It is
the test of spirituality today. Christians should remember the Apostle Peter's
exhortation: "As obedient children, not fashioning yourselves according
to the former lusts in your ignorance: But as he which hath called you is
holy, so be ye holy in all manner of conversation" (1 Pet 1.14-15).

"Remember" (ZAKAR - 2142) not only means to bring to mind, but also to pay attention. They were to bring to mind the Law of Moses and also carry it out (Num 15.40). It is not enough to know the word of God, one must seek to carry it out in one's life. The words "my servant" indicate that the law originated with Jehovah thus adding solemnity to it. Moses was but His servant passing on His law, which consisted of statutes and judgments to Israel. A comparison between Exodus 19 and Deuteronomy 4 establishes that Sinai and Horeb are one and the same place. The expression "for all Israel" indicates that each Israelite was responsible for carrying it out, none was exempt, and it also implies that it was only for Israel.

The future restoration (vv.5-6)

How good to note that in spite of the departure and disobedience of the nation there is a bright future for Israel, and God will fulfil His promises. After the gloom and darkness that permeates the prophecy this last section brings in the theme of the nation's restoration and blessing although it closes with a warning. God's purposes will never be thwarted even by the unfaithfulness and sin of His people. His purposes of grace will be brought to fruition. Whereas v.4 calls upon the people to look back to the Law of Moses, vv.5-6 look ahead to the coming of Elijah. As Moses represents the law so Elijah represents the prophets. The one looks back to the claims of God and the other looks on to the fulfilment of the promises of God. They are mentioned together on the Mount of Transfiguration (Mt 17.3), and some believe they are the two witnesses of Revelation 11.3-11, although others believe these are Enoch and Elijah. The names given to the two witnesses are but suggestions since they are not identified in the passage. As in v.1, the interjection "Behold" demands attention. The words "Behold, I…" occur three times in the prophecy (2.3; 3.1; 4.5) and on each occasion the words emphasise what Jehovah will do. Commentators are divided in regard to these verses. There are two distinct views as to whether or not the coming of Elijah is still in the future.

1. The prophecy here has been fulfilled and therefore there is no future coming of Elijah. C. F. Keil is of the opinion that "The New Testament gives us sufficient explanation of the historical allusion or fulfilment of our prophecy. The prophet Elijah, whom the Lord would send before His own coming, was sent in the person of John the Baptist. Even before his birth he was announced to his father by the angel Gabriel as the promised Elijah…(Lk 1.16,17). This address of the angel gives at the same time an authentic explanation of vv.5 and 6 of our prophecy…The appearance and ministry of John the Baptist answered to this announcement of the angel, and is so described in Matthew 3.1-12; Mark 1.2-8; Luke 3.2-18…Christ Himself also not only assured the people (Mt 11.10ff; Lk7.27ff) that John was the messenger announced by Malachi and the Elijah who was to come, but also told His disciples (Mt 17.11ff; Mk 9.11ff) that Elijah…had already come, though the people had not acknowledged him".

2. The prophecy still has a future and complete fulfilment. C. L. Feinberg states, "John the Baptist himself testified that he was not Elijah (Jn 1.21). He knew by the Spirit that he was referred to in a sense in Malachi 4:5 (Lk 1.17), yet he knew also by divine illumination that he did not completely fulfil all the conditions and requirements of this prophecy. There is a future fulfilment. Even after the transfiguration experience, the Lord in Matthew 17.11 speaks of Elijah's coming as still future, although in the person and ministry of John the Baptist he had come in a certain sense. The mention of the Day of the Lord shows that John cannot be meant exclusively here, for his ministry preceded the day of Christ's grace and not the day of His judgment".

The fact that the Lord Jesus spoke of Elijah's coming after the death of John the Baptist and that he would restore all things, which John did not do, indicates that the second view is correct and that these verses had a partial fulfilment in John the Baptist, but will have a final fulfilment in a coming day. There is also a divided view as to whether, in this future event, Elijah the prophet will come personally or whether one will come, as did John the Baptist, in the spirit and power of Elijah. Jewish interpreters and many christian commentators take the reference to be to the prophet Elijah himself. (For further discussion on this topic, see J. Dwight Pentecost, *Things to Come*).

The expression "the great and dreadful day of the Lord" refers to the commencement of the Day of the Lord when terrible judgment will be poured out on the world prior to the millennial Kingdom (cp. Joel 2.11,31; Zeph 1.14). The ministry of Elijah in that coming day will be to turn the hearts of the people to Jehovah and restore harmony in families. His ministry will be a call to repentance and thus to avert the threatened curse. In that day the ministry of Elijah will fully accomplish a work of grace (Mt 17.11), and apostates will perish under the judgment of Jehovah.

The closing statement of the prophecy seems to indicate that if restoration was not brought about the coming of Jehovah the Messiah would result in a curse upon the earth instead of a blessing. However, in the ministry of Elijah, and of others, restoration will take place - all Israel, represented in the remnant, will be saved (Rom 11.26) and a great multitude of Gentiles will be saved (Rev 7.9) to the blessing of the earth and its families, and to the glory of God. The final message of the prophecy and of the Old Testament itself concerns a curse whereas the closing message of the New Testament is one of grace. The beginning of the Old Testament mentions the entrance of the curse and it closes with the threat of a curse. The beginning of the New Testament unfolds the entrance of the Saviour and it ends with a salutation of grace.

It is fitting to close with the words of H. A. Ironside: "And so with this solemn word, "curse", the Old Testament abruptly comes to a close. The law had been violated in every particular. On the ground of the legal covenant the people had no hope whatever. Wrath like a dark cloud was lowering over their heads. The awful curse of that broken law was all they had earned after long ages of trial. But a Redeemer had been promised; and where there was faith, in any who felt the seriousness of their condition, they looked on to the coming of the Seed of the woman who was to bruise the serpent's head, and Himself be made a curse, that all who put their trust in Him might be redeemed from the doom they had so long and fully deserved". "To him give all the prophets witness, that through his name whosoever believeth in him shall receive remission of sins" (Acts 10.43). Through the Lord Jesus Christ alone can sinners, who repent of their sins and trust Him, be delivered from the judgment of God - "Neither is there salvation in any other: for there is none other name under heaven given among men, whereby we must be saved" (Acts 4.12).

THE INTERTESTAMENTAL PERIOD

(A list of sources from which material has been drawn is given at the end of this Chapter. References to that list are numbered consecutively throughout the text.)

History

The Old Testament closes with Malachi's prophecy and there is a pause in the divinely inspired writings until the New Testament. Thus between Malachi and Luke 1.11-17 there was no further divine revelation recorded. This covered a period of around 400 years (397-4 BC) which is referred to as the Intertestamental Period. It is also referred to as "the dark period of Israel's history in pre-Christian times",[1] because during it there were no prophets and no inspired writers. The words of Psalm 74.9 could well be applied to that period: "We see not our signs: there is no more any prophet: neither is there among us any that knoweth how long". Whatever reasons men might have given for the silence of God during that period, it was part of the eternal plan devised by God in His sovereignty. God had spoken at different times and in various ways through the prophets, but now he has spoken fully and finally in His Son (Heb 1.1-2). It has been suggested that this long and distinctive period emphasised the monumental nature of the revelation of God in the Person of the Son. The ways of God are higher than the ways of men. "O the depth of the riches both of the wisdom and knowledge of God! how unsearchable are his judgments, and his ways past finding out!" (Rom 11.33).

Many think that the teaching of the New Testament is alien to that of the Old. On the surface this seems to be the case. However, both have their origin in God and both are inspired by the Spirit of God. It must be appreciated that the Old and New Testaments complement one another and that the complete message and purpose of God cannot be grasped without both. It is also assumed by some that the Jews in the time of Christ were following strictly the teaching of Moses. That this was not the case is clear in the words of Christ Himself: "Why do ye also transgress the commandment of God by your tradition?" (Mt 15.3), and, "For laying aside the commandment of God, ye hold the tradition of men...Full well ye reject the commandment of God, that ye may keep your own tradition" (Mk 7.8-9). The Lord Jesus Christ would not have charged the religious leaders in this way if they had been observing the Law of Moses. They had drifted far from the law and embraced teachings contrary to the word of God. In fact, the departure from the law had begun prior to the Intertestamental Period: "Even from the days of your fathers ye are gone away from mine ordinances, and have not kept them" (Mal 3.7). However, there was a faithful remnant right through to the Lord's first advent (Mal 3.16-17; Lk 1.5-6, 26-27; 2.25, 36-37).

The general condition of the Jews at the commencement of this 400 year period should be kept in mind. After Judah's seventy years of captivity (605-536 BC), the Babylonian Empire having been replaced by the Medo-Persian Empire (538 BC), Cyrus issued a decree allowing the Jews to return to their land in order to rebuild Jerusalem and the temple (Is 44.28). Only a remnant of about 200,000 Jews returned and a small Jewish nation, dependent upon Persia, was again established in the land. The temple was completed in 516 BC and, under Ezra, the law and the temple rituals were restored. Under Nehemiah the walls of Jerusalem were rebuilt. When the remnant returned they were characterised by devotion to God, by a desire to rebuild the House of God, and by a determination to carry out the word of God. However, declension and departure set in so that in Malachi's day the people in general were characterised by formalism and materialism.

It is advantageous to have a knowledge of the 400 years between the prophecy of Malachi and the advent of the Lord Jesus Christ in order to appreciate some of the events in the New Testament Gospels, and to have a background to conditions and to certain statements in those books. During these 400 years, important historical events occurred and literature was written, both of which significantly affected the Mediterranean area and influenced religious thinking. To understand the Jewish situation at the time of the New Testament we need to look at both the political and the religious developments that had taken place. The changing course of the Jewish nation reflects the different powers which ruled in the land, the one exception being the Maccabean revolt which resulted, for a short time, in an independent Jewish government. During these 400 years there were six dominant groups: the Persians (397-333 BC), the Greeks (333-323 BC), the Egyptians (323-198 BC), the Syrians (198-165 BC), the Maccabees (165-63 BC), and the Romans (63-4 BC).

The Persians (397-333 BC)

Although the Persian era commenced before Malachi it did not end until some 60 years after Malachi's prophecy when Palestine fell under the power of Alexander the Great. To fulfil His word God used the Medes and Persians to deliver the Jews from the Babylonian captivity (Dan 5.30-31). The Persian rule and attitude to the Jews and their way of life was one of tolerance. The priestly form of government was respected with the high priest being given a degree of civil power although he was still responsible to the Persian governor. Internal disputes over the political power of the high priest's office resulted in a partial destruction of Jerusalem by the Persian governor. Apart from this the Persians did not interfere. The Samaritans (a people imported into the land after Israel's captivity - see 2 Kings 17) built a temple at Mount Gerizim in Samaria. This accentuated social and religious differences between Jews and Samaritans.

It has been stated that "The rise of the synagogue as the local centre of worship can be traced back to this period. Scribes became very important for the interpretation of the Scriptures in the synagogue services".[2]

However, some dispute exists as to the commencement of synagogues, even among Jewish writers.

The Greeks (333-323 BC)
Alexander the Great was thrust into leadership when he was just twenty years of age through the assassination of his father. He transformed the face of the world and was the central figure of this short period. He conquered Persia, Babylon, Syria, Egypt and western India. Although he died at an early age, his influence was felt long after his death. He is undoubtedly the notable horn of the he goat in Daniel 8.5-8. In his advance on Jerusalem he spared the city and offered sacrifices to Jehovah. He also had publicly read Daniel's prophecy of Persia's defeat by a Grecian king (Dan 8.1-8, 20-21). He treated the Jews respectfully and gave them full citizenship, along with the Greeks, in certain cities. This created a favourable impression among the Jews. Alexander sought to create a worldwide empire united by language, culture, and religion. He imposed the Greek language, customs, and society on the Middle East and attempted to blend together all religions. This is referred to as Hellenism. This Hellenistic spirit greatly affected the outlook of many Jews. It became so popular that it persisted and continued its influence into New Testament times. The struggle between Judaism and the influence of Hellenism was long and bitter. The widespread acceptance of the Greek language resulted in a Greek translation of the Old Testament known as The Septuagint. Greek continued its influence long after this era and was the language used in the writing of the New Testament.

The Egyptians (323-198 BC)
This period was the longest of the six. After the death of Alexander the Great, the Grecian empire was divided between his four generals: Ptolemy, Lysimachus, Cassander, and Selenus (the four notable ones that came out of the great horn - the four kingdoms - Dan 8.8,22). There was a time of confusion and unrest, and on four occasions Judea was attacked until finally the land came under the control of Ptolemy Soter. He was the first Greek king to reign over Egypt and the first of the Ptolemy dynasty. At first he dealt harshly with the Jews, but later treated them favourably as did his successor Ptolemy Philadelphus. Greek had become the language of the civilized world and in this era the Septuagint translation of the Old Testament Scriptures came into being. With numerous Jews in Egypt, Syria, and North Africa such a translation became necessary. Thus the Septuagint was widely used before New Testament times. Gradually, the influence of Greek culture filtered into Jewish life. "It was at the beginning of this period that Simon the Just was high priest. He was the last of the authorities in the organization founded by Ezra and Nehemiah called 'The Great Assembly' (or 'The Great Synagogue')".[3] "During that difficult time following the sudden death of Alexander the Great, Shimon HaTzaddik

was the uncontested leader of Israel. As one of the Sages of the Great Assembly, Shimon was the spiritual leader of the people. He was also the Kohen Gadol (high priest); and because Alexander had decreed that the Kohen Gadol should be governor of the land, Shimon was the political leader, with the power to enforce his authority. He used this power to strengthen the study and observation of the Torah throughout the land".[4] In this era the Jews were dominated by the Hellenistic Ptolemies in Egypt which profoundly affected their religious beliefs. There was a measure of tolerance during this period which allowed both Hellenism and Judaism to co-exist peacefully with the result that the Hellenistic view of worship, being more outward than inward, had a lasting effect upon Judaism. R. T. Herford states, "There was no escape from that influence (Hellenism). It was present everywhere, in the street and the market, in the everyday life and all phases of social intercourse".[5] The result was the emergence of a strong orthodox section completely opposed to Hellenism. That section was known as the Hasidim or Pious Ones and was the forerunner of the Pharisees. They sought to adhere to the Scriptures and in particular to the Law of Moses.

The Syrians (198-165 BC)

At the death of the fourth Ptolemy, Ptolemy Philopator, Antiochus III invaded Egypt, Judea, and other lands. These were eventually annexed to Syria and came under its rule. At that time Palestine was divided into five sections: Judea, Samaria, Galilee, Peraea, and Trachonitis, which are mentioned in the New Testament. It is stated that "At first Antiochus treated the Jews well. In order to help the city of Jerusalem repair the damage caused by the Ptolemaic-Seleucid wars, he freed the city from paying taxes for three years".[6] However, later he and his successor, Seleucus Philopator, treated the Jews harshly and increased the burden of taxes although they permitted them to live under their own laws which were administered by the high priest and his council. When Antiochus Epiphanes (Antiochus IV) came to the throne things changed. It is said that his courtiers called him Epiphanes (the illustrious) to flatter him, but behind his back called him Epimanes (the madman). His reign was a reign of terror for the Jews. During this time the Hellenists managed to persuade him to depose Chonyo (Onias III) the Kohen Gadol, favoured by the so called orthodox Jews, and appoint instead his brother Yeshua, who had Hellenised his name to Jason, by offering Antiochus a generous bribe. This resulted in conflict and unrest which brought Antiochus to Jerusalem where he commanded his soldiers to slaughter indiscriminately men, women and children. Later he sought to remove the distinctive character of the Jewish faith. Rabbis Nosson Scherman and Meir Zlotowitz state, "A directive was sent expressly to Judea to cease the sacrificial service in the Temple. In its place, altars and temples should be set up everywhere, at which hogs and other unclean animals were to be sacrificed. As if that were not enough, Antiochus commanded that the Holy Temple should be desecrated and converted into a pagan temple!...On the fifteenth of Kislev 168 BCE , an idol was erected upon the altar, and beginning with the twenty-fifth of that month hogs were offered upon the altar to a pagan deity".[7] This final act of sacrilege spelt Antiochus' ultimate ruin. During this time Judaism became divided over the issue of Hellenism. The orthodox section, later known as the Pharisees, and mainly led by the scribes, opposed it and a more pragmatic section, forerunners of the Sadducees, associated with the high priest, embraced it.

The Maccabees (165-63 BC)

Mattathias (Mattisyahu) the Hasmonean (that is from the village of Hasmon), a priest, with his family, left Jerusalem where there was severe persecution and settled in Medein, a Judean village about ten miles from Jerusalem. He had five sons: Judas (Yehudah) the Maccabean, Simon (Shimon), Eleazar (Elazar), Jonathan (Yonasan), and Yochanan. However, the problem followed him to Medein when Syrian authorities appeared and demanded that the people of the village offer a sacrifice in the pagan way. Mattathias remained faithful, and when a renegade Jew approached the altar to offer the sacrifice he killed him and the Syrian emissaries with the sword.[8] He and his family fled to the mountains and thousands of faithful Jews joined them, living in caves, and one of the most honourable demonstrations of jealousy for the honour of God began. They began to make night time raids against the Syrians and to destroy the idolatrous altars. Mattathias did not live to see the result of his revolt, but his sons carried on the conflict. Judas Maccabaeus became the recognised leader and his guerrilla force defeated parts of the Syrian army in the hilly terrain north of Jerusalem. Seron, the commander of the army in Syria, heard of this and set out with a large and well-equipped army to subdue the revolt in Judea. However, Judas and his greatly outnumbered army routed Seron's highly trained force. Hearing of this humiliating defeat of his troops, Antiochus commanded a stronger force, under Lysias, to march into Judea and crush the Maccabean army. This Syrian force was soundly defeated. Judas and his valiant Maccabean men entered Jerusalem. They cleansed the Temple and "On the twenty-fifth day of Kislev, in the year 165 BCE - three years to the day after the terrible moment on which the invaders had sacrificed to a pagan abomination in the Sanctuary - the Hasmoneans rededicated the Holy Temple and renewed the sacrificial services".[9] This event is commemorated by the Jews today in the Feast of Hanukkah (Chanukah). Thus the Maccabean revolt was a great success.

After Judas' death in 160 BC his brother Jonathan became leader of the devout Jews. Fighting continued in parts of Judea as the Syrians, unsuccessfully, sought to defeat the Maccabeans. Simon, the last of the sons of Mattathias, was able to capture other Syrian strongholds (143 BC) and about 142 BC Judea became independent with its own Jewish government. Apart from one short relapse this continued until Judea became a Roman province (63 BC). During the latter part of the Maccabean period there was strong rivalry between the orthodox Jews, then known as Pharisees, and a growing party, descendants of the Hellenists, known as Sadducees, who had the power of the high priestly office.

The Romans (63-4 BC)

In the closing years of the Maccabean era a power struggle between the two sons of Queen Salome Alexandra, Hyrkanus and Aristobulus, took place. After her death open warfare between the two erupted. Aristobulus was under the influence of the Sadducees who supported him in the conflict. Hyrkanus became friendly with Antipater the Edomite whose ambition was to become ruler of Judea. In 63 BC Pompey, a Roman general, was invited to intervene in the civil war between the two brothers. Pompey was a member of a triumvirate (a rule of three men) along with Julius Caesar and Crassus. Pompey responded. Even when the Roman legions approached Jerusalem the two opposing brothers refused to unite. In the process of taking the city the Romans slaughtered thousands. Although Pompey entered the holy of holies the Romans never desecrated the temple. The city walls were torn down and a heavy tax placed upon the people. Thus Judea's independence ceased and it became a Roman province. The high priest was stripped of all civil authority and royal status. Although several attempts were made to regain independence they all failed. Pompey chose to install Hyrkanus as governor, but the real power was with Antipater, his cunning adviser. When Julius Caesar became the ruler of the Roman Empire he appointed Antipater procurator of Judea although he displayed a liberal attitude to the Jews. After Julius Caesar was assassinated Cassius gave Antipater and his sons the office of tax collectors which they efficiently and cruelly pursued gathering great sums of money from the Jews. It is stated that, "Antipater treated the land of Israel as if it were his private property. His older son he appointed governor of the Jerusalem area, and his younger son, Herod, he made governor of Galilee in the north...Herod immediately revealed his brutal nature. He arrested many of the young patriots together with their leader Chizkiyahu, and without any semblance of trial executed them".[10]

In 40 BC the Roman senate proclaimed Herod (known as Herod the Great) king of the Jews although he did not assume total power of the Jews until 36 BC. His rule lasted thirty-two years. In order to please and to be accepted by the Jews, as he thought, he married Marianna (Miriam) the granddaughter of a former high priest, Hyrkanus. He planned and rebuilt the temple making it more beautiful than it was when built in Ezra's day. He also increased the splendour of Jerusalem. Herod was a devout Hellenist and was completely opposed to the Hasmonean family. His cruelty knew no bounds, and he was guilty of murdering every member of that family including his wife's three brothers, his wife Marianna, his mother-in-law, and his two sons by Marianna. This was the Herod who was on the throne when the Lord Jesus Christ was born in Bethlehem. Herod had three other sons by other wives: Archelaus, Antipas, and Philipus between whom the land was divided at the death of their father.

Jewish Writings
There are also a number of Jewish writings, some of which were produced during the Intertestamental Period, which are relevant to our considerations.

The Torah
"Torah" means teaching, and in Jewish thought refers to the divine revelation to Israel. The term is generally restricted to the Pentateuch, the first five books of the Old Testament also called the Law of Moses. In this restricted sense it is preserved in every Jewish synagogue on a hand-written parchment scroll kept inside a compartment which Jewry calls the ark. It is removed and returned to its place with particular reverence. Part of the Jewish services in the Synagogue is a reading from the Torah. However, the term Torah is also used in referring to the whole of the Old Testament called the Torah Shebiksav (the written Torah). The Jewish Torah Shebiksav is divided into three main sections: the Torah, the Nevi'im (Prophets) and Kesuvim (writings) referred to by the risen Lord as the Law of Moses, the prophets, and the psalms (Lk 24.44). In the Torah there are five books: Genesis, Exodus, Leviticus, Numbers, and Deuteronomy. In the Nevi'im there are eight books: Joshua, Judges, 1 & 2 Samuel (one book), 1 & 2 Kings (one book), Isaiah, Jeremiah, Ezekiel, and the twelve minor prophets (one book called Troy Asar). In the Kesuvim there are eleven books: Ruth, 1 & 2 Chronicles (one book), Ezra & Nehemiah (one book), Esther, Job, Psalms, Proverbs, Ecclesiastes, The Song of Solomon, Lamentations, and Daniel. In all there are 24 books in the Jewish written Torah. These three sections are referred to by the acronym TaNaKh (or Tanach).[11]

The Talmud
The Hebrew word Talmud means study or learning and refers to a compilation of ancient teaching of Hebrew civil and ceremonial laws based on the Law of Moses. It was regarded as sacred by all Jews and still is by the Orthodox Jews today. The Jews claim that because many things are not explained in the written Torah (Pentateuch) God gave the explanations to Moses on Mount Sinai along with the written law. These explanations they called the Oral Torah which was handed down from generation to generation. Later, Jewish sages assembled an outline of these explanations in a series of books called the Mishna. The term Mishna means repeated study, and is a collection of the oral law. "The Mishna was primarily an outline and did not include the in-depth analysis and explanation behind

the laws. These explanations are called Gemara".[12] The term Gemara means completion and was put into a written work which is a commentary on the Mishna. The Talmud is the complete collection of the Mishna and Gemara and is made up of six sections dealing with various civil and ceremonial laws. The Talmud is important to Jewish culture, and Orthodox Jewry considers it to be the absolute authority. It is the legal system in certain Jewish communities throughout the world. It is stated that "The jurisdiction of rabbinic courts is voluntarily accepted by Orthodox Jews. These courts continue to exert authority, especially in the areas of family and dietary law, the Synagogue, and the organization of charity and social activity. Conservative Jewry, too, has always been committed to rabbinic tradition".[13.] The Talmud is a compilation of the Rabbis' interpretation and was referred to by the Lord Jesus Christ as "the tradition of men", and "your own tradition" (Mk 7.8-9).

The Targums

The word targum is an Aramaic word meaning translation, or interpretation, and refers to translations of portions or all of the Hebrew Scriptures (Old Testament) into the Aramaic language. These became necessary because the Jews who returned from the Babylonian captivity only spoke the Aramaic language. It is stated that "Aramaic became the official language of the Persian Empire. In the succeeding centuries it was used as the vernacular over a wide area and was increasingly spoken by the postexilic Jewish communities of Palestine".[14] The earliest targums date from the return from Babylon when Aramaic replaced Hebrew as the spoken language of the Jews in that area. Although Aramaic was firmly established in Palestine during that period, Hebrew remained the sacred language. The targums were introduced to meet the needs of the majority of the Jews who could not understand Hebrew and therefore were unable to read the Hebrew Scriptures. Although there are a number of targums of the Pentateuch, the best known, earliest, and most literal is the Targum of Onketos named after the author. It had its origin in Palestine, but was transferred to Babylon where it achieved great authority. The influence of the targums increased and eventually commentary or explanations entered into various portions of the text so that they contained more than a literal translation.

The Dead Sea Scrolls

These are ancient manuscripts discovered in caves and old ruins in the wilderness of Judea and are some of the more important discoveries of modern archaeology. The first manuscripts, accidentally discovered in a cave at Khirbet Qumran on the shore of the Dead Sea in 1947, were called Dead Sea Scrolls. Later finds in the 1950s and 1960s in neighbouring areas were also designated Dead Sea Scrolls. The scrolls and scroll fragments (of leather, papyrus, and copper) recovered in the Qumran region represent a large amount of Jewish documents dating from around the third century BC. It is the largest manuscript find of the twentieth century and displays the rich literary activity of the Intertestamental Period. It was assumed to be part of a library belonging to a Jewish sect called the Essenes who prospered in that region. However, "Some scholars have suggested that the scrolls were not the work of Essene monks but rather a collected library of important Jewish works that was hidden for protection during the Roman invasion of AD 67 to 73".[15] The great variety of literature has led some to question whether a single sect such as the Essenes would have been able to compose or maintain such a vast collection. It contains some works in a large number of scrolls and yet others on only fragments of parchments. It is said that the number of compositions is about 1,000, and they are written in three different languages: Hebrew, Aramaic, and Greek. A variety of literary forms is noted among the texts.

There is no agreement on the specifics of the Dead Sea Scrolls. Some claim that the scrolls and fragments of parchment fall into sections: Biblical texts, commentaries, and pentateuchal stories; legal and ceremonial texts; psalms and poetry; prophecy and visions; wisdom literature; sectarian literature; and miscellaneous. According to many scholars, the chief categories represented among the Dead Sea Scrolls are: Biblical - about 100 manuscripts are taken up with the complete Hebrew Old Testament except for the book of Esther but including copies of Leviticus and a well preserved scroll of the 12 minor prophets which is well-nigh identical to the Hebrew biblical text; Apocryphal or pseudepigraphical texts - those works that are omitted from some canons of the Bible (Jewish and Protestant) and included in others; Sectarian scrolls - these pertain to a strict and pious Jewish sect and include ordinances, commentaries, apocalyptic visions and other works. The Sectarian scrolls are believed by many to have been compiled by the Essenes, but some scholars say that there is not enough evidence to support this view.

The Apocrypha

Some of the outstanding works of Jewish literature during the Intertestamental Period are the fourteen historical books known collectively as the Apocrypha. Apocrypha means hidden writings and refers to the biblical books which were included in the Greek version of the Old Testament (the Septuagint), but not included in the Hebrew Bible. Several writings ranging from the fourth century BC to New Testament times are considered apocryphal. Over the course of centuries it has variously been included in and omitted from different Bible versions. In general, Protestants exclude the Apocrypha, not accepting any part of it as divinely inspired, and therefore as not being a part of the sacred canon. In contrast, the Roman Catholic and Orthodox churches include most of the Apocrypha and refer to those books as Deuterocanonical Books. The Jews do not accept the Apocrypha, claiming that, being uninspired, these books were not part of their Holy Scriptures and thus were of no religious value. It was never part of the Old Testament canon and was never referred to by the Lord Jesus or accepted by the New Testament writers. However, some in Jewry have viewed it as a legitimate part of Jewish literature and it was used to form the basis of an important Jewish prayer called the Amidah. It is stated that "The description of the origins of Hanukkah is also to be found in the Apocrypha; thus while the texts themselves may not be accepted as canonical, some of their contents are still accepted as historical truth. Particularly, 1 Maccabees is cited by Jewish scholars as being highly reliable history. It was used by Josephus in his history of the Maccabean revolt as well". [16]

The Septuagint

The Septuagint, sometimes abbreviated to the numeral LXX, refers to the Greek translation from the original Hebrew Old Testament. It had its origins in Alexandria, Egypt and was translated between 300 and 200 BC although some have disputed that it took place during this period. The translation was necessary because the Greek language became dominant in the region replacing Hebrew among the Jews. It became widely used among the Hellenistic Jews. The word Septuagint is derived from the Latin word *septuaginta* meaning seventy because it was claimed that about seventy Jewish scholars carried out the task of translation. It contains the thirty-nine books of the Old Testament as well as some apocryphal books. It is generally accepted that between seventy and seventy-five Jewish scholars were commissioned by Ptolemy Philadelphus to perform the task. The earliest source in relation to this task is an ancient lengthy document called "The Letter of Aristeas", although some modern scholars have called it an unreliable source. However, it has been established that the Torah (Pentateuch) was translated first and the rest of the Old Testament at a later date because it differs in style. The discovery of the Dead Sea Scrolls has helped to establish the reliability of the Septuagint. It has been stated that "Comparisons of the Dead Sea Scrolls to the Masoretic Text and the Septuagint show that where there are differences between the Masoretic and the Septuagint, approximately 95% of those differences are shared between the Dead Sea Scrolls and the Masoretic text, while only 5% of those differences are shared between the Dead Sea Scrolls and the Septuagint…The majority of the Septuagint, Masoretic Text, and the Dead Sea Scrolls are remarkably similar and have dispelled unfounded theories that the Bible text has been corrupted by time and conspiracy. Furthermore, these variations do not call in question the infallibility of God in preserving His word".[17] During the first century AD, when Greek was widely used, Christians depended upon the Septuagint for their understanding of the Old Testament. It is claimed that it was through it that those Christians understood the prophecies which were fulfilled in the birth, life, death, and resurrection of the Lord Jesus Christ. At that time the Jews objected to what they considered an abuse of Holy Scripture and ceased from using the Septuagint.

Institutions and Groups

It is clear from the New Testament that changes had taken place in the Jewish nation since the close of the Old Testament. There were new institutions and new religious parties which are mentioned in the Gospels.

The Synagogue

"Synagogue" comes from the Greek word *sunagoge* meaning meeting. Because of this it is claimed that the rise of synagogues took place in the third century BC. There is a general agreement that synagogues existed during the Grecian period. However, the Hebrew name for synagogue is Beit Knesset which means House of Assembly and is a meeting place for Jews, where they share the important facets of life. It is the place where they meet to pray, study, celebrate, mourn, and socialize. Even today it is the centre of a Jewish community. Jewish writers claim that such establishments existed long before the Grecian era. Some have claimed that the commencement of synagogues was in Solomon's day, but this is doubtful. Most Jewish scholars accept that the rise of synagogues took place before, or at the beginning of, the Babylonian captivity. The collapse of the Jewish religious system with the Babylonian exile resulted in the rise of another system, in captivity, which replaced the sacrifices and rites of the temple with assemblies for study, prayer, and socializing. There were no longer officiating priests as such, but scribes and scholars called Rabbis. "The synagogue was not constructed in opposition to the temple, but as a complement. It is not surprising therefore that, with the destruction of the temple and then the dispersion of the Jews, the synagogue, initially a complement, became a substitute", and, "according to Megillah 29a, the synagogue is thought to have been founded by exiles taken by Nebuchadrezzar".[18] The synagogue also goes by the Hebrew name Beit Midrash which means House of Study where the Torah and other sacred books, which are the essentials of Jewish life, are studied. Today educational programs for Jews of all ages are carried out in the synagogue. It is also called by the Hebrew name Beit Tefilah which means House of Prayer where Jews meet for prayer. Today the synagogue is the centre for most Jewish prayer services.

The Scribes

The scribes mentioned in the Old Testament must be distinguished from those mentioned in New Testament times. In the Old Testament the word "scribe" is applied to one who carried out correspondence for kings etc. (cp. Esther 3.12), and to those who wrote, copied, and expounded the Scriptures. Thus Ezra was "a ready scribe in the law" as well as being a priest (Ezra 7.6,11; Neh 8.1-13). The new system of Jewish religion, Judaism, which developed during the Intertestamental Period gave rise to a new order of scribes who acquired important status and great power. The very nature of Judaism was to demand that every Jew was responsible for keeping the whole of the law and the traditions that had arisen from their interpretation of the Hebrew Scriptures. They had extracted from the law a rule that covered practically every activity of daily life. Such a detailed regimen was complex and needed clarification. The scribes were trained experts who made a study of this rule the business of their lives. Those who had undergone such training in their school were granted the status of "Scribe" and were respectfully addressed as "Rabbi" (Mt 23.7). The significance of this was that the scribe was a combination of theologian and lawyer. They were considered as professional experts in the interpretation and application of the Old Testament Scriptures and Rabbinical teaching. They wore the long robe of the scholar, sat in seats of honour in the synagogue, and claimed places in the chief rooms at feasts (see Lk 20.46-47).

The Sanhedrin

This term refers to the civil and religious tribunal of the Jews. The word Sanhedrin (sometimes spelled Sanhedrim) comes from the Greek word *sunedrion* meaning Council. It is not surprising, therefore, that this Jewish tribunal is referred to as a council in the New Testament (Mt 26.59; Mk 15.1; Lk 22.66; Acts 23.1). It was the supreme judicial and administrative council of the Jewish people. It was their highest court and its decisions were binding on Jews everywhere. It is claimed that it was first instituted by Moses and consisted of seventy men (Num 11.16-17). This was evidently not so since it is not recorded in the later books of the Old Testament. What Moses instituted was only a temporary arrangement. The name Sanhedrin was first used by the Jewish historian Josephus and it is stated that "it is probable that it was instituted in the time of the Maccabees".[19] According to Talmudic sources the Sanhedrin was made up of seventy-one sages who met on fixed occasions. Its composition is disputed with some saying it was made up only of Sadducees, some saying it was made up only of Pharisees, and others saying it was a mixture of both. The latter seems correct in light of Acts 23.1-10 when there was "a dissension between the Pharisees and Sadducees" in the council. It is clear from Mark 14.53 that it consisted of chief priests, elders, and scribes with the high priest presiding over all. The jurisdiction of the Sanhedrin was curtailed first by Herod and then by the Romans who removed its power to put a person to death (Jn 18.31). It ceased to exist in Jerusalem after the destruction of the temple in AD 70.

The Pharisees

This name was given to a religious Jewish sect who called themselves Hasidim meaning pious ones. The name Pharisee is derived from the Hebrew word PARASH (6567) meaning separate, leading to the Greek derivative *pharisaios* - a separatist. This was because of their strict observance of the Law (written and oral). It was proclaimed as the binding standard for the individual and the nation. They firmly held that the Oral Law was given to Moses at the same time as the Written Law. Placing great importance on adherence to the Law resulted in them applying the Oral Law to everyday life. This insistence on the oral tradition (the unwritten Law) being binding remains a fundamental dogma of Jewish thought today. Josephus records their rise in the reign of Jonathan (161-144 BC). It is generally believed that they were spiritual descendants from the Hasidim. They opposed the hellenistic and social group of Jews called the Sadducees, whose interest was the political side of religion. It could be said that these two opposing groups provoked each other into existence. The Pharisees were ritualists and sought to harmonize the Law (the Torah) with their own ideas. It was because of this progressive tendency that their interpretation of the Law continued to develop, and it remains a powerful influence in Judaism today.

The character of the ritualist is one of adding detail since he is not content with the written word of God and the clear message of the gospel. Thus the importance of salvation is clouded by the ideas, ordinances, and religious ceremonies of men. What started out as a wholesome dependence on the word of God deteriorated into the denial of the true spirit of the Scriptures. The Pharisees became so rigid in the Oral Law and their legalistic interpretations that by the time of the Lord Jesus Christ their teaching had little resemblance to the Scriptures. They had deteriorated into formalism and legalism which the Lord condemned as contrary to the word of God and making it of none effect (Mk 7.6-13).

The Sadducees

The rise of the Sadducees, as well as the Pharisees, took place during the reign of Jonathan the Maccabean. It is stated that "they were disciples of Tzadok and were therefore known as Tzadokim (Sadducees)".[20] They were the party of the aristocratic and wealthy section of the people. They had strong links with the high priest unlike the Pharisees who were strongly connected with the scribes. Whereas the Pharisees made proselytes the Sadducees were too exclusive to do so and were therefore smaller in number though more influential. During the long struggle between the two parties, which lasted until the destruction of Jerusalem (AD 70), the Sadducees dominated the temple and its priesthood. They completely rejected the Oral Law, but claimed allegiance to the Written Law (the Torah). However, they treated parts of the Written Law with scepticism which was evident in their denial of angels, spirits, and the bodily resurrection (Lk 20.27; Acts 23.8). The character of the Sadducee was rationalism, an unwillingness to accept the written word in its entirety because it did not fully meet the criterion of human reasoning. For the same reason rationalists today will not accept the plain and simple gospel. Everything must be tried at the bar of human reason. The readiness of the Sadducees to compromise with the Romans stirred up the hatred of the common people. The Sadducees believed that politics and the law of God could be kept apart and refused to accept that the spiritual condition of the people had an effect on God's dealings with them. They were intolerant of the teaching of the Lord Jesus Christ and in their hatred joined with the Pharisees to put Him to death (Mt 16.1). The Sadducees, being closely linked with the temple and its worship, ceased to exist when the temple was destroyed by the Romans in AD 70.

The Herodians

The Herodians were a political group that appeared during the Roman era. Its main aim was to further the authority and cause of Herod and his government. There is no clear information as to their rise, but it seems to have been during the reign of Herod the Great (40-4 BC). There is no evidence of any direct connection between this party and the household of Herod although it had Herod's approval. It is suggested that fear of the Roman power and the possibility of total destruction if the Jews rebelled against this power stimulated the Herodians in their support of Herod. They were Hellenistic in their outlook and were greatly opposed to the Pharisees, although they were not in any way a religious party. They had no concern for the Written or Oral Laws and considered the cause and belief of the Pharisees to be dangerous for the nation. What did it matter that Herod was a heathen as long as the nation's interests were furthered? Thus they supported the Herodian throne because it had the favour of Rome and the protection of the Roman Empire. This may well have been the reason why they joined forces with the Pharisees, whom they hated, to entrap the Lord Jesus in his words and sought to destroy Him (Mt 22.15-18; Mk 3.6).

The Zealots

The Zealots (spelt Zelotes in the New Testament - Lk 6.15) were marked by a fiery nationalistic spirit as befits their name and were directly opposed to the Herodians. They were zealous for their country and for strict observance of the Law of Moses. Thus they had a deep concern for the national and religious life of the Jewish people. They despised those Jews who sought the favour of the Roman authority. They refused to pay taxes to the Romans and would not conform to Roman rule. Unlike the Pharisees, who waited submissively for the Messiah to come and overthrown the Romans, the Zealots were militant and advocated overthrowing the ruling power on the basis that God alone was their Ruler. They emphasised the need for military deliverance rather than waiting for divine intervention. To this end extremists among them turned to terrorism and became known as Sicarii from the Greek word *sikarioi* meaning dagger men. These, it is claimed, frequented public places, with hidden daggers, to kill those friendly to the Romans. It was Zealots who made a stand at Masada and committed suicide rather than be captured by the Romans. Some scholars see a possible link between them and the Jewish religious community mentioned in the Dead Sea Scrolls.

The Essenes

Although not mentioned in the New Testament the Essenes were a religious group which arose during the period of Roman rule and are mentioned by Josephus and also in the Dead Sea Scrolls. They claimed a greater spirituality, and held that their teacher and founder knew the interpretation of the prophets for their time. They lived apart from society having withdrawn into desert seclusion. They practised a monastic kind of life believing they were the elect of the nation living in the end times. From what is known of them their community was celibate, their laws strict, and their discipline severe. To become a member of this group a long period of probation and initiation was necessary. Ritual purification preceded most of their religious rites, the most important of which was participation in a sacred meal in anticipation of the Messianic feast. Their separation from ordinary society enabled them to concentrate on the study of the Scriptures. They were content to shut out the world with its problems while they waited for the Messiah. They believed that they alone would be saved. It is thought that the Essenes were killed or fled from their wilderness abode in the Roman purge of AD 68-70.

References

1. See http://www.bibleinst.com/BibleSchool/NT-U-11T.htm.

2. McDonald, William. *Believer's Bible Commentary: Old Testament.* Thomas Nelson Publishers, 1992.

3. Associates for Scriptural Knowledge (http://askelm.com/doctrine/d020601.htm).

4. Rabbis Nosson Scherman and Meir Zlotowitz. *ArtScroll History Series: History of the Jewish People, The Second Temple Era.* Mesorah Publications Ltd., 2003; pp.40-41.

5. Herford. R. Travers. *Talmud and Apocrypha.* Soncino Press, 1933; p.77.

6. Rabbis Nosson Scherman and Meir Zlotowitz. *ArtScroll History Series: History of the Jewish People, The Second Temple Era.* Mesorah Publications Ltd., 2003; p.59.

7. Rabbis Nosson Scherman and Meir Zlotowitz. *ArtScroll History Series: History of the Jewish People, The Second Temple Era.* Mesorah Publications Ltd., 2003; p.66.

8. Rabbis Nosson Scherman and Meir Zlotowitz. *ArtScroll History Series: History of the Jewish People, The Second Temple Era.* Mesorah Publications Ltd., 2003; p.64.

9. Rabbis Nosson Scherman and Meir Zlotowitz. *ArtScroll History Series: History of the Jewish People, The Second Temple Era*. Mesorah Publications Ltd., 2003; p.72.

10. Rabbis Nosson Scherman and Meir Zlotowitz. *ArtScroll History Series: History of the Jewish People, The Second Temple Era*. Mesorah Publications Ltd., 2003; p.125.

11. See http://members.aol.com/LazerA/torah.htm.

12. See http://members.aol.com/LazerA/torah.htm.

13. Encyclopaedia Britannica Deluxe Millennium Edition CD - Talmud.

14. Encyclopaedia Britannica Deluxe Millennium Edition CD - Targum.

15. Encyclopaedia Britannica Deluxe Millennium Edition CD - The Dead Sea Scrolls.

16. See http://en.wikipedia.org/wiki/apocrypha.

17. See http://www.Septuagint.nct/Septuagint.htm.

18. Jarrasse, Dominique. *Synagogue - Architecture and Jewish Identity*. Vilo International, 2001.

19. Morrish G. A. *A New and Concise Bible Dictionary*. G. Morrish, 1973; p.692.

20. Rabbis Nosson Scherman and Meir Zlotowitz. *ArtScroll History Series: History of the Jewish People, The Second Temple Era*. Mesorah Publications Ltd., 2003; p.90.

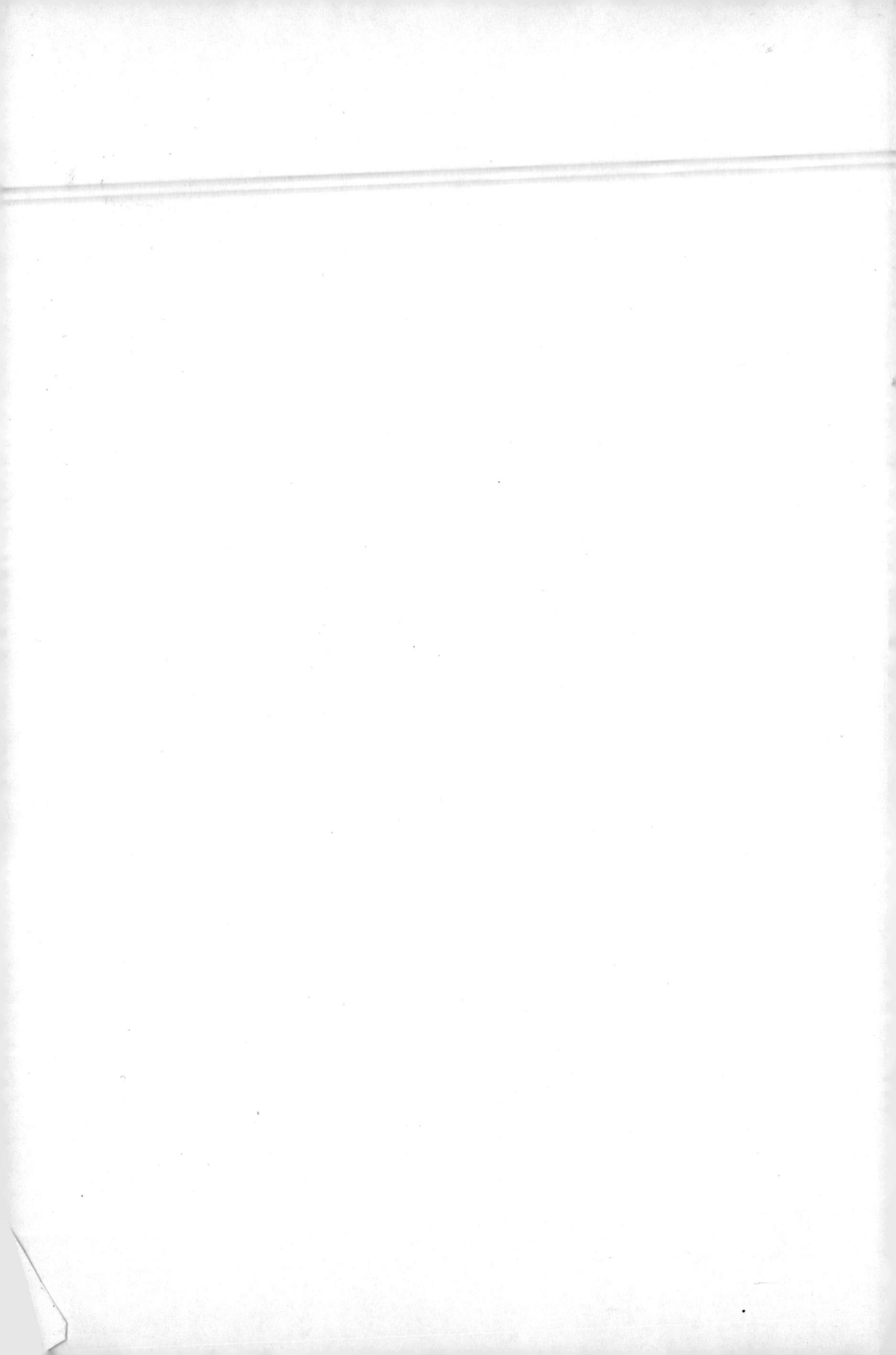